# PRAISE FROM OUR READERS

## Mastering Access 97

"**I read this book from cover to cover and found each page loaded with very practical information and explicit examples.** I commend the authors for their ability to communicate otherwise very technical detail in understandable 'user friendly' language. I highly recommend this book."

*Jim Shannon, Montana*

## Mastering FrontPage 98

"**Best of the 9 FrontPage 98 books I own.** Sybex does it again! I have been reading computer books for the last 10 years and Sybex has been a great publisher—putting out excellent books. After reading 3/4 of the book so far, I know that the publisher and the authors take pride in their product. It's a wonderful book!"

*Mike Perry, New Jersey*

"**This is THE book for mastering FrontPage 98!** I skimmed through 4 other books before deciding to buy this one. Every other book seemed like a larger version of the weak documentation that comes with the software. This book provided the insight on advanced subjects necessary for administering a web. A must buy for FrontPage users."

*Richard Hartsell, Utah*

## Mastering Windows 98

"**The first book I've read that does what it says it will do!** I learned more about Windows 98 in the first one hundred pages of this book than in all of the previous books I had read. My copy lies, dog-eared, beside my computer as a constantly ready source of easy to understand information. It really does show you how to Master Windows 98."

*Steven Dean, Arizona*

SYBEX

www.sybex.com

# MASTERING
## MICROSOFT
# OUTLOOK 2000

# MASTERING™
## MICROSOFT®
# OUTLOOK™ 2000

*Gini Courter*
*Annette Marquis*

SYBEX®

**San Francisco • Paris • Düsseldorf • Soest • London**

Associate Publisher: Amy Romanoff
Contracts and Licensing Manager: Kristine O'Callaghan
Acquisitions & Developmental Editor: Sherry Bonelli
Editor: Andy Carroll
Project Editor: Diane Lowery
Technical Editors: Will Kelly, James Howe
Book Designers: Franz Baumhackl, Patrick Dintino, and
          Catalin Dulfu
Graphic Illustrator: Tony Jonick
Electronic Publishing Specialist: Franz Baumhackl
Production Coordinator: Susan Berge
Indexer: Ted Laux
Cover Designer: Design Site
Cover Illustrator: Sergie Loobkoff

*To Charlotte, our No.1 fan and promoter*

# ACKNOWLEDGMENTS

As always, Sybex brings together the most talented and professional people to complete a book such as this one. We were all very lucky to be led by Sherry Bonelli, who deserves special thanks as acquisitions and developmental editor. She made sure that the material in this book meets your needs. Connor, her son, has a mother he can be very proud of.

Our project editor, Diane Lowery, saw us over every tall hill and through every dense dale and made this experience more enjoyable than it would have been otherwise.

We extend special thanks to Will Kelly, our technical editor, for his input. We also extend additional thanks to James Howe, who stepped in at the last minute and contributed his VB expertise to the project.

Kudos to our crack production team who made this book look as good as it does: Franz Baumhackl, the electronic publishing specialist, Susan Berge, the production coordinator, and Tony Jonick, the graphic artist.

A very special thanks goes to our editor, Andy Carroll. Andy's editorial skills made sure this book was readable.

And finally, another very special thank you goes to the two hard-working and dedicated people who updated this book for Outlook 2000. Tyler and Rima Regas deserve a hearty pat on the back for the work they have done for this edition.

# CONTENTS AT A GLANCE

# TABLE OF CONTENTS

## PART III • EXTENDING OUTLOOK

### 11 Designing Custom Views and Print Styles 317

### 12 Setting User Preferences 349

# APPENDICES

# INTRODUCTION

**S**taying on top of the avalanche of information in today's work world requires a new kind of tool—one that goes beyond traditional methods of communication, that integrates well with other applications, and that provides users and system administrators with the ultimate degree of flexibility. If you find yourself constantly fighting to keep from being buried, Microsoft Outlook 2000 is the tool you've been looking for.

Outlook 2000 combines messaging, contact management, task management, and scheduling with a variety of organizational features that, when put to good use, can actually make your job easier. Outlook lets you track future events, keep records of past activities, notify others of scheduled meetings, and even conduct polls. Whether you want an application that has room to grow with your small business or you want to implement a communication standard across your corporation, Outlook has the features and flexibility to meet your goals.

## What's in This Book

*Mastering Outlook 2000* provides you with the tools and information you need to implement Outlook in your business. We assume that you have some familiarity with Microsoft Office products, but you may or may not have used Outlook previously. If you're familiar with Outlook 98, you will probably be especially interested in those sections of this book marked with a New icon. The New icon identifies some of the features that have been added to the new version of this product.

This book takes you through each of the six components that make up Outlook 2000 and then explores ways to apply Outlook in a variety of business environments. "Part I: Overview of Outlook 2000" takes you on a quick tour of the features and functionality of Outlook 2000. If you're new to Outlook, this will show you the whole picture so you can see how all the components work together. If you've worked with Outlook before, this will show you some of the new and enhanced features of Outlook 2000.

"Part II: Mastering the Outlook Components" takes you on an in-depth tour of each of the six Outlook components: Contacts, Inbox, Calendar, Tasks, Journal, and

Notes. You'll learn about how the components work together and what features are available with the three installation configurations: No E-Mail, Internet Only, and Corporate/Workgroup.

In "Part III: Extending Outlook," you'll see how to make Outlook work for you most effectively. In this part, you'll learn about custom views, filtering and sorting data, setting user preferences, and backing up your all-important Outlook data. If you're interested in how Outlook integrates with other applications, this part will show you how to use Outlook with other Office products and specialty software, such as Microsoft Project, to make workgroup collaboration as easy as clicking a button. In Part III, you'll also see how Outlook interacts with the World Wide Web so you can exchange information with anyone on the Web and set up Web-based meetings with colleagues and business associates.

After you've begun working with Outlook, it doesn't take long to see the value of using Outlook in a workgroup setting. "Part IV: Configuring Outlook for Your Business" shows you how to configure Outlook with Microsoft Mail to set up an inexpensive and effective network for a small office. If you work in a larger work setting and want to install Microsoft Exchange Server, you'll have access to a number of Outlook features that you can only use in an Exchange Server environment. In this part, you'll also find out how to access Outlook from the road or from a dial-up connection in a remote office.

Although building custom applications is not for everybody, Outlook makes it possible for anyone to add fields, add forms to make Outlook keep track of the information you need to know, and even create commercial-grade applications that can extend Outlook to the specific areas you need it. In "Part V: Building Customized Outlook Applications," you'll learn the basics of Outlook customization and delve into the structure of Visual Basic for Applications and VBScript, the programming languages of Outlook. You'll also learn about the Outlook Object model, so you can develop applications that integrate Outlook with other Microsoft Office products.

Installing Outlook correctly takes a little forethought because you are offered three types of installations that determine what features you have available to you. Appendix A walks you through the installation process to ensure you make the right choices.

Appendix B could turn out to be the most valuable section of the book after you learn your way around. In this appendix, you'll find a troubleshooting guide that helps you through many of the most common problems users and system administrators encounter when using and implementing Outlook. With this guide at your fingertips, you'll be an Outlook expert in no time.

# Conventions Used in This Book

Throughout the book, you'll find practical suggestions for making Outlook work for you. Mastering the Opportunities sidebars provide ideas about using Outlook most effectively based on a number of successful Outlook implementations in a variety of settings. Mastering Troubleshooting sidebars provide you with information about how to avoid problems with Outlook and how to recover from problems you may be experiencing.

## MASTERING THE OPPORTUNITIES

This type of sidebar expands on the information in the text by providing some real-life examples of how you can use Outlook 2000 in your everyday work.

## MASTERING TROUBLESHOOTING

This type of sidebar explains some possible pitfalls and provides some tips or tricks that you can use to get around them.

In addition to the sidebars, you'll find Notes, Tips, and Warnings scattered throughout the chapters.

 **NOTE** Notes provide explanations that will help you understand a particular topic better.

 **TIP** Tips show you quick ways to stretch Outlook just a little further, with suggestions for shortcuts and alternate methods.

 **WARNING** Warnings point out potential problems and ways of avoiding them.

All of these extra features are designed to take you a step beyond the typical user and make you an Outlook master.

# How to Use This Book to Master Outlook

Although we would like you to start with page one and devour each word as you work your way through to Appendix B, we recognize that there are some topics that may not apply to your situation. As a result, there is no set formula that all users should follow to make the most of *Mastering Microsoft Outlook 2000*. New users should cover the first ten chapters pretty thoroughly in order to grasp the essential concepts in each of the Outlook components. We have ordered the chapters in the sequence we think will be easiest for you to learn, but if they are not in the order that you need, feel free to skip around. When there is prior knowledge that is essential to the current topic, we have included cross-references to where that topic is covered.

The book is written in narrative form to give you more information about each topic rather than just showing you what to do to accomplish a particular task. However, we've included numbered steps whenever it seemed appropriate, so you can follow along with the specific task at hand.

If you are an experienced Outlook user, you'll find a number of new features in Outlook 2000 and enough design changes to be disconcerting. This book is well-indexed and you should be able to find information about any topic that you want to explore in more detail. Be sure to read the section in Chapter 1 on what's new in Outlook 2000. That will give you a starting place for exploring the critical new features.

If you are a network administrator, you are probably quite interested in Outlook configuration and customization issues. You will find a lot of information about implementing Outlook in a networked environment in Part IV, and Part V gives you in-depth coverage about using Visual Basic for Applications and VBScript to build custom Outlook applications that you can distribute to a workgroup. Information about installation and configuration options is contained in Chapter 1 and in Appendix A. You'll also find Appendix B on troubleshooting Outlook problems especially useful. It contains the questions your users will be asking you and answers that you can give them.

Whatever approach you take to mastering Outlook, this book will answer most of your questions and make you feel comfortable with this powerful and sometimes mind-boggling product. We'd love to hear your comments or answer your specific questions. When you get your e-mail up and running, send us a message. Words of praise and stories of success are always welcome!

Gini Courter and Annette Marquis
triad@kode.net

# PART I

# Overview of Outlook 2000

*LEARN TO:*

- *Navigate in Outlook*

- *Work in Outlook modules*

- *Create Outlook items*

- *Get help in Outlook*

# CHAPTER 1

# A First Look at Outlook 2000

**W**orking in today's fast-paced environment, you know what it's like to keep track of the mountains of information that you deal with every day. Whether or not you're connected to the Internet or you're part of a corporate network, you are handling phone calls, writing reports, and sending and receiving information from clients, customers, and other business associates. If you're like most people, you've tried numerous methods of organization. You have probably used a variety of address books, appointment books, day planners, complex filing systems, and notebooks, trying to fill the gap of a truly integrated system of organization. Well, wait no longer—Microsoft Outlook 2000 has come to the rescue. Outlook 2000 provides a way to manage contacts, communication, scheduling, information sharing, and record keeping in one powerful and easy-to-use package. Whether you're new to Outlook or an experienced Outlook user, you'll find the exciting new features of Outlook 2000 well worth your consideration.

## Outlook Uses and Outlook Users

Outlook 2000 is a flexible tool that can be used in any business environment, and it has many applications for managing personal information. Outlook can be used effectively on a stand-alone computer with no outside access, or as part of a large corporate network with hundreds of computers and multiple sites around the globe. Regardless of your environment, you'll find tools that you can use to organize your information. Outlook is referred to as a *desktop information manager* (DIM) but it's really that and more. You can use Outlook to organize all the information on your desktop, a significant amount of information that you probably kept only in paper form up to now, and some information that you may never have organized at all.

With Outlook 2000, you can:

- Record the names, addresses, and other information related to personal and business contacts.
- Keep your to-do list and organize it by priority, by due date, and endless other ways.
- Manage your appointments and track birthdays, holidays, and other special events.
- Send electronic mail through the Internet or your corporate network.
- Keep notes about telephone conversations, meetings, and other conversations and, if desired, relate them to individual contacts.
- Schedule a meeting with other people in your workgroup or even across the Internet.
- Organize all of your personal information and files through one central interface.

And this is just the beginning. There is only one way to truly appreciate the power of Outlook 2000—you have to start using it. Once you do, you'll experience an increase in personal productivity and actually start to believe that you'll one day be able to control the incredible amount of information that crosses your desk. Maybe it will even improve your outlook!

## Designed to Fit Your Environment

Outlook 2000 comes with three basic configurations, appropriate for different environments. When you install Outlook, you are given a choice of which configuration best fits your situation (for more about installing Outlook 2000, see Appendix A). The three configurations are as follows:

- Internet Only: this option provides e-mail capability for users who have an e-mail service through an Internet service provider or other SMTP/POP3 or IMAP4 mail server. Users can use the Internet vCalendar protocol for sending meeting requests, iCalendar for sharing free/busy calendar information, and vCard for sharing Contact (business card) information. (See Chapter 15 for more about these Internet protocols.)

- Corporate/Workgroup: this is the richest of the three configurations, offering full support for e-mail, group scheduling, voting buttons, and message recall using Microsoft Exchange Server or another network mail server. (However, depending on your mail server, you may still have some limitations. See "Outlook on a Small Network" later in this chapter.)

- No E-mail: this is the configuration for stand-alone computers that do not have access to Internet e-mail or an e-mail server on a network.

 **NOTE** A new feature in Office 2000 is the Setup utility's ability to dynamically install a new feature the first time you use it. We'll look more closely at this feature in Appendix A.

## Outlook as a Personal Information Manager

If you work at home or in a small business, it's possible that you might have a computer that has no connection with other computers or the outside world. Chances are, however, you've taken the plunge and signed up with an Internet service provider for access to e-mail. If either scenario describes you, Outlook 2000 has plenty to offer.

Outlook 2000 is made up of six primary components or modules. Users in a stand-alone (No E-mail or Internet Only) environment have access to the following Outlook 2000 features:

**Inbox**   Your source for sending and receiving electronic mail from home, the office, or while you're on the road. If you have Internet access, you can participate in Internet newsgroups (NNTP) and create private discussion groups.

**Calendar**   Records your appointments, meetings, and other date-specific information, such as birthdays, holidays, vacations, and anniversaries in a date book. You can easily create time in your calendar to work on items in your task list.

**Contacts**   Replaces your manual address book. In Contacts, you keep personal and business contact information, names, addresses, e-mail addresses, and other information related to individuals. You can send contacts through Internet e-mail to other Outlook users.

**Tasks**   Your online to-do list. You can list your tasks, assign due dates, prioritize items, and even include shortcuts to Microsoft Office documents that are related to the task. You can also delegate tasks through e-mail to other people who are running Outlook.

**Journal**   Lets you record what you've done. It can be used as a personal diary, a record of conversations and interactions with a client or customer, a time tracker to analyze how you spend your time, and a place to organize documents and communications related to a specific individual or project.

**Notes**   An electronic notepad to keep track of all those little pieces of paper scattered all over your desk.

## Outlook on a Small Network

If you work in a small-business setting where you have anywhere from two to twenty computers, you're probably running a peer-to-peer network or small LAN (local area network) using a mail client such as Microsoft Mail, or Lotus cc Mail. In this situation, you should install the Corporate/Work Group configuration. In addition to the personal information management tools listed in the previous section, with this configuration you can:

• Exchange contacts with others on the network.

• Assign tasks to other users and accept or decline task requests.

• Store messages in multiple server folders (also available to IMAP4 users); apply Inbox rules, shown in Figure 1.1 (this option is available to SMTP/POP3 users); share public folders; exchange e-mail without dialing up an Internet service provider.

• Use group-scheduling features, such as those shown in Figure 1.2, to send and receive meeting requests and let others have access to your personal schedule.

PART
I

Overview of
Outlook 2000

**FIGURE 1.1**

*Inbox rules can be
applied to e-mail with
the Rules Wizard.*

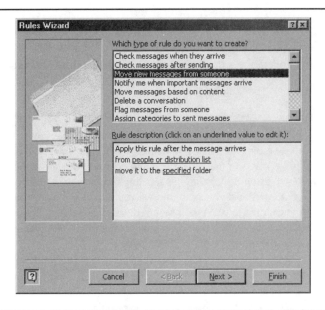

**FIGURE 1.2**

*Using Outlook's Group
Scheduling features*

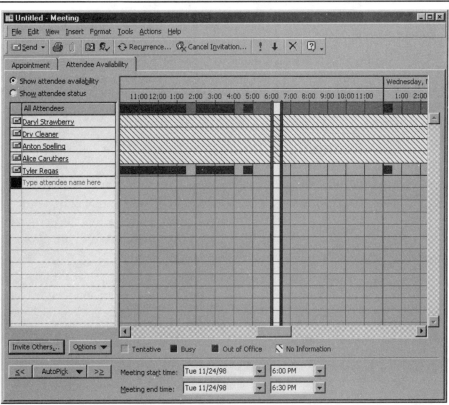

With the advancement of Internet technology, fewer features are only available to networked users. The biggest advantage of running a network is the ability to exchange e-mail and use other Outlook features collaboratively without connecting to the Internet. This reduces the cost of external phone lines and speeds access for users inside the company.

 **NOTE** Though not absolutely necessary, connecting your business to the Internet can make a big difference. It adds new ways of reaching and connecting with your customers, and a Web site makes a great, low-cost way of getting the word out about your product. Also, customers who are researching products or services on the Web will only learn about your Internet-savvy competitors if you don't have a Web site. You can even sell your product over the Internet with secure transaction servers, the security of which is a given these days. Even adding a single e-mail account will offer you another low-cost way of letting your customers get in touch with you.

## Outlook in a Corporate Setting

To experience all the incredible functionality of Outlook 2000, you must be running Outlook as a Microsoft Exchange Server client. You don't have to be a large corporation to use Exchange Server. Many small companies are seeing the benefits of running Exchange Server. It's an ideal system for companies organized around a virtual office. By setting up an Exchange Server, staff can dial in to the server from their homes or hotel rooms and have access to e-mail, to documents stored in public folders, and to shared calendars.

Whether you're in a corporation of thousands or your company is five people working from home, Outlook 2000 running under Microsoft Exchange Server has this additional functionality:

- Calendar lets you see the free/busy information of other users, as shown in Figure 1.2; it opens others' calendars with appropriate permissions; it works with Microsoft Schedule+ for group scheduling; and it lets you delegate access to your calendar to another user for scheduling.

- Inbox stores e-mail on the server in public folders; it uses server-based rules to filter your mail; it uses voting, message flags, and message recall; it defers delivery of e-mail; it receives receipts when mail has been delivered or read; it gives access to the Exchange Server Global Address List; and it accesses mail remotely and uses client/server replication of messages.

- Workgroup Functionality creates private discussion groups (available also to Internet users); and it works with collaboration, workflow, and project tracking applications, such as Microsoft Project, Microsoft Team Manager, and Microsoft Office products.

Outlook was clearly designed with the workgroup in mind. Its primary objective is to make collaboration in a workgroup setting efficient, friendly, and productive.

# Other Outlook Productivity Tools

In addition to the six Outlook modules, Outlook 2000 gives you a number of productivity tools to make your life easier. For example, the AutoDate feature takes descriptions of dates and converts them into actual dates for you: "a week from tomorrow," "two months from now," and "last Friday" are all acceptable dates as far as Outlook is concerned. Outlook's multilevel sorting, grouping, and filtering features and customizable views help you to organize and view your data in the ways that are most beneficial to you on any given day. All data in Outlook can be assigned categories to help you organize data into projects or other useful tracking methods.

If you've been using other Microsoft Office applications, you'll feel right at home with many of the commands and tools available in Outlook 2000. The Office Assistant and the Office Shortcut Bar are already familiar to users of Office 97. You can access the Word Letter Wizard to send a letter to a person in your Outlook Contact list. You can also merge a contact list to create labels and form letters in Word. Outlook's Journal, shown in Figure 1.3, will automatically record Office documents that you are working on and allow you to copy information directly between Outlook and other Office applications.

If you're in need of custom applications that combine messaging, custom data needs, and legacy systems, you'll find that Outlook is fully customizable. In addition to designing custom forms, developers can create add-in programs that read and write Outlook information. Using Visual Basic 6, Microsoft Exchange Client extensions, and the OLE Automation Object Library, it's possible to develop complete Outlook applications that let you use the functionality of Outlook with data in other client/server applications and even on corporate mainframes.

**FIGURE 1.3**

*The Journal automatically records work on Office documents.*

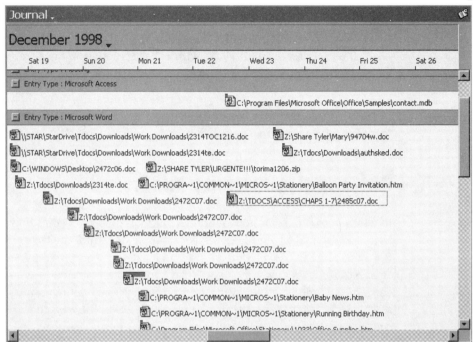

**FIGURE 1.3**

*The Journal automatically records work on Office documents.*

# An Overview of Profiles

When Outlook is installed on a desktop, it creates a default *user profile*. A user profile is nothing more than a group of settings that defines how you are set up to work with Outlook. A user profile identifies how you receive e-mail, where your personal information is stored, and what other information services, such as Microsoft Exchange Server, are available to you.

If you're operating Outlook from your home computer and you are the only user, you can set Outlook to automatically load your user profile. However, if other people use your computer or your network environment, user profiles become much more significant. User profiles can be set up to be mobile, which means that in an office environment you could log on to any computer and have access to your personal information. It also protects your information from being accessed by other users. For more information about user profiles, see Chapter 17 and Appendix A.

# What's New in Outlook

If you used Outlook 97 or the immensely improved Outlook 98, you'll find a lot that's familiar in Outlook 2000. But as with any ambitious product like Outlook, there's always room for enhancement. You may find some features easier and more powerful to use and you may wonder why they ever changed others. The most significant changes are related to organizing your information, working with other applications, and using the Internet to extend the power of Outlook. Outlook 2000 expands on the additions made in Outlook 98 and includes some minor interface tweaks to make things more intuitive, but if you've used Outlook 98, you'll have little trouble adjusting to Outlook 2000.

Jumping from Outlook 97 to Outlook 2000 is an entirely different matter. One of the most significant complaints about Outlook 97 concerned its overall performance. This complaint persisted somewhat through Outlook 98, but Microsoft has seriously addressed this issue and made Outlook 2000 much more responsive when involved in common tasks such as start-up and shutdown. Depending on your computer's capacity, however, you may find that some of the features first added in Outlook 98, such as the Find and Organize features, shown in Figure 1.4, are not as snappy as you might like.

**FIGURE 1.4**

*Outlook's Find feature, first introduced in Outlook 98*

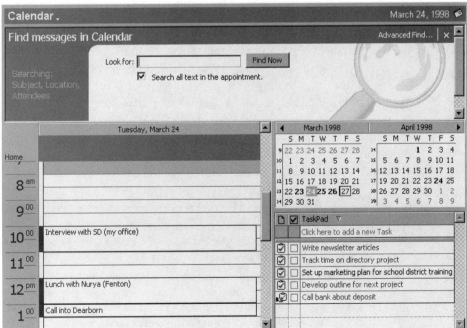

## Productivity Enhancements

Outlook 98 had a refined interface designed to make it easier to navigate and give it a cleaner appearance, and Outlook 2000 only modifies this interface slightly. You'll find that Outlook has simplified menus, toolbars, and dialog boxes—commands and choices are accessible with little clutter. Options actually relocate themselves to the top of their menus when you use them often. The Standard toolbar has been divided into Standard and Advanced toolbars, and more buttons are labeled so you can easily figure out what they are. The downside? Familiar buttons such as Group By, Field Chooser, and Folder List are now relegated to a secondary toolbar. On the other hand, you can now customize toolbars to your personal preferences.

One of the frustrations of working in Outlook 97 was that you had to close one component to open another. As in Outlook 98, Outlook 2000 components open in separate windows so it's possible to check an item in your Calendar without having to close your Inbox to do it.

A step forward for Microsoft and an advancement that helps keep the toolbar clutter to an acceptable minimum is the addition of an Add/Remove fly out to each toolbar. Simply click on the down double-arrow at the right end of the toolbar and point to the Add or Remove Button. A menu opens, presenting a list of buttons with checkmarks beside the ones that are active on the toolbar. Click on a checkmark to remove the button from the toolbar, or click beside a button with no checkmark to add it to the toolbar. Here's the productivity booster: when you click in the flyout, it doesn't close. You can add or remove as many buttons as you need, and then when you are finished, click on the arrow again or anywhere outside of the menu and it will close. This is a concept whose time was long overdue.

Outlook 2000 also improves on the functionality of the toolbars. Figure 1.5 shows two windows. The one on the left shows the Standard toolbar with all of its buttons visible. The window on the right, which is exactly the same size as the one on the left, is showing five buttons and the Add/Remove button that you would not see until you click on the button at the right end of the toolbar (indicated in Figure 1.5).

 **NOTE** The Standard toolbar in Outlook Today contains 9 buttons. The Inbox has 13 buttons on the Standard toolbar. Depending on the size of your window, you may not see all of the toolbar buttons in all windows.

Previously, Microsoft's solution was to have a "scrolling" toolbar. When you clicked on the small arrow button where the obscured buttons should be, they slid into view. This, however, caused the buttons on the opposite end to be obscured, and you had to scroll them back into view when they were needed. Microsoft, as of recently, has started using a new type of toolbar that eliminates the scrolling. When you click on the button at the right end of the toolbar (shown in Figure 1.5), a whole, separate menu appears that contains all of the obscured buttons *and* the Add or Remove Buttons button.

**FIGURE 1.5**

*The new toolbar in
Outlook 2000 is on
the right.*

Toolbar button that shows Add/Remove button
and other hidden buttons and fields

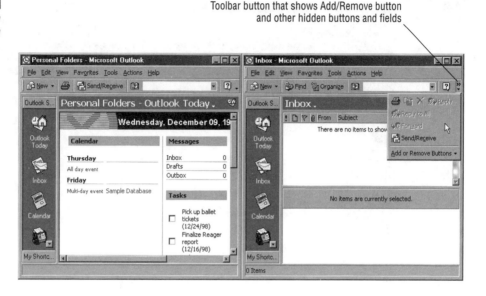

## Information Management Enhancements

Outlook 2000 makes it easy to locate specific data and organize your information so
the things you have to follow-up on jump right off the screen. Another feature of
Outlook gives you an at-a-glance view of your day. This feature is called Outlook
Today (see Figure 1.6), and it shows how many unread messages you have in your
Inbox and gives you a list of tasks and appointments for the next few days.

The Find command (introduced in Outlook 98) allows you to search for messages,
appointments, contacts, and tasks using a Web-like interface. You can even sort different
groups, and change the view of your search results. The Organize dialog box allows you
to create e-mail rules, change views, manage junk e-mail, assign categories to items, color
code messages, and create folders to store messages. When you need to be reminded to
follow up, you can flag a contact to remind yourself to call them, send a letter, or otherwise communicate with them.

**FIGURE 1.6**

*Outlook Today*

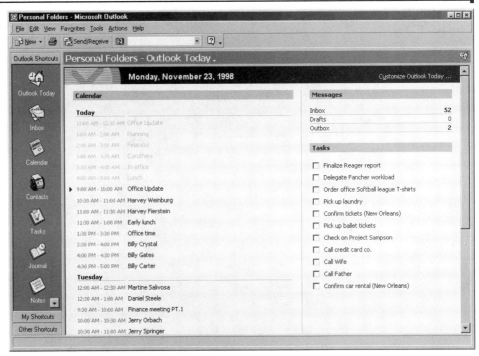

## E-mail Enhancements

With the dramatic increase in the number of people and organizations using Internet e-mail as a preferred form of communication, you'll find a number of exciting Outlook enhancements related to electronic mail. If you've had to configure Internet e-mail to work with a new mail application, you know it can be a challenge. Outlook takes all the frustration away from having to reconfigure it by including a feature in the Import and Export Wizard to detect existing e-mail applications on your system and configure them for you automatically.

After your e-mail is up and running, sending and receiving messages will be better than ever. Outlook 2000 lets you control what happens with your mail and how it looks when you send it. One of the most significant enhancements to Outlook 98 was the addition of the Rules Wizard. The Rules Wizard is built into Outlook 2000, letting you create rules to automatically move, delete, forward, or flag incoming or outgoing messages. You can even set it to automatically change the color of adult content e-mail.

When you don't have time to finish a message you've started, you can store it in the Drafts folder until you have time to complete it and send it out. Another nifty add-on is the Preview Pane that lets you view e-mail without opening a separate window.

If you're tired of sending plain text messages, Outlook 2000 has just what you need to make your e-mail come alive:

- HTML mail gives you the ability to send messages that contain multimedia objects, such as animated graphics, sound, and pictures.

- You can use stationery with images and background colors to jazz up your e-mail.

- You have multiple signatures available to personalize your e-mail messages: one for business, one for your friends, and so on.

- Support for digital IDs assures that e-mail addresses are indeed authentic.

 **WARNING** Not everyone can see your neatly formatted Web page or RTF file (RTF is Microsoft's Rich Text Format, a file format that preserves a subset of Word's formatting capabilities). There are a number of e-mail clients out there that simply don't support these formats. Before spending lots of time creating your HTML masterpiece, find out if the person on the receiving end can actually view it. We know people who have used e-mail for years, but have still not touched a Web browser.

## Internet Information Exchange Enhancements

The growth of the Internet has stimulated the development of exciting new technologies for information exchange, and Outlook is ready to embrace them. Outlook 2000 includes support for the following:

- vCalendar, which lets you exchange meeting request information over the Internet

- iCalendar, which lets you share free/busy information over the Internet by publishing your free/busy information to a Web site for other users to access

- vCard, which lets you send contact information over the Internet

- Internet Mail protocols, such as POP3/SMTP, IMAP4, LDAP, NNTP, and S/MIME

## Integration Enhancements

Outlook works closely with Internet Explorer and installs some components to Internet Explorer during setup, such as adding Outlook to the Quick Launch Bar and Go menu.

Outlook also has access to Internet Explorer's newsreader, and you can share HTML-based information between two applications. If you travel with a computer and are tired of lugging around your heavy laptop, it may be time to purchase a Windows CE 2.0 handheld device. Outlook 2000 integrates smoothly with Windows CE Pocket Outlook, so you can keep up-to-date without straining your back in the process.

 **NOTE** Microsoft has chosen to require the installation of Outlook Express if you want to use Outlook—we're not sure exactly why. Also, if you already have Internet Explorer 5 on your computer, the Outlook installation will not touch it, but if you use Internet Explorer 4, it will ask if you want to upgrade. Keep in mind that upgrading to Internet Explorer 5 is *not* required, but is suggested. Internet Explorer 5 does add some nice new features, but also a few new glitches. If you're comfortable with the version you have, you might want to keep what you already have.

Outlook also integrates with Microsoft NetMeeting, as shown in Figure 1.7. With NetMeeting, you can conduct virtual meetings over the Internet with another person or a group of people using audio, video, text, and data exchange. A person in California can take control of an application running on a desktop in Michigan to share a document or demonstrate a feature. Attach a simple microphone and small video camera to your computer, and you can send voice and video images. NetMeeting does not require Outlook to run, but it comes as part of the Outlook package and makes setting up NetMeetings a snap.

## Performance Enhancements

Although it may only take a few seconds, if you're like a lot of people, you get tired of waiting for applications to open and close. Outlook has been notoriously slow in comparison to other Office applications. Microsoft reported that this had been addressed, and start-up, shutdown, and switching between modules in Outlook 98 was improved. Outlook 2000 is even faster. Downloading e-mail from an ISP is much faster, and you can continue working in Outlook while mail is being downloaded.

If you're synchronizing offline folders using Microsoft Exchange Server, you can continue to work while your offline folders are being synchronized, and you can configure Outlook to automatically synchronize your offline folders at specified times.

Outlook 2000 offers lots of possibilities to both new and experienced users alike. As you work with the product, you're going to run across other changes—some that will be intuitive and some that you may need some help with. This book should provide you with all you need to master this latest version of Outlook.

**FIGURE 1.7**

*Access NetMeeting
from the Outlook
Calendar.*

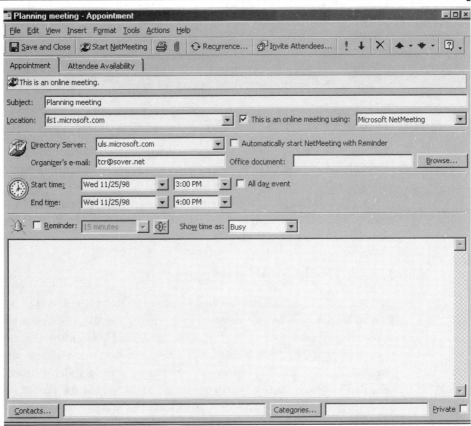

# The Microsoft Mail Client Family

Now that Outlook has become an established product in its own right, Microsoft has
developed several spin-offs to round out the Outlook family. For example, if you purchase a Windows CE 2.0 handheld computer, you'll find you have a product called
Pocket Outlook. If you install Internet Explorer 4 or 5, you also get a product called
Outlook Express. If you're in a position to make decisions or recommendations regarding products in your company or if you are a user who wants to take full advantage of
a new technology, it's helpful to understand the similarities and differences between
the various members of the Outlook family of products. This list provides you with an
overview of each of the products to date.

# Microsoft Outlook 2000

Clearly, Outlook 2000 is considered the head of the Outlook family. Microsoft describes Outlook 2000 as its "premier e-mail and collaboration client." It contains a full range of features, from e-mail to contact management, scheduling, task management, journaling, and integration with other Office products.

# Microsoft Exchange Client

Outlook 2000 has become the only mail client that is included with Microsoft Exchange, replacing the Exchange client and Schedule+ included with previous versions. Running Outlook under Exchange Server adds increased functionality to Outlook, including group-scheduling capability and workgroup functionality. There is also a 16-bit Windows version (for Windows 3.1x) and a Macintosh version of the Outlook Express client for businesses that use Exchange Server 5.5 or later.

# Microsoft Outlook Web Access

Outlook Web Access is a new feature of Microsoft Exchange Server that uses a Web browser to give users remote access to their e-mail, calendar, and information on group scheduling in public folders. Users must be connected to Microsoft Exchange Server via a phone line to use Outlook Web Access. It also provides cross-platform functionality for Macintosh and even UNIX operating systems. It's a useful tool for remote-access users who don't have access to a PC with Outlook. It can also be used on PCs with RAM or hard-drive limitations. Microsoft warns that Outlook Web Access does not have all the functionality and should not replace the Outlook clients for 16-bit Windows or Macintosh. It is, however, the primary client for UNIX users.

# Outlook Express

Outlook Express, shown in Figure 1.8, is a replacement for the Microsoft Internet Mail and News client that was included with Microsoft Internet Explorer 3. Outlook Express is installed automatically when you install Internet Explorer 4 or 5, so you probably already have this on your system. The primary use of Outlook Express is to access e-mail and newsgroups. For users who do not need the full functionality of Outlook, Outlook Express is a worthwhile alternative. Many of the same e-mail features that are included in Outlook 2000, such as HTML mail, stationery, AutoHyperlinks, Inbox rules, and support for multiple e-mail accounts, are included with Outlook Express. Users of Outlook Express should require only Internet e-mail and newsgroup functionality. It offers no advantages for users of Outlook 2000.

FIGURE 1.8

Outlook Express

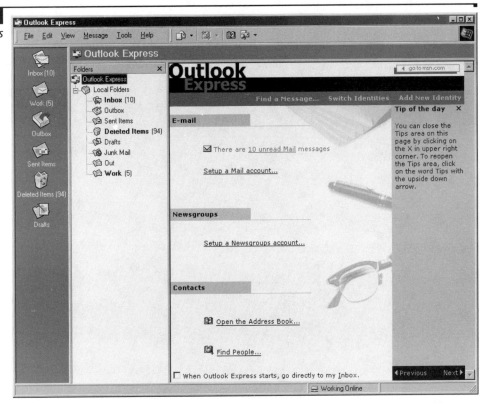

## Microsoft Pocket Outlook

Pocket Outlook is the version of Outlook for people on the go. Designed for the new generation of palm-top computers powered by Windows CE 2.0, Pocket Outlook has four of the six Outlook components: Contacts, Calendar, Tasks, and Inbox. You can enter information on the road and, when you're back at your desk, synchronize the Pocket Outlook with your desktop version. Any changes you made to either data set will be exchanged with the other, so all your data is current. Although you don't have all the functionality of Outlook, Pocket Outlook is a powerful sidekick and beats the heck out of a paper-based system.

### What's Next?

Now that you have an idea of what Outlook is all about, Chapters 2 and 3 will give you all you need to get started entering your own Outlook data. Chapter 2 focuses on the features that are common to all the Outlook modules, and Chapter 3 gives you a first look at using each of the modules individually.

# CHAPTER **2**

# Understanding Outlook Basics

O utlook is a tool that can help you organize the mountains of information that inundate your life. The first few times you launch Outlook, spend some time finding your way around—Outlook has much to offer when you know where to look and how to make it work for you. Outlook has six distinct applications (called *Outlook components*), and you can use all of them or only one, depending on your needs and circumstances. The great part is that once you've learned how to use one module effectively, you know most of what you need to use each of them.

If you are unsure what to do first with Outlook, start working with the module that you have the greatest need for: Contacts, Inbox (e-mail), Tasks, Calendar, Journal, or Notes. Once you are comfortable with one of the components, it will be much easier to move into the next one. Before long you'll be throwing away your paper-based planner and you'll wonder how you ever lived without Outlook.

 **WARNING** To launch Outlook, choose it from the Windows 95/98 Programs menu (Start ➢ Programs ➢ Microsoft Outlook), or if you're using Windows 98, look for an icon directly on the QuickLaunch bar (located to the immediate right of the Start button). Be careful not to select Outlook Express, a more limited e-mail application that is included with Internet Explorer 4 and 5.

 **NOTE** If you are using Windows NT 4.0, you will need to have installed Internet Explorer 4 or 5 to gain the advantages of the QuickLaunch bar (as well as the other Windows 98–style taskbars, toolbars, and the Active Desktop).

## Outlook Today

When you start Outlook for the first time, you will probably start in Outlook Today, again updated for this version of Outlook. Using a Web-browser–type interface, Outlook Today, shown in Figure 2.1, provides you with the day-at-a-glance view of your world by listing your appointments, unread e-mail, and tasks.

In an ideal world, you would spend your day completing these responsibilities and then start fresh tomorrow with a brand new list. Recognizing that few of us live in that ideal world, Outlook Today defaults to displaying appointments for the next five days and includes tasks that are overdue as well as those that are due today. However, if you'd rather focus only on today, or even broaden your today to see more than five days of appointments, you can change some of the basic options that control Outlook Today.

*FIGURE 2.1*

*Outlook Today*

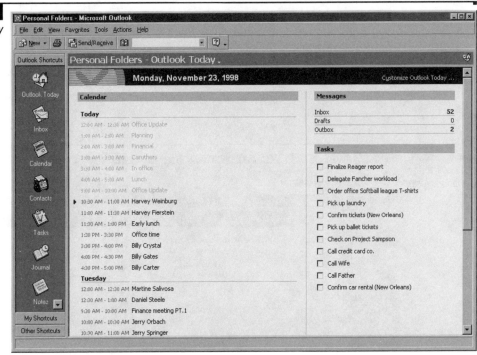

If Outlook Today does not appear automatically when you launch Outlook, you can open it yourself by clicking the Outlook Today icon on the Outlook bar. To change the Outlook Today options, click Customize Outlook Today to the right of today's date.

The Outlook Today Options form, shown in Figure 2.2, opens so you can change the following:

**Startup**  If you like Outlook Today's view of your world, click the check box to have Outlook Today appear every time you launch Outlook.

**Messages**   This option allows you to select the folders from which mail will be displayed in Outlook Today. Only messages that have not been read will be displayed.

**Calendar**   You can choose to display between one and seven days of your calendar by choosing the number from the drop-down list. The default is five days.

**Tasks**   Select either a Simple List, which shows tasks that are due, overdue, and completed; or choose Today's Tasks, which shows only those incomplete tasks that are due today.

**Styles**   Choose between different presentations of Outlook Today.

When you have finished setting your preferences, click Save Changes to save the changes you made.

**FIGURE 2.2**

*The Outlook Today Options form*

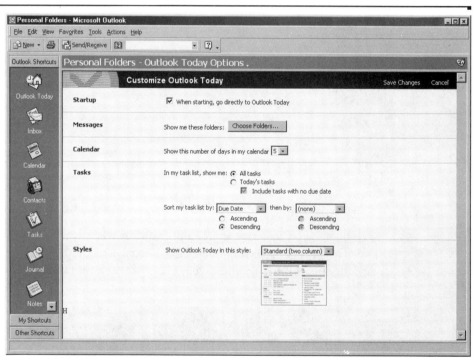

# Finding a Contact

In addition to summarizing your day, Outlook Today provides you with an easy way to locate an item within your Contacts folder. Simply enter a name or part of a name in the text field in the Standard toolbar to ask Outlook to search for the entry. This feature used to be a part of the Outlook Today page, but Microsoft has moved this to the Standard toolbar, making it available at any time.

Outlook will use its powerful Find feature to find all occurrences of the text you entered in the Full Name field of your Contacts folder (see Chapter 4 for more about Contacts fields). If there is only one match for the text you entered, you will be taken directly to the open Contacts form. If there is more than one match, you will see a Choose Contact dialog box like the one shown in Figure 2.3. Select the name you want to use, and click OK. (See Chapter 13 for more information about using Advanced Find, and Chapters 3 and 4 for more about entering contacts.)

**FIGURE 2.3**

*Choose Contact
dialog box*

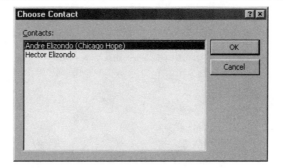

 **NOTE**  The Choose Contact dialog box may look slightly different if you are running Outlook under Microsoft Exchange.

# Parts of the Application Window

The Outlook application window, shown in Figure 2.4, has many elements that should be familiar to Microsoft Office and Windows users. The application window itself has a title bar that identifies the name of the application and the module that is currently active. On the far right side of the title bar are the standard Windows Minimize, Maximize/Restore, and Close buttons that you can use to control the application. Underneath the title bar are two toolbars: one that contains menu options and one with buttons to access the most commonly used features.

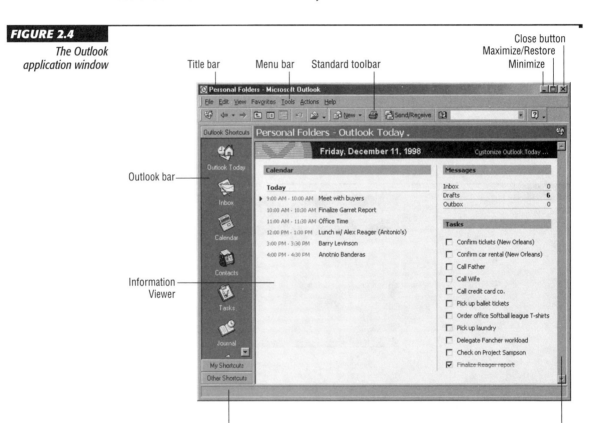

**FIGURE 2.4**

*The Outlook application window*

The bar of icons on the left side of the application window, called the *Outlook bar,* is a feature that is unique to Outlook. These icons let you move between the Outlook components and easily access other folders. Outlook data is displayed in the larger window to the right of the Outlook bar, called the Information Viewer. You can use the scroll bars on the bottom right of the Information Viewer to see data that does not appear in the display. At the bottom of the application window, the status bar tells you how many items are in the particular module you are viewing.

**NOTE** Every record in Outlook, whether a contact, a task, an appointment, an e-mail message, a journal entry, or a note, is referred to as an *item*. Items are stored in folders designated by the component in which the item was created. You can create new folders and then move and copy Outlook items between folders to organize your data. See Chapter 13 for more about organizing items in folders.

## Toolbars

An important part of finding your way around is learning the commands and the easiest way to find them. As with all Microsoft Office applications, commands are found on toolbars located at the top of the application window. The toolbar menu options or buttons are dynamic, which means that they change depending upon which component is active at the current time. If you are in Contacts, for example, the Actions menu, shown in Figure 2.5, has options related to creating a new contact, sending a message to a contact, calling a contact, and so on. If you are in Calendar, the options on the Actions menu relate to creating new appointments, new events, and new recurring appointments.

 **NOTE** The Menu toolbar can be relocated, but, unlike earlier versions of this feature, the Menu toolbar will remain where you put it over subsequent restarts. Although it's okay to move around the other toolbars to fit your needs, we recommend you leave the Menu toolbar in its default position in case you need help from a help desk or IS department.

**FIGURE 2.5**

*The Actions menus of Contacts and Calendar*

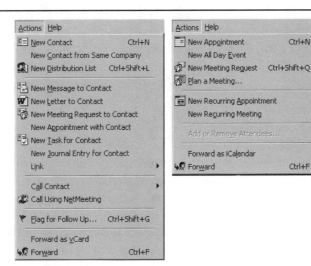

The first button on the Standard toolbar is the New button. The New button is the easiest way to create a new anything—a new task, a new contact, a new appointment, and so on. However, because it is a dynamic button, it changes depending on which component is active. As a result, it's easy to lose track of what the button specifically does (although it always creates a new item in the current module). When you point to the New button, you will see a ToolTip that tells you what new item the button is currently set to create.

So, if you are in the Tasks module, the New button is a New Task button; if you're in Journal, it's the New Journal Entry button. In every module, you can choose to create any new item by clicking the downward-pointing arrow on the right side of the button. This opens up the New menu, shown in Figure 2.6, which gives you all the new item choices available in Outlook.

**FIGURE 2.6**

*The New item menu
on the New button*

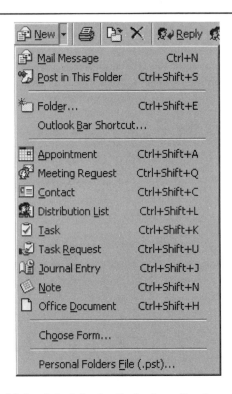

Two toolbars are visible by default in the Outlook application window: the menu bar and the Standard toolbar. The menu bar contains all of the commands available in Outlook. The options on the Tools and Actions menus change depending on which component is active at the current time. For example, if you're in the Inbox (e-mail), the Tools menu has options such as New Mail Message and Flag for Follow-up. If you're in Contacts, these options change to New Contact and Call Contact. If you have difficulty finding a menu option that you know you saw somewhere before, switch to the module where it's most likely used, and you'll probably find it on one of the menus there.

For more options, you can turn on the Advanced toolbar by choosing View ➤ Toolbars and clicking Advanced, or by right-clicking the Standard Toolbar and selecting Advanced from the list. If these aren't enough toolbars to suit you, you can create your own custom toolbars and customize any of the available Outlook toolbars. (In Chapter 12, you can learn how to create and customize toolbars.)

 **NOTE** If you have used Outlook 97 or 98, the Outlook 2000 Advanced toolbar will contain several of the buttons you are used to seeing on the Standard toolbar, such as Folder List, Current View, Group by Box, Field Chooser, and Auto Preview. You may want to turn the Advanced toolbar on and leave it on—otherwise, you'll have to find these useful options hidden in a menu.

## The Outlook Bar

The Outlook bar, shown in Figure 2.7, gives you easy access to the Outlook components and to other folders on your computer. Click one of the icon shortcuts to activate that module. Use the floating scroll button on the bottom of the Outlook bar to see other icons on the Outlook bar that may be located below the window edge.

Shortcuts on the Outlook bar are organized into groups. Click one of the group buttons (see Figure 2.7) at the bottom or top of the Outlook bar to display the shortcuts available in that group.

To make the icons on the Outlook bar smaller, so more can be displayed, right-click anywhere on the bar except directly on a button, and choose Small Icons from the pop-up menu that appears.

If you decide that the Outlook bar takes up too much room on your screen, click Outlook Bar on the View menu to turn it off. Click View ➤ Outlook Bar again to make it visible. In Chapter 12, we'll show you how you can add shortcuts and groups to and remove them from the Outlook bar.

*The Outlook bar*

## The Information Viewer

The Information Viewer is where it all happens—where Outlook displays all of your data. It displays multiple items or records simultaneously and is where you see all of your unread e-mail, a catalog of your contacts, or a list of your tasks. The best part about the Information Viewer is that it displays your data the way you want to see it. You can sort your data, group it together, and select records that meet specific criteria. In the next section, "Working in the Outlook Components," you'll learn more about the Information Viewer.

# Working in the Outlook Components

Each of the Outlook components has features that are unique to it. However, some aspects are common to all six components, such as how you enter and edit text. In this section, we will explore the common features of the Outlook components. In Chapter 3, we will give you an overview of each of the components and describe their unique features.

The two ways to work with Outlook data are in the Information Viewer and in Outlook forms. As mentioned earlier in this chapter, the Information Viewer shows you multiple Outlook items or records. You can enter data directly in the Information Viewer, or you can double-click a particular record to open that item in a form. A form displays an individual Outlook record: all the information about a particular contact, the entire contents of an e-mail message, or the details of a scheduled appointment. The Information Viewer lets you look at your data as a group—all the people from the same company or all of your unread e-mail—while the forms let you focus on one record and see all the data you have on that specific record.

# Viewing Data in the Information Viewer

One of Outlook's greatest strengths is its ability to display your data in a wide variety of ways. Because the Information Viewer lets you look at multiple records at one time, how you view your data here is paramount. Before you can enter or edit data in the Information Viewer, it's necessary to understand what you are seeing as you move between the Outlook components.

## Types of Views

A view is a defined set of fields with a sort order, grouping levels, a filter, and formats. Outlook has five types of views available. Each of the Outlook modules has a default view type, but you can switch to or create different view types for each of the modules.

**Table View**    The default view in Tasks; data in this view is organized in columns and rows.

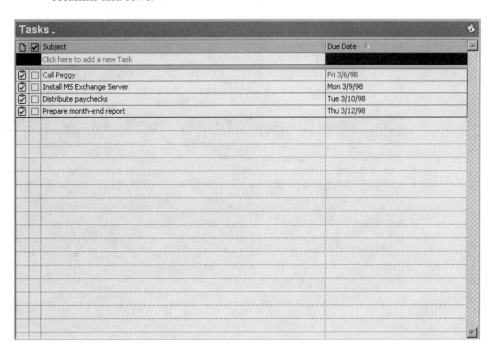

**Card View** The default view in Contacts; this view displays contact data in an address-book fashion, much like the card file sitting on your desk. You can use alphanumeric buttons on the right side of the screen to navigate quickly between records.

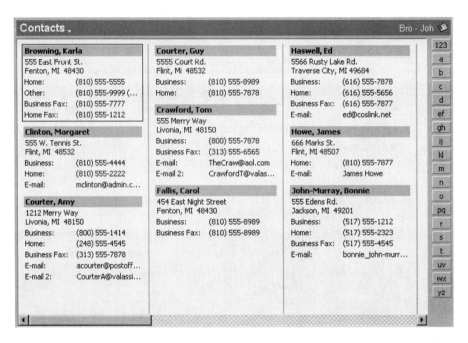

**Timeline View** The default view in Journal; data in this view is seen along a timeline. The emphasis in this view is on when things occurred—for example, when you made a journal entry or received an e-mail message.

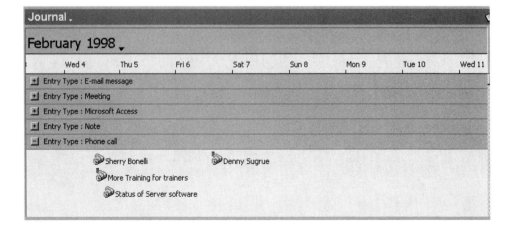

**Day/Week/Month View**    The default view in Calendar; this view most closely resembles a day planner. Data is displayed on a calendar showing a day, a week, or a month. A two-month navigation calendar makes it easy to go to a different time period. In the default Calendar Day/Week/Month view, a list of tasks is also displayed in table format.

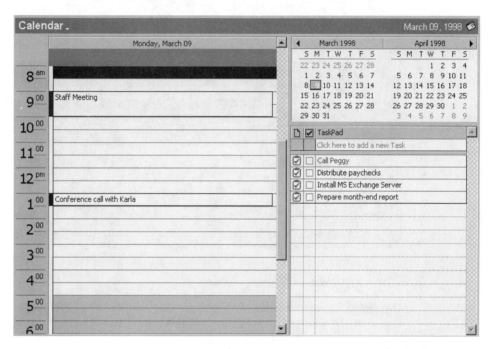

**Icon View**    The default view in Notes; this view display records as icons, much like the icon view in My Computer in Windows or on the Desktop.

Regardless of what view you are in, data is generally sorted alphabetically or in date order. In some views, data is also grouped, which organizes the data according to common values or entries in a field. For example, to see all your contacts within a single company, you could group by company. Grouped views usually are indicated with the word "by" in their name—for example, the By Company and By Category views in Contacts. Figure 2.8 shows an example of contacts grouped By Company.

**FIGURE 2.8**

*Contact data
grouped in the
By Company view*

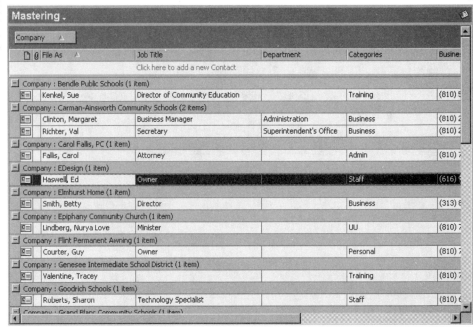

## Changing Your View

Whether you want to switch to one of the predefined views, alter an existing view, or create your own from scratch, Outlook makes it easy to display your data in whatever view most suits your needs or preferences.

**Switching between Views**   To switch to another view, click the View menu, choose Current View, and select one from the list of available views. It's helpful to explore the views available in each module to see which one is closest to the view you want. You may also find that it's valuable to switch to a different view to see your data in a different light—to give yourself a different outlook, so to speak. Figure 2.9 shows the views available in Tasks.

**Rearranging a Table View**   Table views are the easiest view type to alter. (In Chapter 11, you will find more information about defining new views and modifying views.) In Table views, you can rearrange the order of the columns, delete columns, and sort the data with just a few mouse clicks.

To rearrange the order of the columns in a Table view, click the column label in the header row, hold your mouse button down, and drag the column label to its new location. When you see two red arrows pointing to where you want to insert the column, as shown in Figure 2.10, release the mouse button.

PART

I

Overview of
Outlook 2000

**FIGURE 2.9**

*Predefined views available in Tasks*

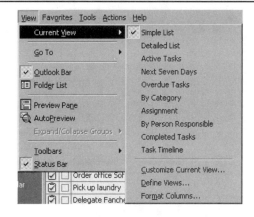

**FIGURE 2.10**

*Dragging a column to a new location*

To delete a column, drag the column off the header row and drop it when you see a large black X appear over the column header, like the one in Figure 2.11.

**FIGURE 2.11**

*Deleting a column*

To sort the data in a different order, click the label of the column on which you want to sort. An upward- or downward-pointing arrow will appear in the label. An upward-pointing arrow, as in the Last Name label shown in Figure 2.12, indicates that the data is sorted in ascending order; a downward-pointing arrow indicates descending order. Click the label again to change the sort direction.

Clicking the column labels is a quick way to sort, but it limits you to one level of sorting. For example, you can order the data by Last Name but not by Last Name and then by First Name. See Chapter 11 for information about how to sort on more than one field.

**FIGURE 2.12**

*Data is sorted in ascending order on the Last Name field.*

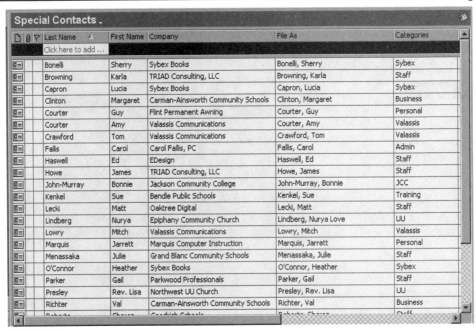

## Entering Data in the Information Viewer

You can enter data directly in the Information Viewer, depending on the particular view that is active. For example, to add a task in Task List view, click at the top of the list where it says Click Here to Add a New Task. Type the task into the text box, and press Enter to add the task to the list.

Not all views allow you to enter new items in the Information Viewer, but you can edit existing data in most of the available views. To edit an item, click once in the field you want to edit. If an insertion point appears, you can edit the data. If it does not, you must edit the data in the corresponding form for that item.

## Using Forms to Enter Data

Creating a new record in any of the modules is as simple as clicking the New button on the Standard toolbar. Remember to switch to the module you want to use before clicking the New button, or to click the drop-down list at the right of the New button to select the desired item. (See the section on toolbars earlier in this chapter for more information about the New button.) The default form for a module contains all of the fields in the module where you can enter data. (It is possible to create custom Outlook forms for any of the modules—see Chapter 20 for more about creating custom forms.)

To open the form for an existing record, double-click the item in the Information Viewer, or right-click the item and choose Open.

## Navigating a Form

When you open a form, such as the Contacts form shown in Figure 2.13, the focus is automatically on the first field in the form. Each form has its own special toolbars with options available only in that module. Use the Tab key to move to the next field and Shift+Tab to move to a previous field. You can also click in any field to activate it.

 **TIP** Each of the default forms has multiple pages that make up the form. Click the tab at the top of the form to move back and forth between form pages.

**FIGURE 2.13**

*The Contacts form*

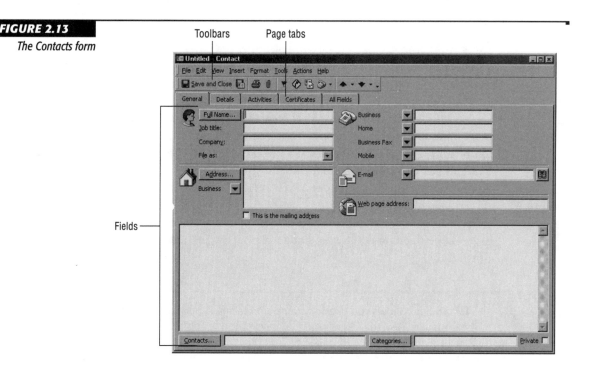

To move from record to record without closing the form, click the Previous Item or Next Item button (the large blue arrows pointing up and down on the far right end of the Standard toolbar)—these buttons move you directly to the next record. Outlook will prompt you to save any changes that you made to the current record before moving on.

The downward-pointing arrows attached to each of these buttons let you move quickly to the first and last records in the module. Click the arrow attached to the Previous Item button and choose First Item in Folder from the menu; click the arrow to the right of the Next Item button and choose Last Item in Folder.

## Entering Text and Numbers

When you enter text in a form, Outlook makes available many of the same options you are used to in Word and other Office programs, such as multiple undos. Other editing options include the following:

- Double-click to select a word, and triple-click to select a line of text.
- Select all text in a field by selecting Edit ➢ Select All.
- Go to the Edit menu to access Cut, Copy, and Paste options, or use the shortcut keys: Ctrl+X to cut, Ctrl+C to copy, and Ctrl+V to paste.

**Using AutoDate**    One of the exciting features of Outlook is the natural-language feature called AutoDate. *Natural-language technology* allows you to enter text in a convenient English sentence or phrase and have the software convert it to regular date format. Outlook applies this technology to the entering of dates and times. For example, if you want to schedule a meeting for three weeks from today but you aren't sure of the date, rather than scrolling through the calendar to find the date, just type **3 weeks from today** into the Date field, and AutoDate will convert the text to the actual date. AutoDate can also convert holidays, but only those with fixed dates. Unfortunately, it cannot convert moveable holidays, such as Hanukkah or Easter, even if you add the appropriate year.

Table 2.1 shows examples of some of the common date descriptions you may want to use. Experiment and you may find more that are particularly useful—or at least entertaining.

**TIP**  Outlook allows you to add national and religious holidays to your calendar, including Christian, Jewish, and Islamic holidays. Choose Tools ➢ Options, click Calendar Options, and then click Add Holidays. Check the holiday groups you will use most often.

**TABLE 2.1: EXAMPLES OF OUTLOOK'S AUTOTEXT FEATURE**

| Dates and Times | Holidays |
|---|---|
| First of Jan | Boxing Day |
| Noon | Cinco de Mayo |
| Next Fri | Christmas |
| Yesterday, tomorrow, today | Halloween |
| One month from today | Independence Day |
| Next month | St. Patrick's Day |
| A week from now | Valentine's Day |
| A month ago | Veterans' Day |

## Saving Data in a Form

Outlook gives you several options for saving data entered in a form. If you have entered some data but you get interrupted and aren't quite finished yet, it's a good idea to choose File ➤ Save to make sure you don't lose your work if something happens to your system before you return. File ➤ Save As lets you save the item as an RTF (Rich Text Format) file on your hard drive or network location. Use this option only if you want to use this item in some other Windows application, such as incorporating the contents into a Word document.

 **TIP** Outlook gives you several file type options, in addition to RTF, when you use the Save As command. You can choose to save as a text file (.txt), an Outlook template (.oft), or a message format (.msg). Contacts can also be saved as vCard files (.vcf) and Calendar items in vCalendar format (.vcs). See Chapter 20 for more information about Outlook templates and Chapter 15 for more about vCards and vCalendars.

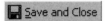    When you have finished entering data in a form, click the Save and Close button on the Standard toolbar or click the Windows Close button (X). If you have made changes to the item, Outlook will prompt you to save it.

# Printing in Outlook

 Printing in Outlook is essentially a WYSIWYG feature (what you see is what you get), which means that whatever is on your screen is pretty close to what will print. If you want to print a list of contacts, display that list in the Information Viewer. If you want to print the contents of an individual e-mail message, open the message before you print. Clicking the Print button on the Standard toolbar will print whatever is in the Information Viewer.

## Special Printing Options

Outlook also has a number of advanced page-setup features, so you can print pages that will fit right into your favorite paper-based planner, such as Day-Timer, Day Runner, and Franklin Day Planner. You can also print attractive schedules and directories from the choices available, such as the directory shown in Figure 2.14.

**FIGURE 2.14**

*A Contacts directory using special printing options*

To access these options, change the view in the Information Viewer to one that most closely matches what you want to print. For example, if you want to print a list of tasks, switch to one of the task list views (View ➢ Current View). When you are ready to print, select File ➢ Page Setup to choose your printing preferences.

In the Page Setup dialog box, shown in Figure 2.15, the first choice you are given is to choose the style of layout that you want. The options presented here depend on the type of items you are printing. Two styles are available in all components:

**FIGURE 2.15**

*The Page Setup dialog box for Tasks*

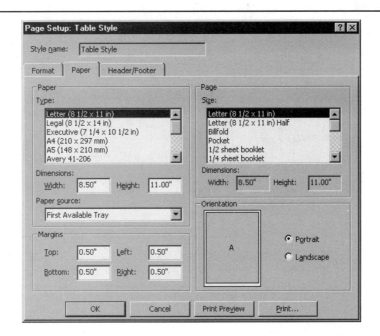

**Table Style**   Data is presented in a traditional format of columns and rows, as shown in Figure 2.16. The biggest drawback is that you have to display the borders, and you can't do anything to make the layout look more attractive.

**FIGURE 2.16**

*An example of the Table Style*

Outstanding Tasks
3/13/98

| ☑ | ! | Subject | Due Date | Cate... |
|---|---|---------|----------|---------|
| ☐ | | Call Peggy | Fri 3/6/98 | |
| ☐ | ! | Install MS Exchange Server | Mon 3/9/98 | |
| ☐ | ! | Abby Referral letters and report changes | Tue 3/10/98 | Abby |
| ☐ | ! | Distribute paychecks | Tue 3/10/98 | |
| ☑ | | Prepare month-end report | Thu 3/12/98 | |
| ☐ | | Order bar code guns | Fri 3/13/98 | Abby |
| ☑ | ↓ | Create Educational Promotional Letter | Fri 3/20/98 | Business |
| ☐ | | Survey DB Reports | Fri 3/27/98 | JCC |
| ☐ | | Order Company Polo Shirts | Thu 4/2/98 | Admin |
| ☐ | | EDD - English Wizard Dictionary | Fri 4/3/98 | JCC |
| ☐ | ! | Submit quarterly sales tax report | Fri 4/3/98 | Admin |
| ☐ | | Make Promotional Bookmarks | Fri 4/17/98 | Business |
| ☐ | ↓ | Develop a "While We Were Here" form | Fri 4/17/98 | Admin |
| ☐ | ! | Database Natural language dictionary for O & Sat | Sun 5/10/98 | HFHS |

**Memo Style** The selected record will print as shown in Figure 2.17. This is the style that will print when you have one item open in a form.

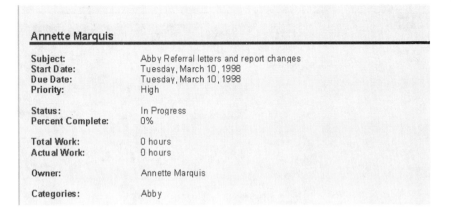

**Annette Marquis**

| | |
|---|---|
| Subject: | Abby Referral letters and report changes |
| Start Date: | Tuesday, March 10, 1998 |
| Due Date: | Tuesday, March 10, 1998 |
| Priority: | High |
| Status: | In Progress |
| Percent Complete: | 0% |
| Total Work: | 0 hours |
| Actual Work: | 0 hours |
| Owner: | Annette Marquis |
| Categories: | Abby |

**TIP** The Calendar has several styles unique to it, such as Daily, Weekly, Monthly, and Tri-fold styles. To find out more about printing calendars, see Chapter 9.

## Using Print Preview

Previewing your document before you print it not only saves time but saves paper. You can get to Print Preview directly from the File menu or from any of the Page Setup dialog boxes. It's helpful to preview the document while you are making Page Setup choices so you can see the results of your selections. The Print Preview toolbar is shown in Figure 2.18.

When you are satisfied with the document's setup, click the Print button from Print Preview, or return to Page Setup and print from there.

# Getting Help When You Are Stuck

Outlook offers a variety of ways to find help with the application in general, or with a specific feature. There are four types of help available within Outlook: Office Assistant, Contents and Index, On-Screen Help, and Online Help.

There is no best way to receive help—it really depends on what you need to know, how detailed the information needs to be, and how badly you want to know it.

## The Ever-Helpful Office Assistants

The Office Assistant was introduced with Office 97 and was a prominent feature in versions 97 and 98 of Outlook. Outlook 2000 changes all that with a completely made-over version of the Office Assistant. The Office Assistant is a dynamic help interface that provides tips, makes suggestions, and helps you search for answers. It's hard to avoid seeing the Office Assistant, so we'll assume you've already been introduced to the default character called Clippit, shown in Figure 2.19.

**FIGURE 2.19**

*Clippit, the Office Assistant*

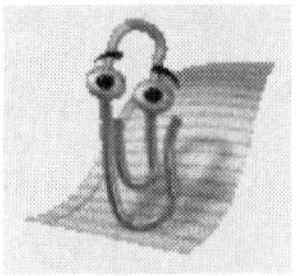

**NOTE** If you have not yet been formally introduced to Clippit, choose Help ➤ Show the Office Assistant, and Clippit will immediately come out to greet you.

Clippit may be cute and cuddly, but there are other interesting Assistants to choose from, the most entertaining of which are The Genius (an Albert Einstein look-alike), Rocky (a perky little puppy), Links (a precious kitty cat), and F1 (a little Spielbergian robot). When you first start Outlook, Clippit will appear and give you some choices, one of which is to simply begin using Outlook immediately. Unless you banish Clippit for good, it will appear either when you meet the help criteria or when you invoke the Office Assistant from the Help menu.

**NOTE** One of Microsoft's goals in creating the Office Assistants was to make our computers seem friendlier, and to help us develop personal relationships with them. To that end, you are welcome to assign a gender to the Office Assistant if you prefer, but we've never been able to figure out whether Clippit is male or female. For now, we'll use the pronoun "it" to refer generally to an Office Assistant.

For example, the Assistant appears with a message whenever there's an easier way to do something, or when you try to use a feature that you haven't installed yet. It also issues warnings and tries to keep you from making irrevocable mistakes. The information box shown in Figure 2.20 is an example of the Office Assistant's desire to help.

**FIGURE 2.20**

*Clippit's AutoArchive message*

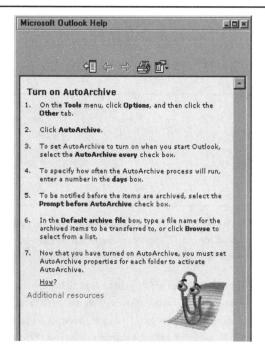

 **TIP** Whenever you see a yellow lightbulb appear over Clippit's head, it means that Clippit has a tip to share with you. Bear in mind, however, that the tip probably has no relationship to anything you are actually doing at the current time—it's just a general way to streamline your work in Office. Click the lightbulb to see the tip.

## Searching the Office Assistant's Memory Banks

When you want to initiate conversation with the Office Assistant, just click Clippit to open a Search window:

The Office Assistant is designed as a natural-language interface, so you can type a normal question in the text box below the question "What would you like to do?" Click the Search button to generate a list of topics related to keywords that the Office Assistant picked up from your question. Figure 2.21 shows the results of the question **How can the Office Assistant help me?**

**FIGURE 2.21**

*A list of related topics from the Office Assistant*

Review the list of topics and choose the one that most closely matches your request. If there are more topics than can appear in the Office Assistant's balloon, click the triangle to the left of See More to move to the second page of the list. You'll find a See Previous option at the top of the second page.

Once you click a topic, you are taken to a normal Help window. To return to the Office Assistant, close the window using the Windows Close button and click the Office Assistant window again. Click the Search button to return to the previous list of topics, or enter a new question in the Search window.

## Closing the Office Assistant

To close the Office Assistant's Help window, click anywhere outside of Clippit's "area." The Office Assistant will stay open but the Help window will close. Just click Clippit again to reactivate it.

If you want to move the Office Assistant off your screen entirely, right-click Clippit and select Hide Clippit or choose Hide the Office Assistant from the Help menu.

While in hiding, the Assistant will gracefully retire to the Office Assistant button on the Standard toolbar. Whenever the Office Assistant thinks you could use some help, it will reappear on the screen. To bring it up yourself, just click the button on the toolbar.

 **NOTE** Some people can't stand the cutesy Office Assistants. If you are one of these people, you may be interested in how to get rid of them completely. Simple: just right-click on the offender and select Options from the menu. In the top-left corner of the resulting dialog box, and under the tabs, is a Use the Office Assistant check box. Uncheck this box, and all items on the Options page will become inactive.

## Customizing the Office Assistant

After you've worked in Outlook for a while, you may want to tone the Office Assistant down a little bit or adjust some of the options to make its interaction more useful to you. The Office Assistant has a number of options that control how involved it is in your work. To access the options, right-click the Office Assistant to open the Office Assistant dialog box.

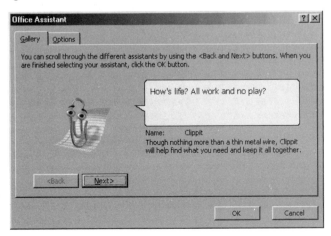

You will find two tabs here: Gallery and Options. The Gallery lets you select the Office Assistant that most appeals to you. In addition to Clippit, you have your choice of Rocky, Links, The Dot, The Genius, F1, Office Logo (animated and inanimate versions), and Mother Nature. None of the Office Assistants is any smarter or more helpful than the others, despite the glowing descriptions under their names. Click OK to select one of the Assistants. You need to have access to the Office 2000 CD or the installation files on your network to install one of the other Assistants. If you don't, all you can do is look at them here. Click Cancel if you don't want to change the Assistant, or click the Options tab to change other Assistant options.

 **WARNING** The Office Assistant is part of Office rather than being specific to each application. As a result, any changes you make in the Office Assistant's options in Outlook will affect the Office Assistant in all of the Office applications.

The Options page, shown in Figure 2.22, is where you can change the Assistant's capabilities and set options regarding tips.

**FIGURE 2.22**

*The Office Assistant's options*

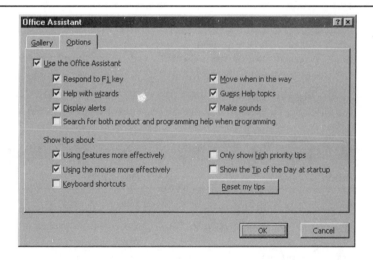

The options with checkmarks in front of them are enabled. Click the check box again to clear an option. To restrict the Assistant to responding only when you specifically request help, clear all the check boxes. The options related to the Assistant's capabilities are described in Table 2.2.

**TABLE 2.2: OFFICE ASSISTANT CAPABILITIES OPTIONS**

| Option | Description |
| --- | --- |
| Respond to F1 Key | Keyboard lovers can press the F1 key to activate the Assistant. |
| Help with Wizards | Provides help with some of the built-in wizards in the Office applications, such as the Letter Wizard. |
| Display Alerts | Shows messages, such as those reminding you to save or to archive your data. |
| Search for Both Product and Programming Help When Programming | When you are programming using Visual Basic, this option makes both product and programming help available. (Outlook uses a different version of Visual Basic called VBScript as well as Visual Basic. See Chapters 21 through 25 for more information.) |
| Move When in the Way | Moves the Assistant out of the way of dialog boxes, and shrinks its window if you haven't used it for five minutes. (Seems to be only the polite thing to do...) |
| Guess Help Topics | Assesses what you are doing and initiates suggestions for doing things more easily, even if you haven't asked for help. |
| Make Sounds | Turn this option off to silence the Assistant's noises. |

The second set of options on the Office Assistant's Options page relates to Tips. Tips are designed to help you get the most out of Outlook. You have the option of having a tip appear each time you start Outlook, or only when you click the Office Assistant's Tip button. Table 2.3 describes the options related to tips.

**TABLE 2.3: OFFICE ASSISTANT TIP OPTIONS**

| Option | Description |
| --- | --- |
| Using Features More Effectively | Displays tips related to program features. |
| Using the Mouse More Effectively | Shows tips related to more effective use of the mouse. |
| Keyboard Shortcuts | Provides you with keyboard shortcuts for operations that can be completed without a mouse. |
| Show Only High Priority Tips | Shows only tips related to vital issues that can help you save time. |

*Continued*

| **TABLE 2.3: OFFICE ASSISTANT TIP OPTIONS (CONTINUED)** | |
| --- | --- |
| Show the Tip of the Day at Startup | Shows you a tip every time you start Outlook. |
| Reset My Tips | Shuffles the deck, so you may see tips you've seen already. |

## Contents and Index

Microsoft has made some rather sweeping changes to the help system in Office 2000. Much of the help is now offered through the Office Assistant; the old way of getting help is still available, but it has been modified. The key difference is that the help is now based on HTML, the language of the World Wide Web. However, this is really only important to developers, because the resulting system works much the same as the old one.

Unless you disable the Office Assistant entirely, the Assistant will take your questions. If the Assistant *is* disabled, then the Help system is displayed when you select Microsoft Outlook Help from the Help menu. This system will take up an entire side of your Desktop and is composed of three tabbed sections: Contents, Answer Wizard, and Index. Microsoft expects most people to use the Assistant to ask English-language questions, but the same functionality is found in the Answer Wizard without having to use the Office Assistant.

The first tab, Contents, displays the list of major content areas available in Outlook Help. Answer Wizard allows a more detailed search of the actual text of the Help topics to locate references to keywords you enter. Index allows you to search for Help topics based on keywords.

To use Contents, click the Contents tab and double-click any of the subject areas, shown in Figure 2.23, to see a list of topics related to that subject. The book icon represents a major subject area. The page with a question mark icon represents an actual Help topic.

Double-click any of the Help topics to open a Help screen that contains information on how to accomplish a particular task, as shown in Figure 2.24. If the Help topic has an item with a double right arrow, click the arrow to move to more detailed help. Click the Back button to return to the previous screen.

Accessing Help through Contents is most useful when you want information about a general topic or when you don't know where to start. If you want to look up a specific topic, you'll probably have better luck using the Index. The Index lets you search for a topic by keyword or phrase, so you can focus in on your topic quickly and easily. To use the Index, just type a keyword in the first text box. As soon as you type a character, the list moves to the topics that begin with that letter. Each letter you type narrows the search even further. In the example shown in Figure 2.25, we typed the letter **A** and then **D**, which was enough to bring up the topic called *Add*. Adding another **D** and an **R** gave us *Address*.

**FIGURE 2.23**

The Contents of
Outlook Help

Contents tab

Subject area

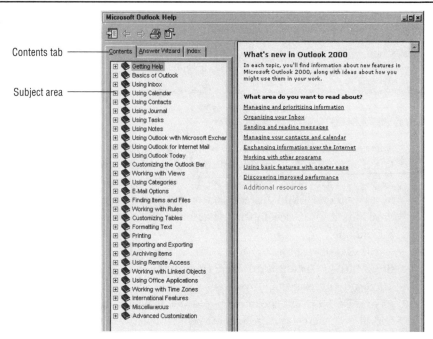

**FIGURE 2.24**

A Help topic

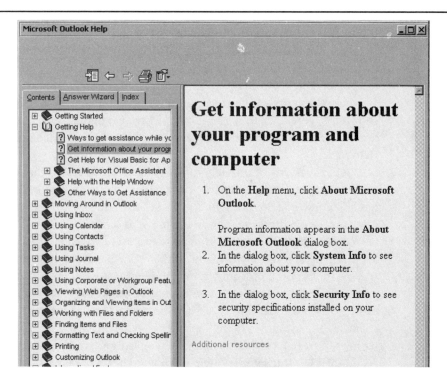

**FIGURE 2.25**

*Zeroing in on a
Help topic*

When you find the topic you are looking for, either double-click the topic or click the Display button to open a list of related topics:

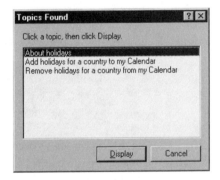

Choose the topic from the Topics Found dialog box, and click Display to see the actual Help topic.

## Help Options

Outlook 2000 offers fewer options than did Outlook 98's Help system. The Options menu no longer exists in Outlook 2000. In fact, there is no longer a menu, period. Microsoft's implementation of HTML-based help leaves a bit to be desired.

Key among the casualties are the ability to Annotate and to easily place bookmarks at commonly visited Help topics and pages. The replacement for bookmarking, which is not immediately obvious, is to drag the link you want to save to the Desktop, which creates a shortcut. Though somewhat useful, it's not nearly as intuitive as the old way of doing things.

Printing remains as easy as ever: just click on the Printer icon when the page you want to print is displayed. Unfortunately, there is nothing else to the new help system. This is all you get.

> **TIP** If you want to print all of the Help topics related to a particular subject, find the subject in Contents and click the Print button. A dialog box will appear, asking you to choose whether to print the selected topic or the selected heading and all of its subtopics.

## On-Screen Help

Sometimes you'll want to know what a particular menu feature does, or what an option on a dialog box is for. You can wade through the Help files, ask the Office Assistant, or access Help that is available right on the screen. There are two kinds of on-screen Help: ToolTips and What's This?

ToolTips are the little yellow notes that appear when you point to a button on a toolbar. They are handy ways to locate a button or to verify that you've selected the correct one. They are optional, so you can choose to display them or not, but they consume only a small amount of your system resources, so you might as well keep them available. To find out more about the options related to ToolTips, see Chapter 12.

 What's This? is a Help option that lets you point to an item on the screen and find a brief definition of the item. It's particularly useful when you want to identify what an option on a menu or a dialog box is for. To access What's This?, choose What's This? from the Help menu, or click the question mark at the top right of a dialog box. When you click the question mark, the mouse pointer changes to an arrow with a question mark attached to it. Click an item on the screen to see a definition of the item.

>  **WARNING** Not all items have definitions attached to them. Don't be surprised if you have to dig up the manual to find out what you were trying to point at.

Unfortunately, What's This? is good for only one item at a time. You have to choose the option again to find out about another item.

## Microsoft Help on the Web

Microsoft has established an incredibly valuable presence on the Web that lets you find out about products, receive technical support, and download add-ons to Outlook and other Microsoft products. As long as you have an Internet connection, you can get to the Microsoft Web site easily by choosing Office on the Web from the Help menu. Unlike previous version of Outlook, Outlook 2000 has only this one link, which takes you directly to the new Office Update Web site.

It's worthwhile spending some time exploring the links related to Outlook. You can find important information here about upgrades, bugs, and service patches to help keep your version of Outlook up-to-date and reasonably trouble-free. You'll find information about how other companies are implementing Outlook in their environments and suggestions for using the features most effectively. You'll also find free add-ons that will help you make the most of Outlook.

Microsoft requires that you register to gain access to technical support and to download software. The only information required, however, is your name, your e-mail address, a password you supply, your country and language, where you use a computer, and what level of search options you want to have available. You don't have to input software registration numbers to access the information. If you try to access the site after you have registered but have forgotten your password, Microsoft will e-mail it back to you.

### What's Next?

Now that you have an idea of the features common to all of Outlook, you're ready to begin working with the individual modules. Chapter 3 will give you a quick overview of each of the six modules so you can actually begin entering your own information.

# CHAPTER 3

# A Quick Tour of Outlook 2000

I f you're like many people, you've waited a long time for a tool like Outlook to get your life in order. Or maybe you already have your life in order and you're excited about adding a powerful tool like Outlook to your organizational system. Whichever description fits you, this chapter will provide a brief overview of each of the six Outlook components that, combined with the general information provided in Chapter 2, will get you started using Outlook in your everyday work and personal life. You can then go on and study the more in-depth chapters of this book with a little experience under your belt.

# Organizing Your Contacts

Life is richer when shared with others, and Outlook is a great tool for communicating and sharing with others. Although you can enter tasks and keep your calendar without entering contacts, Outlook is much more powerful when you are able to relate entries to other people. You probably already keep some sort of address book, whether it's a worn-out, ragged-eared, paper address book, a card file, or an electronic database. Whatever form it's in, it is the best place to start, so keep your address book handy and get ready to see what Outlook can do for you.

 **NOTE** If you currently have an electronic address book in another contact manager, such as ACT or Sidekick, or you have contact data in a spreadsheet or database, skip to Chapter 14 and read the section on importing contacts from other programs before you enter any contacts. If you're interested in using a handheld PC (using Windows CE 2.0), you'll want to take a look at Chapter 18. There you'll find information about synchronizing your Outlook data with Windows CE devices, as well as with other PDAs (personal digital assistants).

When you click the Contacts icon on the Outlook bar, you are taken to a blank Information Viewer with the numbers 123 and the letters of the alphabet down the right-hand side of the window, as shown in Figure 3.1. Once you have entered some contacts, you'll be able to use these buttons to navigate through them.

## Exploring the Contact Form

To enter data about contacts, you must open the Contact form—the easiest way is to double-click a blank row in the Information Viewer. The Contact form is the central storehouse of all kinds of personal information about an individual. It consists of five pages, but most of the data is entered and displayed on the first two.

**FIGURE 3.1**

*An empty Contacts Information Viewer*

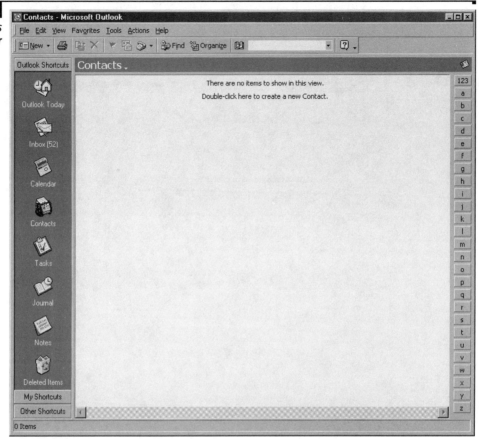

The first page, called the General Page (see Figure 3.2), is where the address book–type information is found: name, address, phone numbers, and other similar contact information. You can enter three different addresses—Business, Home, and Other—and 19 different phone numbers (although only four will display on the form at a time). There's a place for e-mail addresses and even a line for a Web page address for your techno-savvy associates. You'll also find an open text field that allows you to write as much as you would like about the person: where you met, directions to their house, their kids' names, their favorite basketball team—whatever information you want to keep about this person.

The second page, Details, shown in Figure 3.3, is the place to store other kinds of data, such as the department the person works in, their profession, and the names of their manager, their assistant, and even their spouse for those days when you have to reach *someone*. You can also enter important dates, such as birthdays and anniversaries.

Other options on this page allow you to record information so you can communicate with your contact over the Internet in an online meeting or check their online schedule to set up an appointment.

**FIGURE 3.2**

*The General page of the Contact form*

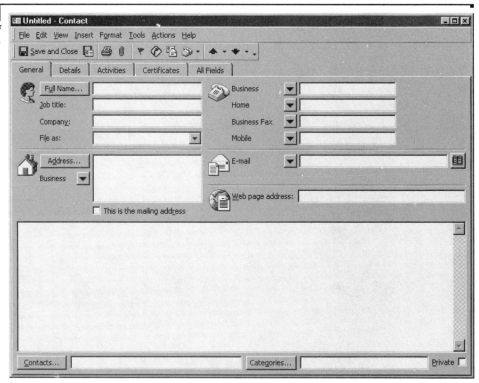

The Activities page, shown in Figure 3.4, is an example of where two of Outlook's modules interact. When you record Journal entries from within the Contact form, they are automatically related to the contact you have open. All of the Journal entries related to the contact can be viewed on the Activities page of the form. You also have the option of viewing the journal entries for this contact in the Journal component, where they will be combined with all your other Journal entries. This is a clear example of the power of Outlook's integration. To find out more about how to integrate the Outlook components, refer to Chapters 4 through 10, which focus on each of the individual components.

The Certificates page, shown in Figure 3.5, is used for importing a contact's digital IDs for use in secure Internet communications. You'll learn more about Certificates in Chapter 4.

**FIGURE 3.3**

*The Details page of the Contact form*

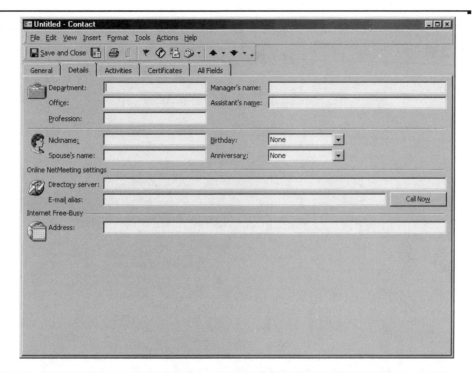

**FIGURE 3.4**

*The Activities page of the Contact form*

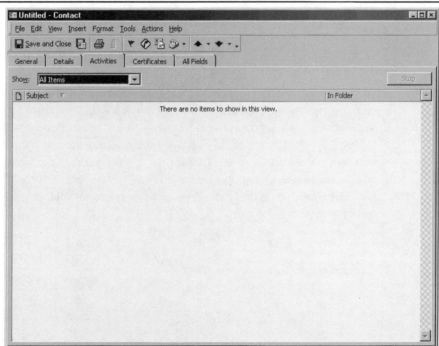

**FIGURE 3.5**

*The Certificates page of the Contact form*

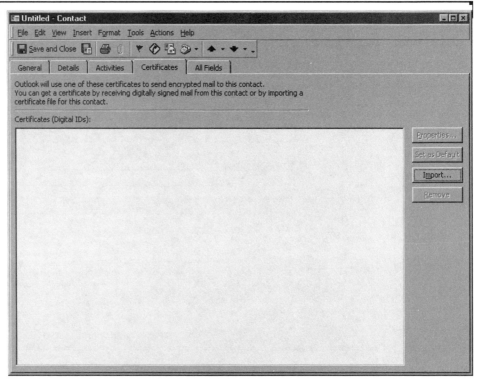

The final page, shown in Figure 3.6, is the All Fields page. Outlook contains literally hundreds of predefined fields—there are 134 fields available in Contacts alone. Only a small number of these are actually displayed on the forms. Contacts, for example, only displays about one-third of the available fields on the Contact form. That doesn't mean you can't enter data in those fields; you just won't have a pretty form to do it in. You can select from several different field lists and enter text directly into the table that is displayed on this page. This allows you to track data that may be less common and therefore does not appear on one of the Contact form's pages. For example, this is a place where you'll find fields for languages, hobbies, children's names, and the contact's personal home page.

**FIGURE 3.6**

*The All Fields page of
the Contact form*

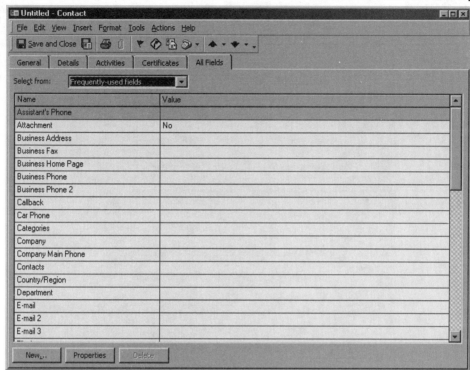

When you've entered all the data for a contact, click the Save and Close button on the Standard toolbar to save your entry in the Contacts folder. This will take you back to the Information Viewer, where you should see an Address Card view of the contact you entered, such as the one in Figure 3.7.

## Now It's Your Turn

Try your hand at entering three or four of your contacts. Even if you just enter their names and e-mail addresses, it will give you something to work with as you learn about other modules in the rest of this chapter. If you come to a field you are unsure about, skip it for now—you can come back to it in Chapter 4, where you'll receive an in-depth look at the Contact form.

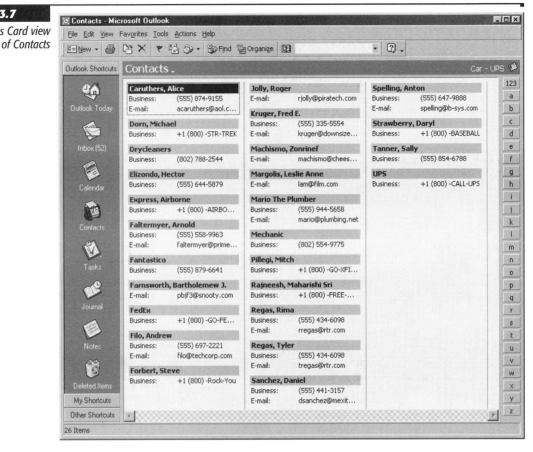

# Sending and Receiving E-mail

E-mail has become one of the most common modes of communication today. From business environments to private homes, more and more people are finding that e-mail is a convenient and productive way to communicate, whether it be within the office or around the globe. Outlook was built as an e-mail messaging system, so this is an area where it really shines.

The e-mail module within Outlook is called Inbox, and it is the only mail-related icon on the Outlook Shortcuts bar, but there are actually four folders directly related to e-mail: Inbox, Outbox, Draft, and Sent Items. You can find the last three by clicking the My Shortcuts button at the bottom of the Outlook bar. Mail that you receive is held in the *Inbox*. Mail that is ready to send is stored temporarily in the *Outbox*; if you're on a network, mail may only stay there for a second or two before it goes on its way. When you are creating an e-mail message but don't quite have it finished yet, you can store it in the *Draft* folder. Copies of mail that you have sent out are stored in the *Sent Items* folder.

Before you can send or receive e-mail messages, you have to have a connection either to the Internet through a modem or to a network server that can process mail, such as a Microsoft Exchange Server. Chapters 17 and 18 and Appendix A will give you more detailed information about configuring Outlook to send and receive e-mail. You also need a your recipient's e-mail address. You can then compose a message using a Message form, shown in Figure 3.8.

**FIGURE 3.8**

*An e-mail
Message form*

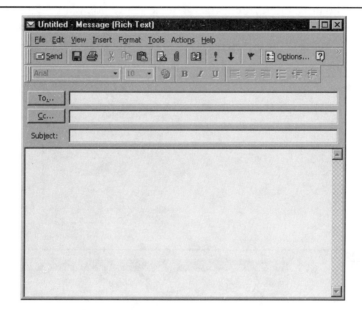

## Composing E-mail

E-mail messages can be short and to the point, or they can go on for pages. If you've never sent an e-mail message before, it's time to take the plunge. If you've entered an e-mail address for one of your contacts, all you have to do is type their first or last name in the To text box. Outlook will search its address lists and try to locate the address for you. If the person has more than one e-mail or fax address, Outlook will let you select the one you want to use, as shown in Figure 3.9. If you haven't entered the e-mail address in Contacts, just type the address into the To box.

You can take files that you created in other applications, such as Word or Excel documents, and send them along as attachments to the e-mail message. The person you've sent the message to can just double-click one of the attachment icons to open the document in their application. (For this to work, the person receiving the file must have a program that can open the file.)

If the person you're sending the message to is also running Outlook, you can send them Outlook items that you've created—contacts, tasks, or calendar events, for example—that they can then copy and paste directly into their Outlook folders.

Outlook gives you a number of useful options through the Message Options dialog box, shown in Figure 3.10, that give you more control over your e-mail messages. For example, you can mark the message as having high importance or being highly sensitive, as would be appropriate for an internal corporate document that contains important financial information. You can indicate that you want a response that tells you the message was delivered or even read (no, they don't attach a camera to the message so you can watch the person read it—all you really know is that someone opened the message).

**FIGURE 3.9**

*Selecting an e-mail address to use when more than one meet the search criteria.*

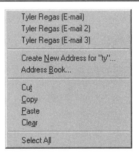

**FIGURE 3.10**

*Message Options dialog box*

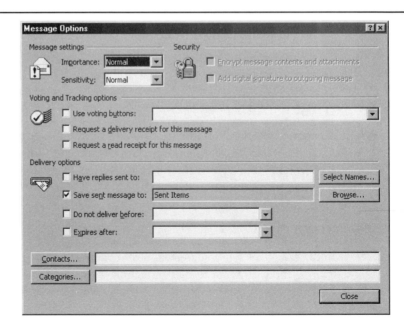

If you're going on a trip and would like someone else to receive the replies to a message you send, you can have the replies sent to anyone of your choosing. You can also choose to have a message delivered after a certain date. This can ensure that your boss doesn't know about the project you left unfinished until you are relaxing on a beach somewhere in the Caribbean.

And when you're working on a team, it sometimes becomes necessary to get the opinions of the other team members about an important issue (like where to go to lunch). Outlook accommodates the democratic process by allowing you to attach voting buttons to your messages, as shown in Figure 3.11. When each person receives the message, they can click a voting button and the message is sent back to you. Outlook automatically tallies the responses for you, so you can immediately see the voting results; you can then decide whether to listen to their opinions or not.

**FIGURE 3.11**

*A message with voting buttons*

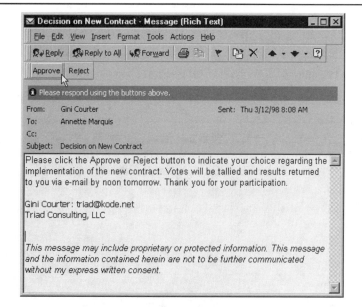

**NOTE** Voting options are available only if all the people you are asking to vote are also running Outlook as a Microsoft Exchange Server client.

When you have your message ready to go, just click the Send button to move the message to your Outbox. Outlook also copies the message and stores it in the Sent Items folder. If you are on a network and working online, the message will be processed from your Outbox automatically. If you have to dial in to your Internet service provider first, you can click the Send and Receive button on the Standard toolbar when you are ready to make the connection. (For more about setting up Internet Services, see Appendix A.)

## Opening the Mail

When mail arrives, it is placed in your Inbox and remains listed in bold type until you double-click it to open it. You can then reply immediately (just click the Reply button) or close it and reply at a later time. If the message might be of value to someone else, you also have the option of forwarding it to as many people as you would like to have see it.

One of the mixed blessings of sending mail is that it improves your chances of receiving some. It's great to hear from old friends, or carry on a conversation with a colleague about a topic of mutual interest, and later be able to refer back to written messages that might previously have been lost in the stream of voice mail. It can also be a bit overwhelming at times when you send out five messages and receive ten in return.

To help you manage the flow of e-mail, Outlook includes the Rules Wizard, shown in Figure 3.12. With the Rules Wizard, you can designate what happens to a message when it is received or after it is sent.

**FIGURE 3.12**

*The Rules Wizard*

As shown in Figure 3.13, the Rules Wizard can evaluate eleven different types of rules. If a message meets the established criteria, such as being from a particular person or looking suspiciously like spam (junk e-mail), a specified action is taken. The Rules Wizard can delete the message, move it to a certain folder, or flag it for special attention, depending on the rules you define.

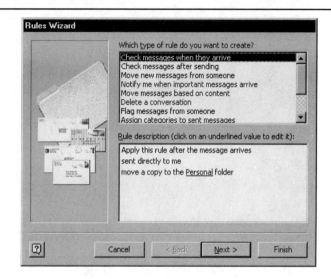

This powerful wizard acts as your personal mail carrier, sorting your messages into useful piles and ultimately helping to bring your e-mail under control.

# Managing Tasks

If you've ever made a list of things you had to do, then you'll love Outlook Tasks. Here you can not only record what you have to do, you can send yourself reminders to make sure you get it done. The task list, shown in Figure 3.14, appears when you click on the Tasks icon on the Outlook bar; there is also a simplified version that is displayed in the default Calendar view.

It's easy to enter tasks right in the Information Viewer; you don't even have to open the Task form. Just click where it says Click Here to Add a New Task.

When you're really serious about managing your tasks, it's time to open the Task form shown in Figure 3.15. Here you can set the due date, the start date, the priority, the status, and how much has been completed. You can set a reminder for the days it's due or, if you prefer, set it for a week ahead of time so you can get started on the task in plenty of time.

**FIGURE 3.14**

*The Tasks list*

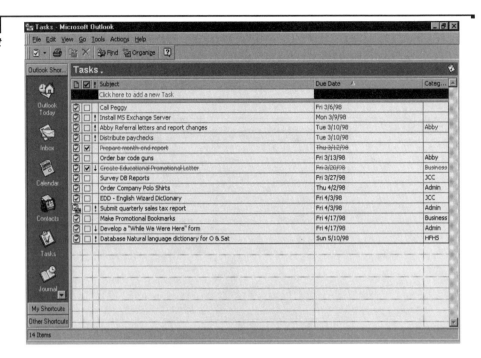

**FIGURE 3.15**

*The Task form*

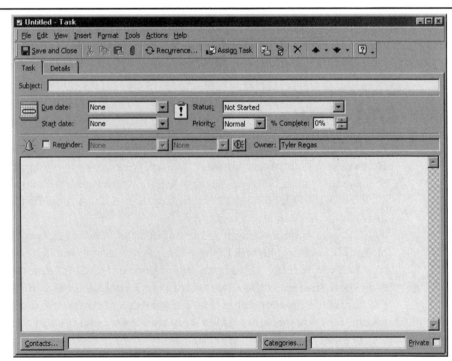

The large text box gives you plenty of space to write a full description. If the task involves working on a document of some sort in another application, you can even create a shortcut to the document right here. Chapter 8 has more details on the procedures involved.

## Passing the Baton

Tasks are often easier to complete if they can be shared. Outlook helps you be even more efficient by allowing you to assign tasks to other people. The downside of this feature is that the other people have the ability to decline your request, but it's better than nothing.

Even when you assign a task to someone else, you can automatically receive updates every time the task is modified (even if the new owner surreptitiously changes the due date). You will also be able to keep a record of when a task was completed and how many hours it took.

Outlook also allows you to pass a task on to more than one person, and for them to pass it along to someone else. This is especially valuable in multilevel organizations, where there is always someone with less seniority to whom you can pass on that less-than-desirable task.

## Staying on Top of Repetitive Tasks

Paper lists are great for portability, but they can't stay ahead of tasks you have to do over and over again, such as a monthly report, your quarterly taxes, or buying a gift for your spouse's birthday. With Outlook, you can enter the task once and use the Recurrence feature, shown in Figure 3.16, to add the task automatically to your list as frequently as you need to do it. You can set a task to recur daily, weekly, monthly, or yearly. It will recur a specific number of times, or from now until forever, if that's what you need.

## It's Your Turn Again

The time has come to gather all those scraps of paper, phone messages, and to-do lists together into one place and start entering them into Outlook. It's a good idea to just start entering your tasks in the Information Viewer. Once you get the hang of it, go to Chapter 8 to learn about all the details.

**FIGURE 3.16**

*Setting a recurring task*

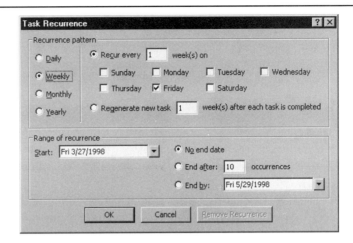

# Keeping Your Calendar

Of all the Outlook modules, the Calendar can be the most valuable tool in organizing your life, but in reality it's often the most difficult for people to get used to. Most people have grown dependent on calendars they can carry with them. The idea of putting important appointments into a computer on a desktop and leaving it there when you have to go somewhere else can be rather disconcerting. It can also be more difficult to look at the big picture on a computer-based system than it is leafing through a calendar a month at a time. Outlook has done a great job of addressing these concerns so that the benefits far exceed the drawbacks in adapting.

The default Calendar view, shown in Figure 3.17, displays a single day's schedule, a date navigator that shows a two-month calendar, and a list of current tasks.

This view is easily changed by clicking the Work Week, Week, or Month button on the Standard toolbar. Clicking any day on the date navigator will take you to that date in the Calendar view.

To enter a new Calendar item, you have to open an Appointment form, shown in Figure 3.18; just double-click the start time of the appointment you want to schedule.

In the Calendar, you are able to track both scheduled appointments and day-long events. The primary distinction between them is that appointments begin and end at specified times; events are day-long occasions that may or may not occupy your time, such as holidays and birthdays.

Whether it is an appointment or an event, you can indicate whether the time is free, busy, tentative, or out-of-the-office. As with Tasks, you can set reminders so that you get to your appointments on time, and you can schedule recurring appointments. All these options are explained in detail in Chapter 9.

PART

Overview of
Outlook 2000

**FIGURE 3.17**

The default
Calendar view

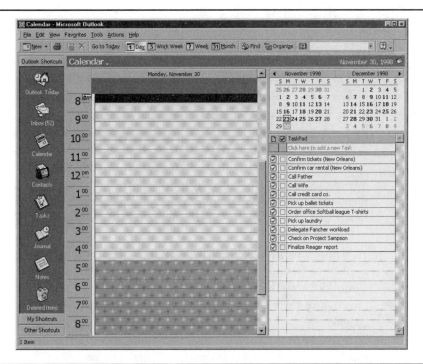

**FIGURE 3.18**

An Appointment form

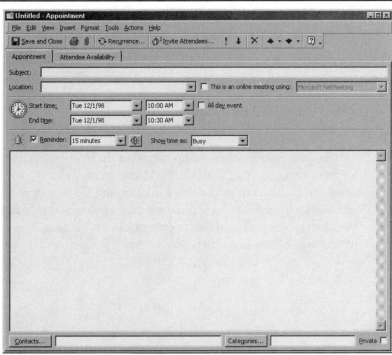

# Scheduling with Others

Time studies in office settings show that secretaries often spend up to 40 percent of their time scheduling and rescheduling meetings; many savvy businesses are trying to reverse that trend. Group scheduling software is one of the hottest desktop applications on the market today. Electronic group scheduling cuts the amount of time spent scheduling meetings from hours to mere minutes. And to top it off, everyone gets a written confirmation of the meeting sent directly to their calendars electronically.

Outlook's group-scheduling features are available when Outlook is running as a mail client under Microsoft Exchange Server. Anyone with an Exchange Server mailbox can use Outlook to schedule meetings with other people on the same network. If meeting rooms and AV equipment are given mailboxes on the network, it's possible to schedule these resources at the same time by inviting them to the meeting along with everyone else.

Many people get nervous when they hear about group scheduling because they don't want everyone else to be able to see their schedule. That fear is totally unfounded because Outlook only lets someone see if you are free, tentatively scheduled, out of the office, or busy during the preferred meeting time—they don't see what you're actually going to be busy doing.

If you are busy during the time someone wants to schedule with you, they can use the AutoPick feature on the Attendee Availability form, shown in Figure 3.19, to search for the next time when you're available. That's all other users can see, unless you've given them permission to actually view your calendar in detail.

 **NOTE** The Attendee Availability form and the Meeting Planner tab of the Meeting form are the same thing. You get to them by different routes, but they are functionally identical. Don't worry about the change of name.

Outlook can even schedule meetings over the Internet using Microsoft NetMeeting or other online meeting software. NetMeeting allows you to place calls to anyone over the Internet, talk with them using a microphone, see them with a computer video camera, work with them in an application on your workstation, use the Whiteboard to sketch diagrams, and send files to everyone in the meeting. It's a fast, efficient way to hold a mini-conference with people who are spread around the world.

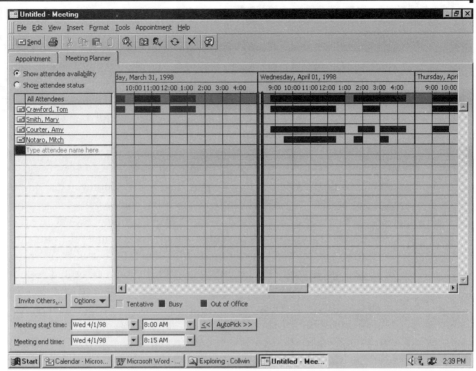

**FIGURE 3.19**

*Viewing meeting
attendee availability*

## Getting Started with the Calendar

If you are new to using an electronic calendar, start by entering your appointments
for the next month or two. Continue to enter your appointments manually into your
paper-based calendar. Begin printing out pages from Outlook's calendar and carrying
them with you. After you get the feel of working with Outlook's Calendar feature, you
can slowly begin to wean yourself off your old system. Chances are that you will still
carry around a printed version of your calendar, but more and more you'll come to
rely on the organization and ease of electronic calendaring with Outlook.

**NOTE** Don't feel like lugging around a sheaf of paper just to keep yourself up-to-the-
minute? You sound like a perfect target for the handheld computer or PDA (personal digital assistant) market. Windows CE-based devices and the wildly popular Palm III handheld
computers are both able to synchronize with Outlook 2000 so you can carry that all important data with you and even read it in the dark (all Palm IIIs and most Windows CE devices
have backlit screens). For more information on PDAs and synchronizing with Outlook, see
Chapter 18.

# Tracking with the Journal

The Journal is an often misunderstood and underused feature of Outlook. Many people are not in the habit of thoroughly documenting phone conversations, meetings, or other work they do, so they often wonder why they need the Journal. The Journal is a tool that helps to make sure you are maintaining appropriate records about your interactions throughout the course of your day. It's an especially useful tool if you spend a lot of time on the phone and need to have some record of your conversations. Rather than jotting down a few notes on a piece of paper and sticking it into a file somewhere, the Journal allows you to enter those notes right into Outlook. The advantages are several, the most obvious being the ability to locate a particular conversation you had months ago by entering a keyword or two into a Search box, or being able to write a report about your contacts with a particular company or contact over a period of several months or even years.

The Journal also can be set to automatically track your work in the other Office applications, so you can determine exactly how much time you spent writing a report or creating a spreadsheet. It's immensely valuable in conducting studies of how employees spend their time, or as a tool to convince your boss you need a raise.

Of course, you can also use the Journal to record the personal secrets you've always kept in one of those blank books with a cat on the cover. Don't worry, each Journal entry can be marked as Private, which prevents other users with whom you share files from having access to it (as long as you choose Exit and Log Off from Outlook's File menu when you leave your computer unattended).

The default view in the Journal is Timeline view, shown in Figure 3.20, which lets you focus on what you accomplished either in a given day or over time.

To create a Journal entry, you must open the Journal Entry form, shown in Figure 3.21, by clicking the New Button drop-down list and choosing Journal Entry. You can select from a number of different entry types, including Phone Call, Task, Meeting, and Conversation. You can also relate the entry to a Contact, although this is easiest to do directly from the Contact form. If you're near your computer when you're on the phone with someone, there's a built-in timer available in the Journal Entry form, so Outlook can clock the length of the conversation automatically.

## Giving It a Try

The best way to get into the habit of using the Journal is to open a person's Contact form every time you place a call to them. Click the Activities tab of the Contact form, and click the New Journal Entry button at the bottom of the page. As soon as you finish the call, record a few notes about your conversation in the Journal. Save and close it and then don't worry about it. It won't be long before you find that you can't recall some critical detail about a conversation you've had. Check in the Journal, and the information you need may be there.

**FIGURE 3.20**

The Journal's
Timeline view

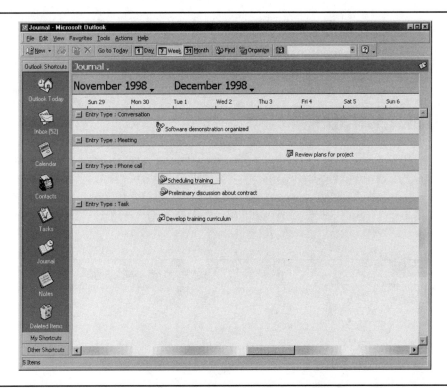

**FIGURE 3.21**

The Journal Entry form

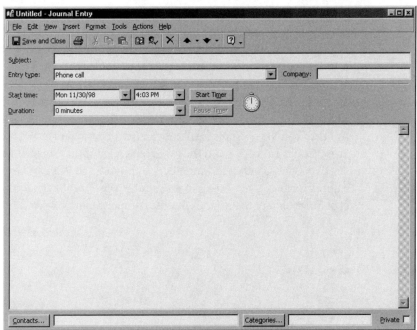

The first time the Journal saves you, you'll be hooked. In the meantime, you will have started to develop the journaling habit, and it won't be long before you'll be giving away those pads of sticky notes by the dozen. Chapter 10 will give you an in-depth look at using the Journal.

# Making Notes

Just to make sure that you never need sticky notes again, Outlook comes with its own form of electronic sticky notes that you can access by clicking the Notes icon on the Outlook bar. These little text windows, shown in Figure 3.22, are designed to let you jot down quick notes, reminders to yourself, phone messages—whatever you don't know where else to put.

**FIGURE 3.22**

*Outlook's electronic
sticky notes*

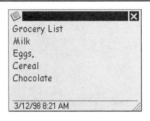

To top it off, Notes can sit outside of the Outlook application, out on the Windows Desktop, as seen in Figure 3.23. Here they can be used as an electronic memo pad where you can jot down the grocery list (yes, you can print Notes), the winning lottery numbers, or directions to someone's house. If you decide that you later want to preserve the note (if you won the lottery, for example), it can easily be converted into a Task or Calendar event. A note can even be moved into the Contacts folder to create a contact from a scrawled phone number or address.

Another benefit of Notes is that it can be used to transfer text to and from PDAs, such as 3Com's PalmPilot and the more recent Palm III. More information on synchronizing data between Outlook and PDAs and handheld PCs can be found in Chapter 18.

Although Notes is not the most powerful of the Outlook modules, it provides an extra level of functionality that rounds out the complete Outlook package.

**FIGURE 3.23**

*Notes can float on the
Windows Desktop.*

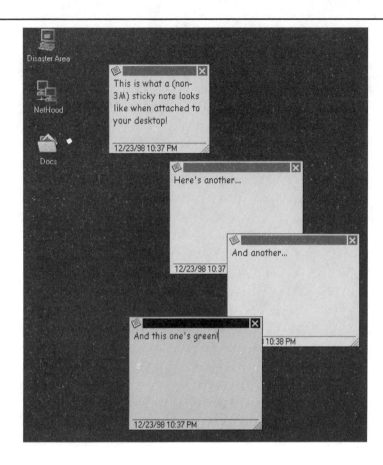

## What's Next

Now that you have an idea of what each of the Outlook modules can do, move on to
Chapter 4 to delve deeper into one of the most crucial building blocks of your information management system: creating contacts.

# PART II

# Mastering the Outlook Components

## LEARN TO:

- *Track your contacts*

- *Send, receive, and organize e-mail and faxes*

- *Manage the things you have to do*

- *Maintain your calendar*

- *Keep records of what you have accomplished and how you spend your time*

CHAPTER **4**

# Managing Contacts with Outlook

O utlook is primarily a communication and organization tool and, as a result, your contacts form the foundation of your Outlook data. Contacts is the place to record name and address information, telephone numbers, e-mail addresses, Web page addresses, and a score of other information pertinent to the people with whom you communicate. If there is a piece of information you need to record about an individual, you can probably find a place for it in Contacts.

## Creating a Contact

In Outlook, a *contact* is an individual or organization you need to maintain information about. The information can be basic—a name and phone number—or include anniversary and birthday information, nicknames, and digital IDs. Outlook is, at its core, a contact management system. The other Outlook components are designed to work in conjunction with your contacts, so the more time you spend developing accurate and useful contact information, the easier it is to use Outlook to schedule meetings, send e-mail and faxes, and document time spent on the phone or visiting in person. You probably have an existing address and phone list in a contact management system, such as a Day Runner, Franklin Planner, or Rolodex. When you start using Outlook, entering data from your current system as Outlook Contacts is the best way to begin. While Outlook is robust enough to help you easily manage business and professional contacts, don't forget to take time to add personal contacts like friends and family members so all your important names, e-mail addresses, phone numbers, and addresses are in one place.

 **TIP** If you have contacts in a computerized contact manager like ACT or ECCO, or in a database like Microsoft Access, you don't have to reenter them. See Chapter 14 for information on how to copy your existing contacts to Outlook.

You enter information about a contact in an Outlook Contact form. A blank form can be opened in several ways. If you're going to be entering a number of contacts, click the Contacts icon in the Outlook shortcut bar to open the Contacts component.

From the menu bar, choose File ➤ New ➤ Contact, or click the New Contact button on the toolbar to open a blank Contact form. If your hands are already on the keyboard, there's no need to grab the mouse: press Ctrl+Shift and the letter C to open a Contact form, shown in Figure 4.1.

**FIGURE 4.1**

*Use Outlook Contact forms to collect and manage information about business and personal contacts.*

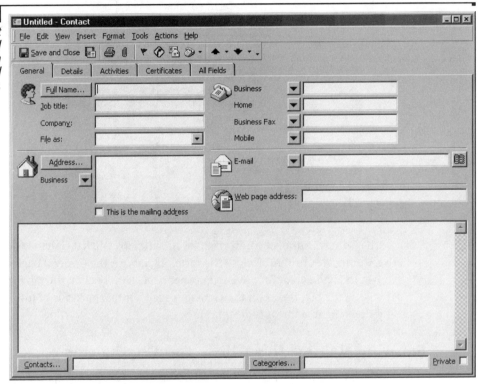

If you're working in another component (for example, the Outlook Calendar), you don't need to switch to Contacts to open a Contact form. You can choose File ➤ New ➤ Contact from the menu bar in any module—you'll just need to look a bit further down the menu selections to find Contact. The same list is attached to the toolbar; click the New Item button's drop-down arrow and select Contact from the menu.

PART

II

Mastering the
Outlook Components

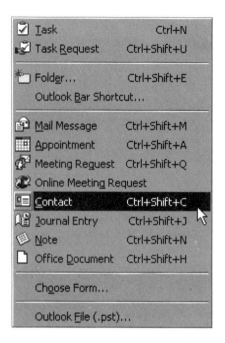

The Contact form is a multi-page form, with tabs labeled General, Details, Activities, Certificates, and All Fields. The form opens with the General page displayed, as shown in Figure 4.1. (To move to another page, simply click the tab for the page.) You'll use the text boxes on the General page to enter the kinds of information usually stored in an address or telephone book.

## Entering Names, Job Titles, and Companies

Begin by entering the contact's name in the first text box on the General page, next to the Full Name button. If you just want to enter the contact's first and last names, that's fine, but you can also include their title, middle name (or initial), and suffix. For example, "Mary Smith", "Dr. Mary Smith", or "Smith, III, Mr. Richard M." are all acceptable ways of entering names.

You don't have to fill all the fields; on the other hand, you can't use information you don't enter. For example, Outlook provides an easy way to quickly create a letter to be sent to a contact. If you might need to send formal correspondence to your friend Bill Jones, take the time to enter Bill's title when you create the Contact. You can always choose to omit the title on a specific piece of correspondence, but you can only include it easily if you've entered it in the Contact form.

When you've finished typing the contact's name, press Enter or Tab to move to the next field. Outlook will parse (separate) the name into parts for storing it. If Outlook can't determine how to separate the parts of the name, or if the name you entered is incomplete (perhaps you entered only a first name in the Full Name field), the Check Full Name dialog box, shown in Figure 4.2, opens so you can verify that Outlook is storing the name correctly.

**FIGURE 4.2**

*The Check Full Name dialog box appears when you need to verify how a name should be stored in Outlook.*

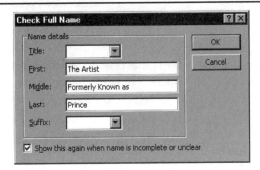

Outlook does a fairly good job of separating names appropriately. However, it doesn't handle some names and titles perfectly. If you enter the titles Dr., Miss, Mr., Mrs., Ms., or Prof., Outlook places them in the Title field. However, if you use other titles—for example, Rev. for a minister, The Honorable for a judge, or Fr. for a priest—Outlook will not recognize them as titles and places them in the First Name field. Names that are composed of two words, such as Jo Anne or von Neumann, may also not be separated correctly into first, middle, and last names. You can edit these fields manually by clicking the Full Name button to open the Check Names dialog box.

**TIP**  To instruct Outlook not to check incomplete or unclear names, clear the check box in the Check Full Name dialog box before clicking OK. To turn checking back on, open a Contact form, click the Full Name button to open the dialog box, turn the option back on, and then click OK.

In the Job Title text box, enter the contact's complete job title. If you don't know the contact's job title, simply leave the field blank. Enter the name of the contact's company in the Company field. If you've already entered another contact from the

PART

II

Mastering the
Outlook Components

same company, make sure you spell and punctuate the company name the same way. Later, you'll probably want to sort your contacts by company. Outlook views each unique spelling of a company name as a separate company. If some of your contacts work for *Sybex* and others for *Sybex, Inc.*, Outlook won't group them together.

In the File As field, either select an entry from the drop-down list or type a new entry to indicate how the contact should be filed.

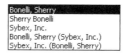

If you choose to file contacts with the first name first, you can still sort them by last name, so it's really a matter of personal preference. If you'll usually look up the company rather than the individual, it's a good idea to file contacts by company name. For example, ABC Graphics assigned Jim as the sales representative to your account, but it might be more useful to file the contact as *ABC Graphics (Jim)* than as just *Jim*—particularly if you have trouble remembering Jim's name.

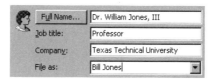

You aren't limited to the choices on the File As drop-down list. Select the text in the File As text box, and then enter the File As text you'd like to use. This allows you to enter formal names for contacts, but store them in a way that makes them easy to retrieve; you can enter Dr. William Jones III as the contact name, but file your friend as Bill Jones so you can find him quickly.

## Entering Contact Addresses

Outlook allows you to store three addresses—Business, Home, and Other—for your contact and designate one of the three as the address you want to use as the contact's primary address. To choose the type of address you want to enter, click the drop-down arrow in the address section, and select the address type from the list. The address type will be displayed to the left of the arrow.

Click in the Address text box and type the address as you would write it on an envelope. Type the street address on the first or first and second lines, pressing Enter to move down a line. Type the city, state or province, country, and zip code or postal code on the last line. If you don't enter a country, Outlook uses the Windows default country.

 **NOTE** The Windows default country is set in the Windows Control Panel under Regional Settings.

When you press Tab to move to the next field, Outlook will check the address just as it did the contact name. If the address is unclear or incomplete, the Check Address dialog box opens, as shown in Figure 4.3. Make sure the information for each field is correct, and then click OK to close the dialog box.

**FIGURE 4.3**

*The Check Address dialog box opens to allow you to verify an incomplete or unclear address.*

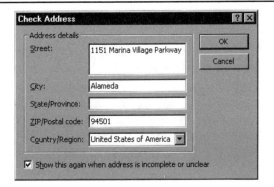

In Outlook, the primary address for a contact is called the mailing address. The mailing address is the address displayed in most views, and is the address used when you merge a Word main document with your Outlook Contacts. By default, the first address you enter for a contact is set as the mailing address. To change the address used as the mailing address, make sure the address you want to use (Home, Business, or Other) is displayed in the Address text box; then click the This Is the Mailing Address check box to make the displayed address the mailing address.

## Entering Contact Telephone Numbers

This is truly the age of connectivity. While three mail addresses are sufficient for nearly everyone you know, it isn't unusual to have five, six, or more telephone numbers to contact one person: home phones, work phones, home and work fax numbers, mobile phones, ISDN numbers, and pager numbers. With Outlook, you can enter up to nineteen different telephone numbers for a contact and display four numbers "at a glance" on the Contact form, as shown in Figure 4.4.

**FIGURE 4.4**

*The Contact form displays four of the nineteen numbers you can enter for a contact.*

When you create a new contact, the four default phone number descriptions displayed are Business, Home, Business Fax, and Mobile. To enter a telephone number for one of those four descriptions, simply click in or tab to the appropriate text box and type in the telephone number. You don't need to enter parentheses around the area code, hyphens, or spaces—just enter the digits in the telephone number, as shown here.

When you move out of the text box, Outlook will automatically format the digits, adding parentheses, spaces, and hyphens. If you enter a seven-digit telephone number, Outlook assumes the phone number is local and adds your area code to the number.

**NOTE** International phone numbers get some rather convoluted treatment. Locate your contact, go to Actions ➢ Call Contact ➢ New Call, and click Dialing Properties. In the Dialing Properties dialog box, check the For Long Distance Calls, Use This Calling Card option and click the Calling Card button. Oddly enough, this does not mean you must have a calling card to make an international call—the default option is None (Direct Dial). Get your call information together and click the International Calls button. In the International Calls dialog box, you will be able to enter all of the information required to make a successful international connection.

**NOTE** If you include letters in your telephone numbers (like 1-800-CALLME), you won't be able to use Outlook's automated dialing program to call this contact.

To enter another type of telephone number, click the drop-down arrow for any of the four text boxes to open the menu of telephone number descriptions.

The telephone number descriptions with checkmarks are those you've already entered. From the menu, choose the description of the telephone number you wish to enter; then enter the number in the text box. When you've finished entering telephone numbers for the contact, the numbers that are displayed in the four text boxes may not be the numbers you use most frequently. That's not a problem—just open the menu next to each text box and, from the menu, select the descriptions for the numbers you want to display. In Figure 4.5, we've displayed the four numbers we use most frequently to reach Bill Jones.

**FIGURE 4.5**

*You can choose to display any four telephone numbers in the Contact form.*

PART

II

Mastering the Outlook Components

# Understanding E-mail Addresses

You can enter up to three e-mail addresses for a contact. The e-mail addresses are labeled E-mail, E-mail 2, and E-mail 3, rather than "Business" and "Home" like mail addresses and telephone numbers. You might think it would be easy to get a contact's home and work e-mail addresses confused, but the e-mail address itself usually contains the information you need.

Internet e-mail addresses have three parts: a username, followed by the "at" symbol (@), and a domain name. The domain name includes the *host name*, and may include a *subdomain name*.

Each e-mail account has its own *username*. In Windows NT, usernames include the owner's name, such as bjones, jonesb, or billjones. Many companies and e-mail providers also add a number to the usernames, so they look like bjones1, or they include the person's middle initial so that Bill Jones and Barbara Jones don't have to fight over who gets to be the "real" bjones.

The username and domain name are separated with the @ symbol. The *domain name* begins with the host name. The *host name* is the name of the server that handles the e-mail account. For example, in the address `bjones@wompus.berkeley.edu`, the host name is "wompus". (On one of the wompus server's hard drives, there's space for Bill Jones to keep his e-mail; the space is called his *mailbox*.) The *subdomain* is "berkeley"— the name or an abbreviated name of the organization that owns the server. The last part of the domain name, following the last period, is the *domain*, which describes the type of organization. Currently, there are six domains used in the United States, and seven additional domains may be added soon (if the politicians make some decisions). Table 4.1 lists the current domains.

**TABLE 4.1: CURRENT DOMAIN NAMES**

| Domain | Type | Example |
|--------|------|---------|
| com | Commercial: for-profit organizations | sybex.com |
| edu | Educational: schools, colleges, and universities | berkeley.edu |
| gov | Governmental: federal, state, and local governmental units | michigan.gov |
| mil | Military: armed services | af.mil |
| net | Network: network access providers | att.net |
| org | Organization: non-profit businesses | uua.org |

Outside of the United States, most domains are a two or three character abbreviation for the country: uk for the United Kingdom, ca for Canada, jp for Japan. An increasing number of educational organizations use us (United States) as their domain rather than edu; the domain name oak.goodrich.k12.mi.us describes a host at Oaktree Elementary in Goodrich Public Schools, a K-12 district in Michigan.

## Entering E-mail Addresses

To enter an e-mail address, enter the entire address, including the username and the domain name. When you move out of the e-mail address text box, Outlook analyzes the address you entered to ensure that it resembles a valid e-mail address. Outlook does *not* check to make sure that the address is the correct e-mail address for this contact, or that the address exists. Outlook just looks for a username, the @ symbol, and a domain name. If all the parts aren't there, Outlook deletes the text you entered.

When you enter inappropriate characters, Outlook is a bit bolder in letting you know about it. Some addresses used within mail systems aren't compatible with the Internet. For example, many CompuServe addresses contain commas: 72557,1546. This is a valid e-mail address for a CompuServe member if you're also a CompuServe member and stay within the CompuServe system, using the CompuServe Information Manager to send your e-mail. However, it's not a valid *Internet* e-mail address. The only punctuation used in Internet addresses are periods and the @ symbol. If you want to send e-mail to this CompuServe address from Outlook or any other Internet mail system, the address must be modified for use on the Internet. (For CompuServe addresses, change the comma to a period and add the CompuServe domain name: *72557.1546@compuserve.com*.)

If you mistakenly enter the CompuServe address as the e-mail address for your contact, Outlook thinks it is two addresses, separated by a comma:

Outlook won't let you save this Contact until you either correct or delete the incorrect e-mail address.

All versions of Outlook support a file format called *Rich Text Format* (*RTF*). With RTF, you can format an e-mail message as you would a Word document, using boldface, italicized text, and different fonts and font colors to provide emphasis in the message. If you're using Outlook on a server at work, your colleagues running Outlook on the network will be able to open RTF messages and see your text in all its formatted glory.

However, not all e-mail services support RTF (and all of your colleagues may not be using Outlook). Services that don't support RTF support *plain text*. If your contact's e-mail service doesn't support RTF, the formatting of the message can make it harder to decipher the actual text of the message because it inserts funny codes. At best, the formatting doesn't appear, and you've spent time formatting for no good reason. If you know that your contact's e-mail service doesn't support RTF, check the Send Using Plain Text check box to send all messages to this contact in plain text. If you leave the check box disabled, messages will be sent in RTF if you choose RTF as your default e-mail format. (You'll find out how to select e-mail formats in Chapter 6.)

The Send Using Plain Text setting is for the Contact and affects all three of the contact's e-mail addresses. What happens when your contact's work e-mail service supports RTF, but their home service does not? In Outlook, you can change an individual e-mail message to plain text or RTF when you create the message. (See Chapter 6 for more information on e-mail options.) If one of the e-mail addresses you use for the contact doesn't support RTF, we suggest that you check the Send Using Plain Text check box.

## Understanding URLs

When you're preparing for a visit, telephone call, or Internet meeting with a contact, you probably have a number of information sources you check. You'll look at your Calendar to see when you met last, check your Task list to ensure that all the tasks related to the contact are complete, and search online for recent news about the contact's organization. The contact's Web site is one of the places you'll want to search. Web sites often contain news about an organization, including recently announced products, promotions, legal actions, press releases, and other information of interest. By adding a *hyperlink* pointing to the URL of the General page on the Contact form, you can access the contact's Web site with one quick click of the mouse.

To find the contact's Web site, you must know the site's Internet address. An individual item you can find on the Internet is called a *resource*. Just as e-mail addresses are used to locate individuals, *Uniform Resource Locators*, or *URLs*, are Internet addresses that contain all the information needed to find a Web site or specific document.

The URL has two parts: the resource and a *protocol* that specifies the method used for retrieving the resource. The protocol for a page on the *World Wide Web* (*WWW*), the graphically based portion of the Internet, is *Hypertext Transfer Protocol* (*http*). Most of the URLs you'll see begin with http, but there are other protocols, including *file transfer protocol* (*ftp*), used on sites where you download files; *gopher*, a search and retrieve protocol used on university database sites; and *file*, used for files located on a local or network drive.

The protocol is followed by a colon and two slashes "://" and then the resource, including directions to the file you want to retrieve. The resource includes the host name and may also include a filename and path.

## Assigning a Web URL to a Contact

When you enter a World Wide Web URL in the Web Page Address text box, you don't need to enter the protocol. Enter the resource name (for example, www.disney.com), and when you leave the text box, Outlook will automatically add http:// to the beginning of the URL. However, if you're entering an address for another type of protocol, such as gopher, telnet, or ftp, you must enter the entire URL, including the protocol and the resource. If you don't, Outlook will still add http:// to the beginning of the URL, and it will be incorrect.

 **NOTE**  If the URL you are pointing to includes standardized components, Outlook can handle things other than WWW links. For instance, ftp.uunet.com will become ftp://uunet.com and gopher.ucla.edu will become gopher://gopher.ucla.edu, which is nice if you need fast access to various different resources. However, if an FTP site begins with a WWW prefix (this is how most ISPs allow access to personal Web space), then it will still be interpreted as a Web address.

To visit the user's Web site, simply point to the URL and the mouse pointer will change to the familiar browser-link hand shape. Double-click to launch your default browser and load the Web page. If the Contact form isn't open, select the contact in any view, and either choose Action ➤ Explore Web Page from the menu bar, or right-click the contact and select Explore Web Page from the shortcut menu.

## Assigning a File URL

File URLs point to addresses on a local area network. A file URL begins with the file:// protocol, followed by the filepath and file name. For example, file://k:\users\BillJones.doc is a file on the K drive in the folder named "users". If there is a space anywhere in the filename or path, you must enclose the address in brackets, using the < and > symbols: for example, <file://c:\My Documents\News About Bill Jones.doc> is a valid URL. Without the < and > symbols, the URL is invalid. There are limitations to the usefulness of assigning URLs to files. You can only access files that you have network permissions for, and if another user moves or renames the files, the URL won't be correct.

# Using Categories

A *category* is a key word or term that you assign to an item. Categories give you a way to sort, group, filter, and locate Contacts, Tasks, and other Outlook items. With the exception of e-mail messages, every type of Outlook item can be sorted and grouped by category. Outlook comes with 20 built-in categories, and you can delete categories or add other categories that reflect your work.

With categories, you can consistently organize items in all modules and use the categories as a way to relate items. If all the contacts, journal entries, tasks, and appointments related to Project XYZ are assigned to the Project XYZ category, you can use Advanced Find (see Chapter 13) or the newly added Categories button located in many forms to locate and display them. You can sort and filter Outlook items based on category within a module. Thoughtful use of categories is a key to Outlook organization.

For example, you can create a category for each department in your organization and assign staff to the appropriate department category. Sorting by category results in a list sorted by department. Print the view, and you've got an employee directory.

To assign a category to a Contact, either type a category description in the Categories text box or click the Categories button on the General page to open the Categories dialog box, shown in Figure 4.6.

**FIGURE 4.6**

*Assign, add, and delete Outlook categories in the Categories dialog box.*

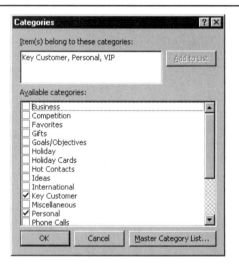

You can add as many categories as you wish to a Contact. Click the check box in front of each category that you wish to assign. Some of the categories, such as Holiday and Time & Expenses don't apply to Contacts. As you click the check boxes, the categories you select are listed in alphabetical order in the Items Belong to These Categories box at the top of the dialog box. When you close the dialog box, the categories are listed in the Categories text box on the General page.

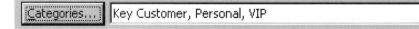

**WARNING** While Outlook allows you to assign multiple categories to items, many Outlook-compatible personal data assistants (PDAs) are more limited. If you intend to synchronize your Outlook Contacts with a PDA, see the owner's manual both for the PDA and the synchronization software before assigning multiple categories to contacts. (See Chapter 18 for more information about PDAs.)

## Adding and Deleting Categories

There are two approaches to changing categories: you can add them one at a time, as you need to use them, or do a bit of planning and add them all at once in the Master Category List. To add a category on the fly, click after the last category in the Items Belong to These Categories list, type a comma and the name of the category, and then click the Add to List button, shown in Figure 4.7. The new category is added to the alphabetized category list.

PART

II

Mastering the
Outlook Components

**FIGURE 4.7**

*Click the Add to List button to add a new category to the Master Category List.*

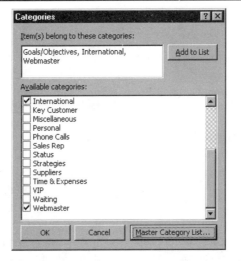

While you can add categories on a whim, we suggest a more planned approach. If you've already entered a hundred Contacts, creating a new category or deleting existing categories often means you'll have to open existing Contacts and change their categories. After you've looked at each of the Outlook components, but before you create too many Contacts, open the Categories dialog box and determine if the categories listed will meet your needs. Delete the categories you don't want to use, and add the categories you require to the Master Category List.

To access the Master Category List from any Outlook form, click the form's Categories button to open the Categories dialog box. Then click the Master Category List button at the bottom of the Categories dialog box. The Master Category List dialog box, shown in Figure 4.8, opens.

To remove a category from the list, select the category and click the Delete button. To add a category, type the category name in the New Category text box and then click the Add button. If you click the Reset button, Outlook returns the Master Category List to the 20 default categories, most of which are visible in Figure 4.8.

**FIGURE 4.8**

*Use the Master Category List dialog box to add or delete Outlook categories.*

Deleting a category from the Master Category List does not delete it from the categories assigned to Contacts. In Figure 4.9, we've opened the Categories dialog box for a Contact after removing two categories, My Friends and Sales Rep, from the Master Category List. The two categories are still assigned to this Contact, but probably won't be assigned to another Contact because they're no longer choices in the list.

This presents a minor problem. When you sort your Contacts by category, every category that's used in a Contact shows up, even after you delete the category from the Master Category List. If you don't want to see Contacts grouped under categories you've deleted from the list, you'll need to open each Contact and delete the category from the Contact.

 **TIP** The same category list is used in all the Outlook modules. So while it might not make sense to have a category for Phone Calls in Contacts, it can be very useful in categorizing Tasks. Create your category list with all the applications in mind.

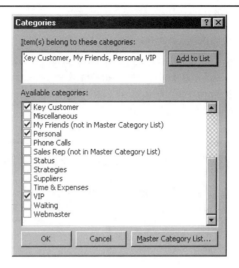

**FIGURE 4.9**

*Categories that have
been deleted from the
Master Category List
are indicated in the
Categories dialog box.*

## Making a Contact Private

If you're using Outlook on a network, other users may have been given permission to share your Contacts folder, or you may place Contacts in a public folder. In the bottom-right corner of the General page, there's a check box marked Private. By enabling the Private setting, you prevent other users from seeing this Contact, even if they have access to your Contacts folder. (For more about shared and public Contact folders, see Part IV of this book, "Configuring Outlook for Your Business.")

## Entering Contact Comments

The large text box at the bottom of the General page is an open area for comments about the contact: anything from quick phrases to eloquent paragraphs. For example, if the contact is your sales representative, you might put your account number in the comments text box. Or you might note hobbies and favorite ice cream flavors. If your company hands out t-shirts, it's a perfect location for shirt sizes.

You can't sort, group, or filter on comments, so don't put information here that you'll want to use to sort views. For example, one Outlook user wanted to be able to organize lists of employees who participated in the company softball league, so they entered the contact's team name as a comment. After entering over seventy team members, they realized the contacts couldn't be sorted by team. (This would have been a good use for categories.)

 **NOTE**  You can use Find to locate text in comments, but it's a time-consuming process.

## Adding Details

On the Details page, shown in Figure 4.10, you'll record less-frequently used information about your contacts. Remember that you can sort and filter your contacts on these fields, so try to use standard entries. If, for example, you want to be able to find all the vice presidents in your Contacts folder, make sure you enter **vice president** the same way for each contact.

**FIGURE 4.10**

*Use the Details page
to record other
information about
your contact.*

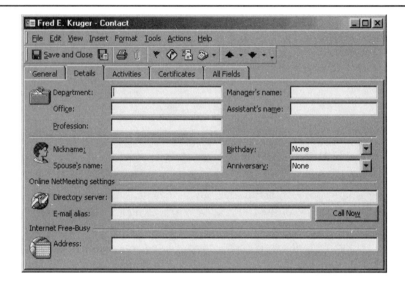

The Birthday and Anniversary fields have a drop-down arrow that opens a calendar. You can type dates in these fields using the *mm/dd/yy* format (3/8/57 for March 8, 1957), or you can select a date from the calendar. The Outlook calendar control is pretty nifty. Click the arrow and the calendar opens, displaying the current month.

To choose the current date, click the Today button on the bottom of the calendar. To enter a different date in the current month, just click the date. Click the arrows in the calendar's header to scroll to the prior month or the next month. This is fairly tedious if you're entering a contact's birthday (unless he was born yesterday!). To scroll more rapidly, point to the name of the month in the header and hold down your mouse button to open a list of calendar pages. Scroll up or down through the list to select the calendar for the month and year you want to display; then select the date from the calendar.

## Entering NetMeeting Addresses

Microsoft NetMeeting is Internet-based collaboration software included with Outlook. With NetMeeting, you can work with one or more contacts "face to face" over the Internet, using video and audio as you would in a video conference call. Some hardware is required to support NetMeeting's high-end video and audio functions.

Even if you don't use these functions, though, NetMeeting has a lot to offer. You can use NetMeeting to send files directly to a meeting attendee, have open chat sessions for brainstorming ideas about projects, diagram ideas on a Net whiteboard, and work with other attendees in real time in shared applications. For information on scheduling online meetings with NetMeeting, see Chapter 15.

NetMeetings are held on an *Internet Locator Server* (*ILS*); each meeting participant must log on to the server, which maintains a list of users so that other participants can find out who is available for a meeting. On the Details page, you can enter two NetMeeting settings. Enter the ILS used for meetings with the contact in the Directory Server text box, and the contact's E-mail Alias (usually their e-mail address), as shown in Figure 4.11.

**PART**

**II**

**Mastering the Outlook Components**

**FIGURE 4.11**

*Enter the ILS and alias the contact uses for NetMeetings in the Details page.*

Online NetMeeting settings

Directory server: ils.microsoft.com

E-mail alias: triad@kode.net      Call Now

## Accessing Your Contact's Schedule on the Internet

*Free/Busy* refers to the times that a user is available (for meetings, including NetMeetings) or unavailable, according to their Outlook Calendar. With Outlook, you can publish your free/busy times in two different ways: in Exchange Server on your local area network, or over the Internet using the iCalendar standard. With Exchange Server, the only people who can see your free/busy times are colleagues who can log on to your network. By publishing your free/busy times on an Internet server, you make the schedule of free time available to people outside your network.

Before users can access your free/busy schedule, you need to tell them where the file that contains the schedule is located. The file can be stored on a server, FTP site, or Web page. If your contact has given you the URL for their free/busy schedule, enter it in the Internet Free/Busy text box on the Details page.

 **NOTE**   For more information on Internet Free/Busy, see Chapters 9 and 15.

# Viewing Journal Entries

After you've entered a contact, Outlook's Journal module helps you track time spent working with or for the contact. Using the Journal, you can automatically record e-mail messages to a contact or manually record information during a phone call or after a meeting with the contact. The Activities page of the Contact form, shown in Figure 4.12, displays both automatic and manual entries related to the contact in a table.

The left column of the table has an icon for the type of entry, which is listed in the second column. The Start column is the start date of the entry; the Subject comes from the Subject line of the Activities form.

## Previewing and Viewing Journal Entries

 If you want to see more detail about each of the entries, right-click anywhere in the Journal window and select the AutoPreview option. The first three lines of the note in each entry will be displayed, as shown in Figure 4.13. It's easy to know if the preview shows all the text in the note, because the end of the note is marked <end>. If the note is longer than the preview, the preview ends with ellipses (…). To turn AutoPreview off, right-click and select AutoPreview again.

To see the entire entry, double-click the entry to open its Journal form.

**FIGURE 4.12**

On the Activities page of the Contact form, you can see all the entries related to the contact.

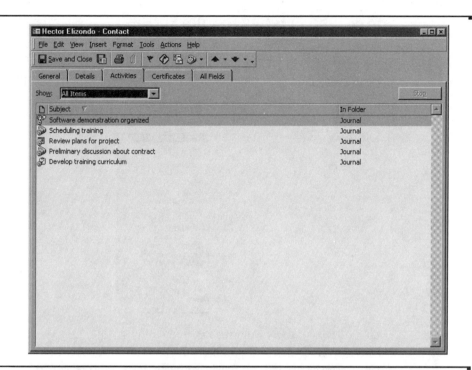

**FIGURE 4.13**

AutoPreview displays the first few lines of the note for the journal entry.

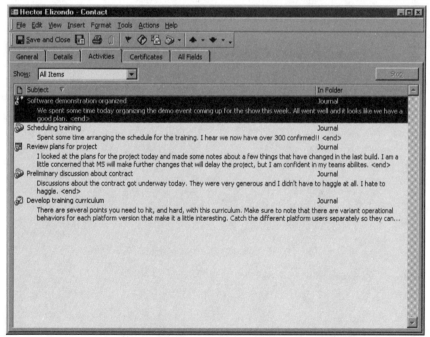

PART

II

Mastering the Outlook Components

## Sorting and Filtering Journal Entries

As with any Outlook view, you can click the heading of a column to sort the entries by the value in the column. For example, to arrange the entries by date and time, click the Start column heading. To filter the entries to show, for example, only phone calls, click the drop-down arrow in the Show control to open the list of types of journal entries, shown here.

Select a type of entry from the list, and Outlook will filter the list to only show the entry type you selected. In Figure 4.14, the journal entries have been filtered so that only Word files are displayed, and they're sorted with the most recent Word file opened first.

**FIGURE 4.14**

*Use the Show drop-down list to filter entries by type.*

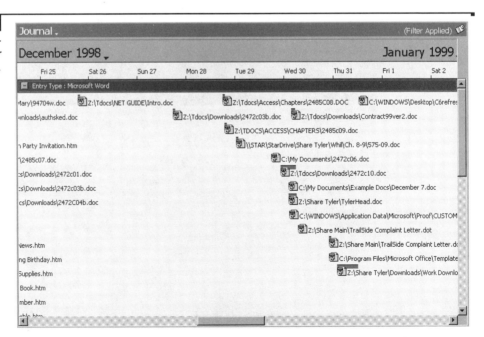

Chapter 10 will give you all the details about manually and automatically recording journal entries.

## Viewing Certificate Information

A *certificate*, or *Digital ID*, is used to verify the identity of the person who sent an e-mail message. Digital IDs have two parts: a *private key*, stored on the owner's computer, and a *public key* that others use to send messages to the owner and verify the authenticity of messages from the owner. The Certificates page of the Contact form shows Digital IDs that you've added for this contact. You can view the properties of the ID, and choose which ID should be used as the default for sending encrypted messages to this contact.

 **NOTE** In Chapter 15, you'll find out how to obtain a personal Digital ID; see Chapter 6 for information on adding other users' IDs to their Contact forms and sending encrypted messages.

## Viewing All Fields

In the Contact form's All Fields page, you can display groups of fields in a table format. The default display is User Defined Fields in this page. Unless someone has customized your Outlook forms and added fields, there won't be any fields displayed—but don't assume that this page is totally useless. Choose Phone Number Fields from the Select From drop-down list, and you'll see all the phone numbers associated with the contact, as shown in Figure 4.15. If you print the form now, you'll get the contact's name and a list of their phone numbers.

## Saving a Contact

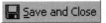 When you've finished entering information in the Contact form, click the Save and Close button, or choose File ➤ Save and Close to save this contact's information and close the form.

 If you're going to be entering another Contact immediately, it's faster to click the Save and New button, or choose File ➤ Save and New to save the current Contact and open a blank form.

PART

**II**

Mastering the
Outlook Components

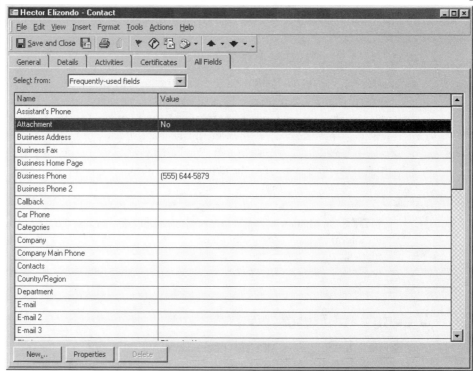

## Adding a New Contact from the Same Company

Once you begin entering Contacts, you'll often have several contacts from the same organization. The contacts have the same business address and the same or similar e-mail addresses and business telephone numbers. Outlook lets you create a Contact based on an existing Contact, so you don't have to enter the business information again. When you've finished entering the first Contact, choose Actions ➢ New Contact from Same Company from the Outlook menu. The first Contact is saved, and the business information for the Contact is held over in the Contact form. Add the new Contact's personal information, and edit the business information as required.

If you've already closed the original Contact, right-click the Contact in the Contact List and choose New Contact from Same Company from the shortcut menu to create a new Contact at the selected Contact's company. When you've entered the last Contact, click Save and Close to close the Contacts form.

## Deleting a Contact

To delete a Contact, select the Contact or open the Contact form. Then choose Edit ➤ Delete from the menu, or right-click and choose Delete from the shortcut menu, or press Ctrl+D. You will not be prompted to confirm the deletion. However, if you immediately notice that you've deleted a Contact erroneously, you can choose Undo Delete from the Edit menu to restore the Contact.

# Using Predefined Views

The Contacts component has seven predefined views: Address Cards, Detailed Address Cards, Phone List, By Category, By Company, By Location, and By Follow Up Flag. To switch to another view, choose View ➤ Current View on the menu bar, and select the view you want to apply.

### Card Views

The Address Card view, shown in Figure 4.16, displays basic information about the contact: File As name, mailing address, e-mail address, and telephone numbers. The Detailed Address Cards display additional data, including full name, job title, company name, and categories. Card views have a handy feature: an index on the right side that lets you quickly go to Contacts by the File By name. Clicking the *S*, for example, takes you to contacts whose File By name begins with the letter *S*. Many users choose either Address Cards or Detailed Address Cards as their default view for Contacts.

### List Views

The remaining predefined views are list views: Phone List, By Company, By Category, By Location, and By Follow Up Flag. All the list views look and function like Excel worksheets. Field names appear at the top of the column, with records below in rows. You use the horizontal and vertical scroll bars to move up and down and pan side to side through the list. The Phone List, shown in Figure 4.17, shows Full Name, Company Name, File As Name, and telephone numbers for each contact.

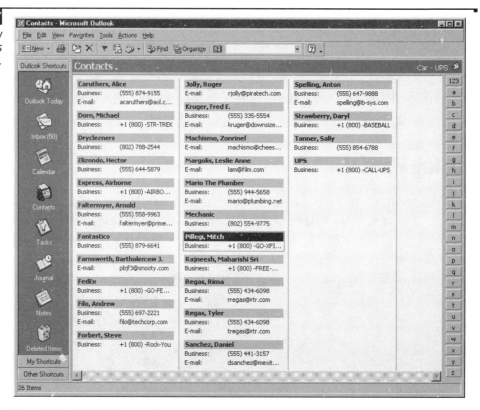

| | | | Full Name | Company | File As △ | Business Phone | Business Fax |
|---|---|---|---|---|---|---|---|
| | | | Click here to add a new C… | | | | |
| | | | | Ameritech Small … | Ameritech Small Business Services | (800) 555-8959 | |
| | | | Glenn Barton | Mission Health Care | Barton, Glenn | (810) 555-5659 | |
| | | | Pamela Barton | Johnson' Electro… | Barton, Pamela | (508) 555-5656 | |
| | | | Karla Browning | TRIAD Consultin… | Browning, Karla | | (810) 555-2284 |
| | | | Peggy Cartoni | Friend | Cartoni, Peggy | (810) 555-7845 | |
| | | | Margaret Clinton | Carman-Ainswort… | Clinton, Margaret | (810) 555-8565 | |
| | | | Amy Courter | Valassis Communi… | Courter, Amy | (800) 555-8959 | (313) 555-8956 |
| | | | Guy Courter | Flint Permanent … | Courter, Guy | (810) 555-8959 | |
| | | | Tom Crawford | Tom's Diner | Crawford, Tom | (800) 555-8956 | (313) 555-8962 |
| | | | Mary Rose Evans | PTR | Evans, Mary Rose | (248) 555-9856 | |
| | | | Kent Fields | Sybex Books | Fields, Kent | (800) 555-5555 | (510) 555-5555 |
| | | | Jacklyn Flocker | Palatine Public S… | Flocker, Jacklyn | (517) 555-4141 | |
| | | | Cindy Graystone | Church | Graystone, Cindy | | |
| | | | Ingrid Guntner | Church | Guntner, Ingrid | | |
| | | | Terrel F. Hatcher | Spring Valley Co… | Hatcher, Terrel F. | (616) 555-4151 | (616) 555-4675 |
| | | | David T. Holstein | Mission Communi… | Holstein, David T. | (616) 555-4545 | (616) 555-1214 |
| | | | Kimberly Mastersons | Mission Health Sy… | Mastersons, Kimberly | (549) 555-8959 | (549) 555-5956 |
| | | | Rosemary Walker | | Walker, Rosemary | | |
| | | | Gloria Wright | Genesee Interme… | Wright, Gloria | (810) 555-4545 | (810) 555-7878 |

The By Category, By Company, By Location, and By Follow Up Flag views are all grouped views. When you open the By Company view, a dark bar with the company name separates contacts from each company. You can expand or collapse the Contact detail for each company. Click the Collapse (minus) button on the company bar to hide the company's contacts and change the Collapse button to an Expand (plus) button. Click the Expand button to see all the Contacts for that company. If you work in a field where employees begin mailing out resumes the second week on the job, Outlook has a feature you'll appreciate. To move a Contact from one company to another, select the Contact and drag it into the new company, as shown in Figure 4.18.

**FIGURE 4.18**

*In the By Company view, you can "transfer" employees from one company to another.*

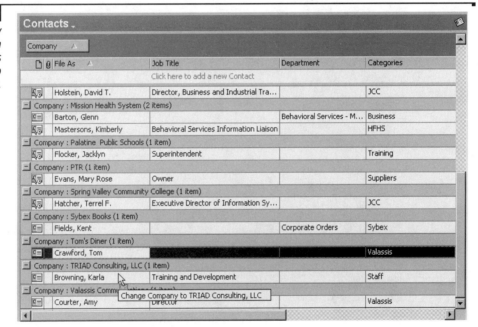

PART

II

Mastering the
Outlook Components

**NOTE** You can create your own views, adding and deleting fields and setting up custom grouping. For information on creating views, see Chapter 11.

## Locating a Contact

The easiest way to search through a long list of contacts is by using Find, which can help you quickly locate items in any view. Click the Find button on the Standard toolbar to open the Find pane at the top of the list, as shown in Figure 4.19. If you're looking for a contact, enter all or part of their name, company name, or address in the Look For text box. To search all the fields in the contact, including the Comments field, leave Search All Text in the Contact check box enabled. Disabling the check box limits the search to the fields displayed at the left and speeds up the search.

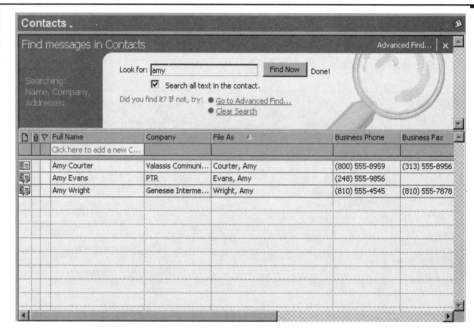

**FIGURE 4.19**

*The Find pane opens at the top of the Contact list.*

Click the Find Now button to find all the contacts that include the text you entered. Figure 4.20 shows the results obtained when searching for "Amy." When you find the contact you're looking for, just double-click on the contact to open the Contact form.

If you can't find the contact you're looking for in the Find pane, or if you're looking for text in specific fields or based on criteria other than text, consider using Advanced Find.

Click the Advanced Find button at the top of the Find pane to open the Advanced Find dialog box. On the Contact page of the dialog box, you can select the type of item, location, and fields to be searched. Open the topmost In drop-down list and select Name Fields Only; then click Find Now. Even if you just remember the person's first name or a part of their last name, Outlook will find every occurrence of those letters in the Name fields, without searching other fields.

Using the Time options, you can search for Contacts that were created or modified within a particular time frame. For example, you can find Contacts you created today or modified in the last week. In Figure 4.21, we're using Advanced Find to locate contacts modified in the last seven days with *Oak* in the company name.

**FIGURE 4.20**

*Use Find to locate a contact based on their name, address, or text anywhere in the Contact.*

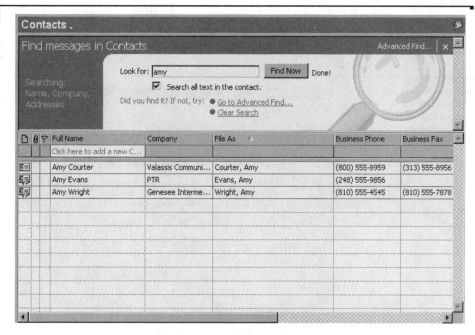

**FIGURE 4.21**

*Advanced Find lets you search for Contacts based on when they were created or modified.*

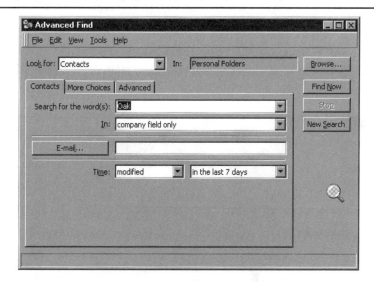

Flip to the More Choices page by clicking its tab, and you can find Contacts by categories. Click the Categories button to open the Categories dialog box. Select the categories you want to search for. If you choose more than one category, Outlook treats the selection as a union and finds Contacts assigned to any of the categories you selected.

PART

II

Mastering the
Outlook Components

Click OK to close the Categories dialog box, and then click Find Now to find the contacts who are assigned to the categories you chose. Figure 4.22 shows a search for Contacts with the Business or Ideas categories.

**FIGURE 4.22**

*Use the More Choices page to search for contacts by category.*

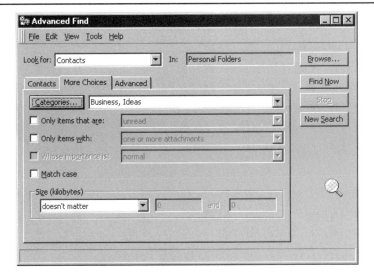

On the Advanced page of the Advanced Find dialog box, shown in Figure 4.23, you can enter multiple, specific search criteria based on the values in fields. To enter a search criterion, click the Field button to open a menu of Outlook field types. Choose a type (for example, All Contact Fields), and then select the field from the menu.

**FIGURE 4.23**

*Use the Advanced page to find contacts based on one or more specific fields.*

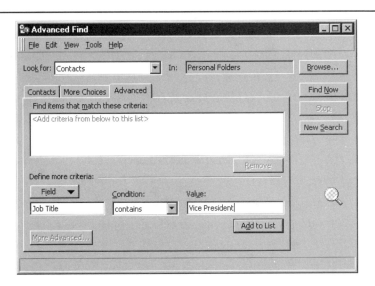

From the Condition text box, choose the appropriate operator. The operators in the list depend on the type of data that will be in the field you selected. For text fields, you'll choose between Contains, Is, Doesn't Contain, Is Empty, and Is Not Empty. Date fields have the same operators as the Time controls in the Contacts page: Anytime, Today, In the Last Seven Days, and so on. In the Value text box, enter the value you're looking for with Contains or Is, or not looking for if you use the Doesn't Contain operator. You don't have to enter a value for Is Empty or Is Not Empty. When you're finished building the criterion, click the Add to List button to add it to the Find Items list. To add another criterion, build it, and then add it to the list. When you've entered all the advanced criteria you need to conduct your search, click Find Now to find the contacts that match all the criteria you entered. In Figure 4.23, we're creating criteria to search for contacts with Vice President in their job title.

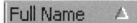

You can enter search criteria on more than one Find page and find, for example, Contacts created in the last seven days in the Business category. If you're finished with one search and want to search for other Contacts, click the New Search button to clear the criteria you entered from all three pages of the dialog box.

When you're finished with Advanced Find, choose File ➤ Close or click the close button on the dialog box title bar to close Advanced Find and return to Contacts. To close the Find pane, click the close button at the top of the pane or switch to another view.

## Sorting Contacts

Sorting is easy in any list view. To sort by a field in ascending order, click the heading at the top of the field. An upward pointing arrow is displayed in the field heading to remind you that it is sorted in ascending order.

> Full Name    △

Click the heading again, and you sort the list in descending order. When the list is sorted in descending order, the heading arrow for the sort-by column points down.

# Printing Contacts

If you've ever been asked to create an employee directory for your organization, you know the potential pitfalls. Someone (probably you) has to enter data, choose a layout for the directory, format all the data, add headings. By the time you actually send the directory to your printer, you've invested a lot of time in design issues. Outlook includes a number of printing options that will help you quickly and easily create directories, phone lists, and other print resources that formerly took hours or days to create.

When you choose File ➤ Page Setup from the Outlook menu bar, you are presented with a list of styles to choose from. The available styles are dependent on the current view, so before you print, select the view that most closely resembles the printed output you want. For a simple employee telephone list, choose one of the list views. For complete names and addresses, choose a card view. Table 4.2 identifies the Contact views and their corresponding print styles.

**TABLE 4.2: PAGE SETUP STYLES**

| Style | View | Default Printed Output |
|---|---|---|
| Table | table | The view as it appears on the screen |
| Memo | table | Data for the selected contact(s), printed in portrait view, with your name at the top of each entry |
| Phone Directory | table | Two-column listing of names and phone numbers, with a heading for each letter of the alphabet (very slick) |
| Card | card | A two-column listing of names and contact information |
| Small Booklet | card | A multiple section listing of names and contact information prepared for two-sided printing |
| Medium Booklet | card | A two-column listing of names and contact information prepared for two-sided printing |

Before you print, it's a good idea to look at each of the styles. Choose File ➤ Page Setup and select the style from the menu.

If you select the medium or small booklet style and your printer prints one-sided output, Outlook will ask if you wish to continue. Click OK to open the Page Setup dialog box, shown in Figure 4.24. The dialog box has three pages: Format, Paper, and Header/Footer.

**FIGURE 4.24**

*Use the Page Setup dialog box to set printing options for the style you selected.*

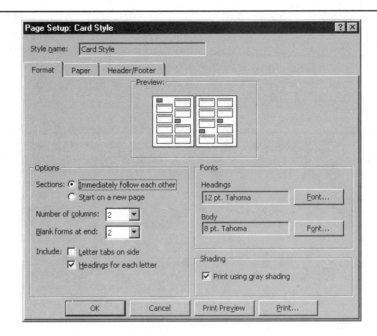

In the Format page, choose the format options you would like to apply to the style:

**Sections**   To have each letter of the alphabet begin on a new page, choose Start on a New Page.

**Number of Columns**   As you increase the number of columns, Outlook decreases the font size.

**Blank Forms at End**   This option allows users to add new entries in the correct section.

**Letter Tabs on Side**   This check box will generate an index, like the index used in Address Card view, with the section's letters highlighted.

**Headings for Each Letter**   This feature gives you a highlighted letter at the beginning of each alphabetic section.

**Fonts**   These lists offer you choices of fonts for the letter headings and body.

**Print Using Gray Shading**   This check box enables or disables gray shading in the letter tabs, letter headings, and contact names.

After you make a change, you can click the Print Preview button to see how the change affects your printed output. In Figure 4.25, we're previewing a booklet with letter tabs on the side and headings for each letter. Click anywhere in the preview to zoom in on the detail; click again to zoom out. To close Print Preview and return to the Page Setup dialog box, choose Page Setup. If you click Close, you close both Print Preview *and* Page Setup.

**FIGURE 4.25**

*Use Print Preview to see how your format change affects the printed document.*

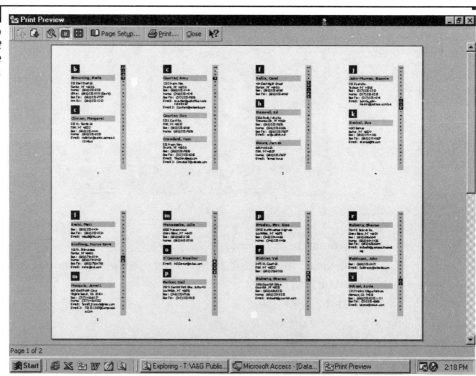

On the Paper page of the Page Setup dialog box (see Figure 4.26), choose the settings that describe the dimensions of the paper you're going to use.

On the Header/Footer page, shown in Figure 4.27, you can create a header and footer that contain text and document information. Headers and footers appear on each page of the finished product. If you're creating a ¹/₄ page booklet, a header will appear four times on the printed sheet, so it will be at the top of each page after it is folded.

**FIGURE 4.26**

On the Paper page of the Print Setup dialog box, specify the size and location of the paper and size of the booklet.

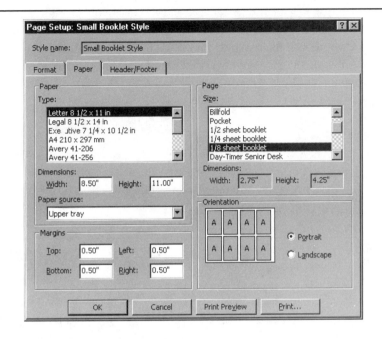

**FIGURE 4.27**

Create custom headers and footers in the Header/Footer page.

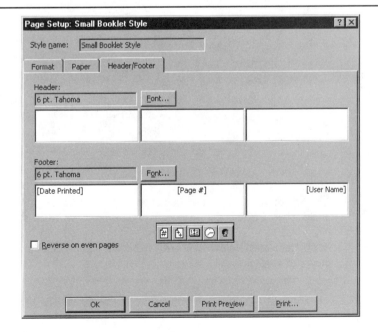

PART

II

Mastering the Outlook Components

The header and footer each have a left-aligned, centered, and right-aligned section. To include text in the header or footer, just click in the appropriate section and begin typing. Use the five buttons on the toolbar below the header and footer sections to include the page number, total number of pages, date printed, time printed, or username in the header or footer.

When you've finished setting print options, click the Print button to open the Print dialog box, shown in Figure 4.28. Select a printer from the Name list, the range of pages to print, and the number of copies. Click the OK button to send the job to the printer.

**FIGURE 4.28**

*Change settings in the Print dialog box to specify the number of copies, range, and number of pages to print.*

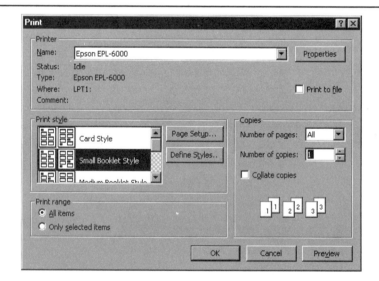

 **TIP** If you want to print a booklet with back to front pages and you have a one-sided printer, choose Odd in the Number of Pages drop-down list, and print all the odd-numbered pages first. Turn the sheets over and reinsert them into the printer. Choose Even to print the rest of the pages. Outlook will order the pages so they can be folded into a booklet when they're all printed.

The printing process is the same in all the Outlook components. Begin by selecting a view that supports the output you want. Preview the output in Print Preview. Change views, if necessary, and then adjust the Page Setup options to further define the final output. Finally, send the job to the printer, and think about how easy this was.

After you've entered your contacts into Outlook, and you can locate the data you need and print your Contact information successfully, you're ready to use Outlook's communication features to stay in touch.

## What's Next

Chapter 5 covers how to call a contact, create a letter to mail to them, and send them a fax. Chapters 6 and 7 will then guide you through the world of e-mail communications.

PART

II

Mastering the
Outlook Components

# CHAPTER 5

# Communicating with Your Contacts

O utlook is much more than a storehouse for your information. You can put Outlook to work dialing phone numbers, sending and receiving faxes, and even drawing maps to your contacts' addresses. Outlook comes equipped with a number of add-on applications and wizards, such as AutoDialer to automatically dial phone numbers, Symantec WinFax or Microsoft Fax to manage your fax correspondence, and the Letter Wizard to help you create a letter using Microsoft Word. If you have Internet access, Outlook will whisk you directly to the Microsoft Expedia Maps Web site, where you can print a map to your contact's exact street address.

## Dialing a Contact

Newer multimedia computers support a full range of telephony accessories, including headsets and built-in or monitor-mounted microphones. You don't need a lot of fancy hardware to use Outlook's telephony features. As long as you have a telephone connected to the line your modem uses, you can place telephone calls from Outlook. You don't need a fast modem to make telephone calls—your voice is simply routed from one port in the modem to the other. Outlook's telephone dialing program is called *Auto-Dialer*. You must be in Contacts to use AutoDialer.

You can begin by opening the Contact form for the contact you want to call. Then, click the drop-down arrow on the AutoDialer button to open the menu of telephone numbers for the contact.

All the contact's numbers are listed, including, but not limited to, the four numbers displayed in the General page of the Contact form. Choose a number from the list, and the New Call dialog box opens.

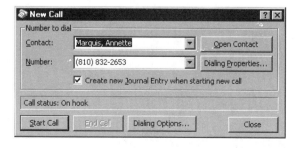

The Contact's name appears in the Contact text box, and the phone number you selected is in the Number text box. You can click the arrow in the Number box to see other numbers.

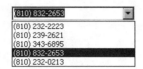

 **TIP** Unfortunately, the numbers in this list have no descriptions. If you need to select a different number and don't know which number is home, business, or pager, click the Open Contact button to close the New Call dialog box. Then you can reopen the AutoDialer menu, which has the descriptions, from the toolbar.

If you know your contact's telephone number, or have it in your telephone's speed dial listing, you could have dialed the number by now. However, AutoDialer is popular because of the check box that appears under the number. One simple click, and Outlook will open a journal entry for the contact while you place the call.

☑ Create new Journal Entry when starting new call

Click the Start Call button to have Outlook dial the number. If the Create New Journal entry check box is enabled, a new Journal Entry form opens automatically, as shown in Figure 5.1.

The New Call dialog box is still open (and remains open during the call). The Call Status reads *Connected*, and the End Call button is enabled.

When you've completed your call, click the End Call button to close the connection. Outlook automatically pauses the timer in the Journal item, and enters the total time for the call in the Duration control. If you'd like to make some notes about the call, enter them in the open notes area in the Journal item. You should also change the subject to describe the contents of the telephone call and assign a category if you wish. When you've finished entering information in the Journal form, click the Save and Close button to close the Journal Entry. If you switch to the Activities page in the Contact form, the entry will appear in the list of Journal Entries for the contact.

PART

**II**

Mastering the
Outlook Components

**FIGURE 5.1**

*You can have Outlook automatically create a new journal entry for an AutoDial call.*

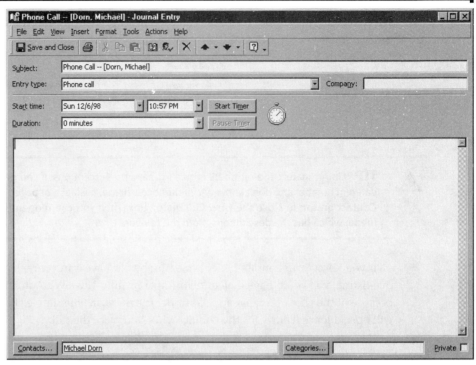

You don't have to open the Contact form to call a contact. In the Contacts view list, select the contact, and then choose the contact's phone number from the Auto-Dialer button's menu. Or right-click on the contact and choose AutoDialer from the shortcut menu:

# Changing Dialing Properties

When you installed Outlook, you were prompted to establish your computer's *dialing properties*—the settings for initiating calls from your number. You may never need to change the dialing properties on a desktop machine; on the other hand, users who travel often need to change dialing properties. You'll need to change the dialing properties if:

- You use your computer in two or more locations with different area codes or numbers to access outside lines
- Your area code changes
- The number you dial to access an outside line changes
- You want to use a calling card from one or more locations
- You add call waiting services to the line connected to your modem
- The numbers used to access an "outside line" at your workplace change

With Outlook, you can create and save a "dialing profile" for each location that you visit or each calling card that you use for long distance calls.

Dialing Properties...

To change dialing properties, click the Dialing Properties button in the New Call dialog box to open the Dialing Properties dialog box, shown in Figure 5.2.

PART

II

Mastering the
Outlook Components

**FIGURE 5.2**

*Use the Dialing Properties dialog box to establish or choose settings for other locations.*

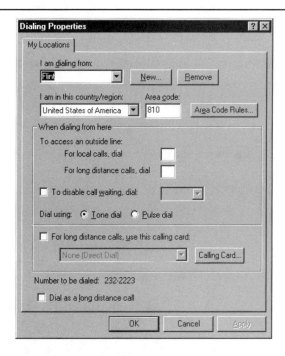

At the top of the dialog box, you'll see the location drop-down list, labeled I Am Dialing From. There is no default location; the location that is displayed when the dialog box is closed is displayed again the next time the dialog box is opened.

A *location* is more than the country and region; it includes all the information in the dialog box: calling cards, call waiting settings, and area code. You can create as many locations as you wish, and edit or remove existing locations. To choose a location, just select it from the I Am Dialing From list.

## Creating a New Location

To create a new location, make sure the Dialing Properties dialog box is open, and then click the New button. A message box appears, indicating that a new location has been created.

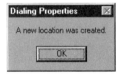

In the Location text box, change the text "New Location" so it describes the location you're creating. The name can be 50 characters long, but only the first 17 characters are displayed in the list, so brief is better.

Choose the appropriate Country/Region for the location from the drop-down list, and enter the location's area code (without parentheses) in the Area Code text box.

**Creating Area Code Rules**   If you make a lot of calls from the location you're creating, it may be worth your time to create area code rules. The rules tell Outlook to skip the "1" when dialing local calls by listing the specific three-digit local prefixes for this location.

Click the Area Code Rules button to open the Area Code Rules dialog box, shown in Figure 5.3. By default, Outlook omits the area code when AutoDialing numbers in this location's area code. For example, when you call another city within your area code, Outlook will only dial the seven digit number. If you want Outlook to precede every number you dial with 1 and the area code, enable the Always Dial the Area Code (10-Digit Dialing) check box. Or you can create a list of prefixes for this location that require 1 and the area code. Click the New button to open the New Area Code and Prefix dialog box, shown here:

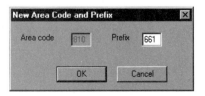

**FIGURE 5.3**

*Area code rules specify how to handle local numbers for this location.*

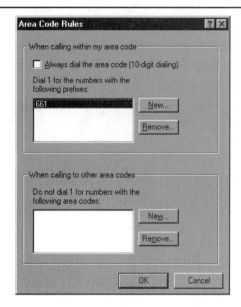

The area code is already entered and disabled, so you can't change it. Enter the prefix in the text box, and then click OK to close the dialog box and add the prefix to the list for this location's area code (see Figure 5.3). To add another prefix, click the New button again, enter the prefix in the New Area Code and Prefix dialog box, and click OK.

## MASTERING THE OPPORTUNITIES

If you're wondering whether there's really a difference between seven- and ten-digit dialing, there is, and the difference is often reflected in someone's telephone bill. Many of the national cellular services have connections in all the major metropolitan areas, so you can call your contact in, for example, Detroit, and their cell phone rings in San Francisco. With some services, the total charge for the call depends on how you dialed it. If you dial the contact's seven-digit number, the contact pays for the call on their cellular phone bill. However, if you precede the cell phone number with 1 and the area code when you dial, there are two possibilities. Either you pay the long distance charge on your telephone bill or there is no additional charge assessed. Billing varies with each cellular service, but if you have widely roaming contacts you frequently dial, it's worth asking about their cellular service to minimize your telephone bill—and theirs.

In some regions, you don't have to dial 1 before a neighboring area code: the adjoining area code is treated like your local area code. To instruct Outlook not to dial 1 before an area code, click the New button in the When Calling to Other Area Codes section of the Area Code Rules dialog box (see Figure 5.3), and you'll open the New Area Code dialog box.

Enter the area code, and click OK to close the dialog box and add the area code to the list in the Area Code Rules dialog box. When you are finished entering prefixes and area codes, click OK to close the Area Code Rules dialog box and return to Dialing Properties.

**Entering Line-Specific Settings**    Use the When Dialing from Here section of the dialog box to specify information about the line you'll use to dial at this location. If you need to dial one or two digits to access an outside line, enter them in the For Local Calls, Dial text box. If the number for long distance and local calls is the same, enter it in both text boxes. Most companies use the same digit(s) to access lines for local and long distance calls, but many hotels use different numbers because they charge a flat fee for local calls and a fee plus time for long distance calls. Outlook lets you enter two different access numbers for local and long distance.

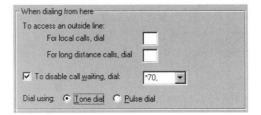

If the line you're using has call waiting service, there is a code you can enter prior to the telephone number to disable it. With call waiting disabled, anyone who dials your number while the line is in use hears a busy signal (or is transferred to voice mail if the line has voice mail service). To disable call waiting, click the To Disable Call Waiting, Dial check box, and enter or choose the code to disable call waiting on the line at this location. If you're not certain which code to choose, a quick call to your local telephone company will provide the answer.

**TIP** When you're primarily using your telephone for personal calls to friends and relatives, you might think call waiting is a nice feature. However, when you initiate business calls, you should disable call waiting for two reasons. First, there is an assumption that "real" businesses don't use call waiting—they have additional lines, voice mail, or another means of coping with multiple calls. The telltale silence created by an incoming call marks your business as a small-time operation. Second, business people are increasingly unwilling to have their conversation placed "on hold" while you chase another call. Giving your attention to the current caller (particularly when you initiated the call) is just good business etiquette.

In the Dial Using option, indicate whether the phone line at this location uses tone dialing or pulse dialing. If you're not sure, dial a number and listen: if each number is a different note, it's tone dialing.

**Using Calling Cards**   Many inns and hotels make a small fortune on long distance calls charged to your room. To have Outlook connect to a calling-card access number, enter your personal identification number (PIN), and then make the call.

To have Outlook use a calling card from this location, begin by enabling the Use This Calling Card check box. Then select the calling card you want to use from the drop-down list.

If the card and access number you want to use aren't listed, you can create a new number. However, double-check the list before creating a new card and access number; other settings are associated with items on the list that make it easier to correctly enter your calling card.

   After you choose a card (or determine that yours isn't on the list), click the Calling Card button to open the Calling Card dialog box, shown in Figure 5.4.

PART

II

Mastering the
Outlook Components

**FIGURE 5.4**

*Enter your calling card
PIN in the Calling Card
dialog box.*

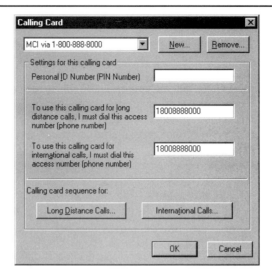

If you need to create a new calling-card access number, click the New button to
open the Create New Calling Card dialog box, shown here. Enter a descriptive name
for the calling card, and click OK to create the name and return to the Calling Card
dialog box.

A personal identification number (PIN) is a security feature used for most calling
cards. If the calling card you selected requires a PIN, enter the number in the PIN
Number text box.

**WARNING**  If you enter your PIN, make sure that your computer requires a login
password in Windows or Windows NT. Once you've saved the PIN in Outlook, anyone who
accesses your computer can charge long distance calls to your calling card.

If you selected a calling card from the list in the Dialing Properties dialog box, the
long distance and international access numbers will already be entered in the Calling
Card dialog box. If you created a new calling card, enter the access numbers that you
dial to use the calling card, including 1 and the area code, in the text boxes.

Now that you've entered your calling card information, you need to let Outlook know the sequence of events that you follow to use the card. Click the Long Distance Calls button to open the Calling Card Sequence dialog box, shown in Figure 5.5.

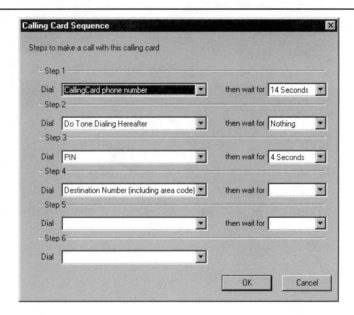

The sequence shown in Figure 5.5 is the default sequence for the MCI calling card we selected earlier. In this sequence, the calling card access number is entered first. Outlook then waits for 14 seconds to ensure that the access number has answered. All further numbers are entered with tone dialing. In step 3, Outlook enters the PIN from the Calling Card dialog box and waits for 4 seconds to allow the calling card service to verify the PIN. Finally, Outlook enters the destination telephone number, including the area code but without the 1, for the contact or new call you're dialing.

If you created a new calling card, or if the calling sequence doesn't work, you'll need to change the sequence. For each step, choose the appropriate dialing action from the Dial drop-down list, and then choose a number of seconds (or Nothing) before the next step from the Then Wait For list. You don't need to enter a Wait for the last step. When you've entered or verified all the steps, click OK to close the Calling Card Sequence dialog box and return to the Calling Card dialog box. If you make international calls from this location, click the International Calls button to enter the calling card sequence for international calls. Then click OK to close the Calling Card dialog box and return to the Dialing Properties dialog box.

**TIP** Haven't used your calling card recently? Don't happen to remember how many seconds it takes to validate your PIN? Your best bet is to examine this dialog box, then grab a stopwatch or a watch with a second hand, make a calling card call, and note the steps and the time between the steps.

The last check box in the Dialing Properties dialog box isn't related to the locations, but to the number you had selected when you opened the dialog box. If you want to dial the number as a long distance call, enable the Dial as a Long Distance Call check box. This check box only appears if you've already selected or entered a number in the New Call dialog box before opening the Dialing Properties dialog box.

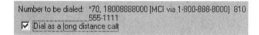

Double-check the settings you chose, and then click OK to save the dialing properties and close the dialog box. To save the properties but leave the dialog box open, so that you can enter another location or choose an existing location, click Apply instead of OK.

## Removing a Location

Removing a location is an easy operation. In the Dialing Properties dialog box, select the location in the I Am Dialing From list, and then click the Remove button. Outlook will prompt you to confirm the deletion of the location:

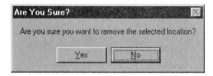

Click Yes to remove the location. Make sure you really want to remove it; you can't undo this operation.

## Editing a Location

You'll want to edit a location when your calling card information changes, when the dialing properties at the location change, or when you and your computer change locations. To edit a location, open the Dialing Properties dialog box, select the location from the I Am Dialing From list, and make your changes. Click the Apply or OK button to update the location settings.

# Setting Dialing Options

The New Call dialog box includes another button, used to open the Dialing Options dialog box. Dialing Options is a bit of a misnomer, because this dialog box has three groups of settings: Speed Dialing, Country Codes, and Modem/Line Properties.

## Using Speed Dial Numbers

Speed Dial numbers should be numbers that you use frequently, because they'll be added directly to the AutoDialer menu.

To use Speed Dial, you don't have to open the Contact you wish to call, or select from the contact's telephone numbers. Just open the menu on the AutoDialer button, and then choose Speed Dial to see the speed dial entries you've created.

Choose a Speed Dial entry, and Outlook automatically opens the New Call dialog box for that entry.

---

⚠️ **TIP** On the menu, speed dial entries are listed in the order in which they appear in the Dialing Options dialog box. If you prefer items listed in alphabetical order, create your entries in alphabetical order.

---

## Creating Speed Dial Numbers

To add a Speed Dial number, first open the New Call dialog box, and then click the Dialing Options button to open the Dialing Options dialog box, shown in Figure 5.6. Type the contact's name in the Name text box. This is a simplified speed-dialer function, and there is no search feature; it is best used for friends, family, and close business contacts whose names you know how to spell.

**FIGURE 5.6**

*Use the Dialing Options dialog box to set up your Speed Dial numbers.*

The contact's telephone numbers will be added to the Phone Number list. Choose the number you want to add from the list, as shown in Figure 5.6. You can then click back in the Name text box and edit the name that will appear on the menu. For example, you might want to add **home** after the contact's name to indicate that it is a home phone number. Click the Add button to add the entry to the Speed Dial list.

 **TIP** Displaying the ampersand (&) we used in Alex & Mary's entry shown earlier was a bit tricky. In Windows applications' text boxes, an ampersand is used to append text. The actual text entered as the Speed Dial Name is *Alex && Mary Courter*, instructing Outlook to append an ampersand.

You can create up to twenty Speed Dial entries. If you try to create a 21st entry, Outlook will prompt you to delete an existing entry before adding the new entry:

## Deleting a Speed Dial Entry

Delete

To delete a Speed Dial Entry, open the Dialing Options dialog box and select the entry you wish to delete from the list. Click the Delete button to delete the entry. You will *not* be prompted to confirm the deletion.

## Using Country Codes

In some regions, you must include the country code as well as the area code when you dial a number. To include the code for local phone numbers, enable the Automatically Add Country Code to Local Phone Numbers check box (see Figure 5.6).

## Choosing Modems

If you have more than one modem or a choice of phone lines and modems on a network, you can select a modem from the Connect Using Line drop-down list.

Clicking the Line Properties button opens the Windows Modem Properties dialog box for the selected modem, as shown in Figure 5.7. For more information on this dialog box, use Windows/Windows NT Online Help (Start ➤ Help).

**PART**

**II**

Mastering the
Outlook Components

**FIGURE 5.7**

*Change modem information in the Windows Modem Properties dialog box.*

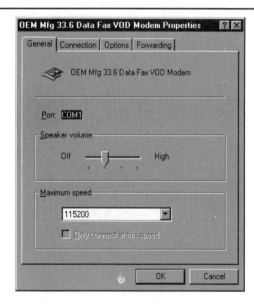

# Creating a Letter to a Contact

Telephony is a grand idea, but nothing replaces the physical artifact: a thoughtfully worded letter on premium, watermarked paper, signed with an ink pen and a flourish. With Outlook and Microsoft Word, you can generate "snail mail" letters using the Letter Wizard for your entries in Contacts.

 **TIP** You don't always have time to write a letter or send a fax to a contact immediately. With Outlook, you can flag a contact so you don't forget to send the communication later. For more information on flags, see Chapter 7.

Begin by selecting the contact you want to write a letter to, either by opening the contact's form or selecting the contact in a view list. Choose Actions ➤ New Letter to Contact from the menu to launch Microsoft Word and the Letter Wizard, as shown in Figure 5.8. This type of action (starting another application to use information from the original program) is called *automation*, and it uses a lot of your computer's resources and will take a moment, so be patient. When you create a New Letter to Contact, Outlook always launches a new session of Word, even if Word is already running.

**FIGURE 5.8**

*Choosing New Letter to Contact in Outlook launches Word's Letter Wizard.*

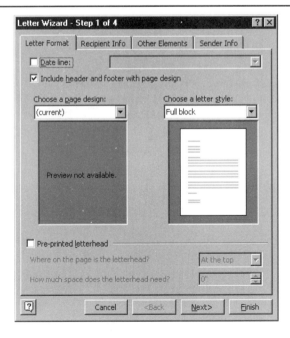

The Letter Wizard has four steps. You can click the Next and Back buttons to move to the next or previous step, or use the page tabs labeled Letter Format, Recipient Info, Other Elements, and Sender Info to move between the steps in the Wizard. In the Letter Format step of the Letter Wizard (see Figure 5.8), format the opening of the letter. To include a date, enable the Date Line check box, and then select a date format from the drop-down list:

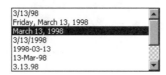

Use the Choose a Page Design drop-down list to select a template. If you haven't created templates in Word, you'll only see two choices: the current design, and Normal, based on Word's `Normal.dot` template.

The Choose a Letter Style drop-down list lets you select the overall format of the letter. There are three styles:

**Full block**   All sections of the letter begin at the left margin, and the first lines of paragraphs in the body of the letter are not indented. This is the default setting.

**Modified block**   The date, closing, and signature lines are set to the right, and the first lines of body text paragraphs are not indented.

**Semi-block**   The date, closing, and signature lines are set to the right, and the first lines of body text paragraphs are indented one tab stop.

When you select a Letter Style, you'll see a preview of the style below the drop-down list, so you can select each in turn and decide which you prefer. You or your employer may already have a preferred style; if not, choose one and stick with it so that the letters you send to a recipient have a professionally consistent look.

If the letter will be printed on preprinted letterhead, enable the Pre-Printed Letterhead check box. Then, grab a ruler and measure the preprinted area of your letterhead. Indicate where the letterhead appears on the page, and use the spin boxes to indicate how much space the letterhead takes up. Next, add an extra $1/_{10}$ or $2/_{10}$ of an inch to provide adequate space between the letterhead and the text of the letter.

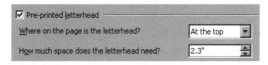

After you've selected a date format and the letter style, set the position of any pre-printed information and click Next to continue to the second step of the Wizard, as shown in Figure 5.9. Your contact's name should appear in the Recipient's Name text box. The Delivery Address is the address you marked in the Outlook Contact form as the contact's Mailing Address.

**FIGURE 5.9**

*Enter recipient information in the Letter Wizard.*

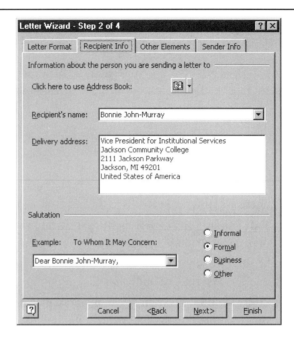

If you selected the wrong contact in Outlook, click the Address Book button to open the Select Name dialog box with your Outlook Contacts, as shown in Figure 5.10. (You'll find out more about using Address Books in Chapter 6.) Enter the contact's name in the Type Name or Select from List text box, or use the scroll bar and mouse to locate and select the contact you wish to correspond with. Click OK to close the Select Name dialog box and move the contact's mailing address to the Letter Wizard. The Letter Wizard automatically includes the country name as part of the address. You can edit the address in the text box, so it's easy to select and delete the country name if you don't want it to appear in the letter.

On the Recipient Info page, you can also select a Salutation type. The Letter Wizard has four groups of salutations. Regardless of which group you select, you'll see multi-purpose salutations, good for any occasion:

- Dear Mom and Dad
- Dear Sir or Madam
- Dear Ladies and Gentlemen
- To Whom It May Concern

**FIGURE 5.10**

*Select a contact from the Select Names dialog box.*

Personalized choices are available in three of the four groups. When you choose the Informal option, the default salutation is Dear First Name, (for example: *Dear Bonnie,*). The default Formal salutation is Dear Title Last Name, (*Dear Ms. John-Murray,*); if you didn't enter a title for the contact in Outlook, the First Name and Last Name are used (*Dear Bonnie John-Murray,*). Choosing Business changes the comma used in the Formal Salutation to a colon (*Dear Ms. John-Murray:*). The Other category only includes the impersonal choices listed above.

To choose a salutation, set the option (Formal, Informal, Business, Other), and then choose the salutation from the drop-down list or leave the default salutation. To create your own salutation, simply enter the text you want to use in the text box, and then click Next to move to the third step of the Letter Wizard.

There are five Other Elements that you can choose to include on the Other Elements page of the Wizard (see Figure 5.11). All of the Other Elements are disabled by default, so you must turn each on in the Wizard to include it in your letter.

**Reference line** Appears directly under the date and indicates a topic for the letter.

**Mailing instructions** Placed directly above the recipient's name in the internal address.

**Attention**   Appears following the address and prior to the salutation.

**Subject**   Placed between the salutation and the body of the letter.

**Courtesy copies**   Follows the closing and signature.

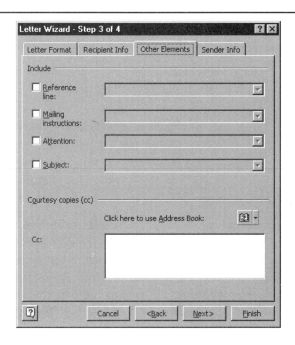

**FIGURE 5.11**

*Add a reference line or subject to the letter on the Other Elements page.*

To add an element to your letter, enable the check box in front of the element, and choose opening text for the element from the element's drop-down list. Then, add any other text in the text box. For example, to add a Reference Line, turn on the Reference Line check box. Next, choose an opening from the list (In reply to, RE, or Reference). Click in the text box and enter additional text about the reference:

For courtesy copies, you can type **Cc:**, followed by the names of the people who will receive courtesy copies. If the recipients are Outlook contacts, click the Address Book button to open the Select Name dialog box. Choose the first recipient, then click the Cc button to add the contact to the courtesy copy list. To add another recipient, choose the contact name and click the Cc button again. When you've added all the recipients from your Outlook Contacts, click OK to close the Select Names dialog box and return to the Letter Wizard.

**NOTE** Cc has its roots in the typewriter age. A *carbon copy* of an original is made by placing a sheet of carbon paper and an additional sheet of blank paper under the original letter or memo in the typewriter. This ensures that the copy is precisely the same as the original. With a computer, you can print the original, and then change the courtesy copy before printing—but don't do this. A courtesy copy should always be an exact reprinting of the original letter. If you need to make additional comments for the recipient of the courtesy copy, hand write them on the copy, or enclose a separate note.

In the final step of the Letter Wizard, Sender Info, you indicate who is sending the letter (see Figure 5.12). This information appears at the top of the letter as a return address, and at the bottom in the closing. From the Sender's Name drop-down list, you can select the user's name entered when Word was installed. If you're typing a letter for a supervisor or colleague, use the Address Book and select the Sender from Contacts. If you're printing this letter on letterhead that includes an address, enable the Omit check box to exclude the internal address in the letter itself.

**PART**

**II**

Mastering the
Outlook Components

**FIGURE 5.12**

*Use the Sender Info page to create the internal address and closing for your letter.*

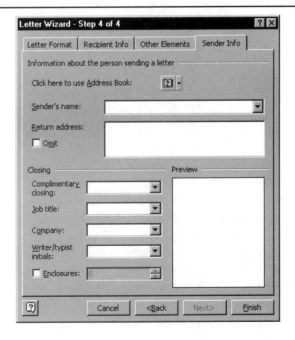

Use the drop-down lists to choose the elements you want to include to end the letter. If additional items will be included with the letter, enable the Enclosures check box and indicate how many items the reader should look for. As you add elements on this page, the Letter Wizard builds a preview of the letter's closing. In Figure 5.13, the letter closes with Regards, blank lines for a signature, the sender's name and job title, and a notice that there is one enclosure with the letter.

**FIGURE 5.13**

*As you add closing elements, Word creates a preview.*

When you click the Finish button, the Letter Wizard adds the elements you selected to a new document. The Office Assistant appears, offering you more choices regarding your letter, as shown in Figure 5.14. The Assistant will help you address an envelope or label. Or, you can rerun the Letter Wizard to create another letter.

In the document window, the words *Type your text here* are selected. Type the body of your letter (the selected words will be replaced). The paragraphs will be formatted according to the letter style you chose in the Letter Wizard. When you've completed your letter, print and save it in Word.

PART

II

Mastering the
Outlook Components

**FIGURE 5.14**

*When you finish the Letter Wizard, the Office Assistant prompts you to create an envelope or label.*

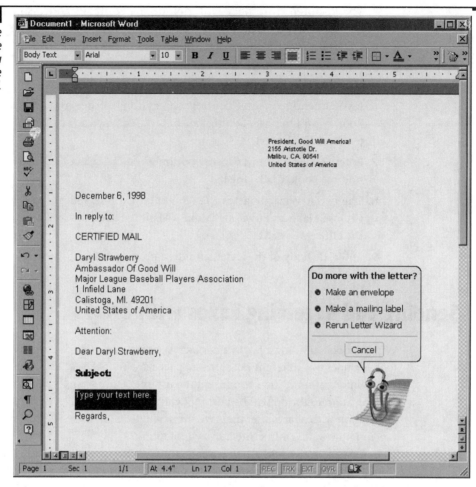

Now that you know about each of the choices in the Letter Wizard, here's a summary of the steps you follow to create a letter to a contact:

1. Select the contact in any view, or double-click the contact to open the Contact form.

2. Choose Actions ➢ New Letter to Contact from the menu to launch Word and start the Letter Wizard.

3. Choose the format you would like to use, including Date Format, Page Design, Letter Style, and choose a preprinted date if you want one. Click Next.

4. The Recipient Info page will include the contact's address information. To change contacts, click the Address Book button and select another contact from Outlook. Enter a salutation in the Salutation field. Click Next.

5. Select Other Elements you would like to include by enabling the check boxes, choosing text from the drop-down lists, and entering text.

6. If you intend to include courtesy copies (Cc) to other contacts, click the Address Book button to select additional contacts, or type each contact's name in the Cc text box. Click Next.

7. Enter Sender Info and Closing options. You can select the Sender Info from the Address Book. Click Finish.

8. The Letter Wizard pastes the elements you selected in the Word document. Choose Make an Envelope, Make a Mailing Label, Rerun Letter Wizard, or close the Office Assistant.

9. Enter the body of the letter, and then print and save it in Word.

# Sending and Receiving Faxes with WinFax

With Outlook, sending a fax to a contact is as easy as sending an e-mail message. Outlook includes two different fax software packages. The fax service you use depends on your configuration. When you install the Internet Only configuration, the Symantec WinFax Starter Edition will be automatically installed. WinFax is an established fax application with a large user base; we think you'll be impressed with WinFax's ease of use and how well WinFax integrates with Outlook.

In the Corporate/Workgroup configuration, Outlook uses a new and improved version of Microsoft Fax. Outlook, like the other Office products, supports fax servers like FaxPress. If you can send faxes in Word, you'll be able to fax from Outlook. Faxing in the Corporate/Workgroup configuration is covered later in this chapter, in the "Sending and Receiving Faxes with Microsoft Fax" section.

## Composing a Fax

To create a fax in the Internet Only configuration, you must be in a folder of Outlook's mail module, such as the Inbox, Sent Items, Outbox, or another mail folder you may have created. Begin by selecting File ➤ New ➤ Fax Message or Actions ➤ New Fax Message from the menu bar to open a new fax message form, shown in Figure 5.15. The WinFax message form closely resembles Outlook's e-mail message form.

Enter the recipient's name in the To text box, or click the To button to open the Select Names dialog box (refer to Figure 5.10). When you open the Select Names dialog box, the settings in the dialog box are based on the type of communication you're creating. In Figure 5.10, the dialog box lets you choose recipients for the original letter (To) and courtesy copies (Cc). The names of the individuals receiving courtesy copies are listed at the bottom of the original letter. With WinFax and e-mail messages, there is a third type of potential recipient: people who receive *blind courtesy copies* (Bcc), as shown in Figure 5.16. Why "blind"? Recipients of blind courtesy copies aren't listed on the original fax or message, so the people who receive the original fax and courtesy copies don't know that copies were also sent to the Bcc recipients.

**FIGURE 5.15**

*WinFax is used in the Internet Only configuration for fax messages.*

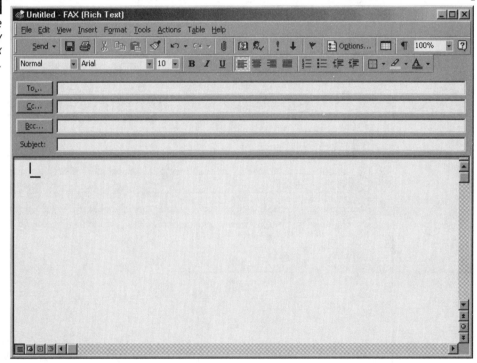

In Figure 5.16, Alice is receiving the original and knows that Bartholemew is receiving a copy. Neither Alice nor Bartholemew are notified that a copy of the fax is also being sent to Maharishi. To send a blind copy, select the contact's name and click the Bcc button.

Type the text you want to fax in the open text area. The text tools you've come to expect in Outlook are included in WinFax:

- Body text is plain text by default; to change to Rich Text Format (see Figure 5.16), choose Format ➤ Rich Text (HTML) from the menu. This enables the other choices on the Format menu—Style, Font, and Paragraph—so you can format the text in the body of the fax.

- In the Format Font dialog box, you can change the text color. However, fax machines don't print in color, so this does not qualify as an incredibly useful option.

- To check spelling, choose Tools ➤ Spelling and Grammar from the menu.

- Use the Edit menu commands or the shortcut menu to cut, copy, paste, find, and select text in the fax.

**FIGURE 5.16**

*You can send blind courtesy copies to fax recipients.*

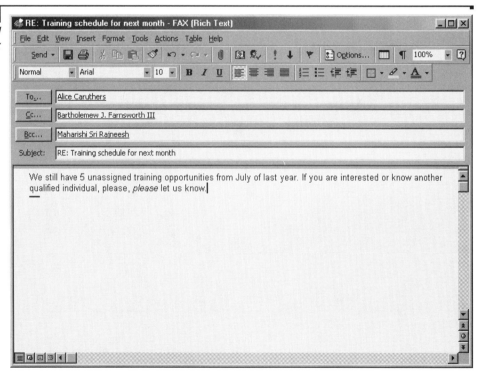

## Attaching a File to a Fax

You can include an entire document from another application by inserting the file in the fax message. Choose Insert ➤ File from the menu, and then locate the file you want to include in the Insert File dialog box.

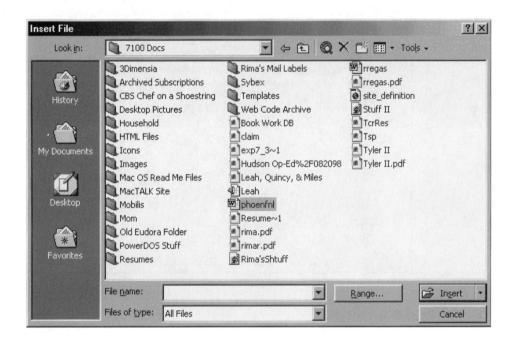

Select the filename, and either double-click on the file or click Insert to close the dialog box and insert the file in the fax message. In the fax message, the file is represented by an icon that appears wherever the cursor was last, as shown in Figure 5.17. When you send the message, WinFax opens the appropriate application and adds the contents of the file to the fax message. You can insert multiple files in a single fax message.

To delete a file from a message, click the icon representing the file to display its selection box, and press the Delete key.

PART

II

Mastering the
Outlook Components

**FIGURE 5.17**

*An inserted file
appears as an icon
in the fax message.*

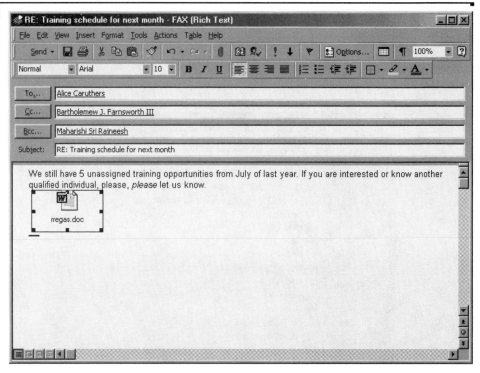

## Sending the Fax

After you've finished composing the fax, it's time to send it to the recipients. Click the Send button on the toolbar (clicking on the pull-down arrow gives you more sending options), or choose File ➤ Send Using ➤ Symantec WinFax Starter Edition, or press Alt+S to begin sending the fax. All of your contacts appear in the Select Names dialog box, not just those with fax numbers. If you choose a contact without a fax number, Outlook will give you the option to insert one for the recipient, as shown here.

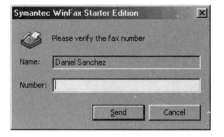

Outlook will present you with a dialog box to enter the fax number for each of the recipients of the fax. Enter the number you want to use for each recipient, but keep in mind that these numbers are not added to the recipient's Contact information. You will have to add those numbers on your own, as shown in Figure 5.18.

**FIGURE 5.18**

*Use the Properties dialog box to add a fax number on the fly.*

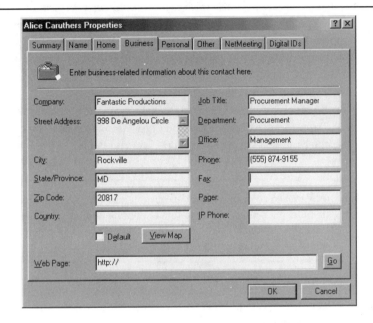

After WinFax verifies that all the recipients have fax numbers, it launches Spelling and Grammar, which checks the spelling and grammar of the text you typed. If it finds words that aren't in the dictionary, the Spelling dialog box opens so you can correct or verify the spelling. Text in inserted files is not checked.

When you've finished with Spelling and Grammar, WinFax will open the application for any file you inserted, and convert the contents of the file to fax text. This process is called rasterizing. For example, if you insert a Word file, WinFax will open Word and rasterize a copy of the Word document. Message boxes keep you informed about the rasterizing process, but you don't need to do anything with these message boxes.

WinFax opens the same dialog box as appears when your recipient has no fax number so that you can verify or change the fax number for the recipient. If the fax number is the number you wish to use, click Send. To change the number, simply edit the contents of the Number text box before clicking Send. If you choose Cancel, the fax will not be sent to this recipient.

WinFax repeats this process for each recipient in the To, Cc, and Bcc text boxes. When you've clicked the Send button for the final recipient, the WinFax Status message box opens and WinFax dials the first recipient. After the first fax has been transmitted, WinFax automatically begins on the next.

PART

**II**

Mastering the
Outlook Components

## Custom Headings and Cover Pages

A cover page is a single sheet that precedes the actual fax pages. You can't create a cover page when you're in the middle of composing a WinFax message; you have to set the cover page options in advance. Choose Tools ➤ Options from the Outlook menu to open the Options dialog box. On the Fax page, you can enter three different types of options: personal information for the fax header and cover page, cover page template, and modem configuration. In the Personal Information area, enter text that you wish to appear in your fax header.

If you choose to add a cover page to your faxes, the name you enter in the Personal Information is automatically added to the cover page. The other information appears in the header at the top of each page of the fax.

 **TIP** While you can enter a department name or other text-based information as the station identifier, it's best to enter the telephone number of the sending fax. Some fax servers track the station ID (also called the CSID) so they can automatically send faxes back to you. If you enter text, they can't respond to your fax.

A cover page is based on a template. Click the Template button to open the Cover Page Properties dialog box, shown in Figure 5.19. To add cover pages to your faxes, enable the Send Cover Page check box. Choose a template from the drop-down list to see a sample in the Preview area of the dialog box.

**FIGURE 5.19**

*Choose a template for your cover pages in the Cover Page Properties dialog box.*

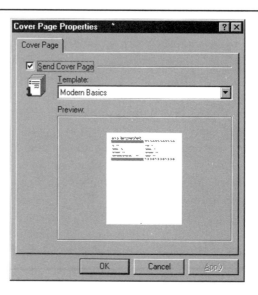

With Send Cover Page enabled, WinFax will automatically add a cover page to every fax you send from Outlook.

# Viewing Received Faxes

Before you can view a fax, you must be able to receive faxes. Fax reception options are set in the Options dialog box (Tools ➤ Options). If you wish your computer to automatically receive faxes (while it is turned on), enable the Automatic Receive Fax check box in the Modem area of the dialog box.

 **NOTE** Outlook does not need to be running to receive a fax document. In fact, some computers don't even need to be on, as they have added self-power-on functionality that allows the system to take messages and faxes while in a sleep-like state. Whether this is a feature your system has or not, be prepared to leave your system on to receive faxes while you are out, as this avoids potential hassles. You'll need to turn on Automatic Receive Fax in the Tools ➤ Options dialog box, as described previously.

In the Answer After __ Rings spin box, set the number of rings WinFax should wait for before answering the line. The Number of Retries and Retries Every __ Seconds controls are for sending, not receiving, and indicate how many times and how often WinFax should attempt to send a fax if the receiving fax machine does not answer or the line is busy. When you've set the answering options, click OK to apply the settings and close the dialog box.

When a fax is sent to you, the WinFax application opens; a WinFax button appears on your Taskbar, and a message box opens to display the fax reception status. Just prior to connection, the status will read "Offering" and will change to "Connected" when the fax is being received.

When the entire fax transmission has been received, WinFax closes and the button disappears from the Taskbar.

To view your fax, switch to Outlook's Inbox. The fax message will be shown in the list as an unread (bold) item, with the subject "Fax Received":

Click on the fax message to open it. The message is separated into two panes: reception information and attached fax files. Double-click on the icon representing the fax to view the fax image.

## MASTERING TROUBLESHOOTING

The first time you open a new type of file attached to an Outlook mail message, you'll be warned about viruses and asked what you wish to do with the file:

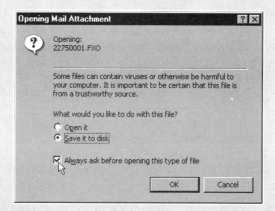

E-mail attachments can contain viruses; files sent from fax machines cannot. If you don't want to be prompted about faxes in the future, clear the Always Ask Before Opening This Type of File check box before closing the Opening Mail Attachment dialog box.

WinFax opens the Quick Fax Viewer so you can see the fax image that you received, as shown in Figure 5.20. A miniature version of the first page of the fax is displayed, in the orientation it was received in. If the fax was sent upside down, the image is upside down.

Use the buttons on the Quick Fax Viewer toolbar to adjust, rotate, or page through the fax. Use the 100, 50, and 25 percent buttons to zoom in on the image, and the four display buttons to rotate the image 90, 180, or 270 degrees from its current orientation. If the fax has more than one page, the Previous Page and Next Page buttons move you backward and forward through the pages of the fax.

To print the fax, choose File ➤ Print from the Quick Fax Viewer menu. You don't have to save the fax, it's still attached to the fax message in the Outlook Inbox. When you've viewed and printed the fax, choose File ➤ Exit or click the Close Button to close the Quick Fax Viewer.

**FIGURE 5.20**

*The Quick Fax Viewer lets you view and print the fax image.*

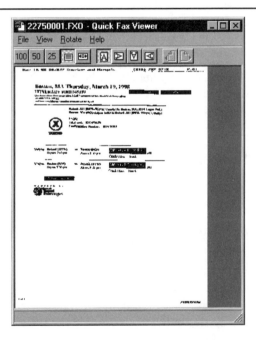

**PART**

**II**

**Mastering the Outlook Components**

**MASTERING THE OPPORTUNITIES**

### Converting Faxes to Text

When you receive a fax, you receive a picture: an image of the document that was transmitted. You can view it and print it, but if you need to use the text that's contained in the fax, you have to retype it. If you spend lots of time reentering text that was originally faxed to you, you should consider optical character recognition (OCR) software.

OCR software is designed to examine an image and translate recognizable characters into text. The WinFax Starter Edition is a basic version of WinFax Pro, a full featured product that includes OCR capabilities. To find out more about WinFax Pro, open the Options dialog box in Outlook (Tools ➢ Options) and click the About the Product button to launch your browser and visit the WinFax Pro site. You can review the features of WinFax Pro and decide whether you want to invest a bit more to have OCR capabilities built in to your Outlook fax product.

WinFax Pro can be used in both the Internet Only and Corporate/Workgroup configurations; product support is provided by Symantec rather than Microsoft. You can download a trial version of WinFax Pro from the Symantec Web site, but the demo does not include OCR functionality.

# Sending and Receiving Faxes with Microsoft Fax

In the Corporate/Workgroup configuration, you can send a fax directly from Contacts. Select a contact, and then choose Actions ➢ New Fax Messages from the Tools menu. The Compose New Fax Wizard opens, as shown in Figure 5.21.

In the first step of the Compose New Fax Wizard, select a location. To verify the dialing settings for the location, click the Dialing Properties button to open the Dialing Properties dialog box, shown in Figure 5.22. (See "Changing Dialing Properties" in "Dialing a Contact" earlier in this chapter for details about the settings in this dialog box.) Close the dialog box after making any changes.

**FIGURE 5.21**

*Microsoft Fax is used in the Corporate/ Workgroup configuration.*

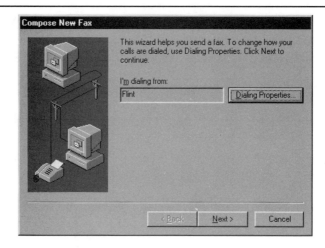

**FIGURE 5.22**

*Use the Dialing Properties dialog box to view and change dialing settings.*

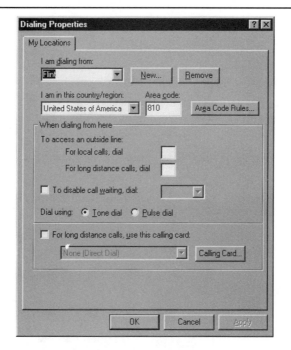

In the second step of the Wizard, shown in Figure 5.23, there are two ways to enter your fax recipients. You can enter a name and fax number in the text boxes, enable or disable the Dial Area Code check box, and then click the Add to List button. You can also click the Address Book button to select recipients from one of your Outlook address books. To delete a recipient, select their name in the list, and then click the Remove button.

**FIGURE 5.23**

*Enter or select recipients in the second step of the Wizard.*

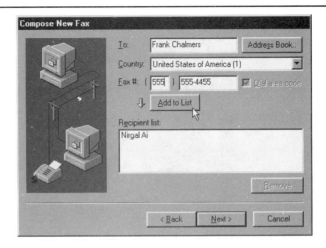

In the third step of the Compose New Fax Wizard, select a cover page design or no cover page. If you want to delay fax transmission or secure the fax, click the Options button to open the Send Options for This Message dialog box, shown in Figure 5.24.

**FIGURE 5.24**

*Use the Send Options dialog box to schedule fax transmission.*

You can secure a fax with a password, encryption, or a digital ID if the recipients use fax/modems rather than fax machines to receive faxes. Click the Security button to open the Message Security Options dialog box, shown in Figure 5.25. To assign a password, just choose the Password-Protected option and click OK. You'll be prompted to enter a password. The recipient must enter the password to view the fax. To use Key Encryption and digital IDs, you must obtain the digital IDs of the recipients. If you don't have digital IDs on file for all recipients, the Key Encrypted option is disabled, as shown in Figure 5.25. For more information on digital IDs, see Chapters 6 and 15.

**FIGURE 5.25**

*Faxes can be encrypted or password-protected.*

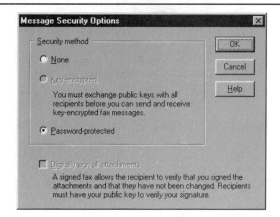

In the fourth step of the Wizard, enter a Subject Line for the top of the fax and a note if you wish. This is the only place to enter a message in Microsoft Fax, so if you aren't attaching a file, you'd better put some text in here. If you don't want the note to start on the cover page, disable the check box.

## Attaching Files to a Fax

In the fifth step of the Wizard, shown in Figure 5.26, you can add files to your fax. As with WinFax, attachments are rendered before they are sent, so the content of the files appears in the fax. Add the files in the order you want them included in the fax, using the Add File button. Click OK to move to the last step of the Wizard, and then click Finish to begin rendering the fax.

Unless you chose to delay the fax, it is sent immediately. On most networks, you'll receive a message letting you know the fax is being queued for delivery. If you use a modem for faxing, Microsoft Fax will render the fax and then initiate the phone calls to the recipients.

**FIGURE 5.26**

*Add files to be rendered in the transmitted fax.*

## Receiving Faxes with Microsoft Fax

If you use a fax/modem, you need to set Microsoft Fax to accept incoming faxes. Click on any Outlook mail folder, and then choose Tools ➤ Microsoft Fax Tools ➤ Options to open the Microsoft Fax Properties dialog box, shown in Figure 5.27.

**FIGURE 5.27**

*Configuring Microsoft Fax for use with a modem*

The dialog box has four pages:

**Message**   Establish default settings for the Compose New Fax Wizard

**Dialing**   Create dialing locations

**Modem**   Select and configure modem options

**User**   Set your personal and station information for the fax header

To receive faxes, go to the Modem page (shown in Figure 5.27), select the modem you wish to use to receive faxes, and click the Properties button to open the Modem Properties dialog box, shown in Figure 5.28. To receive faxes, set the answer mode either to answer automatically after the specified number of rings, or to manual. Use manual when your phone is primarily used for voice; when a fax arrives, Microsoft Fax will ask whether you wish to receive it.

PART

II

**FIGURE 5.28**

*Choose automatic or manual answering to receive faxes.*

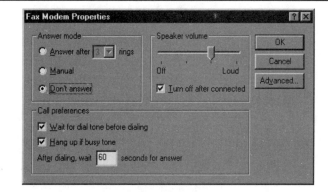

When either answering method is enabled, a fax machine icon appears in the Windows Taskbar. Click the icon to see the current fax status.

**TIP**   The Modem page of the dialog box has one other option worth noting: you can share a fax, just as you would share a folder, hard drive, or printer. If you have the only modem in a small office, sharing it allows other people on your network to use it.

With a modem or a network fax server, fax messages are delivered to the Outlook Inbox. You'll receive the same notification for a fax as you do for e-mail messages. Open the Inbox folder and double-click on the message item to view the fax.

Mastering the
Outlook Components

# Viewing an Online Map for a Contact

You've called, you've written, you've faxed—now the contact wants to see you in person. But where exactly is Beacon Street West in Lanesboro, Minnesota? If your contact's address is in the United States, you can display a map of the address using your Web browser. Open the contact form, select the address you want to see, then click the Display Map of Address button on the contact form toolbar.

Outlook will launch your default browser and connect to the Microsoft Expedia Maps Web site. A map of the address is displayed in the browser window, as shown in Figure 5.29.

**FIGURE 5.29**

*Outlook uses the Expedia Web site to display address maps.*

Use the Zoom level tools to display smaller- and larger-scale maps. Click the Print hyperlink to create a larger, frame-free map in your browser that's more suitable for printing, as shown in Figure 5.30. Choose File ➤ Print or click your browser's Print button to send the map to your printer.

When you've finished using the Expedia Map features, close your browser.

 **WARNING**  We have tested this feature and suggest that the results it returns be treated with caution. Often, the search engine stripped the state information from the query and returned a completely unexpected entry. We entered the address of a friend who lives in Pasadena, California, into the form. Expedia Maps returned a location in Maryland. Not particularly helpful. It did, however, find the White House.

**FIGURE 5.30**

*Print a map to your contact's address directly from the browser.*

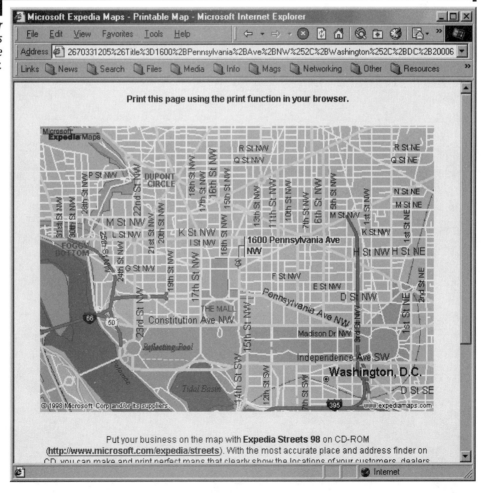

PART
II

Mastering the
Outlook Components

## What's Next

You can write, fax, phone, and even visit your contacts in person. But wait, there's more: e-mail. In Chapter 6, you'll learn how to best use the mail messaging capabilities of Outlook to communicate quickly and efficiently with customers, vendors, and colleagues.

# CHAPTER 6

## Sending and Receiving E-mail with Outlook

I n the 1970s and '80s, the telephone was the lifeblood of many organizations; if your phones weren't working, you weren't doing business. Today, electronic mail has taken center stage. If the phones aren't working, it's no big deal, but cut off e-mail for a few hours, and employees start wandering the halls aimlessly, wondering how to cope with the sudden loss of their primary means of communication. Well, this might be a bit of an exaggeration, but it's not far off the mark. Business depends on e-mail, and the dependence is growing every day.

Outlook was designed first and foremost as an e-mail communication tool, and it offers features that go beyond those of most e-mail software, such as flagging and automatic message decryption. With Outlook, you can work collaboratively, using e-mail messages to distribute documents or to vote on important issues in your company, and you can use Outlook's mail management features to flag and prioritize incoming messages so that these vital communiqués don't get lost in the shuffle. This chapter will get you started with all the daily e-mail functions, and Chapter 7 will go into the details of voting, flagging messages, and other advanced e-mail features.

## Quick Start: Creating and Sending an E-mail Message

If you have experience using another e-mail program or sending faxes in Outlook, you'll have no problem creating and sending e-mail messages in Outlook. This chapter covers all the numerous options for creating and sending e-mail, but to get started quickly, you can create and send a message by following the five simple steps listed here.

1. Choose File ➢ New ➢ Mail Message from the menu bar.

2. Enter the recipient's name(s) or e-mail addresses in the To, Cc, and Bcc text boxes, or click the To, Cc, or Bcc button and select recipients in the Select Names dialog box.

3. Type the subject of the message in the Subject text box.

4. Enter the text of the message in the open text area.

5. Click the Send button to send the message to the recipients.

For detailed information about these steps and other e-mail features in Outlook, read on.

# Outlook Configurations and E-mail

There are three ways to send and receive mail, depending on how Outlook is configured on your PC:

- If Outlook was installed for Corporate/Workgroup use and you are connected to your organization's network, mail from within your organization is delivered directly to your Inbox. Internet mail may also be delivered directly, depending on your organization's connection to the Internet; if it is not, you use a separate dial-up connection to send and receive Internet mail.

- If you have the Corporate/Workgroup setup and are not connected to your company's network (for example, when you are working out of the office with your laptop computer), mail is only delivered on demand when you connect to your organization's server with a dial-up connection.

- If you chose the Internet Only mail option when Outlook was installed, you always need to tell Outlook to send and receive mail, either by changing the Mail Delivery options to automatically connect to your Internet service provider (ISP) at specified intervals, or by telling Outlook to connect to your ISP each time you wish to send and receive mail.

In this chapter we'll focus on the first and third options. For more information on sending and receiving e-mail while working offline, see Chapter 18. Other mail settings are determined by your Outlook configuration; we'll point out the differences between the two configurations throughout this chapter and the next.

PART

II

Mastering the
Outlook Components

 **NOTE** New to Outlook 2000 is a much easier way to change your Outlook mail configuration. Microsoft got smart and added this function to the Options dialog box. Simply go to Tools ➤ Options ➤ Mail Services, and click the Reconfigure Mail Support button at the bottom of the dialog box. Select your new configuration and click OK (if you select Corporate/Workgroup, make sure you can support it with either a local copy of Microsoft Mail or information on how to connect to your Exchange server). Under certain circumstances, the Outlook installer will ask you to insert your CD. When all is said and done, you'll be able to support new features and you won't even have to restart your computer.

# Creating and Addressing E-mail

 To create a message, choose File ➤ New ➤ Mail Message from the menu bar, or open the menu on the New Item button and choose Mail Message to open a Message form, shown in Figure 6.1.

**FIGURE 6.1**

*Open a Message form
to create an e-mail
message.*

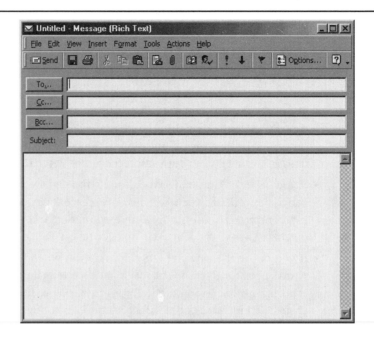

> ⚠ **TIP** There is a fourth installation option besides those listed above: No E-mail. If Mail Message is not a choice on the File ≻ New menu, e-mail has not been installed, and you must install it before you can send messages in Outlook. Choose Tools ≻ Accounts ≻ Mail, and then click the Add button to launch the Internet Connection Wizard and add an e-mail service to Outlook.

There are two view options that determine which text boxes are displayed in a message form: Message Header and Bcc Field. With both turned off, only the To text box is displayed at the top of the form. Enabling the Message Header (choose View ≻ Message Header from the form's menu) also displays the Cc and Subject text boxes. This is Outlook's default setting. With the Message Header displayed, choosing View ≻ Bcc Field from the form menu displays the Bcc text box, as shown in Figure 6.1.

## Entering E-mail Addresses

There are three ways to enter e-mail addresses: from your address books, by typing the address manually, or by searching for the person's e-mail address with a directory service, such as Four11 or WhoWhere?. Enter the recipient's name or e-mail address in the To text box, or click the To button to open the Select Names dialog box, shown in

Figure 6.2. When you open the Select Names dialog box, the choices are based on the type of communication you're creating: To and Cc (courtesy copy) for letters; To, Cc, and Bcc (blind courtesy copy) for e-mail messages and faxes. To and Cc recipients are listed in the header of the message, while recipients of blind courtesy copies are not. Therefore, recipients of the original message and courtesy copies won't know that the message was also sent to the Bcc recipients.

**FIGURE 6.2**

*Select message recipients using the To, Cc, and Bcc buttons in the Select Names dialog box.*

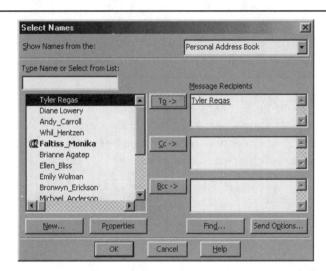

PART

**II**

**Mastering the Outlook Components**

## About Address Books

An *address book* is a list of names that you can select addresses from. You may have only one address book (with the Internet Only configuration), three address books (with the Corporate/Workgroup configuration), or some other number of address books, depending on the services installed to handle mail messaging on your computer. The major address books are:

**Personal Address Book**   This address book can contain personal distribution lists (groups), and is located on your PC. This is the best place to keep your frequently used addresses.

**Global Address Book**   An address book for members of your organization, stored on a server; also called a Postoffice Address List. This address book can contain global distribution lists.

*Continued*

**CONTINUED**

**Outlook Address Book**  The Outlook Address Book automatically contains the entries in your Contacts folder in the Corporate/Workgroup configuration. It only includes contacts that have an e-mail address or fax number listed.

**Contacts**  In the Internet Only configuration, this is your personal address book, and it includes all your contacts, whether or not they have an e-mail address or fax number.

If you have installed other mail services, such as CompuServe, you may have additional address books.

In the Internet Only configuration, you select your recipient from the Contacts folder. With the Corporate/Workgroup configuration, as shown in Figure 6.2, you will have more than one address book, so begin by choosing an address book from the drop-down list in the Select Names dialog box.

Either scroll to the person's name, or begin entering the name in the Find text box and Outlook will find the name in the list. With the contact's name selected in the left pane, click the To, Cc, or Bcc button to add the name to the list of recipients. Or, right-click on the name and select To, Cc, or Bcc from the shortcut menu. You can hold Shift or Ctrl and click to select a contiguous list of names or multiple names before clicking the To, Cc, or Bcc buttons.

The Contacts list is different in the two installation configurations. If you have Internet Only mail, each contact is listed only once. When you choose an address from the list, Outlook uses the contact's default e-mail address (the first address you entered). In the Corporate/Workgroup configuration, each electronic address is listed separately. For example, if Mary Smith has a fax number and two e-mail addresses, she will be listed three times: Mary Smith [Business Fax], Mary Smith [E-mail], and Mary Smith [E-mail2], so you can select either e-mail address.

**TIP**  You can use all of a contact's e-mail addresses in either configuration—it just takes a bit of planning. Instead of beginning with a blank message form, right-click on the contact in the Contacts folder and choose New Message to Contact from the shortcut menu. If the contact has more than one e-mail address, Outlook adds them all to the message and reminds you to delete those you don't wish to use.

After you've added all the recipients, click OK to close the Select Names dialog box and return to the message form. If the intended recipient isn't included in any of your Contacts folders, you can enter the e-mail address directly in the To, Cc, or Bcc text boxes in the message form, and then create a new entry from that information. For more information about adding contacts using e-mail addresses, see "Adding Addresses on the Fly" later in this chapter.

 **WARNING** In the Internet Only configuration, Outlook will let you address e-mail to any contact, even if they don't have an e-mail address. To see if the contact has an address, use the horizontal scroll bar below the list of names to scroll to the second column, e-mail address. If it is blank, there are no e-mail addresses listed for the contact.

## Entering Addresses Manually

You may want to enter e-mail addresses or contact names directly in the message form for two reasons: to send mail to addresses that aren't in the address book, or to save time. Typing an address directly lets you send a message to a contact's temporary e-mail address, for example, or to any address that you may not want to enter into your address book. Typing a contact's name saves the time required to open the Select Names dialog box and locate the name; you need only type enough of the contact's name for Outlook to find the recipient. If you enter an e-mail address, you must enter the entire address.

When you enter text in the To, Cc, or Bcc text boxes, Outlook automatically checks the text against the names in the address books. If Outlook determines that the text is a valid e-mail address, it underlines it.

- If you enter an e-mail address for a contact, Outlook converts the e-mail address to the user's name and underlines it. For example, suppose Bill Jones is in your Contacts folder and the address bjones@abc.com is listed in his contact information. If you type bjones@abc.com in the To text box, Outlook will change the address in the message header to Bill Jones.

- If you enter an e-mail address that is not listed in one of your address books, Outlook checks the syntax of the address. If the text you entered has the proper format for an e-mail address, Outlook underlines the address. For example, if Bill was not in an address book, or his e-mail address was not listed in his contact information, Outlook would simply underline the address you entered: <u>bjones@abc.com</u>.

If you enter a name that is not an exact match for a name in an address book, Outlook underlines the name with a wavy red line (just as Word marks a spelling error). Right-click on the name and select the recipient from the shortcut menu. For example, if you type **John** in the To text box, Outlook will underline the name in red. Right-click on the name, and the menu will include all the entries in the address books that include the text:

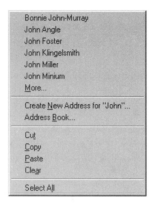

From the menu, select the person you want to send the message to. If you don't identify the recipient before sending the message, Outlook will open a dialog box so that you can select a name.

The next time you enter John as a recipient name, Outlook will automatically select the name you chose from the menu this time. However, the name will have a green, dashed underline so that you know there are other Johns in the address book:

To choose a different John, right-click and select the appropriate recipient from the shortcut menu (who will become the new "default John").

 **TIP** You can tell Outlook which address book or folder to check first when checking names. See Chapter 16 for more details.

 After you've typed the names in the To, Cc, and Bcc text boxes, choose Tools ➤ Check Names from the menu, or click the Check Names button on the message form toolbar.

Outlook's automatic name-checking option is on by default. To turn it off (or back on again) follow these steps:

**1.** Choose Tools ➤ Options from the Outlook menu bar.

**2.** Click the Preferences tab in the Options dialog box.

**3.** Click the E-mail Options button to open the E-mail Options dialog box.

**4.** Click the Advanced E-mail Options button to open the Advanced E-mail Options dialog box.

**5.** Enable or disable the Automatic Name Checking check box.

**6.** Click OK to close each of the three dialog boxes.

 **NOTE** Keep in mind that turning off Automatic Name Checking is just that, turning off the Automatic component. You can still check names manually, but, until you turn it back on, you will not have names checked automatically.

## Using Directory Services

A *directory service* is an address book maintained in an LDAP directory. *LDAP* (*Lightweight Directory Access Protocol*), developed at the University of Michigan, is an emerging Internet/Intranet standard that defines a common format for electronic directories and is used in many networking programs. The directory could be on a local network server running Microsoft Exchange or on a public directory service you access via the Internet, such as Four11 or Bigfoot. You use directory services when you know a person's name but don't have their e-mail address.

 **NOTE** Public directory services are automatically enabled in the Internet Only configuration. In the Workplace/Corporate configuration, LDAP directories are created or enabled by your network administrator. If clicking the Find button doesn't open a Find People dialog box, you don't have access to directory services.

To find an address using a directory service, open the Select Names dialog box, and then click its Find button to open the Find People dialog box, shown in Figure 6.3.

PART

II

Mastering the
Outlook Components

**FIGURE 6.3**

*The Find People dialog box provides easy access to your Contacts list and public directory services.*

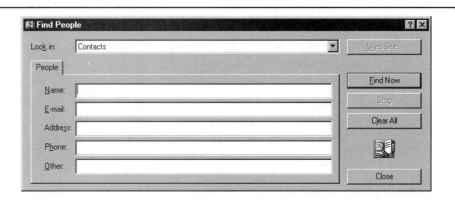

Click the arrow in the Look In text box to open a list of folders and directory services you can search to locate the person you're looking for.

If you're searching a folder that contains Outlook contacts, you can search by name, e-mail address, address, any of the phone numbers listed for the contact, or other information entered in the Contact form, as shown in Figure 6.3. For the directory services, you can usually search only by name or e-mail address.

When you're addressing mail, you'll enter a name and search for an e-mail address. If you receive unsolicited anonymous e-mail, you can use the Find People dialog box to search by the address and find out who sent the e-mail. Figure 6.4 shows the available search fields in the Find People dialog box with the Four11 public directory service selected.

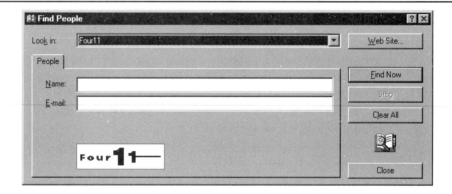

Each of the directory services maintains its own list and provides other types of services on its Web site. Choose a service to search based on the type of information you're looking for:

| Directory Service | Features |
| --- | --- |
| Bigfoot | Free e-mail aliasing and Internet services |
| Four11 and Yahoo! People Search | The most comprehensive lists of individuals; search for telephone numbers on the home page. |
| InfoSpace and InfoSpace Business | Directories of e-mail users, community information, apartment locator, shopping info |
| Switchboard | The "people and business directory," with good lists of companies' e-mail addresses |
| Verisign | People with registered Digital IDs only |
| WhoWhere | Free e-mail and Internet services |

Enter the name of the person whose e-mail address you want to find, and then click the Find Now button. Outlook will connect to the Internet, search the directory service you selected, and find individuals who match the Name text you entered, as shown in Figure 6.5.

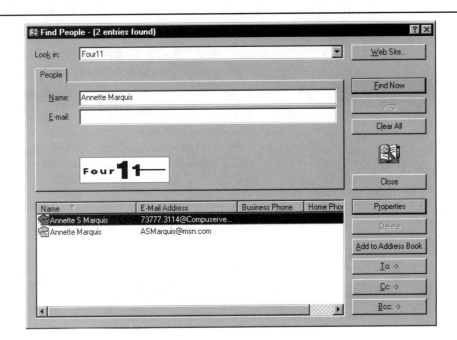

If the name is fairly common, you may see many entries in the list. How do you know which of them, if any, is the person you're looking for? Check the domain for the address. If the person you're looking for works for a company, look for the company's name followed by .com. Do the same for students or employees of educational institutions (.edu), governmental units (.gov), non-profit organizations (.org), and the military (.mil). With addresses from Internet service providers (.net) and the commercial online services (for example, aol.com, msn.com, and compuserve.com) there's no easy way to tell.

If you find the person you're looking for in a directory service, you can click the To, Cc, or Bcc button to add their e-mail address to your message and close the Find People dialog box.

However, if you plan to use this e-mail address again, first click the Add to Address Book button to open the Properties dialog box. The person's name and e-mail address are automatically copied to the appropriate text boxes on the Personal page, as shown in Figure 6.6.

## MASTERING TROUBLESHOOTING

### Troubleshooting Directory Services

If the person you're looking for doesn't appear on the list (or if no potential matches were found), try the following:

- Select a different directory service and repeat the search.
- Enter the person's first initial rather than first name and search again.
- If the person uses both a nickname and their given first name, search both names.

It's possible that the person you're looking for doesn't have e-mail, or that their e-mail address isn't listed in a public directory. Individual accounts with Internet Service Providers typically are not listed unless the person has taken the step of signing up with a directory service. Employees of public institutions in .edu and .gov domains are more likely to be listed than employees of private organizations. Many private institutions keep their e-mail lists private, so employees don't appear in public directories unless they've created an individual listing.

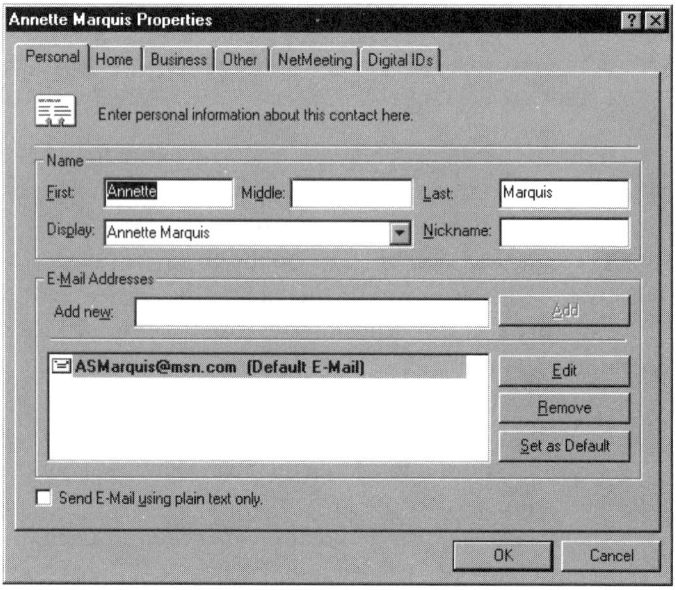

---

**FIGURE 6.6**

*Adding an entry to the address book from the Find People dialog box*

**Annette Marquis Properties**

Personal | Home | Business | Other | NetMeeting | Digital IDs

Enter personal information about this contact here.

**Name**

First: Annette    Middle:    Last: Marquis

Display: Annette Marquis    Nickname:

**E-Mail Addresses**

Add new:    [Add]

ASMarquis@msn.com (Default E-Mail)    [Edit]
[Remove]
[Set as Default]

☐ Send E-Mail using plain text only.

[OK]    [Cancel]

Fill in any other information about the person on the other pages of the Properties dialog box. When you click OK, Outlook closes the Properties dialog box, adds the individual's entry to the currently selected address book, and automatically adds the name to the originally chosen field. To add existing contacts to the recipient list, click the To, Cc, or Bcc button to open the Add Recipient dialog box, select the name of the new recipient, and click the To, Cc, or Bcc button to add the person as a recipient for the current message.

## Adding Addresses on the Fly

You can quickly create a contact from any e-mail address you enter in a message. Right-click on the address in the To, Cc, or Bcc text box and choose Add to Contacts from the shortcut menu. Outlook will open a blank Contact form with the e-mail address in both the Name and E-mail text boxes. Correct the name, enter any additional information you wish, and then click Save and Close to close the form and return to your e-mail message. In the Corporate/Workgroup configuration, you can add the address to your Personal Address Book; the person will appear in your address book, but not in the Outlook Contacts list.

## Creating and Using Distribution Lists (Groups)

When you work with a team or are a member of a committee or task force, you'll find yourself addressing e-mail to the same group of people: the other members of your team or committee. In the infancy of e-mail, you had to address your messages individually to each person on the team. *Distribution lists* streamline this process. With a distribution list, you create a named list in your personal address book and then add all the members of your team or committee to the group. When you address your next e-mail message, you can send it to the distribution list (and all its members) rather than adding each of the members as individual recipients.

In the Internet Only configuration, you create *groups* rather than distribution lists. Groups and distribution lists work the same way, but you create them in a slightly different fashion.

**Creating a Group (Internet Only Users)**     Creating a group is easy. Select Tools ➢ Address Book from the Outlook menu to open the Address Book dialog box. Click the New Group button to open the Group Properties dialog box, shown in Figure 6.7. Type a name for the group in the Group Name text box. Group names can include spaces, hyphens, and other punctuation you would include in a Windows filename. As you enter the name, the dialog box caption in the title bar changes to include the group name before the word *Properties*.

**MASTERING TROUBLESHOOTING**

## Mastering Address Book Icons

In the address book, different icons are used to identify the source for e-mail addresses.

The contact card icon identifies names from your global or personal address book.

When you include an address from a directory service, the remote address icon is displayed. If you add the person to your address book or Contacts, Outlook changes to the contact card icon.

Names of groups (distribution lists) are preceded by the group icon.

---

**FIGURE 6.7**

*Create distribution lists in the Group Properties dialog box.*

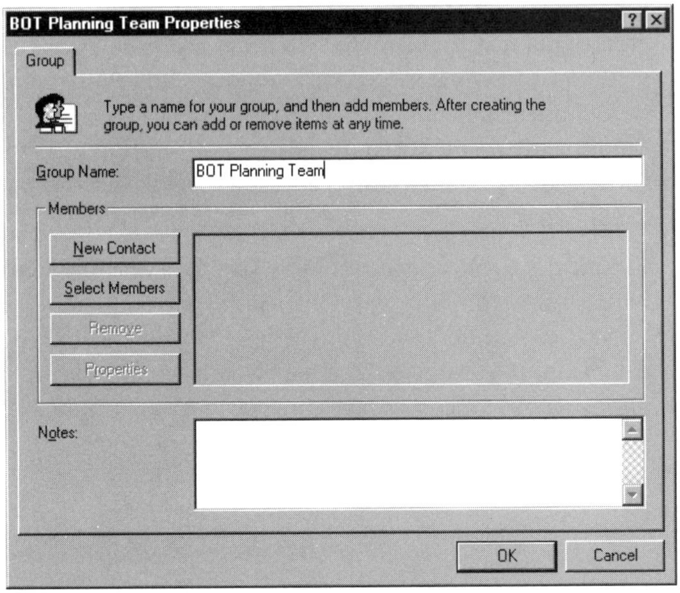

**BOT Planning Team Properties**

Group

Type a name for your group, and then add members. After creating the group, you can add or remove items at any time.

Group Name: BOT Planning Team

Members

New Contact
Select Members
Remove
Properties

Notes:

OK    Cancel

There's a Notes area in the dialog box where you can enter any comments you have about the group. For example, you might note when you created the group, its purpose, and the names of associated groups.

Group members must be included in your address book. If the person you want to add to the group isn't already in the address book, click the New Contact button to open a Properties dialog box. Enter the person's information (including, of course, an e-mail address), and then click OK to create the new Contact, close the dialog box, and add the person to the group.

To add a group member from the address book, click the Select Members button to open the Select Group Members dialog box, which looks much like the Select Names dialog box. Select the entry for the person you want to add in the left pane, and then click the Select button to add the person to the group in the right pane. You can hold Ctrl and click on more than one entry to add multiple addresses to the group at once, as shown in Figure 6.8.

**FIGURE 6.8**

*Use the Select Group Members dialog box to add one or more contacts to the distribution list.*

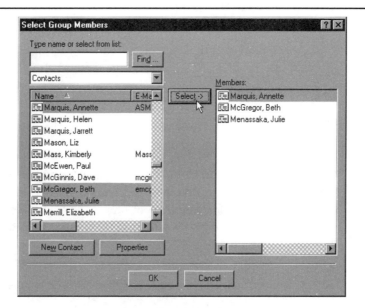

You can also add new contacts in the Select Group Members dialog box, using the New Contact button mentioned previously. After you've added the person as a contact, click Select to add them to the group. Click the Find button to open the Find People dialog box to add group members from a directory service (see "Using Directory Services" earlier in this chapter). When you've added all the group members, click OK to close the Select Group Members dialog box. If you've added any group members from a directory service, Outlook will prompt you to add the person to the address book:

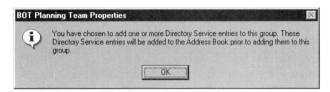

Click OK to close the dialog box. Outlook will open a Properties dialog box for the new contact. Add any other information for the person, and then click OK to add the individual to the address book and the distribution list.

In summary, to create a group in the Internet Only configuration:

1. Choose Tools ➣ Address Book to open the Address Book dialog box.

2. Click the New Group button.

3. In the Group Name text box, type the name for the group.

4. Click the Select Members button to add names from the address book.

5. Select a name in the list and click the Select button to add the address to the group. Hold Ctrl to select multiple names before clicking the Select button.

6. To add people to the distribution list that aren't in your address book, click the New Contact button and create a new contact.

7. Click OK to close the Select Group Members dialog box. Click OK again to close the Group Properties dialog box.

**Creating a Distribution List (Corporate/Workgroup Users)**   In the Corporate/ Workgroup configuration, you create distribution lists in your Personal Address Book. (If you don't have a Personal Address Book on your computer, see Chapter 12 to create one.)

Choose Tools ➣ Address Book to open the Address Book dialog box, and select the Personal Address Book in the Select Names From drop-down list. Then choose File ➣ New Entry from the Address Book menu to open the New Entry dialog box, shown here:

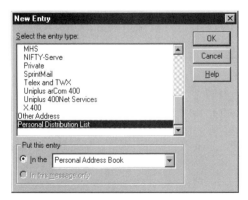

Scroll to the bottom of the Select the Entry Type list, and choose Personal Distribution List. Make sure that Personal Address Book is selected as the location for the entry, and click OK to open the New Personal Distribution List Properties dialog box, shown here:

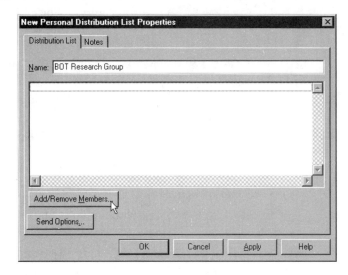

Enter a name for the list, and then click the Add/Remove Members button to open the Edit Members dialog box, shown here:

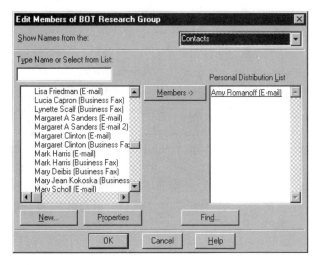

Choose the address book that contains the first member you wish to add. Select the member, and then click the Members button to add the member to the distribution list. To add a member who isn't in an address book, click the New button to open the New Entry dialog box again. Select an address type, and then choose whether you want to add the member to your Personal Address Book, or just to this distribution list. Note that you cannot create a new contact with the New Entry button—only an address book entry.

When you've selected all the members of the distribution list, click OK to close the Edit Members dialog box. Click OK again to close the New Personal Distribution List Properties dialog box and add the distribution list to your Personal Address Book. Close the address book.

In summary, these are the steps to create a distribution list in the Corporate/Workgroup configuration:

1. Choose Tools ➤ Address Book to open the Address Book dialog box.

2. Select Personal Address Book in the Select Names From list.

3. Choose File ➤ New Entry from the Address Book dialog box to open the New Entry dialog box.

4. Choose Personal Distribution List from the list of entry types. Make sure the Personal Address Book is selected under Put This Entry, and click OK to open the New Personal Distribution List dialog box.

5. Enter a name for the Distribution List in the Name text box.

6. Click the Add/Remove Members button to open the Edit Members dialog box.

7. Choose the address book with the member's name in the Show Names from the drop-down list.

8. Select the member's name from the entries in the left pane.

9. Click the Members button to add the selected address to the list. Hold Ctrl to select multiple names before clicking the Members button.

10. To add people who aren't in your address book to the distribution list, click the New button to open the New Entry dialog box. Create a new entry in your Personal Address Book or just in this distribution list.

11. After selecting all members, click OK to close the Edit Members dialog box. Click OK again to close the Group Properties dialog box and add the distribution list to your Personal Address Book.

**Addressing Mail to a Group or Distribution List**   To send mail to all members of a group or distribution list, type the group name in the To, Cc, or Bcc text box on the message form, or click one of the three buttons to open the Select Names dialog box.

Group names are bold in the Select Names dialog box and address books, and they are preceded by the group icon. Select the group name and click the To, Cc, or Bcc button to add the group's members as message recipients. The group name will be bold in the To, Cc, or Bcc text box on the message form.

If you need to check the membership of a group, right-click on the group name in the message's address boxes or in the Select Names dialog box and choose Properties to open the group's properties sheet.

**Adding or Removing a Name from a Group or Distribution List**   The membership of a team or committee can change as members leave the team and new members are added. You can add and remove names from a group in the address book. Choose Tools ➢ Address Book from the menu, and select the address book that contains the group. Double-click the name of the group you want to change, or right-click on a group name and choose Properties to open the group's Properties dialog box.

If you have Internet Only mail, click the Select Members button to add new group members. To remove a member from a group, select the name you want to delete and click the Remove button in the Group Properties dialog box.

In a Workgroup or Corporate setting, click the Add/Remove Members button in the Properties dialog box to open the Edit Members dialog box. Use the Members button to add names to the group. To remove names, select the names in the right pane of the dialog box, and then press the Delete key on your keyboard. When you've finished adding and removing members, click OK to close the Select Names dialog box, and OK again to close the group Properties dialog box.

**Delete a Group or Distribution List**   When a team's work is complete or a committee is disbanded, you probably won't need the group or distribution list any more. You'll keep it for a while so you can send congratulatory messages or commiserate about the group's involuntary dissolution, but eventually you'll be finished with it. To remove a group list, open the address book (Tools ➢ Address Book) and select the group you want to remove.

In the Internet Only configuration, click the Delete button to remove the group. The entries for the individuals included in the group list will not be deleted. With Corporate/Workgroup settings, right-click on the name of the distribution list and choose Delete from the shortcut menu. When you delete the distribution list, any addresses that only existed in the list are also deleted.

PART

II

Mastering the
Outlook Components

**MASTERING THE OPPORTUNITIES**

### Mastering Groups and Distribution Lists

When you address mail to a group (or distribution list), all the members of the group receive the original, or a courtesy copy, or a blind courtesy copy. With some projects, you'll want to create more than one group so you can quickly send messages and copies to the appropriate people. For example, Beth, Jean, and Margaret are members of your planning team, but Denny and John, the team's supervisors, need to be kept "in the loop" as your team makes decisions and implements strategies. By creating two groups—Planning Team (Beth, Jean, and Margaret) and Planning CC (Denny and John)—you can send messages to the team and courtesy copies to Denny and John with two simple clicks. Reports of the team's progress can be sent to Planning CC, with courtesy copies to the Planning Team.

## Entering Message Text

Type the text of your message in the open text area. Text automatically wraps at the end of the line, so you don't need to press Enter unless you are ready to end one paragraph and begin typing another. Use the Edit menu commands or the shortcut menu to cut, copy, paste, find, and select text in the body of the message. To check spelling in a message, choose Tools ➤ Spelling from the menu. Or, you can wait; by default, Outlook will automatically check spelling before sending your message.

E-mail is, in some ways, less formal than traditional correspondence. You don't need a date or internal address—the mail program provides them—and it isn't unusual for messages to end without a closing. When you're entering the body of your message, however, don't mistake casual for less formal. Use appropriate business language in business correspondence and save casual language for e-mail to friends and family. Also, remember that e-mail is read, not heard. Irony and sarcasm are prone to misinterpretation when the audience can't see your facial expression or hear your tone of voice.

# Attaching Items and Files to Messages

You can *attach* a file or an Outlook item to an e-mail message, using the message as you would use an envelope as a container for a letter. It doesn't matter which e-mail editor you use; you can attach items and files to messages in any format. Files and items can be inserted in a message as attachments, as shortcuts, or as text.

**Attachment**   A copy of the file or item is inserted as a separate file alongside the message. Use attachments when the recipient needs to work with a copy of the file or item in its original file format. For example, you could send a colleague a number of Contact items, which they could then use in Outlook, or an Excel worksheet, which they could open in Excel. Note that the attachment is a copy, so changes your colleague makes will not be reflected in the original file.

**Shortcut**   An icon is inserted in the message, which points to the original file. Insert a file or item as a shortcut when you and the recipient both have access to the file. For example, if the Excel worksheet is stored on your departmental server, you could send a shortcut so that your colleague could find the file and both of you could work with the original file.

**Text Only**   The text of the file is inserted in the body of the message. Use this option to send the contents of a file when the recipient doesn't have access to the creating program. For example, send a WordPad file as Text Only to a recipient who doesn't have access to WordPad, or information from a Contact form to a friend who doesn't use Outlook.

**NOTE**   When you send messages with categories like Ideas or Hot Contact as attachments, the categories you used are automatically added to the recipients' categories. Unless you and your recipient use exactly the same categories, you should consider deleting the categories from the attached item before sending the message.

To attach a file to a message, choose Insert ➤ Item from the message menu to open the Insert Item dialog box, shown in Figure 6.9. Select the file, and then choose Text Only, Attachment, or Shortcut from the Insert As option group. Click OK to insert the file.

If you insert the file as an attachment or shortcut, an icon representing the file or file location appears in the message. Text (or something similar) appears for a file inserted as Text Only. In Figure 6.10, an Internet Explorer file has been inserted as a shortcut, a graphics (TIF) file as an attachment, and an executable batch file as text only. When the recipient clicks on the files, the Internet Explorer file will open in Internet Explorer; the TIF will be opened in the recipient's default graphics editor; and the batch file will open in the default text editor. If your recipient doesn't have the program needed to open a file, they can't view it.

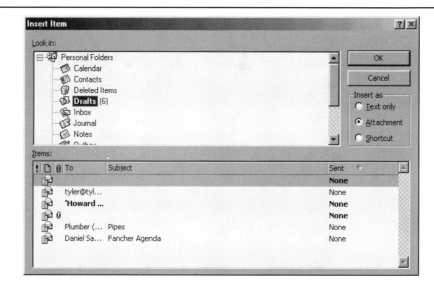

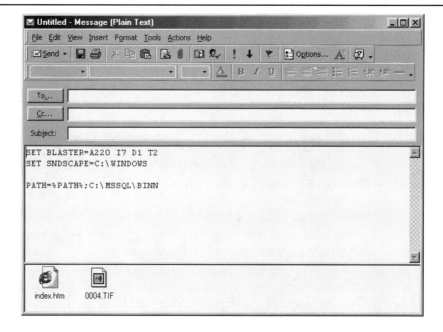

## MASTERING TROUBLESHOOTING

### Troubleshooting File Attachments

Only a few file types can be successfully inserted as Text Only. Files created in plain text editors like Notepad and Rich Text editors such as WordPad insert well; these programs create files with extensions of .txt, .bat, and .rtf. Other files contain formatting that can't be translated as text. For example, Microsoft Word files begin and end with embedded codes that specify the document's properties. If you insert a Word file as Text Only in a plain text or RTF message, it will begin and end with symbols—hundreds or thousands of symbols.

If your intended recipient doesn't have the application to open an attachment, you can send the text of the document in the message without attaching it. For a Word document, for example, open the document in Word, select the text, and copy it to the Clipboard. Open the message in Outlook, position the insertion point, and paste the text into the message. You can also save the Word document using the Text Only or Text Only with Line Breaks format, and then attach the file.

To attach an Outlook item to a message, place the insertion point in the body of the message and choose Insert ➤ Item from the message menu to open the Insert Item dialog box, shown in Figure 6.11. Select the folder that contains the item you want to attach, and then choose the item in the Items pane. You can use Ctrl or Shift and click to select multiple items.

PART

II

Mastering the
Outlook Components

**FIGURE 6.11**

*Use the Insert Item dialog box to select Outlook items to attach to an e-mail message.*

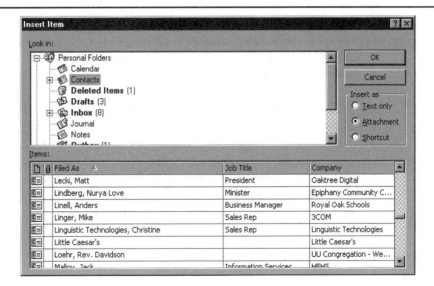

If your recipient uses Outlook, send the item as an attachment. For recipients who don't have Outlook, insert the item as Text Only. Outlook will add the text from the selected item to the message.

 **TIP**  If you send an Outlook item as a shortcut, the recipient must have permission to access the folder that contains the item. By default, other users do not have permission to view items in your personal folders, so you'll generally want to send items as Attachments or Text Only. For more information on folders and permissions, see Chapter 13.

# Sending Your Message

You've selected an e-mail editor, addressed your message, added text, and inserted attachments, and you're ready to send your message to the recipients. But first, take a moment and examine Outlook's message handling options to make sure your message is delivered and received with the same care you took while creating it.

## Setting Message Options

Message Options are available for each message, and you can set them depending on your needs. Some of these options allow you to insert voting buttons or to receive a validation message confirming that a message you sent was received. Some of these options are only available for particular Mail Support configurations. Message options are set for the individual message you're creating now, not for all new messages.

 Click the Options button in the message form's toolbar to open the Message Options dialog box. The Corporate/Workgroup Message Options dialog box is shown in Figure 6.12; the Internet Only version of the dialog box does not include the Voting and Tracking Options.

### Setting Importance and Sensitivity

Both the importance and sensitivity of a message can be set at High, Normal, or Low. Most e-mail programs have a way of marking the importance of incoming messages, so you can use the Importance setting to help the recipient prioritize incoming messages. If you set Importance at High, the recipient will know that the message is not routine; Low says "get to this when you have some free time," and it is generally used for messages you would mark FYI (For Your Information) if they were sent on paper.

**FIGURE 6.12**

*Message options are set for a specific message.*

Message Options

Message settings
Importance: Normal
Sensitivity: Normal

Security
☐ Encrypt message contents and attachments
☐ Add digital signature to outgoing message

Voting and Tracking options
☐ Use voting buttons:
☐ Tell me when this message has been delivered
☐ Tell me when this message has been read

Delivery options
☐ Have replies sent to: [ Select Names... ]
☑ Save sent message to: Sent Items [ Browse... ]
☐ Do not deliver before:
☐ Expires after:

[ Categories... ]

[ Close ]

PART
II

Mastering the
Outlook Components

The default Importance setting for a new message is Normal. To mark a message with Low or High Importance, choose Low or High from the Importance drop-down list in the Mail Options dialog box. Or, you can click the Low Importance (down arrow) or High Importance (exclamation mark) button on the message toolbar.

There are four sensitivity settings: Confidential, Private, Personal, and Normal. You set sensitivity by selecting a setting from the Sensitivity drop-down list in the Mail Options dialog box. This setting is used to help a delegated person handling the recipient's mail know how to deal with incoming items, or route messages to delegates in the recipient's absence. When you use Outlook on a network running Microsoft Exchange, you can give other users permission to view and respond to your messages while you're out of the office (see Chapter 17). You can base your rules for how the delegates should handle your messages on the Importance and Sensitivity settings of the messages. Table 6.1 summarizes the settings for messages with different types of content.

**TABLE 6.1: MESSAGE IMPORTANCE AND SENSITIVITY**

| Importance | Sensitivity | Message Content |
|---|---|---|
| Low | All | Routine information that doesn't require a response, to be reviewed as time permits. |
| Normal | Normal | "Regular" messages that may or may not require a response. |

*Continued* ▶

| TABLE 6.1: MESSAGE IMPORTANCE AND SENSITIVITY (CONTINUED) | | |
| --- | --- | --- |
| **Importance** | **Sensitivity** | **Message Content** |
| High | Normal | Messages that require immediate action or response, or time-value material the sender feels you need to know. |
| All | Personal | Messages that are not work-related. |
| All | Private | Work-related messages that are to be read only by the recipient; private messages cannot be altered after they have been sent. |
| All | Confidential | Messages that should only be opened by the recipient, but which can be altered. |

## MASTERING THE OPPORTUNITIES

## Mastering E-mail Privacy

E-mail can give you a false sense of privacy. You're sitting alone at your computer, creating a message that the recipient will read, alone at their computer. What could be more private, right? Wrong. No message is truly private or confidential. Your e-mail is vulnerable to anyone with high-level permissions on your network or the recipient's network.

Deleting a compromising message isn't enough; a message has a life of its own long after you delete it. Employers regularly back up data, including e-mail messages stored on a server; and backups of messages that defendants deleted from their desktop computers have been used in court as evidence. Employees have been fired for the content of messages sent to coworkers and supervisors. One individual was fired for forwarding sexist and sexually explicit jokes from the Internet to his male coworkers because it created a hostile environment in the workplace. The employer had discovered the messages on the company server.

If a message is marked as Personal, Private, or Confidential, the message may still be opened accidentally by your recipient's assistant if their mail service doesn't note it as private. Some e-mail systems recognize sensitivity settings, but others do not. For home users, anyone with access to the recipient's e-mail account can open the message, regardless of its sensitivity setting.

As an employee, your privacy rights vary in each state, and progressive companies generally have e-mail policies that you can review. But don't get lulled into believing that your messages are confidential or personal; if you wouldn't write it on a paper memo, don't communicate it in an e-mail message.

You can set the default importance and sensitivity for all new messages in the Options dialog box. Choose Tools ➢ Options ➢ Preferences, and then click the E-mail Options button to open the E-mail Options dialog box. In the E-mail Options dialog box, click the Advanced E-mail Options button to open the dialog box shown in Figure 6.13. Choose the default settings in the Set Importance and Set Sensitivity drop-down lists, and then close the open dialog boxes.

**FIGURE 6.13**

*Set default importance and sensitivity in the Advanced E-mail Options dialog box.*

PART

II

Mastering the
Outlook Components

## Directing Message Replies to a Third Party

There are times when you'll want the recipients of your message to reply to another address: your assistant, the person in charge of the help desk or the Habitat for Humanity sign-up sheet, or an alternate e-mail address that you use. You can put "please send replies directly to Mary Smith" in your message, but most people click the Reply button as a matter of habit. You can make sure that all the replies end up in the right place by using the Have Replies Sent To option:

1. Click the Options button on the Message toolbar to open the Message Options dialog box.

2. Enable the Have Replies Sent To check box (see Figure 6.12).

3. Type the name or e-mail address that replies should be sent to, or click the Select Names button to open the Select Names dialog box and choose a recipient for replies.

You can't choose or enter the group name for a distribution list; you can only have replies sent to an address for an individual.

## Saving a Copy of the Message

By default, copies of all messages are kept in the Sent Items folder. If you don't want to save a copy of the message, disable the Save Sent Message To check box in the Message Options dialog box (see Figure 6.12). To save a copy of the message in a different folder, click the Browse button and choose the folder in the Select Folder dialog box.

Don't save sent items in any of the regular Outlook folders except Sent Items unless you like being confused. The assumption is that you've created a new folder to hold certain types of sent items. If you're the point person on a new project, for example, you might want to save the messages you generate in a separate folder so you can easily find the messages related to the project. You'll find more information on creating Outlook folders in Chapter 13.

## Setting a Time Frame for Message Delivery

The Do Not Deliver Before and Expires After settings in the Message Options dialog box allow you to delay mail delivery or stop attempting to deliver a message after a certain date and time (see Figure 6.12). You might delay mail if, for example, you need to send an important announcement to all employees next Monday, and you won't be in the office. Setting an expiration time means that a client who is on vacation this week won't return next week to read about an offer that expires this Friday.

The Do Not Deliver Before and Expires After text boxes both open a calendar control, which you can use to set the delay or expiration date. If you want to include a time as well as a date (other than the default of 5:00 P.M.), choose the date, and then edit the time in the text box:

These are the steps for setting delay and expiration dates:

1. Click the Options button on the Message toolbar to open the Options dialog box.

2. Enable the Do Not Deliver Before and/or Expires After check boxes.

3. Use the calendar controls to set delay and expiration dates. If necessary, edit the time.

4. Click OK to close the Options dialog box.

## Choosing a Delivery Service

If you have more than one e-mail account in the Internet Only configuration, you can select the account you want to use to deliver this message. This may be important, because when a recipient clicks the Reply button, the message is sent to the account that the original message came from. Choose an account from the Send Message Using drop-down list in the Advanced E-mail Options dialog box. This is not an option in the Corporate/Workgroup configuration.

## Using E-mail as a Voting Tool

You're a team player, and you want to know what the other members of your team think about a proposed course of action. You could call them all and keep a tally of their feedback. Or, you could send an e-mail message to each member of the team, wait for their replies, and then open and tabulate them. The Corporate/Workgroup configuration of Outlook has a built-in tool to help you gather opinions and feedback for solid decision-making that will automatically log and tally each team member's vote.

To turn a message into a ballot, open the Options dialog box for the message. In the Voting and Tracking Options section, enable the Use Voting Buttons check box, and then select the voting buttons you want to include in the message from the drop-down list. The choices are:

- Approve; Reject
- Yes; No
- Yes; No; Maybe

If none of these choices meet your needs, you can enter your own button choices, with semicolons between each item. In Figure 6.14, we're asking recipients to vote on a location for a meeting. Replies will be sent to the person in charge of the meeting.

---

**FIGURE 6.14**

*Choose or enter button options to use a message as a voting tool.*

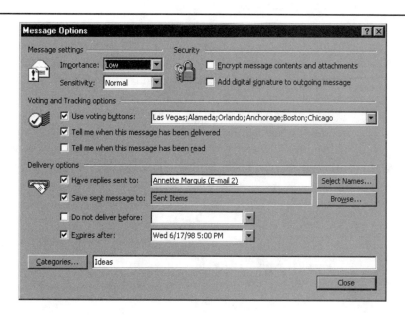

As the recipients vote by clicking one of the buttons on their messages, Outlook sends the replies to the person designated in the message options. Outlook also attaches a tracking form to the original message (in the Sent Items folder) that tallies the responses, as shown in Figure 6.15. You can easily find the original message among the Sent Items; the message icon includes an information symbol.

**FIGURE 6.15**

*Votes are automatically tallied when replies are received.*

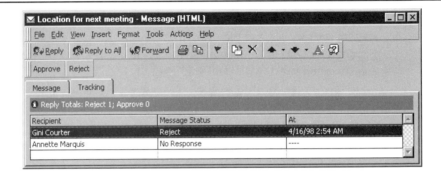

**NOTE** Voting only works for users in your workgroup or company; you can't use voting as an e-mail tool over the Internet.

## Setting Tracking Options

The Corporate/Workgroup configuration also supports tracking for individual messages. Tracking notifies you when your message has been delivered to your recipient; this notification is called a *delivery receipt*. When the recipient opens your message, you are notified with a *read receipt*. The delivery and read receipts are sent by the recipient's mail server; not all mail servers send receipts, so asking for a receipt doesn't guarantee that you'll get one. Another thing to consider: "read receipt" is a bit of a misnomer. The server can't tell you that a message has been read, only that it has been opened. If your recipient opens the message and deletes it without reading it, you'll still receive a read receipt.

The system may be imperfect, but it's still very useful when you need to know, for example, that

- your message to Nancy about Saturday's emergency board meeting was delivered on Friday
- Nancy didn't open it until Monday
- which explains why she didn't come to the meeting

To turn on tracking for a message, enable the Tell Me When This Message Has Been Delivered and/or Tell Me When This Message Has Been Read check boxes (see Figure 6.14).

 **NOTE** You can't set tracking options in the Internet Only configuration, but you can track specified messages using the Rules Wizard. For more information on rules, see Chapter 7.

## Mail Security Options

Outlook includes features that allow you to securely send and receive e-mail messages. There are two ways to secure a message: with a digital signature and with encryption. A digital signature provides corroboration that a message did, indeed, come from you and has not been altered before the recipient opened it. Encryption uses a mathematical algorithm to scramble the message. Only the recipient can unscramble and read the message. Outlook uses S/MIME to secure Internet e-mail messages.

### Adding a Digital Signature to a Message

To send messages with a digital signature, you need a certificate, also called a Digital ID. If you do not have a Digital ID registered on your PC, the Security Message Options will be disabled. When the Security options are enabled, as shown in Figure 6.16, you can add a digital signature to your messages. (For information on obtaining a Digital ID, see Chapter 15.)

**FIGURE 6.16**

*The Security options are enabled if you have a registered Digital ID.*

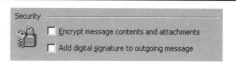

To add a digital signature to your message, open the Message Options dialog box, enable the Add Digital Signature to Outgoing Message check box, and then click OK to close the Message Options dialog box. If some of your recipients may not be able to decode messages with Digital IDs, choose File ➤ Properties from the message menu to open the Properties dialog box, shown in Figure 6.17. Make sure the Send Clear Text Signed Message check box is enabled. If a recipient's mail system doesn't support S/MIME, they'll still get your message, but it won't include a digital signature.

**FIGURE 6.17**

*Open the message Properties dialog box to modify the security settings.*

 **TIP** The security options set in a message's Properties always override defaults set in Outlook's Options dialog box.

To summarize, these are the steps for adding a digital signature to a message:

1. Click the Options button on the message toolbar to open the Message Options dialog box.

2. Enable the Add Digital Signature to Outgoing Message check box.

3. Click OK to close the Message Options dialog box.

To add a digital signature to all new messages, choose Tools ➤ Options from the Outlook menu to open the Message Options dialog box, and then click the Security tab. Enable the Add Digital Signature to Outgoing Messages check box.

## Encrypting a Message

Before you can send an encrypted e-mail message to someone, you must have a copy of that person's digital ID in your contact list. Ask the person to send you an e-mail message that includes their digital signature. Open the message and right-click on the sender's address in the message's From field. Choose Add to Contacts from the short-cut menu. The new contact will include the digital ID. To encrypt a message:

1. Click the Options button on the message toolbar to open the Message Options dialog box.

2. Enable the Encrypt Message Contents and Attachments check box.

3. Click OK.

To encrypt all new messages you send, choose Tools ➤ Options on the Outlook menu, and then click the Security tab. Enable the Encrypt Message Contents and Attachments for Outgoing Messages check box. If you want to send an unencrypted message, choose File ➤ Properties in the message menu and change the settings for the individual message (see Figure 6.17).

## Sending Mail Messages

You're ready to send your message to its recipients. Click the Send button on the mes-sage toolbar, or choose File ➤ Send Using and select a service from the menu to place the message in the Outlook Outbox. You may be wondering how long the message will hang around in the Outbox. The answer: it depends. There are three possible scenarios:

- In a Corporate/Workgroup installation where you are connected to a network, options are usually set to send messages immediately and your outgoing mes-sage will spend very little time in the Outbox.

- In an Internet Only or Corporate/Workgroup installation, you can establish automated Internet mail delivery at specified intervals (see Chapter 12). Out-look connects to the Internet every *N* minutes or hours, and delivers and receives messages.

- On the other hand, you may be using Outlook with the Internet Only configu-ration without automated mail delivery (the default for Internet Only) or you might be working offline in a Corporate/Workgroup configuration. In that case, mail waits in your Outbox until you instruct Outlook to send and retrieve mes-sages.

To move the message out of the Outbox and into the Internet or local mail server, do one of the following:

- Choose Tools ➤ Send from the Outlook menu to send, but not receive, messages from your mail server.

- Choose Tools ➤ Send and Receive ➤ All Accounts (or a specific account) to both send and receive messages.

PART

II

Mastering the
Outlook Components

If you access your mail server with a dial-up connection, a dialog box opens while Outlook is connecting to your server. When connecting to an ISP or company server, Corporate/Workgroup users see the following message box:

This dialog box remains open while messages are being sent and received. Once Outlook has established a dial-up connection, you can move the dialog box to a less central location.

Internet Only users see a different dialog box. When you click the Details button, the dialog box expands to show connection information, as shown in Figure 6.18.

**FIGURE 6.18**

*Click the Details button to watch Outlook send and receive mail.*

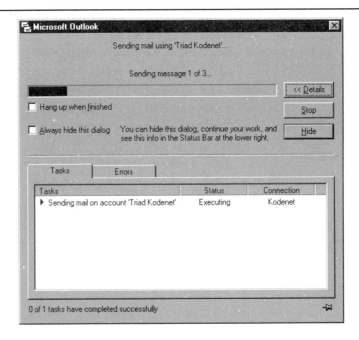

You'll still be able to keep track of Outlook's progress, even with the dialog box hidden. Check the right side of the status bar to see reports as Outlook sends and receives your messages.

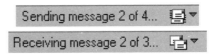

If you need to cancel message sending or delivering, click on the arrow at the right end of the status bar and choose Cancel Mail Delivery from the menu. To redisplay the Details dialog box, choose Details from the menu. After each message has been sent, Outlook moves it from the Outbox to the Sent Items folder, or to another folder you specified in the message options.

# Receiving Mail

One of the best parts of working on a network is automatic mail delivery. You're sitting at your desk typing a short memo, when a bell rings and a small envelope appears in the Windows taskbar tray. You've got mail! Double-click the mail icon in the taskbar and you're automatically moved to the Inbox so you can see your new messages. If your company has an Internet mail gateway, messages from outside the company will also be automatically delivered. Of course, you must have Outlook running to receive messages. If you close Outlook, messages remain on your company's mail server until you start Outlook.

In the Internet Only configuration or the Corporate/Workgroup configuration without an established Internet mail account with automatic retrieval scheduled, you have to tell Outlook to retrieve Internet mail messages.

 **TIP** In either configuration, you can have Outlook display a message box (in addition to playing the sound effect and displaying the envelope icon) when new mail appears. Choose Tools ➢ Options to open the Options dialog box. On the Preferences page, click the E-mail Options button and enable the Display a Notification Message When New Mail Arrives check box.

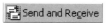

Click the Send and Receive button on the Outlook toolbar, or choose Tools ➢ Send and Receive from the Outlook menu bar. If you have more than one e-mail service or account, you can choose to send and retrieve all messages from the menu, or just messages from one account or service.

In the Internet Only configuration, a large dialog box appears to let you know that Outlook is connecting to your Internet server. You have the option to hide the dialog box or view more details. In the Corporate/Workgroup configuration, you'll see the smaller Deliver Messages message box. With either configuration, you need to wait until Outlook has made the connection and the mail server has verified your password, but then you can continue working in Outlook while messages are retrieved in the background.

# Previewing Mail Messages

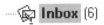

When you look at folders like the Inbox icon in the Folder List, the number of unread messages appears in parentheses after the folder name. (If the folder list is not visible, choose View ➤ Folder List to display it.) In the table view of the messages, unread messages are in boldface, so they are easy to spot (see Figure 6.19).

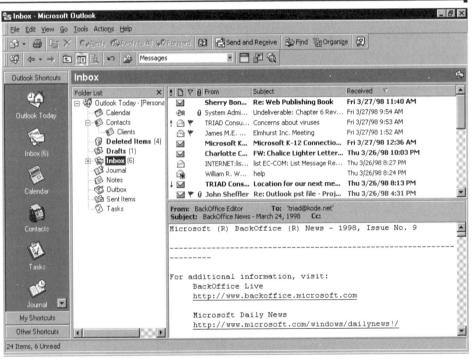

**FIGURE 6.19**

*Unread messages are boldface in the Inbox.*

Select a message, and the beginning of the message appears in the preview pane below the messages. If the preview pane is not open, choose View ➤ Preview Pane from the Outlook menu to display it. You can adjust the size of the preview pane by adjusting the bar at the top of the preview pane up or down with the mouse pointer.

**TIP** You cannot preview encrypted messages.

Right-click in the message list area and select AutoPreview from the contextual menu to display the first three lines of every message. Selecting AutoPreview again turns AutoPreview off.

Using the message icons and the preview pane or AutoPreview, you can quickly decide which messages need your immediate attention and which can wait. The previews usually let you see enough of a message to gauge its urgency. The first four columns of the default Inbox view show the message's Importance, Message Icon, Flag Status, and Attachment information. If the sender set the importance of the message, it is displayed in the first column; high importance is marked with a red exclamation point, low importance with a blue arrow. Table 6.2 shows the icons used in the Inbox.

**TABLE 6.2: INBOX MESSAGE ICONS**

| Icon | Message | Icon | Message |
|------|---------|------|---------|
| ↓ | Low importance | | Encrypted message |
| ! | High importance | | Read |
| ✉ | Unread | | Forwarded |

*Continued* ▶

| Icon | Message | Icon | Message |
|------|---------|------|---------|
| TABLE 6.2: INBOX MESSAGE ICONS (CONTINUED) | | | |
| | Meeting request | | Replied to |
| | Flagged for follow-up | | Rejected by server; can be re-sent |
| | Flagged; follow-up completed | | Includes an attachment |
| | Attached Outlook item (task request, journal entry) | | |

# Replying to Mail

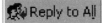

After you read a message, you'll often want to reply to it immediately. You can reply to the sender, or to everyone who received the message and courtesy copies of the message. Select or open the message you wish to reply to, and then click the Reply button to address a reply only to the sender, or the Reply to All button to send a reply to the sender and all the other recipients of the message you received. Outlook opens a message form and enters the recipients' addresses in the To text box. You can add other recipients using the To, Cc, and Bcc buttons on the message form.

The text of the message you're replying to is at the bottom of the open text area of the form; this is called *quoted text*. Each line of quoted text begins with the > symbol so it doesn't get confused with the text of your reply. Enter the text of your reply, and then click Send to send the reply to your Outbox.

**TIP** When you click the Reply or Reply to All button, Outlook opens and addresses the form, but the original message remains open. To have Outlook automatically close the original message when you click Reply, Reply to All, or Forward, enable the Close Original Message on Reply or Forward check box in the Options dialog box (Tools ➢ Options ➢ Preferences ➢ E-mail Options).

# Changing Options for Quoted Text

Quoted text preceded by the > symbol is the norm for replies to plain text messages. If you're exchanging a lot of e-mail messages, or when a number of people are involved in a conversation, it's easy to get lost in the thread of the conversation. When Bob writes "Yes," which of the three proposals was he agreeing to?

You can change the format of quoted text, omit it entirely, omit or change the preceding symbol, or have your reply text preceded with your name. To change the format for replies, choose Tools ➢ Options to open the Options dialog box. On the Preferences page, click the E-mail Options button to open the E-mail Options dialog box, shown in Figure 6.20.

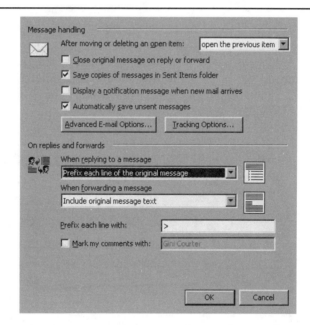

**FIGURE 6.20**

*Change options for message replies in the E-mail Options dialog box.*

There are five options for quoted text in the When Replying to a Message drop-down list:

- Do Not Include Original Message
- Attach Original Message
- Include Original Message Text

PART

II

Mastering the Outlook Components

- Include and Indent Original Message Text
- Prefix Each Line of the Original Message (default)

Prefixing each line of the original message is the default because all mail programs support text, so the prefix is handled just like any other character. Some older programs will remove indenting, or replace it with a symbol. If you prefix each line, Outlook uses the symbol in the Prefix Each Line With text box. The downside of prefixing quoted text is that Outlook's spell check treats it as newly entered text, and checks the spelling of the original messages, as well as the reply text you enter.

There is a trend away from quoted text in business correspondence. If the original text is lengthy, recipients appreciate it if you don't include the full text of the message. Each reply adds another header, and as the conversation continues with replies to replies, you can quickly acquire pages of original text with multiple headers. (It's considered good manners to delete all but the relevant portion of the quoted text.)

When replying to a complex message, comments may provide the best solution. With comments, your name or other custom text appears in brackets to the right of comments you make in the original text. This option won't work if you choose Word as your e-mail editor. Figure 6.21 shows a message reply with comments interspersed in the original text.

**FIGURE 6.21**

*Comments clearly identify your replies within the original text.*

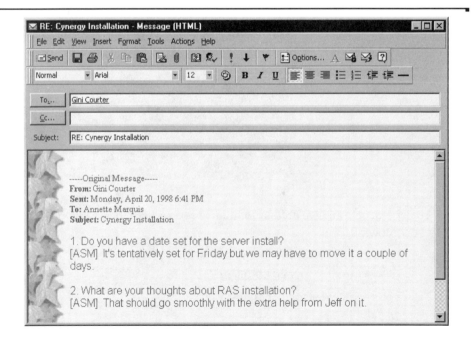

If you want to change how quoted text is handled in your messages, modify the e-mail options for quoted text:

1. Choose Tools ➤ Options on the Outlook menu to open the Options dialog box.

2. On the Preferences page, click the E-mail Options button to open the E-mail Options dialog box.

3. Choose a format from the When Replying to a Message drop-down list.

4. If you choose the Prefix format, enter a prefix symbol or leave the default symbol (>) in the Prefix Each Line With text box.

5. To add comments to replies and forwarded messages, enable the Mark My Comments With check box, and enter your name or other text in the text box.

6. Click OK to close the E-mail Options dialog box.

7. Click OK to close the Options dialog box.

## Changing the Font for Replies

When you reply to a message, Outlook uses the same format as the original message. If the message is plain text, Outlook will use the plain text font you selected for your reply text. However, if the original message was created with an HTML, Word, or Rich Text Format editor, you can use another font for the text you enter in your reply. The same font will be used for text you enter in forwarded messages.

Quoted text will retain its formatting from the original message. As with other Outlook options, changes in the reply font take effect on the next reply you create. To change the reply font:

1. Choose Tools ➤ Options on the Outlook menu to open the Options dialog box.

2. On the Mail Format page, click the Fonts button to open the Fonts dialog box.

3. Click the Choose Font button next to the When Replying and Forwarding text box to open the Font dialog box.

4. Set font options, and then click OK to close the Font dialog box.

5. Click OK to close the Fonts dialog box.

6. Click OK to close the Options dialog box.

# Forwarding Messages

Forwarding a message sends the entire message, and any text you add, to another recipient. To forward an open message, click the Forward button or choose Actions ➤ Forward from the message menu. If the message is not open, right-click the message in the view

Mastering the
Outlook Components

list, and choose Forward from the shortcut menu. As with a reply, the original message is copied into a new message form; you simply need to choose recipients and enter your text before clicking the Send button.

To indicate how the original text and text you add should appear in the forwarded message, open the E-mail Options dialog box. The options for the original message text are:

- Attach Original Message
- Include Original Message Text (default)
- Include and Indent Original Message Text
- Prefix Each Line of the Original Message

If comments are enabled for replies, they are also enabled for forwarded messages. To change options for what's included with forwarded messages:

1. Choose Tools ➤ Options on the Outlook menu to open the Options dialog box.
2. On the Preferences page, click the E-mail Options button to open the E-mail Options dialog box.
3. Choose a format from the When Forwarding a Message drop-down list.
4. To add comments to replies and forwarded messages, enable the Mark My Comments With check box, and enter your name or other text in the text box.
5. Click OK to close the E-mail Options dialog box.
6. Click OK to close the Options dialog box.

## MASTERING THE OPPORTUNITIES

### To Forward or Not to Forward?

Forwarding a message is even easier than replying to a message; all you need to do is pass it on. Forwarding has other implications, however; it's essentially the same as handing a colleague a memo you received or sharing the information from a phone conversation with a third party. Make sure you have the author's permission before forwarding the message.

Some people don't realize that e-mail correspondence is intended to be read by the addressees only, and they forward mail indiscriminately. To lessen the odds of your messages being forwarded without your knowledge, create a custom signature (see Chapter 7) stating that the contents of the message are not to be forwarded without your express written consent. In many companies, this type of signature is required for all messages sent to recipients outside the company.

# Changing the Font for Forwarded Messages

When you forward a message, Outlook uses the same format as the original message. If the message is plain text, Outlook will use the plain text font you selected to display forwarded text. However, if the original message was created with an HTML, Word, or Rich Text format editor, you can use another font for the text you enter in the forwarded message. This font will also be used for text you enter in replies. You can change the font used in forwarded messages by following these steps:

1. Choose Tools ➤ Options on the Outlook menu to open the Options dialog box.
2. On the Mail Format page, click the Fonts button to open the Fonts dialog box.
3. Click the Choose Font button next to the When Replying and Forwarding text box to open the Font dialog box.
4. Set font options.
5. Click OK to close the Fonts dialog box.
6. Click OK to close the Options dialog box.

## What's Next

Once you begin sending and receiving e-mail, you may want to start using the more advanced options that are available in Outlook 2000. In Chapter 7, you'll find out how to create more complex (and better looking) e-mail and manage that slew of incoming mail messages. Outlook includes tools to help you manage the messages you receive, including the Preview Pane and the Rules Wizard.

PART

II

Mastering the
Outlook Components

# CHAPTER **7**

# Advanced Message Formatting and Management

**N**ow that you know how to send and receive your e-mail messages, you'll want to make those messages look good for the right people. Outlook can help you make your messages and other contact material look, breathe, and feel professional. Also, although it's easy to let all of your incoming e-mail pile into one folder, after a while you'll find yourself searching in vain through several hundred messages for that really important one. Outlook can help you by drawing your attention to the important messages and filing the junk mail, all based on criteria that makes sense to you.

# Advanced Message Formatting

One can only go so far with simple ASCII-based messages before one wants more. If you're this kind of person, or if your workflow dictates professionally delivered documents, electronic or otherwise, then Outlook can handle even the most complex formatting. Here, we'll discuss the ins and outs of formatting, including when *not* to do it.

 **TIP** Some Internet users, such as those who still use Pine (a Unix text-based e-mail program) for e-mail, will be annoyed by your neatly formatted messages, chock-full of HTML coding, embedded objects, and such. Formatted messages also cause similar problems when they are sent to some e-mail listservers that distribute in digest format (some know about this problem and strip out the offending HTML and MIME information). For these people (there are a lot more of them than you might think), we recommend avoiding unnecessary formatting. Remember: the larger the message, the larger the recipient's displeasure.

## Formatting Messages

Outlook supports four distinct message formats: plain text, RTF, HTML, and Microsoft Word. The mail editor you select determines the tools you can use to format the text, paragraphs, and background of your mail message. You will select an editor before creating the message, and that editor is used for future new messages you create (until you change editors again).

- Plain text is the default format, created with a plain text editor. With plain text, the text appears in the computer's default e-mail font, usually Courier, and you can't apply formatting.
- Microsoft Outlook Rich Text format (RTF) lets you format fonts, align paragraphs, and use bulleted lists in your message.
- HTML (hypertext markup language) format is the language used to develop pages on the World Wide Web. The HTML format supports an incredibly wide

range of formatting, including backgrounds, horizontal lines, numbered and bulleted lists, and any other formatting you expect to see on a Web page.

- Microsoft Word format uses Word as your e-mail editor and lets you apply any formatting that is valid in Word.

 **TIP** It's easy to confuse Microsoft Outlook Rich Text and HTML, because Outlook refers to both as Rich Text. However, HTML is always listed as Rich Text (HTML); Outlook Rich Text does not include the HTML designation.

Depending on the editor you selected (or didn't select, in the case of the default plain text editor), various tools are available on the Format menu and Formatting toolbar in the message form. For information on choosing an editor, see "Setting a Format for New Messages" later in this chapter.

## Formatting Plain Text Messages

The bottom line here is, you can't format Plain Text messages. When the default Plain Text editor is used to create a message, all the buttons on the Formatting toolbar and most of the items on the Format menu are disabled, as shown in Figure 7.1. You can switch between Plain Text and Rich Text (HTML) editors. To switch to HTML, choose Format ➢ Rich Text from the menu. This enables the buttons on the Formatting toolbar and the Format menu choices that let you change fonts, styles, alignment, and colors. (See "Formatting HTML Messages" later in this section.)

PART

**II**

Mastering the
Outlook Components

**FIGURE 7.1**

*Plain text messages are exactly as described–plain.*

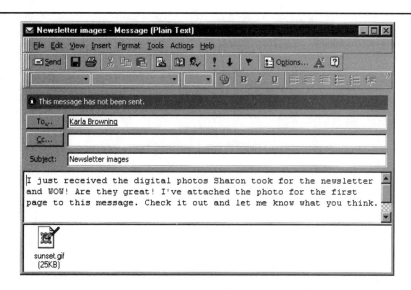

## Adding "Character" to Your Plain Text Messages

The plain text format has been in use for over three decades—long enough for enterprising users to invent ways to add meaning to messages using the characters on the keyboard. Precede and follow a word with an _underscore_ to indicate the word is underlined or italicized. Use asterisks *before and after* a word or words to indicate bold type. Insert emoticons—keystrokes that, when viewed from the side, resemble facial expressions :~) to give recipients an idea of the emotion you're really trying to convey in your message.

## Formatting Outlook Rich Text Messages

Outlook Rich Text Format is the default format for Microsoft Exchange. When the Rich Text editor is used to create a message, Outlook's Formatting toolbar is enabled, and two formatting choices appear on the Format menu: Font and Paragraph. Text can be bolded, underlined, and italicized; you can use different fonts, font sizes, font colors, and alignments to format your message, as shown in Figure 7.2.

**FIGURE 7.2**

*With Outlook Rich Text, you can format the text and paragraphs in your message.*

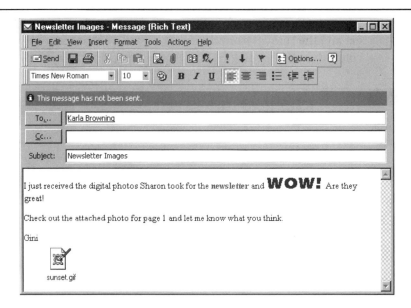

## Formatting HTML Messages

In the HTML editor, Font and Paragraph options are available, so you can format text as you would in an Outlook Rich Text format message. With HTML, you can also apply HTML styles—place horizontal lines, pictures, animated graphics, and multimedia files in the message—and apply a picture or color as a background, as shown in Figure 7.3. Anything that you can place in a Web page, you can include in an HTML message.

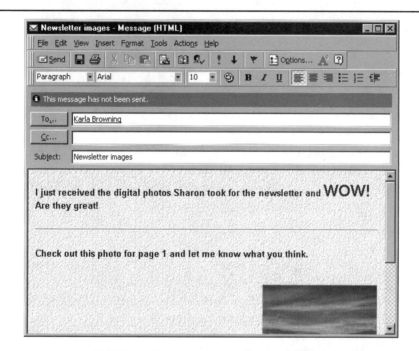

**Adding a Horizontal Line**    Horizontal lines can be an effective way to divide a message into parts. To add a horizontal line to an HTML message, place the insertion point where you want to insert the line in the message body. Then choose Insert ➤ Horizontal Line from the message form's menu bar to insert the line. To delete a line, place the insertion point directly above the line and press the Delete key.

**Applying Paragraph Styles**    HTML supports a number of paragraph styles, including bulleted and numbered lists and six levels of headings. To apply a style, select the paragraph(s) you want to format, and then choose Format ➤ Style to open a menu of paragraph styles. Choose the style you want to apply to the selected paragraphs.

Some aspects of the HTML styles are rigidly defined. For example, the Heading 1 style is bold. If you apply Heading 1 to a paragraph, you can't remove the bolding, but you can change the font. If Outlook won't let you change a text attribute in an HTML message, it's usually a limitation of HTML. You can try switching to the Formatted style and then applying your changes, but be aware that some browsers can't interpret the Formatted style and will simply substitute another font, size, and weight.

**Adding Graphic Elements**    To choose a background color, choose Format ➤ Background ➤ Color from the message form's menu and select a color from the palette. To use a picture as a background, choose Format ➤ Background ➤ Picture to open the Background Picture dialog box, shown in Figure 7.4. The dialog box list includes pictures suitable for use as backgrounds. Select from the list, or click the Browse button and select a picture from your local drive or a network drive.

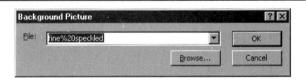

**FIGURE 7.4**

*Use the Background Picture dialog box to apply a background to an HTML message.*

To add a picture to the body of the message, choose Insert ➤ Picture from the message form menu to open the Picture dialog box, shown in Figure 7.5. Click the Browse button to open the Open dialog box. There are two image formats widely used in Web pages—GIF and JPEG—so the Files of Type in the dialog box is set to these two formats. Change the Files of Type if you're looking for a picture saved in another image format. Select the image, and then click Open to return to the Picture dialog box.

**FIGURE 7.5**

*In the Picture dialog box, select either a new file or an existing file to place in the body of the e-mail message.*

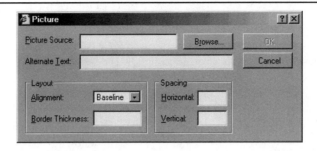

If some of your recipients can't view HTML messages, you can enter text in place of the picture to let them know what they're missing. Enter the text that should be displayed in the Alternate Text text box (see Figure 7.5). In the Layout section of the dialog box, select a position for the picture from the drop-down list. Borders and spacing around the picture are both entered in pixels. To add a border or additional space between a picture and surrounding text, enter a pixel value between 0 and 999. Click OK to close the Picture dialog box and place the image in the message.

 **NOTE** A *pixel* is the smallest displayable unit on a computer's screen. The relative size of a pixel is expressed in the screen's resolution setting; if the resolution setting is set to 640 × 480, there are 640 pixels horizontally on the screen, and 480 vertical pixels.

There is one more graphic element you can apply to Rich Text (HTML) messages. When you use the HTML format, you can use "stationery" to give your messages a distinct look. You can select stationery when you choose the default message format (see "Setting a Format for New Messages" later in this chapter).

## Formatting Word Messages

The last format choice is Microsoft Word. When you install Outlook, you can choose Word as your default e-mail editor; you can switch editors for new messages at any point, so don't worry if you didn't make this choice during installation. Whenever you create a message, a Word session is opened, so you can utilize most of the formatting features available in Word, including:

- AutoCorrect, which corrects mistyped words and expands shortcuts
- Bulleted and numbered lists
- Drawing tools, including WordArt and AutoShapes
- Highlighting for emphasis
- Hyperlinks automatically created from e-mail addresses and URLs

- Images and files inserted into the body of the message
- Spelling and Grammar, to check spelling and grammar as you type
- Tables, for presenting columnar material, such as schedules

The mail message in Figure 7.6 was created in the Word format.

 **WARNING** Only use Word as your editor if you know that your recipient uses Word, too. When you use Word as your e-mail editor, it creates special formatting that is lost if you don't have Word on the other end. More importantly, if you open a Word document in a simple text editor, it's not pretty, nor very easy to read.

**FIGURE 7.6**

*When you use Word as your e-mail editor, you have access to most of Word's formatting features.*

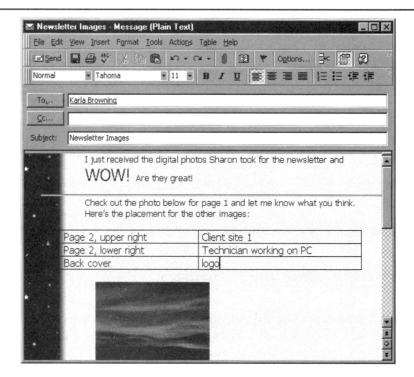

## Setting Mail Format Options

There are three types of mail format options: the default editor, which determines the Message Format; the Stationery and Fonts; and the customized Signatures you can add to your messages.

## Setting a Format for New Messages

With all these choices, how do you choose a format for e-mail messages? The answer depends on a number of factors, including the e-mail editor and other software you and your recipients have. There are four steps to selecting an editor:

1. Choose Tools ➤ Options from the Outlook menu to open the Options dialog box.

2. Click the Mail Format tab.

3. Choose the text editor you wish to use in the Send in This Message Format text box.

4. Click OK to close the dialog box.

Table 7.1 summarizes the advantages and disadvantages of each format.

| **TABLE 7.1: COMPARING MESSAGE FORMATS** | | |
|---|---|---|
| **Format** | **Advantages** | **Disadvantages** |
| Plain Text | Messages can be read with any e-mail editor; supports MIME encoding. | Lack of formatting makes for boring looking, but more universally readable, messages. |
| Outlook Rich Text | Allows font and paragraph formatting, supported by Microsoft Exchange and many PC mail editors. | No cross-platform support, so Unix and Macintosh users get plain text versions of messages. |
| HTML | Language is cross-platform; many users will eventually be able to read HTML messages. Provides support for encoding, graphics, formatting, and custom stationery. | Some e-mail editors don't support HTML messages yet, so a good number of your recipients will receive plain text, at best. Some of the e-mail clients that do support HTML are Eudora Pro and Eudora Light, Netscape's Messenger (a component of Communicator), and Microsoft's Outlook Express. |
| Word | Lots of formatting options and support templates, and Word users see the message exactly as it appears on your screen. If a recipient doesn't have Word but their mail editor supports Rich Text Format, most of the Word formatting is preserved. | You must have Word 97 or later to use this feature. Some of the best formatting features (like tables) are converted to plain text if the recipient doesn't have Word installed on their computer. Custom signatures must be created in Word templates; this format does not support digital signatures. |

When you choose an editor, you're really choosing the potential formatting for new messages. For example, if you create and send an HTML message to a recipient whose e-mail system doesn't support HTML messages, they see the text of your message in plain text. Formatting and graphics are reduced to text strings that look like a lot of garbled text. On the other hand, if your recipient is using a mail editor that supports HTML messages, they get to see your message in all its glory. The potential is there, provided the recipient's mail editor can support the format you choose.

You can choose an editor in the Mail Format page of the Options dialog box. Choose Tools ➤ Options from the Outlook menu to open the Options dialog box, and then click the Mail Format tab, as shown in Figure 7.7.

In the Send in This Message Format text box, select one of the e-mail editors. If you choose HTML or Microsoft Word, you will also be able to select a template or stationery. With HTML and Plain Text, you can automatically encode messages that are sent over the Internet.

**FIGURE 7.7**

*Choose an e-mail editor and set message format options in the Options dialog box.*

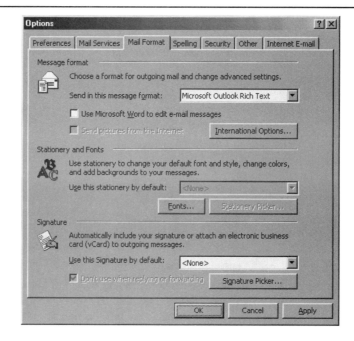

## MASTERING TROUBLESHOOTING

### Troubleshooting Message Backups

Outlook keeps a backup of messages as you create them. If you close a message form after you've entered an address (for example, to change message formats), Outlook will prompt you to save or discard a draft of the message:

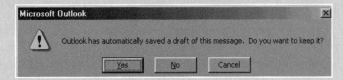

If you save the draft, you can open the message and continue working on it another time. The message will be saved in the Outlook Drafts folder.

If the power goes out while you're creating a message, check the Drafts folder when you restart your computer. The incomplete message may be there.

## Encoding Messages

When you attach a Word document to a message, you're attaching more than just text. Applications add other information to files that is specific to the application. This information can't be translated by text editors—only by the application, in this case Microsoft Word. Encoding translates your message and its attachments into a binary code that your recipient's mail program must then decode. Many mail programs decode messages automatically; if a recipient's mail system does not, there are programs like WinZip that decode encoded messages.

Outlook supports two of the three primary encoding programs: uuencode and MIME. The third program, BinHex, was created for the Macintosh environment, and was not supported by Outlook 98 and is still not in Outlook 2000. To modify the default encoding settings, open a new message, select File ➢ Properties, and click on the Internet E-mail tab. You can either use the default setting or choose between MIME and uuencode. There are advanced settings for each encoding format, but the defaults for each are usually fine.

**TIP** BinHex encoded files, designated by the `.hqx` or `.bin` extension, are pretty common when sharing files with Mac users. Don't feel out in the cold, though. Simply download the freeware Aladdin StuffIt Expander 2.0 for Windows from `http://www.aladdinsys.com` and you'll have access to a wide range of compressed file types that you may not have had before.

Uuencode (which originally meant Unix-to-Unix encode) was designed to allow users of different programs—different word processors and operating systems—to send information back and forth.

MIME (Multipurpose Internet Mail Extensions) was created by the Internet Engineering Task Force (IETF), and is the "official" standard for encoding Internet messages. Uuencode works well for text, but MIME was designed to support a wide range of file types: video, e-mail, audio, and graphics. Most mail programs automatically handle MIME encoding and decoding; other mailers, particularly freeware or shareware mailers, automatically handle uuencode.

 **TIP** Whether you use uuencode or MIME, your recipient must have the appropriate decoding software to decode and read your message. Unless you're sending audio or video files in your message, your best bet is uuencode. With audio and video attachments, use MIME, and choose base64 (an encoding protocol for non-text content) in the Encode Using drop-down list (in the message window select File ➤ Properties and click the Internet E-mail tab to find this list). For more information and help using MIME, visit `http://www.hunnysoft.com/mime/`.

To encode your plain text or HTML messages, click the Settings button on the Mail Format page of the Options dialog box. Choose uuencode or MIME. If you choose MIME, you can also have your message encoded using base64. Click OK to return to the Options dialog box.

## Choosing Stationery and Templates

If you use an HTML editor, you can personalize your e-mail messages by choosing HTML stationery, a scheme that includes a font and a background color or picture. You can create new stationery, or modify stationery by changing fonts and adding background colors or pictures.

To select stationery, you must select HTML as your mail editor in the Options dialog box (see Figure 7.7). Then, choose a stationery pattern from the Use This Stationery by Default drop-down list. To see what the various stationery patterns look like, click the Stationery Picker button on the Mail Format page of the Options dialog box to open the Stationery Picker dialog box, shown in Figure 7.8. Each stationery choice includes fonts and a background picture or color.

PART

II

Mastering the
Outlook Components

**FIGURE 7.8**

*Select a background
for HTML messages in
the Stationery Picker
dialog box.*

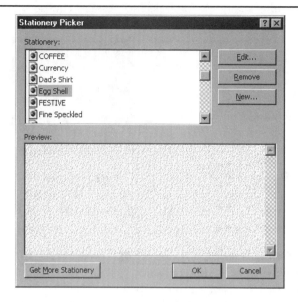

 **WARNING** Not to spoil your fun, but the use of preformatted HTML stationery may not be appreciated by your recipient(s). Even though most people with e-mail also have a Web browser, this does not automatically mean they are willing to load each and every e-mail message from you into it for viewing. If the message requires the formatting of HTML stationery to get your point across and no other way will work, then by all means send it this way. Do, though, try to limit the number of messages you send in this fashion.

Select stationery from the scroll list and you'll see a preview in the lower pane. Make your stationery choice; then click OK to close the Stationery Picker. Click OK again to close the Options dialog box.

 **TIP** Can't find stationery to meet your needs? Just click the Get More Stationery button in the Stationery Picker, and Outlook will launch your browser and visit the Microsoft Web site, where you can download more stationery patterns for free.

The stationery you selected will be the default stationery used for new messages created using the HTML editor. If you choose File ➤ New ➤ Mail Message or click the New Message button on the toolbar, the default stationery is applied. If you want to use other stationery for a specific message, choose Actions ➤ New Message Using to open the following menu:

Stationery that you've used recently is listed on the menu. You can choose a pattern, or No Stationery from the menu. Select More Stationery to open the Stationery dialog box and select stationery for this message. This does not change the default stationery, which will be applied to the next message you create.

**Creating, Editing, and Deleting Stationery**   You can create, delete, or edit stationery in the Stationery Picker. To create new Stationery, open the Stationery Picker and click the New button to open the Create New Stationery dialog box (which acts like a wizard). In the first page of the dialog box, shown in Figure 7.9, enter a name for your stationery and choose whether you want to create stationery from scratch or base it on existing stationery or an HTML file. To base your stationery on an existing HTML file, select the Use This File as a Template option, and click the Browse button to locate the file that you want to use. Click Next.

In the Edit Stationery dialog box (see Figure 7.10), click the Change Font button to open the Font dialog box and select a font to be used for message text in your stationery. Then, set the stationery background. Choose a picture from the list, browse to select another GIF or JPEG image, apply a color, or choose Do Not Include a Background in This Stationery. Click OK to create the new stationery and add it to the Stationery Picker.

**FIGURE 7.9**

*To create new stationery, name the stationery and choose how you'd like to create it.*

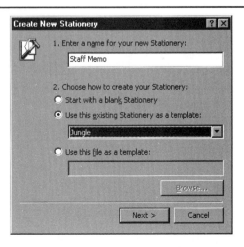

**FIGURE 7.10**

*Select a font and background for the new stationery.*

PART

II

Mastering the Outlook Components

 **TIP** You don't have to be incredibly creative to have great stationery. Wait for one of your artistic friends to send you a well designed HTML message. Open the message, and choose File ➤ Save Stationery from the message form's menu bar. Enter a name for the stationery when prompted, and then click OK to save the stationery pattern. (Asking for your friend's permission is, of course, a good idea.)

To edit existing stationery, select it in the Stationery Picker and click the Edit button. The Edit Stationery dialog box, shown in Figure 7.10, opens. Choose a font and background, and then click OK to save the edits. To delete stationery, select it in the Stationery Picker, and then click the Remove button. You'll be prompted to confirm the deletion:

**Selecting Templates** If you've chosen Word as your e-mail editor, you can select a Word template to serve as the background for your messages. In the Options dialog box of Word itself (Tools ➤ Options ➤ General ➤ E-mail Options ➤ Personal Stationery), you can choose which theme is the default for your WordMail. Figure 7.11 shows the WordMail Themes section of the dialog box where you can choose a default Theme. To browse for other themes, click the Theme button to open the WordMail Theme dialog box.

**NOTE** Keep in mind that all of the WordMail options are available in Word's Options dialog box and not in Outlook.

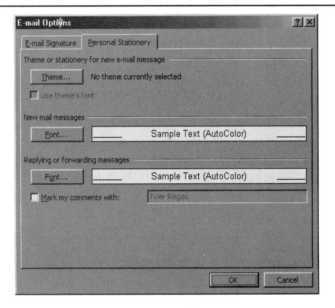

*FIGURE 7.11*

*Select a WordMail theme in the Word E-mail Options dialog box.*

**NOTE** HTML message stationary is not the same as WordMail Themes (although they are included in the list), which gives you a wide range of graphical styles to choose from. If you have stationery selected in Outlook for HTML messages, it will not appear in WordMail.

**TIP** You can't create new WordMail templates in Outlook; they must be created in Word. You'll find help creating templates in Word's Online Help.

## Designing Custom Signatures

A *custom signature* is text you add to the end of a message. Custom signatures are used to:

- Identify the sender:

    Gini Courter, TRIAD Consulting, 810-555-2221

- Reserve rights to your message:

    The content of this message may be proprietary, and cannot be reproduced or forwarded without my express written consent.

- Pitch your products or services:

    Annette Marquis, author of Mastering Outlook 2000, coming soon to a bookstore in your neighborhood

- Advertise your Web site:

    For more information, visit us at www.sybex.com

- Attach a digital ID to your message

Custom signatures have become commonplace e-mail features: ministers advertise their sermon topics, netizens list their favorite (or trash their least favorite) Web sites, managers add an inspirational quote for the week or month, and one of our friends includes a different bread recipe each month.

With Outlook you can create multiple custom signatures, and then select the signature you wish to use with each message you send. This lets you create a formal signature for business messages (like the "all rights reserved" signature) and a more friendly signature for messages to friends and family.

To create a custom signature or to choose a default signature for all messages, go to Tools ➤ Options ➤ General and click the E-mail Options button at the bottom of the dialog box. In the dialog box shown in Figure 7.12, type a name for your new signature in the topmost text box and, in the larger text box below, enter and format your signature. When you're finished, click the New button.

 **TIP** If you are using WordMail to compose your messages, the Signature Picker in Outlook is disabled. You can create and select your signatures in Word itself.

    You may apply hyperlinks to parts of your signature that you want to make clickable, and you can also add pictures to your signature. Simply click the Picture or Hyperlink button, the two buttons at the right end of the toolbar in the E-mail Options dialog box, and enter a URL (for example, http://www.microsoft.com or mailto:bgates@microsoft.com) or select a picture, respectively.

PART

II

Mastering the
Outlook Components

**FIGURE 7.12**

*Create one or more custom signatures in the E-mail Options dialog box.*

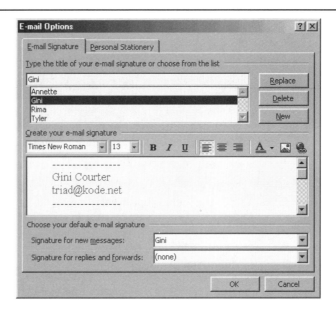

> **WARNING** We strongly suggest that if you must put a picture in your signature, you keep it very, *very* small. Forcing people to wait while your signature-line graphics download can cause friends to become unfriendly. We suggest having a signature line of no more than five lines, the first line being three dashes (---). The dashes signify the end of the message to the mail server.

In the lower section of the E-mail Options dialog box you can select which signatures to use for new messages and which for forwards or replies. You can choose to have no default signature or you can select another signature to insert in the message that will override your default selection. To select another signature while in WordMail, go to Insert ➤ AutoText ➤ Signature and select which signature you would like to use.

**Selecting a Custom Signature** To choose a custom signature for a message, place the insertion point where you want to insert the signature. Choose Insert ➤ Signature or click the Signature button and select a signature from the menu; if the custom signature you want to use isn't displayed on the menu, choose More to open the Signature dialog box. Select a signature, and then click OK to add the signature to the message.

# Managing Your E-mail

Now that we've successfully covered special formatting of e-mail messages, we can move onto a more complex and important aspect of e-mail usage: what to do with it once you get it. There are many factors to successfully managing your incoming messages. You may receive mail from work, and you may need to access your work mail from home. This means you will need to synchronize the mail you get at work with the copies you have at home. And then there's your personal mail to deal with. This can get pretty complicated pretty quickly.

Now suppose you filled out a few forms for information on the Web, and you're starting to get a lot of spam (junk e-mail). You are subscribed to a number of helpful e-mail discussion lists, and you need to keep those messages separate so you don't miss important work messages. If Outlook wasn't at your beck and call to manage your mail for you, you'd spend the entire day filing messages by hand.

This section of the chapter will help you process your Inbox efficiently. In some cases you'll find it useful to flag messages for further action; in other cases you'll want to print them out. And you'll probably want to create e-mail filters to help you sort out your routine business messages from the important messages from friends. You'll learn how to use the Inbox Wizard to let Outlook handle your mail for you.

## Flagging Messages for Further Action

You can't always reply to, forward, or even fully read and review a message when you receive it. You may be busy, need more information before you can reply, or require time to find out who should receive a forwarded message. However, if you let the message languish in your Inbox, it can get lost in the shuffle as new messages are delivered and grab your attention.

By flagging messages, you can ensure that they don't get lost, and it helps you stay organized. When you flag a message, you note the type of action that's required. You can even set a reminder so you don't forget to follow up on the message. The flag descriptions are:

- Call
- Do Not Forward
- Follow-Up
- For Your Information
- Forward
- No Response Necessary
- Read
- Reply
- Reply to All
- Review

To flag an open message, choose Actions ➤ Flag for Follow-Up from the message menu or click the Flag for Follow-Up button on the message toolbar. If the message is not open, right-click on the message in the Inbox and choose Flag for Follow-Up from the shortcut menu.

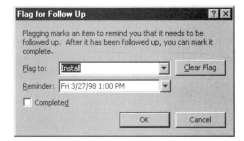

Choose a flag description from the Flag To drop-down list. You can also enter your own description of the action required; for example, Mail Application or Fax FAQ Sheet. You can sort the messages in any folder by flag description, so you should try to stick with the list and a small number of additions, or sorting won't be helpful.

Click the arrow in the Reminder text box to open the calendar control. Choose a date on which you want to be reminded about the message. If you want to be reminded at a specific time, edit the time in the text box. When you're finished entering flag information, click OK to close the dialog box.

 **TIP** You can flag messages that you're sending or forwarding, as well as those you receive.

 In the Inbox, a red flag is displayed in front of the message. In the message form, the flag description and date appear in an information box at the top of the message. The information bar for a flagged message is shown here—it includes a reminder to install the attached file by a specific date.

ℹ Install by Friday, March 27, 1998 1:00 PM.

 When you've completed the follow-up, you can either clear the flag or mark the action complete. To clear the flag, open the Flag for Follow-Up dialog box, click the Clear Flag button, and then click OK. The message will no longer be flagged.

 You may prefer to mark the flagged action as complete, which is indicated with a gray flag. When you mark the action as completed, you know that no further action is needed, but you are still keeping track of that action. To mark a flag as complete, open the Flag for Follow-Up dialog box, check the Completed check box, and then click OK to close the dialog box.

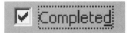

# Printing Messages

To print an open message, choose File ➤ Print from the message form menu to open the Print dialog box, shown in Figure 7.14. Select a printer from the Name drop-down list. The default message print style is Memo Style; if you've defined other styles, you can select them from the Print Style list. If the message has attachments, you can print the attachments with the message by enabling the Print Attached Files with Items check box. In the Copies section, select or type a number of copies. Click the Preview button to preview the printed message before printing, or click OK to send the message to the printer.

To print the open message using the default Print settings, click the Print button on the message toolbar. If the message is not open, right-click the message in the list and choose Print. The message is sent directly to the printer. A message box appears briefly while the print job is being queued; you can click the Cancel button in the message box to cancel printing, but you've got to be quick.

To change formatting for messages, open the message and choose File ➤ Page Setup ➤ Memo Style (or another style that you've created) to open the Page Setup dialog box. Modify the settings on the Format, Paper, and Header/Footer pages as required. To create your own Print Style, see the section on designing print styles in Chapter 11.

PART

II

Mastering the
Outlook Components

---

**FIGURE 7.14**

*Set print options for your message in the Print dialog box.*

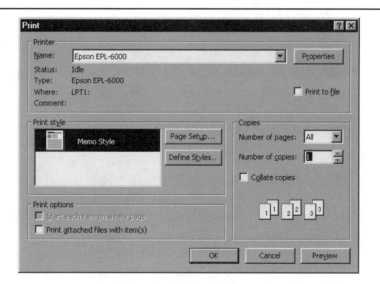

## Printing Multiple Messages and Message Lists

To print multiple messages, select the messages in the list, right-click, and choose Print from the shortcut menu. The Print dialog box opens. Select Memo Style to print all the text of each of the selected messages. Change the Print Options if you want to begin each memo on a new page or to print the attachments with each message.

Choose the Table Style to print the list view. In the Print Options, choose All Rows to print the contents of the folder, or Selected Rows to print or preview the selected messages in a table, as shown in Figure 7.15.

**FIGURE 7.15**

*Use the Table style to print a list of the messages in a folder.*

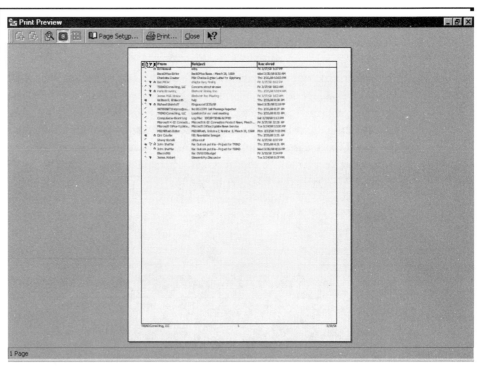

## Setting E-mail Options

The hardest part of setting mail options is finding where to change the settings. Options for sending, receiving, securing, and formatting e-mail aren't in one central location. Options are set in the message form, Outlook Options, or one of the many dialog boxes Outlook provides to set mail management options. For example, you can choose to have a sound played or a message box displayed when new mail arrives at your desktop—but the two settings are found in totally different places. If you're having trouble locating a particular option that you know you've seen before, refer to Appendix B. There you'll find a comprehensive list of mail options to help you wend your way through the maze of mail settings in Outlook.

# Organizing E-mail Messages

One of the most persistent challenges facing the networked business is presented by electronic mail. In most organizations, even unpopular people receive a dozen messages a day. The truly connected may receive scores or hundreds of messages, and the messages compete for time with all the other important tasks in your work life. If you're reading your e-mail messages, you can't be visiting clients, participating in a meeting, building a prototype, or writing code.

Are all these messages important? Probably not. Recent studies indicate that when you advance in an organization, your e-mail volume increases—and so does the percentage of messages that are purely informational and require no action on your part. This makes sense, because, unless instructed otherwise, every person working for you will send you a courtesy copy of nearly every message they create to "keep the boss in the loop." You may like receiving all this information, but even the most controlling personalities can be overwhelmed by the sheer volume of messages hitting the Inbox every day.

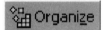

Outlook makes it easy for you to organize and manage your Inbox, and all the tools you need are in one place—the Organize page. Click the Organize button on the toolbar to open the Organize page at the top of the Inbox, shown in Figure 7.16. Using the Organize page, you can create folders for message management, create rules to color-code your messages, change Inbox views, or open the Rules Wizard and automate management of the messages you receive.

PART

**II**

**Mastering the
Outlook Components**

---

**FIGURE 7.16**

*With the Organize page, all your message management tools are right at your fingertips.*

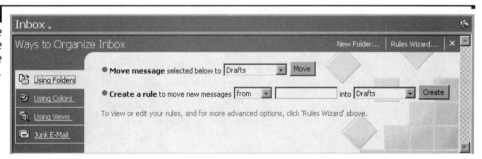

---

The Organize page has four tabs: Using Folders, Using Colors, Using Views, and Junk E-mail. (Information on using Views can be found in Chapter 2.) Find isn't included in the Organize page, but sooner or later you may need to find a message; for details on using Find, see Chapter 13.

## Using Folders to Organize Messages

Outlook has a default set of personal folders, including the Inbox. E-mail messages continue to hang around in the Inbox, even after you've read them and dealt with their content. You can easily create additional personal folders to hold different types of messages. For example, you might create a new folder for a project you're working on, for each major client, for e-mail newsletters, or for updates you receive from vendors.

To create a new folder, click the New Folder button in the Organize page to open the Create New Folder dialog box, shown in Figure 7.17. Enter a name for the new folder and indicate the kind of items that will be stored in the folder. In the Select Where to Place the Folder pane, select a location for the folder. If you'll be using the folder for messages, we suggest you place it in the Inbox or directly in the Personal Folders. It gets confusing when you have mail messages stored in the Journal or Contacts. You can always move the folder later, using drag and drop in the Folder List.

**FIGURE 7.17**

*Creating a new folder for messages in the Inbox*

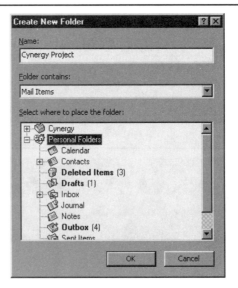

When you create a folder, Outlook asks whether you want to add the folder to the shortcut bar. Click Yes if you want to create the shortcut.

**NOTE** For more information on creating personal, public, and shared folders, see Chapter 13.

To move a message from the Inbox to your new folder, select the message(s) you want to move in the list view. In the Move Message Selected Below To drop-down list, select the name of your folder, and then click the Move button to move the message.

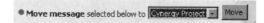

**Creating Rules to Automatically Move Messages**   In the Organizer, you create rules by example. If you want all messages from Karla Browning to be automatically placed in your new folder, select a message from Karla in the Inbox or any other mail folder.

Choose From or Sent To in the first Create a Rule drop-down box to indicate which type of messages should be moved. If you don't have a message from your recipient in any of your mail folders, enter the person's name or something else memorable in the text box. From the Into drop-down list, select the folder you want the messages to/from this person moved to, and then click the Create button to create the new rule. You'll know it worked because you'll see the word *Done* next to the Create button.

In Outlook 2000, the new rules you create can now be retroactively applied to messages you have already received, and to all of your new messages, incoming and outgoing. For more information on rules, see "Using the Rules Wizard" later in this chapter.

## Using Colors to Organize Messages

Message information (sender, subject, etc.) is displayed in the Windows text color by default; this is the color you get when you choose the Automatic color in any Windows application. In the Organizer, click on the Using Colors tab. You can apply one of sixteen different colors to message descriptions based on who sent the message, who it was sent to, and whether or not you are the only recipient.

To set the color based on the sender or recipient, choose a message from the sender, or addressed to the recipient, in the list view. In the Color Messages drop-down lists, choose From or Sent To and a color you wish to apply. Click the Apply Color button to create the color rule.

When you receive a message, that doesn't mean it was "Sent To" you. If you're receiving a courtesy copy, then the message was sent to someone else. Messages that require your personal attention are often addressed directly to you, and you are the

PART

**II**

Mastering the
Outlook Components

only recipient. Coloring these messages so they stand out in the Inbox separates personalized messages from courtesy copies or mail sent to groups. Choose a color in the Show Messages Sent Only to Me In drop-down list, and click the Turn On button to apply this rule.

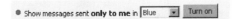

Some color rules are already applied in the mail folders; for example, unread messages are bolded, flagged messages that have passed the reminder date and time are red. To suppress these rules or change the format used for messages meeting different conditions, click the Automatic Formatting button located in the top-right corner of the Organize page to open the Automatic Formatting dialog box shown in Figure 7.18.

**FIGURE 7.18**

*Change the default fonts for conditional message formatting in the Automatic Formatting dialog box.*

This dialog box includes the default formats and any color rules you have created. To turn off automatic formatting for an item in the list, disable the item's check box. For example, to change the formatting used on unread messages, select Unread Messages in the list, and then click the Font button and select a new font for unread messages. Use the Move Up and Move Down buttons to change the order in which user-created rules are applied.

You can create a new Automatic Formatting rule in the Organize page, or here in the Automatic Forwarding dialog box. Click the Add button to create a rule named "Untitled." Type a descriptive name for the rule, click the Font button and choose a font, and then click the Condition button to open the Filter dialog box. In the three pages of the dialog box, set the filter conditions, and then click OK to create the condition. (For more information on using the Filter dialog box, see Chapter 11.) You can't change the conditions for the default items, only for rules you created.

## Using Junk Mail and Adult Content Rules

Businesses have used direct mailing via snail mail to market to individuals and companies for years. What marketing companies call direct mailing, others call "junk mail." Now, direct marketing has moved to the Internet. Internet commerce is booming, with new retailers, wholesalers, and auctions arriving online every day. And while many users still don't purchase goods over the Internet, every Internet user purchases goods somewhere. Why not run a few commercials past us while we're surfing the Net? We can ignore them if we want to.

What users can't ignore is junk mail (spam) sent directly to their Inboxes: unsolicited e-mail messages advertising everything from low-cost hard drives to psychic NetMeeting sessions. For every directory service or Usenet group, there's a company that collects and sorts e-mail addresses, and then rents or sells the lists for use in e-mail–based advertising. If you or your company pay connect time charges, receiving junk e-mail is more than a nuisance, it's a quantifiable expense. While you can't avoid the connect charges, you can have Outlook automatically format junk mail messages so you don't waste your time opening them.

The other type of messages you can format based on content is adult content messages. To format junk e-mail or adult content messages, click the Junk E-mail tab on the Organize page. Choose a color for each type of message (you can apply the same color to both), and then click the Turn On buttons:

PART

II

Mastering the
Outlook Components

## MASTERING THE OPPORTUNITIES

## Mastering Filters for Junk Mail and Adult Content Mail

Outlook recognizes junk mail and adult content mail by filtering message content, searching for phrases commonly used in direct marketing messages and adult content messages. For junk mail, phrases include: "cards accepted," "extra income," "money-back guarantee," and "100% satisfied." Of course, this means that when a client e-mails "I am 100% satisfied with the way your staff handled our concerns," the message will end up in your designated junk mail folder.

With adult content mail, Outlook searches for phrases like "over 18," "adults only," "adult web," and "xxx." We're sure you can think of legitimate messages that would include some of these phrases.

*Continued*

It's worth knowing how Outlook and other programs with content filters determine which messages may be junk mail or have adult content. If you include phrases like "we're brainstorming ways to generate extra income" or "there must be over 18 ways to complete this analysis" in a piece of regular business correspondence, don't be surprised if your recipient never reads the message. To see all the phrases Outlook uses to filter mail, open the file `filters.txt` in the folder where Outlook was installed.

There are other programs you can use to check incoming messages based on sender address that are compatible with Outlook. For more information, visit the Microsoft Web site.

## Using the Rules Wizard

The Rules Wizard is a general-purpose tool to automatically deal with messages based on sender, category, content, or other criteria. You've been using a version of the Rules Wizard to create the folder, color, and content rules in the Organize page.

 With the Rules Wizard, you can automatically move, forward, flag, color, or delete messages. As with the rules created in the Organize page, the Rules Wizard creates rules that are applied to messages you receive or send in the future. From the Outlook menu, choose Tools ➤ Rules Wizard to fire up the Wizard. If you have the Organize page open, switch to Using Folders and click the Rules Wizard button to open the Rules Wizard dialog box. Click the New button to start the Wizard. The first step of the Wizard is shown in Figure 7.19.

**FIGURE 7.19**

*Use the Rules Wizard to automate message handling.*

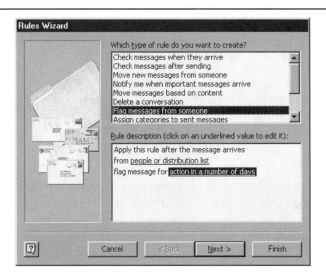

Rules have three parts: conditions that must be met for the rule to be applied, actions you want to occur when the conditions are met, and exceptions to the rule. The conditions are based on message attributes, and allow you to pinpoint exactly the types of messages you're interested in managing. Notify Me When Important Messages Arrive isn't an adequate description for a message management function this powerful, because you can choose to be notified when a message meets one or more of these conditions:

- Sent directly to you or sent only to you

- Marked with a specified importance or sensitivity

- Your name is in the Cc box, the To or Cc box, or is not in the To box (therefore, Cc or Bcc)

- From or sent to specified people or distribution lists

- Contains specific words in: the sender's or recipient's addresses, subject, body, subject or body, or message header

- Flagged for any action, or a specified action

- Assigned to one or more specified categories

- From out of office

- Created using a specific form or with values in form fields you select

- Contains attachments or is within a specified size range (in kilobytes)

- Received within a specified date range

- Suspected to be junk mail or from junk senders, adult content mail or from adult content senders

To create a rule, begin by selecting the primary action you want to occur in the rule. In the Which Type of Rule Do You Want to Create list, look for the action you want the rule to invoke—flag, move, notify—and choose one of the following:

**Check Messages When They Arrive**    Choose this option when none of the other types are what you're looking for and the rule you want to create is for incoming messages.

**Check Message After Sending**    Choose this one when none of the other types fit your requirements and the rule you want to create is for outgoing messages.

**Move New Message from Someone**    Like the Using Folders rules, this option moves incoming messages based on the attributes listed above.

**Notify Me When Important Messages Arrive**    Use this feature to receive notification on the arrival of a message based on attributes.

PART

II

Mastering the
Outlook Components

**Move Messages Based on Content**  This item works the same as Move New Message from Someone, but is based on content.

**Delete a Conversation**  This option deletes all messages based on attributes.

**Flag Messages from Someone**  Choose this option to apply a flag and set a reminder for *N* days from message receipt.

**Assign Categories to Sent Messages**  This item is for outgoing messages.

**Assign Categories Based on Content**  Use this option for incoming messages.

**Move Messages I Send to Someone**  This feature is the same as Move Messages Based on Content for outgoing messages.

**Stop Processing All Following Rules**  If a message meets the criteria here, this is the only rule processed.

After you select a rule, the rule description appears in the lower text box. In Figure 7.19, selecting Flag Messages from Someone inserts this rule description.

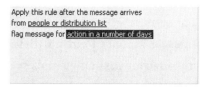

Each underlined term in the description is editable. Clicking People or Distribution List opens the Select Names dialog box, so you can choose the people or distribution list that will trigger this rule. Click Action in a Number of Days to open the Flag Message dialog box, so you can choose a flag and the number of days that should pass before you're reminded of the flag.

When you've finished this initial editing, each of the underlined terms will have been replaced with your choices.

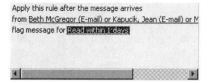

Click Next to continue to the second step of the Rules Wizard, shown in Figure 7.20. In this step, add more conditions to fine-tune your rule.

**FIGURE 7.20**

*Select conditions to indicate when the rule should be applied.*

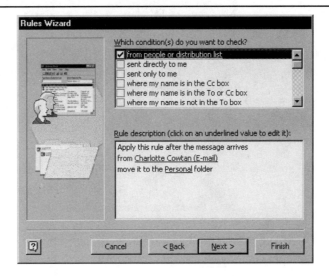

To add a condition, click its check box. The condition is added to the rule description. If you choose a condition with an underlined term, click the underlined term in the rule description to add criteria to the condition. Here we've added two conditions: *with **planning** in the body*, and *received after **3/29/98** and before **4/19/98***.

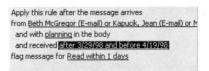

Click Next to proceed to the third step of the Rules Wizard—selecting actions. The action you selected in the first step is already checked, as shown in Figure 7.21.

Choose any other actions you want to happen when a message meets the conditions specified in the Rule Description:

- Flag or clear a flag, change the importance
- Move, copy, forward, or delete it
- Receive notification that it arrived with a message or sound
- Reply with a specific template
- Assign it to a category
- Perform a custom action (add-ins, not part of Outlook)
- Stop processing rules for the message

PART

II

Mastering the
Outlook Components

*Choose all the actions
Outlook should take
when the described
message is delivered
or sent.*

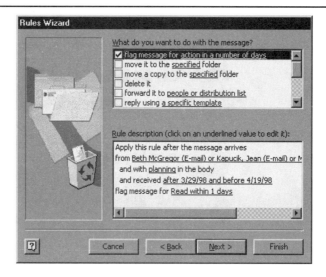

In the rule description below, the message is being flagged and forwarded. Flagging occurs first in the description, so the forwarded message will also be flagged.

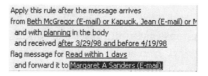

In Outlook, every rule can have its exceptions. Now that you've constructed the rule, you can indicate conditions under which the rule should be ignored. Click Next to move to the next step of the Wizard, and note the conditions under which the rule should not be applied. In this example, we're not going to apply the rule if the specific person we were forwarding the message to already received the message. (This means the message won't be flagged, either.)

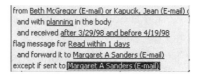

In the last step of the Wizard, shown in Figure 7.22, enter a name for the rule. You don't have to turn the rule on when you create it—you can create rules when you have time to create them and turn them on when you need them. Check the Run This Rule Now on Messages Already in *X* check box (where *X* is the folder group you are currently using) to apply the rule to existing messages. Click Finish to create the rule and return to the Rules Wizard dialog box.

 **WARNING** The Rules Wizard can be a little confusing. When you go to Tools ➤ Rules Wizard, it is actually a Rules Wizard manager dialog box that opens, even though it's called the Rules Wizard. You need to click New to get the "real" Rules Wizard, which walks you through the job of making a new rule to *add* to the Rules Wizard manager.

**FIGURE 7.22**

*Name the rule and turn it on before you click Finish.*

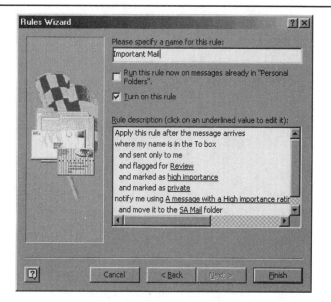

When a rule is turned on, messages that meet the conditions in the rule's description are acted on by Outlook as described in the rule. After you've created a rule, return to the Rules Wizard dialog box to turn the rule off or on, delete the rule, or rename the rule. You can copy the rule, and then modify the copy to create another rule with similar actions or conditions.

 **TIP** You can share your rules with other users. Click the Options button at the bottom of the Rules Wizard dialog box (the one that opens when you go to Tools ➤ Rules Wizard) to export rules to a floppy disk or shared folder. Other users can then open the Rules Wizard, click the Options button, and import the rules.

PART

II

Mastering the
Outlook Components

## What's Next

Now that you are managing your mail and files in the way *you* want them to be managed, you're bound to find a lot of things to do. You have people to call back, projects to work on, reports to turn in, and that week-long to-do list that's been resting comfortably. In the next chapter, you'll learn how to keep track of your tasks so that nothing falls between the cracks.

# CHAPTER **8**

# Managing Tasks in Outlook

**M**aking a list of things you have to do is a time-honored tradition. Many people are great list makers, and some even accomplish the tasks on their lists. With the power of Outlook behind you, you now have the opportunity to become one of those people. However, Outlook's Task component is not just a place to type your to-do list. With Tasks you can actually manage your responsibilities by tracking when they are due, organizing related tasks, reminding yourself of recurring tasks, scheduling time to complete them, and evaluating the progress you are making. Making lists no longer becomes a futile attempt at organization—with Outlook's Tasks, it's a real step toward task completion.

## Creating a Task

To create a task, you simply type the name of the task and its due date. You can also enter more detailed information about the task, taking full advantage of the power that Outlook has to offer.

To enter a task, click the Tasks icon on the Outlook bar. The default view in Tasks is the Simple List view, shown in Figure 8.1. The Simple List view has four columns:

**Icon**    An icon that changes if a task is assigned to someone else or was assigned by someone else

**Complete**    A check box indicating whether the task has been completed

**Subject**    A descriptive name for the task

**Due Date**    The date on which you expect or need to complete the task

You can enter a task directly into the Information Viewer by clicking in the Click Here to Add a New Task text box. The row turns blue, and the box that is active for editing is white. Type a subject in the Subject field. It's helpful if you make the subject descriptive but not too long—less than 30 characters is best so the column doesn't have to be too wide to read it all.

 **NOTE**  You must be in Simple List or Detailed List view to have the Click Here to Add a New Task text box. If you prefer to use another view, then create a new task by choosing Task from the New button.

**FIGURE 8.1**

*The Simple List view of Tasks*

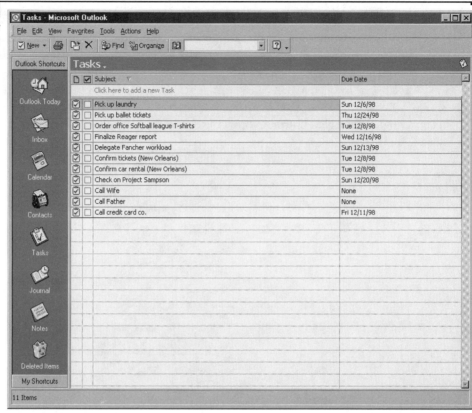

Press Tab to move to the Due Date field (Shift+Tab will move you back to Subject); the text box will turn white. Because Outlook recognizes natural-language dates using its AutoDate feature, you have multiple options for entering dates in this field (see Chapter 2 for more information about the AutoDate feature). Just about anything you type into the field that remotely resembles a date will be converted into a standard date format (Wed 8/18/99). You could type **8-18-99**; **aug 18**; **three weeks from now**; **a week from today**; **tomorrow**; **one month from next wed**. All are legitimate dates in Outlook (of course, they wouldn't all return the same date). Go ahead and try it—it's fun to see what AutoDate's limits are.

If your objective is just to get the task recorded and then come back to it later to add information, you're finished with this task. Click anywhere in the task list to move the task into the list. Where the task appears in the list depends on how the list is currently sorted. You can now enter another task. This is the quickest and easiest way to enter tasks.

PART

II

Mastering the
Outlook Components

## Entering Details about a Task

To take advantage of the powerful features built into Outlook, you need to add more information about the task. The most direct way to do this is to enter a Task form. You can open the form for any existing task by double-clicking the task in the Information Viewer. To open a blank Task form, click the New button on the Standard toolbar (if Tasks is the active module in the Information Viewer); or click the down arrow to the right of the New button to open the New menu, and choose Task from the list.

The Task form, shown in Figure 8.2, is composed of two pages: Task and Details. The Task page focuses on a description of the task (see "Completing a Task" later in this chapter for more information about the Details page). Enter the subject in the Subject text box, and press Tab to move to the Due Date field. Click the down arrow to choose a date from the calendar, or enter a date in the text box. If the task is not scheduled to start right away, enter a Start Date to indicate when it should be started.

## Setting Reminders

Click the Reminder check box to activate a reminder that will be displayed at a specified date and time.

The Time drop-down list has a choice for every half hour around the clock, so be careful to select the correct A.M. or P.M. time. There's nothing like setting a reminder for twelve hours after something was supposed to be done! You can also type an entry in this box if you need a reminder at the quarter hour.

**FIGURE 8.2**

*The Task form*

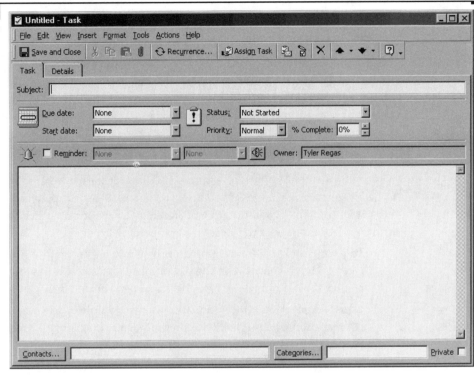

Reminders come with a sound by default. You have the option of disabling the sound or changing the sound file it plays. Click the speaker icon to access the Reminder Sound options.

Clear the Play This Sound check box if you'd prefer your reminders appeared on your screen silently. If you would like to hear a sound but would prefer a different sound file, click the Browse button to locate the file you would like to use. Double-click the filename, and it will appear in the Play This Sound text box.

**TIP** If you change the sound file within a task, it will only be in effect for that specific reminder. To change the default sound file for Reminders, go to Sounds in the Windows Control Panel and change the sound assigned to Microsoft Office Reminders. Sound files, or wave files, are designated by a .wav extension. If you would like to record your own reminder message or sound that plays when it is time to do a task, you can do so using the Windows Sound Recorder.

## Updating Task Status

When you enter a task, Outlook assumes you haven't started working on the task yet. To help you manage your tasks and assess the status of certain projects, you have four other Status options in addition to Not Started available to you. Click the Status down arrow on the Task page of the Task form to open the list of choices:

**In progress**   If a task is in progress, you might also want to indicate the percentage that is complete in the % Complete text box. Use the spin box to change the percentage, or type the actual percentage directly in the box.

**Completed**   In addition to marking a task complete, you might also want to complete some additional fields on the Details page. See "Completing a Task" later in this chapter.

**Waiting on someone else**   It's helpful to set a reminder to yourself to call this person if you don't hear from them in a reasonable amount of time.

**Deferred**   You may want to change the start and end dates so this task doesn't show up on your list of active tasks.

## Setting Priorities

By setting a priority level for a task, you can be sure that your most important tasks receive most of your attention. The default priority is set at Normal. You have additional options of High and Low. High priority items are designated by a red exclamation point in the Information Viewer, and Low priority items are designated by a blue downward-pointing arrow, as shown in Figure 8.3.

## Owning a Task

The Task Owner is the person who creates the task, or the person to whom the task is currently assigned. When you create a task, you are the owner by default. To give up ownership, however, all you have to do is assign the task to someone else. As soon as that person accepts the task, they officially become the new owner.

**FIGURE 8.3**

*Viewing the Priority field in the Information Viewer*

| 🗋 | ☑ | ! | Subject | | Due Date △ | |
|---|---|---|---------|---|-----------|---|
| | ■ | | | | None | |
| ☑ | ☐ | | Call Peggy | | Fri 3/6/98 | |
| ☑ | ☐ | ! | Install MS Exchange Server | | Mon 3/9/98 | |
| ☑ | ☐ | ! | Abby Referral letters and report changes | | Tue 3/10/98 | |
| ☑ | ☐ | ! | Distribute paychecks | | Tue 3/10/98 | |
| ☑ | ☐ | | Prepare month-end report | | Thu 3/12/98 | |
| ☑ | ☐ | | Order bar code guns | | Fri 3/13/98 | |
| ☑ | ☐ | ↓ | Create Educational Promotional Letter | | Fri 3/20/98 | |
| ☑ | ☐ | | Survey DB Reports | | Fri 3/27/98 | |
| ☑ | ☐ | | Order Company Polo Shirts | | Thu 4/2/98 | |
| ☑ | ☐ | | EDD - English Wizard Dictionary | | Fri 4/3/98 | |
| 🗊 | ☐ | ! | Submit quarterly sales tax report | | Fri 4/3/98 | |
| ☑ | ☐ | | Make Promotional Bookmarks | | Fri 4/17/98 | |
| ☑ | ☐ | ↓ | Develop a "While We Were Here" form | | Fri 4/17/98 | |
| ☑ | ☐ | ! | Database Natural language dictionary for O & Sat | | Sun 5/10/98 | |

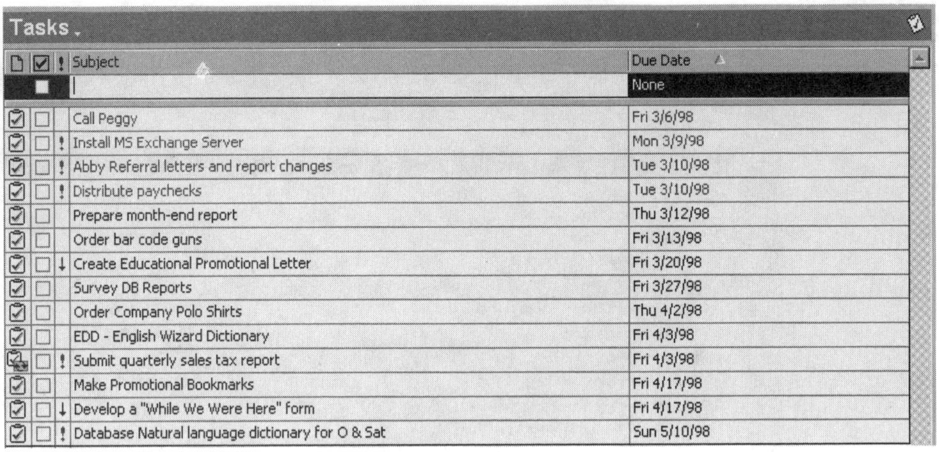

## Assigning Categories to Manage a Project

Categories are user-defined values that help to organize your data throughout Outlook. Chapter 4 provides a thorough discussion of how to create new categories and delete undesired categories. Despite the fact that you have the same list of categories available to you, categories serve a slightly different purpose in Tasks than they do in Contacts or the other Outlook modules.

Categories play a vital role in tracking tasks related to a single project. When you create a task, the more specific you can be, the easier it is to complete the task. For example, if the Task you enter is *Complete database for Goodrich*, you will have a difficult time demonstrating progress toward your goal. When is the database complete—after the application is functioning or after the product is installed? Maybe it's not complete until employees are trained and using the product successfully.

It would be a lot more helpful to break down the various steps of the project into its logical components. In this case, you could list *Complete data analysis*, *Complete database structural design*, *Solicit feedback from client*, and so on as separate tasks in Outlook. Each could have its own description and due date. Status, priority, and % complete could also be assigned to each task.

Categories could then pull all these individual tasks together into one project. Just click the Categories button and assign each one to the same category from the Categories dialog box. (You can't do it as a group, so you have to open each task individually and make the assignment.) When you return to the Information Viewer, you can sort by category, group all the tasks in the same category together, or even filter out just those tasks related to a single category (see Chapter 11 for more about creating custom views). Figure 8.4 is an example of a task list grouped by category (see "Viewing Tasks" later in this chapter).

PART II

Mastering the Outlook Components

**FIGURE 8.4**

*Task list grouped by category*

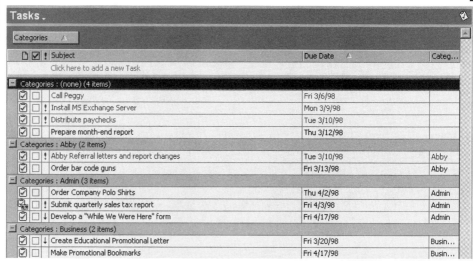

## Making a Task Private

If your Outlook folders are shared on a network, there may be times when you don't want others to see information about a task. Click the Private button on the right-hand corner of the Task form to keep this task in your personal Outlook folders. The task will be hidden, and other users will not be able to view it.

# Setting Up Recurring Tasks

A *recurring task* is a task that you must complete on a regular basis—such as a monthly report, a weekly agenda, a quarterly tax submission. Anything that you have to do periodically qualifies. In Outlook you can enter the task once, and then set a pattern for it to recur on your task list. Outlook doesn't care if you've completed this month's report; when the time comes for next month's, it will add another copy of the task with a new due date to your list.

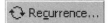

To set up a recurring task, enter the task as you would any other task that needs completion. When you have the data entered for the first occurrence of the task, click the Recurrence button on the Standard toolbar within the Task form. This opens the Task Recurrence dialog box, shown in Figure 8.5.

PART

II

Mastering the
Outlook Components

**FIGURE 8.5**

*Task Recurrence
dialog box*

Here you can set the Recurrence Pattern and the Range of Recurrence. To set the Recurrence Pattern, indicate whether the task needs to be accomplished Daily, Weekly, Monthly, or Yearly. If the task needs to be completed every three days, choose Daily; every two months, choose Monthly; and so on. Each of the four options gives you different choices for defining the actual pattern. For each pattern, you are then asked to indicate how many days/weeks/months/years you want Outlook to wait after a task is marked as complete before it generates a new task.

**Daily**   Choose between Every N Days or Every Weekday.

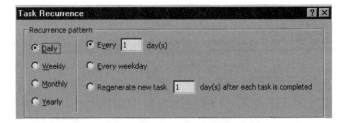

**Weekly**   Indicate how often the task should occur: every week (1), every other week (2), every third week (3), and so on. This is the best option if the task needs to be completed every six weeks or every eight weeks (because some months have more than four weeks). Then mark on which day of the week the task needs to be accomplished.

**Monthly**   Choose between specifying which date of each *N* month(s) or indicating the first, second, third, fourth, or last day of every *N* month(s); for example, the last Friday of every month or the third Thursday of every second month. You could also indicate the first weekday or the last weekend day of the month.

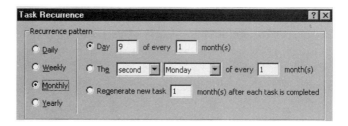

**Yearly**   Indicate a specific date in a specific month (every May 5), or mark the first, second, third, fourth, or last day of a specific month (the first Friday in May).

Sometimes you have to be creative to figure out how often a task really occurs. For example, if a task occurs two times a year on February 28 and August 31, do you use

Monthly or Yearly? Because these dates are six months apart, you could use Monthly and indicate the last day of every six months (as long as the Start date was set to one of the two dates).

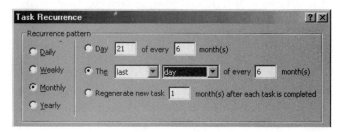

However, if this task is not so evenly spaced—May 31 and August 31 for example—you probably will have to enter two tasks: one for the May date every year, and one for the August date every year.

## Defining the Range of Recurrence

The Range of Recurrence refers to when the first task in the series is due and how long the task will continue.

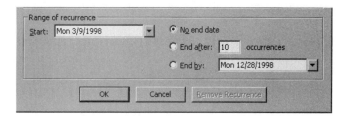

You have your choice of:

**No End Date**   The task will continue into eternity (or until you tell it to stop).

**End after N Occurrences**   You only need to complete the task a specific number of times, and then you are finished with it.

**End By**   You only have to do this task until a certain date, and then you are free.

Once you have set the Range of Recurrence, click OK to return to the Task form. Click Save and Close to save the task and return to the Information Viewer.

### Editing Task Recurrence

To make changes to the recurrence pattern or range that you set, open the task and click the Recurrence Pattern button. Make your changes and then click Save and Close again. You may also edit the Subject of the task, but any changes you make will be made only to future occurrences of the task.

If you want to skip the next occurrence of a task but not interfere with the recurrence pattern, open the task and choose Skip Occurrence from the Actions menu. The due date will automatically change to the next date the task is due.

To delete the recurrence pattern without deleting the task, open the task, click the Recurrence button, and click the Remove Recurrence button on the bottom of the Task Recurrence dialog box. Close the Task Recurrence dialog box and Save and Close the task. The task will still be on your list, but it will be there for one time only.

# Assigning a Task to a Contact

If you work as a member of a team, or if you have people reporting to you, there are times when you may want to create a task for someone else to do. As long as the other person is running Outlook and you both have access to e-mail, you can assign tasks to each other.

To assign a task to someone else, create the task as you normally would, add task Recurrence, if appropriate, and click the Assign Task button on the Standard toolbar of the Task form. This opens a message form with the task included, as shown in Figure 8.6.

 **WARNING** When sending a task to another person through Internet e-mail, make sure the Properties for that person's e-mail address in Contacts is set to Always Send to This Recipient in Microsoft Outlook Rich-Text Format. This way, the recipient will be able to transfer the task directly into their task list using copy and paste. (See Chapter 4 for more information about Microsoft Outlook Rich Text format and address properties.)

Enter the person's e-mail address, or click the To button and choose the name from your address lists (see Chapter 5 for more information about addressing e-mail messages). You have two options related to this assignment:

**Keep an Updated Copy of This Task on My Task List** Even though you have assigned the task to someone else, you may still want to know how the task is going. Every time the new owner of the task revises the task in any way, a message is sent to you indicating that the task was updated and the task is revised in your task list. This option is not available if the task is recurring.

**Send Me a Status Report When This Task Is Complete**   When the new owner marks the task as complete, you receive a message automatically informing you that the task is complete, and it is marked as complete on your task list.

**FIGURE 8.6**

*Assigning a task to someone else*

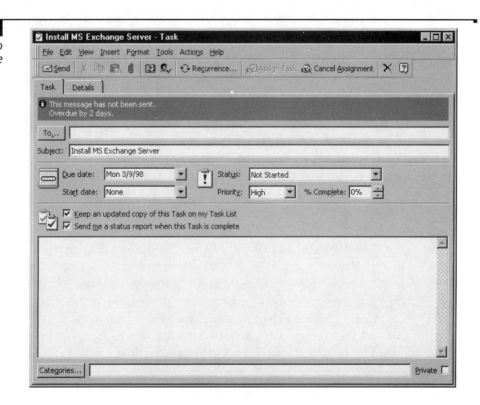

PART

**II**

**Mastering the Outlook Components**

 **NOTE**   Although you can assign a task to anyone who runs Outlook, if the person is not on your network, you will not receive automatic updates when that person makes revisions to the task.

If you would like to send a message along with the task assignment, enter the text in the message box. Click Send to transfer the message to your Outbox.

## Assigning a Task to More than One Person

It's possible to assign the same task to more than one person, but if you do, you cannot keep an updated copy of the task in your task list. To assign the task to an additional person, open the task, click the Details tab, and click the Create Unassigned Copy button.

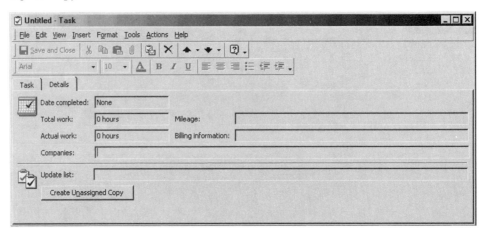

You will be warned that you will become the owner again (the person you originally assigned the task to took over ownership of the task when they accepted it) and will no longer receive updates (unless you want to write them to yourself). Click OK to create the copy and assign the task.

If you really need to receive updates from more than one person about the task, create the task multiple times and assign it individually to each person. Include the person's name in the Subject so you can differentiate the three tasks.

## Receiving a Task Assignment

When someone sends you a task, you will receive an e-mail message labeled Task Request.

When you open the task, you can choose to accept the task or decline the task by clicking the appropriate button on the message form.

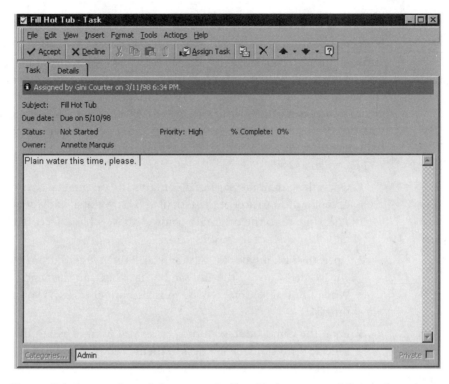

If you click Accept, the task is automatically added to your task list, and you become the owner of the task. If you click Decline, the person who sent you the task retains ownership. Either way, the person who originated the task is sent a message indicating your response. When you click Send, you are given the option of editing the response before sending it, or sending it without editing. If you want to explain why you're declining your boss's request, click Edit the Response Now and enter your explanation in the message.

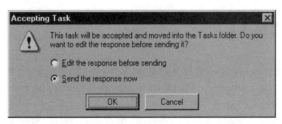

Even after you accept a task, you can change your mind and decline the task. Just open the task and choose Decline Task from the Actions menu.

## Passing the Task Along

If you receive a task from someone, it's possible for you to accept the task assignment and then turn around and assign the task to someone else (commonly referred to as passing the buck). When you accept the task, you become the owner of the task, and changes and updates you make are returned to the task's originator. When you reassign a task to someone else, that person becomes the owner and future updates are returned to you. In order to keep the task's originator up-to-date, you will have to generate updated status reports when an update is returned to you from the new owner.

To reassign a task:

1. Open the e-mail message that contains the original task request, and click the Accept button to accept the task (if you have not already done so). This sends a Task Update to the originator indicating you have accepted the task. You are now the owner of the task.

2. Open the task in your task list and click the Assign button. Make sure the Keep an Updated Copy of the Task on My Task List and the Send Me a Status Report When the Task Is Complete options are both checked so you won't lose track of the task.

3. Enter the e-mail address of the person you want to assign the task to, and click Send to send the Task Request to them. They are now the temporary owner of the task. When they accept the task, they become the task's owner.

4. When you receive a task update from the new owner, click Actions ➤ Send Status Report from the Standard toolbar of the open task. Type in (or copy and paste) your status report. Enter the e-mail address of the task's originator, and click Send to send an update to them.

By following this process, you keep the task's originator informed, and you have someone else doing the work—not bad work, if you can get it!

# Viewing Tasks

One way to stay on top of what you have to do is to review your tasks from different perspectives. The default view for tasks in the Information Viewer is the Simple List (shown in Figure 8.1). This view shows the Subject and Due Date of both active and completed tasks. It's quite simple to switch to another view that shows only active tasks or that organizes the tasks in some other meaningful way. To change to another view, click View ➤ Current View. This opens the list of available views displayed in Figure 8.7.

PART

II

Mastering the
Outlook Components

**FIGURE 8.7**

*Available views in Tasks*

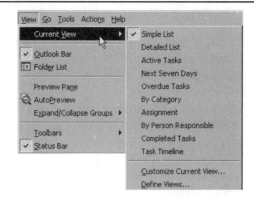

The Detailed List and the Active Tasks are essentially the same view, except the Detailed List includes completed tasks while the Active Tasks includes only those tasks yet to be completed. The Detailed List is shown in Figure 8.8.

**FIGURE 8.8**

*Detailed List view*

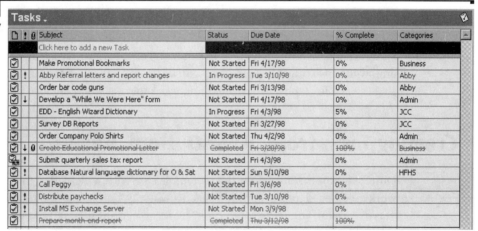

The Next Seven Days view displays the same fields as the Detailed List and Active Tasks views, but it filters the view to only show those tasks with Due Dates within the next seven calendar days.

When a task passes its Due Date, Outlook turns the task red to distinguish it from current tasks. You can then choose Overdue Tasks from the Current View menu to see only those tasks that require immediate attention.

The next three views allow you to examine your tasks by Category, by Assignment, and by Person Responsible. These views are especially helpful in managing the work on a particular project or managing the workloads of personnel, because they group tasks together that have something in common (see Figure 8.4 earlier in this chapter for an example of Tasks grouped by Category).

The final view, Task Timeline view, is designed to let you examine your tasks based on when they are due in relation to each other. Tasks are spread out along the timeline grouped together by due dates. This view, shown in Figure 8.9, can be used to plan your activities for particular days based on the tasks you have to accomplish.

**FIGURE 8.9**

*The Task Timeline view*

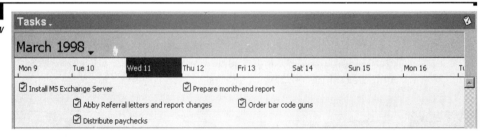

See Chapter 2 for help on how to sort based on any of the visible fields, change column width, rearrange the fields, and remove fields from any of the table views. In Chapter 11, you'll learn how to design custom views to meet your particular needs.

# Creating Tasks from Other Outlook Items

Outlook's power comes from the incredible ease with which all of the components work together to make your life easier. How many times have you received an e-mail message asking you to do something? Unless you print the message and put it in the stack of papers on your desk and hope you run across it before it needs to get done, you may find yourself forgetting it was even asked of you. Outlook changes all that. The next time you receive an e-mail message asking you to do something, all you have to do is drag the message onto the Task icon on the Outlook bar.

Outlook will automatically open a Task form for you with the information already in it, including the actual contents of the e-mail message, as shown in Figure 8.10.

PART

II

Mastering the
Outlook Components

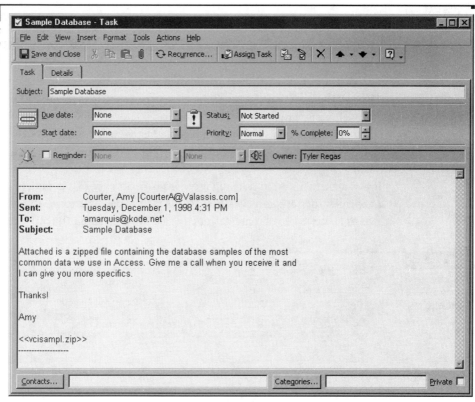

**FIGURE 8.10**

*A Task form opens automatically from an e-mail message.*

All you have to do is add Due Dates, assign the task to a category, and add any other details you want—and your reminder is all set. (You will, however, have to actually do the task yourself.)

You can use this trick to create Outlook tasks with any other Outlook item, such as a Journal entry, a Calendar item, or a Note. Try it after you learn more about these Outlook components in Chapters 9 and 10.

# Completing a Task

When you've finally completed a task, there is nothing more satisfying than checking it off your list. Outlook wouldn't want you to miss out on this pleasure, so it has incorporated a check box into the Information Viewer for most of the standard views. To mark a task complete, just click the check box, as shown in Figure 8.11.

**FIGURE 8.11**

*Completing a task*

The task is crossed off the list. If the view you are using does not include completed items, the item is actually removed from the list altogether. Of course, you can always see it by switching to a view such as Simple List view, which shows all Tasks. If you mistakenly check off a task as complete, just switch to Simple List view and clear the check box.

If you are interested in tracking more information about a completed task, you may want to open the task and click the Details tab of the Tasks form. It has several fields, shown in Figure 8.12, that are designed to be filled in when the task is completed.

**FIGURE 8.12**

*Tracking additional information about a completed task*

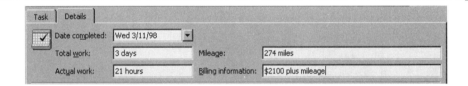

On this page you can record the date the task was completed, the planned number of hours (Outlook will translate to days), the actual number of hours, and other billing information you may want to track, such as the number of miles traveled on the job. If you have to submit an expense or billing statement at the end of the month, this is a great way to track the information you need.

## What's Next

Now that you know what you have to do, you need to figure out when you'll have time to do it. Chapter 9 will show you how to schedule meetings, vacations, and other important events. You can then add tasks to the Calendar to make sure you have time set aside to complete them before they are due.

# CHAPTER 9

# Scheduling Your Time

FEATURING:

**T**iming is everything, and controlling your scheduling often makes the difference between success and failure in this fast-paced world. Whether you keep your own calendar or have an assistant keep it for you, it can be a challenge to schedule your time wisely. Every fall, millions of people search through office supply stores and catalogs looking for the perfect calendar that will keep them organized in the coming year. If you are among them, Outlook's Calendar is for you. Not sure whether to choose a calendar with a daily view or a weekly view? With Outlook you can have both. In fact, you can view your calendar by the day, multiple days, workweek, calendar week, month, and a variety of other ways.

The real power of using an electronic calendar lies in being able to schedule recurring appointments and, if you are on a network, schedule appointments with other people. In this chapter, you'll learn how to make your calendar work for you instead of becoming a slave to it.

## Viewing and Navigating the Calendar

When you first enter the Calendar, either by clicking the Calendar icon on the Outlook bar or by choosing Go ➢ Calendar from the menu, you are shown the Day/Week/Month view, shown in Figure 9.1.

**FIGURE 9.1**

*The Calendar's Day/Week/Month view*

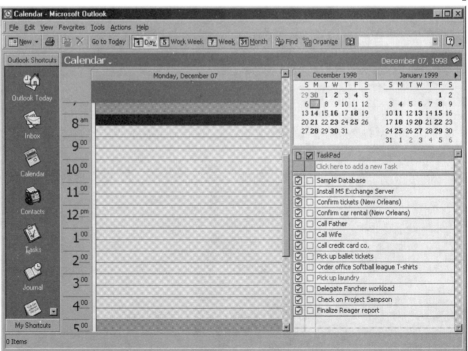

The Day/Week/Month view is actually a combination of a daily calendar, a monthly calendar called the date navigator, and a list of active tasks on the TaskPad. So why, you may be asking, is this called the Day/Week/Month view when there is no week visible? It's because you can easily switch from Day view to Week view to Month view using buttons on the Standard toolbar, as shown in Figure 9.2.

**FIGURE 9.2**

*The Standard toolbar with the  Day button selected*

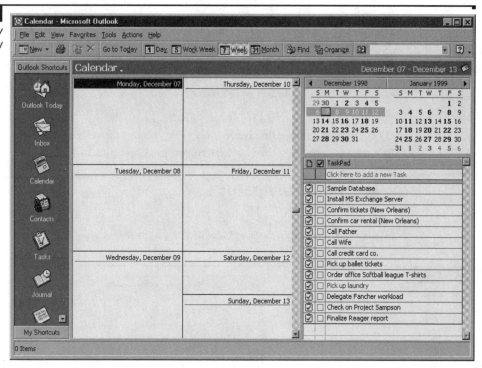

The Day button shows the default view. The next button, Work Week, displays a workweek of five days. If your workweek is made up of different days, you can customize the week, using the Calendar options. (See "Configuring the Calendar" later in this chapter.)

The Week button shows all seven days of the week in the typical week-at-a-glance format, shown in Figure 9.3, which you may be used to from your paper-based calendar.

**FIGURE 9.3**

*The typical seven-day week view*

PART

II

Mastering the
Outlook Components

The Month button displays a month at a time, alternating gray and white backgrounds to differentiate the months, as shown in Figure 9.4.

**FIGURE 9.4**

*The Month view*

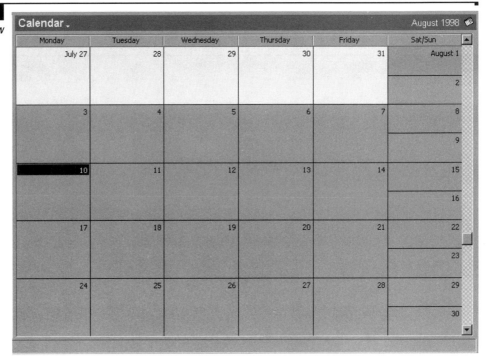

Personal preference dictates which view you use most frequently. Choose the view that gives you the best sense of where you have to be and what you have to do.

## Using the Date Navigator

The date navigator, shown in Figure 9.5, not only shows you the monthly calendar, but also lets you select days to view in the Calendar itself.

**FIGURE 9.5**

*The date navigator*

Click any date in the date navigator, and that date becomes visible in the Information Viewer.

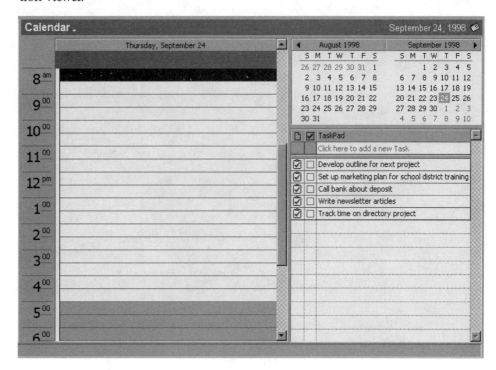

Click the left and right arrows next to the month headings to select a different month.

To select an entire week, move your pointer to the left side of the date navigator. The pointer changes position and points toward the date navigator. Click your mouse to select the week. To select multiple weeks, hold your mouse button down and drag, as shown in Figure 9.6.

To move quickly to a different month, click on the month name and select another month from the list.

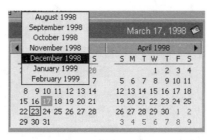

PART

**II**

Mastering the
Outlook Components

**FIGURE 9.6**

*Selecting multiple weeks*

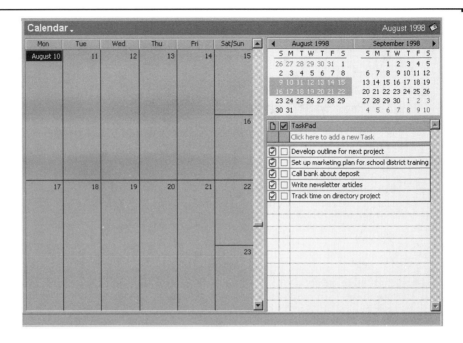

It's also easy to compare nonconsecutive days. Click a day and hold the Ctrl key down before selecting the next day, as shown in Figure 9.7.

**FIGURE 9.7**

*Selecting nonconsecutive days*

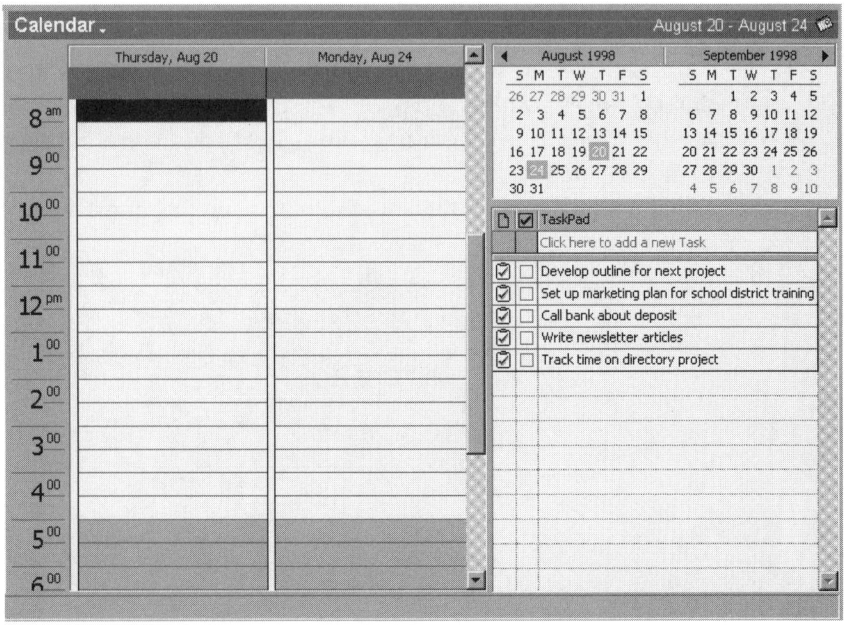

Using this month-selection feature can be a little bit tricky if the month you want is not immediately visible among the months displayed. Pretend there is a scroll bar and hold your mouse button down and drag. You'll find that you have to drag outside of the list in order to activate the scroll feature. Figure 9.8 shows an example of scrolling the month list. Notice the position of the mouse pointer.

---

**FIGURE 9.8**

*Scrolling the month list*

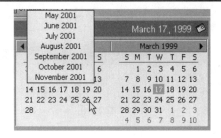

Moving the mouse pointer farther away from the list will increase the speed of the scroll. To slow down the scroll rate, move the mouse pointer closer to the list. To move to a previous month, position the mouse pointer above the list, as shown in Figure 9.9.

---

**FIGURE 9.9**

*Scrolling to a previous month*

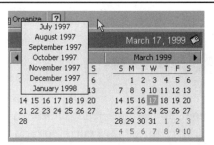

Any time you want to move quickly back to today, click the Go to Today button on the Standard toolbar.

If you prefer to display only one month in the date navigator, move your mouse pointer to the left side of the date navigator—the pointer will change to a resize arrow. Drag the border of the date navigator to the right until only one month is visible, as shown in Figure 9.10.

PART

II

Mastering the
Outlook Components

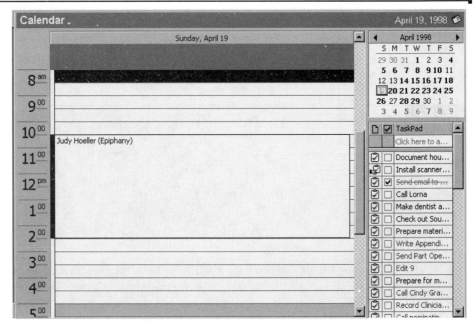

# Scheduling Appointments

Scheduling an appointment is as easy as clicking on the appointment slot in the Day view and typing in the information, as shown in Figure 9.11.

Once you have typed in the entry, point to the lower border of the appointment slot and, with the two-headed arrow pointer, drag down to identify the end time of the appointment. Drop the blue line just above the desired end time.

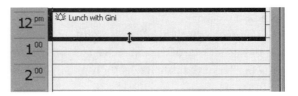

PART

II

Mastering the
Outlook Components

**FIGURE 9.11**

*Entering an
appointment in
the Calendar*

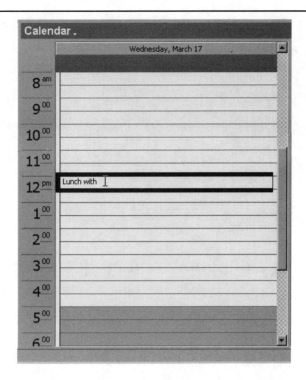

To change the start time of the appointment, drag the blue line above the appointment slot. If you want to maintain the length of the appointment but alter the start and end times, point to the blue line on the left side of the appointment and, with the four-headed arrow, drag the entire appointment to a new time.

Once you begin dragging, the four-headed arrow will change shape to a pointer with a move box.

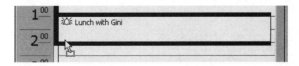

To change the appointment to a different day, it's necessary to first make the new date visible in the date navigator. Switch to the desired month in the date navigator, and drag the appointment to the new date using the four-headed arrow/move box.

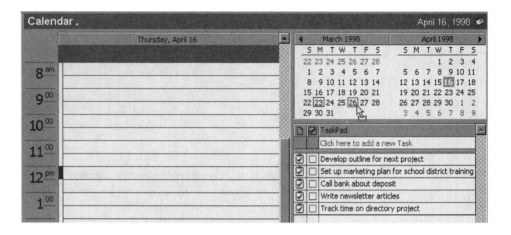

## Entering an Appointment in the Appointment Form

When you want to enter more details about an appointment, double-click the appointment in the Information Viewer to open the Appointment form. (See Figure 9.12)

**FIGURE 9.12**

*The Calendar's Appointment form*

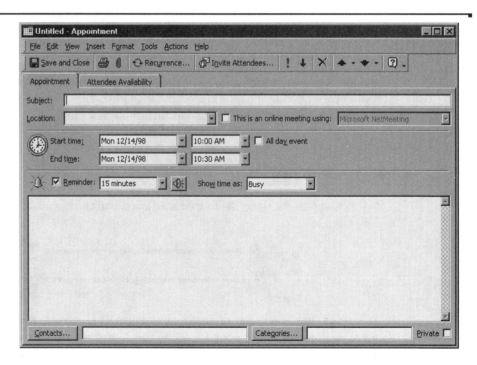

In addition to the Subject and Start Time and End Time, the Appointment form allows you to enter a location, to set a reminder, and to enter other notes about the appointment.

## MASTERING THE OPPORTUNITIES

### Appointments versus Events

Outlook's Calendar feature distinguishes between appointments and events. An appointment has a start and end time and may last for less than one day or may span multiple days. An event, on the other hand, encompasses an entire day or perhaps several days but does not have a specific start and end time. For example, a holiday, a birthday, or a vacation is designated as an event. To change an appointment to an event, click the All Day Event check box to the right of the Start Time on an Appointment form. The Start Time and End Time fields are removed from the form. Because an event does not automatically impact your schedule, the Show Time As field is set to Free. Events appear as a banner in the Day view of the Calendar. See "Scheduling Events" later in this chapter for more information about events.

Click the This Is an Online Meeting check box if the meeting will occur over the Internet (for more information about online meetings, see Chapter 15).

To set the Start Time and End Time in an Appointment form, click the down arrow to the right of the Start Time and End Time fields. The first arrow opens a calendar from which you can select the date for the appointment. Use the left and right arrows next to the month name to select from a different month.

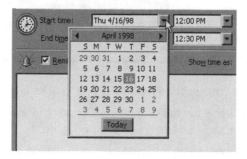

The arrow to the right of the second field opens a list of times on a 24-hour clock. Be careful to select the correct A.M. or P.M. time, or you may be expecting to have lunch some day at midnight.

PART
II

Mastering the
Outlook Components

**TIP** Outlook has incorporated the use of natural language for dates. Rather than typing a date in traditional format or selecting the date from the calendar, you can type in text to describe the date. For example, rather than locating the date for next Friday, you can simply type in the words **next Friday** and Outlook will translate the text to the correct date. For more about natural language dates, see Chapter 2.

## Setting a Reminder

One of the biggest advantages of using an electronic calendar is that it can automatically remind you when it's time to go to your appointments. Assuming that most of your appointments are held in your office, the default reminder is set for 15 minutes prior to a scheduled appointment. For a meeting that occurs out of the office, you can set this reminder from 0 minutes to up to 2 days by selecting a different choice from the drop-down list. As a matter of fact, you can type in a reminder that extends even beyond the two days that are included in the list. To turn off the reminder, click the check box to the left of the Reminder field.

When a reminder is scheduled, it will appear as a small dialog box in whatever application is running at the time (as long as Outlook is at least running in the background). Figure 9.13 is an example of an appointment reminder.

**FIGURE 9.13**

*A reminder for an appointment*

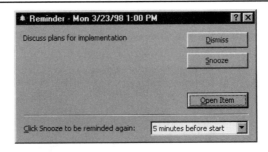

When you receive a reminder, you have several options. You can:

- Dismiss the reminder (click Dismiss), in which case Outlook assumes you are on your way and won't bother you again.

- Choose to be reminded again in a designated amount of time by selecting the desired time interval from the Click Snooze to Be Reminded Again drop-down list and clicking Snooze.

- Open the Appointment form so you can review the appointment or make changes to it.

When the reminder dialog box opens, clicking anywhere outside of the dialog box will move it to the Windows taskbar. You are then free to open it at any time to respond to the reminder.

By default, an appointment reminder is accompanied by a short ding (actually it's the Windows default ding). You can choose to turn the ding off or choose a more dramatic sound to accompany the reminder.

 To change the sound options, click the speaker icon next to the Reminder text box. This opens the Reminder Sound dialog box.

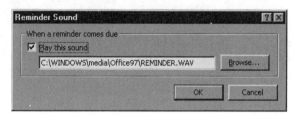

To turn off the sound so that the reminder appears silently on your screen, simply click the Play This Sound check box to clear it. To designate a different sound file, either type the path to the sound file or click the Browse button to access your file list. The file must be a .wav file—the reminder cannot play a MIDI or other type of sound file.

**TIP** You can record your own reminder sound using the Windows Sound Recorder and play that sound file (.wav) when it's time to go to an appointment. You'll find the Windows Sound Recorder in the Accessories program group on the Programs menu.

When you have set the Sound Reminder options, click OK to return to the Appointment form.

## Scheduling Recurring Appointments

You probably have a number of appointments that occur on a regular basis—for example, a weekly staff meeting, a daily project review meeting, or a monthly district sales meeting. With Outlook's Calendar, you can set up a meeting once and it will automatically recur in your calendar.

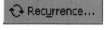 To access the recurrence features, set up the appointment in the Appointment form, and then click the Recurrence button on the Standard toolbar of the Appointment form. This opens the Appointment Recurrence dialog box.

PART

II

Mastering the
Outlook Components

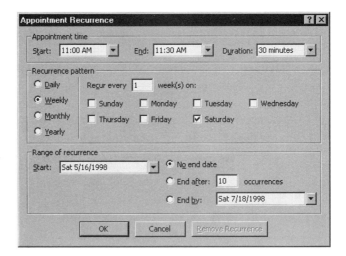

Use the Start, End, and Duration fields to designate the typical time for the recurring appointment. You only have to set two of these three fields—Outlook will calculate the third. For example, if the start time is noon and the duration is three hours, Outlook will automatically set the end time to 3:00 P.M.

Choose the recurrence pattern that most closely matches the recurring appointment's schedule. Each of the four options—Daily, Weekly, Monthly, and Yearly—offer different choices for setting up the pattern. If, for example, the meeting occurs every day, choose Daily as the recurrence pattern and click the Every Weekday check box. If, however, the appointment occurs on the fourth Monday of every other month, set the recurrence pattern to Monthly and enter the fourth Monday of every two months, as shown in Figure 9.14.

**FIGURE 9.14**

*This meeting occurs the fourth Monday of every second month.*

After establishing the recurrence pattern, you'll want to identify the range of recurrence. This tells Outlook when to schedule the first meeting and how many times the appointment will recur. Enter the date of the first meeting in the Start field and choose among the following three options to indicate how many times to add the appointment to your calendar:

**No End Date**    Use this option if it appears that the meeting will occur from now until the end of time.

**End after *N* Occurrences**    With this option you can designate exactly how many times to add the meeting to your calendar.

**End By**    This option allows you to designate a specific end date. The meeting will be scheduled only between the designated start and end dates.

When you have set the recurrence options, click the OK button to assign the recurrence pattern to the appointment. You'll notice that the recurrence pattern is listed on the Appointment form.

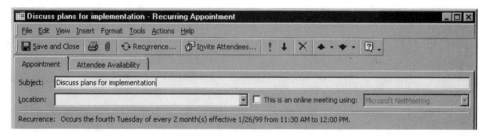

You don't have to have the Appointment form open to recognize a recurring appointment. A recurring appointment is displayed in the Information Viewer with an icon composed of two circular arrows.

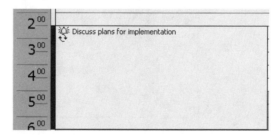

To set a recurrence pattern, then, follow these steps:

1. Open an Appointment form and click the Recurrence button.

2. Choose the frequency of the recurrence (daily, weekly, monthly, or yearly), and then specify the day on which the meeting will occur; for example, the first Friday of every month.

PART

II

Mastering the
Outlook Components

**3.** Identify the range of recurrence, that is, how far in the future these meetings will continue to be held: until the end of time, for three weeks, from now until December 31, 2001, etc.

**4.** Click OK to save the recurrence pattern. A recurring appointment is designated in the Information Viewer by an icon with two circular arrows.

## Scheduling Events

As indicated earlier in this chapter, an event has no start and end times, such as a holiday, anniversary, or any other day that you want to note. To schedule an event, open an Appointment form, enter the Subject and the date information, and click the All Day Event check box. This removes the Start Time and End Time fields from the Appointment form. You can set a reminder for an event and set a Recurrence Pattern just as you would for any other appointment. So when you find out the date of your best friend's birthday, enter it as an event and set the recurrence pattern to yearly. To make sure you have time to buy a gift, set a reminder for one or two days before the birthday. Your friend will be shocked when you actually remember the all-important day.

Outlook assumes that an event does not occupy your time, so it shows your time as Free. However, you may want to change this if, for example, the event you are entering is your vacation. In this case, you could set the Show Time As field to Out of the Office.

Because there are no times associated with an event, events are displayed differently from regular appointments in the Information Viewer. In the Day view, an event appears at the top of the day's schedule. In the Week and Month views, events are displayed in bordered boxes, such as the one in Figure 9.15.

**FIGURE 9.15**

*An event in Month view*

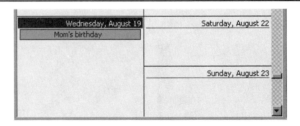

 **TIP** Outlook gives you the option of loading a variety of different holidays into your Outlook Calendar. For example, you can load United States holidays and Christian, Jewish, and Islamic religious holidays. See "Configuring the Calendar" later in this chapter for more information about how to add these holidays to your calendar automatically.

## Scheduling a Multiday Event

Multiday events are scheduled activities that have no set start and end times and span several days. To enter a multiday event, open the Appointment form and set the start and end time dates to coincide with the dates of the event.

# Scheduling Time to Complete a Task

In an effort to help you manage your time more effectively, Outlook displays the TaskPad as part of the default Calendar view. This is not only so you get a sense of tasks that you have to accomplish; it's so you can actually schedule time to work on individual tasks.

To schedule time to work on a task, display the day and select the time in the Information Viewer. Drag the task that you want to work on from the TaskPad to the designated time. Outlook will create an appointment based on the task and will open an Appointment form with the contents of the task already included in it, as shown in Figure 9.16. Set the other options just as you would for any other appointment—the only difference is that this is an appointment with yourself.

PART

II

Mastering the
Outlook Components

**FIGURE 9.16**

*An appointment
created from a task*

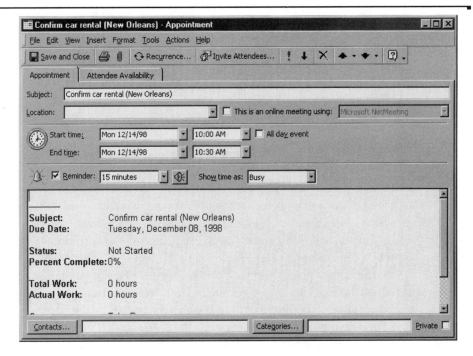

When you complete the task, mark it complete on your Task list just as you would any other task (see Chapter 8 for more information about completing tasks). You'll be surprised at how much easier it is to check off items on your Task list when you schedule time in your daily calendar to complete them.

### Creating a Shortcut to a Task

If you'd rather an appointment were created with only a shortcut to the corresponding task, drag the appointment onto the Calendar using the right mouse button. When you release the mouse button, you will be given options to do the following:

- Copy the task as an appointment with text.
- Copy the task as an appointment with a shortcut.
- Copy the task as an appointment with an attachment.
- Move the task as an appointment with an attachment.

When you copy the task as an appointment with a shortcut, the contents of the task do not occur in both the Calendar and the Task list. When you open an Appointment form, you'll find an icon representing the task. Double-click the icon to open the task in the Task list. This option saves space on your hard drive and reduces the size of your Personal Information Store. The two other options, involving attachments, create copies of the task, which you would also access by double-clicking the icon within the Appointment form. Use one of the attachment options if you plan to share this appointment with someone else using Outlook (see "Using the Calendar in a Workgroup" later in this chapter).

# Configuring the Calendar

Because people work very different schedules these days, Outlook has included a number of options that let you define the days you work, the hours that you want to display in your calendar, and which day is the first in your week. To change the Calendar options, click the Tools menu on the Standard toolbar and choose Options. This opens the Options dialog box, shown in Figure 9.17.

This is your gateway to the options for each of the Outlook components. You can adjust the Calendar option for the Default Reminder time from this initial dialog box. Just choose a different time from the choices available in the drop-down list.

To access additional options, click the Calendar Options button. This button takes you to more specific Calendar options, as shown in Figure 9.18.

**FIGURE 9.17**

The Options dialog box

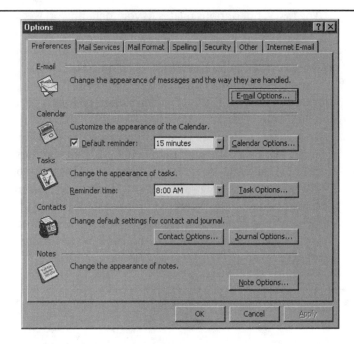

**FIGURE 9.18**

The Calendar Options
dialog box

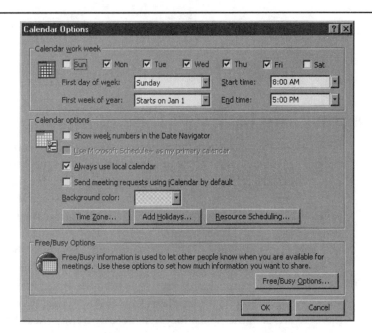

The first set of options relates to your default workweek. Click the check boxes in front of the days of the week to designate the days that make up your workweek. If you would prefer the Calendar to display Monday or any other day as the first day of the week, select the day from the First Day of the Week field.

The Day view of the Calendar is set to display the typical workday. If your workday differs from this, set the start and end times of your typical day using the Start Time and End Time fields.

To keep your calendar in line with your staff schedules, you may want to start your calendar year on a date other than January 1. Perhaps yours starts on the first four-day week or first full week of the year. Choose one of these options from the drop-down list.

The second set of options relates specifically to the Calendar. For many companies it is important to know the week number in order to calculate payroll and benefits for employees. Outlook will let you display the week number in the date navigator, as shown in Figure 9.19, by clicking the Show Week Numbers in the Date Navigator check box.

**FIGURE 9.19**

*The week numbers can be displayed in the date navigator.*

## Showing Two Time Zones

If you are someone who travels frequently across different time zones or has regular phone conferences with people in different time zones, it's helpful to know what time it is in another place. You can choose to show more than one time zone in the Day view of the Information Viewer. Click the Time Zone button to set up an additional time zone or to make adjustments to your current time zone, such as adjusting for daylight savings time.

To set up an additional time zone in the Time Zone dialog box, shown in Figure 9.20, start by giving the time zone a label. This will identify the time zone in the Day view of the Calendar. Select the desired time zone from the Time Zone drop-down list. Indicate if you would like Outlook to automatically adjust for daylight saving time by making sure there is a check in the Adjust for Daylight Saving Time check box. Outlook will display the current date and time based on the Windows Date/Time Properties. If you find that the date or time is wrong, double-click the time in the Windows taskbar and adjust the settings there.

FIGURE 9.20

*The Time Zone
dialog box*

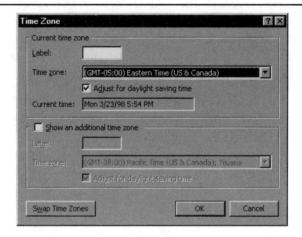

When you would like to display an additional time zone, click the Show an Additional Time Zone check box. This activates the second set of fields so you can enter a label and choose a new time zone. To display both time zones, click OK to close the dialog box. Click OK again to close the Calendar Options, and click OK a third time to close the Options dialog box. The two time zones will be displayed side-by-side, as shown in Figure 9.21.

FIGURE 9.21

*Displaying two
time zones*

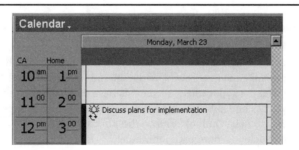

 **TIP** If you'd prefer to only display one time zone at a time but frequently move between the two, re-open the Time Zone dialog box (Tools ➢ Options ➢ Calendar Options ➢ Time Zone) and click the Swap Time Zones button. You can then clear the Show an Additional Time Zone check box to display only the secondary time zone.

PART

II

Mastering the
Outlook Components

## Loading Holidays

We find it a lot easier to remember the date of some holidays than to remember others—the Fourth of July and Christmas are easy ones. However, many holidays are not content to occur on the same day every year; they are constantly moving around the calendar. Outlook makes it easy to load these dates into your permanent calendar. In fact, you have to be careful to not load too many holidays, or your calendar will be overrun with them. To load holidays into your calendar, follow these steps:

1. Select Tools ➤ Options ➤ Calendar Options ➤ Add Holidays.

2. Select from the list of national holidays (from such countries as the United States, Australia, and Canada) and religious holidays (such as those of Christianity, Judaism, and Islam).

3. Click OK three times to close all the option dialog boxes.

Holidays appear on your Calendar as events, so they are displayed in the banner at the top of each day. If you've chosen holidays from a particular country or religious group, that group's name will appear in parentheses after the holiday, as shown in Figure 9.22.

**FIGURE 9.22**

*The source of each holiday is displayed next to the holiday name.*

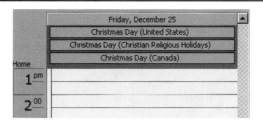

 **WARNING** Many holidays are repeated from country to country and between countries in religious groups. For example, Christmas Day is shared by Christians and people in the United States, Ireland, and numerous other countries. If you choose to add all of these holidays to your calendar, you will have multiple occurrences of these shared holidays on your calendar. Be selective when choosing which groups of holidays to add. There is no way to have Outlook remove the holidays once you've added them, except by selecting and deleting them each individually.

The other Calendar options available from the Options dialog box are specific to using Calendar on a network. For information about the network applications of Calendar, see "Using the Calendar in a Workgroup," later in this chapter.

# Printing the Calendar

Recognizing that it may be difficult at first to part with your paper-based planner, Outlook has set up a wide variety of printing options that allow you to print your calendar so it fits right into your planner. Until you are able to develop a system that no longer depends on carrying around that book, you can rest assured that your Outlook calendar can still go with you.

Before you can print your calendar, you need to decide what style you want to use. If you go directly to Print Preview, you'll see that whatever view is visible on your screen is the view that will print. For example, if you are in Day view, you'll see all your appointments for that day, as shown in Figure 9.23. If you are in the Week or Month views, you will get a weekly or monthly view of your calendar.

FIGURE 9.23

*Print Preview of the Day view*

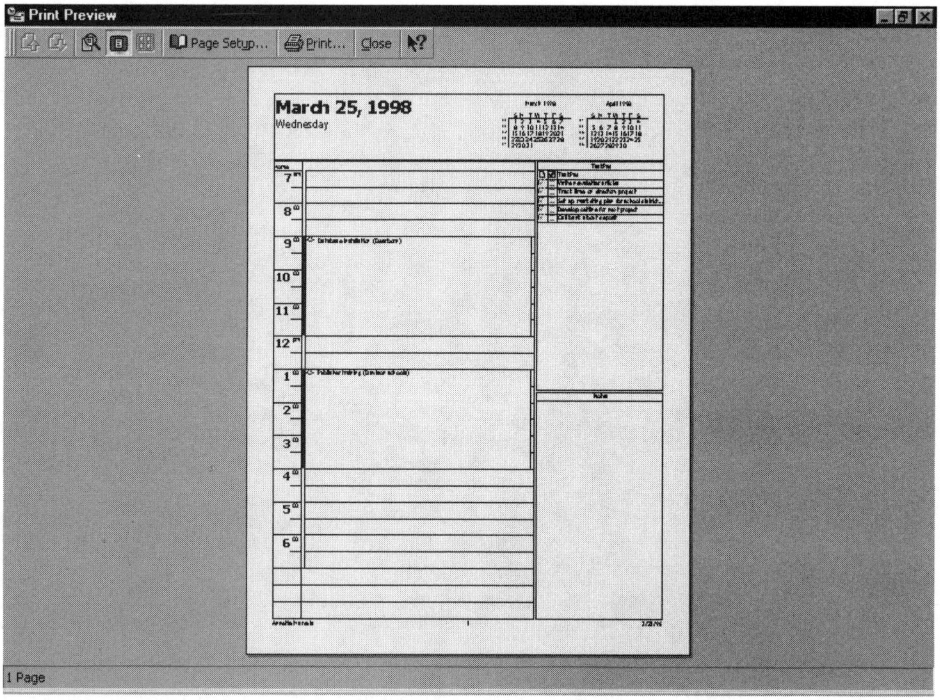

PART

II

Mastering the
Outlook Components

Have you ever struggled over which paper-based planner best meets your needs? Now you can choose whichever style you want whenever you want it. You can print out your calendar in all three views if that will make your life easier.

If you are more particular about your calendar's layout, click the File menu and choose Page Setup to have a world of options available to you. Before a dialog box even opens, you are presented with a list of choices.

Choose the primary layout that you want for your calendar. Depending on which style you choose, you are presented with different page setup options. The page setup options for the Weekly view are displayed in Figure 9.24.

**FIGURE 9.24**

*Page Setup dialog box for the Weekly Style*

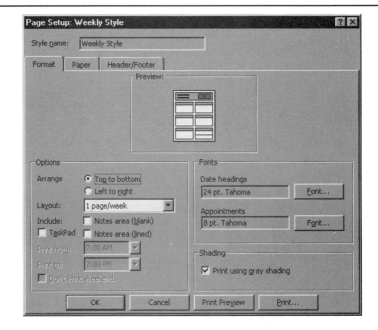

The first page of the Page Setup dialog box presents the Format options. Here you can indicate what sections you want to appear on the page. You can even include a lined or unlined notes area for your handwritten notes. At any point in the Page Setup process you can click the Print Preview button to see how your printed document will appear. If you are satisfied, click the Print button; if it needs more work, click Page Setup and you're brought right back here.

The second page of the Page Setup dialog box, shown in Figure 9.25, is the Paper page. This page is especially critical if you plan to print your calendar on paper other than a standard $8^1/_2 \times 11$ sheet. On this page you can set the paper type, size, dimensions, orientation, and margins, and you can identify what tray of the printer the paper will be in.

**FIGURE 9.25**

*The Paper page of the Page Setup dialog box*

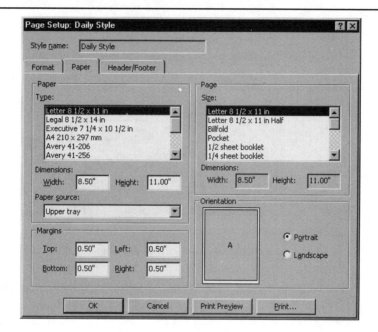

 **TIP** If you are using a planner from the big three: Day-Timer, Day Runner, or Franklin, take special note of the Page Size list. Your planner is probably listed, so you'll be able to select an exact match.

## Headers and Footers

The Headers/Footers page of the Page Setup dialog box, shown in Figure 9.26, closely resembles the header and footer feature of Microsoft Excel. If you're familiar with Excel, this will be a snap. If you are not an Excel user, don't let it scare you—it's easier than it appears.

**FIGURE 9.26**

*The Header/Footer page of Page Setup*

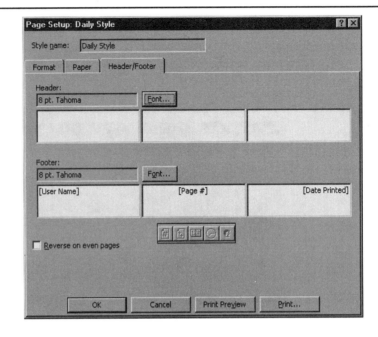

A header appears at the top of every page of your document, which in this case is the Calendar. A footer appears at the bottom of every page. Typically, you'll find the title and subtitle in the header. By default, Outlook includes the User Name (that's generally you), the Page Number, and the Date Printed in the footer. You are not bound by this convention, however. You are free to put any information anywhere you want it.

The header and footer sections are each divided into three subsections: left, center, and right. Click in any of the six text boxes to enter text in that section.

Outlook provides you with placeholders for five variable fields that you can insert in either the header or the footer. To insert a placeholder, click in the section of the header or footer where you want the placeholder to appear, and then click the placeholder button. The following list identifies the function of each of these placeholders, from left to right:

**Page Number**    Inserts the actual page number of the document.

**Total Pages**    Can be combined with the page number placeholder to create the expression "Page 1 of 4" (Page [Page Number] of [Total Pages]).

**Date Printed**   Displays the date the Calendar was printed, regardless of the date that is shown in the Calendar.

**Time Printed**   Displays the actual time the Calendar was printed.

**User Name**   Displays the name of the user currently logged in to Outlook.

 **TIP**   If you're printing the Calendar in booklet form, you may want to reverse the header and footer on pages that face each other. For example, if the date printed appears on the right side on odd pages, it would appear on the left on even pages. This touch can make it look like your document was produced by a professional printer.

When you have finished setting up the Page Setup options, click the Print button to print your calendar.

## Creating a Style for Printing Your Calendar

After you've gone through changing all of the Page Setup options a few weeks in a row, you may find that it's easier to define a Page Setup style you can reuse every time you want to print your calendar. This is a great way to save time and still be able to use a consistent format for your calendar from week to week. Follow the steps below to define your own print style, which will appear in the Page Setup menu list.

1. Select File ➤ Page Setup ➤ Define Print Styles.

2. Choose to edit an existing style or to create a new style by copying an existing style.

3. If you choose to copy an existing style, enter a name for the new style in the Style Name text box at the top of the Page Setup dialog box.

4. Create your custom style using the Page Setup options.

5. Click OK to save your changes.

6. Select your newly created style from the Page Setup menu.

If you want to delete a custom style, choose Define Print Styles, select the style you want to delete, and click the Delete button.

 **TIP**   If you are editing an existing style, the original style will no longer be available. However, you can reset the original style by choosing Define Print Styles from the Page Setup menu, selecting the style, and clicking the Reset button.

PART

II

Mastering the
Outlook Components

# Using the Calendar in a Workgroup

If you've ever worked in an office that holds lots of meetings, then you know firsthand how very much time is spent scheduling and rescheduling meetings. Some office studies have found that nearly 30 percent of secretarial time is spent scheduling meetings for managers and administrators. One of the fastest-growing software markets today is the group scheduling market. Companies all over the globe are recognizing the need to simplify the process of scheduling meetings.

Outlook is ready to address this challenge. With Outlook, you can schedule a meeting with people on your network or over the Internet, using either vCalendar or iCalendar, depending on your compatibility needs. Chapter 15 has details about using these calendar technnologies. You'll also learn how to hold a meeting over the Internet using NetMeeting, but for now let's look at scheduling appointments with people who are part of your internal network.

## Planning a Meeting with Others

Outlook offers several ways to invite others to attend a meeting. The simplest way is to click the down arrow on the New button and choose Meeting Request from the list of choices. This opens the e-mail message form, shown in Figure 9.27, but you may notice that there are some differences between this and the standard message form.

**FIGURE 9.27**

*A Meeting message form*

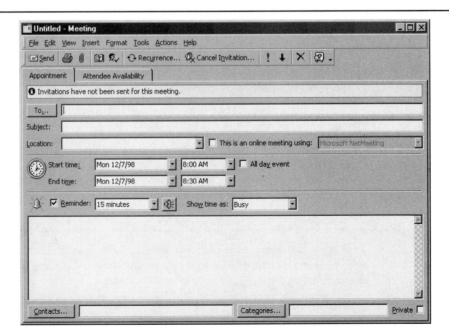

First, there is an informational message telling you that invitations for this meeting have not yet been sent. Of course, you already knew that in this case, but you can always find the status of an invitation here even after you send it.

Second, in addition to the To and Subject fields, there is a Location field for you to identify where the meeting will take place. Clicking the To button will take you to a special version of your Contacts address book, shown in Figure 9.28. Here you can identify those people whose attendance at the meeting is Required, those whose attendance is Optional, and the Resources, such as meeting rooms and AV equipment, that are required for the meeting (for more about scheduling meeting rooms and equipment, see the sidebar "Scheduling Meeting Rooms and Equipment" later in this chapter). Click OK once you have identified all the attendees.

**FIGURE 9.28**

*The Select Attendees and Resources dialog box*

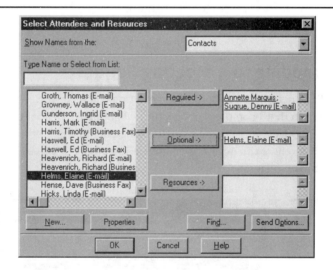

The other fields on the Meeting request form are similar to the standard Meeting form. To create a meeting request on your own, follow these steps:

1. Click the down arrow on the New button and choose Meeting Request.

2. Click the To button to open the Select Attendees and Resources dialog box.

3. Double-click the names of those people whose attendance at the meeting is required.

4. If a person's attendance is optional, click their name and click the Optional button.

5. If you have meeting rooms and other resources set up with their own mailboxes, select the resource you want to assign to the meeting and click the Resources button.

PART

II

Mastering the Outlook Components

6. If the person you want to invite to a meeting is not in your Address book, click the New button and, in the Properties dialog box that opens, enter information about the contact. Click OK to add this person to your Address book.

7. Click OK to close the Select Attendees and Resources dialog box and return to the Meeting request form.

8. Enter the Subject and Location, and click the This Is an Online Meeting check box if it is an online meeting that you are scheduling.

9. Fill in the Start Time, End Time, Reminder, and Show Time As fields, just as you would for any other meeting.

10. If the meeting is going to be regularly scheduled, you can click the Recurrence button and set up the recurrence pattern (see "Scheduling Recurring Appointments" earlier in the chapter).

11. Click the Send button to send out the meeting requests.

## Responding to a Meeting Request

Each person you invited to the meeting will receive an e-mail message labeled *Meeting*. When they open the message, they will be able to read the information about the meeting. Once they've made a determination about whether or not they can attend, they can click one of the Accept, Decline, or Tentative buttons at the top of the Meeting form, shown in Figure 9.29.

**FIGURE 9.29**

*Meeting request response buttons*

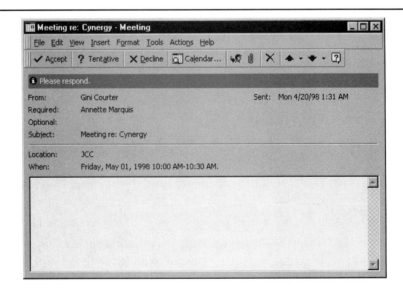

Clicking one of these three buttons generates an e-mail message back to you, the meeting request originator, which indicates to you whether or not this person will attend. If the person accepted the meeting request, it's automatically placed on their calendar. In addition, all of the responses are automatically tabulated for you, so there is no need for you to keep a manual count. It really couldn't be easier. All you have to do is open the appointment in your calendar and click the Attendee Availability tab to see the list of attendees and their responses to date, as shown in Figure 9.30.

**FIGURE 9.30**

*Attendee Availability page of the Meeting form after a meeting has been scheduled*

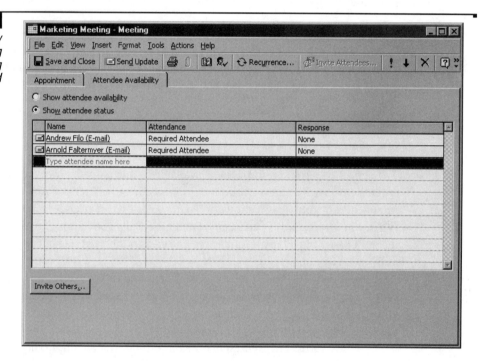

If, after seeing who has accepted your invitation, you decide that you want to invite other people to this thrilling meeting, click the Invite Others button on the Attendee Availability page. You'll then be able to generate new e-mail meeting requests.

That's all there is to it. Never again will you have to make 25 phone calls to get 4 people to attend a meeting. Now you'll actually have time to get some real work done.

## Checking Your Coworkers' Schedules

Even the steps outlined previously for requesting a meeting could backfire, though, if you find that the majority of the people you need at your meeting can't attend at the time you requested. It might be easier to check individual schedules first and schedule the meeting at a time when all of your key people can attend.

PART

II

Mastering the
Outlook Components

A lot of people get nervous when you talk about making their schedules available for other people to see. Outlook has found how to give you the best of both worlds. It allows you to look at what is referred to as the individual's free/busy information. In other words, you can see when an individual is free, busy, out of the office, or tentatively scheduled. You cannot, however, see what they are doing or how they are spending their time (unless the other person has given you permission to do so). This seems to relieve most people's anxiety about Big Brother looking over their shoulders and still allows for the greatest success in scheduling meetings with the first request.

 **WARNING** There is only one caveat to making an electronic scheduling system work: each person on the network has to keep their Outlook schedule up-to-date. If an individual's time is marked as free and you schedule a meeting with them during that time, it's pretty frustrating to find that this key person can't make it after all. Each office has to deal with this problem in their own way, but it's critically important that an expectation be set from the top that each person keep their schedule current.

To check to see when someone is available to meet, open a Meeting Request form, enter the person's address in the To box, and click the Attendee Availability tab. The Attendee Availability page, shown in Figure 9.31, lists all attendees in the left column. When you first open this page, Outlook automatically goes out to the network to gather the most current free/busy information. The grid on the right side of the page shows each individual's free/busy status.

If an individual is free, their time is not marked in the grid. If they are out of the office, a maroon-colored bar extends across the grid to mark the time they will be gone. If they are busy, you'll see a blue-colored bar, and if they are tentatively scheduled, you'll see a light blue bar.

The white vertical bar represents the duration of the meeting. The green border on the left indicates the start time, and the brown border represents the end time of the meeting.

 **TIP** If you're still uncomfortable releasing your free/busy information because you don't want someone booking up your schedule for the next month while you're still working on booking your own appointments, go to Tools ≻ Options ≻ Calendar Options and click the Free/Busy Options button. You can indicate there how many months of your free/busy information you want to make available at one time. You can also indicate how often you would like your free/busy information to be updated on the server. Increasing the frequency will reduce the likelihood that someone might schedule a meeting during a time that you just booked for yourself.

**FIGURE 9.31**

The Attendee
Availability page of
the Meeting form

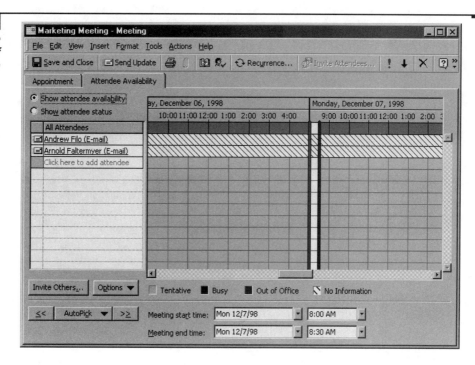

The key to working with the Attendee Availability grid is to start by manually setting your preferred meeting time in the Meeting Start Time and Meeting End Time text boxes. Even if the desired attendees are not available at this time, this action sets a beginning date and the duration of the meeting. Click the AutoPick button to locate the first time when all attendees are available. Notice that the Meeting Start Time and Meeting End Time text boxes change to correspond to the time indicated by the grid. When you find an agreeable time, click the Send button at the top of the form. This will generate the attendees' e-mail messages. Because you've already checked their schedules, you should be pretty confident that the attendees will accept the meeting request.

If you decide to invite others to the meeting, click the Invite Others button. Click the Options button to access the following three options:

• To show only work hours in the Calendar, choose Show Only Working Hours.

• To see more dates at once, choose Show Zoomed Out.

• To force Outlook to update the free/busy information on the server, choose Update Free/Busy.

## MASTERING THE OPPORTUNITIES

## Scheduling Meeting Rooms and Equipment

One of the most common scheduling needs in an office setting is the need to schedule meeting rooms and AV equipment. It's not unusual to spend hours setting up a meeting only to discover that there's no available room for it. Or maybe you get the meeting room scheduled, only to find out there's no way to show your PowerPoint presentation because someone just took the last LCD projector out of the building. Outlook provides a way for you to schedule meeting resources at the same time you schedule people to attend a meeting. To do this, the Microsoft Exchange network administrator needs to set up mailboxes for each of the rooms and each of the pieces of equipment. These can be kept in a separate address book that is made available to all the users on the network. The people or person responsible for maintaining the schedule of resources needs to have access to each of these mailboxes. (For more information about setting up mailboxes and making files in folders available to other users, see Chapter 17.)

When you schedule a meeting, you can then select the meeting room and other resources from the address list in the Select Attendees and Resources dialog box. Now when you check for attendee availability, the availability of the room and required resources will also be considered.

So, you may ask, who's supposed to handle all the e-mail generated by meeting requests? You can have Outlook handle these requests automatically by carefully setting the Calendar options for the resources. To set the options for a resource, you first have to log in to Outlook as that particular resource. For example, if you want to set the options for Meeting Room A, you would log into Outlook under the username Meeting Room A. (If it's your job to maintain the schedule of resources, check with your network administrator to find out the usernames that were set up for the company's resources.) Then go to Tools ≻ Options ≻ Calendar Options and click the Resource Scheduling button. Here you're given three options regarding a resource's mailbox:

- Automatically Accept Meeting Requests and Process Cancellations. This option gives anyone the freedom to schedule any room or other resource as long as it's available.
- Automatically Decline Conflicting Meeting Requests. With this option turned on, no one can schedule a resource if it's already tied up.
- Automatically Decline Recurring Meeting Requests. You may have a policy that recurring meetings must be scheduled in person with the meeting coordinator. This option restricts users from booking a room or other resource for regular meeting time every week or every month.

After you have set these options, scheduling meeting rooms and other resources can happen behind the scenes with very little personal maintenance.

# Canceling a Meeting

After a meeting has been scheduled and everyone has gotten back to you with their enthusiastic confirmations, a situation may arise that requires you to cancel a meeting you've already arranged. Don't despair; you don't have to make a slew of phone calls. Open the meeting in your calendar and click the Cancel Invitations button on the Meeting form's toolbar. This will generate an e-mail to all attendees, indicating that the meeting has been canceled. You'll be given an opportunity to explain why you are canceling the meeting. You can then follow it up with another invitation to the meeting at the new date and time. What used to take hours is now handled in just a few minutes. Everybody's notified, everyone's calendar is updated, and no one had to be interrupted from their work to make it happen.

## What's Next

Maintaining your scheduled appointments in Outlook gives you the peace of mind of knowing that you'll be reminded where you're supposed to be and that other people you've invited have been properly notified. After you are finished with a meeting, the Journal provides a place for you to record what transpired. The Journal is a great place to document phone calls, meetings, and even ad hoc conversations by the watercooler. Chapter 10 will show you around the Journal and introduce you to Notes, the feature that lets you record everything that you have no other place to put.

PART

II

Mastering the
Outlook Components

# CHAPTER 10

# Using the Journal and Notes

**L**et's face it: record keeping is not something that most people do well. Outlook 2000 may just change all that. Outlook has the ability to track items that you enter and also to record certain items automatically. Once you start using the Journal, it won't take long to discover the incredible power that comes with documenting your conversations, phone calls, and other interactions. All it takes is being able to go back and pull up your comments about one critical conversation to be hooked on what the Journal can do for you. And Notes gives you a way to organize every little tidbit of information that you currently have on those scraps of paper scattered all over your desk. With Journal and Notes together, you never knew you could be so organized.

## Understanding the Journal

To use the Journal effectively, it's helpful to have an understanding of what the Journal is designed to do. While Tasks and Calendar are intended to help you plan your upcoming activities, the Journal's purpose is to record the work you've done. You can make notes about telephone conversations, record your impressions after a meeting, organize e-mail communications to and from a contact, and track how long you spent developing an Excel spreadsheet. You can use the Journal to generate reports, to confirm conversations with your clients, and to keep a running history of your daily activities. If you need to prove to your manager that you're overworked, use the Journal to conduct time studies in which you document how you spend your days. You can even use the Journal to track your exercise program. The possibilities are endless.

If you've taken a class on using one of the popular day-planner systems, you probably have learned some things about the value of recording events in your planner. You may appreciate the importance of keeping all your notes in one place so you can refer to them when questions come up down the road. But paper-based systems can never compete with the organization and search utilities that electronic journaling can provide. The Journal has all the powerful tools that make Outlook such an incredible tool, such as Find, views, sorting, filtering, and integration with the other Outlook components and Office applications. These tools allow you to examine and organize your data in ways that have never been possible before.

 **NOTE** In order to use the Journal effectively, it's helpful to have a solid grasp of the other Outlook components, particularly Contacts. If you're a new Outlook user, we recommend that you spend some time working with Contacts before tackling the Journal. See Chapter 4 to learn all about Contacts.

# Manually Recording an Event in the Journal

To access the Journal, click My Shortcuts and then click the Journal icon on the Outlook bar. The Journal will open in its default view, Timeline view. The primary focus of the Journal is on how you've spent your time and what events have occurred on a particular day. Figure 10.1 shows one of this book's author's Journal while working on this book. In this example, you can easily see all the Word documents that were worked on during this time.

PART

II

Mastering the
Outlook Components

**FIGURE 10.1**

*The Journal's
Timeline view*

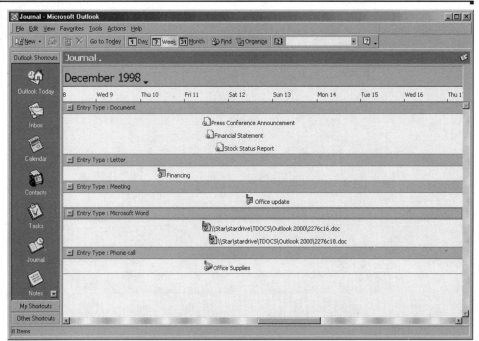

To expand a particular Entry Type so you can see all of the entries underneath it, click the plus button to the left of the Entry Type label. To collapse a group that is already expanded, click the minus button.

**NOTE** The first time you click the Journal icon on the Outlook bar, you may be surprised to find that there are already entries in the Journal. This is because the Journal is working behind the scenes automatically, recording work that you're doing in other Office applications. For a better understanding of these entries, and to learn how to change the automatic settings, see "Automatically Recording Journal Events" later in this chapter.

There are five Journal types visible in Figure 10.1: Document, Letter, Meeting, Microsoft Word, and Phone Call. In all, there are approximately 20 types of Journal entries that you can make. To create a new Journal entry, click the New button on the Standard toolbar and choose Journal Entry from the list. The Journal Entry form shown in Figure 10.2 will open.

**FIGURE 10.2**

*A Journal Entry form*

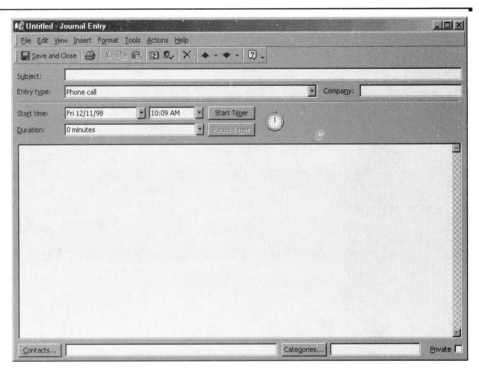

The default entry type is Phone Call. Just click the down arrow in the Entry Type field to see the other available choices.

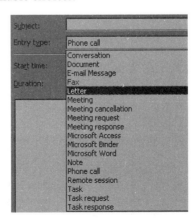

You are probably asking yourself, "Why would I want to record an e-mail message or task in a Journal entry? I've already got a record of that." The answer is simple: Journal entries can be linked directly to Contacts. Instead of searching through all of your files, wouldn't it be nice if you could look in one place for all of your communications with an individual, including e-mail messages, phone conversations, faxes, and even tasks that were completed for this person? This is the power of the Journal.

Recording a Journal entry is really quite simple. If you've used Tasks and Calendar, you're already familiar with most of the fields on the Journal Entry form. Follow the steps below to create a Journal entry:

1. Choose Journal Entry from the New button to open a Journal Entry form.

2. Enter a Subject for the Journal entry and choose the Entry Type from the drop-down list.

3. To associate a Journal entry with an existing contact, click the Address Book button and choose a contact from the Select Contacts dialog box.

4. Enter a Company name, if desired.

5. Enter a date and time in the Start Time fields or, if you're making a phone call, click the Start Timer button to have the Journal automatically time your conversation.

6. Record the length of the communication by selecting from the Duration drop-down list, or type in an entry of your own. If you clicked the Start Timer button, click the Pause Timer button when you've finished your phone call to have Outlook automatically record the call's duration.

7. Type your notes for this Journal entry in the open text box area.

8. Assign the Journal entry to a Category by clicking the Categories button at the bottom of the Journal Entry window. (For more information about assigning Categories to items, see Chapter 4.)

9. If you'd like to make this Journal entry private, to prevent anyone who has access to your Outlook folders from reading it, click the Private check box at the bottom-right corner of the window.

10. Click the Save and Close button to record your Journal entry.

PART

II

Mastering the
Outlook Components

## MASTERING TROUBLESHOOTING

### Troubleshooting the Company Name Field

The Company field in the Journal is a different field from the Company field in Contacts. That's why when you associate a Journal entry with a contact, the Company field is not automatically filled in. (When you create a Journal entry from an e-mail message, the Company field *is* filled in. See "Creating Journal Entries from Other Outlook Items" later in this chapter.)

*Continued*

> **MASTERING TROUBLESHOOTING CONTINUED**
>
> There is a reason for this apparently confusing behavior. You may want to enter a company name in the Journal that's completely different from the one you entered in Contacts. If, for example, you were calling a vendor on behalf of a client, you might associate the Journal entry with your contact at the vendor. On the other hand, you might want to organize your Journal entries by the client you were going to work for. Having separate fields allows you to do that.
>
> If you are making cold sales calls, you might want to wait to add someone to Contacts until you get a positive response of some sort, rather than cluttering up your Contacts with people who are interested but not committed. You can still record the Company of the people you call, so you can track how many people within a company you have contacted.
>
> When you start using the filtering features discussed in Chapter 11, it's important to remember that the Company field in Journal and the Company field in Contacts are distinct fields.

## Inserting Files into Journal Entries

You can insert documents and Outlook items directly into Journal entries. For example, if you had a phone conversation about a proposal you were writing for a client, you could insert a copy of the Word document or a shortcut to the document directly into the Journal entry. In the future, when you want to review what you talked about, you could directly reference the proposal. Follow these steps to insert a file into a Journal entry:

1. Open the Journal entry.
2. Choose Insert ➢ File from the Journal Entry Standard toolbar. The Insert File dialog box opens.
3. Choose between Insert as Text Only, Attachment, and Shortcut (see the "Which Insert File Option Should I Choose?" sidebar, following).
4. Locate the file you want to insert, and select it.
5. Click OK to insert the file. The contents of the file (Text Only) or an icon representing the document (Attachment or Shortcut) appears in the Notes area of the Journal entry.
6. Double-click the icon to open the document.

## Which Insert File Option Should I Choose?

There are significant differences between inserting a file as Text Only, Attachment, or Shortcut; you should make a conscious choice each time you insert a file into an Outlook item. The default choice is Attachment. Be aware that when you insert an attachment, you are making a copy of the original document. When you double-click the icon in the Outlook item to open the document, you are opening and perhaps modifying the copy. The original document remains unchanged. Use this option with an e-mail message if you want to send a file to someone who can open a Word attachment.

The Shortcut option creates a pointer to the document on your local or network drive. Use this option if you are inserting the document for your own reference and do not plan to e-mail the item to anyone else. When you double-click the icon to open this document, you are opening and potentially modifying the original document in its original location.

The Text Only option is useful if you plan to send this item to someone who cannot open a Word document attached to an e-mail message. The actual text of the document (without formatting) is inserted into the Notes area of the item. If the document is formatted (font formatting, headers/footers, and so on), you may get a lot of unreadable characters, but somewhere in the midst of it all you should find your text. Saving the file as Rich Text Format (.rtf) or Text (.txt) before you insert it will eliminate the garbage characters.

# Inserting Other Objects into a Journal Entry

To manually insert an object such as a bitmap image, Word document, or Access database into a Journal entry, follow these steps (you can also follow these steps to see which types of objects your computer will support, because each type is listed in the dialog box):

1. Open the Journal entry.
2. Choose Insert ➢ Object to open the Insert Object dialog box, shown in Figure 10.3.
3. Choose the type of object you would like to insert, and select either Create New or Create from File.
4. Click OK. If you chose to create a new file, the Journal entry window will be modified to show the tools necessary for creating the selected file type. If you chose to open an existing file, an Open File dialog will open.

*The Insert Object dialog box*

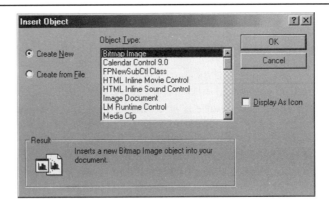

## Creating Journal Entries from Other Outlook Items

When an important e-mail comes through your Inbox, you may find it useful to record that e-mail in your Journal so you can easily find it again when you need it. You can drag items from any of the Outlook modules to the Journal, and Outlook will create a Journal entry from it. For example, Figure 10.4 shows a Journal entry created by dragging an e-mail message to the Journal. Notice that it placed all the information from the message into the corresponding fields of the Journal Entry form.

 **WARNING** When you create a Journal entry from an existing item, Outlook places a shortcut in the Journal entry. If you move the original item, the shortcut will no longer be valid.

## Relating Journal Entries to Contacts

Although you could easily find the entry from Figure 10.4 in the Journal, Outlook makes it even easier to track this communication. You may remember from Chapter 4 that the Contact form has an Activities page. Because the original e-mail message was from a contact, and because the Journal recognizes the relationship to your contacts, you can open the Contact form for that contact, switch to the Activities page, and see a list of Journal entries related to that particular contact. Figure 10.5 shows e-mail messages and other items on a typical Activities page of the Contacts form.

**FIGURE 10.4**

*A Journal entry created
from an e-mail
message*

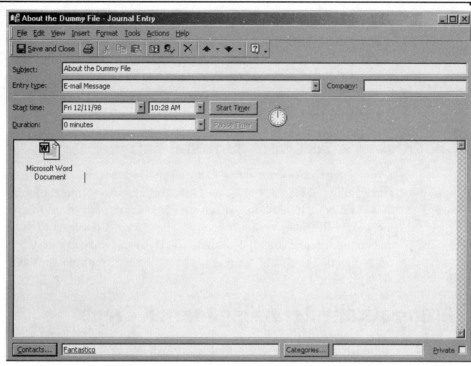

**FIGURE 10.5**

*The Activities page of
the Contact form*

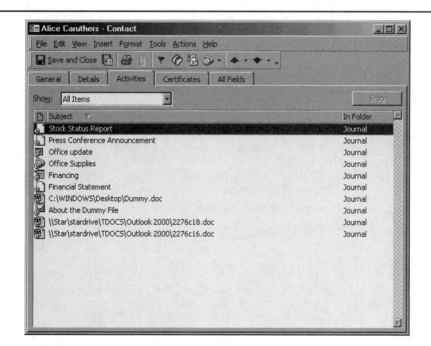

To manually record a Journal entry directly in a Contact form, open the Contact form and switch to the Activities page. Go to File ➤ New and select Journal Entry to open a Journal form.

Record the journal entry and click Save and Close to file it away. Next time you plan to contact this person, open their Contact form and the contents of the last contact will be right there in front of you. To view an existing entry in the Journal, double-click the entry to open it.

### Creating a Task from a Journal Entry

If you agreed to take some action as the result of your discussion with a contact, you'll also want to create an Outlook Task. Open the Journal and drag the Journal item to the Tasks icon or folder. Outlook will create a Task with a copy of the Journal entry already included in the Notes section. You may want to revise the subject so that it is more specific to the Task and enter the details of the Task (start and end dates, for example), but other than that you are all set. (See Chapter 8 for more information about using Tasks.)

# Automatically Recording Journal Events

Although you now know how to record e-mail messages in the Journal by dragging them to create a Journal entry, why not have Outlook do that for you automatically? You can set it up once and Outlook will do the rest for you behind the scenes. Any action associated with a contact, such as sending or receiving e-mail, a meeting response, or a task request, can automatically appear in the Journal for this contact.

1. Choose Tools ➤ Options from the menu and click Journal Options to open the Journal Options dialog box, shown in Figure 10.6.

2. Select the items you would like to automatically record from the list of choices, including:
   - E-mail message
   - Meeting request
   - Meeting response
   - Meeting cancellation
   - Task request
   - Task response

3. Mark the contacts for whom you want to record items automatically (this is an all-or-nothing proposition—if you want to record e-mail messages and task

requests for one contact, you can't choose to record only e-mail messages for another).

4. Select the files you would like to record automatically from the list of application choices, including:

- Microsoft Access
- Microsoft Excel
- Microsoft Office Binder
- Microsoft PowerPoint
- Microsoft Word
- Other programs that are part of the Microsoft Office Compatible program

5. Choose if you want double-clicking a Journal entry to open the Journal entry or to open the item referred to by the Journal entry.

6. Click OK to save the Journal Options dialog box, and click OK again to close the Options dialog box.

PART

II

Mastering the
Outlook Components

**FIGURE 10.6**

*The Journal Options
dialog box*

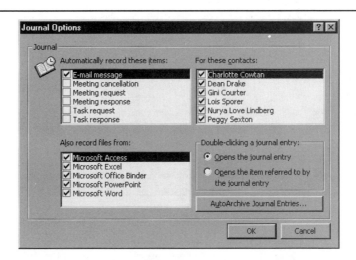

After you have selected the Outlook items that you want to record automatically for a contact in the Journal Options dialog box, you can assign the item to a newly created contact from the referral's Contact form. Switch to the Activities page of the Contact form and click the Automatically Record Journal Entries for This Contact check box. Outlook will create Journal entries for this contact containing shortcuts to original Outlook items, as shown in Figure 10.7.

**TIP** When you double-click a Journal entry, the Journal Entry form opens containing an icon for the referenced item. If you'd like to open the referenced item directly, go to Tools ➤ Options ➤ Journal Options and choose Double-Clicking a Journal Entry Opens the Item Referred to by the Journal Entry.

**FIGURE 10.7**

*A Journal entry with a shortcut to a Word document*

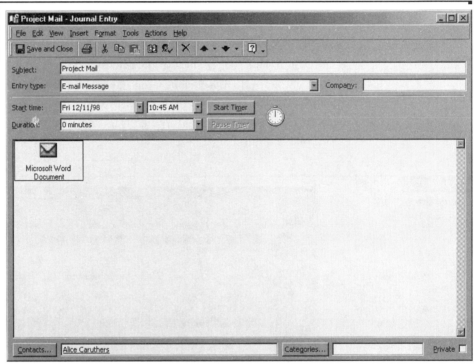

 **TIP** When you set the Journal to automatically record documents that you work on in any of the Office applications, Outlook records the author of the document as the contact it associates with the Journal entry. If you create the document, you are listed as the contact. However, if you open a document created by someone else, their name appears in the Contact field of the associated Journal entry. The author of the document is pulled from the Author field on the Summary page of the document's properties. (To get to the Summary page, open the document in the application, choose File ➤ Properties, and click the Summary tab.)

# Changing Journal Views

Changing the way you look at something can open your eyes to connections and relationships that you previously couldn't see. Journal views let you both examine the minute-by-minute details of your day and step back to review the big picture. You can view your Journal entries according to when they were recorded and also organize them by type, by contact, or by category. This flexibility makes the Journal a tool that can help you analyze your activities, in addition to documenting them.

## Viewing by Day, Week, or Month

The Timeline view is similar to the Day/Week/Month view of the Calendar in that there are three ways to view the timeline. Click the Day, Week, or Month button on the Standard toolbar to change the focus of the timeline. The Day view, shown in Figure 10.8, focuses on the time of day that the Journal events occurred.

PART

II

Mastering the
Outlook Components

**FIGURE 10.8**

*The Day view of the Journal*

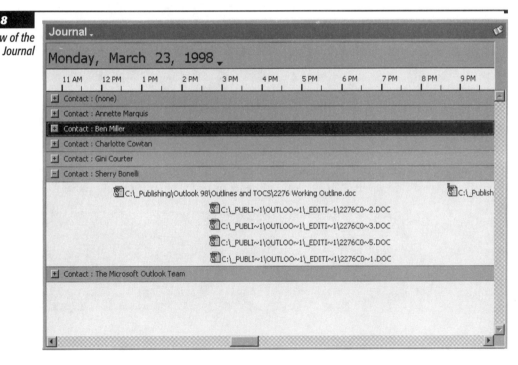

There are several ways you can move quickly to a particular date:

- Select the date you want to see in Week or Month view by clicking the date in the Date row (the selected date will turn blue), and then switch to Day view.

- Right-click anywhere in the timeline (except right on an event) and choose Go to Date from the shortcut menu to open the Go to Date dialog box, shown here:

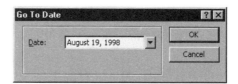

- Click the Month in the top row to open a date navigator.

The Month view, shown in Figure 10.9, focuses on the big picture.

In both the Day view and the Month view, the Journal events are reduced to icons with no labels. Point to any of the icons to see what it represents.

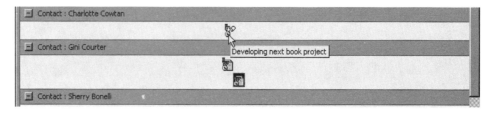

**FIGURE 10.9**

The Month view of the
Journal

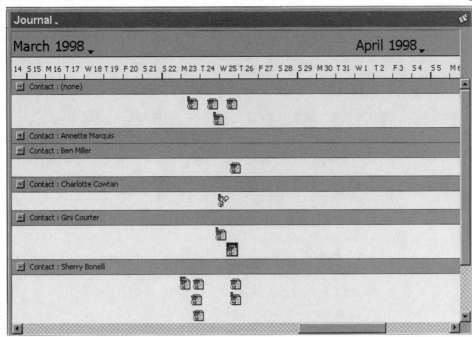

To change the display in Day or Month view, use the Format Timeline View dialog box. You can open it by right-clicking the timeline and choosing Other Settings from the shortcut menu.

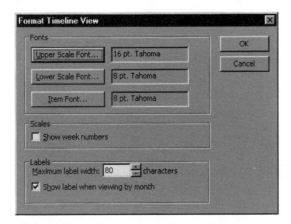

If you have a vision impairment and are having difficulty seeing the text that is displayed in the Timeline, use the Format Timeline View dialog box to change the font. To display the week numbers instead of the dates, click the Show Week Numbers check box. If you would like to display the icon labels in Day or Month view, click the Show

Label When Viewing by Month check box (it turns the labels on for viewing by Days, too). You can also set the maximum number of characters to display in the labels, so they don't get too unwieldy. Click OK to save the new Format options and return to the Journal.

## Other Views

In addition to the Timeline views that group data by entry type, the Journal has several other built-in views. Choose View ➤ Current View and choose from:

**By Type**    This Timeline view groups events and activities by their type.

**By Contact**    Timeline view that groups the events by contact (see Figure 10.8 and Figure 10.9 for examples).

**By Category**    Timeline view that shows events grouped by the assigned Category.

**By Entry**    List view that shows events in a list format, similar to the default Tasks view (see Figure 10.10). In this view, you can sort the events by clicking the column label.

**Last Seven Days**    List view that shows events from the last seven days exclusively.

**Phone Calls**    List view that displays phone calls only.

**FIGURE 10.10**

*The By Entry view of the Journal*

| | | Entry Type | Subject | Start ▽ | Duration | Contact | Categories |
|---|---|---|---|---|---|---|---|
| | | Microsoft Word | C:\_Publishing\Office 98\test docu... | Wed 3/25/98 1:... | 0 hours | Ben Miller | |
| | | Microsoft Word | C:\_PUBLI~1\OUTLOO~1\_EDITI~... | Wed 3/25/98 1:... | 4 minutes | Sherry Bonelli | |
| | | Microsoft Word | C:\_Publishing\Outlook 98\Outlines ... | Wed 3/25/98 1:... | 0 hours | Sherry Bonelli | |
| | | Microsoft Word | C:\_Publishing\Office 98\Office 98 ... | Wed 3/25/98 9:... | 0 hours | | |
| | | Microsoft Word | C:\_Publishing\Office 98\Office 98 ... | Wed 3/25/98 9:... | 0 hours | Annette Marquis | |
| | | Microsoft Word | C:\_Publishing\Outlook 98\Outlines ... | Wed 3/25/98 9:... | 0 hours | Gini Courter | |
| | | Conversation | Developing next book project | Tue 3/24/98 9:... | 15 minutes | Charlotte Cowtan | |
| | | Microsoft Word | C:\_Publishing\Outlook 98\2276c10... | Tue 3/24/98 6:... | 236 minutes | Gini Courter | |
| | | Microsoft Word | C:\_Publishing\Outlook 98\Outlines ... | Tue 3/24/98 4:... | 1 minute | Annette Marquis | |
| | | Microsoft Word | C:\_Publishing\Outlook 98\2276c09... | Tue 3/24/98 4:... | 1 minute | Annette Marquis | |
| | | Microsoft Word | C:\_Publishing\Outlook 98\Outlines ... | Tue 3/24/98 4:... | 4 minutes | Annette Marquis | |
| | | Microsoft Word | C:\_Publishing\Outlook 98\2276c09... | Tue 3/24/98 4:... | 1 minute | | |
| | | Microsoft Word | C:\_Publishing\Outlook 98\2276c09... | Tue 3/24/98 4:... | 9 minutes | Annette Marquis | |
| | | Microsoft Word | C:\_Publishing\Outlook 98\Ch 09\c0... | Tue 3/24/98 4:... | 3 minutes | Annette Marquis | |
| | | Microsoft Word | A:\Auction item.doc | Tue 3/24/98 8:... | 0 hours | | |
| | | Microsoft Word | A:\Auction item.txt | Tue 3/24/98 8:... | 0 hours | Annette Marquis | |
| | | Microsoft Word | C:\My Documents\Auction item.doc | Tue 3/24/98 8:... | 20 minutes | Annette Marquis | |
| | | Microsoft Word | C:\_Publishing\Outlook 98\_Editing ... | Mon 3/23/98 8:... | 1 minute | Sherry Bonelli | |
| | | Microsoft Word | C:\_Publishing\Outlook 98\2276c09... | Mon 3/23/98 7:... | 803 minutes | Annette Marquis | |
| | | Microsoft Word | C:\_PUBLI~1\OUTLOO~1\_EDITI~... | Mon 3/23/98 2:... | 0 hours | Sherry Bonelli | |
| | | Microsoft Word | C:\_PUBLI~1\OUTLOO~1\_EDITI~... | Mon 3/23/98 2:... | 0 hours | Sherry Bonelli | |
| | | Microsoft Word | C:\_PUBLI~1\OUTLOO~1\_EDITI~... | Mon 3/23/98 2:... | 0 hours | Sherry Bonelli | |
| | | Microsoft Word | C:\_PUBLI~1\OUTLOO~1\_EDITI~... | Mon 3/23/98 2:... | 0 hours | Sherry Bonelli | |
| | | Microsoft Word | C:\_Publishing\Outlook 98\2276c09... | Mon 3/23/98 2:... | 5.5 hours | Annette Marquis | |

## Grouping Data

Several of the built-in views group the events in the Journal in various ways: By Type, By Contact, By Entry, or By Category. You can easily change the grouping of any of the predefined Timeline views by right-clicking in the timeline and choosing Group By. This opens the Group By dialog box, shown in Figure 10.11.

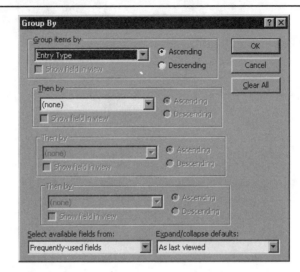

**FIGURE 10.11**

*The Group By
dialog box*

Select the field you want to group by from the Group Items By drop-down list. You can choose up to four levels of grouping. For example, you could group by Contact, then by Date, then by Entry in either Ascending or Descending order.

If the field you want to group by is not in the list, click the Select Available Fields From down-arrow and choose All Journal Fields. Set the Expand/Collapse defaults to display the groups All Expanded, All Collapsed, or As Last Viewed. Click OK to display the new view.

To remove all grouping, open the Group By dialog box and click Clear All.

# Locating Events in the Journal

If you are looking for a particular Journal entry, click the Find button on the Standard toolbar and type a key word or name into the Look For text box. Click the Find Now button to conduct the search. Outlook searches the Subject and Body of the entries for the text you entered and returns the results in a list view in the Information Viewer. Figure 10.12 shows search results for the name *Sherry*.

Click the Find button on the toolbar again to close the Find window. For more information about Find, refer to Chapter 5.

**FIGURE 10.12**

*Using Find to search for key words or names*

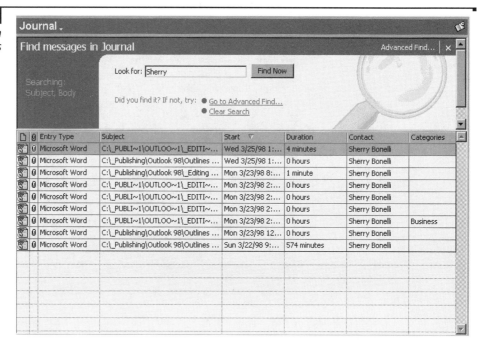

## Making Notes

Even after you are using Outlook to its fullest, you will still run across those odd pieces of information that have nowhere to go, or that you want to keep at your fingertips: your flight information, your sweetie's sizes, or information about your car insurance. They aren't related to a contact, they aren't events, so what do you do with them? Never fear, Outlook has a place for those too. Outlook includes an easy way to computerize your notes. Choose Note from the New Item button (or hold Ctrl+Shift and press N) to open a Note window. Enter your text in the Note window.

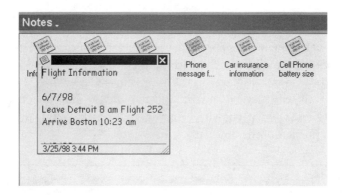

 **TIP** When you are entering a note, enter a title for the note and then press Enter before entering the contents of the note. Otherwise, the entire text of the note will be visible in the Notes Information Viewer.

Each note is automatically time and date stamped. Closing the window automatically saves the note. To view a note, click the Notes icon on the Outlook Bar to go to the Notes window. Double-click a note to open it. Click the Note icon in the upper-left corner of the Note window to access options for deleting, saving, and printing notes.

To make it easier to organize notes, Outlook 2000 brings the Categories a simple right-click away. To apply a category (or two or three) to a note, right click the target note, select Categories from the list, and make your choices.

If a note grows up and it needs to become a task, a Journal entry, or an e-mail message, just drag the Note icon onto the appropriate icon on the Outlook bar or into the appropriate folder in the folder list.

## Notes Views

Even though notes are small, you still have options for viewing them in different ways. Choose Small Icons, Large Icons, or List from the Notes Standard toolbar to change how the icons are displayed in the Information Viewer.

Choose View ➤ Current View to switch to a number of predefined views, such as Notes List view, shown in Figure 10.13, which shows you a list of your notes and gives a preview of the notes' contents.

**FIGURE 10.13**

*Notes List view*

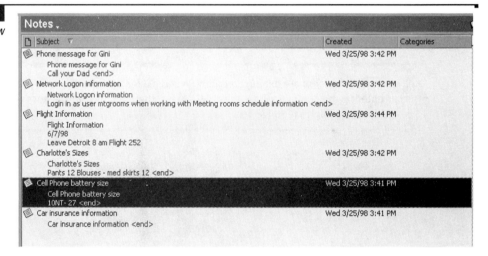

## Taking Your Notepad with You

To provide you with no excuse to continue using sticky notes, you can take a note with you to any application or even let it sit open on the Windows Desktop ready and waiting for you. To place a note on the Windows Desktop, restore the Outlook window (click the Restore button on the Outlook title bar) and drag the note to the Desktop.

Outlook does not have to be open for you to edit the note, make additions to it, or delete the contents. However, if you close the note you'll have to re-open Outlook to view the note again.

### What's Next?

Finishing this chapter is an important milestone. You now have an in-depth view of all of the Outlook components. Chapter 11 focuses on how to make your data work for you by designing useful ways to display it. In that chapter, you'll learn how to sort and group your data, how to apply conditional formatting, and how to filter your data so you're seeing just what you want to see.

# PART III

# Extending Outlook

## LEARN TO:

- **Sort, group, format, and filter your data**

- **Create a new user profile**

- **Manage your computer's files and folders**

- **Archive and back up Outlook data**

- **Import and export Outlook data**

- **Use Outlook on the Web**

# CHAPTER <u>11</u>

# Designing Custom Views and Print Styles

**E**very Outlook component includes predesigned views of the items in the folder. When the predesigned views don't completely meet your needs, you can design your own custom views for messages, contacts, and the other Outlook items. Custom views, like the predesigned views, can be chosen from the View menu, from the View drop-down list in the Organize page or from the View list on the Advanced toolbar.

A view has five attributes: fields, formatting, sorting, grouping, and filtering. You create a custom view by changing any or all of these attributes, either by copying and modifying one of the predesigned views or by beginning from scratch in the Design Views dialog box.

## Quick Start: Creating a Custom View

If you're experienced with sorting and filtering in other Office programs, you'll find it easy to create custom views in Outlook. Name the new or copied view in the Define Views dialog box (before you begin changing the view's options) by doing the following:

1. Create a new view, or copy an existing view (View ➣ Current View ➣ Define Views).

2. In the View Summary dialog box:

   • Click the Fields button to choose fields to display in the view.

   • If you want to insert group headers, click the Group By button.

   • Click the Sort button to sort the items.

   • If you want to display only items that meet certain criteria, click the Filter button to specify the criteria.

   • Click the Other Settings button to format the headings, columns, rows, and panes in the view.

   • Click the Automatic Formatting button to create and apply formatting rules.

3. Click OK to close the View Summary.

4. Click Close to close the Define Views dialog box and save the custom view, or click Apply View to apply and save the view and close the dialog box.

# Creating a View

In Outlook, views are treated something like toolbars in the other Office applications. You can customize them and you can always reset the view to restore the original settings.

To create a new view, begin with a copy of an existing view or a "blank" view. First open the component you want to create a new view for. If you want to begin with a copy, identify the view that's closest to the view you want to create. In Contacts, for example, look at the Table views if you want to create a new Table view, and at Phone Cards if you're creating a Card view. Choose View ➢ Current View ➢ Define Views to open the component's Define Views dialog box. The dialog box for Contacts is shown in Figure 11.1.

**FIGURE 11.1**

*The Define Views dialog box displays all the views for the current component.*

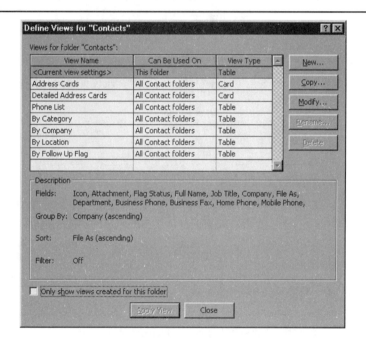

**PART**

**III**

**Extending Outlook**

## Copying a View

To copy an existing view:

**1.** Select the view you want to copy.

**2.** Click the Copy button to open the Copy View dialog box (shown in Figure 11.2).

3. Enter a name for the copy.

4. Choose a Can Be Used On option (see "Assigning a View to a Folder," later in this chapter).

5. Click OK to create the view and open the View Summary.

---

**FIGURE 11.2**

*Create a copy of an existing view in the Copy View dialog box.*

## Starting with a New View

If none of the existing views resemble the view you want to create, you may as well start from scratch.

1. Open the component, and then choose View ➤ Current View ➤ Define Views to open the Define Views dialog box.

2. Click the New button to open the New View dialog box.

3. Enter a name for the view.

4. Select the type of view.

5. Choose a Can Be Used On option (see "Assigning a View to a Folder," following).

6. Click OK to create the view and open the View Summary.

## Assigning a View to a Folder

Choose the folders the view should be displayed in. You have three choices: all folders of this type (all Contact folders, all Journal folders, etc.); the current folder, visible to everyone; and the current folder, visible only to you. Make your choice based on the type of folder you're creating the view in and how likely it is to be used outside the folder or by other users.

• If you're creating a view with widespread appeal in a public or shared folder, then you might make the view visible to all users of the folder.

- If you're the only person who's likely to use the view, why clutter up the View list? Make it visible only to you.

- If the view could be useful in subfolders or other folders that contain the same type of items, choose All folders.

Outlook automatically opens the View Summary dialog box when you click OK in the Copy View dialog box.

## Choosing Fields in the Show Fields Dialog Box

You can see fields associated with the current component in two places: the Show Fields dialog box and the Field Chooser. When you copy or create a new view, Outlook automatically opens the View Summary dialog box, shown in Figure 11.3. If you want to further customize an existing view, choose View ➢ Current View ➢ Customize Current View or, if the Organize page is open, switch to Using Views and click the Customize Current View button to reopen the View Summary dialog box.

**FIGURE 11.3**

*Open the View Summary dialog box to display settings for the current view.*

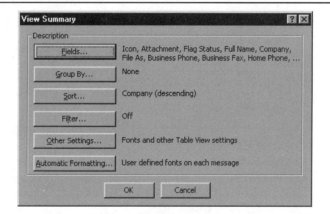

The View Summary dialog box displays all the information about the current view: in this case, the Phone List view for the Contacts component. The description lists some of the fields included in the view. The list ends with an ellipsis (...), indicating that there are more fields that are not shown. To see all the fields that are included in the view, click the Fields button to open the Show Fields dialog box, shown in Figure 11.4.

The left pane shows some of the available fields for this component in alphabetical order. Notice that some of the fields are missing; the fields in the right pane are the ones that are used in the current view. The right pane lists the fields in their order of appearance. The first field will be at the top of a Card view and at the left side of a Table view.

**FIGURE 11.4**

*The Show Fields dialog box lists fields available to and used in the current view.*

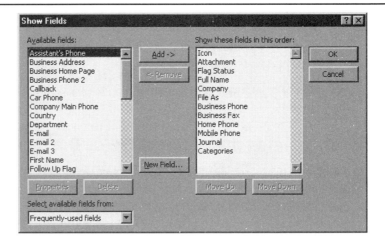

## Adding Fields from the Show Fields Dialog Box

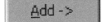

To add a field to the current view, select the field in the left pane. Select the field in the right pane below which the new field should appear, and then click the Add button.

## Removing Fields in the Show Fields Dialog Box

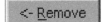

To remove a field from the current view, select the field in the right pane and click the Remove button to move the field back to the list of available fields.

**WARNING** Clicking the New button opens a dialog box where you can create a new field and include it in the view. We don't encourage you to do this. The field you create won't appear on any of the Outlook forms included with the component, and it can get in the way of any customization you'd like to do in the future. If you want to add fields to Outlook items, see Chapter 20.

The fields shown in Figure 11.4 aren't all the fields available in the Contacts component, just those most frequently used in Contacts. For each component, there's a list of frequently used fields, other lists grouped by type (address fields, name fields, and so on), and a comprehensive list of all the fields in the component—108 different fields in Contacts. If you want to add a field that doesn't appear on the frequently used fields list, choose another list from the Select Available Fields From list.

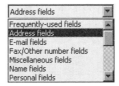

The first few entries in the Select Available Fields From list relate to the Contacts component, followed by lists for other components, such as All Journal Fields. Make sure you're selecting fields from the current component, or fields that make sense in the current component. For example, there is no Created field in Contacts, even though you create the contacts in the folder. If you add the Journal's Created field to a Contact view, it will display the date that a contact was created. On the other hand, if you include the Bcc field from All Mail Fields, you'll get an empty column. Contact items don't have a blind courtesy copy property, so there is no data to display, and you can't enter data in the Bcc column:

| □ | 0 | ♥ | Full Name △ | Created | Bcc |
|---|---|---|---|---|---|
| | | | Click here to add... | | |
| ☐▤ | | | Ben Miller | Tue 3/24/98 4:59 PM | |
| ☐▤ | | | Beth McGregor | Tue 3/24/98 12:35 PM | |
| ☐▤ | | | Betty Smith | Sun 1/4/98 2:13 PM | |
| ☐▤ | | | Bill Piper | Tue 3/25/97 11:35 PM | |
| ☐▤ | | | Bob Beckwith | Wed 12/25/96 4:29 PM | |
| ☐▤ | | | Bob Carlton | Fri 5/23/97 5:21 PM | |
| ☐▤ | | | Bonnie John-Mu... | Sun 2/9/97 11:05 AM | |

### Rearranging Fields in the Show Fields Dialog Box

To rearrange the field order in the right pane, select a field and click the Move Up or Move Down button to change the view's order. You can also select the field and drag it to its new spot in the order. When you're finished adding, removing, and arranging fields, click OK to close the Show Fields dialog box. To see the changes you've made to the view, click OK to close the View Summary dialog box, and then click the Apply button in the Define Views dialog box.

## Using the View List and the Field Chooser

You don't have to use the View Summary or Show Fields dialog box to add, remove, or rearrange fields. You can remove and rearrange fields directly in the View list and add fields with the Field Chooser.

After you've copied a view to serve as the basis for your new view, close the View Summary dialog box and click the Apply button in the Define Views dialog box to apply the new view. To rearrange fields in the view, just drag the field's column heading to a new location. As you drag across the headings, arrows show where the column will be displayed when you drop it:

| 0 | ♥ | Full Name △ | C Categories | Company |
|---|---|---|---|---|
| | | Click here to add... | | |
| | | | Tue 9/16/97 7:58 PM | CompUSA |

To remove a field, right-click its column heading and choose Remove Column from the shortcut menu. Or drag the column heading out of the heading area—up into the Organize page or down into the items—until a large *X* appears on the heading:

Drop the column heading to remove the field from the view.

To add fields, click the Field Chooser button on the Advanced toolbar. (If the Advanced toolbar is not displayed, choose View ➤ Toolbars ➤ Advanced, or right-click in a clear area in any toolbar and select it from the list to turn it on.) The Field Chooser, shown in Figure 11.5, has column heading buttons organized in the same way as the lists in the Show Fields dialog box. Use the drop-down list at the top of the Field Chooser to select the list of fields you want to pick from. Drag a button from the list to the column heading area to add the field to the view.

**FIGURE 11.5**

*Drag column heading buttons from the Field Chooser to add fields to the current view.*

When you're finished with the Field Chooser, close it by clicking its Close button or clicking the Field Chooser button on the toolbar.

# Saving and Modifying Views

Outlook keeps track of the current view in each component, so when you switch components, the view is the same as when you last worked in the component. When you change views within a component, Outlook automatically retains changes you've made to the current view.

To modify a predesigned existing view, switch to the view and make whatever changes you wish; when you switch to another view, your changes will be saved in place of the original view. It's easy to modify a predesigned view, but that also makes it easy to mess up a view that you use on a regular basis. If you intend to delete or add columns to a frequently used view, begin by creating a copy of the view so you retain the original.

To reset the original view, select the view in the Define Views dialog box and click the Reset button. To reset a customized view, open the Define Views dialog box, select the view, and click Apply to reset the view you designed.

# Sorting Items

Sorting orders the items in a column in ascending or descending order. In ascending order, text fields are sorted alphabetically (A to Z), and numerical fields, including dates, are sorted from lowest to highest value (0 to 9). With a descending sort, text fields are shown in reverse alphabetical order (Z to A) and numerical fields from largest to smallest (9 to 0). You can sort columns in the Sort dialog box or the view list.

## Sorting in the Sort Dialog Box

When you're creating a new view, click the Sort button in the View Summary dialog box to open the Sort dialog box, shown in Figure 11.6. In the Sort Items By control, select the first field you want to sort by and choose Ascending or Descending order. If the field you want to sort by isn't included in the drop-down list, choose the appropriate field list from the Select Available Fields From list at the bottom of the dialog box.

**FIGURE 11.6**

*Use the Sort dialog box to establish the sort order for the new view.*

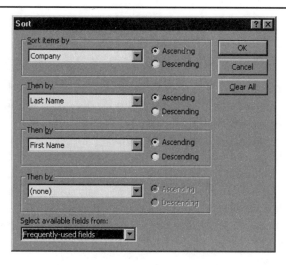

PART

**III**

Extending Outlook

You can sort by a second, third, and fourth field by choosing them in the Then By controls. For example, if you sort by Company, some of your contacts may work for the same company. Within a company, you can sort the contacts by last name, and then by first name.

To remove all the sorting in a view, click the Clear All button in the Sort dialog box.

> **TIP** If you sort by a field that is not included in the view, Outlook will ask whether you want to include it in the view. It's a good idea to click Yes. If the column is not included in the view, it's hard to tell what columns the view is sorted on.

## Sorting in the View List

To sort a column in the view in ascending order, click the column heading you want to sort by, or right-click the heading and choose Sort Ascending from the shortcut menu. An upward-pointing arrow in the column heading indicates that the column is sorted in ascending order:

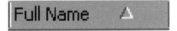

To sort the column in descending order, click the column heading again, or right-click the heading and choose Sort Descending from the shortcut menu. The downward-pointing triangle in the column heading shows that the column is sorted in descending order:

### Sorting the View by Multiple Fields

You'll often want to sort by multiple fields. A telephone book, for example, is sorted by last name, then by first name, middle initial, address, and other information. All the Smiths are sorted by first name.

To sort by more than one field, click the heading for the first column you want to sort by, and then hold the Shift key and click the heading for the column you want to sort by when values in the first column you selected are the same. Continue to hold Shift and click on other column headings to include them as sort columns. If you need to change the direction of the sort in any of the columns, hold Shift, and click on the column heading again.

Clicking any heading while not holding Shift removes the multiple column sort and sorts by the single column heading you clicked.

 **TIP** You can't sort by some fields because they contain multiple values, such as the Categories field. If you can't sort by a field, try grouping by it instead.

# Grouping Items

Grouping is like sorting, but items in a group are clustered together under a group heading. Grouping items helps you manage the items more effectively by arranging items in a logical group that you understand or that helps you. You can move, copy, or delete all the items in a group by moving, copying, or deleting the group header.

## Grouping in the Group By Dialog Box

When you're creating a new view, click the Group By button in the View Summary dialog box to open the Group By dialog box, shown in Figure 11.7. Choose the Group Items By and Then By fields as you do in the Sort dialog box (see "Sorting in the Sort Dialog Box," earlier in this chapter, for more details).

**FIGURE 11.7**

*Use the Group By dialog box to group items under a common header.*

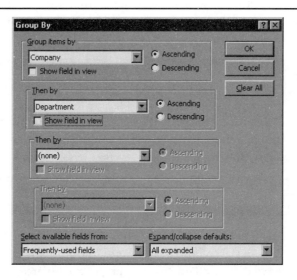

When you group by a field, you don't need to show the field in the view as a column, because the field's value appears in the group header above the items, as shown in Figure 11.8. To remove the Group By field from the view, disable the Show Field in View check box below the field (see Figure 11.7).

**FIGURE 11.8**

A Contacts view grouped by Company and Department creates two levels of headers.

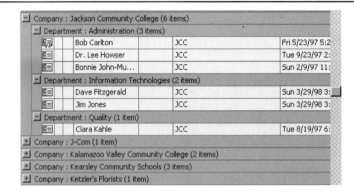

To remove all grouping levels in the view, click the Clear All button in the Group By dialog box.

## Grouping in the Current View

In the View list, there's a Group By box above the table. If it is not displayed, click the Group By button on the Advanced toolbar to show it. The view in Figure 11.8 is grouped by Company and Department in ascending order, so the Group By box shows this relationship.

To group by a field, drag the field's column heading into the Group By box. A triangle on the column heading shows the sort order of the group. Click the column heading button in the Group By box to reverse the sort order.

Drag a heading out of the Group By box to remove the grouping. If you drop the heading in the column heading area, the grouping is removed and the column is added to the view. Drop the heading in the list area, and the grouping and column are removed from the view. For example, if you drop the Company group heading in

Figure 11.8 among the rows in the list, you delete the grouping. But if you drop the Company heading in the column headings, you add the Company column to the view while deleting the grouping.

## Grouping by Multiple Fields in the View List

Just as you can sort by multiple fields, you can group by multiple fields. Drag two column headings into the Group By box. From left to right, the columns are Group Items By, Then By, Then By. In this example, the columns are grouped by Categories, then by Company, then by Department.

Use drag and drop to rearrange the column headings, or double-click in the background of the Group By box to open the Group By dialog box (see Figure 11.7). Set the grouping in the dialog box, and then click OK.

# Filtering Data

Sort and group can arrange all the items in a view. To place limits on the items displayed, create a filter based on one or more criteria. With a filter, only the items that meet the specified criteria are displayed. Examples of filters in the predesigned views include the following:

- Unread Messages (Mail) filters messages based on read status.
- Incomplete and Next 7 Days (Tasks) filters tasks based on completion status and date.
- Phone Calls (Journal) filters items based on type.

To create a filter in the View Summary, click the Filter button to open the Filter dialog box, shown in Figure 11.9. The dialog box that appears is based on the type of folder your view is in. The dialog box in Figure 11.9 begins with a Contacts page because the view is a Contacts view. In a Mail view, the first page of the dialog box is the Messages page.

If you've worked in other Windows applications, this will be a vaguely familiar dialog box. A version of this dialog box is used to enter criteria to find or filter files and items in Windows and the Windows standard applications. For example, Figure 11.10 shows the Windows dialog box that opens when you choose Find ➤ Files or Folders from the Start menu.

*The first page of the Filter dialog box reflects the type of folder you're building a view for.*

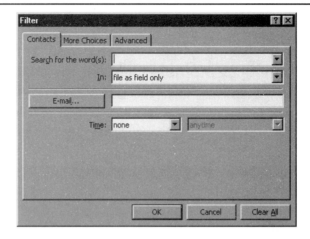

*The Windows Find dialog box is similar to the Outlook Filter dialog box.*

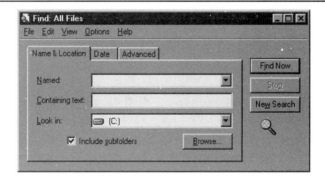

In the first page of the dialog box, shown in Figure 11.9, you can enter criteria to filter items based on values that you entered or that Outlook automatically added to fields in the item. Table 11.1 summarizes the available filter criteria in each component.

**TABLE 11.1: FILTER CRITERIA BY ITEM TYPE**

| Criterion | Item Type | Used to Filter |
|---|---|---|
| Search for the Words | All | Text in fields and logical field groupings: name fields, address fields, subject field, and message body |
| E-mail | Contacts | Contacts with the selected e-mail addresses |
| Entry Type | Journal | Entry type: phone call, e-mail message, etc. |
| Contact | Journal | Contact related to the journal entry |
| Status | Tasks | Based on completion status |
| From/To | Tasks | Tasks received from or delegated to specified people |

*Continued* ▶

| TABLE 11.1: FILTER CRITERIA BY ITEM TYPE (CONTINUED) | | |
|---|---|---|
| **Criterion** | **Item Type** | **Used to Filter** |
| Time | Contacts and Notes | Contacts created or modified in a selected time frame (today, last seven days, etc.) |
| Time | Journal | Journal entries created, modified, starting, or ending in a selected time frame |
| Time | Mail | Messages created, modified, received, sent, due, or expiring in a selected time frame |
| Time | Tasks | Tasks created, modified, due, starting, or completed in selected time frame |

To begin creating a filter, enter text in text boxes and select items from the drop-down lists. When you create a filter, the items displayed in the view must meet all the criteria you enter. For example, the filter shown here will display only phone calls made in the last seven days. E-mail messages sent in the last week and phone calls made eight days ago will not be displayed in the view.

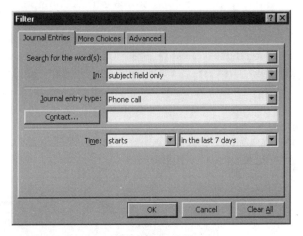

On the More Choices page of the Filter dialog box, shown in Figure 11.11, you can specify criteria for these options:

**Categories**: must include all the categories you select (if more than one)

**Only items that are**: read or unread

**Only items with**: attachments or no attachments

**Whose importance is**: normal, low, high

**Size (in kilobytes)**: is greater than, less than, approximately equal to, or between

PART

III

Extending Outlook

**FIGURE 11.11**

*Enter criteria on
the More Choices
page to further
refine your filter.*

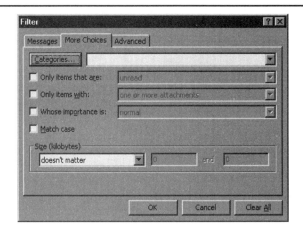

Regarding the Match Case option, if you entered text in the Search for the Word(s) text box on the first page of the dialog box (see Figure 11.9), check the Match Case check box to make the filter case-sensitive.

When a criterion isn't relevant in the current component, the choice is disabled. For example, you can't filter Journal entries on Importance, because there's no way to set importance for a Journal entry.

Use the Advanced page of the dialog box to create field-specific criteria. For example, let's say you'd like to create a filter that shows contacts with a business or home address in Chicago. The first page lets you look for text in all the address fields, so a filter for Chicago will return contacts in the city of Chicago, but will also display contacts on Chicago Boulevard in Detroit, which is a long way from Wrigley Field. In the Advanced page, you can filter based on a text string in a specific field, so you can filter contacts where the Chicago that turns up is in the Business Address City field or the Home Address City field, as shown in Figure 11.12.

**FIGURE 11.12**

*Use the Advanced
page to create filters
you can't build in the
first two pages.*

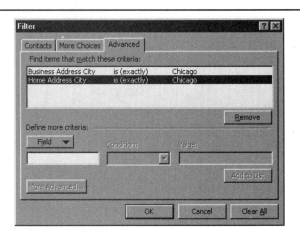

You create an advanced filter by building criteria one at a time and adding them to the Find Items That Match These Criteria list. To create a criterion, click the Field button to open the menu of field lists.

Move the mouse pointer to the list that contains the field you want to create a criterion for, and Outlook opens the field list so you can select the field.

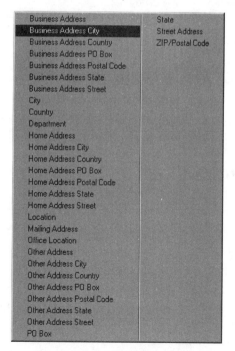

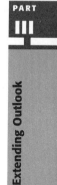

PART

III

Extending Outlook

In the Condition drop-down list, select a condition, and then enter the text string for the condition in the text box:

 When all the required parts of the condition are in place, Outlook will enable the Add to List button. Click the button to move the condition to the Condition list. Create additional conditions until you've created all the conditions for your filter. Click OK to create the filter and close the Filter dialog box.

To remove a condition from the Advanced page, select the condition and click the Remove button. This doesn't affect the conditions on the other two pages. To remove all the conditions from the filter and start again, click the Clear All button at the bottom of the Filter dialog box.

> **TIP** When you return to the View Summary, don't be concerned if the summary doesn't reflect all the filter criteria you entered. It will display only one criterion unless there is no filter applied to the view, in which case it will display "Off." To see all the filter criteria in any view, open the Filter dialog box.

When a view is filtered, Filter Applied appears in parentheses in the Folder name bar.

You can't change a filter directly in the view. You must open the Filter dialog box (View ➢ Current View ➢ Customize Current View ➢ Filter).

# Formatting the View

Three types of formatting are applied to views. You can change:

- Fonts, gridline colors, and other aspects of the view in the Other Settings dialog box
- Rules and automatic formatting applied to items in the view in the Automatic Formatting dialog box
- Alignment, column width, and other field attributes in the Format Columns dialog box

The first two formats are accessible from the View Summary. Column formatting is done in the view itself.

## Specifying Other Settings

To change fonts or gridline colors, click the Other Settings button in the View Summary (View ➢ Current View ➢ Customize Current View). The dialog box that opens varies depending on the component that you are in and the view that you have displayed, but the options are similar. The following description is of the Other Settings dialog box (shown in Figure 11.13), which lets you set font and gridline attributes for the Messages view of the Inbox; the dialog boxes for the other components and views will have similar settings and options.

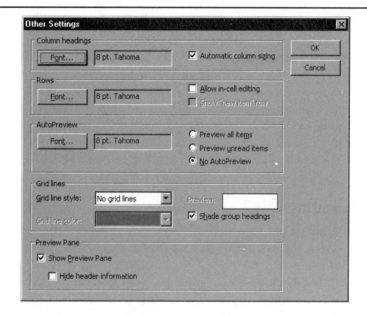

**FIGURE 11.13**

*Use the Other Settings dialog box to select fonts and colors for the view.*

Two or three default fonts are used in a view:

- Font for column headings
- Default row font, used for items displayed in the view
- AutoPreview font, for items such as messages

To change one of the fonts, click the Font button to open the Font dialog box. Select a font, and then click OK to close the Font dialog box and return to the Other Settings dialog box.

## Setting Column Attributes

To have all columns automatically sized to fit their contents, enable the Automatic Column Sizing check box in the Column Headings section.

## Setting Row Attributes

The two row attributes are generally used to create views in custom applications. When you create an application in Outlook (see Chapters 19–25), you can secure the application by protecting the application's forms—opening only forms when a user has the correct password. However, this doesn't do a lot of good when users can edit items or create new items in the views.

To create a "read only" view, disable the Allow In-Cell Editing check box. Users will be able to look at items in the view but won't be able to change the existing items. To prevent users from creating new items in a View list, turn off the Show "New Item" Row check box.

## Setting AutoPreview Attributes

AutoPreview is used in Mail, Tasks, and Journal folders to show the first few lines from the open notes or message area of an item. You can enable AutoPreview for all items, unread items, or no items. Choosing either Preview All Items or No AutoPreview, then clicking the AutoPreview button in the Advanced toolbar, toggles the preview for all items off and on.

However, when you choose Preview Unread Items, clicking the AutoPreview button in the view displays and hides the AutoPreview for unread items only, so choosing Preview Unread Items effectively turns AutoPreview off for read items in the view.

## Setting Gridline Attributes

Gridlines have two attributes: line style and color. The settings appear both on the screen and when you print the view in a table style. Choose both settings from the drop-down lists.

The shading color for group headings is automatically inherited from the Windows system settings. You can turn shading on or off by checking or unchecking the Shade Group Headings check box. You can change the default gridline color by selecting another one from the Color list.

## Setting Preview Attributes

While you can include a Preview Pane in any view, most folders have nothing to preview. In Contacts, for example, the Preview Pane will open below the list, but will be empty. If you display the Preview Pane, you can display or hide the header information for the item displayed in the view.

When you've finished with the Other Settings dialog box, click OK to close the dialog box and return to the View Summary.

## Automatic Formatting

Outlook has Automatic Formatting rules that work in all the components, so when you're creating a view, the rules are on by default. For example, overdue items are red in every component, and unread items are bold.

When you create a view, you can create new rules for the view and modify or disable the default rules. In the View Summary dialog box, click the Automatic Formatting button to open the Automatic Formatting dialog box, shown in Figure 11.14. The default rules are listed in the dialog box.

*The Automatic Formatting dialog box shows the rules available to and enforced in the view.*

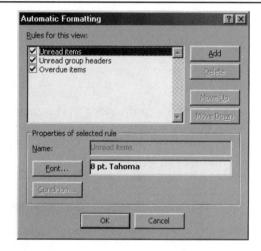

You can't delete the default Automatic Formatting rules, but you can turn them off for this view by disabling the rule's check box. Let's say you're creating a view called Overdue Items, which is filtered to display only overdue items. You might want to turn off the Automatic Formatting for Overdue Items, because it won't help distinguish items in the list.

However, you might also leave the formatting on. The Outlook interface consistently provides the same formatting so that users have visual cues to let them know when items are overdue or unread. If you look at the Overdue Items view in Tasks, you'll notice that all the items have red text. You don't have to look at the name of the view to know what you're looking at. Consistency in the Windows environment has proven to be a powerful tool that flattens the learning curve.

To create a new formatting rule for this view, click the Add button. A new rule named Untitled is created. Enter a new name for the rule, and then click the Condition button to open the Filter dialog box. Enter the conditions for the rule, close the dialog box, and open the Font dialog box to select formatting for items that meet the conditions of the rule.

**PART**

**III**

**Extending Outlook**

**NOTE** See Chapter 7 and "Filtering Data," earlier in this chapter, for more information on automatic formatting rules and creating conditions.

## Formatting Columns

When you format columns in a view, you aren't applying fonts and styles as you would in an Excel worksheet or Word table—that's done in the Automatic Formatting and Other Settings dialog boxes. Column formatting is limited to five options:

- Numerical formats
- Date and time formats
- Column heading label
- Column width
- Alignment

You use the Format Columns dialog box to change column formats, whether you're creating a new view or modifying a view in the view list. Right-click the column heading and choose Format Columns from the shortcut menu to open the Format Columns dialog box, shown in Figure 11.15.

**FIGURE 11.15**

*Set the column alignment, size, and heading label in the Format Columns dialog box.*

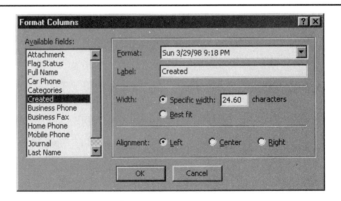

Choose the column you wish to format from the Available Fields list. If there are multiple formats available for the column, select a format from the drop-down list. Text fields have only one format: text. Number and date fields have multiple formats to choose from, as you see below.

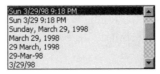

In the Label text box, enter the text that should be used to label the column. For example, you might change File As to Contact Name, or Created to Date Created. Enter a specific width for the column, or choose Best Fit to have the column sized to fit the field's contents. In the Alignment option group, choose Left, Center, or Right alignment for the values in the column.

When you've finished formatting a column, select the next column to format from the Available Fields list. When you're finished making formatting changes, click OK to close the dialog box and apply the new column formats.

# Designing Custom Print Styles

One of the primary reasons you may design a custom view is so you can print the data as a report, a directory, or a simple phone list containing just the information you want to see. After you sort, filter, and group your data, you can design an attractive paper presentation of your data. Outlook already includes a number of nicely designed print styles that require little or no intervention on your part. However, if you decide to modify one of the existing print styles to create your report, you can save the modified style so you can reuse it any time you want. You can also create new styles based on several available print styles:

**Card style** Use this view to print the directory on $8^1/_2 \times 11$ sheets of paper.

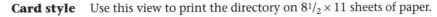
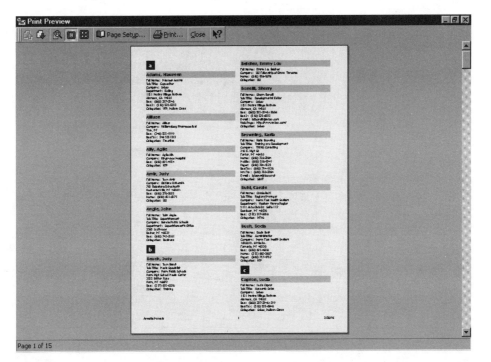

**Small Booklet style**   This style prints a $^1/_8$-sheet booklet that makes an address book, which fits in a breast pocket or purse:

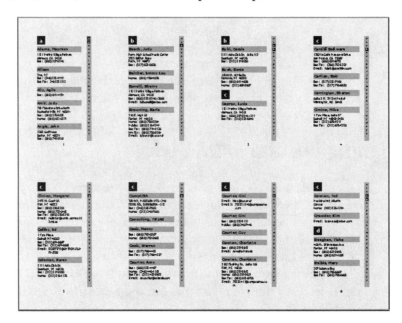

**Medium Booklet style**   This style prints a $^1/_4$-sheet booklet for those who like a larger format:

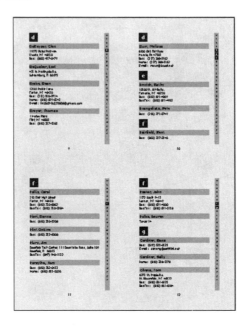

**Memo style**   Use this style to print an individual contact's information. Select the contact you want to print before selecting this style:

**Annette Marquis**

| | |
|---|---|
| **Full Name:** | Bonnie John-Murray |
| **Last Name:** | John-Murray |
| **First Name:** | Bonnie |
| **Job Title:** | Vice President for Institutional Services |
| **Company:** | Jackson Community College |
| | |
| **Business Address:** | 2111 Jackson Parkway |
| | Jackson, MI  49201 |
| **Home Address:** | 2111 Emmons Rd. |
| | Jackson, MI  49201 |
| | |
| **Business:** | (517) 555-7966 |
| **Business 2:** | (517) 555-0800 |
| **Home:** | (517) 555-8540 |
| **Business Fax:** | (517) 555-8630 |
| | |
| **E-mail:** | bonnie  john-murray@jackson.cc.mi.us |
| | |
| **Web Page:** | http://www.jackson.cc.mi.us/JCC WEB/default2.html |
| | |
| **Categories:** | JCC |

**Phone Directory style**   This style, available only in Contacts, displays names and telephone numbers in a catalog style:

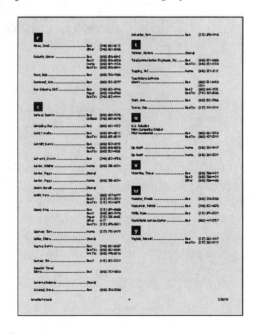

PART

**III**

Extending Outlook

**Table style**  This is the traditional style of columns and rows with borders around every cell:

| 🗋 | ! | 📎 | Subject | Status | Due Date | % Complete | Categories |
|---|---|---|---------|--------|----------|------------|------------|
| ☑ | | | Write newsletter articles | Not Started | Mon 3/23/98 | 0% | |
| ☑ | | | Track time on directory project | Not Started | Mon 3/23/98 | 0% | |
| ☑ | | | Call bank about deposit | Not Started | Mon 3/23/98 | 0% | |
| ☑ | | | Develop outline for next project | Not Started | Fri 3/27/98 | 0% | |
| ☑ | | | Set up marketing plan for school district training | Not Started | Fri 3/27/98 | 0% | |

 **NOTE**  Some styles are tied to specific views. You can't access the Table style, for example, unless you're in a Table view. If you can't find a print style, switch to a view similar to the print style and try again.

Choose these styles from File ➤ Print ➤ Define Print Styles or from File ➤ Page Setup ➤ Define Print Styles. This opens the Define Print Styles dialog box, shown in Figure 11.16.

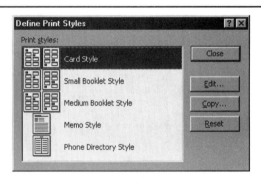

If you want to modify an existing style, select the style and click Edit. Don't worry about destroying one of the default styles; you can always return the style to its original settings by clicking the Reset button if you're not satisfied with the results.

If you'd rather leave the original styles intact, select the style you'd like to base yours on and choose Copy. The Page Setup dialog box, shown in Figure 11.17, will open, and the Style Name text box at the top of the dialog box will be active. Enter a name for your custom style.

**FIGURE 11.17**

The Page Setup
dialog box

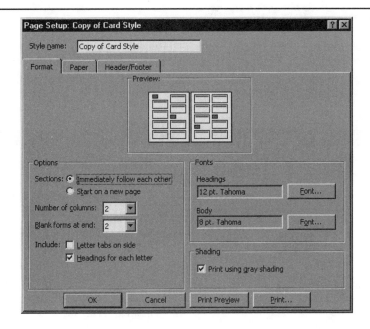

If you click OK, Page Setup closes and you'll be back at the Define Print Styles dialog box. Your new style is added to the list of style choices and a Delete button replaces the Reset button. Click any of the pre-existing styles, and the Reset button reappears.

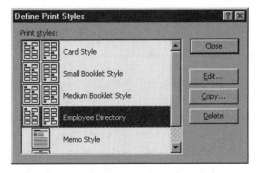

Now that your new style is included with the original five, you can choose to edit it or copy it to make another new style. If you decide you really don't want your new style, click Delete, and it will be removed.

 **TIP** Before designing a custom print style, open the component that contains the data you're creating the style for and set up the view to represent the view you'll want to print. This will ensure that you'll have an accurate representation of what the style will look like when you're finished.

PART

III

Extending Outlook

## Formatting the Style

Click the Edit button to go back to Page Setup and define the settings that will differentiate your style. The first page of Page Setup (refer back to Figure 11.17) focuses on the format of the printed document. For a description of each of the Page Setup options, see Table 11.2.

**TABLE 11.2: PAGE SETUP OPTIONS**

| Option | Choices | Description |
|---|---|---|
| Sections | Immediately Follow Each Other; Start on a New Page | Prints alphabetic sections, A, B, C, etc., either continuously or with page a break before each new section. |
| Number of Columns | 1–6 | Indicates how many columns are on a page. Some page sizes preclude choosing multiple columns. |
| Blank Forms at End | None–20 | Prints blank forms with all the Contact fields listed, so you can enter new contacts manually before entering them into Outlook. |
| Include Letter Tabs on Side | Yes, No | Prints the alphabet as a vertical shaded index strip on the outside of each page. The letters corresponding to the current page are printed white on a black background. |
| Include Headings for Each Letter | Yes, No | Prints a white letter on a black background at the beginning of each new section. |

The default Headings and Body fonts are Tahoma 12-point and 8-point, respectively. Tahoma is an attractive sans-serif font that is bolder than Arial but fairly similar in overall appearance. To choose any other font, font style, or size, click the Font button next to Headings or Body. Click the Print Using Gray shadings check box to clear it if you plan to make copies of the document you're printing. Gray shading can be attractive from a printer but is usually not rendered well by most copy machines.

## Choosing the Right Paper

The options on the Paper page of Page Setup, shown in Figure 11.18, can have the most significant impact on the appearance of your printed document.

**FIGURE 11.18**

*The Paper page of
Page Setup*

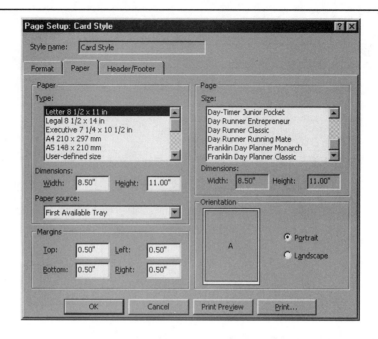

In Outlook, *paper* and *page* have two distinct meanings. *Paper* refers to the physical paper you have in your printer: letter, legal, etc. *Page* refers to the area of the paper that you'll be printing on. If you set Paper Type to $8\,{}^1\!/_2 \times 11$ and Page Size to $8\,{}^1\!/_2 \times 11$, you'll print on the entire sheet of paper (minus the margins, of course). If you set Paper Type to $8\,{}^1\!/_2 \times 11$ and Page Size to Billfold ($3.75 \times 6.75$), your data will print only on a portion of the page, as you can see in Figure 11.19. You will then need a paper cutter to make this a usable addition to your billfold.

The Paper Type options give you different sets of Page Size choices so you can choose the Paper Type and then the Page Size. Check out the results of your selections in the Orientation preview. If you use one of the paper-based planning systems, such as Day-Timer, Day Runner, or Franklin Day Planner, you can choose the exact page size of your planner.

To enter a custom paper type, choose User-Defined Size, and then enter the dimensions in the Width and Height boxes. The default user-defined size is a $3 \times 5$ card. Switch the orientation to landscape, and you'll get a standard index card size.

If you've put custom paper in the printer, indicate which tray to use from the Paper Source list. Change margin settings by typing your choices in the Top, Bottom, Left, and Right boxes. Change the orientation of the page by choosing Portrait or Landscape.

PART

**III**

Extending Outlook

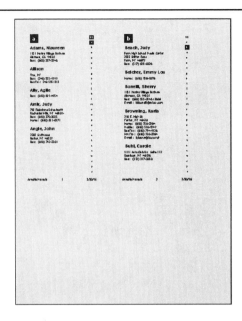

**FIGURE 11.19**

*Billfold page size on an 8½ × 11 paper type*

# Adding Headers and Footers

If you want to print repeating text on each page of your document, click the Header/Footer tab. The Header/Footer page, shown in Figure 11.20, is similar to the Header and Footer feature in Excel, so if you're familiar with Excel, you have it made. If you are not an Excel user, don't let it scare you—it's easier than it appears.

The header and footer sections are each divided into three subsections: left, center, and right. Click in any of the six text boxes to enter text in that section. By default, Outlook includes the User Name (that's generally you), the Page Number, and the Date Printed in the footer. You are not bound by this convention, however. You are free to put any information anywhere you want it.

Outlook provides placeholders for five variable fields that you can insert in either the header or the footer. To insert a placeholder, click in the section of the header or footer where you want the placeholder to appear, and then click the placeholder button. The following list identifies the function of each of these placeholders.

**Page Number**   Inserts the actual page number of the document.

**Total Pages**   Can be combined with the page number placeholder to create the expression "Page 1 of 4" (Page [Page Number] of [Total Pages]).

**Date Printed**   Displays the date the document was printed.

**Time Printed**   Displays the actual time the document was printed.

**User Name**   Displays the name of the user currently logged in to Outlook.

*FIGURE 11.20*

*The Header/Footer
page of Page Setup*

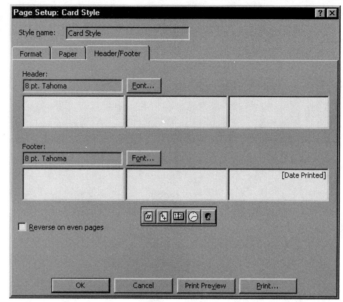

If you're printing a booklet, click the Reverse on Even Pages button to switch the header and footer placement on opposing pages. When you've finished entering the header and footer, click OK. You're taken back to the Define Print Styles page to create another style. If you're ready to use the style you just created, click Close to exit this dialog box. Choose File ➤ Print and choose the new style from the list of Print Style choices.

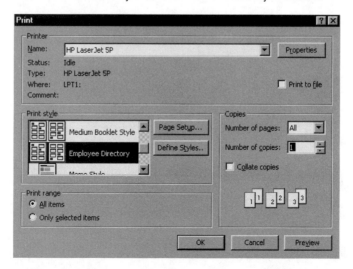

PART

III

Extending Outlook

Everything should be set up exactly the way you want it, so click Print and you're finished. You can now choose this print style any time you want to print your data.

## What's Next

In the next chapter, you'll find out how to customize Outlook itself—with user profiles, services, and toolbars—to make Outlook fit the way you work.

# CHAPTER 12

# Setting User Preferences

**M**uch of Outlook's work behind the scenes is dictated by the settings in your user profile. A *profile* is a file that contains information about your Outlook configuration. The profile, stored on your local computer, links you to particular information services and address books.

An *information service* is a group of settings that tell Outlook how and where to send and receive messages, store and recall items, or connect to address books. Each of the following is an information service:

- Internet mail
- Microsoft Exchange mail
- CompuServe mail
- Personal address book
- Outlook address book

Each profile includes multiple information services. In order to configure a service that interacts with other computers, such as Microsoft Exchange mail or Internet mail, you need to gather additional information. Depending on the specific service, this may include such things as the server name, an access phone number, and your mailbox name.

## Creating a New Profile

If more than one person works on your computer, you should each have your own profile. Profiles help keep your personal computer personal by saving each user's mail and address book settings separately.

 **NOTE** Your profile is not the same as your Windows or Windows NT user account. A workstation may have five different user accounts but only one profile, or *vice versa*. However, when you're adding new profiles for current users, it's helpful if you give it the same name as your Windows user account.

Each user can have more than one profile. For example, your notebook computer might include one profile that you use when you're in your office, connected to a mail server that delivers both internal and Internet mail. A second profile, for use out of the office, could include dial-up information services. You can designate a default profile or have Outlook prompt you to select a profile when you launch Outlook. You create new profiles, whether for yourself or another user, in the Windows Control Panel.

Mail

Choose Start ➤ Settings ➤ Control Panel on the Windows taskbar to open the Control Panel. Then double-click the Mail icon to open the Services page of the Properties dialog box, shown in Figure 12.1.

**FIGURE 12.1**

*The Services page of the Properties dialog box displays information services for the active profile.*

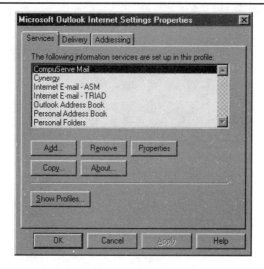

You'll be seeing this dialog box again—it shows the information services included in the current profile. For now, though, click the Show Profiles button to open the Mail dialog box, shown in Figure 12.2. On this workstation, there are two profiles: Microsoft Outlook Internet Settings and Valued Acer Customer. (Guess what kind of PC this is!)

**FIGURE 12.2**

*Open the Mail dialog box to see the profiles set up on the computer.*

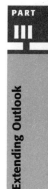
PART

III

Extending Outlook

Click the Add button to launch the Inbox Setup Wizard to add a new profile. In the first step of the Wizard, shown in Figure 12.3, choose the information services you'd like the Wizard to configure for messaging on this workstation, or select Manually Configure Information Services. Manually Configure is the same as "do it later." You can add services to the profile at any time; don't add services until you intend to use them.

**FIGURE 12.3**

*Choosing services in the Inbox Setup Wizard*

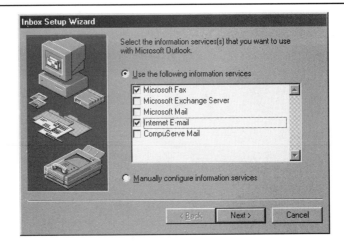

In the second step of the Wizard, you're prompted for a name for the profile. The default name is the username from Windows. If you're creating a profile for another user, enter their name. A second profile for your use might be called Alternate Profile, At Home, or any other descriptive name.

## Configuring Services in the Wizard

If you chose information services in the first step, you're asked to configure each of the services you selected in order. You'll need information (and maybe a disk or CD) for each information service you selected. Windows will prompt you to provide configuration information. For Internet e-mail, for example, you will click a Setup Mail Account button in the Wizard, which opens the Mail Account Properties dialog box, shown in Figure 12.4.

In the General page (see Figure 12.4), you enter a friendly name for the service, which can be any text string you want to use to refer to the service. Enter the user's name, organization, e-mail address, and the address others use to reply to the user. In the other pages of the dialog box, things get a lot more specific. If you've configured your Internet e-mail account previously, you may know the name of the POP server and SMTP server and the server port numbers you need to use. If you don't, call your Internet service provider (ISP) and ask for this information.

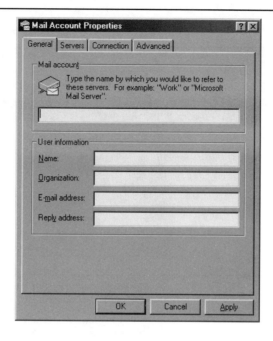

When you're finished configuring services, the Services page of the Properties dialog box (see Figure 12.1) opens again, displaying the services you've just configured.

In the final steps of the Inbox Wizard, you can add Outlook to the Windows Startup group and then click Finish to close the Wizard. The Mail dialog box will still be open, displaying your PC's profiles, including the new profile you created.

# Adding Services

To add a service to a profile, open the Mail dialog box (Start ➤ Settings ➤ Control Panel ➤ Mail ➤ Show Profiles). Select the profile you want to add services to in the Mail dialog box, shown in Figure 12.5.

Click the Properties button to open the Properties dialog box for the service, shown in Figure 12.6.

Click the Add button to open the Add Service to Profile dialog box, shown in Figure 12.7. The dialog box has a list of services you can add. If the service you want to add is listed, select the service from the list and click OK.

If the messaging service you want to add isn't listed, you can insert the disk or CD for the service and click the Have Disk button. You'll be prompted to locate the setup file for the service on the disk or CD, and Windows will install the software for the service.

Properties

PART

III

Extending Outlook

**FIGURE 12.5**

Selecting a profile to add new services

**FIGURE 12.6**

The profile's Properties dialog box displays the services–if any– configured for the profile.

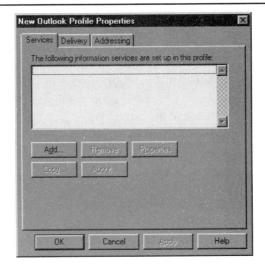

**FIGURE 12.7**

Select a service to add in the Add Service to Profile dialog box.

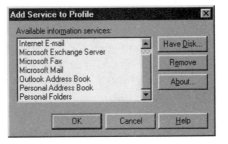

**TIP** Contact your messaging service or visit its Web site to find out if you need additional software to install the service. For example, to install CompuServe mail, you need to add CompuServe and a driver for Outlook called `cismail.exe`, which is available from Compu-Serve, or you need to convert your CompuServe mailbox to a POP3 mailbox. While logged onto CompuServe, do Go:PopMail for instructions on how to activate your PopMail account.

## Adding Personal Folders

At a minimum, a profile should include the Personal Folders service. Personal Folders is the *information store* (one type of information service) for the profile, which is the file where Outlook will keep the Contacts, Tasks, and other items associated with this profile. Personal folders have the `.pst` file extension.

To add a Personal Folders service, select Personal Folders in the Add Service to Profile dialog box (see Figure 12.7) and click the Add button to open the Create/Open Personal Folders File and dialog box, shown in Figure 12.8. Select a file name and location for the `.pst` file, click Open to create the new `.pst` file. Choose a location for the `.pst` file. If you're creating personal folders for one of the users on your PC, consider creating the `.pst` file in the `Windows\Profiles\Username\Application Data` folder for the user. Outlook creates the `.pst` file and opens the Create Microsoft Personal Folders dialog box.

**FIGURE 12.8**

*Configuring the personal folders for a new user*

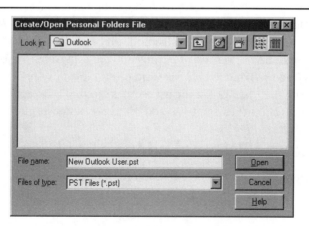

PART

III

Extending Outlook

**TIP** You can connect a profile to an existing set of personal folders by selecting the .pst file for the existing profile. The two profiles will share Outlook items.

The file path and name you entered has "read only" at the top of the dialog box. In the Name text box, enter the name that will appear for this service in the Information Services dialog box. Using part of the user's name, as well as Personal Folders, can help keep things straight when more than one person uses an information store.

## Encrypting Personal Folders

Encryption stores the .pst file in a format that can't be read externally, keeping your data confidential. Choose No Encryption if you don't want to encrypt your data—for example, if you use a desktop computer on a secured network. Choose Compressible Encryption to encrypt your personal folders in the smallest disk space possible. Best Encryption chooses the most secure encryption, but will take up more disk space than Compressible Encryption. If you want to encrypt your files, this is the time to do it. You can't change this option later.

## Assigning a Password to Personal Folders

You do not need to put a password on your personal folders. However, adding a password provides another level of security for your files. If other people use your computer and your .pst file is not password-protected, they can attach your personal folder file to their profiles.

If you add a password, you'll be prompted to enter the password when you either start Outlook or otherwise connect to your personal folders. You can save the password in your Windows password list and not be prompted by Outlook. Be aware that this is the computer version of putting all your eggs in one basket. Anyone who knows your Windows/Windows NT password can get into any application or folder that is protected with that password. If the password is saved, you're prompted to enter it only if you log on as another user or try to add the personal folders file to a profile.

# Creating a Personal Address Book

In the Internet Only configuration, Contacts acts as your personal address book, and you create groups to use as distribution lists. If you want to create distribution lists in the Corporate/Workgroup configuration, you need a personal address book. Creating a personal address book, which has a .pab extension, is much like creating personal folders. In the profile's Properties dialog box, click the Add button, and then select Personal Address Book from the list in the Add Services to Profile dialog box.

The default name for a personal address book is `mailbox.pab`; a `.pab` file is often just called a "pab." You can choose an existing pab file to connect to your personal address book in another profile, or create a file with a different name for a new user's profile. Click OK to open the Personal Address Book dialog box, shown in Figure 12.9. Choose the default display for names in the pab, enter any notes about the pab on the Notes page, and then click OK to add the personal address book to the profile.

**FIGURE 12.9**

*Choose how names should be displayed in the personal address book.*

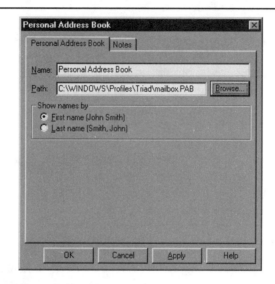

## Deleting Services

If you're no longer using a service, you should remove it from your profile. For example, if your workplace is routing your Internet mail, and you no longer need to connect to an ISP, you should remove the Internet mail service for the ISP from your profile for two reasons. Removing it as a service removes it from the Outlook menus and also ensures that it won't conflict with your other mail services.

To delete a service, open the Properties dialog box for the profile, select the service, and click Remove. You'll be prompted to confirm removing the service:

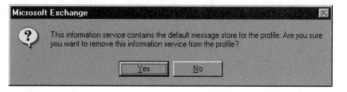

PART

**III**

Extending Outlook

## Modifying Service Properties

Occasionally, you'll need to modify your service properties. For example, your Internet service provider may add a new high-speed line (with a new telephone number) that you'd like to use. To change the properties of any service, open the profile's Properties dialog box (see Figure 12.1), select the information service you want to modify, and click the Properties button. Make the modifications you want in the service's dialog box, and click OK.

## Copying Information Services

You already have a profile you use in the office, and you are creating a second profile for use on the road. You'll use the same personal address book in the new profile, so why re-create it? You can copy an information service to another profile. With complex services like Internet mail services, this increases the likelihood that the service will work in the new profile.

To copy a service, open the Properties dialog box for the profile that contains the service you want to copy. Select the information service and click the Copy button to open the Copy Information Service dialog box, shown in Figure 12.10.

**FIGURE 12.10**

*Use the Copy Information Service dialog box to copy a service to another profile.*

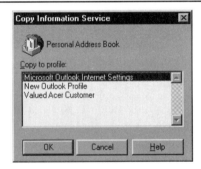

Select the destination profile for the information service, and click OK to copy the service. You won't see a confirmation, but if you look at the properties for the destination profile, you'll see the copied information service on the list. You can't copy an information service that already exists in the destination profile.

# Setting Profile Options

The profile includes options for using the information services configured within it. You set these options in the profile's Properties dialog box. In the Control Panel, double-click the Mail icon to open the Properties for the active profile. (To make changes to a different profile, click Show Profiles, select the profile, and click Properties.)

## Setting Delivery Options

On the Delivery tab of the Properties dialog box, shown in Figure 12.11, choose the information store where messages should be delivered in the Deliver New Mail to the Following Location drop-down list.

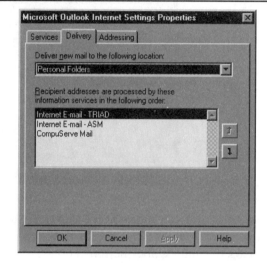

**FIGURE 12.11**

*Choose a location for mail and prioritize your mail services in the profile's Delivery options.*

By default, mail is delivered to your Inbox in the Internet Only configuration, and to the mailbox on your server in the Corporate/Workgroup configuration.

The Recipient Addresses list shows the messaging services in your profile in the order in which they process the mail you send. If you have more than one information service, you may want to change the order in which they process mail. For example, Microsoft Exchange can send Internet mail, so if Microsoft Exchange is higher in the list than an Internet mail service you have on your computer, Microsoft Exchange will handle all the Internet mail you send, as well as the Microsoft Exchange mail. To put the services in your order of preference, click to select the service that you want to use to process mail first. Use the Move Up arrow button to move your primary mail service into the first position. Select the other services in turn and use the Move Up and Move Down arrow buttons to rearrange them as required.

PART

III

Extending Outlook

## Setting Addressing Options

The Addressing options (see Figure 12.12) specify the default address book and the order in which address books are used in Outlook.

*Choose the default address book and address book processing order on the Addressing page.*

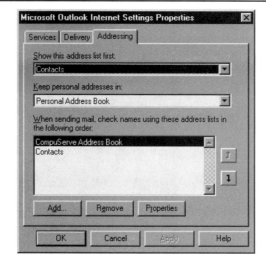

The address book you choose in the Show This Address List First drop-down list is the address book you'll see whenever you open the Select Names dialog box in Outlook or click the Address Book button in other Office applications. Select the address book you choose names from most often.

In the Keep Personal Addresses In drop-down list, you'll probably want to select your Personal Address Book or Outlook Address Book in the Corporate/Workgroup configuration, and Contacts in the Internet Only configuration.

The When Sending Mail list shows the address books in the order in which Outlook and other applications check them to find a name you enter for a message recipient. Use the Move Up and Move Down buttons so that the most frequently used address book is at the top of the list.

# Copying Profiles

You don't have to create a new profile from scratch if you already have a profile with most or all of the services you want to add. In the Mail dialog box (Start ➤ Settings ➤ Control Panel ➤ Mail), choose the profile you want to copy, and click the Copy button.

In the Copy Profile dialog box, enter a name for the copied profile and click OK. Then modify the profile by adding, removing, or modifying services.

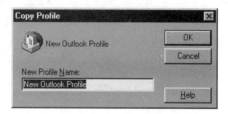

# Deleting Profiles

When someone quits using a workstation, you can delete their profile. Open the Mail dialog box (Start ➤ Settings ➤ Control Panel ➤ Mail), and then click the Show Profiles button. Select the profile you wish to delete, and click the Remove button. Windows will prompt you to confirm the deletion.

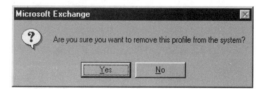

# Selecting a Profile

You set the default profile from the When Starting Microsoft Outlook, Use This Profile drop-down list in the Mail dialog box. When the computer is started, this is the profile that will be used.

But how do you get to the other profiles if this profile is always used? The setting to prompt for a profile is in Outlook. Choose Tools ➤ Options from the menu to open the Options dialog box, and click the Mail Services tab (see Figure 12.13). In the Startup Settings section, choose the Prompt for a Profile to Be Used option, and then click OK to close the dialog box.

PART

III

Extending Outlook

Have Outlook prompt
the user to select a
profile.

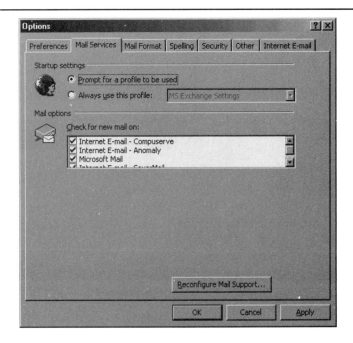

The next time Outlook starts, you'll be prompted to choose a profile.

 **MASTERING THE OPPORTUNITIES**

## Mastering Multiple Computers

In some companies, employees use more than one computer on a regular basis. With Outlook, you can receive mail at any computer you use. On one computer, make sure that your mail is being sent to your server mailbox, not your Inbox on the PC. (Do this on the Delivery page of the profile's Properties dialog box.) Next, create a user profile on another computer you use and connect it to your server mailbox.

# Customizing Command Bars

Outlook has four command bars: the menu bar and the Standard, Advanced, and Remote toolbars. All command bars are fully customizable, and you can create your own command bars with features you use frequently.

To create a new command bar, choose View ➣ Toolbars ➣ Customize from the menu bar, or right-click any command bar and choose Customize from the shortcut menu, to open the Customize dialog box.

Settings in the Options page of the Customize dialog box, shown in Figure 12.14, affect not only all Outlook command bars, but the command bars in all Office applications. If you turn off toolbar ScreenTips in Outlook, they're gone in Excel as well. If you animate menus so they slither or slide here, then you'll have that added functionality in Word and PowerPoint. This is true throughout Office, so, for example, a change in Excel changes what you see in Outlook.

**FIGURE 12.14**

*Change settings in the Options page of the Customize dialog box for all Office applications.*

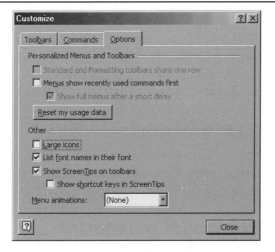

To change the items on a command bar, move to the Toolbars page of the dialog box, shown in Figure 12.15. You can reset an existing command bar to its default buttons and menu items by selecting the bar and then clicking the Reset button.

 **NOTE** Prior to Office 97, there were two different types of bars in Office applications: menu bars with text choices, and toolbars with buttons. Now you can place menus on toolbars and buttons on menus, so both are called command bars, although the customization dialog boxes refer to all of them as toolbars.

**PART**

**III**

**Extending Outlook**

*Create new command bars or reset existing bars on the Toolbars page of the dialog box.*

## Creating Toolbars

To create a new toolbar, click the New button to open the New Toolbar dialog box. Enter a name for the command bar and click OK. A tiny toolbar, just big enough to hold one button, will appear somewhere near the center of your screen.

## Renaming and Deleting Toolbars

The default command bars can't be deleted or renamed. Custom toolbars that you (or other users) create are renamed or deleted on the Toolbars page. Select the toolbar, and click the Rename or Delete button.

## Adding Commands to Toolbars

You add commands to new toolbars and to the default toolbars the same way. Click the Commands tab of the Customize dialog box to see the lists of available commands, shown in Figure 12.16. In the Categories list, select the type of command you want to add. For example, you might want to add a button for the Group By box to your new toolbar. In the Categories list, choose View, and then scroll through the list of commands to find the Group By button.

**FIGURE 12.16**

*Drag commands from the list to a command bar to add a new button or menu option.*

Drag the command from the Commands list and move it to the toolbar. A dark line appears. Move the mouse until the dark insertion line appears in the position where you want the new button, and then drop the button to place it (see Figure 12.16).

After you've added the button, you can click the Modify Selection button in the Customize dialog box to see a list of options for the button. For example, you can select a new image for the button by choosing Change Button Image, or display the name of the button as well as the Group By picture by choosing Image and Text.

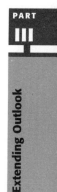

**PART**

**III**

**Extending Outlook**

Continue adding commands by selecting commands and dragging them onto the toolbar.

## Adding Commands to the Menu Bar

When you add commands to the menu bar, be aware of one small difference in the process. You have to wait until the menu opens to place the command on the appropriate menu. For example, you can add the Group By button to the View menu. Drag the command from the Customize dialog box to the View menu, and wait for the menu to open. Drag the command to the desired location on the View menu before dropping it into place.

## Rearranging Commands

Use drag and drop to move commands from one location on a toolbar or the menu bar to another (or from one toolbar to another). To copy a command, hold Ctrl while dragging it to its destination. To delete a command, drag the button off the toolbar. An *X* appears on the command; drop the button to delete it from the toolbar.

 **TIP** This may seem obvious, but if you rearrange the Outlook command bars too much, you'll have a hard time getting appropriate help from other users, your company's help desk, or Microsoft Technical Support. After the third or fourth time you reply "I don't have that there," you'll be on your own. If you want a specialized toolbar or menu, create a new toolbar or add a menu to the existing menu bar (with the New Menu command) and add commands to the new toolbar or menu.

As long as the Customize dialog box is open, you can add, delete, and rearrange commands. When you're finished customizing the command bars, click OK to close the Customize dialog box.

# Controlling Outlook Startup Options

When Outlook launches, the file Outlook.exe runs. You can add command-line parameters to the shortcut you use to start Outlook and change what Outlook does when it opens. There are two approaches you can take:

- Add parameters to the default shortcut.
- Create a new Outlook shortcut on the Desktop with special parameters, and leave the default shortcut in place.

If you change the default shortcut, Outlook will always start with the command-line parameters, whether you launch it from the Programs menu, the Office shortcut bar, or the Start menu. If you create a Desktop icon, you can launch Outlook from the icon when you want the customized behavior, and from the Start menu, Programs menu, or Office shortcut bar otherwise. Table 12.1 lists the actions you can have Outlook automatically follow.

**TABLE 12.1: OUTLOOK STARTUP OPTIONS**

| Action | Parameter |
| --- | --- |
| Create e-mail message | c/ipm.note |
| Create an appointment | c/ipm.appointment |
| Create a journal item | c/ipm.activity |
| Create a contact | c/ipm.contact |
| Create a note | c/ipm.stickynote |
| Open a folder | /select *"path and folder name"* |

## Changing the Default Shortcut

If you always want Outlook to open a folder or create an item, you can change the default shortcut. In Windows Explorer or My Computer, locate the shortcut to Outlook.exe. The shortcut to Outlook.exe is either in the same folder as Outlook.exe or up one folder level.

Right-click the shortcut's icon and choose Properties to open the Microsoft Outlook Properties dialog box, shown in Figure 12.17. In the Target text box, click at the end of the target text, type a space, and add the command parameter you want to use from Table 12.1. The Target shown in Figure 12.17 will cause Outlook to open a new message form automatically.

Click OK to close the Properties dialog box. The next time Outlook is launched, it will behave according to the command parameters you entered.

In Figure 12.17, the Target and Start In paths are enclosed in quotes because there's a space in the path between *Microsoft* and *Office* and between *Program* and *Files*. In Windows, paths with spaces need to be enclosed in quotes.

**FIGURE 12.17**

*Add parameters to the Target to have Outlook automatically open a form.*

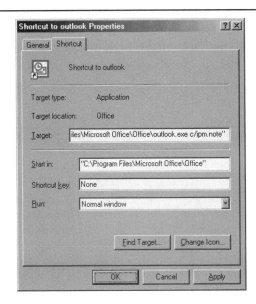

## Adding a New Shortcut

If you only want a new message form (or journal form, or whatever) some of the time, you're better off with a new shortcut that you can use when you want a new form, leaving the default shortcut for use at other times.

To create a new shortcut, find either Outlook.exe or the shortcut to Outlook.exe. Right-click and choose Create Shortcut from the menu to create a new shortcut in the current folder. Drag the shortcut onto the Desktop, and add the parameters you want to use to the new shortcut. You can rename the shortcut (right-click the icon and choose Rename) so that the Desktop shortcut is called Outlook E-mail, reminding you that it creates a new e-mail message when you use it to launch Outlook.

## What's Next

Instead of switching to Windows Explorer or My Computer, you can simplify your file management chores by handling it all through Outlook. In the next chapter, you'll learn how to create folders, move and copy files, and rename and delete files and folders without ever leaving Outlook. You'll also learn how to archive old data and back up those all-important Outlook folders.

# CHAPTER 13

# Organizing Your Outlook Data

ou may remember that in Chapter 1 we referred to Outlook as a desktop information manager. Nowhere does it do a better job of living up to its name than in its folder- and file-management features. You never have to launch the Windows Explorer or My Computer again. All of your file-management needs can be accommodated from within Outlook. And to top it off, all of the features that make Outlook so exciting, such as views, integration, and the powerful new Find feature, give Outlook the edge over Windows as a file management tool.

## Managing Data and Files in Outlook

Whether you've realized it or not, all of the Outlook components are organized as folders, and they each have all of the properties of other folders on your hard drive or network. You can move them, copy them, rename them, create subfolders under them, and view them in different ways. The easiest way to grasp the Outlook folder structure is to choose Folder List from the View menu. This opens a third pane in the Outlook window that clearly shows the folders and subfolders that make up the Outlook components (see Figure 13.1).

**FIGURE 13.1**

*The Folder List view of Outlook*

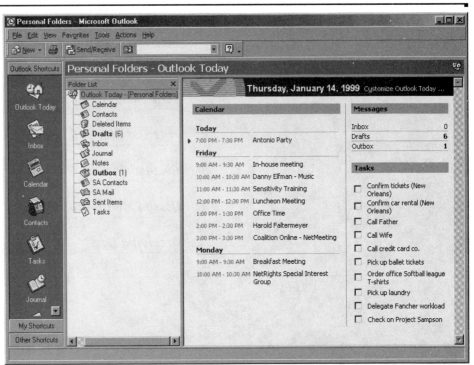

Another quick way to open the Folder List is to click the component name in the banner of the Information Viewer. This opens the Folder List temporarily so you can view it and move between folders. To keep it open, click the push pin in the top-right corner.

At the top of the list is Outlook Today - [Personal Folders]. *Personal folders* is the Outlook information service that contains your personal information. Other information services may contain public folders on a Microsoft Exchange server or Internet folders for sharing information with others on the Internet. The personal folders information service contains your personal information store, Contacts, Calendar, Tasks, and so on. It's possible to have more than one set of personal folders available to you as part of your user profile, or to have a mixture of personal and public folders. (For more about information services and personal folders, see Chapter 12.)

Click on any of the folders to display the contents of that folder. The minus sign or plus sign to the left of Outlook Today - [Personal Folders] (and of other folders, too) is a Collapse/Expand button. If it's a minus sign, you can click it and collapse the folder, so that all of the folders underneath it are hidden, as shown in Figure 13.2. The minus sign changes to a plus sign to indicate that this folder can be expanded to show the folders or files underneath it.

PART

III

Extending Outlook

**FIGURE 13.2**

*Click the Collapse button to collapse all the folders.*

Clicking the plus sign expands the folder again. To change the width of the folder list, point to the right border and, when your pointer changes to a double-headed resize arrow, like the one in Figure 13.3, drag the border to the left or the right. Release the mouse button when you have the desired pane size.

**FIGURE 13.3**

*Change the width of the Folder List by dragging its border.*

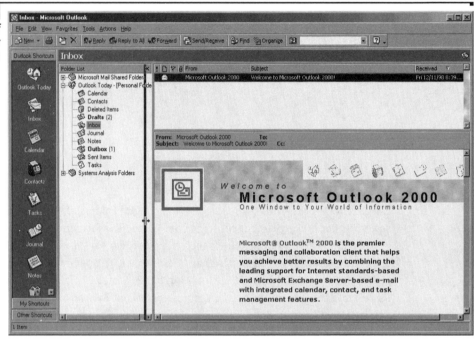

When the list is too narrow to display all of its contents, a scroll bar appears at the bottom of the list.

**TIP** If you prefer using the Folder List instead of the Outlook Bar, you can turn off the Outlook bar by choosing View ➢ Outlook Bar. Turn it back on again by repeating the process. See "Customizing the Outlook Bar," later in this chapter, for more about using the Outlook bar effectively.

# Creating Folders

As your personal folders begin to fill up with information, you may find it valuable to create subfolders to store some of your information. This is especially useful in managing your incoming and outgoing e-mail. To create a subfolder, right-click on the main folder and choose New Folder from the shortcut menu.

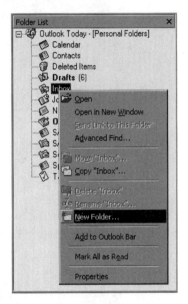

You could also choose File ➤ New Folder or click the New button drop-down list and choose Folder. Any of these options opens the Create New Folder dialog box. The main folder you clicked will be highlighted; the Folder Contains option corresponds to that type of folder. In Figure 13.4, the Inbox is highlighted and the Folder Contains list box is set to Mail Items. You are not bound by these choices. Once the Create New Folder dialog box opens, you can select a different main folder altogether. If you do, however, the Folder Contains option will not change on its own, so you'll have to change it to match the folder type. For example, if you decide to create a Calendar folder instead, just click the Calendar in the Select Where to Place the Folder list, and choose Appointment Items from the Folder Contains list.

**FIGURE 13.4**

*The Create New
Folder dialog box*

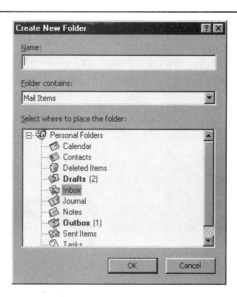

When you have finished entering the folder type and selecting where it will go, enter a name for the new folder. In Figure 13.5, a new Calendar folder called Training is created.

**FIGURE 13.5**

*Creating a new
Calendar folder*

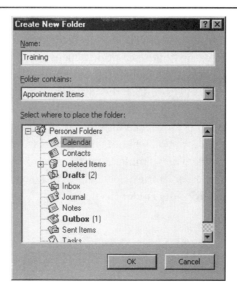

When you click OK, you will be asked if you would like to create a shortcut to this folder on the Outlook bar.

The Outlook bar is fully customizable—you can add to it and remove any of the items on it (see "Customizing the Outlook Bar," later in this chapter, for details). If you would like this folder to be available to you on the Outlook bar, click Yes; if you would prefer not to add this folder to the Outlook bar, click No. The only way you'll be able to access the folder if you choose No is to turn on the Folder List. If you plan to keep the Folder List visible and turn off the Outlook bar (View ➤ Outlook Bar), check the Don't Prompt Me About This Again check box and click No. Figure 13.6 shows the newly created Calendar folder (you may have to click the Expand button (+) to see it).

**FIGURE 13.6**

*A subfolder is displayed under the Calendar folder.*

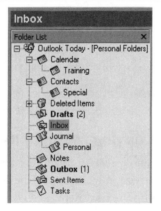

 **TIP** If you decide you'd like to add a folder to the Outlook bar after you've created it, just right-click the folder and choose Add to Outlook Bar from the shortcut menu.

## Moving Items to Different Folders

Now that you have a new folder, it might be nice to have something in it. You can create new items to put in the folder by selecting the folder and clicking the New button. If you want to organize existing items into subfolders, just click on the item and drag it into the new folder. For example, Figure 13.7 shows a Calendar item, Publisher

PART

III

Extending Outlook

Training, which is highlighted on the right (note the thick border), being dragged to the Training folder. Dragging an item places a small, gray rectangle at the bottom of the pointer.

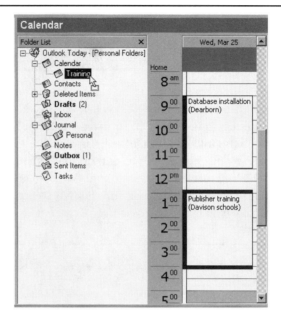

To copy an item instead of moving it, hold down the Ctrl key when you drag. The pointer will include a plus symbol below the Move Document icon.

## Moving or Copying Multiple Items

To select more than one item in a folder for moving or copying, you can use the standard Windows selection techniques. Click on the first item and hold down the Ctrl key before clicking the next item. Keep the Ctrl key held down until you've selected all the desired items.

If you want to select several consecutive items in a list, click the first one and hold the Shift key down before selecting the last item in the list. This will select all the items in between. To select all the items in a list, choose Edit ➤ Select All.

You can move multiple items at once by clicking anywhere in the selected list and dragging them, as shown in Figure 13.8.

 **TIP** If you're confused by whether you are moving or copying, you might find it easier to drag with the right mouse button. When you reach your destination, release the mouse button and a shortcut menu will appear that lets you choose among Move, Copy, or Cancel.

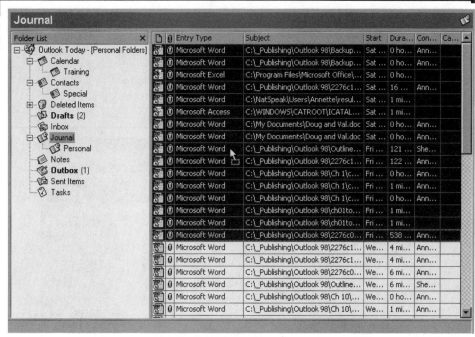

**FIGURE 13.8**

*Dragging multiple items*

## Moving and Copying Items to Folders Using Menus

If you're not proficient at dragging and would like to use menu options to move and copy files, Outlook has not forgotten you. Right-click on any item to open the shortcut menu and choose Move to Folder.

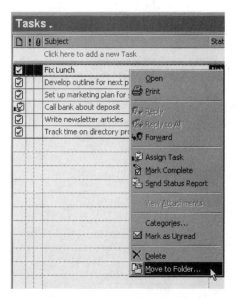

**NOTE** The shortcut menu has different choices on it depending on what type of item you select.

Choosing Move to Folder opens the Move Items dialog box, shown in Figure 13.9. Select the folder you want to move the item to, and click OK.

**FIGURE 13.9**

*The Move Items dialog box*

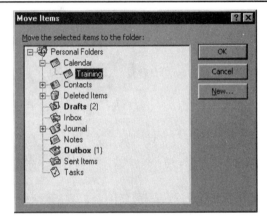

If you want to create a new folder, click the New button in the Move Items dialog box to open the Create New Folder dialog box (shown previously in Figure 13.4).

To copy an item, you must choose Copy to Folder from the Edit menu. This opens the Copy Item dialog box (this is identical to the Move Items dialog box shown in Figure 13.9, except for the title) and creates a copy of the items in the designated folder.

## Moving Items to Folders Using the Organize Page

 The Organize page, opened by clicking the Organize button on the Standard toolbar, has options for moving some items, specifically contacts, tasks, notes, and mail items, to folders (this excludes using this option to move Calendar items or Journal

entries). The Organize page is slightly different depending on which component you are in, but it closely resembles the Contacts version shown here.

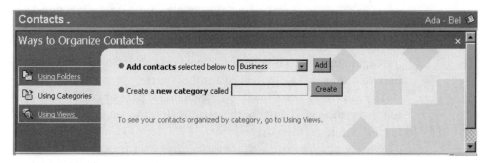

The Organize page has a Web-like interface, so instead of buttons, it uses hyperlinks. Click the Using Folders hyperlink and click the down arrow on the Move Contact Selected Below To field to display the list of available folders.

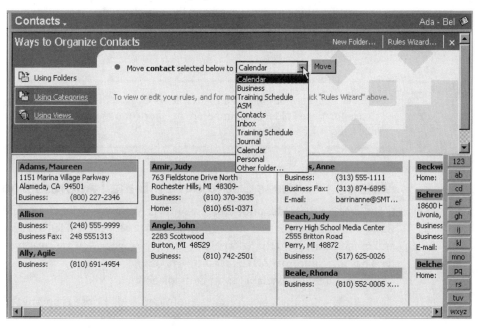

If the folder you want is visible from the Folder List, select it and click Move. If the folder you want is not visible, select Other Folder at the bottom of the list to open the Select Folder dialog box. Select the folder you want from this list and click OK to close the dialog box; then click Move to actually move the item.

Remember to only move an item into a folder that was created to accept it—a mail item into a mail folder, a contact into a Contacts folder, and so on—unless you want to create another type of item. For example, you can schedule time to work on a task by moving a task into a Calendar folder. When you do, a meeting form opens so you can schedule the task. If you move a contact into a mail folder, it creates an e-mail message addressed to that person (Chapters 4 through 10 cover creating an Outlook item that is related to an item of another type).

You can create a new folder on the Organize page by clicking the New Folder button in the top-right corner of the pane. Follow the same process outlined in "Creating Folders" earlier in this chapter.

When you want to close the Organize page, click the Organize button on the Standard toolbar, click the Close button on the Organize page, or switch to another component.

## Moving and Copying Folders

Moving and copying folders is really no different from moving and copying items. Right-click on the folder in the Folder List, and choose Move Folder or Copy Folder. You'll find the same dialog box you saw in Figure 13.9. Select the folder and click OK.

 **NOTE** You cannot move the main folders of each of the Outlook components. The choice for Move Folder is dimmed on the shortcut menus of Contacts, Calendar, Tasks, Inbox, Journal, and Notes.

### Making a Contacts Subfolder an E-mail Address Book

If you create a subfolder underneath Contacts, you have to let Outlook know that you want to make it available as an Outlook address book. This will let you access the e-mail and fax addresses from the Select Name dialog box when you are creating e-mail. (Chapter 4 has more information about address books.)

To make a folder available as an Outlook address book:

1. Right-click the new Contacts subfolder, and choose Properties from the shortcut menu.

2. Click the Outlook Address Book tab of the Special Properties dialog box, shown in Figure 13.10.

3. Click the Show This Folder as an E-mail Address Book check box.

**4.** Enter a different name for the address book if desired. This does not change the folder name—only the name of the address book.

**5.** Click OK to save the changes and close the Special Properties dialog box.

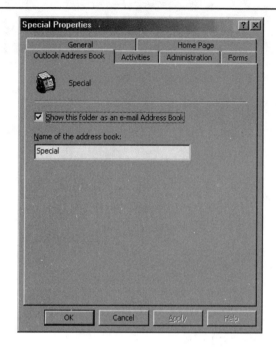

## Opening Folders in New Windows

There may be times when you want to check something *now* while you're in the middle of something else. Maybe you're reading your e-mail and discover that your best friend has front row tickets to a Semisonic concert and is inviting you to go if you are available. You don't want to waste any time getting back to her, so, rather than switch from the Inbox to the Calendar and back again, you can just right-click on the Calendar icon on the Outlook bar (or the Calendar folder in the Folder List) and choose Open in New Window from the shortcut menu. The message automatically minimizes and the Calendar opens in a separate window. To double-check that you have the date right, just click the message on the Taskbar and you can easily see both windows at the same time, as shown in Figure 13.11.

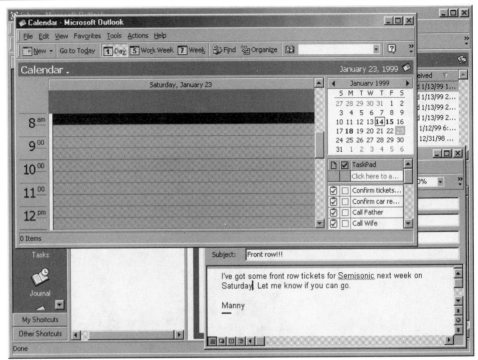

**FIGURE 13.11**

*Choose Open in New Window to have two components open at once.*

## Renaming Folders

As long as you created the folder, you can rename it or delete it whenever you want. To rename a folder, follow these steps.

1. Right-click on the folder you want to rename from the folder list.

2. Choose Rename [Folder Name] from the shortcut menu.

3. The folder name is selected (it becomes blue with a black box around it), and a flashing insertion point appears at the end of the current name.

**WARNING** If you select Rename from a right-click and start typing, you will replace the existing name. If you want to edit the current name, you must deselect the text before making any changes.

4. Enter the new folder name in the text box.

5. Press Enter to save the name or, if you change your mind about renaming the folder, press the Esc key.

## Deleting Items and Folders

To delete a folder, right-click on the folder and choose Delete [Folder Name] from the shortcut menu. To delete an item, right-click the item and choose Delete, or choose the delete button from the Outlook Standard toolbar or the Standard toolbar on the item's form. Don't worry if you delete something by accident—it doesn't go far.

You'll find deleted material in the Deleted Items folder, which is accessible from the Outlook bar or the Folder List. Folders and items remain in the Deleted Items folder until you delete them from the Deleted Items folder. At that point, you are given a warning, like this one:

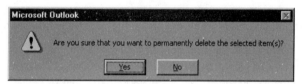

If you delete a folder from the Deleted Items folder, the warning is slightly different.

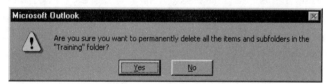

**TIP** You can also delete items and folders by dragging them to the Deleted Items folder on the Folder List or the Deleted Items icon on the Outlook bar. To recover them from the Deleted Items folder, just drag them back to their original locations.

PART

**III**

Extending Outlook

**MASTERING THE OPPORTUNITIES**

## Using the Advanced Toolbar

Whether you are an Outlook 97 user finally migrating to Outlook 2000 or a new Outlook user, there are buttons on the Advanced toolbar that will make your life easier. This is especially true in file management. The Advanced toolbar shown below, in addition to having an Outlook Today button and a New button, includes Back, Forward, Up One Level, Folder List, Undo, Current View, Group by Box, Field Chooser, and AutoPreview.

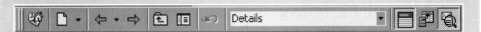

The Back and Forward buttons, which work like buttons on a Web browser, are particularly useful in navigating through your folder structure. The Up One Level button found in Windows Open and Save dialog boxes takes you up your directory tree to the folder above where you began. Undo is only useful in editing, so it doesn't serve much purpose here. Current View can be used to easily switch between views in any of the Outlook components. Group by Box opens a box above the file list that you can drag a field into to group by that field. For example, to see all of the files grouped by Type, drag the Type field into the Group by Box. Field Chooser lets you easily add and remove fields from your view. AutoPreview is most useful in the components where you can see the first couple of lines of e-mail messages, Journal entries, and notes.

To make the Advanced toolbar visible, choose View ➤ Toolbars and choose Advanced. Because the file management Standard toolbar is so small, you can move the Advanced toolbar to the same row as the Standard toolbar (move it by pointing to the two parallel bars on the left side of the toolbar and dragging). When you move back to the Outlook components, the Advanced toolbar will move to a new position below the Standard toolbar.

If you think that having both toolbars on all the time is too much, see Chapter 12 and design your own custom toolbar to meet your personal work habits.

# Managing the Files and Folders on Your Computer or Network

In addition to the folders contained within Outlook, you can use Outlook to access all the folders and files on your computer and network drives. Click the Other Shortcuts button on the Outlook bar. There you'll find three icons: My Computer, Favorites, and My Documents, as shown in Figure 13.12.

**FIGURE 13.12**

*The Other Shortcuts
group on the
Outlook Bar*

Click the My Computer icon to see the drives available on your computer. Notice that the Standard toolbar changes rather dramatically to include icons related to file management, such as Map Network Drive and Disconnect Network Drive.

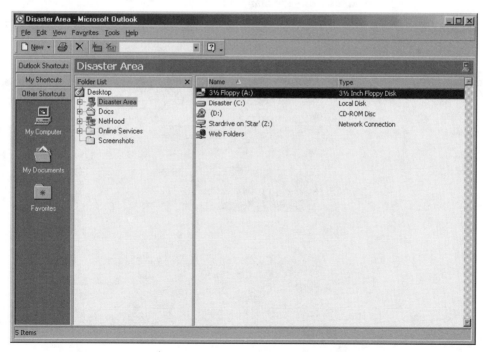

PART

**III**

Extending Outlook

Click any one of the drives in the Information Viewer to see the folders and files on that drive. Right-clicking on any file or folder gives you the same list of choices you get when you right-click on a file in the Windows Explorer.

## Printing a List of Files and Folders

Choosing Print from the shortcut menu opens and prints the document. One of the more exciting things about using Outlook for file management is that you can print a list of the files on your drive or in any folder on your drive. This isn't possible with your traditional Windows file-management tools. To print the file list, choose Print from the File menu or click the Print button on the toolbar. This opens the Print dialog box, shown in Figure 13.13.

**FIGURE 13.13**

*The Print dialog box*

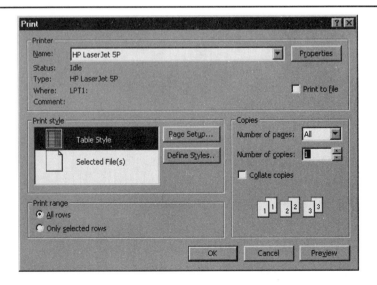

The list prints in Table style. You can choose to print all rows of the list, or you can select only the rows you want to print. If you would like to see what the list will look like before you print it, click the Preview button in the Print dialog box. Figure 13.14 shows an example of what the Windows folder looks like in Print Preview.

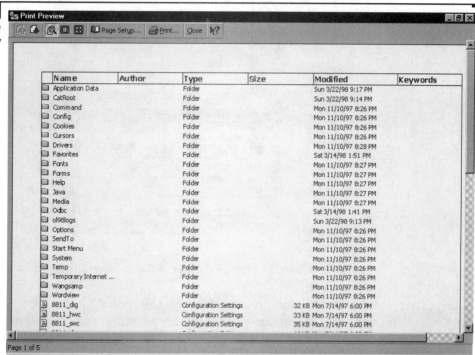

Click the Page Setup button if you'd like to change the paper size, margins, or add a header or footer to identify the file list you are printing and the date you're printing it (for more about Page Setup, see Chapter 2). Click the Print button to return to the Print dialog box, or click Close to return to Outlook without printing.

## Taking a Quick Look at a Document

Rather than having to open a document to see what it is, wouldn't it be nice to be able to preview it first? Right-click any file and choose Quick View to open the document in a miniature application window, as shown in Figure 13.15.

**FIGURE 13.15**

*Viewing a document in Quick View*

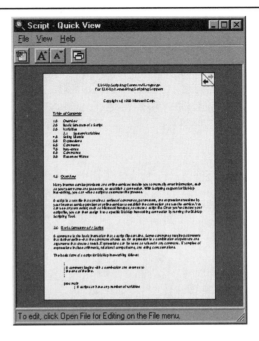

Click the arrows in the top-right corner of the document to scroll through the pages of the document.

If you need to actually read the document to figure out if it's the one you want, click the Increase Font Size button. It's really more like a Zoom—it doesn't really increase the font size of the document, it only makes it look that way so you can read it. Click Decrease Font Size to return it to its full page view.

Another way to read the document is to click the View menu and click Page View to toggle Page View off. This makes the contents readable without having to click the Increase Font Size button repeatedly. Select View ➤ Page View again to return to the full page view.

If you decide that this is the document you want to open, click the Open File for Editing button on the toolbar. This button represents the application the document was created in, so it changes depending on the document.

If you'd like to view another document, you can choose to have the document displayed in the same window or have a new Quick View window opened with the new document. Click the Replace Window button to close the current document and open a new one in the same window. When the Replace Window button is depressed, click it again, and the next document you open will open in a new window.

**NOTE** When you click outside the Quick View window to select another document, the Quick View window minimizes to the Taskbar. If you have chosen the Replace Window option, the window is restored when you select another document to Quick View. If you have chosen to open the document in a new window, the original window stays minimized on the Taskbar.

Click the window's Close button or choose File ➤ Exit to close the Quick View window.

 **NOTE** Quick View is a Windows component. If Quick View is not an option when you right-click on a file, the Quick View component was not installed with Windows. To install it, go to Add/Remove Program on the Windows Control Panel and click Windows Setup. You'll find Quick View in the Accessories group.

## Moving and Copying Files and Folders

Moving and copying files and folders works the same as it does in Windows Explorer. The following lists outline your moving and copying options.

To move a file to a new location:

- Drag the file from one folder to another on the same drive.

- Use Shift+drag to move the file from one folder to another on a different drive.

- Right-click and drag, and then choose Move from the shortcut menu that appears when you release the dragged item.

- Right-click and choose Cut from the shortcut menu, open the new folder, and right-click again to choose Paste.

- Choose Edit ➤ Cut, open the new folder, and choose Edit ➤ Paste.

To copy a file to a new location:

- Drag the file from one folder to another on a different drive.

- Use Ctrl+drag to copy the file from one folder to another on the same drive.

- Right-click and drag, and then choose Copy from the shortcut menu that appears when you release the dragged item.

- Right-click and choose Copy from the shortcut menu, open the new folder, and right-click again to choose Paste.

- Choose Edit ➤ Copy, open the new folder, and choose Edit ➤ Paste.

PART

**III**

Extending Outlook

## Creating New Folders

If you decide that having two hundred documents in your My Documents folder is getting a little unwieldy, you can create a new folder by choosing File ➤ New ➤ Folder. Enter the folder name in the Create New Folder dialog box that opens.

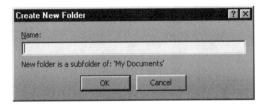

## Renaming a File or Folder

To change the name of a file or folder, all you have to do is right-click it and choose Rename from the shortcut menu. This opens the Rename dialog box where you can type in the new name. Click anywhere in the existing name if all you want to do is edit that name.

## Applying Outlook Views

One of the greatest file organization tools offered by Outlook is the ability to apply Outlook views to your files. In the Windows Explorer, you have your choice of four views: Large Icons, Small Icons, List, and Details. You can also sort (arrange) your files by Name, Type, Size, and Date. Although those options have seemed adequate for years, Outlook views blow them out of the water.

The default view for My Computer in Outlook is Details view. In Details view, as shown in Figure 13.16, you can see the name of the file, what type of document it is, who created it, the size, when it was last modified, and any keywords that have been assigned to help locate it later.

One of the most helpful views that Outlook can offer (and which you can't get anywhere else) is the By File Type view. This organizes all the files in a folder of the same type so you can ignore those system files that just get in your way. The By File Type view is especially useful if you're looking for files in large folders, such as the Windows folder. To see all the files of one type, just click the Plus button next to the type, as shown in Figure 13.17.

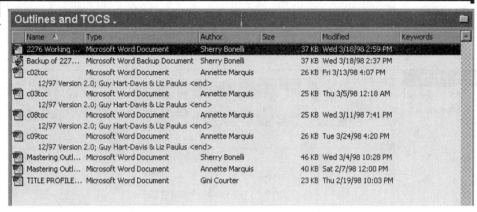

FIGURE 13.16
The default Details view

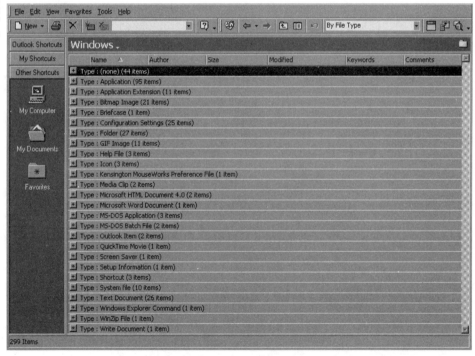

FIGURE 13.17
The Windows folder
organized by file type

Another useful view is the Document Timeline view. This view is similar to the
Timeline view in the Journal, but includes files that you didn't create or that weren't
automatically recorded in the Journal (see Chapter 10 for more information about
how to automatically record documents in the Journal). If you'd like to display the

document name in the Month view, right-click anywhere in the timeline (except on an icon) and choose Formal View. Click the Show Label when Viewing by Month check box and click OK. The results are shown in Figure 13.18.

**FIGURE 13.18**

*The Document Timeline view*

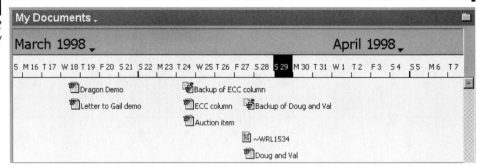

You can combine the Document Timeline view with By File Type by switching to the Document Timeline view and choosing View ➤ Current View ➤ Edit Current View, and selecting Group by File Type (see Chapter 11).

## MASTERING THE OPPORTUNITIES

The other views in files and folders that are available to you include:

**By Author**   Groups files by author (as designated in the file's properties)

**Icons**   The familiar My Computer view of the world

**Programs**   Shows only folders and applications

Of course, if none of these views is exactly what you want, you can always design your own custom views. See Chapter 11 for more details.

# Filtering Files and Folders

When you want to create a view that contains only files that meet certain criteria, you can set up a filter to select the files you want to see. (Filtering is covered in depth in Chapter 11.) You'll want to keep a few considerations in mind when applying filters to Windows folders.

**1.** You cannot apply a filter that will identify files in multiple folders—a filter can only be applied to one folder at a time.

2. Filter is not a menu option when you are in your Windows folders. You have to access it from the shortcut menu. Open the folder you want to filter, move to an empty space at the bottom of the file list, and right-click and choose Filter.

3. A filter can be saved with a view, but it will only apply to the current folder. You can't create a view that filters for a certain file type, for example, and then apply that view to other folders.

For the differences between filtering and finding files, see "Using Find to Locate Items" later in this chapter.

# Customizing the Outlook Bar

The Outlook bar, shown in Figure 13.19, is a relatively new tool in the Microsoft arsenal. Introduced in Outlook 97, this feature received positive responses from user groups, so it has started appearing in other applications. FrontPage 98, for example, uses a similar navigational feature in the FrontPage Explorer.

The concept behind the Outlook bar is simple. It holds shortcuts to the Outlook components and other folders on your computer, so with one click you can easily switch between folders. The Outlook bar is fully customizable, which means you can add shortcuts to your most commonly used folders, rearrange icons, rename icons, add new groups to organize your shortcuts, and, if you prefer, turn it off completely.

The shortcuts on the Outlook bar are divided into three groups:

**Outlook Shortcuts**    Shortcuts to all of the Outlook components, Outlook Today, and the Deleted Items folder

**My Shortcuts**    Shortcuts to the Drafts, Outbox, and Sent Items folders

**Other Shortcuts**    Shortcuts to the My Computer, My Documents, and Favorites folders

You may find that these groups meet your needs, or you may be itching to change them. Stayed tuned to learn more about how to make the Outlook bar more useful to you.

## Customizing the Outlook Bar's Display

One of the first things you might want to do to the Outlook bar is change the size of the icons, so you don't have to scroll to access all of the icons in the Outlook group. To change the size of the icons, right-click anywhere in the Outlook bar (except on an icon), and choose Small Icons from the shortcut menu.

This lets you see all of the Outlook icons and leaves you plenty of room to add new icons.

## Adding New Shortcuts to the Outlook Bar

Whenever you create a new folder, you are prompted to create a shortcut for it on the Outlook bar (unless you've told Outlook not to prompt you again; see "Creating Folders" earlier in this chapter). You can add a shortcut to any existing folder by right-clicking on the folder in the Folder List and choosing Add to Outlook Bar from the shortcut menu.

Outlook adds the shortcut to the bottom of the currently active group. Point to the icon and drag it if you would prefer having it in a different location. Figure 13.20 shows the Training Schedule icon being dragged to below the Calendar.

**FIGURE 13.20**

*Moving an icon by dragging it*

 **NOTE** To move an item to a new group, drag the icon to the group title. When the group opens, drop the icon into the new group. Be sure to move into the group itself before you drop it, or you'll get an error message telling you that you can't drag an icon to a group's title.

You can also click File ➣ New and choose Outlook Bar Shortcut from the list. This opens the Add to Outlook Bar dialog box. Just select the folder you want to add, and click OK.

## Deleting an Icon from the Outlook Bar

To remove an icon from the Outlook bar, right-click the icon and choose Remove from Outlook Bar. Remember, this won't delete the folder—you're only removing a shortcut to the folder. Outlook gives you a friendly prompt to make sure you want to remove it and reminds you how to re-create if later if you change your mind and want it back.

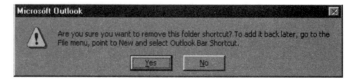

## Adding, Removing, and Renaming Groups

Groups help you organize your shortcuts so you can access them quickly and efficiently. Adding a new group is as simple as right-clicking on the Outlook bar and choosing Add New Group. Enter the name for the new group in the group box and press Enter.

To remove a group, right-click on the group's title and choose Remove Group. Renaming a group is just as simple. You guessed it—right-click again and choose Rename group. Type the new name in the title box and press Enter.

## MASTERING THE OPPORTUNITIES

### Simplifying the Outlook Bar

If you create too many groups, it becomes difficult to remember where you put the shortcut you want, which defeats the whole purpose of the Outlook bar. For one way of simplifying access to your folders, follow these steps:

1. Switch to Small Icons.
2. Move all the icons from My Shortcuts into the Outlook group.
3. Remove the My Shortcuts group.
4. Rename the Other Shortcuts group to My Computer.
5. Add additional commonly used folders to either of the appropriate groups.

This gives you just two groups—one that has all your Outlook folders in it and one that gives you access to the folders on your hard drive or network.

# Using Find to Locate Items

Although it may not happen right away, it won't be long before you have so many Outlook items that you can't easily find the one you want. You know you received two messages from your boss about a particular project, but you can only find one of them—the one that says the project is late. Don't panic. Outlook will scour through all of your folders, reviewing each item thoroughly until it comes up with the one you're looking for.

Outlook has a Find feature that lets you enter key words and phrases, like on a Web search page. Outlook will search the primary fields in a component or, if you prefer, will search the entire text of the items, to find what you're looking for.

You can access Find by clicking the Find button on the Standard toolbar. This opens up the Find page shown in Figure 13.21.

PART

**III**

Extending Outlook

**FIGURE 13.21**

*The Find page*

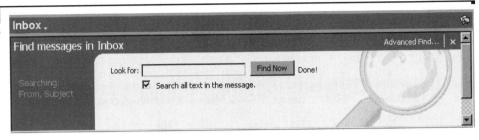

Enter the text you want to search for in the Look For text box, and click Find Now. If you know that what you're looking for is in one of the primary fields indicated on the Find page, it will speed the search to clear the Search All Text in the Message check box.

Your results are returned in a list format below the Find page. Figure 13.22 shows the result of a Find on the Inbox for the word *office*, searching all text in the message.

Click the Clear Search button if you want to conduct another search. If you didn't find the results you were looking for, or if you would like to refine the search more, click Go to Advanced Find.

To close the Find page, click the Find button on the Standard toolbar.

**FIGURE 13.22**

*The results of a search*

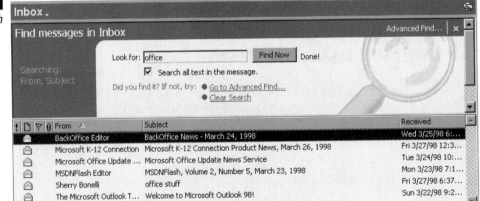

## Advanced Find

Finding something that you've lost is certainly a practical and worthwhile enterprise, but the uses of Find don't stop there. Advanced Find is really a powerful tool that is both similar to and different from Filter (for more about filters, see Chapter 11). The major differences can be summed up this way:

- While both Filter and Find let you establish criteria to search any single Outlook folder, Find lets you search all of the Outlook folders at once.

- You can save a filter with a view, so that you can apply it later. You can save a search (Find) as a file that you can reapply at another time or even send to coworkers who have the need to apply the same criteria to their data.

- Filters can only be applied to Outlook folders. By installing an Outlook add-on component called Integrated File Management, you can use Find within Outlook to search all your Windows files and folders, as well.

For a practical example, let's say you need to know all the communications and all the work you've engaged in for a particular client or customer. You could create a search that showed you every mention of the customer's name in all of your Personal Folders. The results would include communications, meetings, notes, contacts that were related to the customer, and also those correspondences where you discussed the customer with a member of your team. As long as the customer's name was mentioned somewhere, the item would appear in the list.

To use Advanced Find, click the Find button on the Standard toolbar and click Advanced Find or choose Advanced Find from the Tools menu. The Advanced Find window, shown in Figure 13.23, looks almost identical to the Filter dialog box.

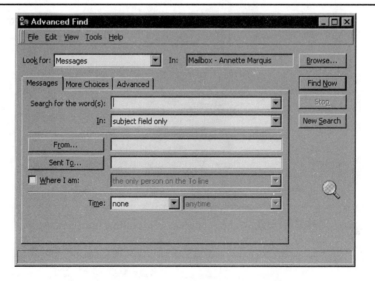

**FIGURE 13.23**

*The Advanced Find dialog box*

All the options for applying criteria that appear in Chapter 11 work the same way in Advanced Find. There are only a couple of exceptions that are noted here.

- When you create a search, click the Look For list to choose from a list of all the Outlook components, from Any Type of Outlook Item or from Files.

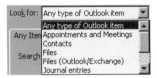

- If you are searching for Outlook items, the default folder to look in is Personal Folders. If you would like to narrow your search or choose a different folder altogether, click the Browse button next to the In field. This opens a Select Folders dialog box. Click the Plus button in front of Personal Folders to expand the list. Click any of the folders you want to include in the search. Clear the Search Subfolders check box if you want to search only the main folders.

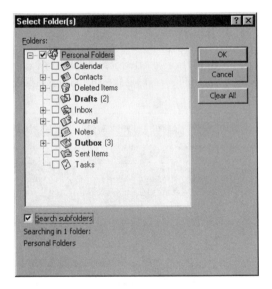

 **WARNING**  You can only select individual folders that are part of the same information service.

Once you identify what you want to search and where you want to search, you can establish your criteria for the search itself using the same methods as you would to set up a filter. (If you still haven't gone back to review Chapter 11, and you don't know what to do here, it's time to go there now. Everything you need to know about setting up criteria is back there.)

- You can sort the search results table by clicking the column headings.
- Click View ➢ Current View and select from By Category, By Subject, or Detailed Items to change the table's view.
- Choose View ➢ Current View ➢ Edit Current View to customize the view the way you want it. You can't apply a Filter to search results, but you can apply any of the other custom view options.
- Use Edit Features to move and copy items in the search results table to different folders. They will stay in the search results table but will show up in a different location (the In Folder column).
- To move an item to the Deleted Items folder, select the item and choose Delete from the Edit menu (this does not delete the item from the search results—it only changes its In Folder location).

## Saving the Search Results

Save the search (but not the results) by choosing File ➢ Save Search. This will save the search criteria and the view, but not the results, as an Office search file (`.oss`). You can re-run the search at any time by choosing File ➢ Open Search and opening the search file.

If you want to save the actual items as a document, choose File ➢ Save As. You are only given the option of saving the document as a text file, but you can then open it in Word to format it.

## Printing the Search Results

Depending on the purpose of your search, you can print the search results table, or, if you are developing a report based on the search results, you can print the details of each item in memo form, even choosing to print attached documents if you want. To print the search results, follow these steps:

1. Highlight the items you want to print. If you want to print them all, choose Edit ➢ Select All.
2. Choose File ➢ Print.
3. Choose Table style and indicate if you want to print the entire table or only the selected rows, or choose Memo style and indicate if you want to start each item on a new page and if you want to print the attached documents.

4. Use the Page Setup and Print Preview buttons to prepare your document for printing (for more about printing, see Chapter 2).

5. Click Print to send the document to the printer.

### MASTERING THE OPPORTUNITIES

## Assigning Categories to Multiple Items at Once

After locating all the items related to a single customer or other search criteria that you establish, you may decide that you'd like to assign all the items to the same category for ease in grouping them in individual Outlook folders in the future. You can do this in one easy step. Just choose Select All from the Find Edit menu, and then select Edit ➤ Categories. Select the category you want to assign, and click OK. There are some items, such as messages in your Inbox, that cannot be assigned categories, but all the others will now roll up to a single category.

This technique can also be applied in any of the Outlook components. For example, you can use Ctrl+click to select several items in your Contacts folder. Choose Edit ➤ Categories and assign them all to the same category. Any of their original categories will be retained, and the new one you assign will be added, unless you clear all the existing categories in the Categories dialog box first.

## Finding Public Folders

If you work in a large company, the number of public folders on the Exchange Server may grow out of control, making it difficult to find the information you are looking for. With Outlook 2000's new Find Public Folders option, shown in Figure 13.24, you can quickly locate and open any public folder you need. To access this feature, follow these steps:

1. Select Tools ➤ Find Public folder.

2. Click Browse to open up a Select Folders list if you want to narrow your search.

3. Enter the text you are searching for in the Contains Text box.

4. Indicate whether you would like to look for that text in the Name or Description, Internet Newsgroup Name, Folder path, Folder name, or Folder Description.

5. Specify a folder creation date if you want to search within a certain date parameter.

6. Click Find Now to conduct the search.

Outlook returns the name of the folder and the path where the folder is located. Just double-click the folder to open it in a separate window.

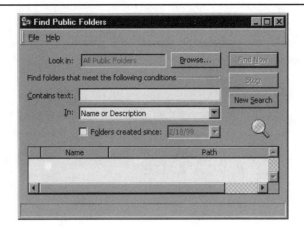

**FIGURE 13.24**

*Use the Find Public Folders option to locate a public folder.*

# Archiving Items

How many times have you gone back and looked at your calendar from two years ago or at a to-do list you completed months before? If you're like most people, probably not very often. A time may arise, however, when you need one piece of information from one of those sources, so, just to be on the safe side, you probably haven't thrown them away just yet. Conceivably, you could keep all of your outdated information in Outlook forever. You'd have to have a lot of extra disk space to store the file, and Outlook would be running so slowly you'd need a fair amount of patience, but it could be done. It makes a lot more sense, though, to decide how long to keep your outdated data around, and store anything that exceeds that time period in another file. This is called *archiving* your data, and it's a built-in Outlook feature.

Calendar items, tasks, Journal entries, and e-mail messages can all be archived, and you can establish different archive schedules for each component. You may have a need to keep Journal entries available longer than completed tasks. If you're really daring, you can also choose just to delete items completely after a certain amount of time. Outlook lets you determine what makes sense to you.

## AutoArchive

The process that governs archiving in Outlook is called *AutoArchive,* and you can guess from the name that it happens automatically (see "Archiving Items Manually" later in this chapter for details on manual archiving). Don't let this make you nervous—there are a number of controls that you can put on AutoArchive to make sure it doesn't do things without your approval. When Outlook archives data, it moves it to a personal folder on your hard drive called `archive.pst`. The default location for this folder is `C:\WINDOWS\Profiles\`*your profile name*`\Application Data\Microsoft\Outlook\`

`archive.pst`. You can change this to any location you'd prefer when you set up the archive options. If you ever need any data that's been archived, you can restore the archive file, pull out the information you need, and send the file back to the attic until the next time.

Several Outlook folders have AutoArchive turned on and default archive periods established when they are originally set up. These folders are Calendar (6 months), Tasks (6 months), Journal (6 months), Sent Items (2 months), and Deleted Items (2 months). AutoArchive is not activated automatically for Inbox, Notes, and Drafts.

## Setting Up AutoArchive

To set up AutoArchive, follow these steps:

**1.** Right-click on Calendar, Tasks, Journal, or any of the message folders, and select Properties.

**2.** Click the AutoArchive tab to open the AutoArchive page shown in Figure 13.25.

**3.** Click the Clean Out Items Older Than check box if it is not already checked.

**4.** Enter the number of Months, Weeks, or Days that you'd like to establish.

**5.** Choose the path and folder name you'd like to move items to (you can enter a name other than `archive.pst`, but retain the `.pst` file extension).

**6.** If you'd prefer to delete old items, select Permanently Delete Old Items.

**7.** Click OK to save the AutoArchive properties for that folder.

**8.** Repeat the process with each folder you want to archive.

---

**FIGURE 13.25**

*The AutoArchive
Properties page*

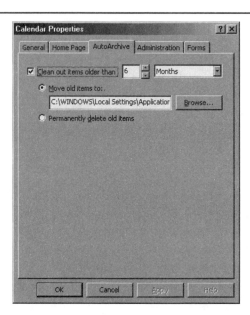

## Setting AutoArchive Options

To control how AutoArchive actually works, there are several options you may want to adjust. To find them, click Tools ➤ Options, click the Other tab, and then click AutoArchive.

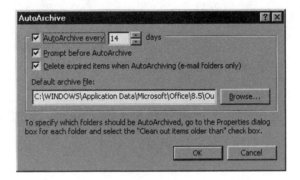

Indicate here how frequently you'd like Outlook to AutoArchive. The default is every 14 days, but you may want to change that to monthly or increase it to once a week, depending on the volume of Outlook items you process each week.

AutoArchive initiates when you log in to Outlook on the designated day. However, if you happen to need a phone number in a hurry that particular day, having to wait until AutoArchive is completed may not be what you want. If you'd prefer that Outlook notifies you before it begins its AutoArchive process, you can click the Prompt before AutoArchive option.

The third option deletes e-mail messages that have expired. This only applies to messages that have a specified expiration date.

The final option lets you designate a default folder for the archive.pst file. If you change the folder here, before setting the AutoArchive options in each component, you won't have to change it in each place.

Click OK to close the AutoArchive dialog box, save your settings, and click OK again to close Options.

## Archiving Items Manually

If you'd rather Outlook left the driving to you, you can archive items when you are good and ready. Follow the steps below to archive items manually.

**1.** On the File menu, select Archive.

**2.** To archive all folders, click the Archive All Folders According to Their AutoArchive Settings option button (see "Setting AutoArchive Options" earlier in this section). To archive one folder only, click Archive This Folder and All

PART

III

Extending Outlook

Subfolders, as shown in Figure 13.26. Click the folder that contains the items you want to archive.

**3.** In the Archive File box, type a filename for the archived items to be transferred to, or click Browse to select from a list.

**4.** In the Archive Items Older Than box, enter a date. Items dated before this date will be archived.

**5.** Select the archive file if you want to change the default.

**6.** Click OK to begin the archiving process.

**FIGURE 13.26**

*The Archive dialog box*

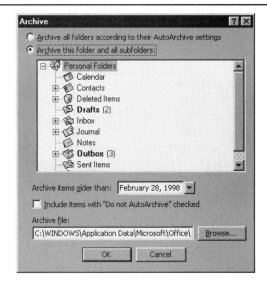

## Restoring Archived Items

There are two ways to recover items from archive.pst. You can:

- Import the items into their original files. If you choose to import the items, you can filter the archive file first to only retrieve the items that you want to recover. (See Chapter 14 for more information about importing a file.)

- Open archive.pst in Outlook. If you are looking for multiple items in the archive file, you may prefer to open the Personal Folders file to find the items you're looking for. To open the archive.pst file, follow these steps:

    **1.** Choose File ➤ Open ➤ Other Outlook File (.pst).

    **2.** Locate the archive.pst file on your hard drive.

**3.** Click OK to bring the Archive folder into Outlook. It will appear as a separate folder above Outlook Today – [Personal Folders].

You can open the AutoArchive personal folders and work with them just as you do your regular personal folders. When you've found the information you're looking for, you can close AutoArchive by right-clicking on the folder and choosing Close ➤ AutoArchive.

 **NOTE** AutoArchive re-creates the folder structure of your personal folders that are being archived, even if the folders are empty. The Inbox may be created, for example, even if you're only archiving folders underneath the Inbox. This is so that Outlook can restore the folders to the same location if you choose to import them back into Outlook.

## What's Next?

Organizing your Outlook data includes being able to use the data in other applications and being confident that your data is safely backed up in another file location. Chapter 14 covers importing data from other sources, exporting data to other Office applications and files, and communicating with project management tools, such as Microsoft Project. Using these features, you'll see the incredible power of Outlook as a versatile and flexible workgroup tool.

PART

**III**

Extending Outlook

# CHAPTER 14

## Integrating Outlook with Other Applications

O ne of the most significant developments in software over the last couple of years has been the improvement in the portability of data. Data entered into one database is rarely trapped there anymore. In this chapter, you'll see how you can import data created in other applications into Outlook and export Outlook data into other formats. You'll also see how data created in one application, such as Microsoft Project, can be communicated using Outlook as the communication vehicle.

# Importing Outlook Items

If you already have data on a computer, you can probably import them into Outlook. Most of the time, these will be contact data: names, addresses, and phone numbers, but you can also import calendar information, tasks, and e-mail messages. The Import and Export Wizard will walk you through the steps to import data from these contact managers:

- ACT! 2.0, 3.x, and 4.0
- ECCO 2.0, 3.0, and 4.0
- Lotus Organizer 1.0, 1.1, 2.1, and 97
- Microsoft Outlook personal folders
- Schedule+ 1.0 and 7.0
- Sidekick 95 and Sidekick for Windows 2.0

It will also convert data from these file formats:

- dBASE database files
- Microsoft Access
- Microsoft FoxPro
- Schedule Plus Interchange
- Microsoft Excel

If the file format you have isn't on either list, don't despair. Outlook will also import files in standard DOS and Windows formats, which most programs can produce:

- Comma-separated values (DOS and Windows)
- Tab-separated values (DOS and Windows)

To import files from any of these formats, begin by choosing File ➢ Import and Export to open the Import and Export Wizard, shown in Figure 14.1. The Office Assistant immediately opens, offering help with the Wizard. To close the Assistant, choose No, Don't Provide Help Now.

*Use the Import and Export Wizard to import contacts from another file format.*

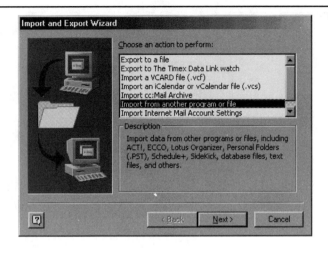

If you want help after you've closed the Assistant, click the Assistant button in the Wizard. In the first step of the Wizard, choose Import from Another Program or File, and then click the Next button.

## MASTERING THE OPPORTUNITIES

### Strategies for Importing Contacts

In actual practice, you can import contacts from nearly any application. If, for example, you keep your contacts in a Lotus 1-2-3 spreadsheet, you can open the spreadsheet in Excel and save it as an Excel worksheet. Are your contacts in a table in Word? Copy and paste the table into Excel. We've converted files from a no-name 64K organizer using the Comma Delimited format. We've combined the contact with fields in two separate Access databases by linking the tables from one database into the other, and then creating a query to display the fields we wanted to put into Outlook. To import another group of contacts from Quattro Pro, the file had to be saved in Quattro as a previous version, then opened and converted in Excel. If Outlook doesn't support the format of the file you're importing, there's invariably another way to convert the file to a supported format.

In the second step of the Wizard, select the format for the information you want to import, and click Next. In Figure 14.2, we're importing contacts from the Windows 95 Schedule+ program.

PART

**III**

Extending Outlook

**FIGURE 14.2**

*Select a file format to
import in Outlook's
Import and Export
Wizard.*

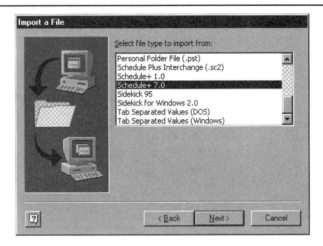

In the third step of the Wizard, shown in Figure 14.3, select the file you want to import. Either enter the path and filename or click the Browse button and select the file in the Open dialog box.

**FIGURE 14.3**

*Choose the file that
contains the contacts,
and tell Outlook how
to deal with duplicates.*

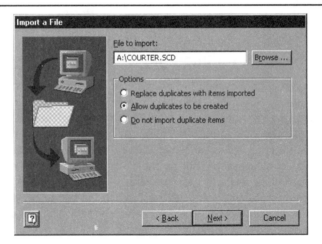

Before you click Next, you need to choose one of three options for dealing with duplicates—data you've entered in Outlook that also exist in the file you're importing. Unless you are importing an Outlook personal folder, you can't select which records you import. The duplicate options are designed to deal with three possible scenarios:

- If you haven't entered any data in Outlook, or if all the information in the imported file is more correct than the Outlook information, choose Replace Duplicates with Items Imported.

- If you've already entered some data into Outlook and kept them up-to-date, you may have correct information in both Outlook and the imported file. For example, if you're importing contact information, Outlook may have Jane Smith's new e-mail address at work, but her home phone number is only in the file you want to import. In this case, choose Allow Duplicates to Be Created. All the contacts in the import file are added to the existing contacts in Outlook. You'll have to check the information in both of Jane Smith's Contact forms, copy either the e-mail address or the home phone number to one of the two forms, and delete the other.

- If the information in Outlook is the most recent information for each contact, choose Do Not Import Duplicate Items. If a contact already exists in Outlook, it won't be imported from the other file. Only data that are missing in Outlook will be added.

**TIP** If you want to import information into a separate folder before mixing it with your data, create the folder before starting the Import and Export Wizard.

You can invest a lot of time opening contacts and copying and pasting information between forms. Often it's easier to decide whether Outlook or the import file has the best, most recent data. Print the other file and manually update the individual records in the best data set with information from the other file. This gives you one excellent data set. If the best data is in Outlook, select Do Not Import Duplicate Items in the Import and Export Wizard. If the best data is in the file you're importing, select Replace Duplicates with Items Imported. Remember, you don't need to worry about items that only appear in Outlook *or* the import file—you only have to alter items that appear in *both* files.

**TIP** When you import and export Outlook items, you can apply filters to the process. For example, you can import only the business contacts from one of your colleagues so you don't have to re-create the contacts. See "Importing an Archive File" later in this chapter for an illustration of importing filtered data.

In the last step of the Import and Export Wizard, select the types of data you wish to import. The Schedule+ file in Figure 14.4 includes Contacts, Tasks, and Appointments. If you know that your Outlook 2000 Calendar is current, turn off the check box so you don't import the appointments.

Extending Outlook

**FIGURE 14.4**

*Select the types of data you want to import.*

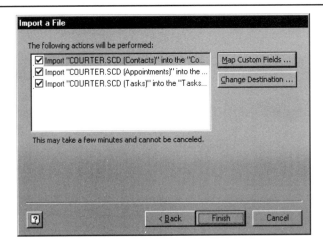

Check to make sure that the data you're importing is going to the correct location: contacts to the Contacts folder, tasks into the Tasks folder. If you want to see, for example, where the Schedule+ contacts will go, select Contacts in the action list and then click the Change Destination button to open the Select a Folder dialog box.

Outlook will place the contacts in the selected folder. If this is incorrect, choose a different folder before clicking OK to close the Select a Folder dialog box and return to the Wizard.

You know where the imported data are going; now you can find out where each field in a contact will be placed in Outlook. Click the Map Custom Fields button to open the Map Custom Fields dialog box, shown in Figure 14.5. The left pane of the dialog box shows the field names and a sample record from the data file being imported. The right pane of the dialog box shows fields in Outlook and the name of the imported field that will be used to fill the Outlook field. For example, the Name field from Schedule+ will be used to fill the Name field in Outlook. Click the plus sign in front of the Name field, and it will expand to show the components of the field. If you're not familiar with the contact shown in the sample record, use the Previous or Next button to move to another record in the import file.

**FIGURE 14.5**

*Use the Map Custom Fields dialog box to assign imported fields to Outlook Contact fields.*

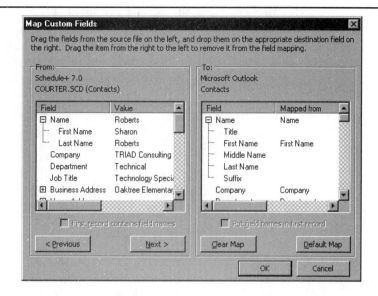

While Outlook was going to import Name to Name, it hadn't assigned Last Name to the Last Name field. To make sure that the parts of the name are imported correctly, you need to map this field. To map a field, drag the field name from the left pane and place it next to the correct Outlook field in the right pane, as shown in Figure 14.6. After you've made sure all the fields are mapped correctly, click OK to close the Map Custom Fields dialog box.

**FIGURE 14.6**

*Use drag and drop to manually map fields from the import file.*

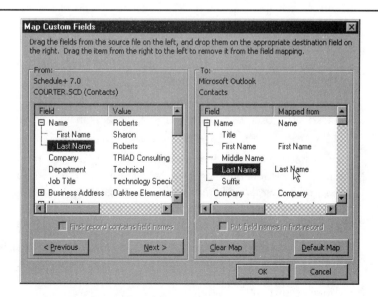

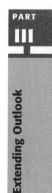

Extending Outlook

Now click Finish to import the data from the import file and create new Outlook items. While Outlook converts the data, a message box appears to show you Outlook's progress. You can't cancel the import, but don't worry, it doesn't take long. You can import hundreds of records in two or three minutes. When Outlook is finished importing records, the dialog box disappears. Your data is now available for you to use in Outlook.

## MASTERING TROUBLESHOOTING

### Tips for Importing Contacts

When Outlook maps the import file, it looks for field names that are similar to those used in Outlook: Name, Address, Department, and so on. If you can change the field names in the import file, you won't need to spend as much time mapping custom fields.

Combined fields don't import well. For example, if the import file lists first and last name in a single field and middle initial in a second field, you'll need to separate the first and last names into two fields in the import table before you can import the data.

If most of the fields are mapped incorrectly, it's easier to begin mapping from scratch. Click the Clear Map button in the Map Custom Fields dialog box to start with a fresh map in the right pane.

You can use the four extra fields for imported data that don't have corresponding Outlook fields. User 1, User 2, User 3, and User 4 appear at the bottom of the list in the right pane of the Map Custom Fields dialog box.

If you have fields you don't want to import, you can either remove them from the import file before importing, or remove them from the map. To remove a field from the map, drag the Mapped From value in the right pane and drop it anywhere in the left pane. Only mapped fields are imported.

If you make a mistake mapping fields and want to start over again, click the Default Map button in the dialog box to return to the map that was displayed when you opened the Map Custom Fields dialog box.

# Importing an Archive File

In Chapter 13, you learned how to archive your data using AutoArchive. Importing the archive file is one of the methods for retrieving archived data.

Before you start the Import and Export Wizard, decide where you want the data to be stored. You can import it into your existing folders and choose whether to overwrite the data, or you can create a new folder to house the imported data. If you plan to use a new folder, create the folder before starting the Wizard. To import your archive file, follow these steps:

1. Choose File ➤ Import and Export.

2. Select Import from Another Program or File and click Next.

3. Select Personal Folder File (`.pst`) and click Next.

4. Enter the path to the archive file, or click Browse to locate it.

5. Choose one of the three duplicates options: replace duplicates, allow duplicates, do not import duplicates. Click Next.

6. Select the folder to import from (see Figure 14.7). Choose Archive Folders to import all the data, or a subfolder to only import part of it.

7. Clear the Include Subfolders check box if you only want to import the parent folder.

8. Choose whether to import items into the current folder (whatever folder was selected when you started the Wizard) or to retain the folder structure in your personal information store or other available folders.

9. If you want to apply a filter to the data, click Filter to open the Filter dialog box (see Chapter 11 for more about applying filters). Click OK to return to the Wizard. Click Finish to import the file.

**FIGURE 14.7**

*Select the folder and subfolders you want to import and where you want to store the imported data.*

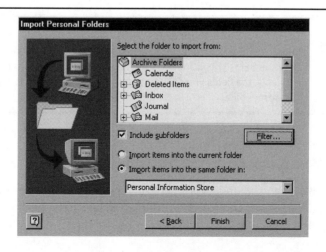

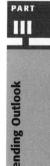

PART

**III**

Extending Outlook

# Exporting Outlook Items to Other Programs

It doesn't take long before you come to rely on Outlook as your primary data source for all kinds of information. If you have to create a report about your activities, conduct an analysis of your time, or use a list of contacts in a spreadsheet you're creating, it makes sense to export the data out of Outlook rather than re-creating it in another application. The Import and Export Wizard works as easily copying data from Outlook as it does bringing it in from other sources.

To export data, follow these steps:

1. Choose File ➤ Import and Export.

2. Select the type of file you want to create, including comma- and tab-separated values, dBASE, Access, Excel, and FoxPro databases, or a personal folder file. Click Next.

3. Choose the folder you want to export. You can only export one parent or sub-folder at a time (unless you are exporting a Personal Folder File; see "Backing Up Your Outlook Files" in the next section). Click Next.

4. Enter the name of the file that is created by the exported data. Click Browse to open a dialog box to help you locate the folder and enter a filename. Click OK to close the dialog box and Next to move to the next step of the Wizard.

5. Click Map Custom Fields to make sure that the data is mapped correctly (refer to "Importing Outlook Items" earlier in this chapter for more about mapping). If the incorrect fields appear in the To column, click Default Map to replicate all the fields in the From column.

6. Click OK to close the Map Custom Fields dialog box, and click Finish to export the file.

 **TIP** To create database tables or spreadsheets that only contain some of the fields in the folder you are exporting, open the Map Custom Fields dialog box and click Clear Fields. Drag the fields you want from the From column to the To column. When you export the data only, the fields you select will appear in the table that gets created in the database or spreadsheet file.

## Backing Up Your Outlook Files

Backing up your data is an essential part of using Outlook successfully. You can do it the hard way and search your drives to locate the .pst files that house your Outlook data, or you can do it easily by using the Export Wizard to create a copy of your data.

Although it's a good idea to know where your personal information files are stored, it's not essential to using the Export Wizard. Follow these steps to create a backup of your Outlook data:

1. Choose File ➤ Import and Export.

2. Select Personal Folder File (.pst) from the list of file types. Click Next.

3. Enter the path and filename of your backup file. (You can store the backup file anywhere you want, but, for ultimate safety, choose a different drive from where your active .pst file is stored.) Click Finish.

If you have a lot of data in Outlook, it may take a while to create the backup file. Outlook uses significant system resources to create the file, so you may want to take a break for a few minutes to let the process finish successfully.

 **NOTE** You may also want to create a copy of your Outlook address book. This file, called mailbox.pab, will probably be found in your Windows folder. Make a copy of the file to the same path you used to export your .pst file.

# Creating High Volume Mailings with Outlook Data

If you're responsible for sending out newsletters or any type of group mailings, you may be used to creating a mailing list in Word or Excel for one group of people and then creating a completely new list for a separate mailing to a different group. If any people cross over both lists, their information has to be repeated in each list. With Outlook, you can import all of these lists into one Contacts folder, and then use filters to select the specific contacts you want to include in a particular mailing.

## Using Mail Merge with Outlook

Outlook does not have its own capacity for creating mail merge documents. It doesn't need to because of its integration with the other Office applications. You can create labels and other main documents in Word. If you need to use only the standard name, address, and phone number fields in a selected Contacts folder, Microsoft Office's Dynamic Data Exchange (DDE) features can link the Word document to the Outlook Contacts folder to create the final merge document. If you need information not in the standard Contacts fields, such as the fields found on a contact's Details page, then you must export the contacts (see "Exporting Outlook Contacts" later in this chapter). Using either option, you can create filters to select only those records that you want to use in the mail merge.

To create a merge using Outlook data, switch to Word and start the Mail Merge Helper by choosing Tools ➤ Mail Merge from the Word menu. (If you're going to use a previously created main document, open it before starting the Mail Merge Helper.) Click the Create button and select the type of main document you are going to create: form letter, mailing label, envelope, or catalog. You'll be asked whether you want to use the currently open document or switch to a new window. If you're creating a new main document and you don't have an existing document open, choosing the currently open (blank) document is fine. Switch to a new window only if the open document is unrelated to the merge you are about to create.

Click the Get Data button and choose Use Address Book. When the Use Address Book dialog box opens, shown in Figure 14.8, select Outlook Address Book from the list and click OK.

**FIGURE 14.8**

*Select Outlook Address Book from the list of available address books.*

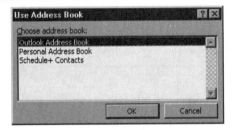

If you have more than one Contacts folder, select the Contacts folder you wish to use.

 **NOTE** Outlook does not have to be open for Word to find the Contacts folder. However, if you have multiple profiles on your machine, it will prompt you for your profile so it can connect to the right Contacts folder.

Word will convert the contacts in the Contacts folder for use in Word. If you are creating a new main document, you'll receive a message telling you that Word found no merge fields in your document and prompting you to add them to the main document. Click OK, and then click the Edit Main Document button to add them.

You are now ready to add Outlook fields to your main document. Enter any nonvariable text into the main document. To add fields to the document, position the insertion point where you want the merge field and click the Insert Merge Field button on the Mail Merge toolbar.

 **NOTE** If the Mail Merge toolbar is not visible, choose View ➤ Toolbars and select Mail Merge.

Select the field you want to insert. Position the insertion point again and repeat the process to insert additional merge fields, as shown in Figure 14.9. After you have inserted all the merge fields you want, save the main document.

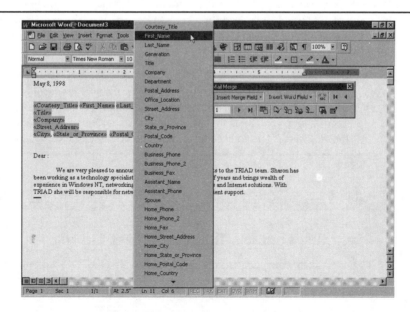

**PART**

**III**

Extending Outlook

You can test the merge by clicking the View Merged Data button on the Mail Merge toolbar. Use the navigation buttons to scroll through the records.

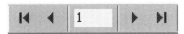

To select records that meet specific criteria, click the Mail Merge Helper button on the Mail Merge toolbar and choose Query Options. Enter your filter and sort criteria here before you complete the actual merge.

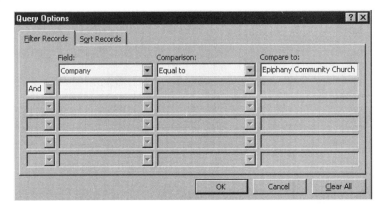

  After you are satisfied that the merge will be successful, click the Merge button on the Mail Merge Helper and then click Merge again in the Merge dialog box, or click the Merge to New Document or Merge to Printer buttons on the Mail Merge toolbar.

---

 **TIP** If you would like to tweak the contents of any of the records without it affecting the original data in Outlook, click the Edit Data Source button on the Mail Merge toolbar. This opens a form containing the merge fields and the Outlook data. Any changes you make in the data here is temporary and will not be reflected in the Outlook Contacts folder.

---

 **MASTERING THE OPPORTUNITIES**

## Selecting Contacts That Don't Meet Criteria

At some point you'll want to merge contacts with a main document, but the contacts may not all meet specifiable criteria. Suppose, for example, that it's time to send thank you letters out to people who volunteered to work on a special community improvement project. They are not all from one department and don't have anything else in common.

*Continued*

You can manually select the records you want to merge by copying the contacts into a new Contacts folder.

**1.** In Outlook, choose File ➤ New ➤ Folder.

**2.** Enter a name for the folder.

**3.** In the Folder Contains box, choose Contacts.

**4.** Choose a location for the folder in the Make This Folder a Subfolder Of control.

After you've created the folder, open your original Contacts folder. Select the contacts you wish to place in the new folder, and use drag and drop (holding Ctrl) to copy them to the new folder. When all the contacts have been copied to the new folder, you have a new data source that you can access directly from Word (as long as you require only the standard address and phone number fields. If you require other fields in your data source, you need to export the contacts). After the merge is complete, you can delete the Outlook folder so each contact only has one Outlook record.

## Exporting Outlook Contacts

If you need to use fields that are not part of the standard Outlook address book fields, you need to export the Outlook data to a file before using it to merge with a Word main document. Select the Contacts folder that contains the items you want to export, and then choose File ➤ Import and Export. Outlook will launch the Import and Export Wizard discussed earlier in this chapter. In the first step of the Wizard, choose Export to a File. In the second step, choose the folder that contains the contact items you wish to export. This can be a personal folder or a public folder to which you have access.

Next, select the type of file you wish to create. Many of the file types listed work well as data sources, including Excel, Access, and the Personal Address Book. Word also handles the comma- and tab-separated values with ease, and both types create files that use a minimum of storage space.

You'll be prompted to name the exported file. Click the Browse button and select a location; then name the file before clicking Next. When the Export to a File dialog box opens, the action you have specified is selected. Unless you want Outlook to dump all the fields for each contact in the export file, click the Map Custom Fields button to open the Map Custom Fields dialog box, and select the fields you want to include (see "Importing Outlook Items" earlier in this chapter). If you want to export only a handful of fields, it's quickest to click the Clear Map button to empty the To pane, and then drag the fields you wish to export from the From pane. When you click the Default Map button, it restores the original map, which includes every possible field. When the fields in the To pane are exactly the ones that you wish to export, click OK to close the Map Custom Fields dialog box. Then click Finish to export the file.

PART

**III**

Extending Outlook

When you're ready to use the file you exported as a data source, open a main document or create a new main document in Word using the Mail Merge Helper. Click the Get Data button and choose Open Data Source. Locate the file you exported and merge as usual.

 **TIP** If you add custom fields to the Contacts form, you won't be able to use them in a merge. You can't export custom (user-defined) Contacts fields.

# Project and Team Management with Outlook

Although importing and exporting are fabulous ways to put your Outlook data to work for you, if you need to manage projects or teams of people, you can extend the power of Outlook to phenomenal proportions. Outlook is not only integrated with members of the immediate Microsoft Office family, it is also integrated with its newer cousins, Microsoft Project 98 and Team Manager 97. Microsoft Project is a comprehensive tool for managing complex projects, including resource allocation, budget management, and scheduling. Microsoft Team Manager is a tool for tracking assignments and the performance of individuals and teams working on projects and other tasks.

With Microsoft Project, Team Manager, and Outlook working together, you can monitor projects, assign tasks to team members, and receive status reports that automatically update the individual tasks. Here are a few of the benefits of using these products together:

- Project tasks can be assigned to team members directly from Project. When a team member accepts a task, it is added automatically to the team member's Outlook task list.

- Team members can update the project manager on their progress by sending TeamStatus reports directly from within Outlook. The report is sent by e-mail to the project manager and can be automatically generated by updating an Outlook task. A team member can also generate a report manually at their discretion or as requested by the project manager. Figure 14.10 shows an example of a TeamStatus report.

- Project managers can set the Outlook Journal to automatically track work on Microsoft Project files (see Chapter 10 for more information).

- Team members don't have to learn another software product to actively participate in updating a project. They can use Outlook to communicate all their reports while project managers and team managers regularly receive up-to-date data. Figure 14.11 shows an active team file in Microsoft Team Manager.

If you would like more information about these products, check out Microsoft Project 98 at http://www.microsoft.com/office/project/ and Team Manager at http://www.microsoft.com/office/teammanager/.

---

**FIGURE 14.10**

A TeamStatus report can be automatically or manually generated from within Outlook.

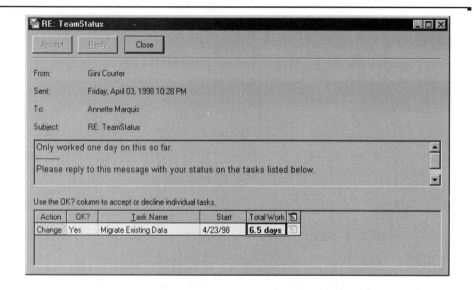

---

**FIGURE 14.11**

Team Manager tracks the activities of a team on the tasks identified as part of a project.

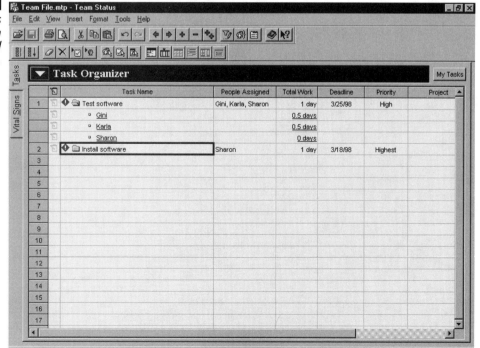

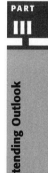

PART
III

Extending Outlook

**NOTE** Microsoft Project and Team Manager work with any MAPI-compliant e-mail system, so users in multiplatform environments can also benefit from sharing and updating project tasks and team assignments.

The ease with which you can move data in and out of Outlook through importing and exporting, mail merging, and sharing tasks and team assignments makes Outlook an indispensable office companion.

## What's Next

Not only does Outlook effectively share data with applications across local area networks (LANs), it allows you to share data around the world using the Internet. Chapter 15 looks at ways to extend your desktop to others through the online newsreader, HTML e-mail, and sharing contacts and calendars across the Internet.

# CHAPTER 15

# Outlook and the Web

**O**utlook 2000 continues the Microsoft Office tradition of supplying increasing levels of support for Internet tools and Web technologies. With Outlook, you can send Contacts and Calendar items and schedule online meetings in a format that crosses platforms and Personal Information Manager (PIM) products. As you increase your Internet use, Outlook's security features ensure that the Web remains a secure environment for all your messaging needs.

## Outlook and Internet Explorer

Outlook is part of the Internet Explorer (IE) family. When you install Outlook on Windows 95, setup checks to see if Internet Explorer is already on your system. If not, it adds it. If you were using Internet Explorer 3, it will be automatically upgraded. Do not remove Internet Explorer 4 from your computer—Outlook needs it.

When installing Outlook on a Windows 98 computer, setup checks the version of Internet Explorer 4.*x* you have (there are several incremental versions) and offers to install Internet Explorer 5. The installation of IE 5 simply updates all of the application files and doesn't touch any of your settings, favorites, or other modifications you have made to IE.

---

 **WARNING** If you choose to install IE 5 over IE 4 or another previous version, you may be in for a surprise when you first start it up. IE 5, just like IE 4, installs a small URL applet that only runs the very first time you start the application (C:\windows\system\runonce .exe). This applet takes you to a special Microsoft Web page. Don't worry, the next time you log on to the Net, your old home page will appear.

---

This doesn't mean you have to use Internet Explorer as your browser, but if you don't, Internet Explorer will nag you about it when it gets the chance. For example, let's say you use Netscape Navigator as your default browser. If you launch Internet Explorer, it will remind you that you leave it alone too often by asking you to select *it* as your default Web browser.

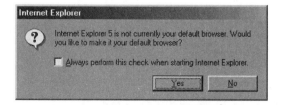

Clear the check box and you won't see this message again.

**TIP** If you're a system administrator or application developer, you'll be interested in another benefit of this integration—Outlook's support for Microsoft's Internet Explorer Administration Kit (IEAK). The kit, which you can download for free from the Microsoft Web site, can be used to automatically configure and upgrade workstation settings in Internet Explorer and Outlook over a network.

# Using the Outlook Newsreader

Another feature of Outlook is its support for the Network News Transport Protocol (NNTP), a standard for transmitting news on the Internet. Internet newsgroups are like bulletin boards where users post messages—called articles—and download and read articles posted by other users. Outlook's implementation of NNTP is Outlook Express, which provides all of Outlook's mail and news handling capabilities, and it can be used to access Internet Usenet groups and newsgroups on your company's intranet.

The first time you use the newsreader, you'll need to configure it. The Internet Connection Wizard will open, and you'll be prompted to enter your name, e-mail account, and the name of the NNTP server you'll use to access news. Contact your Internet service provider (ISP) for the name of their news server.

After you finish the Internet Connection Wizard, the newsreader prompts you to download the list of Usenet groups available through your server. You only need to do this once. The download takes a few minutes; the length of time is testimony to the tremendous number of Usenet and alternative newsgroups—over 36,000 were available at last count. So far, there are already 15,000 in this download alone.

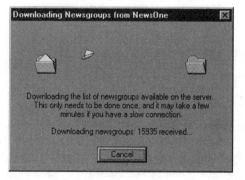

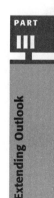

 **WARNING** The number of newsgroups you have available depends on your Internet service provider. In fact, some ISPs don't carry newsgroups at all. Check with your ISP to see if they carry newsgroups and how to access them.

Most users access a news server through their ISP. However, in a company setting, your Microsoft Exchange administrator can provide access to Internet newsgroups or create newsgroups on your network (intranet newsgroups). Figure 15.1 shows the Newsgroup dialog box with a list downloaded from the Internet. If you download the newsgroup list from an Exchange server, the list you see may be shorter and only include company newsgroups or traditional Usenet groups.

**FIGURE 15.1**

*The Newsgroup Subscriptions dialog box displays the newsgroups available from your server.*

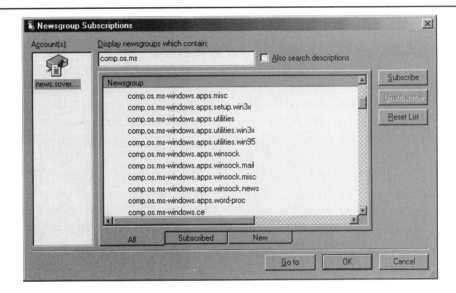

To find a newsgroup for a particular topic, enter text in the Display Newsgroups Which Contain text box. The newsreader filters the list to display groups with names that include the text string you entered.

## What's in a Name?

Traditional Usenet groups have a fixed naming structure. The group name begins with one of the seven Usenet categories: comp, news, rec, sci, soc, talk, or misc. Additional text in the name indicates an increased level of specialization: comp.mail is a newsgroup about computer mail services; comp.mail.mime is a discussion of mime encoding for computer mail. Members of the comp.mail group discussed and voted to create a more specialized Usenet group for MIME.

*Continued*

**CONTINUED**

Alternative groups, beginning with `alt` and other nontraditional categories, don't always follow this structure. Alt names are often more like friendly names, rather than being strictly hierarchical: `alt.this.is.a.test`. Humorous names abound in the alt groups. One of the first, familiar to fans of the Muppet Show, was `alt.swedish.chef.bork.bork.bork`, creating a kind of tradition for humorous naming where the final segment is repeated three times, for example, `hype.hype.hype`.

The groups with traditional names tend to be more long-lived; it took a group to create the subgroup. One individual can create a nontraditional Usenet group, so content often reflects the values of one person; in the nontraditional groups, there's something to offend everyone.

Finding the topic you're interested in can be difficult. Abbreviations are commonly used. If, for example, you enter **operating systems**, you won't find much. Enter **os**, and you're in the right area, but you'll see every name with "os," a common text string.

It helps to think categorically and look for the general heading that might contain the type of discussion you're looking for. A friend was looking for information on rotball, a type of offline baseball league, with no results. Entering **rot** brought up an extensive list, including an alt group on erotic relationships with collectible stuffed toys. Entering **fantasy**, the general category for fantasy baseball, provided an even steamier list, but she finally hit paydirt—`alt.fantasy.sports`.

To subscribe to a newsgroup, double-click the newsgroup name in the Newsgroup list, or select the name and click the Subscribe button. An icon appears next to the name, and it is copied to the Subscribed page of the dialog box. (Double-clicking a subscribed name removes your subscription.)

## Reading Newsgroup Postings

Once you have subscribed to the lists you wish to read, you may now read messages from and post new messages to these lists. Groups you subscribed to are indented underneath the friendly name of the newsreader. Double-click on a newsgroup name to begin downloading headers from the newsgroup, as shown in Figure 15.2.

To view an individual posting, select the posting to see it in the preview pane, as shown in Figure 15.3. Double-click the posting to open it in a separate window.

PART

**III**

Extending Outlook

**FIGURE 15.2**

*The news server and groups you've subscribed to are added to the folder view in the Outlook newsreader.*

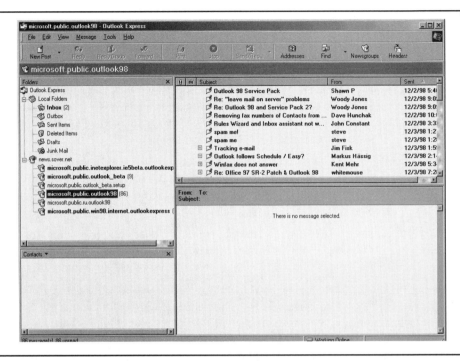

**FIGURE 15.3**

*Select a posting to preview or open it.*

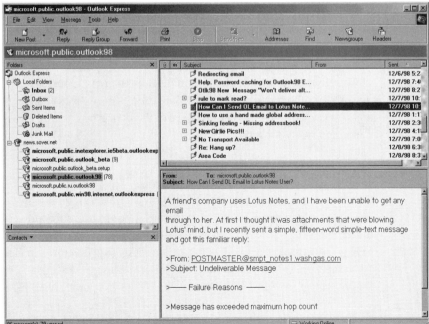

## Spam! Spam! Spam!@#!

If you've wondered what spam is, there's a quintessential example in Figure 15.3 (look at the fourth message from the bottom). Spam is an unwelcome, inappropriate message, advertisement, or other such mail, that is sent to a newsgroup or individual without their consent or prior request, and often without regard to who might read the message. Figure 15.3 shows a newsgroup about Outlook Express, and right there in the middle is a message advertising pornography that was sent to thousands of newsgroup readers. This didn't take a lot of effort on the part of the spammer; the messages were addressed with a spamming program: an electronic bulk mailer.

The message is irrelevant to this discussion; that's part of what makes it spam. If you really wanted to download stolen sex videos, you could find a newsgroup (several actually) to support this activity; you wouldn't need to find out about it in the middle of a newsgroup on Outlook Express.

Most netizens are agreed that spamming is beyond tacky, and there are several newsgroups dedicated to anti-spamming strategies. There are also several legal cases being fought. America Online recently won a large case against a commercial spammer and has provided its users with a number of options that can significantly reduce messages, either in e-mail or newsgroup posts, that are even remotely related to advertising, much less spam.

## Posting and Forwarding Messages

You can send a new post to the newsgroup, reply to all newsgroups that the selected message was addressed to, or reply to the individual who wrote the selected message. If you want to send the message to a mail recipient outside the newsgroup, you can forward the message. Click the appropriate button on the Newsreader toolbar to open a message form.

When you've finished composing your message, click the Post or Send button to post, send, or forward the message.

PART

**III**

Extending Outlook

**TIP** Outlook Express is filled with useful features. As with Outlook information services, you can configure the newsreader to retrieve messages or headers as you desire. You can filter newsgroup headers using the Newsgroup Filters dialog box, a stripped-down version of the Rules Wizard. For more information, choose Help ➢ Contents and Index on the Outlook newsreader menu.

# Exchanging Internet Business Cards

It's your first face-to-face meeting with a client or vendor, and the big question is: do you shake hands or swap business cards first? While you can't shake hands over the Net, you can swap virtual business cards, or vCards, even when you don't meet face-to-face.

The vCard standard, created by a computer industry group called the Versit Consortium, was developed to allow users of contact management systems to receive text, images, and other contact information over the Internet. When your recipient has a vCard-compliant contact manager, they don't have to reenter your name, phone numbers, and other information. They simply drag the vCard into their contact manager to add your contact information; vCards are even easier to use than business card scanners. A large number of contact managers support vCards, including ACT! (Symantec) and Lotus Organizer (Lotus Development Corporation), so recipients don't have to use Outlook to use the vCard you send them. The Internet directory service Four11 also supports vCards.

 **NOTE** For more information regarding the vCard and vCalendar initiative and the nonprofit standards organization that manages vCard and vCalendar, Internet Mail Consortium, visit their Web site: http://www.imc.org.

## Creating a vCard from a Contact

In Outlook, you create vCards from contact items. The contact's name is used as the vCard filename. vCards have the .vcf file extension and are stored by default in the Signature folder on your hard drive. You can attach a vCard file to a message or include a vCard file in an AutoSignature.

Follow these steps to create a vCard:

**1.** Select the contact you want to save as a vCard.

2. Choose File ➤ Save As from the menu bar, or right-click and choose Export to vCard File from the shortcut menu.

3. In the Save as Type drop-down list, choose vCard Files.

4. Select a location for the file.

5. Click Save.

## Adding a vCard to a Mail Message

Creating and adding vCards to messages is much faster and more accurate than looking up a contact and typing that information into a message form. A vCard is a fast and helpful response to many of the requests you'll receive in the course of a business day:

- What cleaning service does your company use?
- Can you recommend someone to analyze our data needs?
- How do I get in touch with the person who worked part-time for us last summer?

Sending a vCard note delivers the information in a way that's convenient for the recipient as well as for you. You can also add a vCard to a mail message:

1. In the body of the message, choose File ➤ Insert from the menu bar.

2. Locate and select the contact's vCard file.

3. Click OK to insert the vCard.

 **TIP** You don't have to create the vCard in advance. To forward a contact as a vCard, select the contact, and then choose Actions ➤ Forward as vCard from the Outlook menu. Outlook will open a message form, create the vCard file, and attach it to the message. The vCard file will not be saved separately.

## Creating an AutoSignature with a vCard

For contacts that you regularly forward, you should consider an AutoSignature that includes a vCard. (For more information on creating AutoSignatures, see Chapter 7.) An obvious candidate is your own vCard, so this is a good time to add yourself as an Outlook contact.

 **TIP** The plain text, HTML, and Outlook Rich Text editors support vCards, but WordMail does not. If you want to use vCards, don't choose Word as your e-mail editor.

To create an AutoSignature with a vCard:

1. Choose Tools ➤ Options from the Outlook menu bar to open the Options dialog box.

2. Click the Mail Format tab.

3. Click the Signature Picker button to open the Signature Picker dialog box.

4. Click the New button to create a new AutoSignature.

5. Enter options in the first page of the New Signature dialog box. Click Next.

6. In the Edit Signature dialog box, enter any text you wish to include in your AutoSignature.

7. Click the New Contact as vCard button to open the Select Contacts to Export dialog box.

8. Choose the contact whose vCard you want to add to the AutoSignature, and click the Add button.

9. Click OK to close the Select Contacts dialog box and return to the Edit Signature dialog box. Finish creating your AutoSignature, and then click Finish.

10. Close the Signature Picker dialog box.

11. To use this signature as your default, select it in the Signature drop-down list. Click OK to close the Options dialog box.

## Adding a vCard to Contacts

When you receive a vCard in a mail message, it looks a lot like it does when you send a vCard: a file with an attachment, as shown in Figure 15.4.

**FIGURE 15.4**

*This message includes a vCard.*

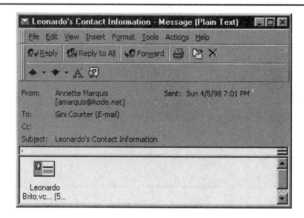

Drag the vCard from the message and drop it on a Contacts folder, as shown in Figure 15.5. Outlook will create and open the contact so you can add or correct any information. If you make changes or additions to the new contact, you'll be prompted to save the changes when you close the Contact form.

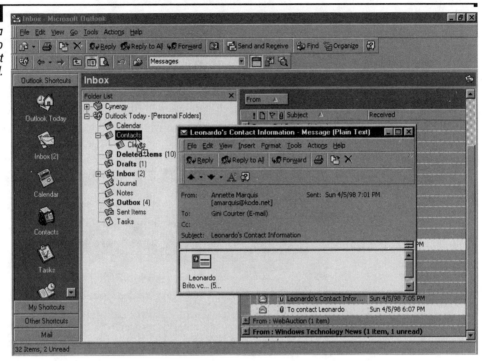

**FIGURE 15.5**

*Drop the vCard into a Contacts folder to create a new contact from the vCard.*

## Using vCalendar for Meeting Requests

vCalendar is another brainchild of the Versit Consortium. vCalendar supports both calendaring (creating a calendar) and scheduling (comparing calendars) on the Internet. As with vCard, the recipient of the meeting invitation can drag the meeting request directly into Outlook or any vCalendar-compliant PIM. Dropping the request in the Calendar creates a new Calendar item.

PART

**III**

Extending Outlook

**TIP** As stated previously, both vCard and vCalendar are part of Versit's Personal Data Interchange (PDI) technology. The Versit companies—Apple Computer, IBM, Lucent Technologies, and Siemens—transferred their rights to PDI to the Internet Mail Consortium (IMC) in 1996. Developers can download PDI software development kits from the IMC's Web site at `http://www.imc.org/pdi/pdiproddev.html`.

## Sending a vCalendar Meeting Request

Begin by creating the appointment or event request in Outlook. Choose Actions ➤ Forward as vCalendar from the Meeting menu, and Outlook opens a new message form with the vCalendar embedded, as shown in Figure 15.6.

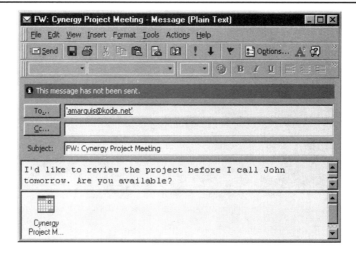

When your recipient gets the meeting request, they can drag it into their electronic calendar.

 **TIP** You can save any appointment as a vCalendar item. Select the item, and then choose File ➤ Save As and choose vCalendar format from the Save as Type drop-down list. You can import vCalendar and vCard files using the Import and Export Wizard.

# Holding Meetings on the Internet

Microsoft's NetMeeting online collaboration tool, included with Outlook, includes an entire toolkit for remote meetings:

- Chat, a text-based interface
- Whiteboard, for illustrating concepts
- NetMeeting Video, which lets you see other participants in their natural environment
- NetMeeting Audio, which lets you talk with other participants
- Sharing, which displays files in any open application
- Collaboration, which lets you work together on open files

You need a camera and video card in order to send video, but no extra hardware is required to see video sent by other participants. You'll need a sound card and speakers to use any of the audio capability of NetMeeting and a microphone to add your own voice to the discussion. But you can use NetMeeting even without video or audio. Meeting participants can work together on documents using Sharing and discuss them in a Chat window. NetMeeting was included with Internet Explorer 4, and a lot of people are comfortable using it to do group work when it isn't possible or convenient to gather at one location.

 **NOTE** If you didn't install NetMeeting with Outlook, you can download it from the Microsoft download site, `http://www.microsoft.com/msdownload/`. If you need more information about using NetMeeting after installing it, choose Help on the NetMeeting menu.

# Setting Up an Online Meeting

With Outlook, you can invite participants to an online meeting from the Calendar. In the Meeting Request form, enable the This Is an Online Meeting check box before sending the meeting request, as shown in Figure 15.7.

 **WARNING** If you send a meeting request over the Internet (even as a vCalendar item), This Is an Online Meeting gets turned off. Make sure you let Internet users know that it is an online meeting in the text of the message.

From the Appointment page of the Meeting Request form, as shown in Figure 15.8, select a Directory Server for the meeting from the drop-down list of servers. There is no charge for using these servers.

PART

III

Extending Outlook

**FIGURE 15.7**

Inviting attendees to an online meeting

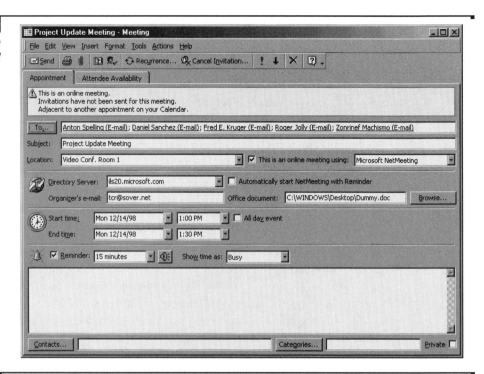

**FIGURE 15.8**

Setting the meeting location

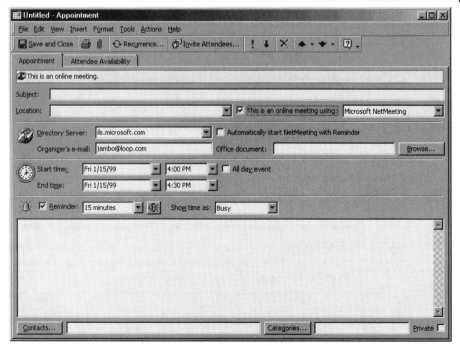

**NOTE** You can start an immediate NetMeeting with a contact. Select the contact, and then choose Actions ➤ Call Using NetMeeting from the Outlook menu bar.

If you haven't used NetMeeting before, the NetMeeting Wizard opens so that you can create a directory listing and test your sound card, speakers, and microphone. Work through the steps in the Wizard so you're prepared for the meeting.

Follow these steps to schedule an Online Meeting:

1. Open a new Meeting Request form.

2. Enter the meeting information on the Appointment page and enable the This Is an Online Meeting check box.

3. Enter the names of the invitees in the To, Cc, and Bcc text boxes.

4. Type the name of the meeting in the Subject text box.

5. Check the This Is an Online Meeting check box. The NetMeeting-specific section will be added to the Appointment tab.

6. Choose a server from the list, or specify one for the meeting.

7. Enable the Automatically Start NetMeeting with Reminder check box to have Outlook automatically start NetMeeting.

8. Click Save and Close.

9. If you have not previously used NetMeeting, the NetMeeting Wizard will open.

At the interval you set in the Reminder box, Outlook will remind you that you have a meeting, as shown in Figure 15.9. Choose Snooze to be reminded again in a few minutes. If you don't delay the reminder, be prepared for Outlook to fire up NetMeeting and connect to the server you selected.

PART

III

**FIGURE 15.9**

*Outlook reminds you that the online meeting is about to begin.*

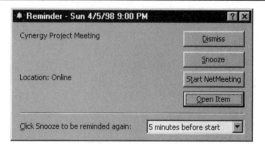

Extending Outlook

**MASTERING THE OPPORTUNITIES**

## Mastering Collaborative Work on the Internet

If you haven't used NetMeeting, the idea of holding a meeting on the Internet can be intimidating. When Internet workgroup tools first came out, only a few brave souls used them. Today, it isn't unusual for team members in separate cities to suggest meetings on the Internet as casually as they'd suggest a telephone conference call. It makes sense to practice ahead of time with a friend or colleague so you can participate smoothly in your first NetMeeting with clients or vendors.

Make a NetMeeting trial run as a product evaluation. You don't need additional hardware to give it a try. You can use Chat and the Whiteboard with the hardware required for Outlook. Once you've experienced a NetMeeting, you'll be able to evaluate its potential use in your business and decide whether you want to invest in video cameras, sound cards, microphones, and fast modems.

# Sharing Calendars on the Internet

When you need to schedule a meeting with other users on your Microsoft Exchange network, you can easily check their free/busy times. Microsoft and Lotus developed an Internet free/busy standard called iCalendar, which has been submitted to the Internet Engineering Task Force (IETF). Outlook was one of the first applications to support this emerging standard, although there are many others now. With iCalendar, you can post your free/busy time on a Web page, allowing other Internet users to schedule meetings with you more efficiently. In an Internet Only configuration, you must specify the Web page URL and update frequency. When you use the Meeting Planner in the Calendar, it checks the attendees' free/busy information. (In an Exchange Server setting, the location for iCalendars is set by your system administrator, and you choose how often the settings on the server should be updated.)

To publish your free/busy information on the Internet, choose Tools ➢ Options to open the Options dialog box. Click the Calendar Options button, and then click the Free/Busy Options button to open the Free/Busy Options dialog box, shown in Figure 15.10.

# Using Internet Security Features

The Internet is the modern equivalent of the Wild West, but with fewer marshals. No one polices the population, so there are scofflaws, criminals, and cutthroats sprinkled in with the law-abiding netizens. Fortunately, you can deputize Outlook to keep guttersnipes from invading your small portion of the Information Highway.

## Setting Warning Levels for Mail with Attachments

Plain old text can't contain viruses. For someone to send you a virus, either intentionally or accidentally, the virus code has to be included in a script, attachment, or link, either embedded in a document or sent as a freestanding program. Outlook can check incoming messages and warn you when they contain attachments or links that could potentially contain viruses. You can then choose to open the file, save it, or do neither if it is not from a trusted source.

Attachment security is an option. If you prefer, you can turn it off. Choose Tools ➣ Options to open the Options dialog box. On the Security page, shown in Figure 15.11, click the Attachment Security button to open the Attachment Security dialog box. Choose the security level you wish to employ, and click OK.

Attachment security is only a warning; Outlook cannot check files for viruses. You're fairly safe opening files created in Word, PowerPoint, and Excel if you have virus checking enabled in these applications, but Access and other applications do not check files before opening them. In addition to attachment security, you should have a good virus-checking program on your computer and download the virus update files regularly. You can find links to download evaluation copies of two antivirus programs on the Microsoft Web site (see Table 15.2 later in this chapter).

**PART**

**III**

**Extending Outlook**

**FIGURE 15.11**

*Set Outlook security options in the Options dialog box.*

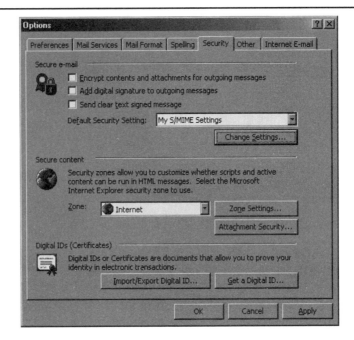

## Setting Security Zones for HTML Messages

HTML is a page description language, so HTML itself cannot contain viruses; however, embedded scripts and active content components can, often producing disastrous results. *Security zones* let you control the way incoming HTML messages and Web pages that you access in your browser interact with your computer. Security settings in Outlook affect Outlook Express and Internet Explorer. The four different security zones are:

**Local Intranet**   Sites on your local intranet (default: Medium security)

**Trusted Sites**   For messages and pages from Web sites that you are confident are well protected against viruses (default: Low security)

**Restricted Sites**   For sites and messages that do not inspire your confidence (default: High security)

**Internet**   Any site not placed in one of the other zones (default: Medium security)

You set security levels of High, Medium, Low, or Custom for each zone, and then add Web sites and HTML messages to a zone. For information on adding Web sites to zones, see Security in Internet Explorer Help.

To set security levels for the zones, open the Options dialog box and click the Security tab. On the Security page, click the Zone Settings button. You'll be reminded that these settings are used by different applications:

Click OK to open the Security dialog box, shown in Figure 15.12. Select a security zone by clicking on the appropriate zone icon, and its settings will be displayed below.

**FIGURE 15.12**

*Set security options for each zone, and then assign sites to the zones.*

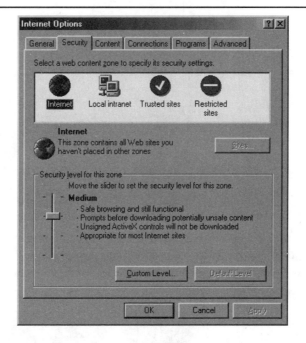

Choose High, Medium, or Low Security for the zone. With security set on High, potentially damaging content is summarily excluded. Potentially damaging content includes Java applets, scripts, and ActiveX components in Web pages and HTML messages. With Medium security, messages are checked for potentially damaging content, and you are warned before the message is opened so you can decide whether or not you want to proceed. With Low security, anything in the message is assumed to be safe.

PART

III

Extending Outlook

## Customizing Security for a Zone

The Custom security level allows you to pick and choose between potentially damaging items. Choose the security zone you want to create custom settings for, and then click the Custom Level button to set a custom security level. Click the Settings button to open the Security Settings dialog box, shown in Figure 15.13.

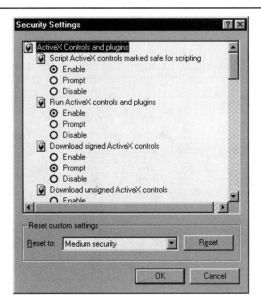

For most of the items listed in the scroll box, there are three choices: Enable, Prompt, and Disable. Enable executes the action for the item; Disable rejects the action. With Prompt, you're always prompted to allow or disallow the content. The messages are very specific, as shown here:

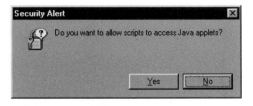

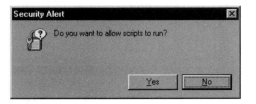

You might think, "Well, I'll just have Outlook and my browser prompt me about all active content." But on an active Web site, you'll receive frequent messages if you choose Prompt for too many settings. When browsing *Revealing Things*, the Smithsonian's first exhibit designed for the World Wide Web, prompting was incessant; as soon as we closed one message box, another opened. On the other hand, this is a great way to find out how each of the active elements in a good Web site was created.

 **TIP** *Revealing Things* can be found at http://www.si.edu/revealingthings/. If you're interested in what an incredibly well-implemented site looks like, check it out.

The list in the Security Settings dialog box includes both signed and unsigned active items. *Signed* means signed with a certificate. If you choose Prompt for Signed Items, the message box will let you know who digitally signed the item. For example, if you download an ActiveX component from the Microsoft Web site, the message box will indicate that the component is signed by Microsoft Corporation. Table 15.1 lists all of the security settings; some are only relevant in your browser, but you may want to change them while you're customizing the settings for messages.

**TABLE 15.1: SECURITY SETTINGS FOR ZONES**

| Action/File/Program/Download | Choices |
| --- | --- |
| Script ActiveX Controls Marked Safe for Scripting: allows scripting for controls that have been downloaded | Enable, Prompt, Disable |
| Run ActiveX Controls and Plug-Ins: run controls from your computer | Enable, Prompt, Disable |
| Download Signed ActiveX Controls: download new signed controls | Enable, Prompt, Disable |
| Download Unsigned ActiveX Controls: download new unsigned controls | Enable, Prompt, Disable |
| Initialize and Script ActiveX Controls Not Marked as Safe: allows scripting for downloaded controls | Enable, Prompt, Disable |
| Java Permissions: groups of settings for signed and unsigned content, including scripting and file size limitations | Custom, Low Safety, Medium Safety, High Safety, Disable Java |
| Active Scripting | Enable, Prompt, Disable |

PART

**III**

**Extending Outlook**

*Continued*

| TABLE 15.1: SECURITY SETTINGS FOR ZONES (CONTINUED) | |
| --- | --- |
| **Action/File/Program/Download** | **Choices** |
| Scripting of Java Applets | Enable, Prompt, Disable |
| File Download: with download enabled, you'll be prompted | Enable, Disable |
| Font Download | Enable, Prompt, Disable |
| User Authentication Logon: choose when you would like to be prompted for your name and password | Automatic Logon Only in Intranet Zone; Anonymous Logon; Prompt for Name and Password; Automatic Logon with Current Username and Password |
| Submit Non-Encrypted Form Data: allow or disallow submission of your personal data in a non-secured Web user form | Enable, Prompt, Disable |
| Installation of Desktop Items: from messages or a site | Enable, Prompt, Disable |
| Drag and Drop or Copy and Paste Files | Enable, Prompt, Disable |
| Software Channel Permissions | Low Safety, Medium Safety, High Safety |

Choose the security option for each item for the selected security zone. When you've finished tweaking security for the zone, click OK to close the Security Settings dialog box.

To reset the security for all zones, click the Reset button in the Security dialog box. To reset security settings for a specific zone, choose the zone, open the Security Settings dialog box, and click Reset.

 **NOTE** If you choose Custom for Java Permissions, a Java Custom Settings button appears at the bottom of the Security Settings dialog box. Clicking the button opens another dialog box to customize Java settings. Combinations of the Java settings form the Low Safety, Medium Safety, and High Safety choices in the Security Settings dialog box, just as combinations of the settings in the Security Settings dialog box create the High, Medium, and Low levels in the Security dialog box. If you're not a Java programmer, don't choose custom Java permissions.

## Obtaining a Digital ID to Secure Sent Messages

With a digital ID, you can open messages encrypted for your eyes only and add a digital signature to verify your messages to the recipients. This is the same type of certificate you trust to validate sites in the Security Settings. Digital IDs have two parts: the private key, stored on your PC, and the public key that you send to other people to validate your digital signature. You obtain your digital ID from a company that issues certificates, such as VeriSign. Your company's network administrator may also be able to issue your digital ID.

 **NOTE** Information on using your digital ID to encrypt and add digital signatures to messages is in Chapter 6.

Personal digital IDs are inexpensive; you can obtain a free 60-day trial ID from VeriSign; a full-featured one-year subscription is less than $10. To get a digital ID from VeriSign, go to the Security page of the Options dialog box and click the Get a Digital ID button. Outlook will launch your browser and open a digital ID information page on the Microsoft site.

Click the VeriSign Get Your ID Now button to go directly to the VeriSign Web site and obtain either a full-featured or trial ID.

 **TIP** To add a digital signature to all of your messages, choose Tools ➤ Options from the Outlook menu to open the Options dialog box, and then click the Security tab. Enable the Add Digital Signature to Outgoing Messages check box.

# Outlook Resources on the World Wide Web

Most of the Outlook resources on the Web are, not coincidentally, on the Microsoft Web site. The site has add-ins that you can download for no charge other than what you pay your ISP for connect time. Additional resources are posted on a regular basis, so we encourage you to browse the site regularly to see what's available. Choosing Help ➤ Office on the Web will take you to the Outlook users download area. Table 15.2 is a list of other pages that include resources for deploying, using, and customizing Outlook.

PART

III

Extending Outlook

**NOTE** Some of the sites that follow did not have updated information regarding Outlook 2000 by the time this book went to press. Just keep in mind that some of these resources are for Outlook 97/98; these sites may be updated to cover Outlook 2000.

**TABLE 15.2: OUTLOOK RESOURCES ON THE WEB**

| Site/Page | Resources |
|---|---|
| http://www.microsoft.com/office/org/office97.htm | Decision-making and deployment information for Outlook and Microsoft Exchange Server for large organizations |
| http://198.107.140.12/office/sbe/v2/demo/welcome.htm | Decision-making and deployment information for small businesses |
| http://www.microsoft.com/office/000/viewers.htm | File viewers and converters for all Office products; training and certification information including Outlook Expert User certification |
| http://officeupdate.microsoft.com/ | Microsoft Office Update page, with links to new Office Assistants, Office Sounds, and subscription to a monthly Office Update newsletter |
| http://www.microsoft.com/outlook/evalres.htm | Pre-implementation decision-making resources, including information on moving to Outlook from other mail services |
| http://www.microsoft.com/office/Outlook/outsolres.htm | Links to synchronization software (see Chapter 18), VeriSign, and third-party vendors, including virus-checking software |
| http://www.microsoft.com/exchange/guide/papers/collabsolutions.asp?A=2&B=6 | White paper on using Outlook with Exchange Server |
| http://www.mous.net | Facts about the Microsoft Outlook certification and Office User certification programs |

You can create custom applications in Outlook to meet the particular needs of your office or business. If you don't want to start your new applications from scratch, Microsoft has created several customized applications that you can download for free and further customize with the skills you'll learn in Chapters 20 through 25.

Microsoft is constantly adding new goodies to their new Office Update Web site at `http://officeupdate.microsoft.com/updates/updOutlook.htm`. Add it to your list of Favorites and check regularly to see what's new and exciting. These add-ons and information pages can significantly enhance your work with Outlook, allowing you to take advantage of new technology without having to buy additional software.

## What's Next

Sharing contacts and calendar events with people across the World Wide Web extends the value of Outlook beyond the confines of your office. Using Outlook between computers within your office makes it a powerful tool for managing your intraoffice communications. The next couple of chapters show you how to set up Outlook on a local area network using Microsoft Mail and Microsoft Exchange Server.

PART

III

Extending Outlook

# PART IV

# Configuring Outlook for Your Business

## *LEARN TO:*

- *Configure Microsoft Mail service*

- *Configure other mail services, such as CompuServe Mail and Lotus cc:Mail*

- *Set up a postoffice*

- *Create Microsoft Mail and Exchange shared folders*

- *Set permissions for users*

- *Set Outlook to work offline*

- *Synchronize offline folders*

- *Use Outlook with PDAs and CE devices*

# CHAPTER 16

# Setting Up Outlook for a Small Office or Home Office

The features and functionality you can access in Outlook depend on how Outlook is configured. This is the first of two chapters on configuring Outlook in a corporate or workgroup environment. In Chapter 17, you'll see Outlook at its best—acting as the client for Microsoft Exchange Server. But you don't have to run Microsoft Exchange to reap the benefits of Outlook's workgroup features. Any network allows you to share tasks and appointments with your coworkers, as you'll see in this chapter.

# Creating a Small Office Network

In the Internet Only configuration, Outlook acts as a stand-alone personal information manager. That's fine when you're the only person working in an office, but as soon as you hire an assistant or take on a partner, you'll want to be able to share information with your colleague.

If you don't have a network, you can still use many of Outlook's features over the Internet. The biggest problem with using an ISP for internal communications is that messages you send to your coworker in the next office can languish on your ISP's server for hours until your coworker dials up and retrieves them. It's more efficient to walk to the next office and say "Hey, Joe"—at least you know the message has been received.

With a simple network and Microsoft Mail, messages that originate in your office are delivered automatically, and quickly, to your colleagues. The smallest network you can create is a peer-to-peer network, connecting two PCs. A peer-to-peer network is suitable for up to 20 users, but you can start small.

For the cost of two network adapters (about $30 to $50 each), some twisted pair or ThinNet cable, and a few hours of your time configuring adapters and protocols, you can connect your computers and run a network mail service. The good news is, if you're running Windows 95 or 98 on your desktop, you already have a suitable network mail service: Microsoft Mail. So, for less than $200, you can build a small office network and take advantage of many of Outlook's Corporate/Workgroup features.

---

 **TIP**  You'll find help setting up a peer-to-peer network at the Microsoft Web site. Go to SupportOnline (http://support.microsoft.com/support/kb/articles/q152/5/62 .asp) to read article Q152562: *How to Use Windows 95 to Connect Computers on a Network.*

---

## Outlook on a Larger LAN

If you already have a network mail service, don't start downsizing. Outlook works with any MAPI-complaint mail server. MAPI (Messaging Application Programing Interface) is the messaging standard underlying products like Outlook and Microsoft Exchange. Outlook's Corporate/Workgroup configuration supports other popular network mail services, such as Lotus cc:Mail, OpenMail, and Lotus Notes. The Lotus cc:Mail driver is on the Outlook CD and is available at the Office Update Web site.

 **TIP** Office Update is a great resource for a lot of helpful things. You may note that we mention it a lot. Go to http://officeupdate.microsoft.com/welcome/outlook.htm for the latest and the greatest.

Outlook includes drivers for Microsoft Mail, CompuServe, and the Microsoft Network. Lotus cc:Mail and Microsoft Mail can only be configured in the Corporate/Workgroup configuration. The two Internet-based services can be added to either the Internet Only or the Corporate/Workgroup configuration.

Installation requirements for other mail services vary. For information on using Outlook with other services, contact your network administrator. If you are the network administrator, check with your mail service software company and/or the Microsoft Web site for information on installing your software.

# Adding Mail Services to Your Small Office Network

If you've just set up your network and are wondering what it would be like to be a postmaster, this is your chance. You, or someone in your workgroup, needs to install and manage your mail services. Microsoft Mail is easy to install:

1. Locate or create a shared folder to hold a postoffice file.
2. Set up the postoffice.
3. Create a mailbox for each user.
4. Add Microsoft Mail information services to the users' Outlook profile.

After you create and configure Microsoft Mail, users in your office can begin sending mail to each other without accessing the Internet.

**WARNING** This chapter assumes you are administering your network or workgroup. If you are not, do not add mail services to your network without contacting your system administrator.

Other users have to be able to access the postoffice file. Therefore, the file must be in a shared drive or a folder on a shared drive. The peer-to-peer architecture is a bit unusual; it doesn't have a central server and client workstations. Instead, any workstation can act as a server, client, or both. However, it's not a bad idea to have at least one workstation with a substantial hard drive that can hold the Microsoft Mail postoffice and shared mail folders for your network.

## Creating a Windows Shared Folder for the Postoffice

Network

The postoffice needs to be in a shared folder so users can access it. Before you can create a shared folder, you must enable sharing privileges on the computer that will hold the postoffice. Choose Start ➤ Control Panel to open the Control Panel, shown in Figure 16.1.

**FIGURE 16.1**

*Open the Control Panel to access Network and Postoffice programs.*

Double-click the Network icon to open the Network dialog box. Click the File and Print Sharing button to open the File and Print Sharing dialog box, shown in Figure 16.2.

**FIGURE 16.2**

*Before you can share
a folder, you must
enable sharing on
the workstation.*

Make sure the I Want to Be Able to Give Others Access to My Files check box is enabled. Click OK to close the dialog box; you may be prompted to insert your Windows CD or disks and to restart your computer. Click OK again to close the Network dialog box.

With sharing enabled, create a new folder on a drive that has some excess capacity. Create the folder in My Computer, the Windows Explorer, or Outlook. Then right-click on the folder and choose Sharing to open the folder's Sharing properties, shown in Figure 16.3.

**FIGURE 16.3**

*Sharing a folder for
the postoffice file*

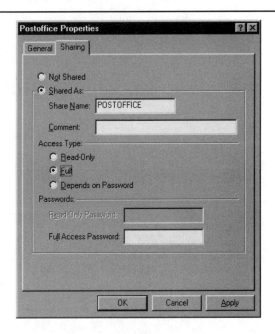

Choose the Shared As option, and enter a name for the folder that other users will see. Under Access Type, select Full; you can choose to assign a password, if you want to. (If you assign a password, network users will need to know what it is, so don't use a password you use for other access.) Click OK to share the folder and close the dialog box.

## Creating the Microsoft Mail Postoffice

To create the postoffice, open the Control Panel (Start ➤ Control Panel) and double-click the Microsoft Mail Postoffice icon to open the Microsoft Mail Postoffice Admin dialog box, which acts like a wizard. In the dialog box, indicate that you want to Create a New Workgroup Postoffice, as shown in Figure 16.4. When you need to administer the postoffice to create mailboxes for your users, you'll choose Administer an Existing Workgroup Postoffice.

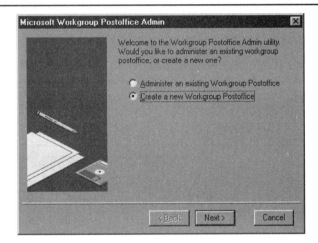

In the second step, shown in Figure 16.5, choose the shared folder as the location for the postoffice. Click the Browse button to open the Browse for Postoffice dialog box. Select the folder and click OK to close the Browse dialog box.

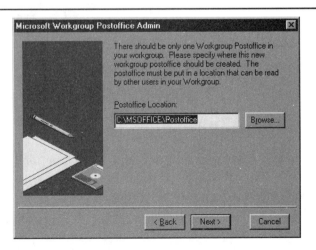

In the next step, Windows displays the path to the new postoffice file. You can't change the name of the file, so all you need to do is check to be sure the folder is correct. When you click Next, Windows opens the Enter Your Administrator Account Details dialog box, shown in Figure 16.6.

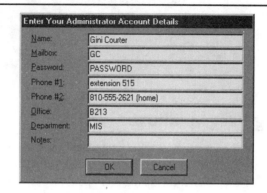

**FIGURE 16.6**

*Enter information about the postoffice administrator.*

Enter your name, a mailbox name, and a password in the appropriate text boxes. The text you enter in the Mailbox text box is the user's address for Microsoft Mail. You should use the same rules to create each mailbox name so that it's easy to figure out someone's mailbox name if you know their first and last name. Typical combinations include:

- first initial, last name: kbrowning
- last name, first initial: browningk
- either of these, plus a digit: kbrowning1 or browningk1
- four characters from each name: karlbrow

These last two combinations are often used in larger organizations or small family offices to provide a way to create different mailbox names for Mary Smith, Marc Smith, and Margaret Smith.

Don't follow this rule, however, for the Postoffice administrator mailbox. You'll want to create a separate mailbox for yourself to receive regular e-mail. The administrator mailbox is where other users will send mail about the postoffice. You could, for example, name this postoffice PostAdmin, postmaster, or just use your initials, as shown in Figure 16.6.

**WARNING**  Note the mailbox name and password that you create in this dialog box. If you forget the password, you won't be able to manage the postoffice and will have to delete this postoffice and create a new one.

As soon as you click OK on the administrator information, a Windows message box lets you know that the postoffice has been created and that the folder must be shared (which you knew already!).

## Creating User Mailboxes

The major task for the postoffice manager is adding and removing mailboxes for individual users. To add a mailbox, double-click the Microsoft Mail Postoffice icon in the Control Panel. When the dialog box opens (see Figure 16.4), select Administer an Existing Workgroup Postoffice, and click Next. You'll be prompted to confirm that Windows found the correct postoffice file; then enter the mailbox name and password that you set when you created the postoffice to open the Postoffice Manager dialog box, shown in Figure 16.7.

**FIGURE 16.7**

*Use the Postoffice Manager dialog box to set up new users.*

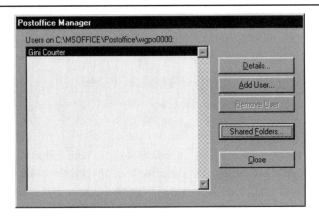

Click the Add User button to open the Add User dialog box and create a mailbox for a user. In this dialog box (shown in Figure 16.8), all that's required is the user's name, mailbox name, and the password. The phone number and office number text boxes are to help you manage the postoffice. If you need to locate the owner of the postoffice in a large organization, it helps to have some basic information.

**FIGURE 16.8**

*Add a mailbox for
each person who
needs internal e-mail.*

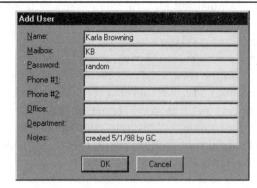

Click OK to add the new mailbox to the postoffice list. Continue creating mailboxes, one for each person who needs to receive e-mail in your office or workgroup. Keep a list of names, mailboxes, and passwords so you can let each person know their mailbox information. When you've created all the mailboxes, close the Postoffice Manager dialog box and the Control Panel.

**TIP** If several employees share a computer, give each employee their own mailbox, and then create a separate profile for each employee on the shared computer.

## Removing and Modifying Mailboxes

When someone leaves your workgroup or office, use the Postoffice Manager dialog box to remove their mailbox. Select the user's name (see Figure 16.7) and click the Remove User button. You will be prompted to confirm the deletion.

To modify mailbox information, double-click on the user's name in the Postoffice Manager to open the Edit Mailbox dialog box. You can change any of the information and view all information except the password. If a user forgets their password, you can delete the existing password and enter a new one. As the Postoffice administrator, you don't need to know the old password to assign a new one.

# Setting Up Workstations for Microsoft Mail

If you've gotten this far, congratulate yourself. You've created the infrastructure to support messaging on your network. There is at least one more step: every user's profile must include the Microsoft Mail information service before they can send messages to each other on your new mail service.

Your PC is a good place to begin. First, check to see how Outlook is configured. Select Tools ➤ Options ➤ Mail Services and click the Reconfigure Mail Support button. Look at the list in the resulting dialog box to see which configuration is active. To change configurations, just select another configuration, click OK, and read the warning window before commiting to the change.

After the Corporate/Workgroup configuration is installed, take a look at the information services in your profile. Choose Tools ➤ Services to open the Services dialog box, shown in Figure 16.9. If Microsoft Mail is already included as a service, you'll just have to configure it. If not, click Add, and then choose Microsoft Mail to add the service.

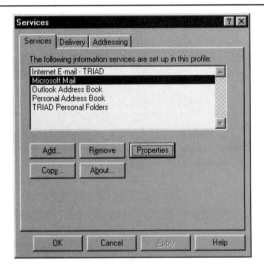

 **TIP** See Chapter 12 for help with information services and profiles.

## Configuring Microsoft Mail for Network Users

You can now connect to your postoffice and specify how Microsoft Mail should behave in this profile. If you're adding Microsoft Mail to the profile, the Microsoft Mail dialog box opens automatically. If Microsoft Mail was already included in the profile, select it in the Services dialog box (see Figure 16.9) and click the Properties button to open the Microsoft Mail dialog box, shown in Figure 16.10.

**FIGURE 16.10**

*Connecting the
user profile to the
postoffice.*

In the Connection page, enter, or browse to locate, the path to your postoffice. In the Select How This Service Should Connect at Startup option group, there are four choices. The two ways to connect are LAN and remote. Offline is the same as no connection. Select the option that describes how you will connect in the active profile:

**Automatically sense LAN or Remote**   For notebook users who are connected to the network when they are in the office and always dial up from remote locations. Additional hardware and configuration are required.

**Local Area Network (LAN)**   For desktop computers in the office. This is the option you'll be choosing for your network.

**Remote Using a Modem and Dial-Up Networking**   For remote users who never connect directly to the LAN; before you can enable this option, additional hardware and configuration are required.

**Offline**   For notebook users who will never be connected to the network.

You can create another profile if you need, or prefer, to use more than one connection option. For example, users who connect their laptops to the LAN in the office, but work offline at home, can have a LAN profile and an Offline profile.

 **TIP**   If the postoffice file isn't on your local hard drive, you may have to map the drive in Windows. Select the drive in the Network Neighborhood, right-click, and choose Map Network Drive.

On the Logon page, shown in Figure 16.11, enter your mailbox name and password. Users can enable the When Logging On, Automatically Enter Password option to store their mailbox password in Windows. Don't enable this now; the required login will help remind you (and your users) to change passwords.

**FIGURE 16.11**

*Identify your mailbox by name and password.*

On the Delivery page, shown in Figure 16.12, specify delivery and sending options for Microsoft Mail. To be able to send and receive mail, enable both of the check boxes at the top of the page. (If you just enable outgoing mail delivery, you can make people feel very lonely.)

Click the Address Types button to open the Address Types dialog box, shown in Figure 16.13. All the types of mail are automatically enabled for Microsoft Mail, but this probably is not what you want.

On a small network, users will often use other services for faxes and Internet mail. If you're only using Microsoft Mail for your workgroup mail, the only address type you want to select is Postoffice/Workgroup. If you select other types, mail won't be delivered. SMTP mail, for example, is Internet mail; your users will probably send Internet mail through an Internet information service. When you've deselected the services you aren't handling with Microsoft Mail, close the Address Types dialog box.

In the Check for New Mail Every *N* Minute(s) control (on the Delivery page shown in Figure 16.12), enter how frequently Outlook should check for mail on Microsoft Mail services. Users can always check more frequently in Outlook (Tools ➤ Check for

New Mail); this setting indicates the amount of time between automatic deliveries. The default setting is usually fine.

When the Immediate Notification check box is enabled, the recipient is notified when mail is delivered by whatever notification method they choose in the mail options—a sound, a little envelope in the taskbar, and/or a message box.

**FIGURE 16.12**

*Choose delivery and sending options on the Delivery page.*

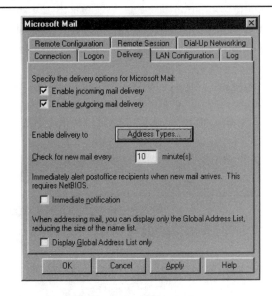

**FIGURE 16.13**

*Select the types of addresses Microsoft Mail should handle.*

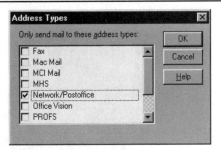

**NOTE** For immediate notification to work, you have to include NetBEUI, the enhanced Windows version of NetBIOS, as a protocol for your network. You may have done this when you installed your network adapter. See Windows Help for more information on NetBEUI.

The Microsoft Mail program included with Windows is the client side of a larger program called Microsoft Mail Server, so there are a few options that aren't relevant for the small network. The global address list is one of these options. Because there isn't a global address list in Microsoft Mail, it doesn't matter whether it's enabled or not.

With Microsoft Mail, users can specify different mail settings for use in the office and when dialing up to access their mail remotely. The LAN Configuration (see Figure 16.14) and Remote Configuration pages have exactly the same choices:

**Use Remote Mail**    When this setting is disabled, messages are delivered in their entirety. With Use Remote Mail enabled, users can download headers and determine which messages they want to receive. Turn this off in the LAN configuration.

**Use Local Copy**    This setting creates and uses a local copy of the Postoffice Address Book. The copy must be manually updated (synchronized) by the user. Turn this off in the LAN configuration.

**Use External Delivery Agent**    This option assumes a Microsoft Mail Server delivering Internet mail. Do not enable this check box.

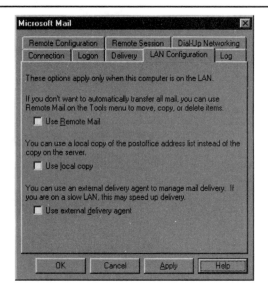

**FIGURE 16.14**

*On the LAN Configuration page, specify options for the workstation when connected to the network.*

You don't need to configure anything else for a PC on your network. Click OK to close the Microsoft Mail dialog box, and then close the Services dialog box. Exit and re-launch Outlook before you use Microsoft Mail for the first time. You'll be prompted to enter your password when you restart Outlook.

When Outlook opens, you may notice an addition in the Folder List, shown in Figure 16.15. Adding Microsoft Mail automatically added a new information store: the Microsoft Mail Shared Folders.

**FIGURE 16.15**

*A set of shared folders automatically created by Microsoft Mail*

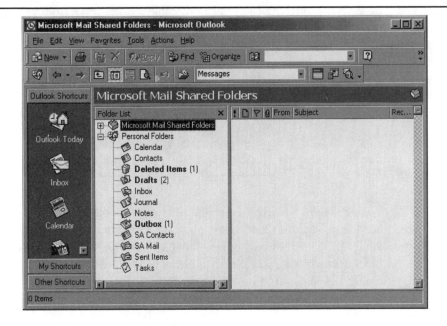

Here's a quick review of the steps to configure Microsoft Mail on a workstation:

1. Choose Tools ➤ Services on the Outlook menu bar to open the Services dialog box.

2. Select Microsoft Mail and click Properties to open the Microsoft Mail dialog box. If Microsoft Mail is not on the list, click Add, select it in the Add Services dialog box, and click OK.

3. On the Connection page, enter the path to the postoffice file. Choose the Local Area Network (LAN) connection option.

4. On the Logon page, enter the user's mailbox name and password.

5. On the Delivery page, enable outgoing and incoming mail. Set other options as you wish.

6. Click Address Types to open the Address Types dialog box. Disable all choices except Network/Postoffice. Click OK to close the dialog box.

7. On the LAN Configuration page, make sure all three check boxes are disabled.

8. Click OK to close the Microsoft Mail dialog box.

## Changing User Passwords

The first time the user starts Outlook with Microsoft Mail services enabled, they'll be prompted to enter their password as shown in Figure 16.16. Users should change the password for their mail account so that it is private—even from you.

*The user is prompted for a mailbox name and password.*

To change a password, open the Microsoft Mail dialog box by choosing Tools ➤ Services ➤ Microsoft Mail and clicking the Properties button. On the Logon page (see Figure 16.11), click the Change Mailbox Password button to open the Change Mailbox Password dialog box, shown in Figure 16.17. Enter the current password, and then enter a new password in the New Password and Verify New Password text boxes. Click OK to close the Change Mailbox Password dialog box.

*Entering a new password for your mailbox*

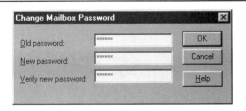

Microsoft Mail will confirm that the password has been changed. Once a user has created a private password, they can choose to save it with their other user configuration information by entering the password in the Password text box in the Logon page of the Microsoft Mail dialog box and enabling the When Logging On, Automatically Enter Password check box. Click OK to apply the changes and close the dialog box.

# Being a First-Class Postoffice Manager

There aren't a lot of duties for a Microsoft Mail postoffice manager. In some companies, this isn't a high-profile position; the manager knows they're doing a fine job when users don't complain. The postoffice manager generally does the following:

- Promptly creates mailboxes for new users
- Promptly deletes mailboxes when users leave the workgroup
- Ensures Microsoft Mail is configured properly at the workstation level
- Reminds new users to change their passwords
- Creates and manages shared folders for use by multiple users

As manager, you can also help your coworkers leverage the power of Microsoft Mail Shared Folders to enhance workgroup communications. To be a first-class postoffice manager, add one more task to your job description:

- Promotes the use of shared folders for flexible internal communications

This will, of course, give you more folders to manage, but the potential payoff is tremendous.

## Managing Microsoft Mail Shared Folders

When you create the Microsoft Mail postoffice and add users, the Microsoft Mail Shared Folders root folder is created. You can't place items in the root folder; it's just a container for the subfolders that you create for your users.

To create a subfolder, right-click on the Microsoft Mail Shared Folders and choose New Folder from the shortcut menu to open the Create New Folder dialog box, shown in Figure 16.18. Enter a name for the folder (24 characters or fewer), make sure Microsoft Mail Shared Folders is selected in the lower pane, and click OK to create the folder.

Outlook will ask if you want to add the folder to your shortcut bar. If you choose Yes, the folder will only be added to the Outlook bar on your desktop in your current profile. Users have to add the folders to the Outlook bar on their own workstations.

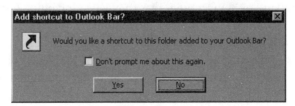

**FIGURE 16.18**

*Creating a new folder
for shared items*

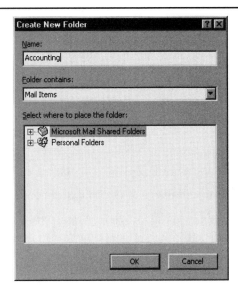

Create folders that will work in your organization. The company in Figure 16.19 has a folder for each functional area. Some folders include subfolders to further organize the items placed in the folders.

When you create a subfolder, you're the owner of the folder—the only person who can change the permissions for the folder. By default, other users have more limited rights. To view a folder's permissions, right-click on the folder and choose Properties to open the folder's Properties dialog box. You can't set permissions for individuals; on the Permissions page, shown in Figure 16.20, enable the permissions you'd like all users to have:

**Read**  Users can open and read items in the folders.

**Write**  Users can add items to the folders.

**Delete**  Users can permanently remove items from the folders.

Even though the folders are mail folders, users with Write permissions can place any kind of item in the folder they wish, including Post items, which are messages placed directly in a folder. Clicking the Post button on the toolbar or choosing File ➤ New ➤ Post in This Folder from the menu opens a post form, as shown in Figure 16.21. When the user clicks the Post button, the message is placed in the indicated folder, to be read and deleted according to the folder's permissions.

**FIGURE 16.19**

*Create shared folders for departments, teams, or functional areas of your workgroup or office.*

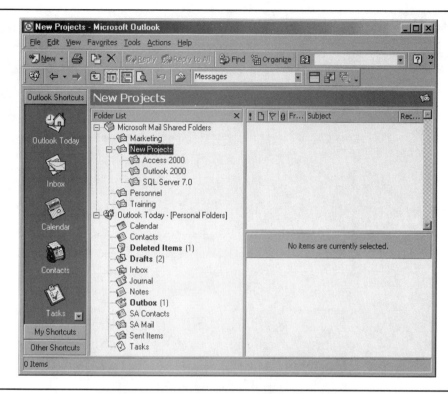

**FIGURE 16.20**

*Enabling or disabling user permissions for a shared folder*

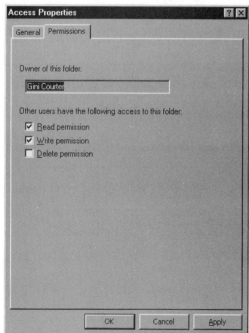

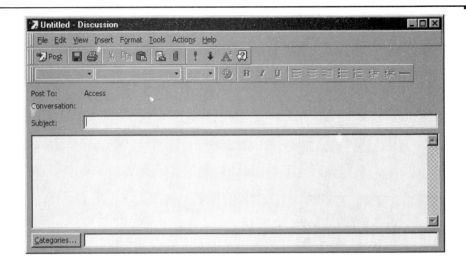

**FIGURE 16.21**

*A post form is a message, pre-addressed to a shared or public folder.*

By enabling and disabling permissions, you can create folders for a variety of uses. If you help other users create folders, you can give those users administrative access and they can manage their own shared folder, deleting items whose time value has expired or reading posts and messages. Useful combinations of permissions include:

**Read only**   A message board that only the owner can post items in. Each department could have a folder to post their fast-breaking news.

**Write only**   A suggestion box, where any Microsoft Mail user can leave a post, but only the owner can review the suggestions. Help your Quality Assurance manager or President create a feedback folder.

**Read and Write**   Conversation folders for discussions on various topics; common folders for messages that should be communally accessible.

**Read, Write, and Delete**   Department or team folders for items that need to be handled, then removed.

To recap, in order to set permissions for a shared folder, follow these steps:

**1.** Right-click on the folder in the Folder view.

**2.** Choose Properties from the shortcut menu.

**3.** Click the Permissions tab in the Properties dialog box.

**4.** Enable or disable Read, Write, and Delete permissions.

**5.** Click OK.

When items are deleted from folders, you can gain some space on the hard drive that holds the shared folders by compressing the folders. To view the current status of the shared folders, open the Control Panel and double-click the Microsoft Mail Postoffice icon to launch the Postoffice Manager. Log in, and then click the Shared Folders button to open the Shared Folders dialog box, shown in Figure 16.22.

**FIGURE 16.22**

*The Shared Folders dialog box shows you the space used and space available in the shared folders.*

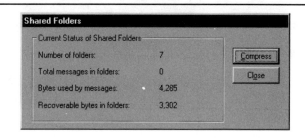

The dialog box shows you the number of folders and the total bytes used by all shared folders. Monitor this on a periodic basis. When you want to compress shared folders, follow these steps:

1. Open the Control Panel.
2. Double-click the Microsoft Mail Postoffice icon.
3. Choose Administer an Existing Workgroup Postoffice. Click Next.
4. Specify or verify your postoffice file location. Click Next.
5. Enter your mailbox name and password. Click Next.
6. In the Postoffice Manager, click the Shared Folders button.
7. In the Shared Folders dialog box, click the Compress button.
8. Close the Shared Folders dialog box, the Postoffice Manager, and the Control Panel.

If you notice that the total bytes are increasing quickly, you can check individual folders to find out where the growth spurt is. It may be that the owner needs to delete or archive older items. To check the size of an individual folder, right-click on the folder and choose Properties. Click the Folder Size button to see a report on the folder and its sub-folders in the Folder Size dialog box, shown in Figure 16.23.

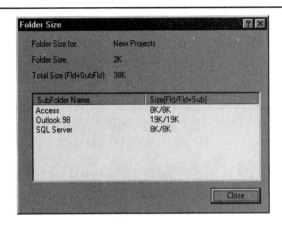

## Upsizing Your Network Mail Service

When you have more than 20 users on your peer-to-peer network, you need to start thinking about moving to a larger network and a more capable mail service. The obvious choice is Windows NT for networking software, with Microsoft Exchange for messaging. The move from Microsoft Mail to NT is relatively easy, and you can keep using your Microsoft Mail system within Exchange until you're satisfied with the way Microsoft Exchange is configured. When you are ready to switch over, Exchange will help you convert your Microsoft Mail system.

Outlook has a wealth of features geared for the mid-sized to large office or workgroup. For a preview of what you and your colleagues will be able to do in the Exchange environment, see Chapter 17.

**TIP** The move to NT and Exchange represents an additional commitment of financial resources for hardware and software (about $5,000) and human resources to install and maintain your network. When you're considering upsizing your network, there are online and print resources that can help. The Microsoft Web site has white papers that detail the total cost of implementing NT and Exchange: http://www.microsoft.com. *Mastering Microsoft NT Server* and *Mastering Microsoft Exchange Server*, both from Sybex, are thorough yet easy to understand, with all the information you need for the installation and configuration processes.

## What's Next

If you have the need for a larger network and a more capable mail service than Microsoft Mail can offer, Microsoft Exchange is a high-powered solution. Chapter 17 will help you configure Outlook to work with all the features of Microsoft Exchange.

# CHAPTER 17

# Setting Up Outlook as an Exchange Server Client

S tarting with Microsoft Exchange Server Version 5.5, Outlook took its place as the undisputed Exchange Server client application, leaving Microsoft Exchange Client and Microsoft Schedule+ in its wake. Outlook combines and significantly extends the features of both of these programs, making it a logical choice for any Exchange Server environment.

When using Outlook in an Exchange environment, you have access to many great features that other products don't offer. Although MS Mail and other similar mail servers provide access to some of these features, it takes an Exchange Server to experience Outlook at its fullest. As you might expect, most of the additional features available under Exchange have to do with messaging and collaboration—after all, the primary reason for a mail server is to improve office communications. Outlook's additional features fall into three general categories: messaging, scheduling, and sharing folders. Obviously, when you begin talking about sharing data, you also introduce concerns about security. Exchange Server offers some excellent controls to ensure that your data is secure and only available to those who have your permission to access it. In this chapter, you'll learn how to set up Outlook as an Exchange client, how to establish permissions, and how to use the application features that make Outlook an excellent Exchange Server client.

# Setting Up Outlook as a Microsoft Exchange Client

Before you can take advantage of the features of Exchange Server, it must be set up as a service in your user profile. To check to see if it's there, choose Tools ➤ Services. If Microsoft Exchange already appears in the list of services that make up your profile, select it from the list and click Properties to review the Microsoft Exchange Server properties. If it is not listed, click Add to open the Add Service to Profile dialog box, shown in Figure 17.1.

**FIGURE 17.1**

*Add additional services to your Outlook profile using the Add Service to Profile dialog box.*

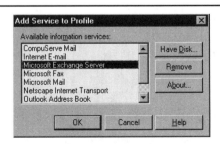

Select Microsoft Exchange Server from the list of available services and click OK. This opens the Microsoft Exchange Server properties sheet, shown in Figure 17.2. Enter the name of the Exchange Server and your mailbox name. Click Check Name to verify that the mailbox name is an active Exchange Server mailbox. Outlook will go out to the Exchange Server and check the name. If it finds it, the name will be underlined. If it doesn't find it, check the spelling of the name or check with the Exchange Server administrator to make sure the mailbox was set up correctly.

**FIGURE 17.2**

*Use the Microsoft
Exchange Server
properties sheet to
configure Exchange
Server for your
profile.*

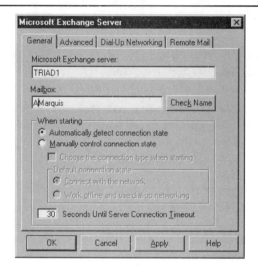

 **NOTE** Before a user can set up Microsoft Exchange Server as an Outlook service, they must have a mailbox on the Exchange Server network. If you are a system administrator and are new to Exchange Server, the Sybex book *Mastering Microsoft Exchange Server* can help you learn how to set up mailboxes and give users appropriate access rights.

Choose Automatically Detect Connection State if you want Outlook to check to see if you're connected to the Exchange Server computer each time you log in to Outlook. This is the preferred method if your computer is a stationary workstation on the network. If you're a mobile user and you'd like to manually control when Outlook checks to see if you are connected to the server, choose Manually Control Connection State. This choice activates a couple additional choices:

**Choose the Connection Type When Starting**    This choice opens a dialog box each time you start Outlook that lets you select whether you want to connect to the server or work offline:

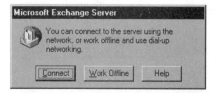

**Default Connection State**    This option sets a default connection state; you can either Connect with the Network (leave this as the default if you are on the network) or Work Offline and Use Dial-Up Networking. This setting determines which option Outlook will try first.

(To find out more about working offline with Exchange Server, see Chapter 18.)

The last option, *N* Seconds until Server Connection Timeout, tells Outlook how long to wait after attempting to connect with the Exchange Server.

Click the Advanced tab of the Exchange Server properties, shown in Figure 17.3, to set the following additional properties:

**Open These Additional Mailboxes**    If you can delegate access permission to other user mailboxes, you can choose to display those mailboxes with this option. Click Add to specify a mailbox to display. (You can find out more about delegating access later in this chapter.)

**WARNING**    The Add button on the Open These Additional Mailboxes option is not available if you select Work Offline and Use Dial-Up Networking or if your mailbox name was not verified by clicking Check Name on the General page.

**Encrypt Information**    Use this option to encode information you send over the internal network. When you are using dial-up networking, choose this option to encode information during transmission.

**Logon Network Security**    Your network administrator should tell you how to set this option. If you want to use the same network security password that you used when you logged in to NT, choose NT Password Authentication. Choosing None means that you'll be prompted for a password when you log in to Outlook.

**Enable Offline Use**    This option must be selected to set up Outlook to work offline. It also allows automatic offline synchronization. This button is not enabled until you create offline folders for remote access (see Chapter 18).

If you're going to be connected to the network the majority of the time, click the Dial-Up Networking tab and make sure that Do Not Dial, Use Existing Connection is selected. You don't have to worry about the properties on the Remote Mail page unless you're setting Outlook up to dial in to access mail (see Chapter 18 for more about Remote Mail). Close the properties dialog box and close Services. Your Exchange service is now set up.

**FIGURE 17.3**

*Open the Advanced
page to set additional
offline file folder
properties.*

# Messaging Features

One of the first differences you'll experience when you start working with Outlook as
an Exchange client is that you'll have access to an Exchange Server Global Address List,
such as the one shown in Figure 17.4.

This address list includes anyone who has a mailbox on the server. You can send
e-mail to anyone on this list and create distribution lists to make it easy to send messages to several people at once. Message features that are available in an Exchange environment include message-tracking options, such as read and delivery receipts, voting,
message recall, message flags, deferred delivery, and message expiration. These options,
shown in Figure 17.5, are found by clicking the Options button on a message form.

Message Tracking will report that your message was received and that the recipient
at least opened it on their machine. If you're looking for opinions about a job candidate or taking a poll of employees to find out how they like the new catering service,
Voting gives you the ability to send out a message that contains voting buttons. One
click and the vote is sent back to you (or to a designated recipient), and votes are automatically tabulated for your review. You'll know who voted and how (no secret ballots
here, folks), and you'll also be able to read any additional comments that voters chose
to include with their votes.

**FIGURE 17.4**

*Exchange Server gives you access to the Global Address list.*

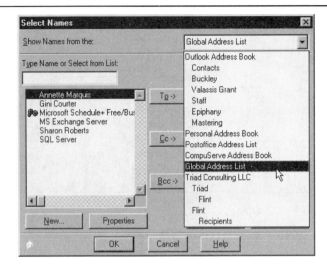

**FIGURE 17.5**

*Message tracking options are available to apply to your e-mail messages.*

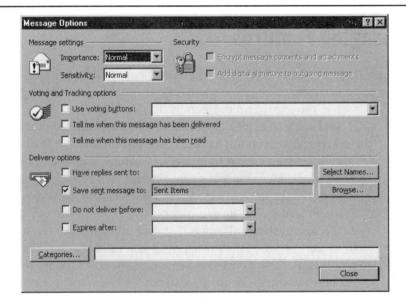

Have you ever changed your mind about that letter you sent to your manager? Or maybe you just learned that the information you sent was inaccurate. Message Recall lets you retrieve messages that you sent out and either dump them or re-send them with the revised information. The only restriction is that the recipient can't have already opened the message. Deferred Delivery lets you set the date that you want a message delivered, and Message Expiration sets a date when it expires if it hasn't been delivered. If you want to make sure you don't forget to follow up with a message that deserves attention, you can attach a message flag and set a reminder to make sure you don't let it fall through the cracks.

Microsoft Exchange Server also extends the power of Outlook with server-based Inbox rules. Using the Outlook Rules Wizard, you can establish rules that apply to e-mail on the server, so they work even when Outlook is not running on your computer. These powerful features make it easy to control how, when, and where your messages are delivered.

## Scheduling Features

Although you can send and receive meeting requests through Internet Only, MS Mail, or other mail servers, with Exchange you can access the free/busy information of other users on your network, as shown in Figure 17.6, so you can schedule a meeting with a reasonable certainty that key people can actually attend.

**FIGURE 17.6**

*When you arrange a meeting in Outlook, it can check the free/busy information of other attendees to see when they are available.*

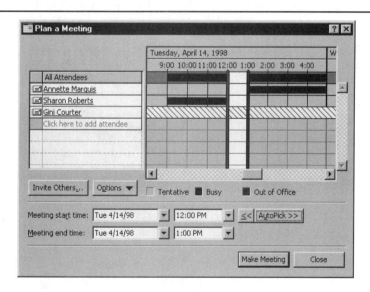

**TIP** With appropriate permissions, you can view the details of the free/busy information of other users. Right-click on another user's blue bar (indicating they are busy) on the Attendee Availability page of an Appointment or Meeting Request form. A ScreenTip will appear, showing you what they are busy doing at a particular time. See Chapter 9 for more about scheduling meetings using free/busy information.

# Sharing Folders

Being able to share a document with your colleagues for their input before it goes out to a client ensures that you make the best possible impression. Although there are a number of effective ways to share documents, one of the easiest is to set up public folders that anyone with the appropriate Exchange Server permissions can access. All you have to do is tell your associates which folder the document is in, and they can open it at their own workstation or even dial in and get it remotely. With Public Folders, you can share documents, folders, and Outlook items across a workgroup. You can also participate in online discussions with your team members or with individuals across the company. Figure 17.7 shows a typical Outlook/Exchanger Server folder structure.

**FIGURE 17.7**

*Exchange Server provides access to shared public folders.*

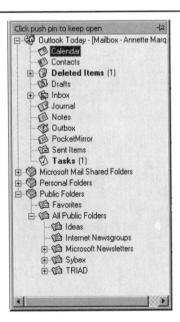

Open the Folder List in Outlook by clicking the Folder List button on the Advanced toolbar or by choosing View ➤ Folder List from the menu. You should see a folder called Public Folders. Double-click on this folder to expand Public Folders, displaying two additional folders: Favorites and All Public Folders.

A public folder is accessible to anyone on the network who has been given permission to access it by the folder's owner. Typically, the owner is the person who creates the folder, but they could also designate someone else to have owner permissions. You must be an owner to delete the folder and assign rights to other users. (For more about permissions, see "Setting Permissions for Others" later in this chapter.)

In All Public Folders, users can create new folders to share with others. These folders can contain files or Outlook components. You might create a shared Contacts folder or a shared Calendar in All Public Folders. Any information that you need to share with a group is appropriate to include in a public folder.

Favorites is a folder similar to your hard drive's Favorites folder. Drag the public folders that you use most often to the Favorites folder. If you are in a large organization, you'll appreciate not having to wade through a gigantic folder structure to find your frequently used public folders. Favorites are the only public folders you have available when you are working offline (see Chapter 18). If you plan to share Outlook items with other users who will be taking them on the road, copy the Outlook component to the Favorites folder.

**MASTERING THE OPPORTUNITIES**

## Making a Folder Do All the Work

If you are an Exchange Server administrator, you can make a folder visible to the Global Address list so others can send messages directly to the folder, using it like a bulletin board. Open the Exchange Server Properties of the folder and clear the Hide from Address Book check box on the Advanced tab. This folder can then become the foundation of a custom application—users can send messages on a custom form directly to the folder for team review. You can also apply Inbox rules to the messages so they are handled automatically (see Chapter 7 for more on applying Inbox rules). To find out more about custom applications, visit Microsoft's Web site, http://msdn.microsoft.com/developer/ news/feature/120197/exchange/outsolu.htm and download the paper *Building Solutions with Microsoft Exchange and Microsoft Outlook.*

## Creating Exchange Folders

Creating Exchange Folders is no different than creating folders for other Outlook items. Select All Public Folders or a folder in All Public Folders and right-click to open the shortcut menu. Choose New Folder, enter a name for the folder, and designate what kind of Outlook items you want the folder to contain, as shown in Figure 17.8.

**FIGURE 17.8**

*You can create a new public folder to hold Outlook items you want to share.*

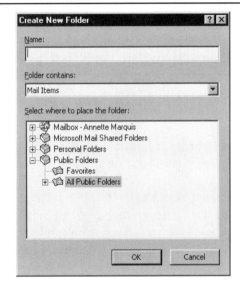

If you want to copy items from one of your folders to the new public folder, select the items, hold Ctrl, and drag them to the new folder. After you create a public folder, you can drag that folder to Favorites so you can access it easily. Any changes you make to the Favorites copy will also appear in the original folder.

**TIP** You can post an Office document to a public folder by opening the file in its native application. On the File menu, point to Send To, and then click Exchange Folder. In the folder list, double-click the folder you want to post the file to. Now anyone who has access to Public folders can share the posted document.

## Creating Online Discussion Groups

An online discussion group or bulletin board system is a public folder that contains threaded messages. Threaded messages are messages connected together by a conversation topic. Individuals can respond to any message in the topic and their response is related to the message they responded to. Figure 17.9 shows a public folder discussion group.

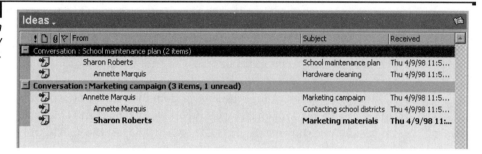

**FIGURE 17.9**

*A threaded discussion joins messages by conversation topic.*

To create a discussion-based folder, create a public folder and change the view on the folder to By Conversation Topic (View ➤ Current View). Instead of sending an e-mail message, users use New Post in This Folder to send messages to the folder. The subject of a new post becomes a conversation topic that others can respond to, as shown in Figure 17.10.

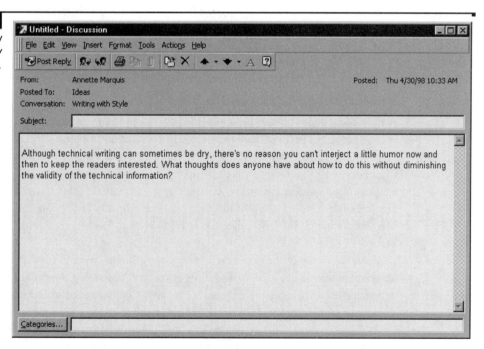

**FIGURE 17.10**

*Introduce a new conversation topic by creating a new post.*

**TIP** To change the opening view on the discussion folder, right-click on the folder and choose Properties. Change the Initial View to Group by Conversation Topic.

To reply to a posting, double-click the message you want to open and click Post Reply. If you are saving your sent messages to the Sent Items folder, you will receive a message that says you can't save sent items to a public folder and asks if you want to save the sent items to your Sent Items folder instead. Click Yes if you want to save your reply in your Sent Items folder.

Although you can change the subject from the original message in the thread, the conversation topic will not change. Enter the new subject and enter your message in the Discussion form shown in Figure 17.11. When you post the item, it will appear indented underneath the message you responded to. If other people respond to your message, it will indent even further under your message.

**FIGURE 17.11**

*Create a new subject in the same conversation.*

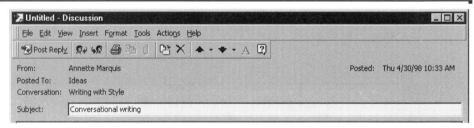

## Moderating a Discussion

A threaded discussion can be set up so that someone can moderate the discussion and review messages before they are posted. In a discussion open to the public, this may be desirable so you can maintain standards and avoid vulgarity and obscenity. In a discussion within a team or workgroup, a supervisor may moderate the discussion to make sure everyone stays on topic. To set up a moderated folder, right-click on the discussion folder and choose Properties. Click the Administration tab and choose Moderated Folder. Click the Set Folder Up as a Moderated Folder check box, as shown in Figure 17.12.

Enter the name of the person who will screen the messages in the Forward New Items To box. You have your choice of sending no response, sending a standard response to the sender, or creating a custom response. Choose Custom Response and click Template to create a custom message. Leave the To field blank and enter a subject and your message in the message box. Choose File ➢ Save and close the message. This message will now be sent out automatically to anyone who posts a message to the folder.

**FIGURE 17.12**

*The Moderated Folder properties let you designate a public folder as a moderated discussion group.*

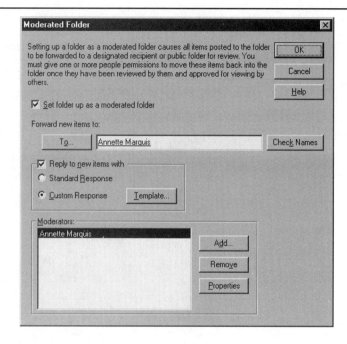

Click Add to add yourself or anyone else as a moderator. Only a moderator can move messages into the moderated folder. Click OK to save the Moderated Folder properties and OK again to close the Properties dialog box.

When a participant sends a message, the message goes to the designated Inbox. The moderator can then decide if the message is appropriate for posting. If it is, they can copy the message to the Public folder. If it is not, they can send a message back to the originator, indicating why the message won't be posted.

# Setting Permissions for Others

When folders become public, you need to be aware of who might have access to the information stored in the folders. By default, anyone who has access to public folders can:

- View folder contents
- Create and read items and files
- Modify and delete items that they create

If you want to limit these rights, you need to modify the permissions assigned to the folder.

To access folder permissions, right-click on the folder and choose Properties. Click the Administration tab and choose between This Folder Is Available to All Users with

Access Permission and Owners Only. The second option immediately limits access to only those users to whom you have granted the highest level of permissions. To adjust permissions individually, click the Permissions tab. This page is shown in Figure 17.13.

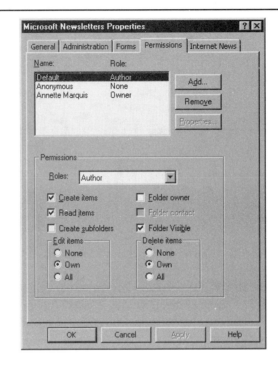

**FIGURE 17.13**

*On the Permissions page, you can assign individual permissions to users to access the folder.*

Before assigning permissions, it's important to have an understanding of the various roles you can assign.

**Owner**   The highest level of permissions; Owner grants all permissions in the folder. Owners can create, read, modify, delete all items and files, and create subfolders and change permission levels others have for the folder.

**Publishing Editor**   Grants permission to create, read, modify, and delete all items and files and create subfolders.

**Editor**   Grants permission to create, read, modify, and delete all items and files.

**Publishing Author**   Grants permission to create and read items and files, create subfolders, and modify and delete items and files the user creates.

**Author**   Grants permission to create and read items and files, and modify and delete items and files the user creates.

**Reviewer**   Grants permission to read items and files only.

**Contributor**   Grants permission to create items and files only. A contributor does not see the contents of the folder.

**Custom**   Lets the folder owner designate the activities a user can conduct. This option only appears in the Role field if you choose individual permissions from the check boxes below the Role box.

**None**   Grants no permission in the folder. Users can see the folder but cannot open it. Use this as the default permission when you want to limit the folder audience to users you specifically add to the Name/Role box.

When you create a public folder, three types of users are automatically created and the following roles assigned (see Figure 17.13):

- Default permissions (Author) are assigned to everyone unless designated otherwise.
- Anonymous permissions (None) are available to anyone with access to the public folders who does not have a mailbox on the system—for example, someone you've given Web access to.
- Owner permissions are given automatically to the creator of the folder.

To change the permissions for one of these three types of users, select the user and select the new role from the Roles drop-down list. To customize the role you assign, select from any of the check box choices: Create Items, Read Items, Create Subfolders, Edit Items, Folder Owner, Folder Contact, Folder Visible, and Delete Items.

If you want to assign permissions to individual users or a distribution list, click the Add button. This opens the typical address list dialog box. Select the users or distribution lists you want to add and click OK. By default, these new users will be given Author permissions. Select each user to change the permissions. When you have set all the permissions you want, click OK to apply the new permissions.

 **WARNING**   If you want to limit access to a folder to select individuals, be sure to change the default permissions to None.

With permissions established, if users try to access folders they don't have permission for, they will receive a stern message telling them to keep out:

> Unable to display the folder.  You do not have sufficient permission to perform this operation on this object.  See the folder contact or your system administrator.

The *folder contact* referred to in this message is the person who receives automated messages when there are problems with the folder, such as replication conflicts. It's also the person users contact to receive additional permissions. You can find out who the folder contact is by viewing the Permission properties for the folder.

# Assigning Delegates to Handle Your Work

If you work with an assistant or a team, you can make someone a delegate, which gives them permission to access your folders, send messages out in your name, and revise or modify items in your Outlook folders. You can assign various levels of permissions depending upon how much access you want the individual to have to your information.

To make someone a delegate, choose Tools ➤ Options and click the Delegate tab. Click Add to select the person or people you want to make your delegate. If you would like your delegate to receive your meeting requests and responses, click the Send Meeting Requests and Responses Only to My Delegates, Not to Me check box.

**NOTE**   If the Delegate tab is not visible, click Other ➤ Advanced Options and Add-In Manager. Select Delegate Access from the list of choices and click Install. Choose `Dlgsept.cgf` from the list of available add-ins and click Open. If this file does not appear in the list, you must install it by using the Outlook Setup program (see the appendix for information about installing add-ins).

To assign specific permissions to your delegates, select the delegate and click Permissions. You must grant individual permissions for each Outlook component, as shown in Figure 17.14. Delegates can be Reviewers, Authors, or Editors of your Outlook items. Select the appropriate permissions from the list next to each component. If you are granting someone delegate access to your Calendar, you can have any meeting-related messages copied automatically to your delegate.

*Grant permissions to delegates in each of the Outlook components.*

**Delegate Permissions: Gini Courter**

This delegate has the following permissions

| | | |
|---|---|---|
| Calendar | Editor (can read, create, and modify items) | ▼ |

☑ Delegate receives copies of meeting-related messages sent to me

| | | |
|---|---|---|
| Tasks | Editor (can read, create, and modify items) | ▼ |
| Inbox | None | ▼ |
| Contacts | None | ▼ |
| Notes | None | ▼ |
| Journal | None | ▼ |

☐ Automatically send a message to delegate summarizing these permissions

OK     Cancel

If you have been granted delegate access to someone else's folders, click File ➢ Open and choose Other User's Folder. Enter the name of the person whose folder you want to open, and select the folder you want to see. Click OK to open the folder in a separate window.

# Adding Another Person's Mailbox to Your User Profile

To add another person's mailbox to your user profile so you can access it quickly, the owner must first share the mailbox. To share a mailbox, set Reviewer permissions for the user you want to share with. After the mailbox is shared, the person with Reviewer permissions can add the mailbox to their profile, following these steps:

1. Click Inbox.

2. On the Tools menu, click Services.

3. Select Microsoft Exchange Server.

4. Click Properties, and then click the Advanced tab.

5. Click Add, and then type the mailbox name of the person whose mailbox you want to add to your user profile.

## Keeping Items Private

If you have granted someone delegate access to your Outlook folders, you can still keep items out of their view. Open the item and click the Private check box in the bottom-right corner of the item's form.

### MASTERING THE OPPORTUNITIES

## Choosing the Best Sharing Option

When you want to share your folders with other users, you have these three options:

- Share private folders by granting permission to others to read, modify, create, or delete information in your private folders.
- Grant Delegate Access to someone.
- Create public folders and grant users permissions to access them.

*Continued* ▯▶

> ◄ **MASTERING THE OPPORTUNITIES CONTINUED**
>
> Deciding which option to use depends on what you want to do and what level of control you want to grant. Share private folders if you want someone to have access to your task list or be able to see the details of your calendar. Grant Delegate Access if you have an assistant who helps you manage your e-mail and your schedule and you want them to be able to respond on your behalf. Create and share public folders if you are working with a group and want multiple users to be able to have access to the information contained in the folders. Public folders can be active within a workgroup or be available to the entire company.
>
> Each of these options allows you to share information with other users. Review the benefits of each option before deciding which one best fits your situation.

# Using Your Own Out of Office Assistant

If you receive tons of e-mail, one of the worst consequences of going on vacation is returning and dealing with all the people who didn't know you were gone. The Out of Office Assistant can handle those people for you, so you can return with everyone knowing it's going to be a few days before they hear from you. To access the Out of Office Assistant, shown in Figure 17.15, click the Inbox and choose Tools ➤ Out of Office Assistant.

**FIGURE 17.15**

*The Out of Office Assistant takes the burden out of returning to the office after some time away.*

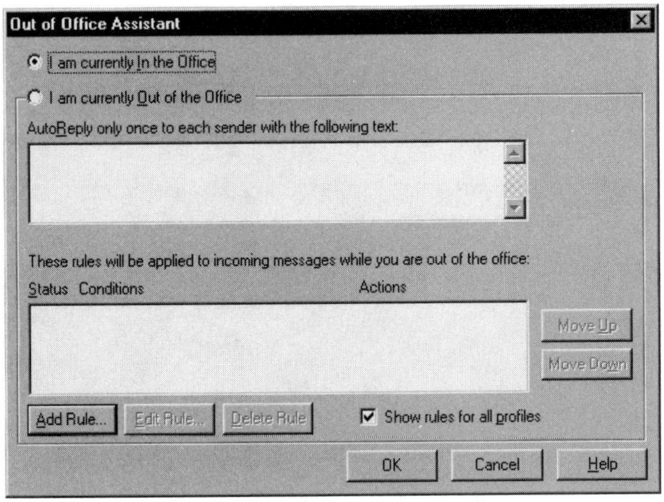

Click I Am Currently Out of the Office, and enter the message you'd like people to receive. Anyone who sends you e-mail will automatically receive this message in response.

 **WARNING** If you subscribe to any e-mail discussion lists that distribute each person's messages to all list members, be careful about using the Out of Office Assistant to send automatic responses to your incoming e-mail messages from these lists. If you do not unsubscribe or place your list accounts on hold while you're away, your auto-responder will dutifully answer each and every message you receive; those responses will be posted to the list, and your Out of Office Assistant will reply to them again, and then again, and then again. You'll be surprised to return home to a large number of very nasty notes concerning your abusive treatment of the list. Making a list of the groups you are involved in helps, and the list administrator is often very happy to temporarily place your account on hold until you return from your trip.

If you would like to apply specific rules to incoming messages, click the Add Rule button. This opens the Edit Rule dialog box shown in Figure 17.16. Select the From, Sent To, Subject, or Message Body condition at the top of the dialog box. Enter the rule you'd like to apply in the Perform These Actions section.

**FIGURE 17.16**

*Add rules to your incoming messages when you are out of the office.*

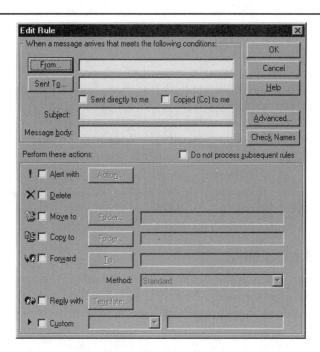

For more advanced options, such as identifying messages of a certain size or messages within a specific date parameter, click the Advanced button.

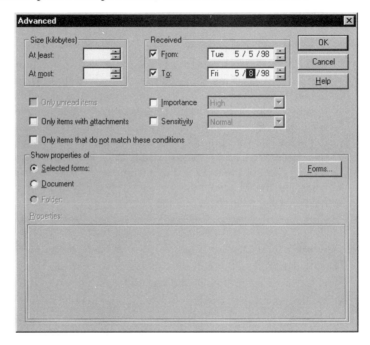

Once the rules are established, click OK and they will be displayed in the Out of Office Assistant dialog box.

When you return to the office, open the Out of Office Assistant and click I Am Currently in the Office. No further messages will be sent; however, the message will be retained for future use.

It often takes a while after an organization migrates to an Outlook/Exchange environment for individuals within the organization to adjust their work habits sufficiently to benefit from all that the program offers. These tools can change corporate cultures because they raise expectations about how people should communicate and to whom they are accountable. Teamwork takes on an entirely new meaning when data and information can be so easily shared and teams can collaborate on projects from across the room or around the world.

## What's Next

For many people, spending a day in the office where they can catch up on mail and exchange messages with colleagues is a luxury. As more people take to the roads, it becomes an increasing challenge to stay on top of things. Outlook's Remote Mail features can make all the difference to someone who travels. In Chapter 18, you'll learn how to use remote mail to communicate with your Outlook folders and Exchange Server even after you leave the office.

# CHAPTER 18

## Taking Outlook on the Road

L eaving work at the office seems to be a thing of the past for millions of people today. Even what used to be free time waiting at the airport or sitting on a plane is now just another couple of hours in which you can get some work done. Notebook computers, pagers, mobile phones, cellular fax/modems, and the latest craze, handheld computers (also known as handheld PCs, or HPCs) and personal digital assistants (PDAs), make it all too easy to stay connected. Whether or not you support this new work ethic, chances are you are faced with the dilemma of how to make your data portable. Outlook was designed with this challenge in mind and, as a result, provides you with several useful options for staying in touch. You can:

- Synchronize with offline folders
- Access your Inbox using Remote Mail
- Synchronize with a PDA or handheld computer

# Using Offline Folders

*Offline folders* are folders that can be synchronized to matching folders on a Microsoft Exchange server using a dial-up connection. Data stored in an offline folder and in its matching folder on the server can be revised and manipulated in any way. The changes only become evident, however, when the two folders are synchronized. If changes are made to the same data stored in both the server and offline folder, a conflict is reported that can then be rectified manually. Offline folders can be set to synchronize automatically at regular intervals, or they can be synchronized manually at random times.

To work offline, you must:

- Set Outlook to work offline
- Establish a dial-up networking connection
- Synchronize the offline folders

---

 **NOTE** Offline folders are stored in the offline folder (.ost) file on your computer's hard drive.

---

## Setting Outlook to Work Offline

Before you can set Outlook to work offline on your notebook or offsite computer, Microsoft Exchange Server has to be set up as one of the services in your profile. If you are a user, your system administrator may have already done this for you when Outlook was installed on your computer, or you may be able to request that they do it now (tickets to a ballgame or concert may help). If you are the system administrator, or if you're a poor soul abandoned in some lonely hotel room and need to connect to your office network, click Tools ➤ Services to see if Microsoft Exchange is listed in your profile. If Microsoft Exchange already appears in the list of services that make up your profile, you're in luck. Select it from the list and click Properties to review the Microsoft Exchange Server properties. If it is not listed, follow the steps in Chapter 17 on setting up Outlook as an Exchange Server client.

You are now ready to create your offline folder file. Click the Offline Folder File Settings button on the Advanced page of the Microsoft Exchange Server properties dialog box to create your offline folder file. In the Offline Folder File Settings dialog box, shown in Figure 18.1, enter the path where you want to store your offline folder file. If you have no particular preference, accept the default C:\Windows\Application Data\Microsoft\ Outlook\outlook.ost.

**FIGURE 18.1**

*Use the Offline Folder File Settings dialog box to create your offline folder file.*

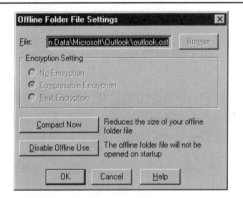

Set the level of encryption you would like on the folder with one of the following choices:

**No Encryption**   Your offline folder file is not encrypted or compressed.

**Compressible Encryption**   Choose this option if you are concerned about saving space on your hard drive and plan to use Windows DriveSpace or another disk compression program on your drive. This allows you to compress your data and still encrypt it for security.

**Best Encryption**   This option offers the best security and still allows you to use a disk compression program, but it does not compress the files as much as the Compressible Encryption option allows.

**WARNING** You must set the encryption level before you create the offline folder file. Once you set it, it cannot be changed.

The last two options on this dialog box are not activated until you have offline folders. Although Outlook automatically compacts the offline folder file while you work, if you delete a large number of items, clicking Compact Now will compact the file immediately, making it faster and more responsive. If you're going to be back at the office and connected to the network for a while, you may want to turn off offline folders by clicking the Disable Offline Use button.

 **NOTE** Compacting and compressing are not the same thing. Compacting a database file fills in the blank spaces in the file left when items were deleted or moved. Compressing files changes the storage structure to minimize the space they take on the drive. Compressed files must be decompressed before they can be used.

You've made it—click the OK button and Outlook will create the offline folder file. Of course, it first tells you that it can't find the .ost file you want to create (which is good news because it doesn't exist yet) and asks you if you want to create it.

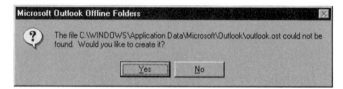

Click Yes and voilà! You have an offline folder file. Click the Enable Offline Folders button on the Advanced page to activate your offline folders. You are now ready to create a dial-up networking connection with the server.

## Establishing a Dial-Up Connection with the Server

If you've already created a Windows dial-up networking connection for your company's Exchange Server, there is nothing much to do in the next step except tell Outlook which connection to use. You can do that by clicking the Dial-Up Networking tab of the Exchange Server properties and selecting the connection from the drop-down list. Enter your user name, password, and domain name, as shown in Figure 18.2.

**FIGURE 18.2**

*Create a dial-up
networking connection
in the Microsoft
Exchange Server
properties dialog box.*

If you have to create a new dial-up networking connection, follow these steps:

1. From Outlook, choose Tools ➢ Services, select Microsoft Exchange Server, and click Properties.

2. Click the Dial-Up Networking tab and click New.

3. Follow the steps of the Make New Connection Wizard, shown in Figure 18.3, to set up the connection.

    a. Enter a name for the computer you are dialing. This doesn't have to be an official name—just so you know what computer this refers to.

    b. Select the modem you are going to use to connect.

    c. Click Configure if you need to change modem properties. If the modem has worked on this phone line and computer before, these settings are probably fine. Click Next.

    d. Enter the number of the server you are calling. Enter a country code if appropriate. Click Next. Click Finish to create the connection and return to the Exchange Server properties sheet.

4. Select the new dial-up connection from the list in the Dial Using the Following Connection box.

**FIGURE 18.3**

*The Make New Connection Wizard walks you through the steps of creating a dial-up networking connection.*

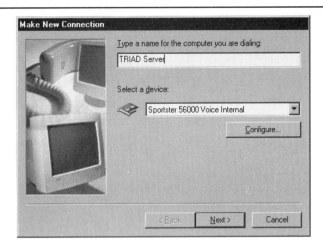

To change the properties of the dial-up networking connection, such as the telephone number or modem, click the Properties button. To change the dialing properties, such as disabling call-waiting or entering a calling card number, click the Location button to open the Dialing Properties dialog box.

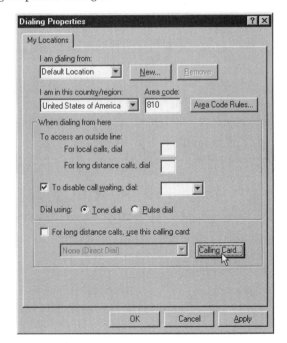

If you want to synchronize your offline folders and are connected to the Exchange Server directly, click the Do Not Dial, Use Existing Connection check box in the Microsoft Exchange Server dialog box. Click OK to close the Microsoft Exchange Server properties sheet and OK again to close the Services dialog box.

## Synchronizing Folders Offline

If a salesperson is on the road traveling from place to place, she needs to be able to synchronize with the Exchange Server on her schedule rather than at specified intervals. On the other hand, if you work out of your home office and need regular updates from the Exchange Server, you may prefer Outlook to synchronize automatically. Outlook provides options for both of these scenarios.

To synchronize manually, follow these steps:

1. Select the folder you want to synchronize.

2. Choose Tools ➤ Synchronize and click This Folder or, to synchronize all folders, click All Folders.

3. A dial-up networking session is launched, and you may be requested to log in to the Windows NT server before the synchronization begins.

4. If the login is successful, an animated synchronize icon, or progress symbol, appears in the bottom right of the screen above the Task bar. When it disappears, the synchronization is complete and the dial-up networking connection closes.

5. To cancel the synchronization, click the small arrow on the animated progress symbol and choose Cancel Synchronizing.

 **TIP** The first time you synchronize your offline folders with the Exchange Server, it's an excellent idea to have your system administrator's help. The first synchronization can be quite lengthy as you copy all the address book information and public folders to your computer. If you can do it while connected directly to the Exchange Server network instead of using a modem, it will save a lot of time and potentially significant long-distance telephone charges.

**TIP** To set the number you want to use to dial into the Exchange Server, choose Tools ➤ Dial-Up Connection, and choose the connection you want to use. You can use this menu to change your Dial-Up Location and add or modify Location Settings.

## Synchronizing Offline Folders Automatically

To set Outlook up so it will automatically synchronize with the server at specified intervals, you have to change a few settings that control how often the synchronization happens. To access these options, follow these steps:

1. Choose Tools ➤ Options and click the Mail Services tab, shown in Figure 18.4.

2. Click the Enable Offline Access check box.

3. Click the When Online, Synchronize All Folders upon Exiting check box if you want to always synchronize with the server before you exit Outlook.

4. Click When Online, Automatically Synchronize All Offline Folders if you want to be in control of how often you receive and share updated data. Enter the time interval in the Every *N* Minutes box.

5. If you're working offline and want to automatically dial in every so many minutes to have Outlook synchronize in the background, click the When Offline, Automatically Synchronize All Offline Folders check box, and enter a time interval in the Every *N* Minutes box.

6. Click OK to apply the changes and close the Options dialog box.

**FIGURE 18.4**

*Open the Mail Services options to set up Outlook to automatically synchronize at specified intervals.*

# Resolving Synchronization Conflicts

If you and another person both make changes to the same Outlook item and then one of you synchronizes, you will see a crossed set of swords next to the item.

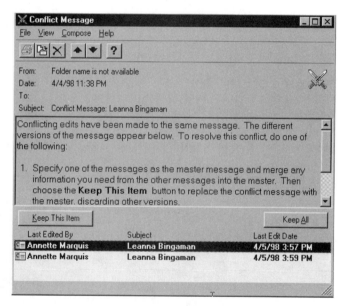

This indicates that there is a conflict that Exchange Server cannot resolve—it requires human intervention. Double-click the item to open it, and a Conflict Message opens instead. Click the diagonal hash marks (Resize Tool) in the bottom right corner of the window to expand the message. This shows who last edited the item and the date and time it was last edited.

Double-click each message to open it and see for yourself where the differences are. If it is clear which information is most accurate, click the item you want to save and choose Keep This Item. If you are unsure which information is most accurate, choose Keep All. When you are certain, you can delete the less accurate contact from your offline folder.

# Troubleshooting Connection Problems

When you dial in to your server, it's easy to tell if you are actually connected. Look for the animated connection icon (two connected computers) on the Windows task bar. If it's there, you are connected. Double-click the icon or right-click and select Status to open the Connected To dialog box.

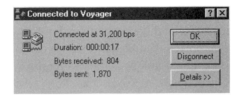

This will show that you are connected, and will also indicate the connection speed, the duration, and the number of bytes received and sent. Click OK to close the dialog box or Disconnect if you want to go offline.

## Checking Connections in the Network Neighborhood

You may find that you have a dial-up connection but you are not able to see the public folders in Outlook. This probably means that something is wrong with your permissions to access the Windows NT network. To test this, double-click the Network Neighborhood icon on the Windows Desktop. If you have access to the network, you will be able to see other computers in the Network Neighborhood dialog box.

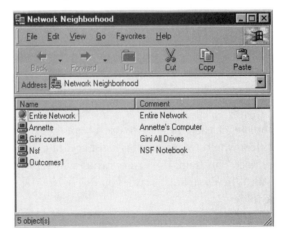

If the dialog box is blank, you are not connected to the network. Disconnect using the Connected To dialog box. Choose File ➤ Exit and Log Off from the Outlook menu bar and restart Outlook. Attempt to reconnect. If you still cannot see the Public Folders in Outlook or other computers in the Network Neighborhood, there may be a problem with your Windows NT permissions. Contact your system administrator or help desk for assistance.

## Other Connection Factors

Modem speed, volume of network activity, or noise on the telephone line can all be factors in making a trouble-free connection. If you are having difficulty connecting or maintaining a connection, stay offline for a while and try it again in an hour or so. If the problem persists or is intermittent but frequent, report the problem to your system administrator or help desk.

## Making a Folder Unavailable for Offline Use

Keeping company files secure is a growing concern for the corporate world. Every year, more and more critical data travels around the globe on notebook computers instead of remaining secure on the corporate mainframe. Due to this risk of theft, extremely sensitive company data should never be stored on a mobile computer. This doesn't mean you can't access this information while you're on the road. You can dial in to the Exchange Server, view the data you need, and leave it there when you disconnect. By making folders available only for online viewing, you prevent the dangers that accompany taking storehouses of data with you when you leave the office.

To make a folder unavailable for offline access, right-click on the folder and choose Properties. Open the Synchronization page shown in Figure 18.5.

Click the Only When Online option to make the folder available for use only when you're logged on to the server. This option does not affect the standard Outlook folders, such as Inbox and Calendar, but can be applied to any folder or subfolder that you create. To make the Outlook folders unavailable, you must disable or delete the offline folder file you created earlier in this chapter. It's a better option to move sensitive data into folders that can be made unavailable while still allowing you to access some folders offline.

### Selecting Records to Synchronize

Rather than copying what could amount to thousands of records to your mobile computer, you might prefer to create a filter to apply to the data that is being synchronized. This will allow you to only copy records that you need and leave the others on the server. To create a filter, click the Filter button on the Synchronization page of the folder's properties. To find out more about creating filters, see Chapter 11.

**FIGURE 18.5**

*The Synchronization page of a folder's properties lets you make a folder unavailable for offline use.*

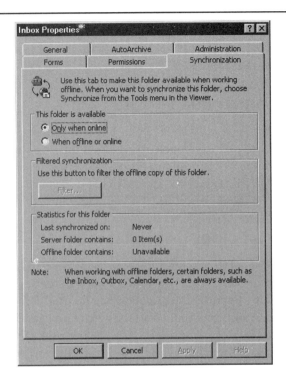

**FIGURE 18.5**

*The Synchronization page of a folder's properties lets you make a folder unavailable for offline use.*

# Using Folders Offline

If you are a mobile user, you may want to work with your data offline and then only connect to the Exchange Server when you want to synchronize your data with the server. To have access to a folder offline, you need to copy the online folder you want to work with to the Favorites folder and set the folder's properties. You only need to do this once, but it's important that you follow a few careful steps to make your folder available offline:

**1.** To copy the folder you work with most often, connect to the Exchange Server and locate the folder you want to copy.

**2.** Click on the folder and drag it to the Favorites folder.

**3.** When the Favorites folder turns blue, drop the folder onto the Favorites folder.

**4.** After a copy of your folder exists in the Favorites folder, right-click on the folder and choose Properties from the shortcut menu.

**5.** Click the synchronization tab of the Folder Properties dialog box.

**6.** Change the property setting from Only When Online to When Offline or Online.

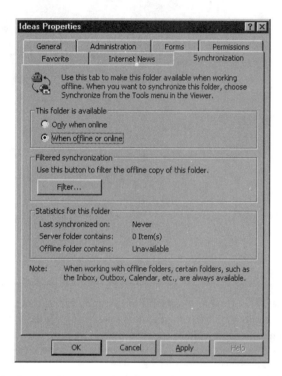

**7.** Click the Outlook Address Book tab of the Folder Properties dialog box and click the Show This Folder as an E-mail Address Book check box. If you're in a hurry and only need to check your e-mail to see if a message has arrived, you can still access your mail using the Remote Mail feature of Outlook.

# Managing Remote Mail

Using remote mail, you can dial into a server, your computer, or an Internet service provider to download the headers of all your e-mail messages. You can then choose which messages you want to retrieve by dialing back in, downloading the messages you want, and deleting the rest. To access Remote Mail, choose Tools ➤ Remote Mail to open the Remote Mail menu.

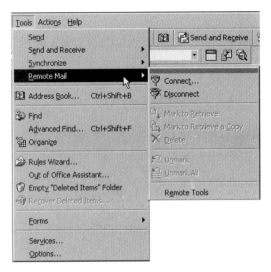

 **NOTE** The Remote Menu is a floating menu that can be freed from its position and become a toolbar. Drag the dark gray bar across the top of the menu. You can also turn it on using View ➤ Toolbars ➤ Remote.

Click Connect to connect to your mail service. The Remote Connection Wizard greets you with two questions. First, it asks which information service you want to connect to. It also asks what you want to do when you get there. Step 1, shown in Figure 18.6, lists the information services you have available to you—select the one you want to use. Click the check box if you would like a confirmation of your request before the connection is made.

Step 2, shown in Figure 18.7, lists the actions the Wizard will take on your behalf. Choose to send and receive all mail, or check the items you would like to complete. Click Finish to initiate the connection.

**FIGURE 18.6**

*In the first step of the
Remote Connection
Wizard, check the
information services to
which you want to
connect.*

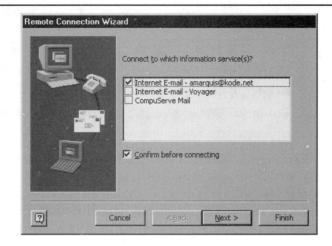

**FIGURE 18.7**

*When you send
remote mail, you can
choose the actions you
want to complete.*

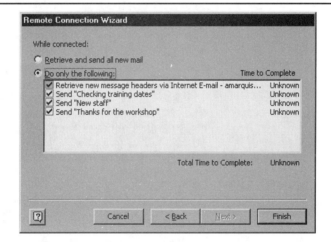

When the connection is underway, you are updated as to the status of the connection.

After you download the message headers, open each message and select one of the following options:

**Mark to Retrieve Message**  Retrieves the message the next time you connect.

**Mark to Retrieve a Copy**  Leaves a copy of the message on the server.

**Delete**  Deletes the message from Outlook.

**Unmark**  Unmarks a message previously marked for retrieval.

**Unmark All**  Unmarks all messages marked for retrieval.

If you receive a deluge of e-mail each day and want to have more control over your remote mail messages than to retrieve or not retrieve them, check out the additional Remote Mail settings in the Microsoft Exchange Server properties dialog box (Tools ➤ Services ➤ Microsoft Exchange Properties). Click the Remote Mail tab of the properties sheet to change settings regarding what to retrieve and to schedule remote connections.

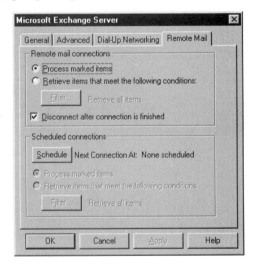

The first connection option, Process Marked Items, downloads all the items you marked for retrieval. If you want to select messages that meet certain criteria, click the second option. This activates the Filter button. Click Filter to set up your criteria.

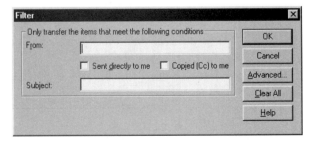

If you only want to retrieve mail from a particular individual, enter a name, or names separated by a semicolon, in the From box. Check the Sent Directly to Me check box if you only want mail that lists your name in the To field. This would preclude any message sent to you as part of a personal distribution list. Click the Copied (Cc) to Me option if you only want mail that was copied to you—this would include mail where your name appeared in a personal distribution list. In the Subject field, enter any text that must be included in the subject of the message. Use semicolons to separate multiple entries. As long as one of the entries appears, the message is retrieved. If you have any stricter requirements, click the Advanced tab to set parameters around the size of the messages, message dates, importance, sensitivity, read status, and attachments.

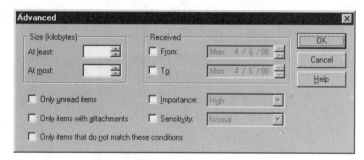

If you can't quite get the filters to work the way you want them to, try setting the criteria for the messages you don't want and clicking the Only Items That Do Not Match These Conditions check box. For example, if you're going on vacation and you want to be able to retrieve any messages except those about a particular project that you'd rather forget about, enter appropriate text in the Subject box on the Filter dialog box, click Advanced, and check this check box. You can have a trouble-free vacation without having to be reminded of what's waiting for you when you get back. When you've set all your criteria, clicking OK will return you to the Remote Mail dialog box.

Remote Mail is set to disconnect when the mail has been retrieved. Clear the Disconnect after Connection Is Finished check box if you want to stay connected. To retrieve mail at a set time every day or at regular intervals, click the Schedule button to open the Schedule Remote Mail Connection dialog box. Enter a time in the At box or a number of hours or minutes in the Every box. Click OK to save the schedule.

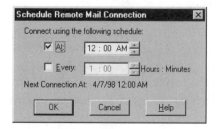

If you schedule Remote Mail and want to apply a filter to the connection, choose the Retrieve Items That Meet the Following Conditions option under Scheduled Connections on the Remote Mail page. Click the Filter button and enter your criteria (follow the same steps as those described in "Selecting Records to Synchronize" earlier in this chapter). Close the Filter, the Exchange Server Properties, and the Services dialog boxes to save all your new settings. The next time you make the connection or Remote Mail connects automatically, your messages will be retrieved as directed.

### The Pros and Cons of Using Remote Mail

Remote Mail is an alternative to offline folders, but you should give careful consideration to when you want to use it. If you don't have an Exchange Server, then using offline folders isn't an option. Remote Mail provides you with a way to pick up only the messages you want to deal with and leave the others to handle another time. But while offline folders give you access to all of your Outlook information and public folders, Remote Mail only gives you access to e-mail messaging. Offline folders synchronize with matching server folders to give you up-to-date data, but the connection may be costly if you have to use expensive hotel telephone lines. Remote Mail gives you access to your mail at a fraction of the connect time. So although Remote Mail may not be for everyone, it's a useful feature for those who need to manage e-mail messages while on the road.

Because you can also use Remote Mail to retrieve messages from an Internet service provider, it's a valuable tool in avoiding e-mail–transmitted viruses. If you're concerned about viruses, download only your message headers and delete any messages that are from anyone you don't recognize. This way you can download only those messages that you feel are relatively safe.

# Using Outlook with Windows CE Devices and Other PDAs

By the time you've been stopped by airport security enough times and asked to open and turn on your seven-pound notebook computer, which, by the way, you've been carrying for two miles from the parking lot along with your suitcase and all your other bundles, the idea of a computer that will fit in your coat pocket begins to sound pretty appealing. Handheld computers are one of today's fastest-growing computer markets.

Although they range dramatically in features and functions, on average, handheld computers are more powerful than our desktops were only a few short years ago. The only downside seems to be how to input data into something so small that your fingers can't fit on the keys. In response to this dilemma and the concerns of people who don't want to have two computerized sources of data—one on their desktop back at the office and one they carry with them—considerable attention has been paid to ways to synchronize these devices with desktop computers, which we'll get to shortly.

There are two major trends in the handheld computer market: those that call themselves personal digital assistants (PDAs), such as 3Com's Palm series (including the Palm III and the upcoming wireless Palm VI), and Windows CE–based handheld computers, also called palm PCs. PDAs, such as the Palm III and its predecessors, are designed to provide controlled access to specific applications: address books, calendars, to-do lists, mail, and notes. Users have somewhat less freedom to customize and, as a result, report fewer problems with them than with the more flexible palm PCs. PDAs, which are primarily Palm OS–based devices these days, are programmable and have an enormous selection of third-party software available to meet every need from diagnostic manuals for physicians, to baseball stats for sports enthusiasts, to games. PDAs tend to be smaller than their Windows CE counterparts and often use a form of handwriting recognition as their primary method of input.

## Synchronizing with Outlook

Both types of handheld device are designed to synchronize with a desktop computer. When these devices first started to appear, they only used a desktop computer to provide a backup system for their data. More recently though, users of these devices have been seeing the benefits of being able to input data into their handheld computer on the road and return it to their desktop computer while they are at the office. No one wants to enter the same data twice, so users have demanded ways to synchronize their data to keep both systems up-to-date.

Some handheld computers connect to the desktop by way of a cable and a desktop serial port. Others use infrared to transfer data between the two systems (of course, this requires that you have an IrDA-compliant infrared port on your PC). Regardless of the hardware interface, they all use some type of synchronization software called a *conduit* to share data with a desktop computer. Most of these devices come with their own desktop software that is closely tied to the handheld versions for easy data exchange. Several third-party vendors have developed conduits that bypass the software applications that come with the devices and synchronize directly with popular information managers, such as Outlook. Figure 18.8 shows an example of how you control synchronization with PocketMirror from Chapura, Inc., one of the leading conduits for the PalmPilot.

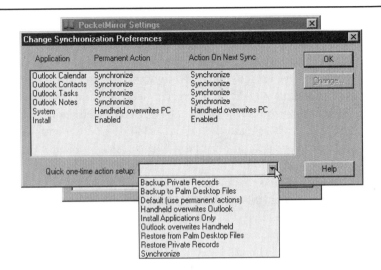

**FIGURE 18.8**

*PocketMirror synchronizes the 3Com PalmPilot with Outlook.*

 **NOTE** Each handheld device maker includes a set of software with each machine. Commonly, this set includes synchronization, communications, and productivity titles. Chapura's PocketMirror is only one synchronization software package—your device may contain other software.

Each of these conduits have their own idiosyncrasies, so it's important to review the features of the products carefully before deciding which features you can live with and which you can't live without. For example, one conduit may not allow you to synchronize with subfolders, while another lets you choose the folder you want to use but only lets you assign one category to an item. Some have more trouble than others resolving conflicts that arise when the same item is changed on both the handheld and desktop computers. None of the products synchronize directly with the Outlook Journal. However, you can create notes or documents that you can then use to create Journal items once you get them into Outlook. All of the conduits are available for download over the Internet, and visiting the developers' Web sites is a great way to compare the various features of their products. Three of the leading conduit developers and their Web addresses are:

- DataViz, http://www.dataviz.com

- Chapura, http://www.chapura.com

- Puma Technology, http://www.pumatech.com

## MASTERING TROUBLESHOOTING

### Before Synching to a Handheld Device

The first time you synchronize with a handheld device there are a few precautions that can help make the experience painless.

First, make sure that you make a backup of your Outlook data. We have cleaned up several messes when users didn't back up before synching and didn't follow the directions about synching the first time. When they got their device, they started playing around with it by entering a few items here and there. When they synched the first time with Outlook on their desktops, the synchronize program saw the handheld data as more current and completely wiped out their Outlook data. Theoretically, this should not happen, but we've encountered it too many times for them each to be flukes.

Second, make sure you read the directions about how to synchronize the first time. Depending on how much data you have in either of the two systems, you may want to have the desktop overwrite the handheld, or have the handheld overwrite the desktop, or synchronize the two.

Finally, be certain you know how the conduit handles multiple user profiles, custom fields, multiple categories, multiple addresses, and synching with different folders. Some of the conduits on the market can't handle these things very well at all, while other programs make these adjustments easily. With a good backup, you have room to experiment and see what options work best for your situation.

## The Palm

The Palm series, from 3Com, has captured a market that was at one time considered impossible to win in. Palm PDAs have outsold every other brand of PDA since their release. Even in the face of Microsoft's Windows CE–device push, the Palm still dominates in sales and popularity, perhaps because it is remarkably easy to use. Its general simplicity, flexibility, wide-spread adoption, large third-party software library, and attractive cost entry point have all come together to make it a smash in the previously dismal PDA market. In essence, the Palm has *created* the PDA market.

**NOTE** Not to be relegated to a footnote in PDA history, Apple's Newton MessagePad was the first PDA to gain acceptance in what was, at the time, a very small PDA market. Early adopters were treated to desktop connectivity, handwriting recognition, lots of extra software, and an easy-to-use interface in a somewhat larger package. Apple canceled the Newton line, but is at work on a new compact device that will be faster, more compatible, and much less expensive.

PART

IV

Configuring Outlook
for Your Business

The Palm series jumped into the desktop connectivity arena immediately, offering one-touch synchronization, called HotSync. This allows a user to set their Palm in a cradle connected to a desktop computer and press a single button. The software on the desktop computer synchronizes the data specified on the Palm. There are a large number of packages—commercial, shareware, and freeware—that are available for synchronizing the Palm with just about everything.

## Outlook Compatibility

The Desktop 3.0 software that's included with the Palm III organizer is able to synchronize data with many desktop applications, including Outlook. Synching with the applications requires that you map the fields to equivalent fields in the Palm III's built-in applications. Though not extraordinarily difficult, most busy people don't have time for this. This problem has been an opportunity for many third-party software developers.

Two of the most popular commercial packages are Chapura's PocketMirror and Data-Viz's Desktop To Go synchronization packages. Among the applications that they work with is Outlook. Desktop To Go works particularly well with Outlook and can perform the following functions:

- Synchronize public folders
- Filter private records
- Prioritize important phone numbers
- Synchronize Date Book alarms
- Handle contacts with more than one address
- Synchronize records with multiple categories
- Record Outlook Journal entries for new contacts added to the Palm III

This is above and beyond what the built-in applications offer. PocketMirror is similar in many ways. You can get more information about these applications at their respective Web sites:

- Chapura, `http://www.chapura.com`
- DataViz, `http://www.dataviz.com/Products/PIM-PDA/DTG/DTGpilothome.html`

## The HotSync Process

The HotSync process is really quite simple. The basic idea is that you attach the cradle's cable to the back of your PC, load the Desktop 3.0 software, and do a bit of setting up. (The setting up is, as we've stated before, mapping Outlook fields to Palm III fields.) Once that's done once, all you have to do to synchronize data is set the Palm III in the cradle and tap the HotSync button.

# Windows CE

Windows-based handhelds (based on the Windows CE operating system) are the only real competitor the Palm currently has in the handheld market, and they make more of an attempt to mimic their desktop parents. These powerful little devices are loaded with familiar software titles, such as Pocket Word, Pocket Excel, Pocket PowerPoint, Internet Explorer, and you guessed it, Pocket Outlook—all scaled down versions of these popular applications. Windows CE devices have much of the functionality of desktops, including built-in modems and color displays, at a fraction of the size. These handheld wonders are also fraught with most of the issues that affect your desktop model—they can crash from memory overload, they freeze up on occasion, and the applications can conflict with each other.

 **NOTE**  Microsoft's latest endeavor to insert itself into a new market is the tablet-style device, controversially called Palm-sized PCs, designed to compete directly with the Palm III. Microsoft has not seen as large a market penetration for these new devices, or anything based on the Windows CE operating system, as they would like. As a result, Palm III devices are still the market leader by a wide margin.

Despite all of this, however, the Windows CE device market is one of the fastest growing segments in computer technology, primarily because of the dominance of Windows on the office desktop. Here's where things stand as far as availability goes.

- Windows CE is at version 2.11, which includes many improvements over 1.0, most markedly its extended feature set, more powerful connectivity capabilities, and support for color displays. Windows CE 2.1, referred to as Windows CE Professional Edition, adds support for larger displays, more recognized peripherals, and more features.

 **NOTE**  Windows CE Pro devices, two notable ones being Hewlett-Packard's Jornada 820 and the Sharp Tripad/Vadem Clio dynamic duo, have large color screens and more powerful processors. The HP 820 even has a trackpad. At nearly $1,000 each, these devices lack the capabilities of slightly larger laptops for almost as much money. If you have to get work done in a more limited environment than will permit a laptop, these might be just what you need.

- Most Windows CE devices are used as communication appliances, and manufacturers have responded to this. Two in particular are NEC's MobilePro 750c and LG Electronics Phenom Express, both of which have built-in modems, as well as large 640 × 240 color displays and touch-type keyboards.

- Several models from various makers include full-sized VGA video-out ports and external monitor support for up to an amazing 1024 × 768 display size (although 800 × 600 is much more common). The devices with these ports can be put to use displaying PowerPoint presentations using Pocket PowerPoint, saving the presenter from lugging heavy equipment around.

The above-mentioned collection of trimmed down Office applications makes these devices attractive enough to consider as a replacement for that old 10 lb. laptop and 30 lb. projection device that people can't see anyway.

**NOTE** At the time of this writing, Royal, the inexpensive digital address-book people, has released the daVinci, a $99 Palm III clone that actually recognizes handwriting (though, from what the reviewers say, just barely). It comes with a synchronizing dock that works with certain desktop-based applications, such as Outlook, ACT!, Schedule+, Organizer, and GoldMine, although that functionality requires buying a copy of WindowsLink ($39.99). There's even a $19 butterfly keyboard that can be used for more intensive data entry. Even buying everything for the daVinci makes the price an affordable $160, far less than the $329 Palm III. This may be the event that will bring the PDA market into the mainstream. Keep an eye out for price drops from Palm if the daVinci takes off.

## Synching Outlook and Pocket Outlook

This is, by far, the simplest way to synchronize your Outlook data between your desktop and your Windows CE device. Pocket Outlook is a small collection of the primary components in Outlook. Unlike its more mature sibling, Pocket Outlook is actually four separate applications: Inbox, Contacts, Calendar, and Notes. Each of these applications are feature-trimmed versions of the desktop versions.

**NOTE** Pocket Outlook can store information that is specific only to the desktop version, even though it can't display it. This is helpful when you synchronize with more than one desktop computer.

As there are many ways to synchronize data, we won't go into details. Here are some helpful links, however:

- PDA Central, `http://www.pdacentral.com`
- Microsoft Windows CE site, `http://www.microsoft.com/windowsce/default.asp`
- Weekly Windows CE newsletter from YourInfo, `http://www.yourinfo.net/`
- Windows CE Technical Journal, `http://www.cetj.com/`

## What's Next

In this chapter, you saw how you can exchange Outlook data with other applications. The power of any application is significantly enhanced when the data becomes portable. As you move on to Chapter 19, you'll see how to enhance the power of Outlook even further by developing custom applications in the Outlook environment.

# PART V

# Building Customized Outlook Applications

## LEARN TO:

- *Determine which component to use for an application*

- *Implement network and enterprise Outlook applications*

- *Create and publish custom forms*

- *Create templates for reuse*

- *Reference Outlook from other Office applications*

- *Use and debug VB code in Outlook forms*

- *Automate forms with VB and VBScript*

- *Create a Visual Basic application*

# CHAPTER **19**

# Improving Your Outlook

O utlook, today's best desktop information manager, is a general tool for use in a wide variety of organizations. But can Outlook handle the more specialized data and communications requirements of your organization? The answer is yes—with some help from you. In this chapter, you'll see how Outlook can be customized to track your critical information.

# Types of Outlook Applications

Outlook customization ranges from simple applications to complex office solutions using Microsoft Exchange and ODBC database connectivity. The amount of work required to create an Outlook application depends on the level of complexity. For example, you can:

- Add a few data fields to an existing component and create custom views that include the fields
- Construct new forms in existing components
- Build new forms from scratch
- Create an entirely different level of functionality in a public folder by adding new controls or modifying existing controls

Outlook is a robust tool for rapid development of user-friendly applications. If you want to let users view contact data in a number of combinations and sort orders in a traditional database (for example, Access), you can create queries and forms to display information or reports to print each data combination. With Outlook, you create and save one or more new views. There are four advantages to developing your projects in Outlook.

First, it's faster to create a view in Outlook than to create a good-looking tabular form in Access or another database tool. Second, the finished product is accessible. In a completed database application, users are kept at arm's length from the tools used to manipulate data. In Outlook, you can encourage users to customize views. The third benefit is a result of the second: because Outlook users can enhance the views you create, you don't have to anticipate and create every view users will ever need.

The fourth benefit is that Outlook automatically supplies a lot of the functionality that's the hardest to create in a programming language or database development tool. For example, an Outlook application that you base on a message form automatically supports forwarding, replying, and the other mail features. Use the form, and you get instant access to all the actions that belong to the form. Inherited functionality is a major reason increasing numbers of Office users and developers are creating office productivity tools in Outlook: you don't have to understand the ins and outs of messaging to create mail applications or be intimate with threading to create post and reply bulletin boards. Imagine building a mail application from scratch using a programming language, and you immediately recognize the massive head start Outlook provides.

## Workgroup Applications Created in an Afternoon

If you create new views and forms for use on your desktop, you have a stand-alone application. Publish the forms and views in a Microsoft Exchange Server public folder and you have instant groupware. Collaboration is one of the strengths of Exchange that you can extend to your workgroup with Outlook. With Exchange public folder applications, you can set permissions to allow only specific people to add newsletter subscribers tasks or to schedule classes, so your application can be as open as you want it to be.

For example, say you're responsible for tracking subscriptions to your company's Office Tips newsletter. Three months before a subscription expires, you notify the Customer Service department, which contacts the subscriber about renewing. To make your job easier, you create an Outlook Contacts folder called Newsletter that contains contact information for subscribers and some new views. If you copy your Newsletter folder to a public folder, you can grant other users on your network access to the Newsletter folder. Instead of e-mailing contacts to the Customer Service Department, you can let your colleagues in the department access the information directly.

Collaborative Calendar applications are popular tools. Create a public folder for Calendar items, and you have a scheduling application for training classes, a speakers' bureau, or personnel development opportunities. Trainees can check to see when specific classes are available or see the entire schedule of opportunities, simply by changing Calendar views. If you're managing a project for your workgroup, create a public folder for the project's tasks. Team members can check the views in the folder to get an update as tasks are assigned, started, and completed.

## Applications Based on Calendar, Contacts, and Tasks

If you need to track additional information that isn't included in an Outlook component, create a new form so users can collect and view the data. There are four types of forms you can create in Outlook:

- Calendar, Contacts, or Task forms
- Mail message forms

PART

**V**

Building Customized
Outlook Applications

- Post forms
- Office document forms

Before you create a form from scratch, see if you can identify an Outlook component that contains most of the fields you need and has the desired functionality. For example, if you want to keep track of people in a database type of application, consider simply adding fields to the default Contacts form. Figure 19.1 shows a newsletter form based on the Contact form. Two fields, Beginning Date and Ending Date, were added to the Contact form.

**FIGURE 19.1**

*The Newsletter Circulation form is based on the Contact form.*

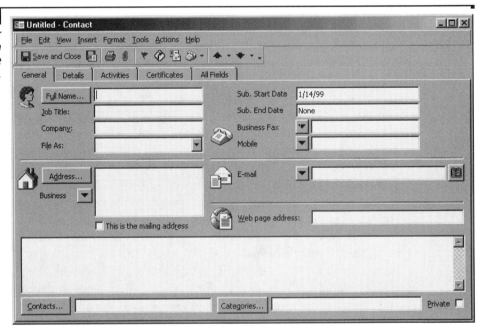

The form allows users to enter or view beginning and ending date information for individual contacts. The existing Contacts views didn't include the added fields, so two new views were created: Subscriber Since and Expiring Subscriptions (see Figure 19.2). Now users in the Customer Service Department can concentrate on reaching subscribers before their subscriptions run out. These modifications to the Contacts component took less than an hour to complete.

**FIGURE 19.2**

*The Customer Service Department contacts customers whose subscriptions are expiring.*

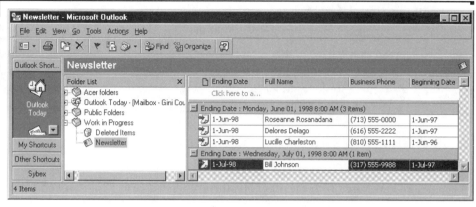

## Mail Message Applications

Mail message applications are used for internal and external communications. Forms can be pre-addressed so that, for example, the Suggestion form is automatically delivered to the Quality Control Department and the Newsletter Subscription form is sent to Customer Service. Mail message items can be sent to a public folder or a distribution list as well as to an individual user. Figure 19.3 shows a customized message form used to send a training request to a company's training coordinator. The message is pre-addressed by the application.

PART

V

Building Customized
Outlook Applications

**FIGURE 19.3**

*Mail message applications send and receive customized mail forms.*

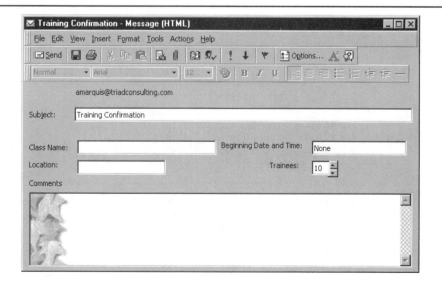

## Post Applications

A Post form is like a message form, but the recipient is a public folder. Other users can read a posted message and reply to the message in the same folder, creating a threaded discussion. Post applications are popular for internal bulletin boards, online brainstorming sessions, and other forums. The discussion group application shown in Chapter 17 is a Post application.

## Office Document Applications

When you need tools from Word, Excel, or PowerPoint, you can rely on Outlook's integration with the other members of the Office family. Office document forms are containers that hold Office documents so they can be mailed or posted. The Weekly Timesheet application's main form, shown in Figure 19.4, includes part of a Microsoft Excel worksheet.

**FIGURE 19.4**

*The Weekly Timesheet form includes part of an Excel worksheet.*

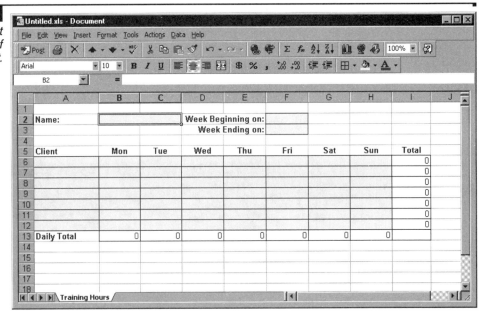

 **TIP** You can place Access information in an Outlook form, but it's a more challenging endeavor to use a custom control and ODBC to link the Outlook form with an Access database.

You have access to the actions in the default forms when you create a new form based on one of the default forms. If you want to add other bells and whistles to your Outlook application, you can use Microsoft's popular Visual Basic programming language. You'll learn how to create new form functionality with Visual Basic and VBScript in Chapters 21 through 25.

---

 **NOTE** Don't worry if Visual Basic is not up your alley. Its use in Outlook makes the application much more powerful, but the changes are relatively simple. You don't need to prepare yourself for late nights and lots of coffee.

---

# Beyond the Boundaries of Outlook

It's easy to get excited by the ease of development and the professional look of Outlook applications. Eventually, you'll begin to wonder why you can't create anything you want in Outlook—why anyone would bother to develop applications using Access, Excel, Visual Basic, Java, or any of the other tools at hand. The answer is that there are a few things Outlook is *not* designed to do. Outlook isn't the only tool you'll need, for example, when you need to:

- Relate data entities. When your data application includes two or more types of entities (classes and students, customers and orders, employees and skills), you'll probably want to use Access, or SQL Server, or both. Outlook databases are not relational databases.

- Sort and filter huge quantities of data. Outlook's Contacts component handles hundreds and even thousands of contact records with decent speed. But Outlook is not the place to store your company's 250,000 customers. For large-scale data storage, look to Access for desktop applications and SQL Server when multiple users need to access the data.

- Use form- or control-level permissions. In databases like Access, security is at the form or control level. You can, for example, give one user or group read-only permissions for data displayed in a particular database form and full permissions for a different form in the same database. In Outlook, permissions are set at the folder level, so a user who can delete one type of item in a folder can delete any item in the folder.

Outlook can't be the only solution in these scenarios, but it can be part of your customized solution. With the addition of user-defined form fields and Visual Basic, you can check to see who is editing or deleting an item and allow or disallow the edit or deletion. Or you can set permissions on groups of folders, and then add Visual Basic code to user forms to copy items from folder to folder.

You can connect customized Outlook forms to data stored in Access. For example, your users can view and enter data in an Access database from a form in Outlook. They will use the familiar tools from Outlook, but the data they're manipulating is stored in Access. Outlook and Microsoft Exchange Server connect to SQL Server for your larger databases. (See Chapter 25 for information on using Outlook with other databases.)

## What's Next

This chapter provided an overview of the types of applications you can create using Outlook. In the following chapters, you'll find out how to create applications for yourself and other users in your office or workgroup.

# CHAPTER 20

# Creating Custom Forms

I n this chapter, we'll look at how to create, modify, and manage custom forms in Outlook. We'll begin by recapping what forms are. We'll then look at the three classes of forms that Outlook supports, and we'll discuss the reasons why creating custom forms is useful. We'll then go through the process of customizing forms and publishing them for use. Finally, we'll look at how to manage your forms and how to create a template for reuse.

## What Is a Form?

A form is essentially a window or container for working with information within Outlook. Each form contains a number of *controls*—interface elements such as text boxes, option buttons, and command buttons—that you use to interact with the form. You'll be familiar with most (if not all) of these controls from your work with other Windows applications and with the eight built-in forms that Outlook provides: the Appointment, Contact, Journal Entry, Mail Message, Meeting Request/Online Meeting Request, Note, Task, and Task Request forms.

As you've seen, the forms vary tremendously in complexity, with the Note form being the simplest. Most of the forms contain more than one *page*—different areas of the form that you reach by clicking the tabs at the top of the pages. For example, the standard Contact form shown in Figure 20.1 contains five visible pages, identified by the tabs General, Details, Activities, Certificates, and All Fields. The form also contains a number of other, hidden pages that you can reveal by customizing the form.

## Understanding the Three Classes of Forms

Outlook has three classes of forms: personal forms, organization forms, and folder forms. These forms are stored in different forms folders, also referred to as *forms registries* or *forms libraries*:

- Forms in the *personal forms folder* or *personal forms library* are personal to the current user of Outlook and can be accessed only by that user. Outlook stores personal forms in the individual user's mailbox.

- Forms in the *organizational forms folder* or *organizational forms library* are shared across the Exchange enterprise and can be accessed by anyone in the enterprise who has the appropriate permissions; by default, all users can access forms in an organizational forms library. Outlook stores organizational forms on the server. You can replicate organizational forms libraries between Exchange sites in an organization so that each site has access to the organizational forms.

- Forms in the *folder forms folder* or (more understandably) *folder forms library* can only be accessed from that folder, no matter whether the folder is a public folder or a private folder. The folder forms library is useful for attaching forms to public folders, so that those people with access to a public folder can use the forms associated with it.

As you'll see later in the chapter, you can copy or move forms from one forms library to another, which gives you flexibility regarding where you decide to store your forms. For example, you might initially create a form for your own use and store it in your personal forms library, and only copy it to the organizational forms library when you've established that your colleagues could use it, too.

PART

V

Building Customized
Outlook Applications

**FIGURE 20.1**

*The standard Contact form contains five visible pages—General, Details, Activities, Certificates, and All Fields.*

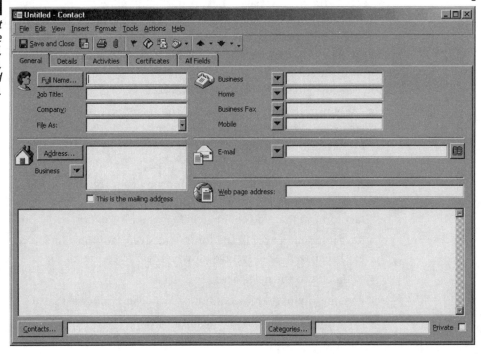

# Why Create Custom Forms?

Outlook's built-in forms provide a great deal of flexibility and functionality straight out of the box. But for many business purposes, you will need to extend or modify their functionality. For example, if you work in sales, you might need to store extra information on your contacts, such as details on their recent orders, fulfillment, and payments. By using custom forms, you can do this easily. Likewise, you might be able to speed up the creation of frequent task requests and appointments by creating custom forms that already contain or automatically enter part of the information for you. If you need to create an application with solid mail or post functionality, Outlook is the place to do it. You can create an e-mail–based application in hours rather than days, because Outlook 2000 handles the mail features for you.

You can customize any of the forms except for the Note form, perhaps because it is too simple to be customized. Each built-in form, apart from the Note form, contains a number of extra, unused pages that are normally hidden from view; you can use these to extend the form. Each built-in form also contains one or more special pages, such as Actions and Properties, that are normally hidden as well. We'll look at how to use these pages later in the chapter, in "Setting Properties for the Form" and "Choosing Actions for the Form."

You can customize a form in several ways:

- Preset information in the form so that you don't have to fill it in each time you create an item based on the form. For example, if you regularly need to send a message to 15 different people, you can create a custom form that contains their addresses in the To box.

- Add fields to or remove them from the pages the form normally displays. For example, you might choose to add one or two extra fields to the standard Contact form so that you could include extra information with your contacts.

- Reveal hidden pages in the form (effectively, adding pages to the form) or hide existing pages (effectively, removing them from the form).

- Add fields to the new pages.

- Rename any page that does not have a default name assigned.

- Alter how the controls on the form work.

 **NOTE** In the next few chapters, we'll look at Visual Basic and how you can use it and VBScript to automate and program customized forms.

The main way of creating a custom form in Outlook is by basing it on one of the existing Outlook forms. For minor customizations, you can simply extend the existing components of a form by adding new pages, custom fields, and features. For more radical customizations, you can remove most of the existing components of a form, providing yourself with an almost clean slate for designing your own form.

You can also create a custom form in Outlook by basing it on an Office document, such as an Excel chart or worksheet, a Word document, or a PowerPoint presentation. The following are a couple of possible uses:

- Distributing interactive questionnaires with embedded PowerPoint slides to employees for training purposes.

- Automating departmental approval of budget expenditures by including spreadsheet views and Exchange Server voting features.

These forms are less customizable than forms based on the existing Outlook forms. We'll look at how to create Outlook forms based on Office documents at the end of this chapter.

# Opening a Form for Customization

To open a form for customization:

**1.** From the main Outlook window or from a form window, select Tools ➢ Forms ➢ Choose Form, or File ➢ New ➢ Choose Form, to display the Choose Form dialog box (see Figure 20.2).

---

**NOTE** To open a form in Design mode from an open form, you can choose Tools ➢ Forms ➢ Design a Form to display the Design Form dialog box, which is the Choose Form dialog box in disguise. If you want to exploit a neat shortcut from an empty form, go to Tools ➢ Forms ➢ Design This Form and you will directly enter Design Mode for the form from which you chose this option.

---

**2.** In the Look In drop-down list, choose the forms library in which the form you want to use is stored. You can choose from the Standard Forms Library (which contains the standard Outlook forms: Appointment, Contact, Journal Entry, and so on), the Organizational Forms Library (which contains organizational forms available to you), the Personal Forms Library (which contains personal forms stored in your mailbox), Outlook Folders, Templates in File System, Tasks, Calendar, Inbox, Mailbox, and Contacts.

**FIGURE 20.2**

*In the Choose Form dialog box, select the type of form you want to create or customize and click Open. This view of the dialog box shows some custom forms available for use or modification.*

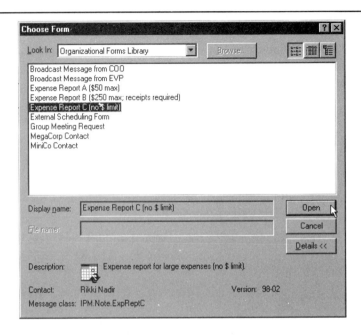

If the folder you need to access is not displayed, click Browse to display the Go to Folder dialog box. Select the appropriate folder and click OK to display it. The Browse button is not available when one of the forms libraries is selected in the Look In drop-down list.

3. In the main list box, select the form you want to work with. The Choose Form dialog box has a number of features to help you locate the form you want:

- You can click Details to toggle the display of the details panel at the bottom of the Choose Form dialog box. This panel, which you can see in Figure 20.2, shows the Contact, Version, and Message Class information for this form.

- Description describes the purpose of the form. For example, the Description for the Meeting Request form is "This form is used to create meeting requests." For the forms you're familiar with, these descriptions may be too obvious to be useful, but for custom forms stored on an enterprise network, they can be helpful in identifying the precise purpose of each form.

- Contact specifies the designated contact for the form. This information is more useful for custom forms than for the standard Outlook forms, which have Microsoft listed as the contact.

- Version is the version number allotted to the form. Again, this is primarily useful for custom forms.

- Message Class shows Outlook's classification of the form. The message class controls the icon allotted to the form. Each class description starts with the letters IPM, followed by a period and the type of form on which the form is based (for example, Appointment or Contact), followed by another period and the file name of the form. As you'll see when you create a custom form, Outlook assigns the class description automatically; you cannot change it.

4. Click Open. Outlook will open a copy of the form in a new window.

5. Choose Tools ➤ Forms ➤ Design This Form to display this form in Design mode so that you can change its design. Figure 20.3 shows a Contact form open in Design mode.

PART

V

Building Customized
Outlook Applications

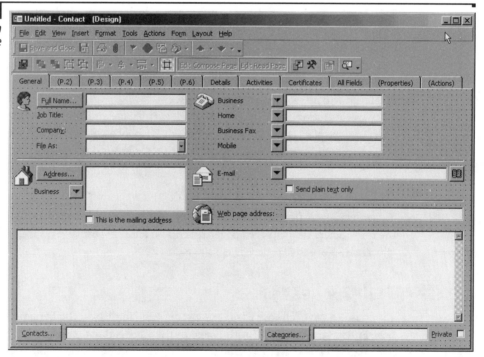

When you display a form in Design mode, Outlook displays all the pages that the form contains—the pages that are normally displayed, the blank pages that are normally hidden, and the special pages (such as Properties and Actions). You can then change the form as discussed in the next section.

# Customizing a Form

In this section, we'll look at the ways in which you can customize a form: by adding, removing, and renaming pages; and by adding, removing, and altering controls on those pages.

 **NOTE** By design, Outlook prevents you from changing the first tab of a custom form based on the standard Appointment form, Journal form, or Task form. The only workaround for this limitation is to hide the first page of the form and use the second page in its stead.

## Adding Pages to a Form

Each form contains a number of unused pages that are normally hidden when the form is displayed. You can activate any of these pages so that they are visible when the form is displayed.

When you display a form in Design mode, the names of pages that are hidden will appear within parentheses on their tabs: (P.2), and so on. The names of pages that are displayed will appear without parentheses.

To cause Outlook to display a page, select the page and choose Form ➤ Display This Page. The Display This Page menu item will display a checkmark to indicate that it is active, and Outlook will not display parentheses around the page's name on its tab.

## Removing Pages from a Form

To remove a page from a form, you simply tell Outlook not to display it when it displays the form. Select the displayed page and choose Form ➤ Display This Page to remove the checkmark from the Display This Page menu item.

## Renaming a Page

To rename a page, choose Form ➤ Rename Page to display the Rename Page dialog box. Enter the new name for the page in the Page Name text box, and then click OK. Page names can be up to 32 characters long (including spaces and punctuation), but usually you'll do better to keep them shorter for legibility—particularly in forms that use more than two or three pages.

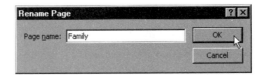

# Adding Fields to a Form

As you've seen from the standard forms, Outlook has a bewilderingly large number of different fields available. You can add any of these fields to a form.

To add fields to a form:

**1.** Display the Field Chooser window (see Figure 20.4) by clicking the Field Chooser button on the Form Design toolbar. Alternatively, you can right-click a blank space in the form and choose Field Chooser from the shortcut menu, or choose Form ➤ Field Chooser.

**FIGURE 20.4**

*The Field Chooser provides access to all the fields that Outlook offers.*

**2.** Use the drop-down list at the top of the Field Chooser to select the set of fields you want to use. This drop-down list offers a choice of field sets, depending on the form. The noteworthy field sets are the following:

- Frequently-Used Fields include Outlook's assortment of fields most frequently used for the form you're working on. A Message form in Design mode will have a different set of frequently used fields in the Field Chooser than a Contact form in Design mode.

- Address Fields, E-mail Fields, Date/Time Fields, and so on are self-explanatory.

- User-Defined Fields in Inbox/Folder include all user-defined fields available in the library or folder containing the form.

- The Forms item at the bottom of the drop-down list displays the Select Enterprise Forms for This Folder dialog box (see Figure 20.5). In the left-hand list box, select the form or forms that contain the field or fields you want to use, and then click Add to add the forms to the Selected Forms list box on the right-hand side of the dialog box. (Use the Remove button to remove selected forms from the Selected Forms list box.) Click the Close button to close the Select Enterprise Forms for This Folder dialog box.

*Use the Select Enterprise Forms for This Folder dialog box to select one or more forms containing fields you want to use.*

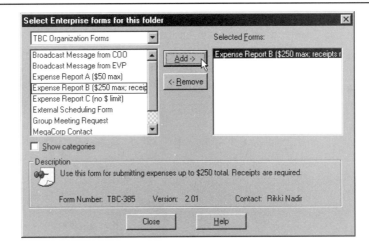

3. To place a field on the form, click its button in the Field Chooser and drag it to where you want it to appear on the form, as shown in Figure 20.6.

*Dragging a field from the Field Chooser to a form*

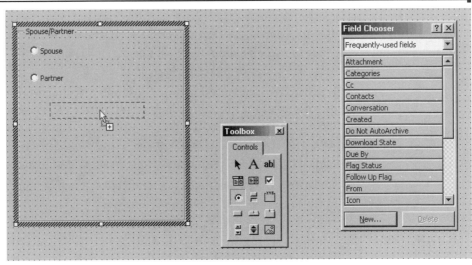

## Creating a New Field

If Outlook doesn't provide the type of field you need for your custom forms, you can easily create a suitable field. To do so:

**1.** Click New at the bottom of the Field Chooser to display the New Field dialog box (see Figure 20.7).

**FIGURE 20.7**

Creating a new field
in the New Field
dialog box

**2.** In the Name text box, enter the name for the field. Avoid reusing the name of an existing field (Outlook will stop you if you try to do this).

**3.** In the Type drop-down list box, choose the type of field this will be. The choices are:

| Type | Contains |
| --- | --- |
| Text | A string of text |
| Number | A number in any of nine numeric formats |
| Percent | A percentage, rounded or unrounded |
| Currency | A dollar amount, in either of two currency formats |
| Yes/No | A two-position choice: Yes/No; On/Off; True/False; or Icon |
| Date/Time | A date/time, date, or time value in any of a number of formats |
| Duration | A length of time, specified in any of four formats |
| Keywords | A text string limited to certain words |
| Combination | A combination formula consisting of either fields and text fragments or the first non-empty field in a series of fields |
| Formula | A formula consisting of fields, functions, or both |
| Integer | An integer in any one of four formats (three computer formats, one conventional integer format) |

**4.** In the Format drop-down list box, choose the format you want for the field. The formats available will depend on the field type. For example, a field of the Text type can have only the Text format, while a field of the Number type can be one of nine number formats (All Digits, Truncated, 1 Decimal, and so on).

**5.** Click OK to create the new field. Outlook will close the New Field dialog box and will add the new field to the User-Defined Fields in Inbox set.

You can now use the new field in your forms by selecting the User-Defined Fields set in the Field Chooser.

## Deleting a Custom Field

To delete a custom field, select it in the Field Chooser and click Delete. Outlook will display the message box shown here to warn you that the field will be removed from the list of available fields but will remain in the items in which it has already been used. Choose Yes to delete the field.

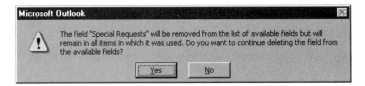

 **NOTE** You cannot delete any of Outlook's built-in fields or change the type of any field.

# Working with Controls

In addition to Outlook's built-in standard fields and the new fields you create, you can also use custom controls to customize forms in Outlook. You'll be familiar with most, if not all, of these controls from your work with Outlook and other Windows applications.

In the following sections, we'll discuss how to add custom controls to a form, how to lay them out, how to change their properties to control their appearance and behavior, and how to connect controls to fields.

## Adding Custom Controls to a Form

Like the Visual Basic Integrated Development Environment and the Visual Basic Editor for the Office applications, Outlook provides a Toolbox (see Figure 20.8) of custom controls that you can add to a form. To display the Toolbox, click the Control Toolbox icon on the Form Design toolbar.

FIGURE 20.8

The Toolbox provides custom controls that you can use on your forms.

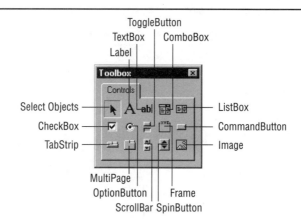

As you can see, all except one of the buttons in the Toolbox represent controls. The odd one out is the Select Objects button, which restores the mouse pointer to Selection mode; you typically use it when you've selected a control and then find that you need to work with another control before placing the current one. Here's what the controls in the Toolbox are:

| Control | Creates |
|---|---|
| Label | A label—text used to identify a part of a form or provide information on the form. |
| TextBox | A text box (also known as an edit box) for text entry or editing. |
| ComboBox | A combo box—a control that consists of a text box at the top of a list box. Use a combo box to present existing choices (in the list-box section) but also let the user enter a different value. |
| ListBox | A list box—a box control that lists a number of values. |
| CheckBox | A check box and a label to identify it. |
| OptionButton | An option button (also known as a radio button) and a label to identify it. Only one option button out of a group of option buttons can be selected at any one time (like a radio, which can be tuned to one station at a time). |
| ToggleButton | A toggle button—a button that shows whether an item is selected. A toggle button can have any two settings, such as On/Off or Yes/No. |
| Frame | A frame—an area of a UserForm or dialog box surrounded by a thin line, also called a group box—and a label to identify it. Use frames to group related elements in your dialog boxes. |

PART

V

Building Customized Outlook Applications

| Control | Creates |
| --- | --- |
| CommandButton | A command button—a button used for taking action in a dialog box. Buttons such as OK, Cancel, Close, or Send are command buttons. |
| TabStrip | A tab strip for creating multipage dialog boxes whose pages share the same layout. |
| MultiPage | A multipage control for creating multipage dialog boxes whose pages have different layouts. |
| ScrollBar | A stand-alone scroll bar for scrolling a custom control. (Combo boxes and list boxes have built-in scroll bars.) |
| SpinButton | A spin-button control for incrementing and decrementing the value of another control. |
| Image | An image control for displaying a picture on the form. |

To add a control to a form:

1. If the Toolbox isn't displayed, display it by clicking the Control Toolbox icon on the Form Design toolbar.

2. Click the button for the control in the Toolbox. The mouse pointer will take on the icon for the item.

3. Place the control on the form:

   - To place a standard-sized control, click where you want the upper-left corner of the control to appear.

   - To place a custom-sized control, click where you want one corner of the control to appear, and then drag the mouse until the outline for the control is the size you want. Release the mouse button, and Outlook will create the control.

   - To simply dump the control on the form (for example, if you're intending to use the alignment commands to arrange a number of controls), drag the control from the Toolbox to anywhere on the form.

4. For a control that has a text label, click in the control to place the insertion point, and then type the text for the label. Click outside the control or press the Enter key to accept the text.

You can customize the Toolbox by adding new pages and new controls to it. Briefly, to create a new page, right-click the tab of an existing page and choose New Page. Right-click the new page (which will be named New Page) and choose Rename from the shortcut menu to rename it. You can then drag custom controls (for example, controls with their properties set to suit you) from a form to the Toolbox, where they will be available for reuse.

## Laying Out the Controls on a Form

Once you've placed a number of controls on a form, you'll typically need to work on their layout. Outlook provides a lot of help for laying out the controls on a form, with many layout commands accessible from both the Form Design toolbar and the Layout menu.

All the layout commands work on the active control or active group—the control or group with white selection handles on it. To select one control or group, click on it. To select a range of contiguous controls, select the first control, hold down the Shift key, and then select the last control in the range; Outlook will select all the controls in between as well. To select multiple noncontiguous controls, select the first control, hold down the Ctrl key, and then select the other controls one by one.

Here's what the buttons on the Form Design toolbar (see Figure 20.9) do:

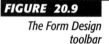

**FIGURE 20.9**
*The Form Design toolbar*

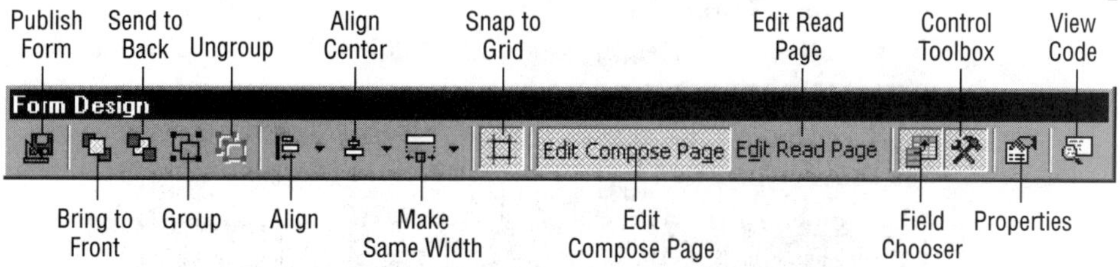
Publish Form
Send to Back
Ungroup
Align Center
Snap to Grid
Edit Read Page
Control Toolbox
View Code
Form Design
Edit Compose Page
Edit Read Page
Bring to Front
Group
Align
Make Same Width
Edit Compose Page
Field Chooser
Properties



**Publish Form** Displays the Publish Form As dialog box, which you use for publishing a form for use by your workgroup.

**NOTE** Keep in mind that users can't use your custom form until you publish it. Once you do, it's available for general use and can be reached by all people with the appropriate access.

**Bring to Front** Brings the selected control or controls to the front of the form (i.e., displays them on top of any controls they overlap).

**Send to Back** Sends the selected control or controls to the back.

**Group** Makes a group of the selected controls. This allows you to work with the group as one unit.

**Ungroup** Disbands the selected group of controls.

**Align** Aligns the selected controls horizontally and vertically depending on your choice from the Align drop-down list, as described in the following list.

The alignment in each case is relative to the active control—the control with the white selection handles around it.

- Left alignment aligns the controls with the left side of the active control.
- Center alignment centers the controls on the horizontal midpoint of the active control.
- Right alignment aligns the controls with the right side of the active control.
- Top alignment aligns the controls with the top of the active control.
- Middle alignment aligns the controls with the vertical midpoint of the active control.
- Bottom alignment aligns the controls with the bottom of the active control.

**Align Center**   Centers the selected controls either horizontally or vertically, depending on your choice from the drop-down list.

**Make Same Width**   Makes the selected controls the same width as the active control. The Height item in the Make Same Width drop-down list makes the selected controls the same height as the active control. The Both item in the drop-down list makes the selected controls the same width and height as the active control.

**Snap to Grid**   Toggles the Snap to Grid feature on and off. When the Snap to Grid feature is on, Outlook automatically aligns controls you place or move with the grid pattern in the form. This makes for quick and accurate alignment of controls, but can mean that you cannot place controls precisely where you want them. The Snap to Grid button appears highlighted (pushed in) when the Snap to Grid feature is active, and appears normal when Snap to Grid is not active.

**TIP**   To gain more control over the placement of controls when you're using the Snap to Grid feature in Design mode, you can change the spacing of the dots that form the grid. Choose Form ➢ Set Grid Size to display the Set Grid Size dialog box. Enter the width and height measurements in the Width and Height text boxes, and click OK to apply them.

**Edit Compose Page**   Displays the *compose page*—the page that the user will see when composing an item based on this form. The Edit Compose Page button is available only when you have chosen to create a separate read layout for the form (by choosing Form ➢ Separate Read Layout). We'll discuss creating forms with separate compose pages and read pages in "Creating Forms with Separate Compose Pages and Read Pages," later in the chapter.

**Edit Read Page**   Displays the *read page*—the page that the recipient of an item based on this form will see. As mentioned in the previous paragraph, you can create a separate read layout for a form.

**Field Chooser**   Toggles the display of the Field Chooser window.

**Control Toolbox**   Toggles the display of the Toolbox.

**Properties**   Displays the Properties dialog box for the selected control.

**View Code**   Displays the Script Editor for the current form.

The Layout menu offers many of these commands, together with the following:

**Size to Fit command**   Sizes the selected control or controls to fit its contents.

**Size to Grid command**   Sizes the control to the nearest gridline.

**Horizontal Spacing submenu**   Provides adjustments to the horizontal spacing of controls.

**Vertical Spacing submenu**   Provides adjustments to the vertical spacing of controls.

**Arrange submenu**   Offers Right and Bottom options useful for arranging groups of command buttons.

**AutoLayout command**   Automatically places controls relative to existing controls as you drag them onto the form.

# Changing the Properties for a Control

Each control has a number of *properties*—attributes—that govern its appearance and behavior. Different controls have different properties—for example, a list box needs different properties than a command button, though both share common properties such as Height and Width.

Outlook provides two ways of changing the properties for a control: by using the Properties dialog box and by using the Properties window. In the next two sections, we'll look at each way in turn.

## Changing the Properties of a Control by Using the Properties Dialog Box

Here's how to use the Properties dialog box to change the most frequently used properties of a control:

**1.** Right-click the control and choose Properties from the shortcut menu, or select the control and choose Form ➤ Properties to display the Properties dialog box (see Figure 20.10).

PART

**V**

Building Customized
Outlook Applications

**FIGURE 20.10**

*Use the Properties dialog box to set the most commonly used properties for a control.*

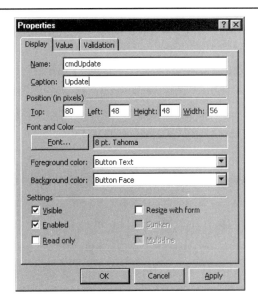

**2.** On the Display tab, choose settings for the properties that affect how the control appears. For different types of controls, different fields will be available in the Properties dialog box.

- In the Name text box, enter the name by which the control will be known by Outlook (and in your code). For example, if you added a command button that bore the text *Mortgage Payments*, you might use *cmdMortgagePayments* as the Name property.

- In the Caption text box, enter the text that should appear on the control. For example, the command button mentioned in the previous point would have a Caption property of *Mortgage Payments*. To set an access key for the control, enter an ampersand (&) before the appropriate letter. (The *access key*, also known as the *accelerator key*, is the underlined letter that you can press to quickly access a control.) For example, to set an access key of *M* for the Mortgage Payments button, you would enter a Caption property of **&Mortgage Payments**.

- In the Position area of the Display tab, set the values of the Top, Left, Height, and Width text boxes to the measurements you want for the control. These properties give you fine adjustment over the size and placement of the control. It's usually easiest to place controls approximately where they belong by dragging them about the form with the mouse and using the options on the Layout menu (discussed earlier in this chapter), and then make fine adjustments as necessary in the Properties dialog box (or the Properties window, which we'll look at next).

- If you need to change the font used in or on the control, click the Font button to display the Font dialog box. Choose suitable font settings and click the OK button to close the Font dialog box. The grayed-out text panel to the right of the Font button will reflect your changes.

---

**WARNING** If you change the font on a control, be sure to use a font that will be available to all users of the form. For most purposes, you'll do best to stay with the default font on controls, both to ensure the font is available and to present a consistent and readable interface.

---

- If you want to change the foreground or background of the control, select the color you want in the Foreground Color drop-down list or the Background Color drop-down list.

- The Visible check box (which is selected by default) governs whether the control is visible when the form is displayed (in some situations, you may want to keep certain controls invisible until the need for them arises).

- The Enabled check box (which is selected by default) governs whether the control is enabled or disabled (if a control is disabled, it is displayed grayed out, and the user cannot use it).

- The Read Only check box (which is cleared by default on most controls) governs whether the user can make changes to the control. If a control is read only, the user can select information in it and copy that information, but they cannot change the information.

- The Resize with Form check box (which is cleared by default) controls whether the control resizes itself when the user changes the size of the form.

- The Sunken check box (whose state varies by control) gives suitable controls (such as a text box) a sunken, 3-D appearance.

- The Multi-line check box, which applies only to text boxes, controls whether the text box can contain only one line (when the Multi-line check box is cleared) or multiple lines (when it is selected).

---

**NOTE** To view the effect that the changes you have made will have on the form, click the Apply button.

---

**3.** On the Value tab, set the field to which the control is *bound*—the field whose information the control displays—as follows:

- To bind the control to an existing field, click the Choose Field drop-down list button and choose the field from one of the submenus on the drop-down list: Frequently-Used Fields, Address Fields, and so on.

- To bind the control to a field available in an enterprise form, select Forms from the drop-down list to display the Select Enterprise Forms for This Folder dialog box. In the left-hand list box, choose the form containing the field, and click Add to add the form to the Selected Forms list box. Click Close to close the dialog box. Outlook will add the form as a submenu to the drop-down list of available fields; click the Choose Field drop-down list button again and choose the field from the submenu for the form.

- To bind the control to a new field, click New to display the New Field dialog box. Create the field as discussed in "Creating a New Field," earlier in the chapter.

 **NOTE** The Properties dialog box for the Frame control and the MultiPage control has only a Display tab—it does not have a Value tab or a Validation tab.

**4.** The Value tab of the Properties dialog box will display the Type, Format, and List Type of the field as appropriate. If these are grayed out, you cannot change them; if they are displayed in black on white, you can change them if necessary.

**5.** If necessary, change the property of the field to use by selecting a different property in the Property to Use drop-down list. If the Possible Values text box is available, check the possible values it displays.

**6.** If the Initial Value section of the Value tab is available, you can set the initial value of the field when the form is created:

- Select the Set the Initial Value of This Field To check box.

- In the text box, enter the value for the field. To enter a function or a formula, click the Edit button and build the function or formula in the resulting dialog box.

- Choose the Calculate This Formula When I Compose a New Form option button or the Calculate This Formula Automatically option button.

**7.** On the Validation tab, choose the validation required for the field:

- Select the A Value Is Required for This Field check box if you need to have the user enter a value for the field. If the user tries to close, save, or send the form without having entered a value in the field, Outlook will prompt them to enter a value.

- To have Outlook validate the field, select the Validate This Field before Closing the Form check box and enter the validation formula in the Validation Formula text box. You can either type the validation formula or click the Edit button to display the Validation Formula dialog box, in which you can build the form using formulas or functions. In the Display This Message If the Validation Fails text box, enter the message that Outlook should display if the value fails the validation. Again, you can click the Edit button to display the Validation Text dialog box, in which you can build the text using formulas or functions.

- Select the Include This Field for Printing and Save As option if you want to include the field's information when the user prints or saves the form.

**8.** Click OK to apply your choices and close the Properties dialog box.

## Changing the Properties of a Control by Using the Properties Window

To set properties that do not appear in the Properties dialog box, or to set a slew of properties all together, display the Properties window by right-clicking on the control and choosing Advanced Properties from the shortcut menu or by selecting the control and choosing Form ➢ Advanced Properties. Figure 20.11 shows the Properties window for a command button.

PART

V

Building Customized
Outlook Applications

**FIGURE 20.11**

*Use the Properties window to set less frequently used properties for a control, or to have quick access to all the properties for controls.*

To change a property in the Properties window:

1. Click in the list of properties to select the property you want to change. The box at the top of the Properties window (to the right of the Apply button) will display any current value for the property. For a property with a predefined set of values (such as True or False, or a set of values regarding, say, scroll bars), the box will become a drop-down list box; for a user-definable property (such as the Caption property, which governs the text displayed on a control), the box will be a text box.

2. Choose the value you want for the property:

   • For a property with a predefined set of values, choose the value from the drop-down list box.

   • For a user-definable property, enter the value in the text box. For example, to set a Caption property, enter the appropriate text string in the text box.

3. Change other properties as necessary by repeating steps 1 and 2.

4. Click Apply to make the change.

You can now either click the close button on the Properties window to close it, or leave the Properties window open so that you can make further changes to this control or to other controls as you work.

Working with the Properties window rather than the Properties dialog box has three advantages:

• The Properties window presents all the properties for a form, rather than a subset.

• You can resize the Properties window to present more or less information to suit your needs.

• Because the Properties window is a window rather than a dialog box, you can keep it open on-screen as you work (at the expense of some screen real estate, of course). This gives you quick access to all the properties associated with the controls you're working with.

## Creating Forms with Separate Compose Pages and Read Pages

You can create forms that display different pages to the sender (or creator of an item based on the form) and to the recipient. The *compose page* is the version of the form that the sender sees, and the *read page* is the version of the form that the recipient sees. You can create these separate *read layouts* page by page for each displayed page in the form. For example, if you customize a Contact form by adding a page named Contact History, you can choose to have separate read layouts for the Contact History page (so that your colleagues to whom you send the form will see a different layout than you) but share the read layout for the General page (so that your colleagues will see the same layout as you). The compose page and read page have the same name, but apart from that, the contents can be entirely different.

To create a separate compose page and read page for the form, select Form ➤ Separate Read Layout. Outlook will create the separate pages and will activate the Edit Compose Page button and the Edit Read Page button on the Form Design toolbar. You can then use these buttons to toggle between the read layouts.

 **TIP** When you use separate compose and read pages, the compose page is only displayed when the item is being composed—before it is posted or sent. If you add custom fields to the compose page, you will need to add the same fields to the read page if you want to be able to display the information later.

## Viewing the Code on a Form

To view the code on a form, click the View Code button on the Design toolbar or choose Form ➤ View Code. Outlook will display the Script Editor window containing the VBScript code for the current form. We'll discuss the Script Editor and how to work with VBScript code in Chapter 23.

## Changing the Tab Order of a Form

The *tab order* of a form is the order in which you move through the fields by pressing the Tab key (to move forwards) or Shift+Tab (to move backwards). (Other forms let you use the Page Down key to move forward and the Page Up key to move backwards.) Most Windows dialog boxes have a tab order arranged in logical groupings starting at the upper-left corner of the dialog box and moving towards the lower-right corner (following the way we read in English and most Western languages).

In UserForms you create, you should try to arrange the controls in a tab order that allows the user to move through them in the most logical way and with the least effort. This usually means putting the controls that the user will need to work with first in the upper-left area of the form, where the user's eye will be drawn first.

The tab order of controls in a form is initially set in the order in which you place the controls on the form, but you can change the tab order at any time. To do so:

**1.** Choose Layout ➤ Tab Order to display the Tab Order dialog box (see Figure 20.12).

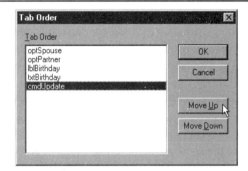

**2.** In the Tab Order list box, select the control whose position in the tab order you want to change.

**3.** Click Move Up or Move Down until the control appears where you want it in the tab order.

**4.** Adjust the position of other controls in the tab order as appropriate.

**5.** Click OK to close the Tab Order dialog box.

# Setting Properties for the Form

The Properties page for the form contains a number of property settings that you can adjust to influence how the form behaves and the information that the user can access about it. Figure 20.13 shows the Properties page for a message-based form.

The following sections describe what you can do on the Properties page of a form. To access the Properties page of a form, click the Properties tab when the form is in Design mode.

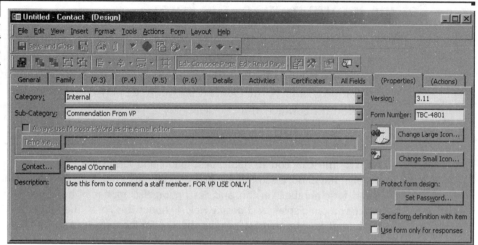

**FIGURE 20.13**

*Use the Properties page of a form to set information about the form—and to protect it if necessary.*

## Setting the Category and Subcategory for the Form

The first choice to make on the Properties page is to assign the form to a category and subcategory by entering the information in the Category and Subcategory text boxes. Use the category and subcategory to manage your forms. For example, you might create several forms relating to business trips and group them in a Business Trip category, with subcategories such as Expenses, Contacts, Reports, and Authorizations.

## Choosing the E-mail Editor

For a message-based form, deselect the Always Use Microsoft Word as the E-mail Editor check box (also on the Properties page) to prevent the user from using Word as the e-mail editor rather than Outlook. There are limitations to using Word (there's no guarantee that the recipient has Word installed, you're limited to the Word file format, and it is difficult to revert back to a non-Word-based form). You would have to completely redesign the form to use it anywhere else.

 **WARNING** If Word is not installed on the computer, Outlook will display an error message when the user starts a form with the Always Use Microsoft Word as the E-mail Editor property selected. Outlook will then default to the Outlook editor for the form.

PART

**V**

**Building Customized Outlook Applications**

# Setting Information for the Form

You can set the following information for the form on the Properties page:

- Assign a contact name for the form—usually the person in charge of administering and troubleshooting the form. Either type the name of the contact into the text box; or click the Contact button to display the Select Contact dialog box, select the contact, and click OK.

---

 **NOTE** The icon, contact name, description, and version for a form appear in the Details panel of the Choose Form dialog box when the user selects a form to open. The contact name, form number, version, and description also appear in the About Form dialog box, which you can display by choosing Help ➢ About This Form. The Properties dialog box for the form (File ➢ Properties) includes the icon for the form, its type, and its location.

---

- Enter a description for the form in the Description text box. Your description should help the user identify the form, understand its purpose, and fill it in correctly with a minimum of effort.
- Enter the version number of the form in the Version text box and the form number in the Form Number text box.
- Choose a different icon for the form by clicking the Change Large Icon button or the Change Small Icon button. In the File Open dialog box, choose the icon to use and click Open.

# Protecting the Form

The Properties page of a form is where you choose protection for the form. To protect the form against changes, first select the Protect Form Design check box on the Properties page. Then click the Set Password button to display the Password dialog box (shown here).

Enter a password in the Password text box, enter it again in the Confirm text box, and click OK. The password can be up to 32 characters long.

Once the password is set, Outlook will prompt for a password when the user tries to enter Design mode from the form. If the password is incorrect, Outlook will not switch the form to Design mode.

## Sending the Form Definition

If you publish the form to your personal forms library rather than to the organizational forms library or a public folder, you will need to send the form definition information with the form so that the recipient can see all the components of the form. If you do not send the form definition information, the recipient will see a vanilla version of the form on which the customized form was based—without any of the customizations. To include the form definition information, select the Send Form Definition with Item check box on the Properties page of the form.

If you publish the form to the organizational forms library, other users will be able to see all of the components of the form without being sent the form definition information. You can still send the form definition information, but it increases the amount of information Outlook is sending and has no practical benefit.

## Use Form Only for Responses

The final choice to make on the Properties page of the form is whether to use the form only for responses. Select the Use Form Only for Responses check box to have the form used only when a user chooses one of the Reply actions for a form.

Forms used only for responses are not listed in the forms library in which they are stored (to prevent users from choosing them in the Choose Form dialog box).

# Choosing Actions for the Form

The Actions page of a form lists the user actions that the form supports. You can use this list to check the actions, to adjust the actions, to enable and disable actions, or to create new custom actions for your forms. Figure 20.14 shows the Actions page of a form.

The Appointment, Contact, Mail Message, Meeting Request, Task, and Task Request forms support the Reply, Reply to All, Forward, and Reply to Folder actions by default. The Journal Entry form supports the Forward action and the Reply to Folder action by default. The Note form supports no actions.

PART

**V**

Building Customized
Outlook Applications

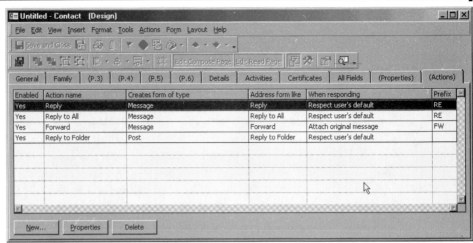

## Creating a New Action

To extend the use of a form beyond the standard actions available for it, you can create a new action for a form. For example, you might create a Broadcast action and form for forwarding a message to everyone on your Exchange system.

To create a new action:

1. Display the form in Design mode by choosing Tools ➤ Forms ➤ Design This Form when the form is open.

2. Click the Actions tab to display the Actions Page.

3. Click New to display the Form Action Properties dialog box (see Figure 20.15). Alternatively, double-click in a blank row in the table of actions.

4. In the Action Name text box, enter the name for the new action.

5. To enable the action, make sure the Enabled check box is selected.

6. Use the Form Name drop-down list to enter the name of the form to be used when the user chooses this action. Click the Form Name drop-down list button and select Form in the drop-down list to display the Choose Form dialog box. Select the form as usual, and click Open to return to the Form Action Properties dialog box. The Message Class text box will display the message class of the form you chose. You cannot change the message class from the Form Action Properties dialog box.

7. In the Characteristics of the New Form section, choose how the form created by the action should behave. In the When Responding drop-down list, choose how

the original message should be handled: include the original message, attach it, prefix it, and so on. In the Address Form Like A drop-down list, choose Reply, Reply to All, Forward, Reply to Folder, or Response, as appropriate.

8. In the Show Action On section, decide how to present the action in the user interface of the form. To have the action appear, select the Show Action On check box. Select the Menu and Toolbar option button to have the action appear on both the Actions menu and the item's toolbar. Select the Menu Only check box to have the action appear only on the Actions menu.

9. In the Subject Prefix text box, enter any text that should appear as a prefix for the message in the Subject line. For example, for a broadcast message, you might enter **BROADCAST** or an abbreviation for it.

10. In the This Action Will section, choose whether to open the form, send the form immediately, or prompt the user. Open the Form, the default setting, is the most widely useful; for procedural forms, such as acknowledgments or receipts, Send the Form Immediately comes in handy.

11. Click OK to close the Form Action Properties dialog box. Outlook will create the new action and enter it on the Actions page for the form.

PART

**V**

Building Customized
Outlook Applications

**FIGURE 20.15**

*Use the Form Action
Properties dialog box
to adjust the actions
supported by a form.*

## Changing an Existing Action

You can also change an existing action for a form by using the Form Action Properties dialog box:

1. Display the form in Design mode.

2. Click the Actions tab to display the Actions page.

3. Select the action you want to change.

4. Click the Properties button to display the Form Action Properties dialog box. (Alternatively, you can press Enter or double-click the action.)

5. To disable the action, clear the Enabled check box. To enable the action, select the Enabled check box.

6. To change the type of form that the action creates, click the Form Name drop-down list button and choose Forms from the drop-down list. In the Choose Form dialog box, select the form to use and click Open.

7. To change the way the form behaves when the user responds, select another action from the When Responding drop-down list. The default setting is Respect User's Default, but you can also choose actions such as Do Not Include Original Message, Attach Original Message, and Prefix Each Line of the Original Message. These enable you to override the user's choice of settings.

8. For a built-in action, you cannot change the Show Action On settings. For a custom action, you can change the Show Action On settings as necessary.

9. Change the Subject Prefix setting if you want.

10. Change the selection in the This Action Will section as necessary.

11. Click OK to close the Form Action Properties dialog box and apply your changes.

### Deleting a Custom Action

To delete a custom action, select it in the table of actions on the Actions page and click Delete or press the Delete key. Click Yes in the confirmation message box that Outlook displays.

You cannot delete a standard action from a form—the best you can do is to disable it. If you try to delete a standard action, Outlook will ask if you want to disable it instead. Click Yes or No as appropriate.

# Using the All Fields Page

The All Fields page of a form (see Figure 20.16) presents a tabular view of all the fields of a particular type contained in the form. This is useful for getting quick information on the fields and checking their properties:

- Use the Select From drop-down list to choose which fields to display.

- To view the properties of a field, select it in the table of fields and click the Properties button to display the Field Properties dialog box.

- To create a new field, click New to display the New Field dialog box. Create the field as described in "Creating a New Field," earlier in this chapter.

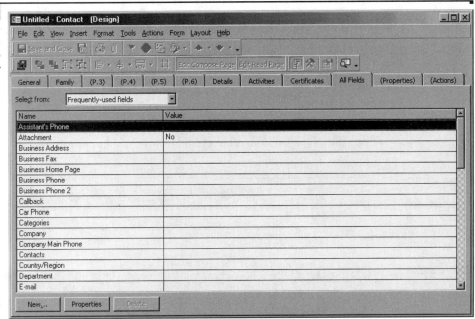

## Publishing a Form

Once you've created a form, you need to *publish* it to make it available for use. You can publish a form to any of the form folders available to you. Which folders are available will depend on the permissions set by your network or Exchange administrator.

To publish a form:

1. Click the Publish Form button on the Form Design toolbar, or choose Tools ➤ Forms ➤ Publish Form, to display the Publish Form As dialog box (see Figure 20.17).

2. In the Look In drop-down list, choose the location in which you want to store the form: the Organizational Forms Library, the Personal Forms Library, Outlook Folders, or one of the folders.

**3.** In the Display Name text box, enter the name by which the form will be identified (when the user opens it) and listed in forms-related dialog boxes (for example, in the Choose Form dialog box). Outlook will duplicate the name you enter in the Display Name text box in the Form Name text box.

**4.** In the Form Name text box, specify the name under which the form should be saved. You can leave the name that Outlook has automatically entered or enter a different name. For example, you might use a descriptive naming convention for the display names of forms so that users could easily identify them, but a more formal or condensed naming convention for the form names. So a form might have a display name of `Meeting with Outside Company`, but a form name of `Mtg_Ext_2`. Outlook will add the text you enter in the Form Name text box to the end of the Message Class description at the foot of the Publish Form As dialog box.

**5.** Click the Publish button to publish the form to the location you chose.

**FIGURE 20.17**

*In the Publish Form As dialog box, specify the location in which to store the form, the display name for the form, and the form name.*

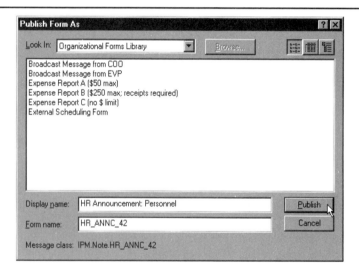

Once you have published the form, you will be able to access it via the Choose Form dialog box (File ➤ New ➤ Choose Form).

To publish an already-published form under a different name, choose Tools ➤ Forms ➤ Publish Form As to display the Publish Form As dialog box. Specify the location, display name, and form name for the form, and click the Publish button.

## MASTERING TROUBLESHOOTING

### "My Colleagues Can't See the Custom Fields in My Forms"

If the three classes of forms cause your eyes to glaze over, read this sidebar. For one thing, it's easy to get confused about the results of having multiple forms libraries available. For another, there's a complicating factor: when designing a form, you can choose whether to send the *form definition*—the information about how the form is constructed and what customizations it contains—with the form. This ensures that the recipient will see all the customized parts of the form as well as the standard parts. But when sending an item based on a form, you cannot choose whether to send the form definition or not; Outlook simply applies the setting that the form's designer chose when designing the form. (By default, Outlook does not send the form definition. For details on how to include the form definition, look back at "Sending the Form Definition," earlier in this chapter.)

If you send an item based on a custom form to a colleague, and the form does not include its form definition, the recipient must have the form available in order to see the customized parts of the form. If you send an item based on a custom form to a colleague, and the form *does* contain its form definition, your colleague will see all the customized parts of the form whether or not the form is available to them.

The disadvantage to always including the form definition is that doing so significantly increases the size of the message you are sending. For small-office environments with plenty of network bandwidth and server power, this may not be a serious worry. But in enterprise environments in which the network and servers are handling many thousands of messages a day, transmitting the form definition with custom forms can degrade performance appreciably.

If you choose not to include the form definition when designing a form, you need to understand the interaction between the personal forms library and the organizational forms library. For example, say you create a custom e-mail message form with two extra pages, and choose to store it in your personal forms library. You then create a message based on the form and send it to a colleague. Here's what happens:

- If your colleague does not have the form available, they will see only the uncustomized parts of the form, so it will appear as a regular e-mail message.
- If your colleague has the same version of the form available in their personal forms library, they will see the same form as you sent.
- If your colleague has a *different* version of the form available in their personal forms library, they will see that version of the form rather than the form you sent. Under certain carefully coordinated circumstances, this behavior can be useful—for example, if the recipient needs to access sensitive areas of the form that the form's original sender should not see. But under most normal circumstances, this behavior is liable to cause confusion.

*Continued*

**MASTERING TROUBLESHOOTING CONTINUED**

- If your colleague has a different version of the form available in their personal forms library *and* a version of the form available in the organizational forms library, they will see the version of the form stored in their personal forms library.

Generally speaking, it's seldom a great idea to have multiple copies of forms with the same name available. Here are our recommendations for where to store forms:

- Store forms that you share with your colleagues in the organizational forms library. For example, if you create a customized e-mail message or meeting request form that your colleagues need to use, store the form in the organizational forms library so that your colleagues can access it and see all the customizations to it.

- Store forms that you do not share with your colleagues in your personal forms library. For example, if you create a customized contact form that only you use, store it in your personal forms library.

- When creating and testing a form, store it in your personal forms library or in another location where your colleagues will not be able to access it unintentionally. Once the form is viable, move it into the organizational forms library.

- If, in your personal forms library, you keep copies of forms posted to the organizational forms library, keep the forms in sync. Otherwise, you may find yourself seeing a different version of a form than do people sending you items or receiving items from you.

In most cases, with proper planning and management of your forms, you should not need to send the form definition. Under special circumstances, or for testing purposes, you may choose to send the form definition—preferably on a form-by-form basis.

# Changing a Published Form

Once you've created and published a form, you may need to make changes to it. You may also need to create new forms based on a form. For example, say you need to create a dozen variations on a human resources form. You'll save a lot of time if you create a template form that you can use as a base for the other forms rather than creating each of the forms from scratch.

To change a form you've created and published, open it as usual: choose Tools ➣ Forms ➣ Choose Form, or choose File ➣ New ➣ Choose Form; then select the form in the Choose Form dialog box, and click Open. You can then modify the form as discussed earlier in this chapter. When you've finished modifying it, publish the form again to make it available.

 **WARNING** You can open two or more copies of the same form at the same time, make changes to each, and then publish both. The changes in the last-saved version of the form will overwrite changes in the previous version of the form—even if the previous version is still open.

## Making a Form the Default Form

If you customize the standard Outlook forms, you may want to use them by default when you create new items. For example, if you customize the Task Request form, you may want to use the customized form rather than the standard form by default when creating a new task request.

To make a form the default form:

1. In the Outlook bar or the Folder List, right-click the folder for which you want to make the form the default, and choose Properties to display the Properties dialog box for the folder.

2. In the When Posting to This Folder, Use drop-down list, choose Forms to display the Choose Form dialog box.

3. Select the form that you want to make the default form for the folder and click Open. Outlook will enter the name of the form in the drop-down list. (If you choose an unsuitable form for the folder, Outlook will warn you to that effect and will refuse to enter the form's name in the drop-down list.)

4. Click OK to close the Properties dialog box for the folder.

When you create a new item based on this folder, Outlook will use the form you chose by default.

## Managing Your Forms with the Forms Manager

Outlook provides a Forms Manager dialog box for managing your forms. You can use this dialog box to perform the following tasks:

- Delete a form
- Check or change various properties of a form

PART

**V**

Building Customized
Outlook Applications

- Save a form as a separate file (for example, to distribute it to other users)
- Install (add) a form to a forms library
- Copy a form from one forms library to another
- Move a form from one forms library to another
- Update a form with a newer version

To perform many of these actions—for example, updating or deleting a form—you need to have owner permission in the forms library that contains the form.

## Displaying the Forms Manager Dialog Box

To display the Forms Manager dialog box, you have to tunnel through several other dialog boxes as follows:

1. Choose Tools ➤ Options to display the Options dialog box.
2. Click the Other tab.
3. Click the Advanced Options button to display the Advanced Options dialog box.
4. Click the Custom Forms button to display the Options dialog box.
5. Click the Manage Forms button to display the Forms Manager dialog box (see Figure 20.18).

**FIGURE 20.18**

*Use the Forms Manager dialog box to manage your forms.*

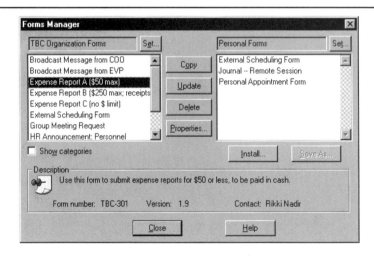

## Changing the Forms Library Displayed in the Forms Manager Dialog Box

Before you can perform most operations with the Forms Manager dialog box, you need to display the appropriate forms library. To change the forms library displayed in the Forms Manager dialog box:

1. Click one of the two Set buttons to display the Set Library To dialog box (see Figure 20.19).

**FIGURE 20.19**

*Use the Set Library To dialog box to change the forms library displayed in the Forms Manager.*

PART

**V**

Building Customized
Outlook Applications

2. Select the forms library you want to use from either the Forms Library drop-down list or the Folder Forms Library list box. Outlook will automatically select the Forms Library option button or the Folder Forms Library option button to suit your choice.

3. Click OK to close the Set Library To dialog box. Outlook will return you to the Forms Manager dialog box and will display the forms library you chose in the list box attached to the Set button.

The default view of the forms in the forms libraries displayed in the Forms Manager dialog box is by form name, but you can select the Show Categories check box to display the forms grouped by categories. You can then expand and collapse the categories and subcategories by clicking on the Expand (+) or Collapse (–) buttons next to them to display or hide the forms in them. Figure 20.20 shows the Forms Manager dialog box with categories and subcategories displayed.

**FIGURE 20.20**

*Select the Show Categories check box in the Forms Manager dialog box to display the forms in the forms libraries grouped by categories and subcategories.*

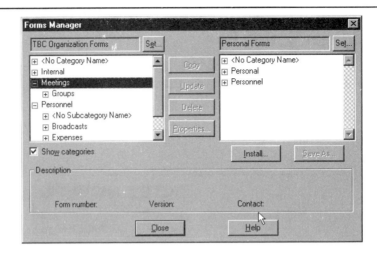

## Removing a Form from a Forms Library

To remove a form from a forms library, select the form in one of the list boxes in the Forms Manager dialog box and click Delete. Click Yes in the confirmation dialog box that Outlook displays.

## Copying or Moving a Form to a Different Forms Library

To copy a form to a different forms library, select the form in the left-hand list box or the right-hand list box in the Forms Manager dialog box and click Copy. Outlook will copy the form to the selected forms library.

To move a form to a different forms library, copy the form as described in the previous paragraph, and then remove the form from the original forms library, as described in the previous section.

## Updating a Form

When a form has changed, you will often need to update the older versions contained in different forms libraries. For example, you might change your personal copy of a form, test it, and then need to update the copy of the form stored in the organizational forms library or in a public folder on the network.

To update a form, select it in the left-hand list box or the right-hand list box in the Forms Manager dialog box. When you have selected the version of the form that requires updating, Outlook will make the Update button available. (If the version of the form you have selected cannot be updated, the Update button will be dimmed and unavailable.)

Click the Update button. Outlook will update the form with the latest version of the original form.

## Installing a Form

You can install (add) a form to a forms library from either a form configuration file or a form message file. Form configuration files have a `.cfg` extension, while form message files have an `.fdm` extension.

To install a form:

1. Select the forms library to which you want to install the form.

2. Click the Install button to display the Open dialog box.

3. Select the form file to install. (If necessary, change the selection in the Files of Type drop-down list from Form Setup Files to Form Message Files.)

4. Click Open. Outlook will display the Form Properties dialog box. If the forms library already contains a version of the form you are installing, Outlook will display a message box asking whether to replace the existing form. Click Yes if you want to replace the form.

5. Check the form's properties, and make changes and updates as appropriate.

6. Click OK to close the Form Properties dialog box. Outlook will install the form to the forms library and apply the properties you specified.

## Saving a Form as a Separate File

You can save a form as a separate file, so that you can share the form with other users or install it in a different forms library. To do so:

1. Select the form in the left-hand list box or the right-hand list box in the Forms Manager dialog box.

2. Click Save As to display the Save As dialog box.

3. Specify the name and location for the form message. Outlook will automatically add an `.fdm` extension to the name.

4. Click Save to save the form.

## Changing the Properties of a Form

Using the Forms Manager dialog box, you can change the following properties of a form:

- Display name
- Category (under which the form is listed)

- Subcategory (under which the form is listed)
- Contact name
- Comment (which appears with the form to describe the form and its purpose)
- Whether the form is hidden or displayed in forms dialog boxes

You cannot change these properties:

- Version number
- Form number
- Platforms the form is available for
- Design tool (the program or tool used to create the form)
- Message class

To change the properties of a form:

1. Display the Forms Manager dialog box.
2. Select the form whose properties you want to display in either of the list boxes.
3. Click Properties to display the Form Properties dialog box (see Figure 20.21).

**FIGURE 20.21**

*Use the Form Properties dialog box to check or change the properties of a form.*

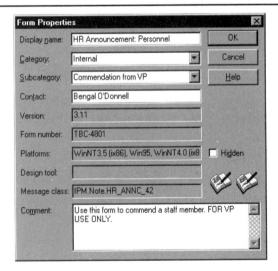

4. Check or change the properties of the form as appropriate.
5. Click OK to close the Form Properties dialog box.
6. Click Close to close the Forms Manager dialog box; then click the OK buttons of the Options dialog box, Advanced Options dialog box, and the main Options dialog box to close each in turn.

# Creating and Using a Template

As you saw earlier in this chapter, you can reuse a form by placing it in a suitable folder. Another way of reusing a form is to save it as a template. Not only can you then reuse it, but you can easily share a template with another Outlook user.

To save a form as a template:

1. Open the form (for example, by choosing File ➢ New ➢ Choose Form).
2. Choose File ➢ Save As to display the Save As dialog box.
3. Enter the name for the template in the File Name text box.
4. Make sure that Outlook Template is selected in the Save as Type drop-down list.
5. If necessary, specify a different drive or folder for the template by using the Save In drop-down list and list box. Often, you'll want to save the template in your \Templates\Outlook\ folder so that it is available via the Templates in File System selection in the Choose Form dialog box.
6. Click Save.

To create a new item based on the template:

1. Select File ➢ New ➢ Choose Form to display the Choose Form dialog box.
2. In the Look In drop-down list, choose Templates in File System if you stored the template in your \Templates\Outlook\ folder. (If you stored the template in a different folder, choose that folder from the Look In drop-down list, or use the Browse button to navigate to the folder.)
3. Choose the template in the list box and click Open.

# Creating a Custom Form Based on an Office Document

Instead of creating a form based on an Outlook form or creating an Outlook form from scratch, you can also create a form based on an Office document, such as a Word document, an Excel spreadsheet or chart, or a PowerPoint presentation. By doing so, you can quickly leverage the capabilities of such a document. For example, if you need a form to contain spreadsheet information, you can save time by basing the form on an Excel spreadsheet rather than creating a new form from scratch in Outlook.

To create a custom form based on an Office document:

1. Click the New drop-down list button on the Standard toolbar and choose Office Document, or choose File ➢ New ➢ Office Document, or press Ctrl+Shift+H to display the New Office Document dialog box.

PART

V

Building Customized
Outlook Applications

**2.** Choose the type of document on which you want to base the new form. Typically, you'll get the choice of Microsoft Excel Worksheet, Microsoft Excel Chart, Microsoft Word Document, and Microsoft PowerPoint Presentation. (These choices will vary depending on the applications installed on your computer.)

**3.** Click OK to proceed. Outlook will display the Microsoft Outlook dialog box shown in Figure 20.22.

*In the Microsoft Outlook dialog box, choose the Post the Document in This Folder option button.*

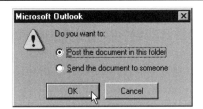

**4.** Choose the Post the Document in This Folder option button and click OK. Outlook will display a new window containing a new document of the type you chose. The window will display a mixture of the host application's toolbars and menus with the Outlook toolbars and menus. For example, the Excel window shown in Figure 20.23 contains a Standard toolbar that combines the Outlook Standard toolbar and the Excel Standard toolbar, along with the Excel Formatting toolbar. The menu bar displays an Actions menu instead of the Excel Window menu, and the menus themselves contain different commands from the regular Excel menus. The window will be identified as follows:

**Untitled.xls - Document** for an Excel chart or spreadsheet

**Untitled.doc - Document** for a Word document

**Untitled.ppt - Document** for a PowerPoint presentation

**5.** Choose Tools ➤ Forms ➤ Design This Form to enter Design mode. The window will display the Form Design toolbar and a tab strip identifying the different pages of information available in the form: Document for the document itself, (Properties) for the properties page, and (Actions) for the actions page. The title bar of the window will display (Design) in parentheses after the title. The title of a Word window will change from "Untitled.doc - Document" to "Untitled - Document," but Excel and PowerPoint windows will remain the same.

**6.** Set Properties and Actions for the form as described earlier in this chapter.

**7.** Enter information in the form as necessary.

**8.** Choose Tools ➤ Forms ➤ Publish Form to display the Publish Form As dialog box, and publish the form as described earlier in this chapter. The form will then be available for posting in the folder to which you published it.

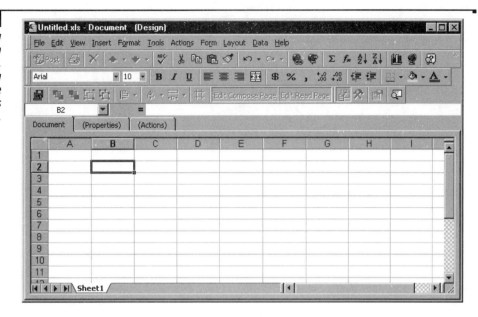

**FIGURE 20.23**

*When you create a new form based on an Office document, Outlook displays a window with a mixture of the application's toolbars and its own.*

## What's Next

In this chapter, you've seen how to create custom forms by modifying the standard forms that Outlook provides. The next step in creating custom forms is to use Visual Basic and VBScript to program them—automating actions and adding custom actions. In the next two chapters, we'll discuss what Visual Basic is and how it works; in the two chapters after that, we'll look at adding simple functionality to Outlook forms with VBScript.

PART
V

Building Customized
Outlook Applications

# CHAPTER 21

# An Introduction To Visual Basic

**A**utomation has always been the promise of computers: get more work done as the computer toils away at repetitive tasks. However, in order to have your computer perform a series of actions when you click a button, you need to tell it what to do in words that it understands. What if your company has a need for a specialized contact sheet, or needs to speed up the budget approval system, or needs to collect disparate versions of a Word document and create a report on the changes as quickly as possible? You can't simply tell your computer to go do these things as you would tell an assistant. You need to write a program.

This is where Visual Basic and VBScript come in. Now, don't shy away. Microsoft has worked hard to make programming with these two languages relatively easy, using English language terms strung together to tell your computer what to do.

 **TIP** Computers are perfectly literal, so when writing a program, you have to tell the computer exactly what to do, where to find things, and what to do if something unexpected happens. If you've programmed in the past, you should find Visual Basic fairly easy to learn. If you haven't programmed before, the learning curve will be a little steeper because you also have to learn to think like a computer.

 Throughout the next several chapters, we will be discussing Visual Basic and its offspring. The family is comprised of Visual Basic (VB), Visual Basic for Applications (VBA), and Visual Basic Script (VBScript). Prior versions of Outlook only supported VBScript. Outlook 2000 has both VBScript and VBA built in, allowing you to automate or accommodate most tasks that you need Outlook to perform. This allows you to add fields and forms that are specific to your business or the job at hand.

 **NOTE** VB and VBA are identical in syntax. Microsoft, however, felt it would be smart to ship VBA with a trimmed down version of the VB programming interface, called the Integrated Development Environment (IDE), which focuses on augmenting the capabilities of a host application (in this case Outlook) rather than on creating freestanding applications, which it cannot do. We think they're right, but because of this we will refer to VB and VBA separately on occasion.

# What is Visual Basic?

To understand what VB is, we need to understand what it does. Within the scope of its abilities, VB will perform the tasks you ask of it. VB cannot be used to tell your computer to make coffee at 7:00 A.M. every morning *unless* your computer is actually capable of controlling a coffee maker. (No Java jokes, please.)

However, you will probably *not* be seeking a programming solution for coffee making unless you're spending time at a ubiquitous computing shop. You'll use VB to automate tasks and extend the capabilities of Outlook 2000. Outlook is already very good at a number of tasks, such as maintaining contacts, managing messages and other forms of communication, and offering access to informational services and archival data. Microsoft realized, though, that there was no way they could anticipate the exact needs of all their users, so they allow you to do it. Most often you will do this by modifying an existing *form*.

 **NOTE** A *form* is very much like a window; forms are the basis of all programming in Visual Basic.

When you add a contact, send a message, or announce a meeting, you are using a form. Before we get into any programming, let's take a brief look at how Outlook lets you customize forms. As you'll see, the "visual" part of Visual Basic comes from the fact that most of the code is generated by *drawing* the controls onto a virtual canvas, the aforementioned form. Start up your computer and follow these steps:

1. Open Outlook and click Inbox.

2. Select File ➤ New ➤ Message. What appears is the New Message form. Take a brief look at the form to get a feel for it.

3. Now select Tools ➤ Forms ➤ Design This Form. What appears now is something that *looks* like the New Message form, but it has more tabs and a new toolbar. To the right of the form appears another window called the Field Chooser.

4. Choose Attachments from the top of the list in the Field Chooser and drag it to the New Message form. Note the small + sign that appears next to the mouse pointer. This indicates a copy operation, just like in Windows. You are simply copying the Attachments control to the Form.

When you drag the item over to the form, you'll see that the message area, the large blank area, moves and resizes on the form to accommodate the new control. You have just placed a new control on an existing form to modify it.

 **NOTE** A *control* is an object, like a button or a text field, that you add to a form and that can modify the form's behavior. For example, the OK buttons that show up in most dialog boxes are controls. When you place a control on a form, you must also add programming code to tell the control what to do. We will examine coding later in this and the next chapter.

Behind each control, you add code that makes the control do what you wish. If the control you placed on your form was a CommandButton (one of the control choices), you could, for example, program that button to open a Save dialog box to automatically let you retain an additional copy of outgoing documents in a folder of your choice.

An *event* is a user- or system-generated action, such as the user clicking a button or a CD-ROM activating the AutoPlay software. Visual Basic is called an event-driven programming language because it responds to events. You place control objects on your forms and then program them to handle specific events. In the case of a command button, you would program it to respond to a Click event: the event that happens when a user mouses over to and clicks a button. All of this is created in the Visual Basic Integrated Development Environment, or IDE, shown in Figure 21.1.

**FIGURE 21.1**

*The Visual Basic environment.*

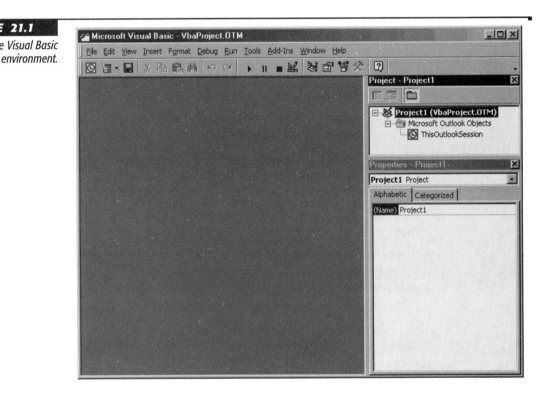

In essence, each control has its own capabilities and can be coded to operate independently of everything else on the form. As an example, we'll look at the ubiquitous OK button, present on most dialog boxes. To create an OK button in VB you would simply click on the CommandButton button in the toolbox, drag the cursor to the form, and drop. This procedure creates a button called *CommandButton1*, as shown in Figure 21.2.

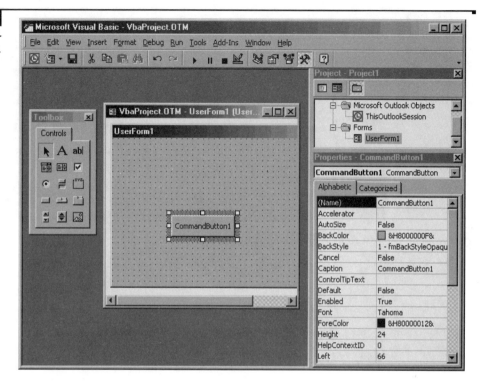

**FIGURE 21.2**

*A new Command-Button on a form.*

For each control there are *properties* that define how the control works. The properties for the CommandButton control are simple, and you use them to define the way the control presents itself. In Figure 21.3, the Default property of CommandButton1 is set to True, meaning that if you were to open this Form in an application and press the Enter key, this button would be clicked by default.

If we created a simple form, placed a CommandButton control and a TextBox control on it, and programmed it to put something in the TextBox control when the CommandButton is clicked, we would be looking at a simple example of programming in action. If, on the other hand, we only included the controls and omitted the code, nothing would happen. Why? Because there is no code to tell the button control what to do. You would click the button, and nothing would happen. It's safe to say that users don't really appreciate this type of form very much.

You can think of writing code as sending a letter of instructions to someone. Assuming we were in the VBA IDE, we would begin that letter by double-clicking the CommandButton control to open the Code Editor, which automatically adds the following code (which, in the world of programmers, is called a *snippet*):

```
Private Sub CommandButton1_click()

End Sub
```

PART

V

Building Customized
Outlook Applications

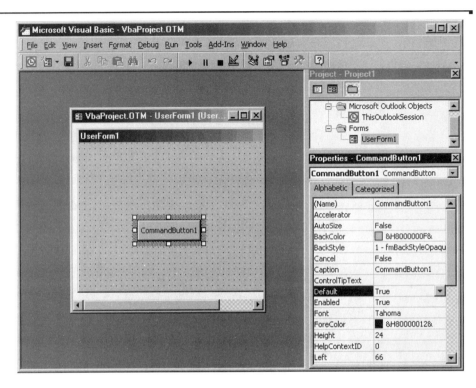

FIGURE 21.3

*CommandButton
showing the Default
property to True*

The IDE assumes that you want to add code to the control you just double-clicked to open. This snippet is a procedural framework, a structure that defines the beginning and the end of what is called a *procedure*.

**NOTE** A procedure is a complete and independent piece of working code. Procedures can be triggered by an event or from other procedures.

In that code snippet, `Private` tells the control that this code will only be available to the form that it is being constructed in. Sub is short for subroutine and identifies the code as a procedure.

**NOTE** Before confusion sets in, the terms *subroutine* and *function* both refer to types of *procedures* in VB. The difference is that a function returns information to a variable and subroutines do not.

CommandButton1_Click identifies the CommandButton by name and indicates what the procedure expects of the control: a click. Each control receives a unique name when it is created so it can be individually identified later. You can rename your controls anything you like, as long as each name is unique. It is also a good idea to make the names easily recognizable so that you can readily recognize their purpose when you go back to the code next year. End Sub indicates the official close of the procedure.

To get the command button to close the window when it is clicked, we just need to add one command between the Private Sub and End Sub lines: Unload Me. The whole completed procedure will look like this:

```
Private Sub CommandButton1_click()
    Unload Me
End Sub
```

If you were writing this as a letter of instructions in English, it might read something like this:

```
RE: Confidential To Do List

Dear CommandButton1,

If you get clicked, close the window you occupy.

Sincerely,
Programmer
```

 Now that we've added a command in language that VB can understand, it will perform the action we ask of it. Clicking the small blue arrow button on the toolbar causes the form to run. This is the same as selecting Run ➤ Run Macro. If we clicked the button, we would see that the form disappears.

**NOTE**  You can create code without first creating a button. To create a new macro, choose Tools ➤ Macro ➤ Macros and type a name for the macro. Make sure that the names you give macros are short, descriptive, and contain no spaces (you can, however, use underscores). If the name you enter meets these criteria and isn't already used in the current VBA module, the Create button will be enabled. Click the Create button to open the Visual Basic Editor.

# Making Use of Visual Basic

We just took a quick look at what VB is and how easy it can be to use it. Now, we're going to examine what VB can be used for. To begin, let's further examine what VB can do as a language.

VB is a complete and powerful event-driven language, which means that each component, like our example button, can operate independently of the rest of the program. When an *event* occurs, VB responds by running the procedure that was defined for that specific event, if any; if no procedure was defined for the event, nothing happens. These *event procedures* are tied to the controls that you place on your forms to permit users to interact with the application (for example, the Common Dialogs control, which adds the ability to use system-based Open and Save dialog boxes with only a few lines of code).

Going back to our example in the previous section, we told CommandButton1 to execute the code related to it when it was clicked. The click was the event and the code executed is the event procedure.

**NOTE** Event-driven programming should not be confused with object-oriented programming languages. A programming language can be event driven, object oriented, or both. For example, programs like Visual C++ and Delphi are both. Those languages, which can be much more complicated to understand and use, allow programmers to create functions, or independent segments of code, and then make use of them across multiple applications. Those languages also allow objects to define the parameters of children objects through inheritance. VBA doesn't support this level of object-oriented functionality, but it is nevertheless a very powerful programming environment used to create commercial applications.

Generally, VB is considered a Rapid Application Development (RAD) tool, with which custom solutions can be prototyped, debugged, and built in a much shorter period of time than with other languages. One of the more common reasons VB is deployed is to provide fast development of database front-end applications. Here are two uses that specifically relate to Outlook:

- You can automate how forms work, specify customized handling of new data, or create new data.
- You can create customized Outlook forms and personalized applications.
- You can access data from Outlook while in other applications.

VBScript, included in Outlook 97, 98, and 2000, allows you to extend the functionality of Outlook forms. VBScripts are stored in the form, which makes them portable.

This allows you to send custom functionality to another user merely by clicking the Send/Receive button. It's important to recognize the differences between VBScript and VBA, as it will help you determine which to use when faced with a problem to be solved. Let's look at that now.

 **WARNING** Code written for VBA will very likely not work in VBScript without significant alteration.

## The Differences between VBScript and VBA

Sometime after Microsoft created Visual Basic, it created VBA, a subset of the original language geared toward complex and complete automation of Office applications.

When Microsoft recognized that the Internet was to become very important, it created *another* subset of VB called VBScript, a simplified programming language that they hoped would become the scripting language of the Internet, allowing Web browsers to do things HTML couldn't. VBScript was direct competition for Netscape's JavaScript programming language. VBScript can be used just about anywhere, but mostly appears in HTML files on some Web sites.

To create VBScript, Microsoft trimmed what was not necessary in VB and left only the most essential components. As a result, VBScript does not support all of the VB syntax, specifically I/O, financial and statistical functions, intrinsic constants, and intrinsic data types. In other words, VBScript is leaner, trimmer, and cannot access the host computer's files, which improves security.

## Converting: Should I or Should I Not?

If you created customized solutions in Outlook 97 or 98, they were created using VBScript. Since VBScript is simply a version of VB, you can retain your existing code in VBScript form. However, in some cases it is better to convert the code to VBA. Here are some cases in which we *would* convert VBScript code to VBA:

- Your VBScript code is large and slow.
- You use VBScript to retrieve but cannot modify and save data from another application.

- You need access to the Windows Win32 API (application programming interface), or a way to talk directly to the operating system and tell it to do things.

Let's look at the reasons behind each one of these items.

Perhaps you've created a script that performs a number of actions that are very important to you, but it often slows down your system and can even slow traffic on the network. This happens at times when you have implemented a VBScript solution in a workgroup. The best way to solve this is to migrate it to VB.

VBScript is also not well suited to retrieving data to display in another application; it cannot perform true file I/O operations, so you've most likely worked around this limitation by publishing your data to a Web page and used VBScript to parse the data for the viewer. This is a cumbersome approach and VBScript is not well suited to this type of task.

If you need access to the local machine's files, VBScript is not very helpful. Since VBScript does not have all of the capabilities of VB or VBA, it cannot perform certain tasks, specifically file I/O. If you need Outlook to access files on a local or remote disk, you should convert to and expand your code in VBA.

## What's Next

In the next chapter, we'll look more closely at VBA as a language, gain a greater understanding of VBA by creating our first application, and point you to some valuable resources that can give you a hand up with Visual Basic—both books and information that is available for free on the Web.

# CHAPTER 22

# A More Complete Introduction to Visual Basic

**W**e realize that the example in the previous chapter was not quite enough to let you really show off your application development skills. In this chapter, we'll build and run a small Visual Basic application; small applications in any language are called *applets*. The applet is called Hello World! and has a long history in the world of programming as the first program many people create when learning a new language. Then we'll point you to some great VB resources that are available over the Internet and some books that can teach you everything you want to know about VB. We'll turn to VBScript in Chapter 23.

# The Big Picture

Before we do anything at all with the computer, we need to determine exactly what we want the computer to do and how we are going to accomplish this using VB. Very few professional programmers sit down and start coding with no idea of what their goal is. If you want to develop a good program in the most efficient way, you need a process.

There are several steps in the program development process:

1. Define the application.

2. Define the programmatic requirements.

3. Define the interface.

4. Compose the application.

5. Debug and test the application.

6. Build and distribute the application.

Let's take a closer look at this to-do list, which is generally referred to as a development cycle. The term *cycle* implies that this process happens more than once, and it does in the course of developing a large application or improving an application. You finish testing your application, release it to users, and then begin planning extensions or improvements.

First we need to define the application. This is when you hammer out the most important details of your application and nail down just what your application will do. In this case, we've already decided what we're going to do.

For the purposes of this exercise, we'll be using the classic beginners program, Hello World! This little application performs a minor task, but provides an easy framework for understanding Visual Basic. The task is simple: create an application that displays a message when you click a button.

Second, we need to define the programmatic requirements. At this point we need to take inventory of our needs and trim them down to the most necessary. It's a cycle, so we can always go back and add functionality; initially, we want to separate the requirements from the fluff. For our project, our basic requirements are the following: display a button to click, a text box so users can view the message, and a window (form) to display them on.

Third, we need to define the *interface*: the part of the application that the user interacts with. Interface design is a critical component, so don't jump into it until you understand the concept behind the application. If you are not entirely clear on what your program will do, you can't be clear on an interface design. (Programs with an outstanding interface but no real functionality are referred to "smoke and mirrors.") Our applet has a simple but easy to understand interface: a CommandButton control and a TextBox control.

The fourth step is to actually compose the application. Only after you've set down what you want your application to do, what programmatic components it should contain, and how the user will interact with it can you really start to create it. This is the step in which you'll create the interface that you decided on in the previous step. As you place each control, you will modify its properties to suit your needs. Once this is completed, you can create the operational code that makes the application work. For our project, we've included a step-by-step tutorial on the construction of the Hello World! program.

The fifth step is to debug and test the application. As you are working on your application you will run it from time to time to make sure you have not missed anything or made an error. When you do this in VBA's IDE, you are not actually compiling the code (translating it into a form that the computer can read more easily) as you are required to do with many IDEs. The code you have written is actually interpreted as it's read by the computer. Interpreting the code allows the application to run without waiting for all of your code to compile. This also allows you to debug your source code while the application is running.

---

 **NOTE** When VB compiles your code, it actually strips out all formatting and comments and creates a more streamlined version of the program for the computer to run. The result is called P-Code. Unlike compiling in languages such as C/C++ or Pascal, this process does not convert the program code into another language.

---

Although this can be the end of the development process, that's only if your application is perfect the first time around—an unlikely event except in the case of very simple applications like Hello World! If you find a bug, you go back one or more steps depending on whether minor or major changes are needed to fix the problem. At a minimum, you need to repair the problem and run and test the application again. Some applications actually work with minor or occasional bugs in them until a user notes the combination of events that triggers the bug. Most commercial applications ship this way, despite exhaustive beta testing.

The bugs that affect operation or that damage files are the most important to fix. Then come the less problematic operational bugs, which make the application less usable but do not cause it to crash. Finally, you can deal with the relatively minor cosmetic bugs, which are unpleasant to look at but don't cause any actual programmatic problems.

Our Hello World! applet is small enough that an experienced programmer could create it with no bugs the first time round. However, we will slip a few deliberate errors into the code so you can see how VBA handles them and reports their activities to you. And no matter how experienced you become, you always need to test even simple programs.

Finally, we will build and distribute our application. The term *build* refers to the process of making a program ready for an end-user to use. In other languages, projects must be built before the user can even run them. In VB, however, the code is interpreted, as we mentioned previously, so when we talk about compiling VB code what we really mean is that the code is *pre*-interpreted, allowing it to run somewhat faster. Compiling will also identify any lingering syntax errors, because every line of code is interpreted and checked for syntactical accuracy.

 **NOTE** Until you compile the program, VBA runs an application interpretively. That means it only compiles the lines of code that it uses and nothing else.

# Hello World!

We're now ready to begin with the fourth step: composing the program, which will consist of a dialog box with a TextBox and a CommandButton control. When the button is clicked, the program will display a text string in the TextBox control.

We'll use the Visual Basic IDE to create our program. Visual Basic's integrated development environment is a programming environment in which you manage, create, and compile your projects. The IDE provides you with the windows and tools you need for programming. The VBA IDE is somewhat trimmed down from the full VB version, but it maintains most of the same functionality.

To get to the VBA IDE, follow these two steps:

**1.** Start up Outlook.

**2.** Select Tools ➢ Macro ➢ Visual Basic Editor.

This opens the VBA IDE as shown in Figure 22.1. To the right, there are two panes: the top one displays the Project Explorer, and the bottom one is the Properties window, which displays the selected object's properties and makes them available for editing. The large gray area is where you'll actually create your form, and the relatively familiar toolbars are just up above.

**FIGURE 22.1**

*The VBA IDE for Outlook*

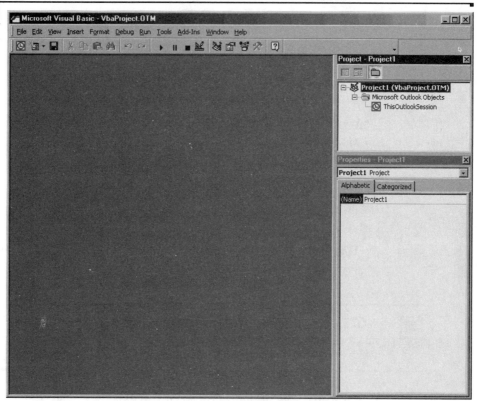

PART

**V**

Building Customized
Outlook Applications

**NOTE** When you start a new project in VBA, you do so within the host application, in this case Outlook. In the Project Explorer, you'll see an entry at the top called Project1 (VbaProject.otm) linked to Microsoft Outlook Objects and then to ThisOutlookSession. This simply indicates that whatever you create will be attached to Outlook.

## Creating the Application Interface

Our project calls for a text box and a command button, but before we can create them, we have to create the UserForm that they will sit on. The UserForm is our canvas, onto which we will "paint" our controls.

### Adding the UserForm

To add a UserForm, go to the toolbar and look at the second icon from the left, which is the Insert Object button. Click the pull-down menu attached to the button to see the objects you can add. These options are also available from the Insert menu.

The choices, as shown above, are the following:

- UserForm
- Module
- Class Module
- Procedure (currently unavailable)

We'll only be using the UserForm for our application, but here's a brief explanation of each of the types:

**UserForm**    A dialog box or window that is used to provide or collect information in an application's user interface.

---

**NOTE**  You can attach VB code to a UserForm; the code is stored in a form module built into the UserForm. This form module is not to be confused with modules or class modules, which are described below.

---

**Module**    Modules are also known as standard modules. They are where procedures and declarations are stored for your project. In essence, this is a code stockpile.

**Class Module**    This is the first hint of object-oriented programming (OOP) in Visual Basic. Class modules are used for complex applications and other operations that are only possible through Visual Basic code. For example, class modules are used to define functions that no control or add-in already provides or to call functions directly from the Windows 32-bit application programming interface (API).

**Procedure**   Procedures are used to break VB code into components that perform specific functions so that repetitive tasks do not need to be written over and over again. Using procedures eases your coding work because each procedure can be written, tested, and debugged independently, rather than as one part of a much larger whole. You can also reuse your procedures in other applications if you keep the code homogenous (avoiding references or calls to application-specific variables).

**NOTE**   The Procedure item is only available when you have a UserForm code module, (standard) module, or class module window open.

Now that you've seen the options, select Insert ➤ UserForm from the VB Editor toolbar to create a UserForm for your application. The form will appear in the large gray area of the VB Editor. You'll notice that you get *two* windows: a UserForm object and a window to hold it, as we see in Figure 22.2.

*FIGURE* **22.2**

*The default UserForm
object*

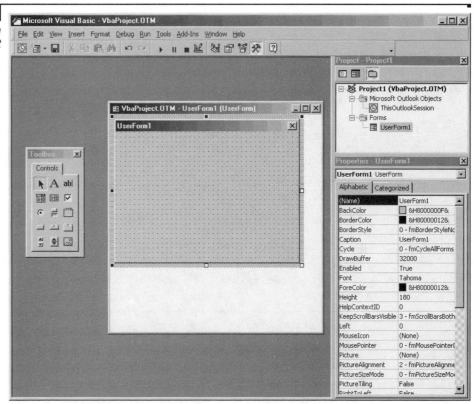

This form, as you can see from Figure 22.2, is named UserForm1. The Properties window shows the properties of the form and the current values of each property. And to the left of the UserForm, you can see the Toolbox. This Toolbox is where you select the controls to add to your UserForm, which we'll do next.

## Adding the Controls

A control is a pre-programmed object that the user can interact with or get information from. Controls include buttons, pull-down lists, and check boxes. Every time you see a dialog box warning you of something and you click the OK button, you have used a control.

To add a CommandButton control to the form, follow these steps:

1. Click the CommandButton button on the Toolbox (the small, gray rectangle, shown here). The button remains depressed once you have clicked it, indicating that the CommandButton is selected.

2. Move your mouse pointer to the form area and point to where you would like the top-left corner of the button to be; then click and drag down and right until you've outlined a rectangle the size you want the button to be.

The other way of creating a CommandButton on your form is to click on the button in the Toolbox and drag it to the UserForm. The default size and shape of the Command-Button control will be illustrated by a gray box.

---

 **TIP** The best way to think of the interface design process is to equate it with painting a picture. If you've used Microsoft Paint or any of the Office drawing tools, you'll have a good idea of how this works. Just select a tool from the Toolbox and click and drag on the form to define its size.

---

**3.** Resize and relocate the control to look something like Figure 22.3 below. To resize a control, select it, point to one of the handles that appear around the control, and drag the handle. Moving the control is simple, too. Point near the center of the selected control and drag it to the new location.

**FIGURE 22.3**

*Congratulations, your first control!*

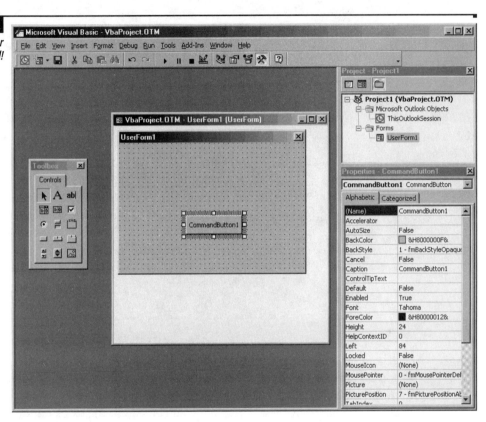

This takes care of the first control, the CommandButton with its default name of CommandButton1. We'll change the name in a moment, but first we're going to add the TextBox control.

Go back to the Toolbox and select the icon with "ab|" on it. Follow the same steps that you used to create the CommandButton control, but place the TextBox *above* the button control. Your end result should look something like Figure 22.4.

**PART**

**V**

**Building Customized Outlook Applications**

**FIGURE 22.4**

*Adding the TextBox control*

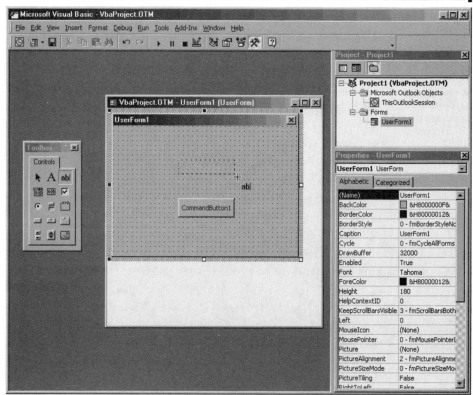

After placing the TextBox, you can also resize and relocate it to meet your needs. You can do that by clicking the control and dragging the nodes around, as you did with the CommandButton, but the VB Editor can perform this task for you. There are two tools that can resize and relocate your controls so they look uniform. First, let's size our two new controls in relation to each other.

1. Select the two controls by clicking on the form and dragging across both of them to "lasso" them. Both controls will have handles when they're selected. In Microsoft products, you don't have to drag completely around controls to select them; any control that you drag across will be selected.

2. Select Format ➤ Make Same Size ➤ Height.

3. Select both controls again.

4. Select Format ➤ Align ➤ Centers to align the centers of the two controls.

**5.** While the two controls are still selected, choose Format ➤ Center in Form ➤ Horizontal. Do *not* center them vertically in the form or you'll simply place one object on top of the other in the very center of the form.

Now that you've created the interface, we'll move on to setting properties and other options.

## Changing Properties

It's one thing to add controls to your form, but it's another to make those controls *look* and *act* as you want them to. This is where properties come in. In this section, we'll look at the properties for each of our controls and examine what they can do for us.

 **NOTE** We're not going to list all of the properties for each control because there are a great number of them. If you're curious about a control's properties, place the control on a form following the steps we've outlined above, and look in the Properties window, which gives you access to all of the properties for the selected control.

First, we'll look at the properties for our UserForm. The Properties window, which is in the lower-right part of the VB Editor window, sorts the list alphabetically by default. You can also click the Categorized tab to see your control's properties organized by type.

 **NOTE** To select the UserForm itself, click any area on the UserForm that is *not* occupied by a control. When the object handles appear around the form itself, it is selected, and you can see and modify the UserForm's properties.

The left column of the list shows the name of the property; the right column shows the value for that property. There are two ways to change a property:

- Type a new value
- Select an option from a list

### The UserForm

For our Hello World! project, we need to rename our UserForm. Locate the Caption property in the Properties window, and click the property name (Caption) to highlight it. When you begin typing, even though the text "UserForm1" is not selected, your new text will replace it. You will note that your new text also appears in the UserForm at the same time. Type **Hello World!** and press the Enter key to change the Caption property.

To add some individuality to our UserForm we'll also define its SpecialEffect property. Locate the SpecialEffect property near the bottom of the list and select its name. You'll note that a pull-down arrow appears in the value column. This property has preset values. You can choose from the following:

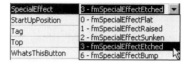

- fmSpecialEffectFlat
- fmSpecialEffectRaised
- fmSpecialEffectSunken
- fmSpecialEffectEtched
- fmSpecialEffectBump

Take a look at the form in each of these modes and decide which one you like better. We're particularly fond of the etched look, so we'll use that ourselves. You can choose what you like; choosing a different value will not affect the operation of the applet—it's only the caption, after all.

## The CommandButton Control

Now we can move on to the next control, the CommandButton. We're going to do two things to the CommandButton control:

- Change the Caption property to "Hi, my name is World."
- Set the newly named CommandButton as the default button for the UserForm.

First, select the CommandButton in your form; then locate the Caption property in the list and select it by clicking on the word Caption. As with the UserForm, the Caption changes as you type the new caption. If your caption text is larger than the button itself, simply drag one of the side handles until the button is large enough to show all of the text in one line.

---

 **NOTE**  If you resize your CommandButton, it will probably be out of alignment with the TextBox. Simply drag-select both controls and select Format ➢ Align ➢ Centers to fix it.

---

When that's done, go back to the Properties window and locate the Default property. From the pull-down list, select the True value. This sets the button to be the default when the UserForm is run, which allows it to be "clicked" with the Enter key or space-bar as well as the mouse.

There are no properties we need to set for the TextBox control, but it's helpful to be familiar with the properties for this very common control. Take a look at its properties to see what is available.

## Writing the Code

Now that we have a pretty face on our project, we need to write some code so that clicking the CommandButton will cause a text string to appear in the TextBox control.

Here is the code for the CommandButton that will start our procedure when we click on it.

```
Private Sub CommandButton1_Click ()
    TextBox1.Text = "Hello World!"
End Sub
```

Once you've added the second line of code, your code window should look like Figure 22.5.

**FIGURE 22.5**

*The code editor window showing our program code*

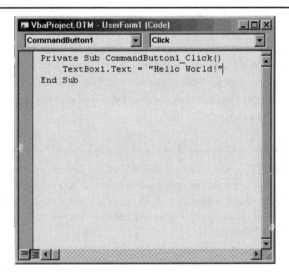

The easiest way to add code to a control is to double-click the control. This opens the Code Editor window. As you can see when you try this yourself, most of your code is already there. All you have to do is add the second line of code. This is just one of the ways that VBA makes it easy for you to create applications.

**TIP** There are a few conventions in programming that are accepted by most programmers. Your program will still work if you don't follow them, but most programmers follow these conventions because it makes code easier to read. When you add the new code above, you can add it without indenting the second line, but it would be harder to distinguish the subroutine from the surrounding statements. Adding tabs at the beginning of lines that are controlled by the previous line simply shows that the tabbed line is subordinate to the preceding one. It won't make much difference in this program, but in larger ones it makes your logic easier to follow and your bugs easier to find.

Let's look at each line of the code so we can get a better understanding of how it works. The first line reads like this:

```
Private Sub CommandButton1_Click ()
```

We already explained this code briefly in the previous chapter, but let's look at it again.

First, `Private` indicates that this procedure is available only to the form that it is on. If you want to make the procedure available to other forms in this application, you would substitute `Public` for `Private`.

Second, `Sub` indicates that the code following is a subroutine. Subroutines are the building blocks that make up programs. Our subroutine here, which includes a single line of code, performs a single task.

Third, `CommandButton1_Click` does two things. The first part of the name tells the subroutine which control is expecting an event; the `Click` part of the name tells the subroutine what *kind* of event to expect, in this case a Click event. When we run the application, we will see that clicking the button *does* cause the text "Hello World!" to appear in the TextBox control.

 **NOTE** You probably noted the lonely parentheses apparently doing nothing at the end of the first line. They are used to surround any values you need to pass into the procedure from another function, or to apply a static value that is always used. These values are called variables. You need the parentheses, even if you don't have any variables to pass into the procedure.

The next line, which is indented for easier reading, is a *statement*. A statement is a line that contains instructions for the program to follow.

The first item is `TextBox1`, which performs the same function as `CommandButton1` in the previous line. It is the name of the TextBox control we placed on our UserForm, and it was given the name TextBox1 for identification purposes. Its presence here indicates that when we click the button, the result will happen in the TextBox control.

The period (.) tells the program that the next item (Text) is a property of the first item, TextBox1. This sets up the Text property to be ready to accept input of some sort.

**NOTE** The Text property of the TextBox control is used to set the default text in the control when the form opens. If you place nothing in the Text property field, the TextBox control will be empty.

You can probably already figure out how the rest of the line works. The equal sign (=) sets the Text property equal to the next bit of information. In this case the Text property is set to "Hello World!" When we run the program and click the button, the text string "Hello World!" will replace the existing text in TextBox1's Text property.

The last line, End Sub, simply tells the program that it has finished its subroutine and can return control to Windows. Every time you click the button, the program runs and puts the text string "Hello World!" into the TextBox control. You won't actually see this unless you change or delete the text in the TextBox.

Now that we understand how the program works, let's run it and see it in action.

## Proof of Concept

Click the Run Macro button on the toolbar and, unless an error exists, your form should appear on your screen. Click the CommandButton and watch as the phrase "Hello World!" appears in the TextBox control.

This was a very basic project, but it is indicative of the process required to add to or modify the functionality of Outlook with VBA. There are, however, a few things that can trip up even the simplest applications.

## To Err is Human

Computers take everything literally, so if you made a typing mistake, your program won't work properly. For example, if instead of this line:

```
TextBox1.Text = "Hello World!"
```

you had entered this line:

```
TextBox1.Txt = "Hello World!"
```

the program would return an error. (Try it yourself and see what happens.)

To fix this problem, you simply need to fix the typing error. However, it's good to know what happens when VBA detects that something is not quite right. When we run the program with the error and click the button, we get an error dialog box with the following message:

```
Compile Error: Method or Data member not found
```

If we go and look at the code after dismissing this dialog box, we'll see that the first line of code is highlighted in yellow and that the text we changed is marked in blue. This tells us that the yellow line was the one that the compiler stopped on when it detected something wrong, and that the error comes from the misnamed property, Text.

## Compiling and Distributing Your Program

Because VBA is dependant on the application it lives in to run (in this case Outlook), that is where the code you create is stored. If you don't *build* your project, VBA will compile your procedures from the code when the user runs a macro, which can be significantly slower, depending on the size of your application. To confuse the issue slightly, VBA refers to building a project as compiling it (though, as we mentioned previously, what it really does is pre-interpret it). To compile your project, go to Debug ➣ Compile Hello World!

This wraps up our VBA tutorial, but that's not all there is. The next section points you to some books and online resources for programming and Visual Basic.

**MASTERING THE OPPORTUNITIES**

### Outlook VBA Distribution Quirks

Outlook uses VBA a little differently than do other Office products. For example, in a Word document, you would distribute the application by distributing a copy of the document that contains the macros—this is the way we distributed our VBScripts when we published a form (see Chapter 20). However, Outlook attaches the VBA macros to users' profiles, not directly to documents. To distribute our project we will have to export all the forms and modules from the project, and users will have to import them into their Profile project, a user's local code storage file. You can only export one file at a time.

To export a module or form, follow these four steps:

1. Open the Visual Basic Editor in Outlook.
2. Select a module or form in the Project Explorer by clicking it.
3. Select Tools ➣ File ➣ Export.
4. Select the destination for the module and enter a filename for it in the dialog box.

To import a module or form follow these steps:

1. Open the Visual Basic Editor in Outlook.
2. Select Tools ➣ File ➣ Import.
3. Select the file you want to import in the dialog box.

# Going Further with Visual Basic

Here is a list of some resources—print and Internet-based—that can help point you in the right direction if you're interested in going further with VB.

**Visual Basic 6: In Record Time** *by* **Steve Brown (Sybex)**    Learn Visual Basic programming quickly and effectively. This book offers clear, practical coverage of the Visual Basic environment, insightful instruction in the principles of Windows programming, and tested, easy-to-follow tutorials that let you quickly learn the language's essential skills.

**Visual Basic 6 Developer's Handbook** *by* **Evangelos Petroutsos and Kevin Hough (Sybex)**    Written by leading VB developers whose enterprise-level VB applications are used by COMPAQ, Exxon, Texas Instruments, and NASA, this book offers high-end coverage of the advanced topics you have to master in order to take your work and your career to the next level.

**Visual Basic 6.0 Programmer's Guide** *by* **Microsoft (Microsoft Press)** This comprehensive and exhaustive guide to programming in Visual Basic 6.0 straight from the horse's mouth is a great help when learning the intricacies of this occasionally complex and powerful language. This book comes with the complete collection of programmer's guides for Visual Studio 6 from Microsoft Press.

**Microsoft's Visual Basic Technical Resources site**    Plenty of technical information, tutorials, and other helpful material that's freely available. `http://msdn.microsoft.com/vbasic/technical/default.asp`

**Developer.Com**    A large network of resources for developers from all walks and languages. They also cover Visual Basic very well. `http://www.developer.com`

**Visual Basic Web Directory**    An immense collection of pointers and links to a huge amount of information about VB. It is organized in categories, which makes it simple to find what you're looking for, including learning from the bottom up. `http://www.vb-web-directory.com/`

**VBOnline Magazine**    An online magazine with lots of helpful material and tutorials that can help get you up to speed with VB. `http://www.vbonline.com/vb-mag/`

## What's Next

Coming up in Chapter 23 we're going to take a look at VBScript and how we can use it to enhance Outlook, but on a much simpler and less powerful level.

# CHAPTER 23

# Getting Started
# with VBScript

**A** s you've seen throughout the book, Outlook provides full e-mail and group-ware features straight out of the box. We've also seen in the last two chapters that Outlook can be enhanced and modified by using Visual Basic for Applications. The other tool for customizing Outlook is VBScript.

VBScript, as we mentioned previously, is a simplified version of the full-fledged Visual Basic programming language; it was intended to provide a universal scripting language for Windows applications and to compete against JavaScript for Web scripting. In Outlook 98, Microsoft included VBScript but not VBA. Outlook 2000 supports both VBScript and VBA, so you can choose between them based on what you need to achieve. VBScript is usually a better tool for developing relatively simple solutions.

 **NOTE** Outlook 2000 maintains the VBScript functionality that Outlook 98 had, so you don't need to convert all of your scripts. If you know VBScript, though, you've got a big head start when learning Visual Basic, the language that VBScript was derived from.

In this chapter, we'll discuss what VBScript is, what its components are, how it works, and how it works with VB; we'll also look briefly at what you can do with it. The bad news is that you need to know quite a bit about VBScript before you can do anything much with it, so if you're starting from scratch, there's a bit of a learning curve ahead of you. Expect to put some time into understanding what VBScript is and how it works with Outlook before you can create powerful scripts. The good news is that for a scripting language, VBScript is easy to learn.

If you've worked with Visual Basic before, you'll probably find you know most if not all of the elements that VBScript uses, so you should be able to work through this chapter more easily. Take a close look at the end of the chapter, however, where we'll point out areas in which VBScript differs significantly from Visual Basic and VBA, and vice versa.

 **NOTE** Adding to forms with VBScript is easier and less time-consuming than using VB.

If you haven't worked with VBScript, or you skirted the VBA chapters thinking that VBScript would be easier to learn, we're facing a little chicken-and-egg problem here: Before you can use VBScript with Outlook, you need to know a certain amount about VBScript. But before you can do anything with VBScript in Outlook, you need to know how VBScript interacts with Outlook. So here's how we'll proceed: We'll start by looking at how VBScript fits into Outlook and where you create VBScript scripts in Outlook. We'll examine a script containing a straightforward sample procedure so that you can see what a script page and a procedure look like. Then we'll discuss the components of VBScript, explaining what each is and what it does, and the syntax that you use for writing VBScript scripts. Toward the end of the chapter, we'll look at some of the common programming structures that you will need for creating scripts to manipulate Outlook.

By the end of this chapter, you'll know the basics of VBScript. Then, in the next chapter, we'll put VBScript into action by adding scripts to customized Outlook forms.

# Where Does VBScript Fit into Outlook?

Outlook is a complex application, and Microsoft worked very hard to make sure that everything you might need would be there if you needed it. The Microsoft engineers knew, however, that they would never be able to provide all people with everything, so they did the next best thing. They added support for VBScript. VBScript is a slimmed-down version of the more complete Visual Basic programming language, and it allows you to add functionality to Outlook's forms with less overhead than VB.

Outlook 2000 differs from the other Office applications in one significant way: it was built primarily to support communications. E-mail, telephony, and Web programs use scripting languages like JavaScript, BASICScript, and VBScript. These scripting languages are streamlined subsets of larger language command sets. Fewer commands mean less overhead, which is important when programs have to be e-mailed or downloaded.

VBScript is the script language that's similar to Visual Basic. Office 2000 has carried the script/full language migration in both directions. Outlook 2000 now supports Visual Basic on the desktop, and you can also add scripts to Web pages created in the other applications.

Learning VBScript is a good way to start automating Outlook. Unless you need to make significant changes to the way Outlook works, VBScript is probably powerful enough for you to accomplish your goals. VBScript does not support most of the advanced features of VB, which means that it is easier to learn, but it does have some tricks up its own sleeve (which we detail later on in this chapter). VBScript is very useful when you need a simple language to take care of a simple problem or to fill a relatively simple need.

## Starting the Script Editor

To create or work with scripts, you use the Script Editor application. Start the Script Editor as follows:

**1.** Choose File ➤ New ➤ Mail Message to create a new message.

**2.** In the To box, enter your name as the recipient for the message. This will serve as a demonstration; for practical use, this message would be addressed to a group of users (for example, everyone at a particular company location).

**3.** Choose Tools ➣ Forms ➣ Design This Form to display the form in Design mode (as discussed in Chapter 20).

**4.** Click the View Code button on the Form Design toolbar, or choose Form ➣ View Code, to display the Script Editor (see Figure 23.1).

**FIGURE 23.1**

*You use the Script Editor application to create VBScript scripts for Outlook.*

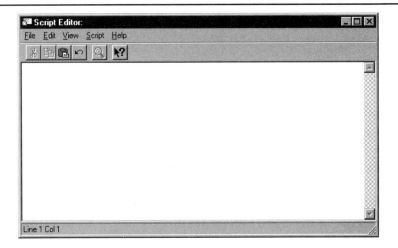

Look over the interface and run your mouse quickly along the menu bar to display each menu in turn. As you can see, the Script Editor is a minimalist application with very few commands. On the plus side, this means that you can get started with it without having to learn a lot. On the minus side, this means that the Script Editor doesn't provide much help in creating code.

**NOTE** If you've used other programming environments, such as Visual Basic's Integrated Development Environment or the Visual Basic Editor for the other Office 2000 applications, you'll find the Script Editor painfully spartan.

## Creating a Sample Procedure

We'll explore the Script Editor's features more fully in the next chapter. For the moment, start a simple procedure as follows:

1. Choose Script ➤ Event Handler to display the Insert Event Handler dialog box (see Figure 23.2).

2. Make sure the Open event is selected in the list box (it should be selected by default).

3. Click the Add button to start creating a procedure attached to the form's Open event. The Script Editor will close the Insert Event Handler dialog box and will insert the following lines of code in the Script Editor window:

```
Function Item_Open()

End Function
```

4. Type in the commands for the procedure so that you have the following code.

```
Function Item_Open()

    'Declare (create) a variable to contain the subject of the message
    Dim strSubject

    'Make sure the item is new (has a CreationTime of 1/1/4501)
    'so that a reply to or forward of this message does not
    'cause this code to run
    If Item.CreationTime = "1/1/4501" Then
```

```
'Assign to strSubject variable the text from an input box
strSubject = InputBox("Enter the subject for the message:", _
"Send Company Event Message", "Company Event: ")

'Assign the contents of the strSubject variable
'to the Subject property of the item
Item.Subject = strSubject

'Set the ReadReceiptRequested property to True
Item.ReadReceiptRequested = True

'Set the OriginatorDeliveryReportRequested property to True
Item.OriginatorDeliveryReportRequested = True

'Set the VotingOptions property to two buttons:
'"Will Attend" and "Will Not Attend"
Item.VotingOptions = "Will Attend; Will Not Attend"
End If

End Function
```

Figure 23.3 shows what you should be seeing now. The code sheet now contains one procedure. As you'll see later, you can add other procedures to the same code sheet.

## What Does the Code Mean?

The following paragraphs describe briefly what you've just created. For now, focus on the general picture without worrying too much about the specifics; we'll go through each of the components of VBScript code in more depth later in the chapter.

This code is a function procedure that starts with the Function Item_Open() statement and ends with the End Function statement. All the code between these statements is part of this function procedure. The function procedure runs when the user triggers the Open event by opening the message.

The procedure begins by declaring (creating) a variable, strSubject, to contain the subject of the message. As you'll see later, it's considered good practice to declare variables at the beginning of a procedure.

*FIGURE 23.3*

*The Script Editor with lines of code entered*

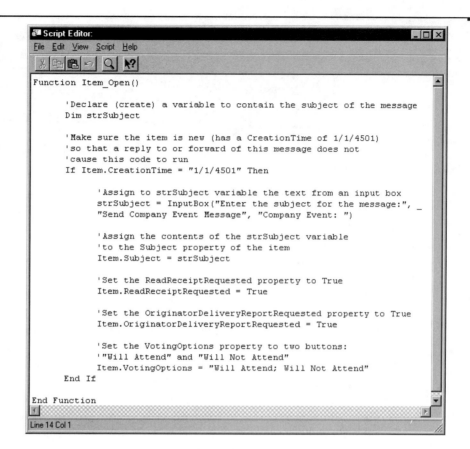

PART

V

Building Customized
Outlook Applications

Then the procedure uses an If... Then statement to check the CreationTime property of the current item (the mail message) to make sure the item being opened is new. Take this for granted for the moment (we'll explain later how it works). We check this because we want the procedure to run only when creating a new message—not when opening it to reply to it or forward it to someone else. If the item is new, the rest of the code runs. If not, VBScript moves from the If... Then statement to the End If statement and continues executing the code from there. Because there are no statements after End If, nothing else happens if the item is not new.

Assuming the item is new, the code displays an input box (see Figure 23.4) prompting the user for the subject of the message. The input box suggests the default text "Company Event: " (with a space after the colon), which the user can add to, replace, or amend as they see fit. When the user clicks the OK button on the input box, VBScript assigns the contents of the text box in the input box to the strSubject variable.

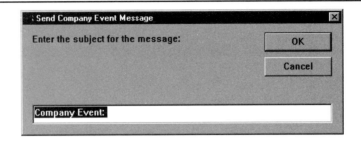

The procedure then assigns the contents of the strSubject variable to the Subject property of the item, thus placing the text the user entered in the input box into the Subject box of the message. Note how this assignment (and the previous assignments) works: you use an equal sign to designate the assignment (here, Item.Subject = strSubject), setting what appears before the equal sign (here, Item.Subject) to equal what appears after the equal sign (here, strSubject).

The procedure then sets the ReadReceiptRequested property of the message to True, which is the VBScript equivalent of selecting the Tell Me When This Message Has Been Read check box in the Message Options dialog box for the message. (Conversely, setting the property to False is equivalent to clearing the check box.) The procedure follows up by setting the OriginatorDeliveryReportRequested property of the message to True as well —the equivalent of selecting the Tell Me When This Message Has Been Delivered check box in the Message Options dialog box. Finally, the procedure sets the VotingOptions property of the message to "Will Attend; Will Not Attend," the equivalent of selecting the Use Voting Buttons check box in the Message Options dialog box and specifying Will Attend and Will Not Attend buttons.

## Using Comments, Blank Lines, and Indentation

The lines that start with single quote marks (') are *comment* lines (also known as *remark lines*) explaining to the human reader the purpose of the code. The single quote tells VBScript to ignore everything on this line after the single quote. You can use rem (short for *remark*) in any capitalization to indicate a comment line. You can also add comments to the end of a line of code, as in the example below, but this typically makes the comments harder to read unless the lines of code are as short as the one in the example:

```
Dim strChair  'declare a variable to contain the chairperson's name
```

Commenting your code is good programming practice. It has three main purposes:

• It can help clarify your thinking when you're creating your code.

- It helps others understand your code.

- It helps *you* understand your code when you revisit it six months later.

About 95 percent of programmers hate commenting their code and resist it at almost all costs. Typically, the most effective way to comment your code is to start by writing a description of what each part of the code should do. Then, as you create the code, describe particular actions in more detail; even add thoughts to yourself about workarounds you might have to take or alternatives worth trying. When you've finished the code, go back through and clean up the comments to make them as clear and concise as you can bear.

You'll see that we've used blank lines to separate the code into logical blocks (here, into comments and the commands they explain). This is a visual convenience for humans; VBScript simply ignores the blank lines.

Likewise, we've used indentation to indicate the hierarchy of the statements. The `Function Item_Open()` and `End Function` statements mark the beginning and end of the code, and so appear at the left margin. Everything else is indented one or more tabs. The statements within the `If... Then` statement are indented further to indicate that they are contained within that condition; if the condition is not true, execution moves from the `If` statement to the `End If` statement without troubling any of the lines of code in between. The indentation helps your eye move quickly from one to the next.

You don't need to indent any of your code—but as you can see, it makes it far easier to read. Typical practice is to indent one tab, or four or five spaces, for each level of indentation. Because the Script Editor does not offer automatic indentation of subsequent lines the way more evolved programming environments do, in the Script Editor it's much easier to use tabs than spaces for indentation.

You'll notice that some of the statements are broken over two lines of code using the line-continuation character—an underscore preceded by a space. This also is for visual convenience only, so that you don't have to scroll horizontally back and forth in the Script Editor window. VBScript reads a line of code broken like this over two or more lines as one logical line.

## Running the Procedure

Now that you've created this procedure, run it so that you can see it working:

1. Activate the Message window by clicking it or by pressing Alt+Tab until it is selected. (You can leave the Script Editor open for the time being.)

2. Choose Form ➤ Run This Form. This will cause Outlook to create a new form based on this form. Because the form is new, the code will run. Outlook will display the Send Company Event Message input box.

**3.** Add to or alter the text in it as appropriate, and click the OK button. Outlook will create the form and will enter the text from the input box in the Subject text box.

**4.** Click the Options button to display the Message Options dialog box (see Figure 23.5).

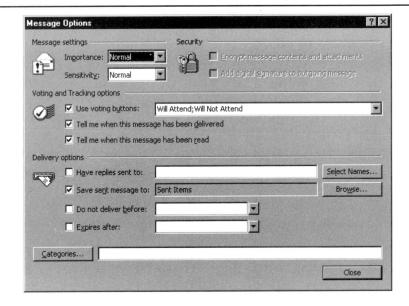

**5.** In the Voting and Tracking Options section, verify that the Use Voting Buttons check box is selected and that "Will Attend;Will Not Attend" appears in the drop-down list text box, and that both the Tell Me When This Message Has Been Delivered check box and the Tell Me When This Message Has Been Read check box are selected.

**6.** Click the Close button to close the Message Options dialog box.

**7.** Click the Send button to send the message to yourself.

You can then open the message and choose one of the voting buttons to reply to it. Note that when you open the message, the Open function procedure will not run because the message has a creation date other than 1/1/4501.

# Understanding VBScript Syntax

To work with VBScript, you need to know a little about the syntax—the rules that govern how the language works. Just as most human languages have widely recognized parts (such as nouns, verbs, adjectives, and so on), scripting and programming languages break down into a number of parts that you put together in *statements*, arrangements defined by the syntax of the language.

You put together statements by using combinations of keywords, objects, properties, methods, constants, and variables, together with required arguments and optional arguments specifying information. In the next sections, we'll look at what these terms mean and how you work with them.

## Keywords

A *keyword* is a word defined as having a meaning in Visual Basic. Keywords include object names, properties, methods, and argument names. It's possible to create variables, constants, and procedures that have the same names as Visual Basic keywords. This is called *shadowing* a keyword and isn't usually a good idea, as it becomes easy to get confused. For example, there's an object called `ContactItem` that represents a contact, so it's a bad idea to create a variable, constant, or procedure named `ContactItem`.

As we'll see in a little while, you can name your variables, constants, and procedures pretty much anything that strikes your fancy, so there's no real reason to shadow a keyword—but it's surprisingly easy to do unintentionally.

## Objects

An object is one of the elements that make up an application. You can look at Outlook as being made up of a collection of objects that allow you to access different parts of the application. For example, Outlook uses the `AppointmentItem` object to represent an appointment in the Calendar. The `ContactItem` object represents a contact in the Contacts folder, the `NoteItem` object represents a Note, and so on.

As you'll see in a moment, objects can contain other objects, which makes for both power and confusion. Outlook has a much flatter structure than the other Office applications, such as Word, Excel, and PowerPoint, which are constructed rather like Chinese boxes, with one object inside another inside another. (For example, in Word, within the `Application` object you find the `ActiveWindow` object; within the `ActiveWindow` object you find the `Selection` object; within the `Selection` object you find the `Font` object; and finally you reach properties that you can use to set the size and typeface of the font.) In Outlook, on the other hand, most of the objects are available at or near the top level—the outermost of the Chinese boxes, if you will.

Objects are organized into a theoretical hierarchy known as an *object model*. We'll look at the Outlook object model in detail in Chapter 25.

# Collections

Groups of objects are organized into *collections*, which provide an easy way to access them. For example, the Attachments collection contains a collection of Attachment objects, each of which represents an attachment contained in an Outlook item, such as a message. Usually, the name of a collection is the plural of the object, as in the previous example, but there are some exceptions. For example, Outlook uses a Folders collection that contains all the MAPIFolder objects. These MAPIFolder objects represent the folders available in Outlook. Outlook also has an Items collection that you can use to retrieve all the items in a specified folder.

 **TIP** Collections themselves are objects, too. To avoid confusion, from now on, we'll refer to any collection as a "collection" rather than a "collection object."

# Properties

Each object has a number of *properties*—named characteristics that define the object. For example, the MailItem object that represents a mail message has a number of properties that range from a Body property that represents the text of the message, to the CreationTime property we used earlier in the chapter to find out when the message was created and the VotingOptions property we used to specify voting options for the message. As you saw, a property appears after the name of the item it refers to, separated by a period. For example, to refer to the CreationTime property of a MailItem object, you would use MailItem.CreationTime. To refer to the current item, you can use the Item keyword instead—Item.CreationTime, as we used earlier in the chapter.

To find out the current settings of an object, you *return* (get) its properties by specifying the property you want to return. So to find out the body text of a message, you would return its Body property. The following statement returns the Body property of the current item and displays it in a message box:

```
MsgBox Item.Body
```

To change the settings of an object, you adjust its properties. So to change the text of the message, you would change the Body property. The following statement changes the Body property of the current item to "Your dinner is in the dog."

```
Item.Body = "Your dinner is in the dog."
```

As you might imagine, Outlook has a large number of objects, and each object has a distinct set of properties. In this chapter and the following chapters, we will examine only the relevant properties of the relevant objects needed to perform certain tasks. Once you understand the principles by which objects work, you'll have little difficulty finding the objects and properties you need.

## Methods

A *method* is a built-in action that you can perform on an object; more technically, a method is a *procedure* (a set of instructions) for an object. For example, the Attachment object that we met a moment ago has a Delete method that deletes the specified attachment, and a SaveAsFile method that saves the specified attachment as a file, while the MAPIFolder object has methods including CopyTo (for copying a folder and its contents to another folder) and MoveTo (for moving a folder and its contents to another folder).

Like a property, a method appears after the name of the item it refers to, separated by a period. For example, the Delete method appears like this:

```
Item.Delete
```

Most methods take one or more *arguments*, parameters that supply pieces of information necessary to the method. Some arguments are required, while others are optional. For example, the SaveAsFile method takes a required Path argument that specifies the path in which to save the attachment:

```
Item.Attachments.SaveAsFile "d:\temp\Example Saved Attachment.ppt"
```

Other methods take no arguments. For example, the Delete method takes no arguments because none are needed—Outlook is deleting the specified item, and that's all the information it needs to do so.

## Constants

A *constant* is a named item in memory that keeps a constant piece of information while a program is executing. You can specify the appropriate constant in your code instead of the corresponding value, which provides an easy way of handling complex information or information that may change from computer to computer, such as the location of a particular Outlook folder. Outlook uses constants to signify frequently used information, such as the day of the week (for example, the constant olThursday in the OlDaysOfWeek group of constants represents Thursday) and its default folders (for example, the constant olFolderInbox in the OlDefaultFolders group of constants represents the Inbox). Each constant has a numeric value associated with it; for example, the constant olFolderInbox in the OlDefaultFolders group has the numeric value 6 associated with it.

When using VBScript to automate Outlook procedures, you need to specify the numeric values rather than the descriptive constants. (When using VBA to automate

Outlook procedures, you can use the descriptive constants instead of the numeric values.) For example, to specify the Sensitivity property of a message, you need to specify the numeric value for the appropriate `OlSensitivity` constant rather than specifying the `Sensitivity` constant itself—1 instead of `olPrivate`, for instance. However, when checking the Sensitivity property of a message, you can use the constant to retrieve the value.

 **NOTE** VBScript implements constants much less thoroughly than Visual Basic and VBA do. For many actions using VBScript to automate Outlook, you need to specify the value for a constant rather than the descriptive constant itself.

# Variables

A variable is a location in memory that you set aside for storing a piece of information while a procedure is running. In the sample procedure earlier in the chapter, we used the variable `strSubject` to store the user's input via an input box. We then used the information in the variable later in the procedure.

You can create as many variables as you need, and you can give them any name that meets Visual Basic's naming rules (see the "Visual Basic Naming Rules" sidebar). As we mentioned before, it's a bad idea to shadow a keyword by giving a variable the same name.

## Visual Basic Naming Rules

Briefly, the rules for creating names for variables in Visual Basic, VBA, and VBScript are simple. A name:

- Can be up to 40 characters long
- Must begin with a letter (after that, it can include letters, numbers, and underscores in any combination)
- Cannot include spaces or symbols (such as % or *)
- Must be unique within its context so that it is not confused with another variable (you'll find out more about context in the next section, "Scope")

## Scope

You can specify the *scope* of a variable—the area of the script in which the variable is available. Variables can have one of three levels of scope:

- *Procedure-level scope* limits a variable to the procedure that creates it; this is also referred to as *local scope*.

- *Script-level scope* makes a variable available to all procedures within the script. This is also referred to as *module-level scope*.

- *Public scope* makes a variable available to all the scripts based on the current document. Outlook items contain only one module or "script." HTML supports multiple VBScripts in a single document, so items based on a stationery document that includes scripts can have global scope, but normal Outlook items do not.

A variable's scope defines the context in which it must be unique. For example, say you're working with the code sheet we created earlier in this chapter. The code sheet already contains the Item_Open function procedure that uses the variable strSubject. Say you add a second procedure to the code sheet and call it myProcedure. If you use local scope for your variables, each procedure can have a variable with the same name (for example, strSubject). But if you use the broader script-level scope for a variable on the code sheet, you can have only one variable with a particular name on the code sheet; because the variable is available to any procedure in the code sheet, it will conflict with any other variable that has the same name. And if you use public scope for a variable on the code sheet, no other active variable can have the same name. We'll look at how to specify the scope of a variable in "Creating a Variable," a little later in this chapter.

## Data Subtypes

Most programming languages (including Visual Basic and VBA) offer different *types* of variables. For example, you would store a string of text, such as a word or phrase, in a string variable, while you would store an integer (whole number) value in an integer variable. Unlike Visual Basic and VBA, which use strong data-typing and have multiple data types for variables, VBScript uses weak data-typing and has only one data type—the variant. Every variable you create is a variant. However, there are a dozen variant *subtypes*—different types of information contained in the variant variable.

Having only variant variables is both good news and bad news. The good news is that you don't have to explicitly declare variable types; most of the time you can simply assign information to a variable and let VBScript deal with it. This is much easier than worrying which of a dozen data types a particular variable is. The bad news is that, when you need to know the data type of a variable, you need to jump through a couple more hoops.

PART

**V**

Building Customized
Outlook Applications

In this section, we'll discuss the different data subtypes that VBScript supports, together with functions for determining which data subtype a variable has and functions for converting one subtype to another subtype. If you're just getting started with VBScript, you may want to skip right ahead to "Creating a Variable," leaving this information for when you've worked with VBScript a little more.

Table 23.1 lists the data subtypes VBScript supports.

**· TABLE 23.1: VARIANT DATA SUBTYPES**

| Data Subtype | Description |
|---|---|
| Empty | A variable that has not yet been initialized, or an empty string (""). |
| Null | A variable assigned a Null value (the variable contains no valid data). |
| Integer | An integer value. Integer variables can contain integer numbers between −32,768 and 32,767. Integers outside this range need to use the Long subtype. |
| Long | A long integer value (from −2,147,483,648 to 2,147,483,647). |
| Single | A single-precision floating-point (i.e., noninteger) number. Single-subtype variants can contain negative values from −3.402823E38 to −1.401298E−45 and positive values from 1.401298E−45 to 3.402823E38. |
| Double | A double-precision floating-point (noninteger) number. Double-subtype variants can contain values from −1.79769313486232E308 to −4.94065645841247E−324 for negative values and positive values from 4.94065645841247E−324 to 1.79769313486232E308 for positive values. |
| Currency | An 8-byte integer with 4 digits of decimal places, designed for working accurately with large and complex numbers. Currency values can range from −922,337,203,685,477.5808 to 922,337,203,685,477.5807. |
| Date/Time | A date and/or time value. VBScript can handle dates from 1/1/100 to 12/31/9999. |
| String | A text string. |
| Object | An object (such as an application or an ActiveX control). |
| Boolean | A two-position variable: True (−1) or False (0). |
| Byte | An integer value between 0 and 255. |
| Array | A collection of information identified by a single indexed variable. |

**Checking the Data Subtype of a Variable**    To tell which type of data a variant contains, you can use the VarType function. VarType returns an integer value (i.e., a whole number) representing the type of data in the variable.

Table 23.2 lists the data subtypes with the identifying number that VarType returns and the corresponding constant.

| Data Subtype | VarType Constant | VarType Value |
|---|---|---|
| Empty | VbEmpty | 0 |
| Null | VbNull | 1 |
| Integer | VbInteger | 2 |
| Long | VbLong | 3 |
| Single | VbSingle | 4 |
| Double | VbDouble | 5 |
| Currency | VbCurrency | 6 |
| Date/Time | VbDate | 7 |
| String | VbString | 8 |
| Object | VbObject | 9 |
| Error | VbError | 10 |
| Boolean | VbBoolean | 11 |
| Variant | VbVariant | 12 |
| Object (non-OLE) | VbDataObject | 13 |
| Byte | VbByte | 17 |
| Array | VbArray | 8192 |

**TABLE 23.2: VARIANT DATA SUBTYPES AND THEIR VARTYPE NUMBERS**

PART

V

Building Customized
Outlook Applications

For example, you could test the variable dteTestDate against the vbDate constant by using a structure such as this:

```
If VarType(dteTestDate) = vbDate Then
    MsgBox "The variable dteTestDate has the Date/Time subtype."
End If
```

**Testing a Variable for Subtype**   VBScript provides the following functions to test for particular subtypes of variables:

- IsNumeric to test for numeric data
- IsDate to test for a valid date
- IsEmpty to test for an empty variable
- IsNull to test for a null value assigned to the variable
- IsObject to test for an object
- IsArray to test for an array

For example, you could test to see if the variable arrRiches was an array by using a statement such as this:

```
If IsArray(arrRiches) Then MsgBox "It's an array."
```

**Converting a Variable to a Different Type**   VBScript automatically assigns a subtype to a variable when you assign data to the variable. You can also convert a variable from one subtype to another by using the conversion functions listed in Table 23.3.

### TABLE 23.3: VBSCRIPT CONVERSION FUNCTIONS

| Function | Returns |
| --- | --- |
| Abs | Absolute value of the number or expression |
| Asc | ASCII value of the first character in the specified string |
| Chr | Character representing the ASCII value entered |
| CBool | True if the expression is nonzero, otherwise False |
| CDate | Date representation of the expression or number |
| DateSerial | Date variable of the date specified by year, month, and day |
| DateValue | Date variable from a text expression or a string |
| TimeSerial | Date variable of the time specified in hours, minutes, and seconds |
| TimeValue | Date variable from a text expression or a string |
| CByte | Byte representation of the expression or number |
| CInt | Integer representation of the expression or number |
| CLng | Long representation of the expression or number |
| CSng | Single-precision representation of the expression or number |
| CDbl | Double-precision representation of the expression or number |
| CStr | String representation of the number; also returns a string from a Boolean, Date, or error value |
| Fix | For positive values returns the next lower whole number; for negative values returns the next lower whole negative number |
| Int | For positive values returns the next lower whole number; for negative values returns the next higher whole negative number |
| Sgn | 1 for positive value, −1 for negative value (the sign of the expression or number) |
| Hex | String containing hexadecimal representation of the expression or number |
| Oct | String containing octal representation of the expression or number |

Here are several examples using these conversion functions:

- Asc(strCity) returns the ASCII value of the first character in the string strCity.
- CBool(1000-900) returns True.
- DateSerial(1998, 10, 31) - DateSerial(1998, 9, 19) returns 42, the number of days between the two dates.
- Hex(16) returns 10, the hexadecimal representation of the decimal 16.

## Choosing Consistent Names for Variables

Because VBScript uses only the variant data type, it's doubly important to use clear names for your variables in VBScript—if you don't, it's all too easy to become confused about which variable is which and what type of information each variable should contain. Mistaking a variable containing the string data subtype for a variable containing a numeric subtype can cause problems in your scripts. And because VBScript lacks many of the development features found in rich development environments, such as the Visual Basic Editor for the Office applications and the Visual Basic Integrated Development Environment, tracking down the source of such confusion is much more laborious in VBScript than in VBA or Visual Basic.

**NOTE** The VBScript development environment is much less sophisticated than the Visual Basic Integrated Development Environment (IDE) used for Visual Basic 6 and the Visual Basic Editor for the Office applications that support VBA. These environments provide a number of tools for monitoring the data type and contents of variables: the Locals window for monitoring the value of all local variables in a procedure, the Watch window and Quick Watch dialog box for monitoring Watch expressions, the Immediate window for Debug.Print statements, and the Data Tips feature for quickly checking the value of a variable or an expression by holding the mouse pointer over it for a moment.

To make clear the data subtype you intend each variable to contain, use a naming convention for each variable you create. Table 23.4 shows a suggested naming convention of three-letter prefixes for VBScript variables.

**TABLE 23.4: SUGGESTED NAMING CONVENTIONS FOR VBSCRIPT VARIABLES**

| Data Subtype | Prefix | Example Name |
|---|---|---|
| Array | arr | ArrScores |
| Boolean | bln | BlnDisplayWarning |
| Byte | byt | BytReps |
| Currency | cur | CurGilts98 |
| Date | dte | DteTomorrow |
| Double | dbl | DblTan |
| Integer | int | IntDaysLeft |
| Long | lng | LngCompanies |
| Object | obj | ObjExcel |
| Single | sng | SngProjIntRate |
| String | str | StrLocation |
| Variant | var | VarMyVariant |

As in the above examples, try to make your variable names comprehensible at a glance without making them absurdly long. If you can condense a description of the variable's function into six to a dozen or so letters (plus the three-letter prefix indicating the subtype), you'll create variables that are easy to understand without being a chore to type. VBScript is not sensitive to capitalization, but intercapping variable names almost always makes them easier to read and is worth the additional effort.

## Creating a Variable

You can create a variable in two ways: by declaring it explicitly (creating it formally, so to speak), or by creating it implicitly (creating it by implication, as it were).

**Declaring a Variable Explicitly**    To declare a variable explicitly, you use a Dim statement, a Private statement, or a Public statement, as follows:

- To declare a variable with procedure-level scope, use a `Dim` statement within the appropriate procedure. The following statements contain a procedure named `GetUserName`. The first statement starts the subprocedure, and the last statement ends it. The second statement declares a variable called `strFirstName` (whose name indicates that it is intended as a string variable). The third statement displays an input box and assigns its result to the `strFirstName` variable.

```
Sub GetUserName()
    Dim strFirstName
    strFirstName = InputBox("Enter your first name.")
End Sub
```

- To create a variable with script-level scope, use a `Private` statement outside any procedure in the script page. You can also use the `Dim` statement outside of any procedure in Outlook, but other applications that use VBScript or VBA may interpret a `Dim` statement as meaning global scope. The first of the following statements creates a script-level Boolean variable named `blnClockOn`. The first group of three statements contains a procedure named `SetClockTrue` that sets the `blnClockOn` variable to True. The second group of three statements contains a procedure named `ToggleClock` that uses the `Not` operator (discussed later in this chapter) to toggle the value of the `blnClockOn` variable to its opposite state:

```
Private blnClockOn

Sub SetClockTrue()
    blnClockOn = True
End Sub

Sub ToggleClock()
    blnClockOn = Not blnClockOn
End Sub
```

- To create a variable with public scope, use a `Public` statement outside any procedure in the script page. The following statement creates an object variable named objMyWord with public scope:

```
Public objMyWord
```

**Creating a Variable Implicitly**   Instead of declaring a variable explicitly, you can create it implicitly as needed in a script. The following statement implicitly creates the variable intMyValue by assigning the value "123" to it. (This example assumes the variable has not been explicitly declared elsewhere in the script or on the script page.)

```
intMyValue = 123
```

When you create a variable implicitly, it has procedure-level scope. To create a variable with script-level scope, private scope, or public scope, you need to declare the variable explicitly.

**Should You Declare Variables Explicitly or Create Them Implicitly?**   You're probably wondering whether you should create procedure-level variables implicitly or declare them explicitly. While both methods are valid, declaring variables explicitly helps make your code easier to understand, easier to debug, and more professional looking.

To force yourself to explicitly declare all the variables in your code, you can place an `Option Explicit` statement in the first line of any script. When a script begins with the `Option Explicit` statement, VBScript will stop with a *Variable is undefined* error at any variable that is not explicitly declared in your code.

You can place variable declarations anywhere in your code—they don't have to occur before the variable is used in the code—but generally accepted practice for local variables is to place them at the beginning of the procedure in which they occur. For example, if the subprocedure myProcedure uses the string variables strVar1, strVar2, and strVar3, you might declare them as follows:

```
Sub myProcedure()
    Dim strVar1, strVar2, strVar3
    'the rest of the subprocedure takes place here
    'including use of the variables
End Sub
```

For variables with script-level, private, or public scope, accepted practice is to place the declarations at the beginning of the script page that contains them, after the `Option Explicit` statement (if you use one).

## Assigning a Value to a Variable

To assign a value to a variable, use an equal sign after the variable name, followed by the value. The following statement assigns the string "This is an example." to the variable strMyString:

```
strMyString = "This is an example."
```

PART V

Building Customized Outlook Applications

The following statement assigns the value 2025 to the variable `intCount`:

```
intCount = 2025
```

To assign an object to a variable, you need to use a `Set` statement (using the `Set` keyword) rather than a simple assignment (one using the equal sign). The following statements declare the variable `objMyExcel` and assign the Excel application object to it:

```
Dim objMyExcel
Set objMyExcel = CreateObject("Excel.Application")
```

# Procedures

A *procedure* is a set of instructions for performing a particular action. The types of procedures we're interested in here are subprocedures, macros, and functions.

## Subprocedures

A *subprocedure* is a named unit of code that performs an action. You can create your own subprocedures in Outlook to perform custom actions on objects. For example, you could create a subprocedure that runs automatically when the user closes an item; the subprocedure might warn the user if they had not saved the item and ask if they wanted to do so, or the subprocedure might save the item without consulting the user. Typically, subprocedures do not use arguments, as functions do.

Subprocedures start with a `Sub` statement and end with an `End Sub` statement. The lines of code below show a procedure named `Greeting` that displays a message box greeting the user:

```
Sub Greeting()
    MsgBox "Hello, and welcome to the show!"
End Sub
```

## Macros

A *macro* is a type of subprocedure. People disagree sometimes about what differentiates macros from other subprocedures; there's certainly room for debate. Macros are often understood to be subprocedures that you record (using an automatic device, such as the Macro Recorder in Word, Excel, and PowerPoint) rather than subprocedures you write, but the term *macro* is also applied sometimes to written subprocedures. You cannot record macros in Outlook because Outlook does not have a Macro Recorder.

Like subprocedures, macros start with a `Sub` statement and end with an `End Sub` statement.

## Functions

A *function* is a unit of code that performs an action and typically returns a value. For example, most dialects of Visual Basic have a function named `Left` that returns the specified number of characters at the left end of the given text string, and a corresponding `Right` function that returns the specified number of characters at the right end of the given text string.

Functions are easy to recognize in code because they start with a `Function` statement and end with an `End Function` statement. The lines of code below show the skeleton for a function named `myFunction`, with a comment line (`'Actions here`) indicating where the actions would take place:

```
Function myFunction()
    'Actions here
End Function
```

You can create your own functions in Outlook. Functions are especially useful for handling events.

## Events

An *event* is an action that happens to an object—typically, an action that the user takes with the application. For example, the `ContactItem` object supports events such as `Close` (closing the `ContactItem` object) and `Open` (opening the `ContactItem` object). You can create procedures that respond to events. For example, you could create a procedure that demanded a password when the user tried to open a particular object.

PART

**V**

Building Customized
Outlook Applications

### Methods, Properties, and Events for the Dog Object

Here's an absurd analogy that you may find useful in straightening out objects, methods, properties, and events. Say you have a dog. Consider your dog as a Visual Basic object called `Dog`. Here's how the `Dog` object works:

- The dog has various properties, such as its type (`Dog.Type = "Doberman"`), size (`Dog.Size = Large`), and age (`Dog.Age = 7`).
- The dog has various methods—actions you can specify it perform—such as barking (`Dog.Bark`) and walking (`Dog.Walk`). Some of these methods take one or more arguments. For example, to specify how many times and how loudly the dog should bark, you might use a `HowManyTimes` argument and a `Loudness` argument (`Dog.Bark HowManyTimes:=4, Loudness:=11`).
- The dog responds to various events, such as your patting it (`Dog_Pat`) or calling its name (`Dog_OnNameCall`).

*Continued*

**CONTINUED**

- In a complex object model, the `Dog` object might contain multiple other objects (`Dog.Stomach.Contents = "Bone"`), some of which in turn might contain further objects (which we won't explore here).

Pushing the analogy past the absurd, you could say the dog fits into the object model of your household in much the same way that Outlook objects fit in the Outlook object model.

# VBScript Operators

VBScript provides a full complement of *operators*—items used for comparing, combining, and otherwise working with values. The operators fall into four categories:

- *Arithmetic operators* (such as + for addition and / for division) for mathematical operations.
- *Logical operators* (such as Or for disjunction and XOr for exclusion) for building logical structures (ways of deciding programmatically which of two or more courses of action to take). Logical operators work with Boolean expressions.
- *Comparison operators* (such as = for equality and >= for greater than or equal to) for comparing values.
- *String operators* (such as & for joining two string variables together).

Table 23.5 lists the operators in their categories, with brief examples of each and comments on the operators that are not self-explanatory.

**TABLE 23.5: OPERATORS IN VBSCRIPT**

| Operator | Meaning | Example | Comments |
|---|---|---|---|
| | | **Arithmetic Operators** | |
| - | Subtraction | x = y - 1 | Straightforward subtraction. |
| - | Unary negation | y = 100<br>x = -y | Sets x to the negative of y. The example returns x = -100. |
| + | Addition | x = y + 1 | |
| * | Multiplication | x = y * 2 | |
| / | Division | x = y / 2 | |

*Continued* ▶

**TABLE 23.5: OPERATORS IN VBSCRIPT (CONTINUED)**

| Operator | Meaning | Example | Comments |
|---|---|---|---|
| | | **Arithmetic Operators** | |
| \ | Integer division | x = y \ 2 | Integer division truncates any remainder. |
| ^ | Exponentiation | x = y ^ 2 | |
| Mod | Modulo arithmetic | 10 Mod 7 | Modulo returns the non-integer part of the division. The example returns 3. |
| | | **Logical Operators** | |
| And | Conjunction | If x > 1 And y > 1 Then | Both conditions must be True for a True result. |
| Not | Negation | x = Not x | Not reverses the value of x (True becomes False). |
| Or | Disjunction | If x > 1 Or y > 1 Then | If either condition is True, the result is True. |
| XOr | Exclusion | If x > 1 XOr y > 1 Then | If one condition is True and the other is False, the result is True; the result is False if both conditions are True or both are False. |
| Eqv | Equivalence | If x Eqv y Then | Similar to And, but results True if both values are False as well as when both values are True. |
| Imp | Implication | If x Imp y Then | True if both values are True or the right-hand value is True. |
| | | **Comparison Operators** | |
| = | Equality | If x = y Then | The two variables have the same value. |
| <> | Inequality | If strTest <> "Cool" Then | |
| < | Less than | If x < y Then | |
| > | Greater than | If x > y Then | |
| <= | Less than or equal to | If x <= y Then | |
| >= | Greater than or equal to | If x >= y Then | |

*Continued* ▶

| **TABLE 23.5: OPERATORS IN VBSCRIPT (CONTINUED)** | | | |
| --- | --- | --- | --- |
| **Operator** | **Meaning** | **Example** | **Comments** |
| | | **Comparison Operators** | |
| `Is` | Object equivalence | `If x = y Then` | The two variables refer to the same object. |
| | | **String Operators** | |
| `&` | Concatenation | `strTest = "Hello."` `& " How are you?"` | `strTest` becomes `"Hello. How are you?"` |
| `+` | Concatenation | `strTest = "Hello."` `+ " How are you?"` | `strTest` becomes `"Hello. How are you?"` The + operator works fine for concatenating strings, but is potentially confusing because of VBScript's weak data-typing—it can look like addition instead of concatenation. |

# VBScript Programming Structures

In this section, we'll discuss some of the VBScript programming structures that you can use in your scripts. These programming structures fall into three types:

- *Sequential structures*, in which one command is executed after another
- *Looping structures*, in which a group of commands is repeated for a set number of times or a variable number of times
- *Conditional branching structures*, in which program flow is directed depending on conditions

## Sequential Structures

Sequential structures are the simplest form of programming structure—statements that perform operations. Most of the sample statements that have appeared so far in this chapter are sequential structures. Sequential structures include calls to subprocedures and functions. (A *call* is when one procedure runs another procedure.)

## Looping Structures

VBScript provides several looping structures for repeating groups of statements. These looping structures include For... Next loops, For Each... Next loops, and various flavors of Do loops. We'll look at these in turn.

### For... Next Loops

A For... Next loop repeats for a specified number of times controlled by a counter variable. The syntax for a For... Next loop is:

```
For counter = start To end [Step stepsize]
    [statements]
[Exit For]
    [statements]
Next
```

Here's how it works:

- *counter* is a numeric variable. The loop runs from the *start* value specified until it exceeds the *end* value specified.

- If the current value of *counter* is less than or equal to the *end* value, VBScript executes the statements in the loop. If the current value of *counter* is more than the *end* value, VBScript branches to the next statement after the loop. The following statements display a message box containing the name of each recipient of the current item (for example, a message or a task request) in turn:

```
For i = 1 To Item.Recipients.Count
    MsgBox Item.Recipients(i).Name
Next
```

- On reaching the Next keyword that ends the loop, VBScript increments the counter by 1 or by the value of the optional argument *stepsize*, which is introduced by the Step keyword. The following statements contain a loop that counts upwards from 100 to 200 in steps of 25 (100, 125, 150, 175, 200):

```
For intMyCounter = 100 To 200 Step 25
    MsgBox intMyCounter
Next
```

- If *stepsize* is a negative number, VBScript decrements the number until it is less than the *end* value. For example, the For... Next loop in the following statements counts down from 100 to 0 in steps of 10:

```
For q = 100 To 0 Step -10
    Msgbox q
Next
```

**NOTE** Unlike VB and VBA, VBScript does not support placing the counter variable after the `Next` keyword to indicate which loop the `Next` keyword refers to. If you place the counter variable after the `Next` keyword (`Next x`), VBScript will stop with an *Expected end of statement* error.

You can exit a `For...` `Next` loop before `counter` reaches the end value by using an `Exit For` statement. Typically, you would use an `Exit For` statement after a certain condition was met. If necessary, you can use multiple `Exit For` statements to evaluate multiple conditions while the loop is running.

## For Each... Next Loops

The `For Each...` `Next` loop is essentially a `For...` `Next` loop linked to a collection. The loop repeats once for each of the objects in the collection and then terminates. A `For Each ... Next` loop looks like this:

```
For Each object In collection
    [statements]
      [Exit For]
    [statements]
Next [object]
```

VBScript evaluates the number of objects in the specified collection and (provided there is at least one object) executes the statements in the loop for the first object. On reaching the `Next` keyword, it returns to the start of the loop, evaluates the number of objects in the collection again, and repeats the loop if necessary.

For example, the following statements display a message box containing the `LastName` property of each contact in the `Items` collection in the Contacts folder in turn:

```
For Each objContact in olContacts.Items
    MsgBox objContact.LastName
Next
```

## Do... Loops

While a `For...` `Next` loop is controlled by a counter, and a `For Each...` `Next` loop by the objects in the specified collection, a `Do` loop is controlled by a condition and enables you to repeat statements while or until the condition is `True`.

There are four types of `Do` loops: `Do While...` `Loop` loops, `Do...` `Loop While` loops, `Do Until...` `Loop` loops, and `Do...` `Loop Until` loops. In the following sections, we'll look at each type in turn.

**TIP** Technically, there's a fifth type of Do loop: one without an Until condition or a While condition. This Do loop will run forever (or until you forcibly terminate it) and has little—if any—practical use outside burning-in a computer or component. You'd be well advised to avoid this type of Do loop.

### Do While... Loop Loops

The Do While... Loop loop repeats the statements in the loop while the specified condition is met. This loop tests the condition before running the statements in the loop for the first time. It uses the following syntax:

```
Do While condition
    [statements]
        [Exit Do]
    [statements]
Loop
```

As long as the condition is met, VBScript executes the statements in the loop. After each loop, the Loop keyword returns execution to the Do While line, and the condition is evaluated again. The following statements show an example of a Do While... Loop loop:

```
Function Item_Close()
    Do While Item.EmailAddress = ""
        Item.EmailAddress = InputBox("Enter the primary e-mail
                address for the contact.", "Missing Contact Information")
    Loop
End Function
```

If necessary, you can use an Exit Do statement (usually tied to a different condition) to terminate the loop before the While condition becomes False. The following statements show an example of using an Exit Do statement. You can use multiple Exit Do statements to evaluate multiple conditions if you want.

```
Function Item_Close()
    Do While Item.EmailAddress = ""
        Item.EmailAddress = InputBox("Enter the primary e-mail
                address for the contact.", "Missing Contact Information")
        If strUserName = "John Kroger" Then Exit Do
    Loop
End Function
```

**Do... Loop While Loops**    The Do... Loop While loop runs the statements in the loop once, and then evaluates the specified condition at the While keyword and repeats the loop as long as the condition is met. The Do... Loop While loop uses the following syntax:

```
Do
    [statements]
    [Exit Do]
    [statements]
Loop While condition
```

The following statements show an example of a Do... Loop While loop. The loop runs a procedure named CreateForm, and then displays a message box asking if the user wants to create another form. As long as the user chooses the Yes button, returning the vbYes value, the loop continues.

```
Do
    CreateForm
Loop While MsgBox("Create another form?", vbYesNo) = vbYes
```

Again, you can use one or more Exit Do statements to terminate the loop before the While condition becomes False.

**Do Until... Loop Loops**    The Do Until... Loop repeats the statements in the loop until the specified condition is met. Like a Do While... Loop loop, the Do Until... Loop loop tests the condition before running the statements in the loop for the first time; unlike a Do While... Loop loop, the Do Until... Loop loop repeats until the condition becomes True (that is, while the condition is False) rather than while the condition is True (until it becomes False).

 **TIP**   You can essentially use a Do Until... Loop instead of a Do While... Loop by inverting the appropriate condition—and vice-versa.

The Do Until... Loop loop uses the following syntax:

```
Do Until condition
    [statements]
    [Exit Do]
    [statements]
Loop
```

The following statements show a `Do Until... Loop` loop that repeats until the user has reduced the number of recipients on a message to three or fewer:

```
Do Until Item.Recipients.Count <=3
    MsgBox "You may not send this message to more than 3 people.", _
    vbOKOnly + vbExclamation, "Server Congestion Error"
Loop
```

You can use one or more `Exit Do` statements to terminate the loop before the `Until` condition becomes `True`.

**Do... Loop Until Loops**   The `Do... Loop Until` loop runs the statements in the loop, and then evaluates the specified condition and repeats the loop until the condition is met. The `Do... Loop Until` loop has a similar relationship to the `Do... Loop While` loop as the `Do Until... Loop` loop has to the `Do... Loop While` loop: it works in the same way, but until the condition becomes `True` rather than while the condition is `True`.

The `Do... Loop Until` loop uses the following syntax:

```
Do
    [statements]
    [Exit Do]
    [statements]
Loop Until condition
```

Again, you can use one or more `Exit Do` statements to terminate the loop before the `Until` condition becomes `True`.

# While... Wend Structures

The `While... Wend` structure provides another way of repeating a number of statements while a condition is met. `While... Wend` uses the following syntax:

```
While condition
    [statements]
Wend
```

VBScript evaluates the condition and, if it is met, executes the statements. On reaching the `Wend` keyword, VBScript returns to the `While` statement, reevaluates the condition, and continues the loop as appropriate.

The following statements use a `While... Wend` loop to increment the counter `intCounter`. The loop terminates when `intCounter` has a value greater than 10.

```
intCounter = 5
While intCounter <= 10
    intCounter = intCounter + 1
    MsgBox intCounter
Wend
```

PART

V

Building Customized
Outlook Applications

## Avoid Infinite Loops by Using a Condition to Terminate the Loop

Because VBScript doesn't implement any kind of reality checks on the logic you supply, you can easily create infinite loops in your scripts by using For... Next loops and Do loops. For example, the following statements produce an infinite loop that will run until you stop it:

```
Sub Infinity()
    For x = 1 to 2
        x = x - 1
    Next
End Sub
```

The error here is obvious: because the action in the loop reduces the counter variable x by the same amount that the loop is incrementing it, x will never reach 2, the end value that will terminate the loop. You'll never write something like this (other than for fun). But it's regrettably easy to produce code that has this effect—particularly if you get confused about the value a variable contains.

Likewise, Do loops can easily become infinite. The loop shown below is not infinite, but it will repeat until the user enters Timbuktu in the input box.

```
Sub Infinite_Do()
    Dim strAbsurdExampleText
    Do While strAbsurdExampleText <> "Timbuktu"
        strAbsurdExampleText = InputBox("Where were you born?")
    Loop
End Sub
```

Again, this is an absurd example that you're unlikely to emulate in practice. But again, it's easy to unintentionally create a loop that has this effect.

It's much harder to create infinite loops in For Each... Next loops, because in most cases the collection on which the Each is based puts a cap on the loop—but it is possible if you try hard enough.

In other languages, you can also create infinite loops with distressing ease by using labels and Goto statements. Fortunately, VBScript spares you this embarrassment by not supporting labels and Goto statements.

# Nesting Loops

You can nest one or more loops within another loop to create the pattern of repetition you need; you can nest For loops, While... Wend loops, and Do loops pretty much to your heart's content. Keep in mind that with every loop you nest, you increase your chances of creating an infinite loop.

 **NOTE** If you're used to Visual Basic or VBA, be careful when nesting For loops inside each other. VBScript's lack of support for placing the counter argument next to the Next keyword can make it hard to tell which loop is ending where. Use indentation and comment lines to make clear which For statement each Next statement refers to.

# Using Conditional Branching Structures

Conditional branching structures enable you to direct the flow of a program depending on conditions you set. In this section, we'll look at the most important conditional branching structures for working with VBScript: assorted types of If statements and the SelectCase structure.

## If Statements

VBScript supports the full gamut of If statements: If... Then, If... Then... Else..., and If... Then... ElseIf... Else.

**If... Then Statements**    The If... Then statement is the simplest type of If statement. You use it to take one or more actions if a condition is True. The syntax is as follows:

```
If condition Then
    [statements]
End If
```

For example, the following statements compare the value of the string variable strUserName to "Traci Jones" and display a message box if the value matches:

```
If strUserName = "Traci Jones" Then
    MsgBox "Hello, Traci!"
End If
```

If the condition is not met, execution continues at the statement following the End If statement.

Simple If... Then statements can be written on one line without the End If statement. For example, the previous If... Then statement could be written like this instead:

```
If strUserName = "Traci Jones" Then MsgBox "Hello, Traci!"
```

However, unless the If... Then statement is very short (as in the previous example), it's usually easier to read code broken out into a block If statement on multiple lines and using the End If statement.

**If... Then... Else... Statements**    The If... Then... Else... statement provides an easy way of branching between two courses of action, depending on whether a condition is met. The syntax is as follows:

```
If condition Then
    [statements1]
Else
    [statements2]
End If
```

If the condition is True, VBScript executes the first group of statements, statements1; if the condition is False, VBScript executes the second group of statements, statements2. For example, the following statements display the "Hello, Traci!" message box if the string variable strUserName is "Traci Jones" and a different message if the user name is anything else:

```
If strUserName = "Traci Jones" Then
    MsgBox "Hello, Traci!"
Else
    MsgBox "Hello, " & strUserName & "!"
End If
```

**If... Then... ElseIf... Else Statements**    The final type of If statement is the If... Then... ElseIf... Else statement. By using this statement, you can evaluate multiple conditions and choose a course of action accordingly.

The syntax for the If... Then... ElseIf... Else statement is as follows:

```
If condition1 Then
    [statements1]
ElseIf condition2 Then
    [statements2]
ElseIf condition3 Then
    [statements3]
Else
    [statements4]
End If
```

If condition1 is True, VBScript executes the first group of statements, statements1; if condition1 is False, VBScript evaluates the first ElseIf statement. If condition2 is True, VBScript executes the second group of statements, statements2; if condition2 is False, VBScript evaluates any further ElseIf statements in turn, executing the statements after the first condition to be True. If no condition is True, VBScript executes the statements that follow the Else statement (here, statements4).

Continuing our example, the straightforward If... Then... ElseIf... Else statement shown below checks the string variable strUserName against three names in turn. If one of the names matches, VBScript displays a message box greeting the user. If none of the names matches, VBScript displays a message box greeting the user by the strUserName string.

```
If strUserName = "Traci Jones" Then
    MsgBox "Hello, Traci!"
ElseIf strUserName = "Gareth Llewellyn" Then
    MsgBox "Hello, Gareth!"
ElseIf strUserName = "Shelly Ramirez" Then
    MsgBox "Hello, Shelly!"
Else
    MsgBox "Hello, " & strUserName & "!"
End If
```

Note that as soon as VBScript finds a condition that is True, it executes the statements following the condition and then resumes execution at the line after the End If statement; it does not evaluate any condition after the one that was true. In the above example, if strUserName is "Gareth Llewellyn", the statement ElseIf strUserName = "Shelly Ramirez" Then is not evaluated. So in building your If... Then... ElseIf... Else structures, make sure that the conditions you evaluate are mutually exclusive.

 **TIP** You can use the If... Then... ElseIf... Else statement without an Else statement if you need to take different actions if one or the other of two conditions is met but no action if neither condition is met.

## Select Case Structures

The Select Case structure provides a way of taking action based on conditions linked to a single value. Select Case takes the following syntax:

```
Select Case testexpression
    Case expression1
        [statements1]
```

```
        Case expression2
                [statements2]
        Case Else
                [statementsElse]
    End Select
```

The Select Case structure begins with a Select Case statement and ends with an End Select statement. *testexpression* is a value or expression providing the information to be evaluated. expression1 and expression2 (and further expressions not shown here) are expressions or values to be compared to *testexpression*. VBScript evaluates each Case statement in turn, only executing the first that evaluates to True.

The following statements evaluate the test expression Item.GetInspector.Modified-FormPages.Count, which returns the number of modified pages in the current item. The Case statements compare this number to 0, 1, 2, and 3, respectively, adding the corresponding text string to the strMsg string variable declared in the first line and initialized in the second line. The Case Else statement takes care of any value greater than 3, again adding a text string to strMsg. After the End Select statement ends the Select Case structure, the last statement displays a message box containing the strMsg string.

```
Dim strMsg
strMsg = "The form contains "
Select Case Item.GetInspector.ModifiedFormPages.Count
    Case 0
        strMsg = strMsg & "no modified pages."
    Case 1
        strMsg = strMsg & "one modified page."
    Case 2
        strMsg = strMsg & "two modified pages."
    Case 3
        strMsg = strMsg & "three modified pages."
    Case Else
        strMsg = strMsg & "more than three modified pages."
End Select
MsgBox strMsg, vbOKOnly + vbInformation, "Modified Pages"
```

# Using Message Boxes and Input Boxes

In the examples so far, we've used a number of message boxes and input boxes. You're no doubt familiar with both, given how extensively both are used in many Windows applications. In this section, we'll look at how to use message boxes and input boxes in your scripts.

# Using Message Boxes

In your scripts, you can use message boxes to display information to the user, as we've done so far in this chapter. You can also use message boxes to enable the user to make simple choices, choosing between two or three buttons in the message box. By using an If structure or Select Case structure linked to the value the message box returns, you can determine which button in the message box the user has chosen. You can use this value to direct the program flow appropriately.

The syntax for displaying a message box with VBScript is as follows:

```
MsgBox(Prompt[, Buttons] [, Title] [, Helpfile], [, Context])
```

Prompt is the only required argument for the MsgBox statement. Prompt is a string that is displayed as the text in the message box.

Buttons is an optional argument specifying the buttons that the message box displays, the icons that the message box displays, the default button, and the modality of the message box. Each of these four elements can be specified with either a value or a constant. You use the + operator to join the values or constants together.

Your first choice is which buttons the message should display. Your options are as follows:

| Value | Constant | Buttons |
|---|---|---|
| 0 | vbOKOnly | OK (the default if you omit the *Buttons* argument) |
| 1 | vbOKCancel | OK, Cancel |
| 2 | vbAbortRetryIgnore | Abort, Retry, Ignore |
| 3 | vbYesNoCancel | Yes, No, Cancel |
| 4 | vbYesNo | Yes, No |
| 5 | vbRetryCancel | Retry, Cancel |

Next, you can choose which (if any) of the standard four message box icons to display. These are your choices:

| Value | Constant | Buttons |
|---|---|---|
| 16 | vbCritical | Stop icon |
| 32 | vbQuestion | Question-mark icon |
| 48 | vbExclamation | Exclamation-point icon |
| 64 | vbInformation | Information icon |

Next, you can set a default button for the message box. If you choose not to set a default button, VBScript makes the first (leftmost) button in the message box the default—the Yes button in a vbYesNo message box, the OK button in a vbOKCancel message box, and so on. These are your choices of default buttons for a message box:

| Value | Constant | Buttons |
|---|---|---|
| 0 | vbDefaultButton1 | The first button |
| 256 | vbDefaultButton2 | The second button |
| 512 | vbDefaultButton3 | The third button |
| 768 | vbDefaultButton4 | The fourth button |

Finally, in theory you can choose whether to make the message box application modal (the default) or system modal. Application modality means that you can take no further actions in the application until you dismiss the message box; system modality means you can take no further actions *on your computer* until you dismiss the message box. In practice, this system modality does not work—even if you use the vbSystem-Modal argument, the resulting message box will be application-modal.

| Value | Constant | Modality |
|---|---|---|
| 0 | vbApplicationModal | Application modal |
| 4096 | vbSystemModal | System modal |

Title is an optional string argument specifying the text to appear in the title bar of the message box. In most cases, it's a good idea to specify a Title argument to make it clear which procedure has caused the message box to appear. If you do not specify a Title argument for the message box, VBScript will display Visual Basic in the title bar, which is singularly uninformative.

Helpfile is an optional argument specifying the Help file to invoke if the user summons help while the message box is displayed.

Context is an optional argument specifying the topic to display in the Help file. If you use the Helpfile argument, you must use a corresponding Context argument.

VBScript displays a separate Help button when you specify the Helpfile and Context arguments for a message box. For three-button message boxes, such as Yes/No/Cancel and Abort/Retry/Ignore, the Help button appears as the fourth button; for two-button message boxes, as the third button; and for an OK-only message box, as the second button.

For example, the following statement specifies the message box shown in Figure 23.6. This message box has Yes and No buttons (with the No button as the default) and displays the question-mark icon.

```
MsgBox "Delete all contents of the current folder?", vbYesNo _
  + vbDefaultButton2 + vbQuestion, "Delete Contents of Folder"
```

The following statement displays the message box shown in Figure 23.7. This message box includes the Helpfile and Context arguments, which cause it to display a Help button:

```
MsgBox "Choose the Help button to display the Help file.", vbOKOnly +
vbDefaultButton2, "Message Box with Help", "c:\Demos\MyHelp.hlp", 22
```

PART

**V**

Building Customized
Outlook Applications

**FIGURE 23.6**

*A custom message box using a vbDefaultButton2 setting and a question-mark icon*

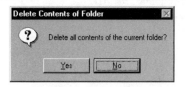

**FIGURE 23.7**

*A custom message box that includes a Help button*

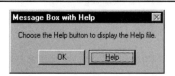

The previous statements simply display the message boxes described; they do not return a value from them. To return a value from a message box, declare a variable for it and set the value of the variable to the result of the message box:

```
Dim Response
Response = MsgBox "Delete all contents of the current folder?", vbYesNo
```

VBScript stores the user's choice of button as a value. Here are the values and their corresponding constants:

| Value | Constant | Button Selected |
|-------|----------|-----------------|
| 1 | vbOK | OK |
| 2 | vbCancel | Cancel |
| 3 | vbAbort | Abort |
| 4 | vbRetry | Retry |
| 5 | vbIgnore | Ignore |
| 6 | vbYes | Yes |
| 7 | vbNo | No |

The following statements use a Select Case structure to establish which button the user chooses in an Abort/Retry/Ignore message box:

```
Dim AbortRetryIgnore
AbortRetryIgnore = MsgBox("Abort, retry, or ignore?", vbAbortRetryIgnore +
vbCritical
Select Case AbortRetryIgnore
Case vbAbort
    'Abort the procedure
```

```
    Case vbRetry
        'Retry the procedure
    Case vbIgnore
        'Ignore
    Case Else
        'Nothing should produce a Case Else here
    End Select
```

For simple Yes/No or OK/Cancel message boxes, you can use a straightforward If statement:

```
If MsgBox("Is it raining?", vbYesNo + vbQuestion, "Weather Check") Then
    MsgBox "It's raining."
Else
    MsgBox "It's not raining"
End If
```

## Use the Buttons Arguments in Order for Easy Reading

The *Buttons* arguments do not have to be in the order discussed here—they will work in any order. For example, VBScript is smart enough to work out that the *1* in the following statement, rather than either of the *0*s, refers to the type of message box:

```
MsgBox "Proceed?", 0 + 16 + 1 + 0, "Bad Value"
```

Better yet, you can mix values and constants if you wish. So the following three statements are functionally equivalent:

```
MsgBox "Proceed?", 1 + 32 + 256 + 4096, "Bad Value"

MsgBox "Proceed?", vbOKCancel + vbQuestion + vbDefaultButton2 +
vbSystemModal, "Bad Value"

MsgBox "Proceed?", 4096 + 32 + vbOKCancel + 256, "Bad Value"
```

That said, your code will be easier to read if you use the standard order: type of message box, icon, default button, and then modality. It will also be easier to read—though a little longer—if you use the constants rather than the values.

## Using Input Boxes

You can use input boxes to gather single pieces of information from the user. By using an If structure linked to the value the input box returns, you can determine whether the user has entered valid information and direct program flow accordingly.

The syntax for an input box is as follows:

```
InputBox(Prompt, Title, Default, XPos, YPos, Helpfile, Context)
```

`Prompt` is a required string argument that specifies the text prompt to be displayed in the input box.

`Title` is an optional string argument that specifies the text for the title bar of the input box. As with `MsgBox`, if you don't specify a `Title` argument, VBScript will display `Visual Basic` in the title bar of the input box.

`Default` is an optional string argument that specifies the default text to display in the text box inside the input box. Often, you'll want to omit the `Default` argument. At other times, you may want to use a `Default` argument to provide text likely to be suitable for the user (for example, the current username in an input box asking for the user's name) or text that may need adjustment.

`XPos` and `YPos` are measurements in *twips* (a twip is 1/1440") for specifying the horizontal and vertical positioning of the input box on the screen. It's usually best to omit these arguments and have VBScript use the default positioning for the input box, which is centered horizontally and a third of the way down the screen, right where the user is used to seeing input boxes.

As for `MsgBox`, `Helpfile` and `Context` are optional arguments specifying the Help file and topic to use. When you specify `Helpfile` and `Context`, VBScript adds a Help button to the input box.

To display an input box and return the text string the user enters, declare a variable for it and set the value of the variable to the result of the input box:

```
Dim strUserName
strUserName = InputBox("Enter your name.", "User Name")
```

You can then check the value of the variable (here, `strUserName`) to make sure that it is not an empty string (""), which will result if the user either clicks the Cancel button in the input box or clicks the OK button without entering any text in the text box. Figure 23.8 shows this input box.

**FIGURE 23.8**

*A custom input box*

PART

V

Building Customized
Outlook Applications

# Dealing with Errors

Unless you can plan your code perfectly, execute it impeccably, and predict every single action that users may try to take with it, your code will result in errors from time to time. And because VBScript provides a relatively poor development environment with few tools, it's easy to inadvertently write code that causes errors when you run it.

In this section, we'll discuss briefly some causes of errors in VBScript and how to avoid them. We'll show you how to use the Err object to trap errors and get information on them. Finally, we'll present a table of the most common error messages, with an explanation of what each means and how to fix the problem.

## Handling Errors

If no error-handling is in place, when VBScript encounters an error, it displays a Script Error message box, such as the one shown here, giving the error description and indicating the line of code in which the error occurred. Many of the error messages are cryptic, while others are more self-explanatory.

You can avoid having VBScript display such error messages by including code in your scripts to trap errors and deal with them. Because VBScript does not support labels and Goto statements, you need to handle all errors inline rather than having a separate section of code for handling errors. This means that you need to check for an error straight after any statement that might produce one.

---

 **NOTE** Compared to Visual Basic and VBA, VBScript's error-handling is weak and restrictive. Unlike Visual Basic and VBA, VBScript supports only the On Error Resume Next and On Error Goto 0 error-handling statements. VBScript does not support labels and Goto statements (other than On Error Goto 0), which means that you need to handle all errors inline rather than using a separate error-handler. Handling errors inline gives you less flexibility in your coding but can make it easier to pinpoint where an error occurs.

---

To trap an error, you use an On Error Resume Next statement with the Err object. The On Error Resume Next statement causes VBScript not to display the error message but to store the error in the Err object and to continue with the next statement. The Err object has various properties that return information about the current error:

- The Description property returns a string containing a brief description of the error.
- The HelpFile property returns a string containing the path of the Help file associated with the error. The HelpContext property returns a number identifying the topic associated with the error in the Help file.
- The Number property returns the number by which VBScript identifies the error.
- The Source property returns the name of the object that caused the error. With Outlook objects, Source returns Microsoft VBScript runtime error.

Typically, you use the Number property to identify which error has occurred. For example, error 11 is a divide-by-zero error. So to check if error 11 had occurred, you would test the current error level against 11. The fourth line of the following statements attempts a division operation involving the variables dblGrossReceipts and intNum-Products, which the second line assumes have been assigned values. The error-handling code in the fifth through eighth lines will trap the divide-by-zero error that occurs if intNumProducts is 0, prompt the user to enter a valid number for intProducts, and repeat the division.

```
Dim dblGrossReceipts, dblUnitCost, intNumProducts
'assign values to dblGrossReceipts and intNumProducts here
On Error Resume Next
dblUnitCost = dblGrossReceipts/intNumProducts
If Err = 11 Then
    intNumProducts = InputBox("Enter a non-zero number of products:")
    dblUnitCost = dblGrossReceipts/intNumProducts
End If
MsgBox "The unit cost is " & dblUnitCost & ".", vbOKOnly, "Unit Cost"
```

To cause errors in your code so that you can debug the code, you can use the Raise method of the Err object with the number of the error. For example, to cause a type-mismatch error, error 13, you could use the following statements:

```
On Error Resume Next
Err.Raise 13
```

After trapping an error and dealing with it, use an Err = 0 statement to reset the error level to 0 (no errors) before testing for further error conditions.

To turn off error-trapping, use an On Error Goto 0 statement. After this, VBScript will display error message boxes as usual if and when an error occurs.

## Common VBScript Errors

Table 23.6 lists the error messages you're most likely to run into, together with explanations of what the error messages mean and suggestions about how to fix your code.

**TABLE 23.6: COMMON ERROR MESSAGES IN VBSCRIPT**

| Description | Error # | Explanation | Suggestions |
|---|---|---|---|
| Syntax error | N/A | The offending line contains a statement or expression that VBScript does not support. You'll see this error if you use a Visual Basic or VBA statement that VBScript does not support. | Remove the offending statement or expression. |
| Invalid character | N/A | The offending line contains a character that VBScript cannot use, such as smart quotes (for example, if you paste sample code from the Help file into the Script Editor). | Replace the offending character with a valid character. |
| Expected end of statement | N/A | The code contains an incomplete statement. This error may indicate a statement that is missing the opening parenthesis on an argument list, or an uncommented comment line. This error also results if you specify the *counter* variable for a loop with its Next keyword (which works in Visual Basic and VBA, but not in VBScript). | Complete the incomplete statement, comment off the comment, or remove the *counter* variable from after the Next keyword. |
| Could not complete the operation. One or more parameter values are not valid. | N/A | One or more of the parameters is incomplete or incorrect. | Correct the offending parameter or parameters. |
| Object doesn't support this property or method: 'Item .Width' | 438 | You have specified a property or method that the object does not have. | Use a property or method that the object has, or an object that has the property or method. |
| The object does not support this method | -2147352567 | This error often means that you've omitted an equal sign from a statement assigning a value. For example, the statement Item.Body "Hello" instead of Item.Body = "Hello" produces this error. | Insert the missing equal sign. |

*Continued*

**TABLE 23.6: COMMON ERROR MESSAGES IN VBSCRIPT (CONTINUED)**

| Description | Error # | Explanation | Suggestions |
|---|---|---|---|
| Variable is undefined: *variable* | 500 | You've included an Option Explicit statement but failed to declare the offending variable. | Declare the undeclared variable—and check for other undeclared variables while you're at it. |
| Type mismatch | 13 | VBScript cannot parse the offending line. This can be any of a variety of problems, including a short comment line missing its comment designator. | Check the statements, syntax, and spelling. If the line is a comment line, comment it off. |
| Unterminated string constant | N/A | A string is missing its ending double quotation marks. | Add the missing double quotation marks to the string. |
| Expected ')' | N/A | A closing parenthesis is missing. | Add the missing closing parenthesis. |
| Invalid procedure call or argument: 'procedure' | 5 | You've called a procedure that the script cannot access. This message also results from failing to specify the *Context* argument for a message box with the *Helpfile* argument specified. | Change the procedure call, or specify the *Context* argument for the *Helpfile*. |
| Name redefined | N/A | You've declared a variable twice. | Remove one of the variable declarations. |
| Division by zero | 11 | Your divisor is zero. | Use a valid divisor. |

PART

V

Building Customized
Outlook Applications

# What's the Difference between VBA and VBScript?

There are no very large differences between the two languages, but there are a few small ones, and they do make a difference.

First, we'll look at what *is* in VBA but is *not* in VBScript. Table 23.7 lists the features (by category) that you'll have to manage without in VBScript.

**TABLE 23.7: VISUAL BASIC FEATURES NOT IN VBSCRIPT**

| Category | Omitted Feature/Keyword |
|---|---|
| Array handling | `Option Base` |
| | `Declaring arrays with lower bound <> 0` |
| Collection | `Add, Count, Item, Remove` |
| | `Access to collections using ! character (e.g.,` |
| | `MyCollection!Foo)` |
| Conditional compilation | `#Const` |
| | `#If...Then...#Else` |
| Control flow | `DoEvents` |
| | `GoSub... Return, GoTo` |
| | `On Error GoTo` |
| | `On... GoSub, On... GoTo` |
| | `Line numbers, Line labels` |
| | `With... End With` |
| Conversion | `CVar, CVDate` |
| | `Str, Val` |
| Data types | `All intrinsic data types except variant` |
| | `Type... End Type` |
| Date/Time | `Date statement, Time statement` |
| | `Timer` |
| DDE | `LinkExecute, LinkPoke, LinkRequest, LinkSend` |
| Debugging | `Debug.Print` |
| | `End, Stop` |
| Declaration | `Declare (for declaring DLLs)` |
| | `New` |
| | `Optional` |
| | `ParamArray` |
| | `Property Get, Property Let, Property Set` |
| | `Static` |
| Error handling | `Erl` |
| | `Error` |
| | `On Error...Resume` |
| | `Resume, Resume Next` |
| File input/output | `All traditional Basic file I/O` |
| Financial | `All financial functions` |
| Object manipulation | `TypeOf` |
| Objects | `Clipboard` |
| | `Collection` |

*Continued*

| TABLE 23.7: VISUAL BASIC FEATURES NOT IN VBSCRIPT (CONTINUED) | |
|---|---|
| **Category** | **Omitted Feature/Keyword** |
| Operators | Like |
| Options | Deftype |
| | Option Base |
| | Option Compare |
| | Option Private Module |
| Select case | Expressions containing Is keyword or any comparison operators |
| | Expressions containing a range of values using the To keyword |
| Strings | Fixed-length strings |
| | LSet, Rset |
| | Mid statement |
| | StrConv |
| Using objects | Collection access using ! |

Believe it or not, VBScript can do a few tricks that Visual Basic can't. Table 23.8 lists these features.

| TABLE 23.8: VBSCRIPT FEATURES NOT IN VISUAL BASIC | |
|---|---|
| **Category** | **Feature/Keyword** |
| Formatting strings | FormatCurrency |
| | FormatDateTime |
| | FormatNumber |
| | FormatPercent |
| | MonthName |
| | WeekdayName |
| Intrinsic constants | vbGeneralDate |
| | vbLongDate |
| | vbLongTime |
| | vbShortDate |
| | vbLongDate |
| | vbTristateFalse |
| | vbTristateMixed |
| | vbTristateTrue |
| | vbTristateUseDefault |

*Continued* ▶

**TABLE 23.8: VBSCRIPT FEATURES *NOT* IN VISUAL BASIC (CONTINUED)**

| Category | Feature/Keyword |
|---|---|
| Objects | Dictionary |
| | FileSystemObject |
| | TextStream |
| Rounding | Round |
| Strings | Filter |
| | InstrRev |
| | Join |
| | Replace |
| | Split |
| | StrReverse |
| Script engine identification | ScriptEngine |
| | ScriptEngineBuildVersion |
| | ScriptEngineMajorVersion |
| | ScriptEngineMinorVersion |

As you can see, there are not too many differences for you to consider. In fact, there's a reasonable chance that your VBScript macro may actually recompile in VBA with only minor changes. It's possible! For more details on which to use and why, head on over to Microsoft's Developer Web site: `http://premium.microsoft.com/msdn/library/backgrnd/html/msdn_ouvbsvba.htm`.

## What's Next

In this chapter, we've looked at the basics of using VBScript, the scripting language you can use for programming Outlook forms. The next step is to see how you attach VBScript code to Outlook forms and how to take actions in Outlook by using VBScript. Turn the page, and we'll get right down to work.

# CHAPTER **24**

# Automating Forms with VBScript

I n the previous chapter, you created a simple script attached to an Outlook form and ran the script. In this chapter, we'll discuss how you can use VBScript to automate a form. We'll start by looking more closely at how you create scripts in Outlook in the Script Editor. We'll discuss how to work with events, which form your first line of attack for automating forms in Outlook, together with examples of using the events. Finally, we'll look at a sample applet consisting of a moderately complex Outlook form that uses events and controls to automate a straightforward but tedious business process.

 **NOTE** An applet in VBA is a small application that must have some sort of host to operate. An example of a host for VBScript is Outlook or Internet Explorer.

In this chapter, you'll see some practical examples of how you work with the Outlook object model to set information in forms and retrieve information from forms. In the next chapter, we'll look more closely at the Outlook object model and how you access it with VBScript and Visual Basic for Applications.

# Creating a Script

As you saw in the previous chapter, each form has a code sheet attached to it. You use the Script Editor application to create VBScript scripts on this code sheet. Unlike Word or Excel, Outlook doesn't have a macro recorder, so you have to create every script by hand.

Go ahead and fire up the Script Editor so that we can look more closely at how you work with it: open a form to work on, choose Tools ➤ Forms ➤ Design This Form to display the form in Design mode, and then choose View ➤ Code.

## Using the Script Editor

The Script Editor is the main tool that Outlook provides for working with scripts. When you install Outlook, you can also install the Microsoft Script Debugger, which you'll use for examining code. We'll look at the Script Debugger later in this chapter.

**NOTE** If you've worked in the Visual Basic Editor for Outlook—or in the Integrated Development Environment (IDE) that Visual Basic provides—you'll find the Script Editor short on both feedback and assistance. For complex procedures, you may want to create the code in the VB Editor or the Visual Basic IDE and then move it to the Script Editor when it's done. You'll need to make a few changes to accommodate the differences between VBScript and VBA or Visual Basic (for example, substituting numeric values for constant names and removing data types from variable declarations), but the code-creation tools in the other development environments may be worth this trade-off when you need to generate a lot of code.

## Using the Script Editor's Toolbar and Menus

The Script Editor's toolbar (see Figure 24.1) is simplicity itself, offering the standard Windows commands for editing text.

PART V

Building Customized Outlook Applications

**FIGURE 24.1**

*The Script Editor's toolbar provides standard Windows commands.*

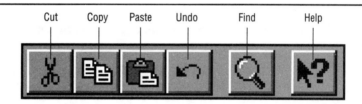

Likewise, the Script Editor's menus are very straightforward. The File menu contains only the Close command for closing the Script Editor. The Edit menu contains standard editing commands, such as Undo, Cut, Copy, Paste, and Select All, together with the following items:

- The Go To item displays the Go To dialog box (shown here) that you can use to move quickly to a specific numbered line of code. This is useful only if you have long scripts and an approximate idea of the line number you need to go to—otherwise, you're better off scrolling down until you find what you need.

- The Find item and Replace item display the Find dialog box and Replace dialog box, respectively. These basic dialog boxes offer a Match Whole Word Only check box and a Match Case check box. The Find Next command (also accessible via the F3 key) finds the next instance of the previous item you searched for; it does not display the Find dialog box.

The View menu contains only two items—View ➤ Status Bar and View ➤ Toolbar. These items toggle the display of the status bar and toolbar, respectively. If you don't use the toolbar, or if you don't need the sparse information (the line number and column number indicating where the insertion point is located) displayed on the status bar, you can toggle them off to gain more space to work with in the Script Editor window.

The Script menu contains only two items—Event Handler and Object Browser. The Help menu contains only one item—Microsoft Outlook Object Library Help.

## Using the Event Handler to Start Creating a Function

The Script Editor provides the Event Handler to help you quickly create functions tied to events. To begin a function tied to an event in a script:

1. Choose Script ➤ Event Handler to display the Insert Event Handler dialog box (see Figure 24.2).

2. In the list box, select the event you want. The Description box at the bottom of the Insert Event Handler dialog box will display an explanation of when the event occurs.

3. Click the Add button to insert the event in your code.

**FIGURE 24.2**

*Use the Insert Event Handler dialog box to quickly insert the shell of a function tied to an event.*

The Event Handler will insert the *stub* (the framework) of a function for the event in your code. For example, if you choose the Send event, the Event Handler will insert the following lines:

```
Function Item_Send()

End Function
```

If the event function requires arguments to be passed to it, the Event Handler will insert those, too. For example, if you choose the Reply event, the Event Handler will insert the following lines:

```
Function Item_Reply(ByVal Response)

End Function
```

You enter the code for the function procedure within the stub. For example, to display a simple message box saying "Hello, Cleveland!" when the user opens a form, you could use code such as the following:

```
Function Item_Open()
    MsgBox "Hello, Cleveland!"
End Function
```

 **NOTE**  The Insert Event Handler dialog box is purely a convenience—you can achieve the same result by typing the code yourself, if you prefer.

## Finding the Items, Properties, and Methods You Need

The Script Editor provides two ways to find the items, properties, and methods you need for your code. The first is the Object Browser; the second is the Outlook Object Library Help file. We'll look at these in turn in this section.

 **TIP**  Another source of information on the objects that Outlook uses are the controls on an existing form. To check the properties of an existing control, display the form that contains it in Design mode and display the Properties dialog box or Properties window for the item. This is also a good way to see which fields the controls on the standard Outlook forms are bound to.

### Using the Object Browser

The Object Browser (see Figure 24.3) provides quick reference to the objects that Outlook uses.

To use the Object Browser:

**1.** Choose Script ➢ Object Browser or press the F2 key to display the Object Browser dialog box.

2. In the Classes list box, select the class (the item) you want to investigate. The Members list box will display the members of the class—the properties, procedures, and functions associated with the class. The description text box at the bottom of the Object Browser dialog box will list the class (for example, "Class ContactItem" if you select the ContactItem class).

3. In the Members list box, select the property, function, or procedure you want. The description box will list a description of the member, together with its type. For example, the Companies property for the ContactItem class is a string data type, so it is listed as "Property Companies As String." If a property is read-only, the description box will display "read only" after the description.

4. To insert the member in your code at the current position of the insertion point, click the Insert button. To move directly to the Help screen for the member, click the Object Help button.

5. Click the Close button to close the Object Browser dialog box.

---

**FIGURE 24.3**

*Use the Object Browser to look up objects, properties, and methods.*

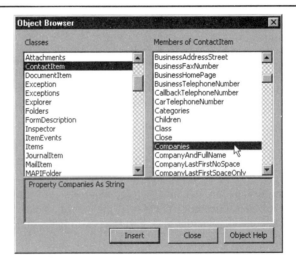

## Using the Outlook Object Library Help File

As you just saw, the Object Browser provides one way of finding the information you need. Also, the Microsoft Outlook Object Library Help file contains a huge amount of information on Outlook's objects, properties, and methods. As you might guess, you access this information by choosing Help ➤ Microsoft Outlook Object Library Help. In this section, we'll look quickly at the information available through the Help file and how you get to it.

When you choose Help ➤ Microsoft Outlook Object Library Help, Outlook displays the Help Topics: Microsoft Outlook Visual Basic dialog box:

- The Contents page (see Figure 24.4) contains information about the various events, methods, objects, and properties that Outlook uses.

**FIGURE 24.4**

*Use the Contents page of the Microsoft Outlook Visual Basic Help file to access information about Outlook's events, methods, objects, and properties.*

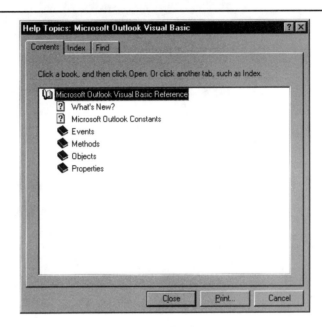

PART

**V**

**Building Customized Outlook Applications**

- The Index page (see Figure 24.5) provides an alphabetical listing of topics in the Help file. In the upper text box, type the first letters of the word you want help on; then select the item you want to see in the main list box and click the Display button.

- The Find page (see Figure 24.6) provides access to an indexed list of the words in the Help file. This provides a different way of searching for the information you want. The first time you access the Find page of the Help Topics dialog box, Help will display the Find Setup Wizard dialog box. Choose the Minimize Database Size (Recommended) option button to create the smallest possible database of search terms, the Maximize Search Capabilities option button to create the largest possible database of search terms, or the Customize Search Capabilities option button to choose options, such as which Help files to include, untitled topics, phrase searching, and matching phrases, as you create the database. We recommend choosing the Maximize Search Capabilities option in order to get maximum use out of the resulting Help database without undue fuss.

**FIGURE 24.5**

*Use the Index page of the Microsoft Outlook Visual Basic Help file to find information by using an alphabetical listing of topics.*

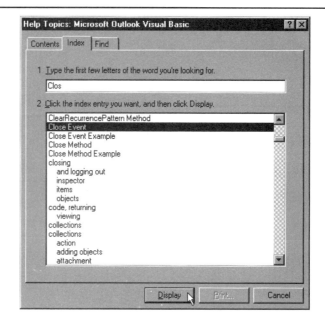

**FIGURE 24.6**

*Use the Find page of the Microsoft Outlook Visual Basic Help file to search for information by a word of your choice.*

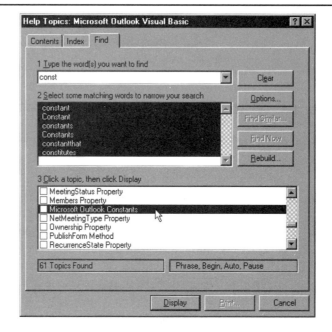

For example, to find information on the MailItem object, you might proceed as follows:

**1.** From the Script Editor, choose Help ➤ Microsoft Outlook Object Library Help to display the Help Topics: Microsoft Outlook Visual Basic dialog box.

**2.** Double-click the Microsoft Outlook Visual Basic Reference main topic to display its subtopics (see Figure 24.7).

**FIGURE 24.7**

*The Help Topics: Microsoft Outlook Visual Basic dialog box with subtopics displayed*

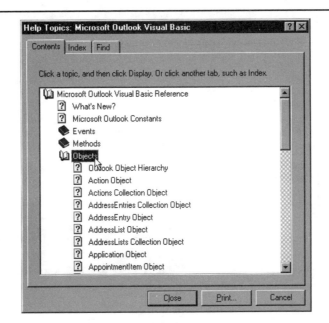

PART

V

Building Customized
Outlook Applications

**3.** Double-click the Objects item to display the list of objects.

**4.** Scroll down if necessary, and double-click the MailItem object to display its Help in a separate window (see Figure 24.8).

**5.** Click the Properties hyperlink to display a Topics Found dialog box (see Figure 24.9) containing a list of the Help topics found for the item you chose. Alternatively, click the Methods hyperlink to display a Topics Found dialog box containing a list of the topics for the item.

**FIGURE 24.8**

*Displaying Help
information*

**FIGURE 24.9**

*The Topics Found
dialog box displays
Help topics associated
with the item.*

**6.** Choose one of the items in the Topics Found dialog box, and click the Display button (or double-click the item) to display the Help associated with it. Figure 24.10 shows the Help information for the Body property.

The Help screens typically offer some of the following hyperlinks to further information:

- The See Also hyperlink displays a Topics Found dialog box containing topics associated with the Help topic you were viewing.

- The Example hyperlink displays the example of VBScript for the item (see Figure 24.11). If there is more than one example, Help displays a Topics Found dialog box listing the choices.

FIGURE 24.10

FIGURE 24.10

*The Help information for the Body property*

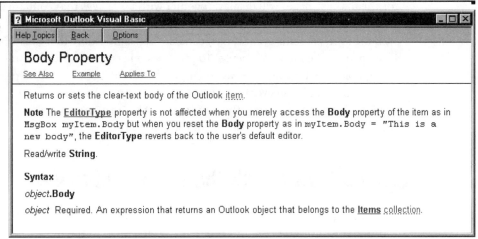

FIGURE 24.11

*Click the Example hyperlink to reach the Help file's example of VBScript for the item.*

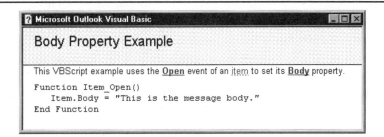

- The Applies To hyperlink (which appears for properties and methods) displays a Topics Found dialog box listing the objects to which the property or method applies.
- The Events hyperlink (which appears for objects) displays a Topics Found dialog box listing the events associated with the object.

# Running a Form

To run a form, choose Form ➤ Run This Form. This puts the form into *Run mode*: Outlook will interpret the form and will display an instance of it, showing each original page and each custom page that you have chosen to display. For example, if you have added controls to pages two and three of a form and chosen Form ➤ Display This Page for them, those pages will display, together with any pages that contained controls in the original form (assuming you didn't remove them).

If the form contains event-driven code, such as a procedure that runs when the form is opened, that code will execute. To prevent code from executing in response to an event, hold down the Shift key as you trigger the event. For example, to prevent a procedure linked to the Open event of a form from executing when you start the form running, hold down Shift as you click the Run item on the Form menu. When you've finished testing the form, close the instance of the form by clicking its Windows close button.

# Debugging a Script with the Script Debugger

Once you've created a script, you need to make sure that it works. You can do so by running the form that contains the script, as described in the previous section. If the script works, well and good. If it doesn't work, you can step through the script command by command in the Script Debugger, see which lines of code are causing problems, and then fix them back in the Script Editor. (You cannot edit code in the Script Debugger.)

 **WARNING** You cannot use the VBA IDE's debugger to debug VBScript applets.

The Script Debugger, which ships as part of Internet Explorer, provides tools to help you locate and suppress errors in scripts, and it works both with VBScript and with JScript (Microsoft's Java scripting language). The Script Debugger displays the source code of the script that you are debugging. This means you can watch the flow of the script as you run it, and you can interrupt the script as necessary. Likewise, you can monitor the values of variables and properties, which helps identify when things go awry.

To work with the Script Debugger, open it when the form you want to debug is in Run mode. To open the Script Debugger, choose Tools ➤ Forms ➤ Script Debugger. Outlook will display the Microsoft Script Debugger window with the script from the form displayed in a window (see Figure 24.12). If the code is running, the current line will be indicated by a yellow highlight with an arrow in the margin.

 **TIP** You can also display the Script Debugger by placing a Stop statement in a script at the point at which you want to open the Script Debugger.

**FIGURE 24.12**

*Use the Microsoft
Script Debugger to
identify problems in
your code.*

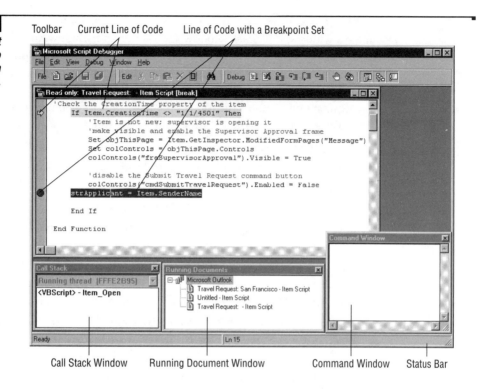

Toolbar   Current Line of Code   Line of Code with a Breakpoint Set

Call Stack Window   Running Document Window   Command Window   Status Bar

The Script Debugger has a straightforward interface with six menus and a tripartite
toolbar. The toolbar's three sections are File (which contains file-related commands), Edit
(editing commands), and Debug (debugging commands). By default, the Script Debugger
displays one section of the toolbar at a time, together with buttons for the other sections,
but you can rearrange the sections, either along the main toolbar or stacked above each
other. For working with Outlook scripts, you'll probably find it most useful to arrange the
toolbar so that both the Edit section and the Debug section show; the File section is more
useful if you're debugging HTML scripts with JScript. The New, Open, Save, Save As, and
Save All commands are primarily for working with HTML files.

You'll spend more time in the Edit menu and Edit section of the toolbar (see Figure 24.13), which offer Cut, Copy, Paste, Delete, Select All, and Find commands. The
latter displays the Find dialog box, which offers a Match Case check box and a Direction drop-down list (Up or Down) but is otherwise unremarkable.

**FIGURE 24.13**

*The Edit section of
the toolbar*

Cut   Copy   Paste   Delete   Select All   Find

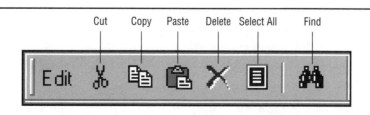

The View menu allows you to toggle the display of the toolbar, status bar, Running Documents window, Call Stack window, and Command window; the Debug section of the toolbar also contains buttons for displaying the last three. The Options command displays the Debug Options dialog box, which controls Java debugging and is not of interest to us here.

The Debug menu contains the following commands for debugging scripts. Most of these are also accessible via the Debug section of the toolbar (see Figure 24.14).

- Run starts a procedure running.

- Break At Next Statement causes the script to enter *Break mode* (suspended Run mode, as it were) at the next statement.

- Stop Debugging stops the current debugging process.

- Step Into executes the next statement in the script. Use the Step Into command to go through a script statement by statement.

- Step Over runs the whole of a procedure or function called from the current procedure (instead of stepping through the called procedure one statement at a time). This button is unavailable until you enter Break mode.

- Step Out runs the rest of the current procedure. This button is unavailable until you enter Break mode.

- Toggle Breakpoint toggles a breakpoint on or off at the line the insertion point is in. (We'll discuss breakpoints and their use in a moment.)

- Clear All Breakpoints removes all breakpoints from the script.

**FIGURE 24.14**

*The Debug section of the toolbar provides commands for debugging scripts.*

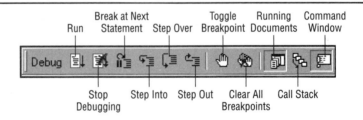

The Window menu provides the standard window-related commands (Next, Previous, Cascade, etc.), together with Close and Close All commands.

The Help menu contains commands for accessing HTML-based Help and Script Debugger–related Web sites.

## Stepping through a Script

To see what is happening in a script, step through its commands one by one, watching the results. To step through a script, display it in Break mode in the Script Debugger, and then:

- Use the Step Into command to step through the code line by line.

- Use the Step Over command to run a whole subprocedure called from the current procedure without stepping through it command by command. This is useful when you believe (or—preferably—*know*) that the problem you're trying to isolate is in the procedure itself rather than the subprocedure it calls.

- Use the Step Out command to finish execution of the current procedure.

## Using Breakpoints to Identify Trouble

One of the benefits of the Script Debugger is that it enables you to use breakpoints to identify problems in your code. A *breakpoint* is a mark you place on the code to tell the Script Debugger to enter Break mode (stop executing) at that statement. Typically, you use a breakpoint to stop execution just before code you want to step through line by line. The breakpoint saves you from having to step through the whole script line by line to reach the part you suspect of malice.

To set a breakpoint, click to place the insertion point in the line of code, and then click the Toggle Breakpoint button. The Script Debugger will display a liverish spot in the margin next to the statement and will display the statement in reverse video with a brown highlight, as shown in Figure 24.15. To remove the breakpoint, click the Toggle Breakpoint button again; the Script Debugger will remove the liverish spot and will restore the statement to normal. To remove all the breakpoints in a script, click the Clear Breakpoints button.

PART

**V**

**Building Customized Outlook Applications**

**FIGURE 24.15**

*Use a breakpoint to tell the Script Debugger where to stop in your code.*

```
Function Item_Open()
    'Check the CreationTime property of the item
    If Item.CreationTime <> "1/1/4501" Then
        'Item is not new; supervisor is opening it
```

 **TIP** Breakpoints are not saved with the code, so you don't need to remove them if you're about to close the script that contains them—you need to remove them only if they're in the code you're about to run in the Script Debugger. You can set as many breakpoints as you want, one per active line of code; you cannot set breakpoints on non-active lines of code, such as declarations or comments.

## Opening a Script

To open a script, display the Running Documents window by choosing View ➤ Running Documents or by clicking the Running Documents button on the toolbar. Click the + sign next to the Microsoft Outlook entry to display the open forms, and then double-click the form whose scripts you want to display.

## Executing a Command while a Script Is Running

Although you cannot change any code in the Script Debugger, you can use its Command Window to execute commands while the script is running. For example, take a look at Figure 24.16. The Item_Open procedure displays a message box containing the variable strTest, which is not assigned a value in the procedure. By executing a command in the Command Window, you can supply the missing variable. (More ambitiously, you can also return properties, execute commands that create or delete items, and so on.)

**FIGURE 24.16**

*Use the Command Window to execute commands while a script is running.*

## Using the Call Stack Window to See What's Running

To see which procedure is running at a particular point, display the Call Stack window by choosing View ➤ Call Stack or clicking the Call Stack button on the Debug section of the toolbar. The Call Stack window (see Figure 24.17) lists the running procedures, with the current procedure at the top of the stack. In the figure, the OpenForm procedure is currently running, having been called by the GetApplicantName procedure, which itself was called by the Item_Open procedure.

 **TIP** You can double-click a procedure in the Call Stack window to move to that procedure.

PART

V

Building Customized
Outlook Applications

**FIGURE 24.17**

*Use the Call Stack dialog box to see which procedure is currently running.*

# Working with Outlook Events

As discussed in Chapter 21, an *event* occurs when the user performs a particular action in an application. For example, an Open event occurs when an Outlook item is opened in an inspector, and a Close event occurs when an Outlook item is closed. By working with the right event, you can automatically run an *event procedure*—a procedure keyed to that particular event—when the user takes the action.

Outlook supports the events listed in Table 24.1. As you can see, the names describe the actions the user takes to trigger the events.

**TABLE 24.1: VBSCRIPT EVENTS SUPPORTED BY OUTLOOK**

| Event | Applies To | Occurs When the User |
|---|---|---|
| AttachmentAdd | Attachments | Adds an attachment to an item. |
| AttchmentRead | Attachments | Opens an attachment for viewing. |
| BeforeAttachmentAdd | Attachments | Adds an attachment to an item. |
| BeforeAttachmentSave | Attachments | Saves changes to an attachment. |
| BeforeCheckNames | Recipients | Leaves focus of a recipient field (shortly before Outlook begins resolving names). |
| Click | Controls | Clicks the control. |
| Close | Items | Closes the item. |
| CustomAction | Items | Performs a custom action on the item. |
| CustomPropertyChange | Custom properties | Changes a custom property of an item. |
| Forward | Items | Forwards the item. |
| Open | Items | Opens the item. The Open event occurs before the Inspector object is displayed. |
| PropertyChange | Standard properties | Changes a standard property of the item. |

*Continued* ▌▶

| TABLE 24.1: VBSCRIPT EVENTS SUPPORTED BY OUTLOOK (CONTINUED) | | |
|---|---|---|
| **Event** | **Applies To** | **Occurs When the User** |
| Read | Items | Opens an existing Outlook item for editing. |
| Reply | Items | Chooses the Reply action for the item. |
| ReplyAll | Items | Chooses the ReplyAll action for the item. |
| Send | Items | Chooses the Send action for the item. |
| Write | Items | Saves the item. |

As you can see, most of the events apply to Outlook items. The exceptions are the Click event, which occurs when the user clicks the control (for example, a command button); the CustomPropertyChange event, which occurs when the user changes a custom property of an object; and the PropertyChange event, which occurs when the user changes a standard property of an object.

Because events provide an easy way to automate Outlook by customizing the user interface, they should form an important part of your programming in Outlook. In the next sections, we'll look at using each of these events in turn. We'll group the events together logically, rather than going through them in alphabetical order. Where appropriate, we'll discuss special considerations for using the events, and we'll look at examples of how to use the most widely useful events.

## The Click Event

The Click event occurs when the user clicks a control such as a command button, option button, check box, or even a label on a form. It also occurs when the user performs an action equivalent to a click—for example, pressing the spacebar when the focus (the current selection in a form or dialog box) is on a command button, or pressing the access key (the underlined letter on the control, also known as the accelerator key) for a control.

 **WARNING**  The Click event is the only event of its type that Outlook's implementation of VBScript supports.

You'll notice that the Insert Event Handler dialog box in the Script Editor omits the Click event; you have to insert it by hand. In fact, until you create the code for it, the Click event technically does not occur; the user can click the control until kingdom come, but nothing will happen.

We'll use the Click event in the sample application later in the chapter, so for now just a couple of notes:

- First, you cannot define a Click event for the TabStrip object or the MultiPage object.

- Second, if you bind a ListBox control, a ComboBox control, an OptionButton control, or a CheckBox control to a field, the Click event for that control will no longer work. To track a user's changes to bound controls, use the Property-Change event or the CustomPropertyChange event (both described later in this section).

 **TIP** To some extent, you can use the Click event to track the user's progress in a form—for example, to make sure that they have filled in earlier areas of a form before they move to later areas.

## The Read Event

The Read event takes place when the user either opens an existing item or selects an existing item for editing in a view that supports in-cell editing (for example, Contacts or Tasks in a row view). If the user is opening the item, the Read event is triggered before the Open event. Note that creating a new item does not trigger a Read event.

## The Open Event

The Open event occurs when the user chooses to open an item and when the user creates a new item. Because the Open event takes place before Outlook displays the item, you can use the event to drive what happens when the user displays the item, or even to prevent the user from displaying the item.

For example, suppose you're lucky enough to have an executive assistant (named Tom Finn in this example) to whom you can delegate a good half of your Task Requests. By customizing the Task Request form with code such as the following, which displays the simple message box shown here, you could save yourself the step of manually assigning tasks to him:

```
Function Item_Open
    If MsgBox("Assign the task to Tom Finn?", _
```

```
        vbYesNo, "Assign Task") = vbYes Then
              Item.Recipients.Add("Tom Finn")
        End If
End Function
```

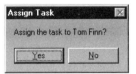

## Simulating a Create Event

Outlook doesn't provide a Create event that runs only when a new item is created. But you can simulate a Create event by using the Open event coupled with the CreationTime property of the object being opened.

Outlook displays 1/1/4501 as the CreationTime property for an item that does not have a valid creation time assigned. So by checking the CreationTime property against this value, you can tell whether the item is being created or being reopened. The following subprocedure checks the CreationTime property of the item being opened; the comment line indicates where you could run code if a new item was being created.

```
Sub Item_Open()
    If Item.CreationTime = "1/1/4501" Then
        'Item is new
        'Run code for new item here
    End If
End Sub
```

 **TIP** To prevent an Open event from being triggered when you open a form, hold down the Shift key as you open the form. This is especially useful when you need to reopen a complex form—for example, a form that uses an Open event to open another form and to close itself—to make adjustments to it.

## The Close Event

The Close event occurs as the user closes an item—more precisely, it occurs before the item inspector is closed. The Close event is especially useful for making sure that the user has saved information in the form they were working on.

The following statements show how you could use the Close event to make sure that the user has filled out appropriate information in a form before closing it. If the user has not filled out the Job Title field of the contact form (if it is an empty string—""), the following statements display an explanatory message and keep the contact form open (by setting the return value of the Close function to "False"):

```
Function Item_Close
    If Item.JobTitle = "" Then
        MsgBox "You must fill in the job title before closing this item.", _
            vbOKOnly + vbCritical, "Incomplete Contact Item"
        Item_Close = False
    End If
End Function
```

## The Send Event

The Send event occurs when the user sends a message, meeting request, task request, or task assignment, typically by issuing a Send command (for example, by clicking the Send button on the Standard toolbar, by choosing File ➢ Send, or by pressing Ctrl+Enter).

The following statements show how you could use the Send event to make sure that every message included a Subject line, to prevent your coworkers from sending unidentified messages.

```
Function Item_Send()
    If Item.Subject = "" Then
        MsgBox "Please include a subject to identify the message.", _
        vbOKOnly + vbExclamation, "Send Operation Canceled"
        Item_Send = False
    End If
End Function
```

## The Write Event

The Write event occurs when the user takes an action that causes the Outlook item they have been working with to be saved. These actions include:

- Issuing a Save or Save As command (for example, by choosing File ➢ Save or File ➢ Save As, or by clicking the Save and Close button).

- Issuing a Send command.
- Closing an item and choosing Yes in response to an Outlook prompt asking whether to save changes to the item.
- Moving to the next or previous item after editing the current item.

Because the Write event only fires when the user has changed the data in the item, you may want to use this event to check the data in the item—for example, to make sure that the user has filled in all required fields, or that a particular field has a suitable value.

## The Forward Event

The Forward event occurs when the user issues a Forward command on an item that supports forwarding (for example, a mail message or a contact item). You might use the Forward event to remind a user not to forward messages flagged as confidential to people outside the company. (More practically, you could use the Send event to prevent people from doing so.)

## The Reply Event

The Reply event occurs when the user replies to an Outlook item (for example, a mail message, a meeting request, an online meeting request, or a task request). You can use the Reply event to automatically insert information in the reply—for example, to insert boilerplate text that will enable you to complete the message faster.

## The ReplyAll Event

The ReplyAll event occurs when the user replies to all recipients of an Outlook item (for example, a mail message, a meeting request, an online meeting request, or a task request). As with the Reply event, you can use the ReplyAll event to automatically insert information in the reply.

## The PropertyChange Event

The PropertyChange event occurs when the user changes a standard property of an item—for example, by changing the value of one of the controls built into a form.

The following statements work with the Contact form and check that the BusinessTelephoneNumber property of the form, when changed, contains a 14-character number—ten digits of number, plus opening and closing parentheses for the area code, plus a space after the closing parenthesis, plus a hyphen separating the exchange from the number (for example, (800) 555-1202). If the telephone number is too short, the procedure puts together a message detailing a problem, and a heading for the message box (shown here), which is displayed in the second-last line.

The `Select Case... End Select` statement, which lets you check a number of different conditions (each identified by a `Case` statement), contains comment lines indicating where you might choose to perform checks on the HomeTelephoneNumber property, the BusinessFaxNumber property, and the MobileTelephoneNumber property of the form. (You might well want to perform different types of checks on these numbers than you perform on the business telephone number.)

```
Sub Item_PropertyChange(ByVal myTest)
    Dim strComplaint
    Dim Msg
    Select Case myTest
        Case "BusinessTelephoneNumber"
            If Len(Item.BusinessTelephoneNumber) < 14 Then
                Msg = Msg + "The business telephone number is too short:" _
                & vbCr & Item.BusinessTelephoneNumber
                strComplaint = "Incomplete Telephone Number"
            End If
        Case "HomeTelephoneNumber"
            'add appropriate checks here
        Case "BusinessFaxNumber"
            'add appropriate checks here
        Case "MobileTelephoneNumber"
            'add appropriate checks here
        Case Else
    End Select
    If Msg <> "" Then MsgBox Msg, vbOKOnly + vbCritical, strComplaint
End Sub
```

## The CustomPropertyChange Event

The `CustomPropertyChange` event occurs when the user changes a custom property of an Outlook item—a property that you create. The following subprocedure traps custom property changes to a form and takes action if they are changes to the property named Smoker. The form contains a check box named chkSmoker that is bound to the property Smoker, a label named lblCigarettesPerDay that displays the text "Cigarettes per Day:", and a text box named txtCigarettesPerDay that is bound to a field named "Cigarettes per Day."

```
Sub Item_CustomPropertyChange(ByVal myProperty)
    If myProperty = "Smoker" then
        Set objCustomPage = _
        Item.GetInspector.ModifiedFormPages("Personal Habits")
        Set objSmoker = objCustomPage.Controls("chkSmoker")
        Set objCigarettes = objCustomPage.Controls("txtCigarettesPerDay")
        Set objCigarettesLabel = _
        objCustomPage.Controls("lblCigarettesPerDay")
        If objSmoker.Value = True Then
            objCigarettes.Visible = True
            objCigarettesLabel.Visible = True
        Else
            objCigarettes.Value = ""
            objCigarettes.Visible = False
            objCigarettesLabel.Visible = False
        End If
    End If
End Sub
```

Here's what happens:

- The name of the property is passed through the argument myProperty on the Sub line and evaluated on the second line. If it matches "Smoker", the rest of the procedure runs.
- The first Set statement uses the GetInspector method to return the customized page named Personal Habits, storing it in the variable objCustomPage.
- The second Set statement returns the chkSmoker control from the Controls collection on objCustomPage, storing it in the variable objSmoker.
- The third Set statement returns the txtCigarettesPerDay control from the Controls collection on objCustomPage, storing it in the variable objCigarettes.
- The fourth Set statement returns the lblCigarettesPerDay control from the Controls collection on objCustomPage, storing it in the variable objCigarettesLabel.
- If the Value property of objSmoker is True (that is, if the property change the user has made was to select the Smoker check box), the subprocedure sets the Visible property of objCigarettes and objCigarettesLabel to True, displaying

the label and the text box it accompanies. Otherwise (Else—the property change was to clear the Smoker check box), the subprocedure sets the Value property of objCigarettes to "" (thus clearing any value set for the text box) and sets the Visible property of objCigaretttes and objCigarettesLabel to False, hiding the label and the text box.

The effect of the subprocedure is that when the user selects the check box, the label and the text box appear; when the user clears the check box, the label and the text box disappear, and any text in the text box is removed (so that the next time it is displayed, it will have no contents). You can adapt this code to set the property of any object based on a change in the property of another object.

## The CustomAction Event

The CustomAction event occurs when a custom action (one created on the Action page of the form) is executed on an Outlook item. For example, in Chapter 20 we created a custom action named Broadcast from EVP for a form. The following statements display a message box when the user takes this custom action.

```
Function Item_CustomAction(ByVal myAction, ByVal myResponse)
    MsgBox "The user chose the Broadcast from EVP action."
End Function
```

## The AttachmentAdd Event

The AttachmentAdd event occurs after an attachment has actually been added to the item. This event has a single parameter that provides access to the attachment that triggered the event. For example, you could use this event to set the subject of a message to the name of the attachment if the user has not provided a subject yet.

```
Sub Item_AttachmentAdd(ByVal NewAttachment)
    'If there is no subject
    If Item.Subject = "" Then
        'Set subject to the display name of the attachment
        Item.Subject = NewAttachment.DisplayName
    End if
End Sub
```

## The AttachmentRead Event

The AttachmentRead event occurs after the user selects the option to open an attachment but before the attachment has actually been opened. Like the AttachmentAdd event, this event provides access to the attachment that triggered the event.

## The BeforeAttachmentAdd Event

The `BeforeAttachmentAdd` event occurs after the user selects the option to add an attachment but before the attachment has actually been added to the item. This event can be used to prevent the addition of an attachment.

## The BeforeAttachmentSave Event

The `BeforeAttachmentSave` event occurs after the user selects the option to save changes to an attachment but before the attachment has actually been saved. You could use this event to prevent attachments from being modified after the item has been created.

## The BeforeCheckNames Event

The `BeforeCheckNames` event occurs shortly before Outlook begins resolving names in the recipients collection (that is, names entered into the To, Cc, and Bcc fields).

# An Example: The Travel Request Application

In this section, we'll walk you through the creation of an Outlook-based application, the Travel Request application. To be honest, this is more of a mini-application than a full-strength application. But while Travel Request is far from complex, it provides an example of how you can use Outlook's events to automate forms and to simplify tedious business processes.

The Travel Request process at our mythical company, Matrix Industries, is as follows:

- An individual fills out a form giving details of their proposed business travel. The individual then submits this form to their supervisor.

- The supervisor reviews the proposed travel and approves it or denies it. If the supervisor approves the trip, the form is forwarded to the travel coordinator, who at Matrix is attached to the Operations department. At the same time, a message is sent automatically to notify the applicant of the approval. On the other hand, if the supervisor denies the travel request, the form returns to the applicant, who can learn the reason for the supervisor's decision.

The Travel Request process has several clear benefits. By processing travel requests electronically rather than on paper, it lessens paperwork and helps spare the occasional forest. It also enables you to check that the form is properly completed. As you'll see shortly, you can implement checking to make sure that at each step of the chain, the person using the form has filled in all the necessary information—something impossible with paper forms, in which incomplete information is a major time-waster. Finally, assuming basic competence on the part of all involved, it also saves time.

The Travel Request application uses two forms, one customized and one standard:

- The Travel Request form (see Figure 24.18). This is a one-page form heavily adapted from the standard message form. The form contains two frames: one for the applicant to fill in and one for the supervisor to approve or deny the travel request. The applicant sees only the first frame and its controls; the second frame and its controls are hidden and are displayed only when the supervisor opens the form.

- The standard Outlook message form. This is used for creating a message sent to the applicant notifying them of their supervisor's decision.

PART

V

Building Customized
Outlook Applications

**FIGURE 24.18**

*The Travel Request form is the first form used in the Travel Request application. Here you see the first frame of the form—the frame the applicant sees when they initially create the form. The Supervisor Approval frame at the foot of the page is hidden.*

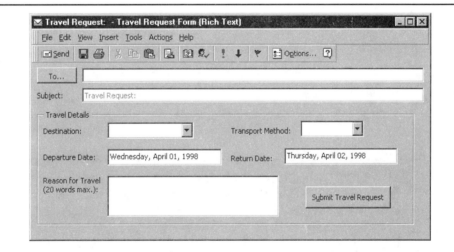

# Creating the Travel Request Form

Create the Travel Request form as described in the following sections.

## Creating the Form and Clearing Space

First, create the form and clear space in it:

1. Start a new message by choosing File ➤ New ➤ Mail Message from the main Outlook window.

2. Choose Tools ➤ Forms ➤ Design This Form to display the form in Design mode (see Figure 24.19).

**FIGURE 24.19**

*Start by creating a new message and switching it to Design mode.*

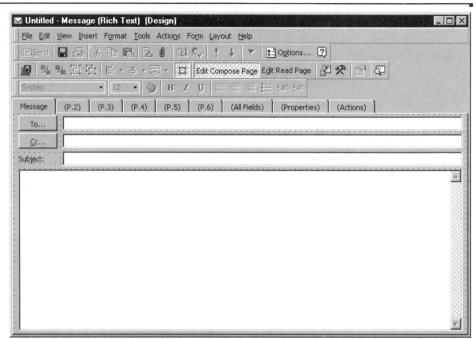

**NOTE** In this example, we used Outlook's e-mail editor rather than the WordMail feature. If you choose to build the form using WordMail, the menus and toolbars will look a little different, but the functionality will be the same.

3. Click to select the Cc command button, and then Ctrl+click to select the text box to the right of it. Right-click either of them and choose Delete from the shortcut menu, or simply press the Delete key, to delete them.

4. Select the message box (the large text box at the bottom of the form) and delete it. This clears a gratifying amount of space in the form.

5. Click the Subject label to select it, and then Ctrl+click the text box to the right of it to select it as well. Move the mouse pointer over one of the horizontal selection borders (*not* over a selection handle), click, and drag the fields up to just below the To command button and its text box. (If you mess up the alignment, select the Subject label and the To command, and use the alignment commands to align them. Then align the two text boxes.)

**6.** Right-click the Subject text box and choose Properties from the shortcut menu to display the Properties dialog box. Click the Value tab to display the Value page of the dialog box. Click in the Set the Initial Value of This Field To text box and enter **Travel Request:** (with a space after the colon).

## Creating the First Frame and Its Controls

Next, create the first frame and the controls it contains:

**1.** If the Toolbox isn't displayed, display it by clicking the Control Toolbox button on the Form Design toolbar.

**2.** Click the Frame button in the Toolbox and drag a frame that takes up most of the bottom part of the form. Don't worry about sizing it exactly; we'll do that when we've placed the other controls.

**3.** Right-click within the frame and choose Properties from the shortcut menu to display the Properties dialog box (see Figure 24.20). Enter **fraTravelDetails** in the Name text box and **Travel Details** in the Caption text box. Select the Resize with Form check box, so that the frame can expand if the user adjusts the size of the form. Then click the OK button to close the Properties dialog box and apply your changes.

PART

**V**

Building Customized
Outlook Applications

**FIGURE 24.20**

*Use the Properties dialog box to set properties for the first frame.*

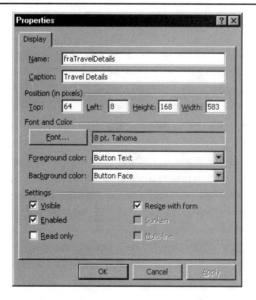

**4.** Click the Label button in the Toolbox, and then click to place a label toward the upper-left corner of the Travel Details frame. Right-click the label and choose Advanced Properties from the shortcut menu to display the Properties window. Set the AutoSize property to `True` (to have Outlook automatically size the label depending on its contents) and the WordWrap property to `False` (to prevent the words from wrapping from the first line onto subsequent lines). Drag the Properties window to where it doesn't interfere with your work in the frame, but leave it displayed. (If your screen isn't big enough for this, close the Properties window for the moment.)

**5.** Select the label, hold down the Ctrl key, and drag to make a copy of the label. Repeat this three times, so that you have five labels. Set the Name and Caption properties of these labels as follows:

| Label | Name | Caption |
|---|---|---|
| First | `LblDestination` | Destination: |
| Second | `LblDepartureDate` | Departure Date: |
| Third | `LblReturnDate` | Return Date: |
| Fourth | `LblTransportMethod` | Transport Method: |
| Fifth | `LblReasonForTravel` | Reason For Travel (20 words max.): |

**6.** Set the WordWrap property on the `lblReasonForTravel` to `True` so that you can break this label over two lines.

**7.** Select the `lblDestination` label, and then Ctrl+click and select the `lblDeparture-Date` and `lblReasonForTravel` labels as well. Use the commands on the Layout menu to left-align the labels at the left-hand side of the frame. Then select the `lblTransportMethod` and `lblReturnDate` labels and left-align them about halfway across the frame.

**8.** Click the ComboBox button in the Toolbox and place a combo box in the frame to the right of the `lblDestination` label. Display the Properties dialog box and set the properties of the combo box: Set **cmbDestination** as the Name property on the Display page; then click the View tab to display the View page. Click the New button to display the New Field dialog box. Create a text field named Destination and click the OK button. In the Possible Values text box, enter the list of the company's office locations, separated by semicolons but without extra spaces: **San Francisco;Dallas;New York;Anchorage;London;Paris;Milan;Vienna**. Click the OK button to close the Properties dialog box.

**9.** Create a second combo box to the right of the `lblTransportMethod` label. Set its Name property to **cmbTransportMethod** and create a new text field named Transport Method for it. Enter **Airplane;Car;Train** as possible values for the field and close the Properties dialog box.

**10.** Click the TextBox button in the Toolbox and place a text box to the right of the lblDepartureDate label. Right-click it and choose Properties from the shortcut menu to display the Properties dialog box. Set the Name property to **txtDepartureDate**; then click the Value tab to display the Value page. Again, create a new field; this time, name it Departure Date, and make it a Date/Time field. In the Format drop-down list in the New Field dialog box, choose a suitable date-only format (we chose the Saturday, August 29, 1999 format as the easiest to understand). Click the OK button to create the field and return to the Properties dialog box. Click the Edit button to display the Initial Value for Departure Date dialog box (see Figure 24.21). Click the Function button to display a drop-down list of available functions, select the Date/Time submenu, and choose Now() from it. Outlook will enter Now() in the Formula text box. Type **+1** after it (so that you have Now()+1—a formula that returns the date of the day after the current day) and click the OK button to close the Initial Value for Departure Date dialog box and return to the Properties dialog box, with the formula entered in the text box to the left of the Edit button and the Set the Initial Value of This Field To check box selected. Click the OK button to close the Properties dialog box.

PART

V

**Building Customized Outlook Applications**

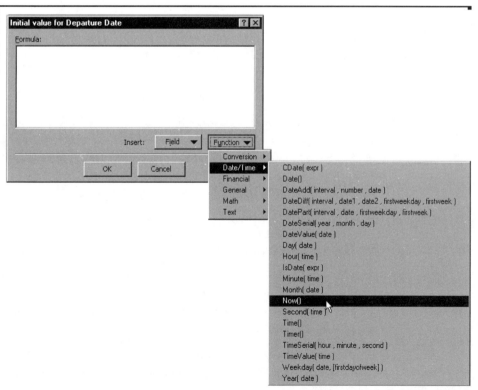

**FIGURE 24.21**

*Create the formula for the Departure Date field by using the Initial Value for Departure Date dialog box.*

**11.** Using the technique just described, create a similar text box named `txtReturn-Date` next to the `lblReturnDate` label. Create a new Date/Time field for it named Return Date, and set the formula for the field to **Now()+2** (two days after the current day).

**12.** Create a third text box, placing it to the right of the `lblReasonForTravel` label and dragging it to a depth of several lines. Right-click and choose Properties from the shortcut menu to display the Properties dialog box. Set the Name property of the text box to **txtReasonForTravel**, select the multiline check box (on the right-hand side, at the foot of the Display page) to make this a multi-line text box, and bind the text box to a new text field named Reason for Travel. Close the Properties dialog box.

**13.** Click the CommandButton button in the Toolbox and create a command button in the lower-right corner of the frame. Right-click and choose Properties from the shortcut menu to display the Properties dialog box. Set the Name property to **cmdSubmitTravelRequest** and the Caption property to **S&ubmit Travel Request** (the letter after the ampersand (&) becomes the access key for the button). Click the OK button to close the Properties dialog box. In a moment, we'll create the code attached to this command button's `Click` event. Before that, we have a couple more controls to create.

Now that you've created all the controls for this frame, resize the frame as necessary, adjusting the spacing of the controls so that each has plenty of room. You should be looking at something like Figure 24.22.

## Creating the Second Frame and Its Controls

Next, create a second frame below the first with the same width as the first. Name it **Supervisor Approval** and set its Visible property to `False`; we want this frame and its contents to be hidden when the form is first displayed, and hiding the frame hides its contents as well. In the frame, place the following controls:

- A label named `lblComments` with a Caption property of **Comments:** (with a space after the colon)

- A multiline text box named `txtComments` bound to a new text field named **Supervisor's Comments**

- A command button named `cmdApproveTravelRequest` with a Caption property of **&Approve Travel Request**

- A command button named `cmdDenyTravelRequest` with a Caption property of **&Deny Travel Request**

When you've done this, adjust the spacing and alignment of the controls, and resize the frame as necessary. You should be seeing something like Figure 24.23.

**FIGURE 24.22**

*The form with the first frame completed*

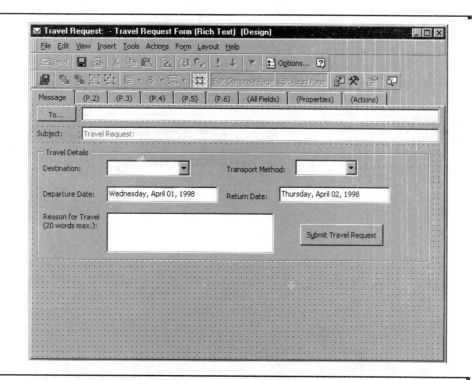

**FIGURE 24.23**

*The form with the second frame completed*

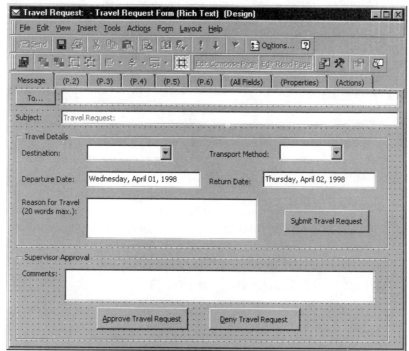

## Checking the Tab Order of the Form

Now that you've got all the controls on the form, check the tab order of the form to make sure the controls are arranged logically for easy movement using the Tab key. Choose Layout ➤ Tab Order to display the Tab Order dialog box (see Figure 24.24).

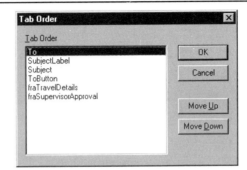

For the whole form, set the following tab order: To; fraTravelDetails; fraSupervisor Approval; ToButton; SubjectLabel; and Subject. Normally, Subject would appear after To because the user is used to filling in the Subject field after designating the recipient. In this form, though, we disabled the Subject field because the form fills it in automatically, so from the To field, the user needs to move to the Travel Details frame, and from there to the Supervisor Approval frame.

Next, right-click in the Travel Details frame, choose Tab Order from the shortcut menu to display the Tab Order dialog box, and set the tab order for the controls it contains: lblDestination, cmbDestination, lblTransportMethod, cmbTransportMethod, lblDepartureDate, txtDepartureDate, lblReturnDate, txtReturnDate, lblReasonFor-Travel, txtReasonForTravel, and cmdSubmitTravelRequest. Here, we've placed the labels before the controls they go with for ease of understanding; because Outlook skips the labels in the tab order (the user doesn't interact with labels—they just sit there on the form displaying words), where they appear in the tab order doesn't actually make any difference.

Finally, right-click in the Supervisor Approval frame, choose Tab Order from the shortcut menu to display the Tab Order dialog box, and set the tab order for its four controls: lblComments, txtComments, cmdApproveTravelRequest, and cmdDenyTravelRequest.

## Adding the Code to the Form

Now it's time to add the code that will drive the form. Choose Form ➤ View Code to display the code sheet for the form in the Script Editor.

The Travel Request application uses seven separate procedures:

- The `Item_Open` function
- The `Item_Send` function
- The `cmdSubmitTravelRequest_Click` subprocedure
- The `cmdApproveTravelRequest_Click` subprocedure
- The `cmdDenyTravelRequest_Click` subprocedure
- The `ForwardTravelRequest` subprocedure
- The `SendNotification` subprocedure

We'll look at each of these procedures in turn—after discussing briefly the declaration of the private variables.

## Declaring the Private Variables

Before the start of the first subprocedure, the code sheet declares the three private variables used to transfer information between the subprocedures:

```
'Declare Private variables strApplicant, strMsg, and strMSubj
'to be available to all the procedures linked to the form
Private strApplicant, strMsg, strMSubj
```

The variable `strApplicant` will contain the name of the applicant; the variable `strMsg` will contain a message to be inserted in the notification message that goes to the applicant; and the variable `strMSubj` will contain the subject of the notification message.

Because these variables are declared as private, they exist while the form is running and are available to all the subprocedures. For example, the `Item_Open` function stores the applicant's name in the `strApplicant` variable; later on, the `SendNotification` subprocedure uses that information when sending the notification message.

## The Item_Open Function

Here is the code listing for the `Item_Open` function:

```
Function Item_Open()
    'Check the CreationTime property of the item
    If Item.CreationTime = "1/1/4501" Then
        'Item is not new; supervisor is opening it
        'Return the Message page of the form
        Set objThisPage = Item.GetInspector.ModifiedFormPages("Message")
        'Return the Controls collection for the page
        Set colControls = objThisPage.Controls
        'Make visible and enable the Supervisor Approval frame
        colControls("fraSupervisorApproval").Visible = True
```

```
        'Disable the Submit Travel Request command button
        colControls("cmdSubmitTravelRequest").Enabled = False
        'Set the strApplicant variable to the sender of the application
        strApplicant = Item.SenderName
    End If
End Function
```

Here's what the `Item_Open` function does:

- The function checks the CreationTime property of the item against 1/1/4501 to find out whether the item is new (being opened for the first time) or not.

- If the item is new, the person opening it will be the applicant; in this case, no action is necessary.

- If the item is not new, the person opening it will be the supervisor, who needs to see the second frame of controls at the foot of the form. The code returns the Message page of the form by using a variable named `objThisPage` to return the Message page from the `ModifiedFormPages` collection, and then sets the variable `colControls` to represent the `Controls` collection on `objThisPage`. Next, the code sets the Visible property of the `fraSupervisorApproval` frame to `True`, displaying it, and sets the Enabled property of the `cmdSubmitTravelRequest` command button to `False`, disabling it.

- Finally, the code assigns to the private variable `strApplicant` the SenderName property of the `Item` object—that is, the name of the applicant who sent the Travel Request form.

## The Item_Send Function

Here is the code listing for the `Item_Send` function. The `Item_Send` function runs when the user invokes a command that initiates the Send event—in this case, when the user chooses the Send button or chooses File ➤ Send.

```
Function Item_Send()
    'Prevent the user from sending the form without
    'supplying the necessary information.
    'Return the Message page of the form
    Set objThisPage = Item.GetInspector.ModifiedFormPages("Message")
    'Return the Controls collection for the page
    Set colControls = objThisPage.Controls
    'Make sure the Destination, Transport Method, and
    'Reason for Travel controls have a value
    If colControls("cmbDestination").Value = "" _
    Or colControls("cmbTransportMethod").Value = "" Or _
```

```
        colControls("txtReasonForTravel").Value = "" Then
            'Display a message box explaining the problem
            MsgBox _
            "Please complete the form and click the Submit Travel Request button.", _
            vbOKOnly + vbExclamation, "Travel Request"
            'Do not send the form
            Item_Send = False
        End if
End Function
```

Here is what the Item_Send function does:

- It uses the GetInspector method to return the customized form page named Message, and assigns it to the variable objThisPage.

- It returns the Controls collection on objThisPage and assigns it to the variable colControls.

- It checks that neither the Value property of the control cmbDestination, nor the Value property of the control cmbTransportMethod, nor the Value property of the control txtReasonForTravel, is an empty string ("")—that is, that the user has made a choice in the Destination drop-down list and the Transport Method drop-down list, and has entered text in the Reason For Travel text box. If any of these is empty, the form is incomplete, so the procedure displays a message box enjoining the user to complete the form, and uses the Item_Send = False statement to prevent the Send event from occurring.

- Otherwise—if the three controls checked in the form all have values—the Send event occurs without hindrance, and the form is sent on its way.

## The cmdSubmitTravelRequest_Click Subprocedure

Here is the code listing for the cmdSubmitTravelRequest_Click subprocedure. This sub-procedure runs when the user clicks the Submit Travel Request button in the Travel Details frame of the form. As you saw from the Item_Open code listing a couple of pages earlier, the Submit Travel Request button is available only for the applicant who creates the form; when the applicant's manager opens the form after receiving it, Outlook deactivates the Submit Travel Request button to prevent the manager from inadvertently clicking it at an inappropriate moment.

```
Sub cmdSubmitTravelRequest_Click()
    'Declare a variable to hold missing information
    Dim strMissing
    'Return the Message page of the form
    Set objThisPage = Item.GetInspector.ModifiedFormPages("Message")
```

```
'Return the Controls collection for the page
Set colControls = objThisPage.Controls
'Make sure the Destination, Transport Method, and
'Reason for Travel controls have a value
If colControls("cmbDestination").Value <> "" Then
    If colControls("cmbTransportMethod").Value <> "" Then
        If colControls("txtReasonForTravel").Value <> "" Then
            'Set the Subject for the form
            Item.Subject = Item.Subject & _
            colControls("cmbDestination").Value
            'Send the form
            Item.Send
        Else
            'Specify the missing information
            strMissing = "Fill in the Reason for Travel text box."
        End If
    Else
        'Specify the missing information
        strMissing = "Fill in the Transport Method drop-down list."
    End If
Else
    'Specify the missing information
    strMissing = "Fill in the Destination drop-down list."
End If
'If information is missing, display a message box telling the user
If strMissing <> "" Then MsgBox strMissing, vbOKOnly + vbExclamation,
"Travel Request Incomplete"
End Sub
```

Here's what happens in the cmdSubmitTravelRequest_Click procedure:

- The procedure starts by declaring the variable strMissing to contain information on what (if anything) is missing in the form.

- Like the previous procedure, it uses the GetInspector method to return the customized form page named Message and assigns it to the variable objThisPage; it also returns the Controls collection on objThisPage and assigns it to the variable colControls.

- It uses nested If statements to check that the cmbDestination, cmbTransportMethod, and txtReasonForTravel controls all have values other than a blank string (""). If they do, it sets the Subject property for the item to the current contents of the Subject property (which was "Travel Request: ") and the contents of the `cmbDestination` control (for example, "Travel Request: Paris"), and then uses the `Send` method to send the form. If one of the controls still has an empty string, the procedure assigns to `strMissing` a text string indicating the offending control.

- At the end of the procedure, if the variable `strMissing` is not an empty string, the procedure displays a message box containing `strMissing` to explain the problem to the user.

## The cmdApproveTravelRequest_Click Subprocedure

Here is the code listing for the `cmdApproveTravelRequest_Click` subprocedure. This subprocedure runs when the supervisor clicks the Approve Travel Request button after opening the Travel Request form they have received from their subordinate. When the supervisor approves the travel request, it needs to be forwarded to the Travel Coordinator, and a notification message needs to be sent to the applicant.

PART

V

Building Customized
Outlook Applications

```
Sub cmdApproveTravelRequest_Click()
    'Return the Message page of the form
    Set objThisPage = Item.GetInspector.ModifiedFormPages("Message")
    'Return the Controls collection for the page
    Set colControls = objThisPage.Controls
    'Set the appropriate string for the txtComments field
    If colControls("txtComments").Value = "" Then
        strMsg = _
        "Your supervisor approved the travel request but added no comments."
    Else
        strMsg = _
        "Your supervisor approved the travel request and added the following
        comments: " & _
        colControls("txtComments").Value
    End If
    strMSubj = "Approved: Travel Request to " & _
    colControls("cmbDestination").Value
    'Call the ForwardTravelRequest subprocedure
    ForwardTravelRequest
    'Call the SendNotification subprocedure
    SendNotification
End Sub
```

Here's how the `cmdApproveTravelRequest` procedure works:

- As in the previous procedures, the procedure returns the customized form page named Message, and assigns it to the variable `objThisPage`; and it returns the `Controls` collection on `objThisPage` and assigns it to the variable `colControls`.

- It then checks the Value property of the `txtComments` control. If the supervisor has entered no text in the text box, the procedure assigns to the private variable `strMsg` a suitable text string; otherwise, the procedure assigns a text string together with the Value property of `txtComments`.

- It then assigns to the private variable `strMSubj` a text string and the Value property of the `cmbDestination` control, to produce a string such as "Approved: Travel Request to Milan".

- It calls the `ForwardTravelRequest` and `SendNotification` procedures (which we'll discuss in a minute) to forward the message to the Travel Coordinator and notify the applicant, respectively.

## The cmdDenyTravelRequest_Click Subprocedure

Here is the code listing for the `cmdDenyTravelRequest` subprocedure. This subprocedure runs when the supervisor clicks the Deny Travel Request button after opening the Travel Request form they have received from their subordinate. When the supervisor denies the travel request, nothing is forwarded to the Travel Coordinator, but a notification message still needs to be sent to the applicant.

```
Sub cmdDenyTravelRequest_Click()
    'Return the Message page of the form
    Set objThisPage = Item.GetInspector.ModifiedFormPages("Message")
    'Return the Controls collection for the page
    Set colControls = objThisPage.Controls
    'Set the appropriate string for the txtComments field
    If colControls("txtComments").Value = "" Then
        strMsg = _
        "Your supervisor denied the travel request but added no comments."
    Else
        strMsg = _
        "Your supervisor denied the travel request and added the following
        comments: " & _
        colControls("txtComments").Value
    End If
    strMSubj = "Denied: Travel Request to " & _
    colControls("cmbDestination").Value
    'Call the SendNotification subprocedure
    SendNotification
End Sub
```

Here's what happens in the `cmdDenyTravelRequest_Click` procedure:

- As in the previous procedures, the code returns the customized form page named Message and assigns it to the variable `objThisPage`, and it returns the `Controls` collection on `objThisPage` and assigns it to the variable `colControls`.

- As in the `ApproveTravelRequest` procedure, it checks the Value property of the `txtComments` control. If the supervisor has entered no text in the text box, the procedure assigns to the private variable `strMsg` a suitable text string; otherwise, the procedure assigns a text string together with the Value property of `txtComments`.

- It then assigns to the private variable `strMSubj` a text string and the `Value` property of the `cmbDestination` control to produce a string such as "Denied: Travel Request to Milan".

- It calls the `SendNotification` procedure to notify the applicant that the travel request has been denied.

## The ForwardTravelRequest Subprocedure

Here is the code listing for the `ForwardTravelRequest` subprocedure. This subprocedure is called by the `cmdApproveTravelRequest_Click` subprocedure—it runs when the supervisor has clicked the Approve Travel Request button on the Travel Request form they have received from their subordinate.

```
Sub ForwardTravelRequest()
    'Forward the form to the Travel Coordinator
    Set objForward = Item.Forward
    'Set the To property for the forwarded message
    objForward.To = "Travel Coordinator"
    'Set the Subject property for the forwarded message
    objForward.Subject = "Forwarded Travel Request"
    'Send the forwarded message
    objForward.Send
End Sub
```

Here's what this straightforward subprocedure does:

- It uses a `Set` statement to assign the Forward method of the `Item` object to the `objForward` variable.

- It sets the To property of `objForward` to "Travel Coordinator" (addressing the forwarded message to the Travel Coordinator).

 **TIP** For testing, change the Travel Coordinator to yourself.

PART V

Building Customized Outlook Applications

- It sets the Subject property of objForward to "Forwarded Travel Request" (setting the subject for the forwarded message).
- It uses the Send method to send objForward on its way.

## The SendNotification Subprocedure

Here is the code listing for the SendNotification subprocedure. This subprocedure is called by both the cmdApproveTravelRequest_Click subprocedure and the cmdDenyTravelRequest_Click subprocedure—it runs when the supervisor has clicked either the Approve Travel Request button or the Deny Travel Request button on the Travel Request form they have received from their subordinate.

```
Sub SendNotification
    'Create a new mail item based on the MailItem form
    Set objNotice = Application.CreateItem(0)
    'Set the To property to the contents of strApplicant variable
    objNotice.To = strApplicant
    'Set the Subject property to the contents of strMSubj variable
    objNotice.Subject = strMSubj
    'Set the Body property to the contents of strMsg variable
    objNotice.Body = strMsg
    'Send the message
    objNotice.Send
    'Close the form
    Item.Close 1
End Sub
```

Here's what the SendNotification subprocedure does:

- It uses a Set statement to assign to the variable objNotice a new mail item (type 0) created by using the CreateItem method.
- It sets the To property of objNotice to the private variable strApplicant, thus addressing the notification method to the applicant.
- It sets the Subject property of objNotice to the private variable strMSubj, thus entering a subject for the notification message.
- It sets the Body property of objNotice to the private variable strMsg, entering the approval or denial, together with the supervisor's comments (if any), in the body of the message.
- It uses the Send method to send objNotice.
- It uses the Close method on the Item object with the Discard (1) argument to close the form without saving changes or prompting to save changes.

# Running the Form

Once you've finished adding code to the code sheet in the Script Editor, run the form to see it working:

1. From the Outlook window containing the form, choose Form ➤ Run This Form to display a copy of the form.

2. Click the To button to display the Select Names dialog box; choose your name (you'll stand in for your supervisor here) and click the To button, and then click the OK button to close the Select Names dialog box.

3. In the Travel Details frame, make a selection in the Destination drop-down list and the Transport Method drop-down list; then set dates in the Departure Date text box and Return Date text box, and enter some text in the Reason for Travel text box.

4. Click the Submit Travel Request command button to send the request.

5. In your Inbox, open the Travel Request you've received. If you receive a Warning dialog box, choose the Enable Macros button. The form will appear with the Supervisor Approval frame displayed.

6. Enter a comment in the Comments text box; then click the Approve Travel Request button or the Deny Travel Request button as appropriate. If you chose Approve Travel Request, the request will be forwarded to the Travel Coordinator (you). Whichever button you chose, an appropriate notification message will be sent to the applicant (you again), and the form will be closed.

7. Open the notification message and make sure it's correct. If you chose Approve Travel Request, examine the forwarded travel request as well.

8. Close all the test messages.

# Publish the Form

Now that the form runs, publish it to an appropriate folder:

1. Choose Tools ➤ Forms ➤ Publish Form to display the Publish Form As dialog box.

2. Choose a suitable folder (probably the Organizational Forms Library) in the Look In drop-down list.

3. In the Display Name text box, enter the display name for the form.

4. In the Form Name text box, adapt the automatically generated form name if necessary.

5. Click the Publish button. If you chose the Personal Forms Library in step 2 and did not select the Save Form Definition with Item check box on the Properties

PART

**V**

Building Customized
Outlook Applications

tab of the form, Outlook will display the message box shown in Figure 24.25, offering to select it for you if you intend to send the form to other people. Choose Yes, No, or Cancel as appropriate (Cancel returns you to the Publish Form As dialog box).

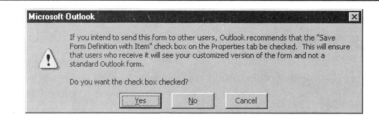

**FIGURE 24.25**

*If you publish the form to the Personal Forms Library but do not select the Save Form Definition with Item check box on the Properties page of the form, Outlook will offer to select it for you.*

The form will now be available for use in the forms library to which you published it.

# Beyond the Travel Request Application

Unless we've miraculously divined the structure of your organization and its internal processes, the Travel Request application is unlikely to be of use to you immediately. However, it illustrates how easily you can take Outlook's existing forms and create automated custom forms that streamline business processes.

To deploy the Travel Request application in a business setting, you would probably need to extend its functionality by adding further procedures (or further pages) to handle what happens when the form reaches the Travel Coordinator. For example, the Travel Coordinator would plan and book the travel requested, and then send details of the dates, times, and reservations to the applicant, with a cc going to the applicant's supervisor.

## What's Next

In the next chapter, we'll discuss how you can use VBScript and VBA to make Outlook interact with other Office applications, such as Word, Excel, and Access.

# CHAPTER **25**<u> </u>

# Automating Outlook with Other Applications

I n this chapter, we'll discuss how to use automation to transfer information between Outlook and the other Office applications. We'll start by looking at the Outlook object model, the logical structure that describes how the components of Outlook fit together. We'll then look at some of the key properties and methods for accessing and manipulating Outlook's objects, both from within Outlook and from other applications. In the second part of the chapter, we'll look at examples of using automation to integrate Outlook with Word, Excel, and Access.

# The Outlook Object Model

The Outlook object model is the logical structure that describes how the Outlook objects—the components of Outlook—fit together. As we mentioned in Chapter 23, Outlook has a relatively flat object model compared to other Office applications such as Word and Excel, which resemble a set of Chinese boxes, with one object inside another inside another.

Figure 25.1 shows the representation of the Outlook object model provided in the Outlook Visual Basic Help file. To display the object model, open the Visual Basic Editor (Tools ➤ Macro ➤ Visual Basic Editor) and select Microsoft Outlook Help from the Help menu. On the Index page of the Microsoft Visual Basic Help dialog box, enter **object** as your keyword and then choose the topic titled Microsoft Outlook Objects. All the objects in the collection are hyperlinked to their Help topics, so you can access the Help topic for an object by clicking the picture of the object.

 **NOTE** Viewing the object model will not work unless you have the Help files installed for Outlook. You can add these files by going to Start ➤ Settings ➤ Control Panel ➤ Add/ Remove Programs and double-clicking the Office 2000 item. This will start the installer and give you a few options to choose from. Click the Add/Remove Components button and follow the instructions. You'll have it running in no time.

In the following sections, we'll discuss the most important objects in the Outlook object model and how to access them programmatically in your scripts and subprocedures. Because the Outlook object model contains a large number of objects and this chapter has a limited number of pages, we will not discuss every object, and for most the objects we discuss, we will not examine every property and every method. However, you will be able to apply the principles you learn from the discussion in this chapter to the other objects you need to use and to access their properties and methods.

**FIGURE 25.1**

*The Outlook object model, as shown in the Outlook Help file. Click an object to see its Help topic.*

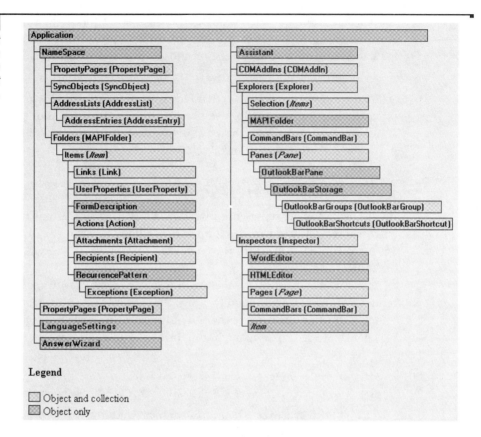

Legend

☐ Object and collection
▨ Object only

PART

**V**

Building Customized
Outlook Applications

Generally speaking, to work with an object, you access it through the object model, starting from the top. For example, to access the Item object, you could work through the Application object to the Explorer object, from which you can reach the Item object.

When you're using VBA or Visual Basic to access the Outlook object model from another application, this is how you would proceed. But for working within Outlook, you can often access an object more directly, because the path to the object is implied. For example, instead of going through the Application object to the Inspector object and thence to the Item object, you can simply refer to the Item object, because the Application object (Outlook 2000) and the Inspector object are implied.

## Using the Application Object

At the top of the Outlook object model is the Application object, which represents the Outlook application. You typically use the Application object to access Outlook from another application; for example, when using a `CreateObject` statement to start an Outlook session or a `GetObject` statement to return the current Outlook session. The following statement starts an Outlook session and assigns it to the variable `objMyOutlook`:

```
Set objMyOutlook = CreateObject("Outlook.Application")
```

Briefly put, this creates an `Automation` object of the class `Outlook.Application`. In other words, it starts an Outlook session that you can then access programmatically.

You can also use the `Application` object to access the `Explorer` and `Inspector` objects in the current session of Outlook. We'll look at these objects next.

## Using the Inspector Object

An `Inspector` object represents a window containing an Outlook item. You use an `Inspector` object to refer to a form in the Outlook object model. To work with an `Inspector` object, you return it using either the `ActiveInspector` method or the `GetInspector` method.

As you might guess, you use the `ActiveInspector` method with an expression that returns the Outlook application to return the currently active `Inspector` object. For example, to return the name of the currently active `Inspector` from Outlook and display it in a message box, you might run the following code from VBA in Word:

```
Dim myOl As Object
Set myOl = GetObject(, "Outlook.Application")
MsgBox myOl.ActiveInspector, vbOKOnly, "Active Inspector"
```

If a task titled `Organize Planning Meeting` is running, the message box will display "Organize Planning Meeting."

To return an `Inspector` object for a specific object other than the currently active object (or indeed for the currently active object, but not by identifying it as such), you use the `GetInspector` method with an expression that returns the Outlook application. The following statements declare one object variable named `objOutlook`, a second named `objNote`, and a third named `objInspector`. They then assign to `objOutlook` the Outlook application and to `objNote` a note created by using the `CreateItem` method. The `GetInspector` method then returns the inspector for `objNote` and assigns it to `objInspector`, which the final statement displays by using the `Display` method.

```
Set objOutlook = GetObject(, "Outlook.Application")
Set objNote = objOutlook.CreateItem(olNoteItem)
Set objInspector = objNote.GetInspector
objInspector.Display
```

To return the `Inspector` object for the current item, you can use a straightforward `Item` reference, such as this:

```
Set objInspector = Item.GetInspector
```

The properties of the `Inspector` object are, in general, less immediately useful than its methods (which we'll look at in the next section). The two most useful properties are the ModifiedFormPages property and the CurrentItem property. The ModifiedFormPages property returns the `Pages` collection, which contains the modified (customized) pages in the object in the inspector. (If the form contains no modified pages, the `Pages` collection is empty.) The CurrentItem property returns the current item that the user is viewing; this is primarily useful when you're working with Outlook from another application.

The following sections describe what you can do with the methods of the `Inspector` object.

## Displaying a Form

Use the `Display` method of an `Inspector` object to display a form. For example, the following subprocedure linked to the `Click` event of a command button named cmd-FirstContact returns the Outlook application's `NameSpace` object and the Contacts folder (identified by its constant, 10) and then uses the `Display` method to display the first contact form in the Contacts folder:

```
Sub cmdFirstContact_Click()
    Set objNameSpace = Application.GetNameSpace("MAPI")
    Set objContacts = objNameSpace.GetDefaultFolder(10)
    objContacts.Items(1).Display
End Sub
```

## Closing a Form

Use the `Close` method to close a particular form. (This closes the inspector for the form; the effect is to close the form.) The `Close` method takes an option SaveMode argument as detailed in the list below:

| olInspectorClose Constant | Value | Effect |
|---|---|---|
| olDiscard | 1 | Closes the inspector and discards any changes without prompting the user. (This is the default value for SaveMode.) |
| olPromptForSave | 2 | Closes the inspector. If the item contains unsaved changes, Outlook prompts the user to save them. |
| olSave | 0 | Closes the inspector and saves any changes without prompting. |

For example, you could close the current inspector and prompt the user to save any changes by using statements such as the following:

```
Set objInspector = Item.GetInspector
objInspector.Close olPromptForSave
```

PART V — Building Customized Outlook Applications

## Displaying a Particular Page of a Form

Use the SetCurrentFormPage method to display a particular page of a form. For example, say you've created a custom contact form that contains a page named Sales History. For existing contacts, you want to display that page whenever you open the form. For new contacts, you want to display the General page of the contact form so that you can fill in all the contact's information as usual. The following statements use the Open event with a check of the CreationTime property against "1/1/4501" (the creation time returned by an item that does not have a real creation time) to achieve this effect.

```
Function Item_Open()
    If Item.CreationTime <> "1/1/4501" Then
        Set objInspector = Item.GetInspector
        objInspector.SetCurrentFormPage("Sales History")
    End If
End Function
```

## Showing and Hiding Form Pages

Use the ShowFormPage method to make a form page visible and the HideFormPage method to hide a form page. For example, the following subprocedure linked to the Click event of a command button named cmdHideCertificatesPage hides the Certificates page of a contact form:

```
Sub cmdHideCertificatesPage_Click()
    Set objInspector = Item.GetInspector
    objInspector.HideFormPage("Certificates")
End Sub
```

## Checking Whether a Message Uses WordMail

Use the IsWordMail method to determine whether a mail message is using WordMail or not. The following subprocedure returns an object named objInspector representing the inspector for the current item, tests for WordMail, and displays a message box announcing what it finds:

```
Sub TestForWordMail()
    Set objInspector = Item.GetInspector
    If objInspector.IsWordMail = True Then
        MsgBox "This message is using WordMail."
    Else
        MsgBox "This message is not using WordMail."
    End If
End Sub
```

## Using the Explorer Object

The `Explorer` object represents an explorer, a window that displays the contents of a folder. This doesn't necessarily mean an Explorer-style window—it can also be an explorer showing, say, the Inbox in its regular Outlook view.

As with the `Inspector` object, you use the `ActiveExplorer` method to return the active `Explorer` object, and the `GetExplorer` method to return a specified `Explorer` object. For example, to display the name of the active explorer in a message box, you could use the following statements from VBA:

```
Dim objOutlook
Set objOutlook = GetObject(, "Outlook.Application")
MsgBox objOutlook.ActiveExplorer
```

If no explorer is active, the `ActiveExplorer` method returns `Nothing`. For example, you could check to see if any explorer was active by using the `TypeName` function, as in the following code:

```
If TypeName(Application.ActiveExplorer) = "Nothing" Then
    MsgBox "No Explorer is active."
Else
    MsgBox TypeName(Application.ActiveExplorer) & " is active."
End If
```

To display a folder in its explorer, use the `Display` method. For example, to display the Contacts folder, you could use VBScript statements such as the following. The first statement uses the `GetNameSpace` method, which we'll examine in the next section, and the `GetDefaultFolder` method, to assign the variable `objContacts` to the Contacts folder. The second statement uses the `GetExplorer` method to return the `Explorer` object for `objContacts`. The third statement uses the `Display` method to display the `objExplorer` explorer.

```
Set objContacts = Application.GetNameSpace("MAPI").GetDefaultFolder(10)
Set objExplorer = objContacts.GetExplorer
objExplorer.Display
```

Use the `Close` method to close an `Explorer` object without saving changes. For example, to close the `objExplorer` explorer used in the previous example, you could use the following statement:

```
objExplorer.Close
```

## Using the NameSpace Object

Considering how you use them, the `Explorer` and `Inspector` objects are named logically enough; the `NameSpace` object, on the other hand, is much harder to wrap your brain around. Technically, the namespace represents the MAPI (Messaging Application Programming Interface) message store in which all Outlook items are stored; in practice, the namespace presents your way of getting a grip on the folders that Outlook uses. For example, to get at the default Contacts folder in an installation of Outlook, you would return the namespace for Outlook and then use the `GetDefaultFolder` method on the namespace to return the Contacts folder.

To return the `NameSpace` object, use the `GetNameSpace` method with an expression that returns an `Application` object—either the Outlook `Application` object itself or an object set to refer to it. The syntax for returning the `NameSpace` object is as follows:

```
expression.GetNameSpace(Type)
```

As we mentioned, *expression* is an expression that returns an `Application` object. *Type* is a required string argument specifying the type of namespace to return. This is less complicated than it looks, because Outlook automation currently supports only MAPI as the *Type*, so typically you'll be using a statement such as `Application.Get-NameSpace("MAPI")` to return the namespace.

For example, the following statements create an object variable named `objNameSpace` that references the `NameSpace` object. They use `objNameSpace` to create another object variable named `objContacts` that references the Contacts folder, and they then use the `Display` method to display the Contacts folder:

```
Dim objOutlook As Object, objNameSpace As Object, objContacts As Object
Set objOutlook = GetObject(, "Outlook.Application")
Set objNameSpace = objOutlook.GetNamespace("MAPI")
Set objContacts = objNameSpace.GetDefaultFolder(olFolderContacts)
objContacts.Display
```

# Using the FormDescription Object

The `FormDescription` object contains the properties for a form—the description of the form, if you will. These are mostly the properties you see on the Properties page of the form in Design mode, and you can set them programmatically as well as you can interactively.

## Returning and Setting Properties for the FormDescription Object

These are the most useful properties of the `FormDescription` object:

- The Category property sets or returns the category assigned to the form description. The CategorySub property returns the subcategory.

- The Comment property sets or returns the comment (the description) of the form.

- The ContactName property sets or returns the name of the contact for the form.

- The DisplayName property sets the form's display name—the name that is displayed in the Choose Form dialog box and the Design a Form dialog box.

- The Hidden property controls whether the form can be used to create a message or whether it is only used as the response form for a custom form. When Hidden is True, the Use Form Only for Responses check box on the Properties page of the form is selected; when Hidden is False, this check box is cleared.

- The Icon property sets or returns the filename of the form's icon. Likewise, the MiniIcon property sets or returns the filename of the form's miniature icon.

- The Locked property corresponds to the setting of the Protect Form Design check box on the Properties page of the form. If Locked is True, the check box is selected; if Locked is False, the check box is cleared.

- The Name property sets or returns the caption of the form.

- The Number property sets or returns the form number—the number contained in the Form Number text box on the Properties page of the form.

- The Password property sets or returns the password for locking and unlocking the form.

- The ScriptText property returns a text string containing the contents of the form's code sheet.

- The UseWordMail property sets or returns the setting of the Always Use Microsoft Word as the E-mail Editor check box on the Properties page of the form: True indicates that the check box is selected, False that it is cleared.

- The Version property sets or returns the version number of the form.

To return the FormDescription object for an item, use the FormDescription property. For example, to return the FormDescription object for the first item in the mail folder identified as objMail and find out if it used WordMail, you could use the following statement:

```
If objMail.Items(1).FormDescription.UseWordMail = True Then
    MsgBox "This item uses WordMail."
Else
    MsgBox "This item does not use WordMail."
End If
```

## Publishing a Form Programmatically

The FormDescription object has only one method, PublishForm, which is used to publish a form programmatically. The syntax for using the PublishForm method is as follows:

```
expression.PublishForm(Registry, Folder)
```

Here, *expression* is an expression that returns a FormDescription object.

*Registry* is a required Long argument specifying the form class:

| olFormRegistry Constant | Numeric Value | Explanation |
| --- | --- | --- |
| olDefaultRegistry | 0 | The default registry |
| olPersonalRegistry | 2 | The Personal form registry; makes the form accessible only to the user of the message store |
| olFolderRegistry | 3 | The Folder form registry; makes the form accessible only from that folder |
| olOrganizationRegistry | 4 | The Organization form registry; makes the form accessible to anyone in the enterprise |

*Folder* specifies a MAPIFolder object. This argument is used only with the olFolder-Registry argument, when it is required. For the other *Registry* arguments, omit this argument.

The following example, run from VBA (for example, from Word or Excel), creates a form named objNewTaskForm. It then sets the Name, Version, ContactName, and Number properties of the form and publishes it to the Personal form registry.

```
Dim objOutlook As Object, objNewTaskForm As Object
Set objOutlook = GetObject(, "Outlook.Application")
Set objNewTaskForm = objOutlook.CreateItem(olTaskItem)
objNewTaskForm.FormDescription.Name = "Heavy-Duty Task"
objNewTaskForm.FormDescription.Version = "1.0"
objNewTaskForm.FormDescription.ContactName = "Bengal O'Donnell"
objNewTaskForm.FormDescription.Number = "TBC-138"
objNewTaskForm.FormDescription.PublishForm olPersonalRegistry
```

# Using the MAPIFolder Object

Outlook uses the MAPIFolder object to represent an Outlook folder. To refer to an item in a folder, you need to use the MAPIFolder object. Any given MAPIFolder can contain other MAPIFolder objects and Outlook items (such as e-mail messages, tasks, and contacts).

To return one of the default Outlook folders, you use the GetDefaultFolder method with the appropriate olDefaultFolder constant (when working from VBA or Visual Basic) or the constant's numeric value (when working from VBScript). Table 25.1 lists the default folders, their olDefaultFolder constants, and their numeric values.

**TABLE 25.1: OUTLOOK'S DEFAULT FOLDERS, THEIR CONSTANTS, AND THEIR NUMERIC VALUES**

| Folder | olDefaultFolder Constant | Numeric Value |
|---|---|---|
| Calendar | olFolderCalendar | 9 |
| Contacts | olFolderContacts | 10 |
| Deleted Items | olFolderDeletedItems | 3 |
| Drafts | olFolderDrafts | 16 |
| Inbox | olFolderInbox | 6 |
| Journal | olFolderJournal | 11 |
| Notes | olFolderNotes | 12 |
| Outbox | olFolderOutbox | 4 |
| Sent Items | olFolderSentMail | 5 |
| Tasks | olFolderTasks | 13 |

The key properties of the MAPIFolder object are the following:

- The DefaultItemType property returns the type of the default Outlook item associated with the folder. Table 25.2 lists Outlook items, their OlItemType constants, and their numeric values.

**TABLE 25.2: OUTLOOK ITEMS, THEIR CONSTANTS, AND THEIR NUMERIC VALUES**

| Item | olItemType Constant | Value |
|---|---|---|
| Appointment | olAppointmentItem | 1 |
| Contact | olContactItem | 2 |
| Journal | olJournalItem | 4 |
| Mail Message | olMailItem | 0 |
| Note | olNoteItem | 5 |
| Post | olPostItem | 6 |
| Task | olTaskItem | 3 |

- The Items property returns the collection of items in the folder. For example, to display the first item in the folder `objMyFolder`, you could use the following statement:

  ```
  objMyFolder.Items(1).Display
  ```

- The Name property returns the display name for the folder. For example, to display the name of the folder `objMyFolder` in a message box, you could use the following statement:

  ```
  MsgBox objMyFolder.Name
  ```

- The Folders property returns the folders in the folder.

- The UnReadItemCount property returns the number of unread items the folder contains.

We've met the key methods of the `MAPIFolder` object already: `GetExplorer` and `Display`. The `MAPIFolder` has three other methods:

- The `CopyTo` method copies a folder and its contents to the specified folder.

- The `MoveTo` method moves the folder and its contents to the specified folder.

- The `Delete` method deletes the folder.

# Integrating Outlook with the Other Office Applications

In this part of the chapter, we'll discuss how to use automation to integrate Outlook with the other Office applications. Because this chapter and this book have a finite length, we will assume that you are familiar with the other Office applications and have had some experience working with VBA in them.

As you saw earlier in the chapter, you use the `Application` object with the `CreateObject` or `GetObject` method to create an Outlook object from another application:

```
Set objOutlook = CreateObject("Outlook.Application")
```

## Automating Word from Outlook

In this section, we'll look at an example of how to automate Word from Outlook. In this example, we'll import information from a custom Word form (see Figure 25.2) into an Outlook contact form. The Outlook contact form (see Figure 25.3) is lightly customized to provide a command button for the user to click to run the subprocedure; the only other customization is the code on the code sheet.

**FIGURE 25.2**

*The Word form from
which we transfer
information to a new
contact form*

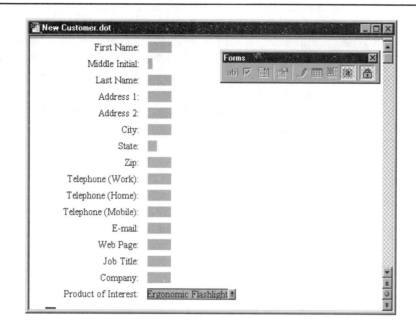

**FIGURE 25.3**

*The customized
Outlook contact form*

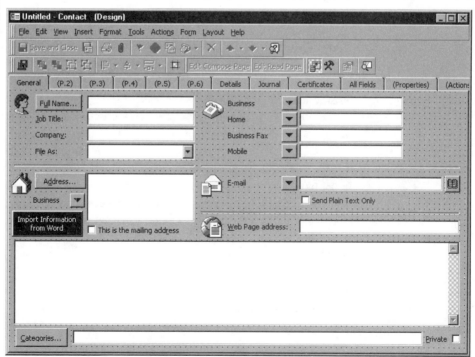

The subprocedure starts Word, opens the Word form the user specifies, retrieves the contents of several form fields, and enters that information in the Contact form. When the information has been successfully entered, the subprocedure closes Word and hides the command button (which has served its purpose). The user can then review the contents of the Contact form, change or add information as appropriate, and then save it as they would any other contact.

Here is the code that appears on the code sheet attached to the form:

```
Option Explicit


Sub cmdImportFromWord_Click()

    'Declare the variable to represent Word
    Dim objWord
    'Declare the variable to represent the ActiveDocument object
    Dim objADoc
    'Declare the variable to represent the Controls collection of the form
    Dim objControls
    Dim strDocToOpen

    'Declare variables for the contact's information
    Dim strFirstName, strMiddleInitial, strLastName

    'Start Word
    Set objWord = CreateObject("Word.Application")

    'Prompt user for the name of the customer to open
    strDocToOpen = InputBox("Enter the name of the form to open:", _
    "Import Contact from Word Form", ".doc")

    'Create the full file name by adding the path
    strDocToOpen = "f:\Customers\New\Registration\" & strDocToOpen
    'Add .doc to the end of the file name if necessary
    If LCase(Right(strDocToOpen, 4)) <> ".doc" Then
        strDocToOpen = strDocToOpen & ".doc"
    End If

    'Begin error trapping
    On Error Resume Next
```

```
'Open the document
objWord.Documents.Open(strDocToOpen)

'Check for an error opening the document
If Err <> 0 Then
    'Display a message box informing the user of the problem
    MsgBox "The file " & strDocToOpen & " does not exist.", _
    vbOKOnly + vbCritical, "File Not Found"
    'Quit the Word session
    objWord.Quit
    'Release the memory held by the objWord variable
    Set objWord = Nothing
    'Terminate the procedure
    Exit Sub
End If

'Assign ActiveDocument to objADoc variable
Set objADoc = objWord.ActiveDocument
'Unprotect the document
objADoc.Unprotect

'Return the telephone numbers and assign them to the appropriate
'properties
Item.MobileTelephoneNumber = _
    objADoc.FormFields("TelephoneMobile").Range.Text
Item.BusinessTelephoneNumber = _
    objADoc.FormFields("TelephoneWork").Range.Text
Item.BusinessFaxNumber = objADoc.FormFields("TelephoneFax").Range.Text
Item.HomeTelephoneNumber = _
    objADoc.FormFields("TelephoneHome").Range.Text

'Return the first name, middle initial, and last name
strFirstName = objADoc.FormFields("FirstName").Range.Text
strMiddleInitial = objADoc.FormFields("MiddleInitial").Range.Text
strLastName = objADoc.FormFields("LastName").Range.Text

'Create the full name and assign it to the FullName property
Item.FullName = strFirstName & " " & strMiddleInitial & ". " & _
    strLastName
```

```
'Return the street address and assign it to the BusinessStreetAddress _
'property
Item.BusinessAddressStreet = objADoc.FormFields("Address1").Range.Text
'If the Address2 field contains text, add that to the address
If objADoc.FormFields("Address2").Range.Text <> "" Then
    Item.BusinessAddressStreet = Item.BusinessAddressStreet & _
    vbCr & objADoc.FormFields("Address2").Range.Text
End If

'Return the City, State, and Zip, and assign them
Item.BusinessAddressCity = objADoc.FormFields("City").Range.Text
Item.BusinessAddressState= objADoc.FormFields("State").Range.Text
Item.BusinessAddressPostalCode = objADoc.FormFields("Zip").Range.Text

'Return the Job Title, Company, Email, and Web page, and assign them
Item.JobTitle = objADoc.FormFields("JobTitle").Range.Text
Item.CompanyName = objADoc.FormFields("Company").Range.Text
Item.Email1Address = objADoc.FormFields("Email").Range.Text
Item.WebPage = objADoc.FormFields("WebPage").Range.Text

'Return and assign the result of the Products of Interest drop-down list
Item.Categories= _
    objWord.ActiveDocument.FormFields("ProductOfInterest").Result

'Close the Word document
objWord.ActiveDocument.Close
'Quit the Word session
objWord.Quit
'Release the memory held by the objWord variable
Set objWord = Nothing

'Assign Controls collection from General page to objControls variable
Set objControls = _
    Item.GetInspector.ModifiedFormPages("General").Controls
'Hide the Import Information from Word button
objControls("cmdImportFromWord").Visible = False
End Sub
```

The preceding code begins with an Option Explicit statement to make sure that all variables are declared explicitly. This is not strictly necessary, but it helps avoid potential problems caused by misspelled variables.

The cmdImportFromWord_Click subprocedure begins by declaring the variables it uses:

- objWord will be used to represent the Word application.
- objADoc will be used to represent the ActiveDocument object.
- objControls will be used to represent the Controls collection of the Outlook form.
- strDocToOpen will be used to contain the name of the Word document to open.
- strFirstName, strMiddleInitial, and strLastName will be used to contain the new customer's first name, middle initial, and last name, respectively.

The subprocedure then uses the CreateObject method to start the Word Application object, assigning it to the objWord variable.

Next, the subprocedure displays an input box (see Figure 25.4) prompting the user for the name of the customer form to open. The text box in the input box displays .doc by default, to suggest to the user that they should include the Word document extension in the file name they type. The subprocedure assigns the result of the input box to the variable strDocToOpen.

PART

V

Building Customized
Outlook Applications

**FIGURE 25.4**

*The input box suggests the .doc extension to the user, but the code adds the extension if the user omits it.*

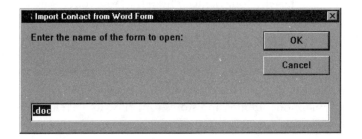

**Import Contact from Word Form**

Enter the name of the form to open:

OK

Cancel

.doc

**NOTE**   In this example, we used the input box as a way of allowing the user to choose which document to open; in the real world, you would most likely provide a more sophisticated way of choosing the document, such as a form or dialog box. As you can easily see, the input box has various disadvantages: the user cannot see the documents available (unless they display a separate Explorer window), and they have every chance of typing an inappropriate name. As a concession to reality, this procedure traps any error that results from the document-opening operation.

The subprocedure then manipulates the variable strDocToOpen, building a full path and filename out of it by adding the path (f:\Customers\New\Registration\) and then using the Right function with the LCase function (which lowercases the string it is fed) to check that the last four characters of strDocToOpen are .doc; if they are not, the subprocedure adds them.

The subprocedure then uses an On Error Resume Next statement to begin error trapping for the document-opening operation. As mentioned in the nearby Note, the user can easily specify an incorrect document name, which will cause an error. The objWord .Documents.Open(strDocToOpen) statement then opens the document.

The If statement that follows checks whether an error has occurred. If an error has occurred (if the value of the Err object is not 0), the subprocedure displays a message box informing the user of the problem, uses the Quit method to close the Word session, and then uses a Set objWord = Nothing statement to release the memory occupied by the objWord variable. The Exit Sub statement then terminates execution of the subprocedure; no further statements are executed.

If the document-opening operation succeeds, the subprocedure assigns the Word ActiveDocument object (which represents the active document—the document that the user just chose to open) to the variable objADoc. It then unprotects the document (which is a protected form) by using the Unprotect method.

From here on, the subprocedure is plain sailing for a while. The next four statements return the telephone numbers from the Word form, which are stored in the text form fields identified by the TelephoneMobile, TelephoneWork, TelephoneFax, and Telephone-Home bookmarks. The text is stored in the Text property of the Range object for the appropriate FormField object, which is accessed through the FormFields collection. For example, Item.MobileTelephoneNumber = objADoc.FormFields("TelephoneMobile").Range .Text returns the Text property of the Range object for the FormField object named "TelephoneMobile" and stores it in the MobileTelephoneNumber property of the Item object (which, you'll remember, represents the current item—the Outlook Contact form).

Next, the subprocedure returns the contents of the FirstName, MiddleInitial, and LastName text form fields from the form, storing them in the strFirstName, strMiddle-Initial, and strLastName variables, respectively. It then sets the FullName property of the Item object to the full name that it builds by concatenating (joining) the strFirst-Name, strMiddleInitial, and strLastName variables, with the obligatory spaces between the components and the period after the middle initial.

**NOTE** We used the variables `strFirstName`, `strMiddleInitial`, and `strLastName` to store the results of the form fields for variety and to produce somewhat shorter and more readable statements. Instead, the procedure could perfectly well assign the `FullName` information by using a statement such as:

```
Item.FullName = _
objADoc.FormFields("FirstName").Range.Text & _
""&objADoc.FormFields("MiddleInitial").Range.Text _
& "." & objADoc.FormFields("LastName").Range.Text
```

This statement is harder for the human eye to read, but the computer is quite happy with it.

Next, the subprocedure transfers the address information from the Word form to the Outlook Contact form. First, it returns the contents of the text form field named `Address1` and assigns it to the BusinessAddressStreet property of the `Item` object. So far so good; but the Word form also has a text form field named `Address2`. If `Address2` contains text, it needs to be assigned to the BusinessAddressStreet property with a carriage return (`vbCr`) separating it from the `Address1` information; if not, the Business-AddressStreet property needs to remain untouched. The `If` statement performs this operation.

The rest of the address information is more straightforward: the subprocedure returns the contents of the text form fields named `City`, `State`, and `Zip` in turn, and assigns them to the BusinessAddressCity, BusinessAddressState, and BusinessAddressPostalCode properties, respectively.

Next come the text form fields `JobTitle`, `Company`, `E-mail`, and `WebPage`, which the subprocedure assigns to the JobTitle, CompanyName, Email1Address, and WebPage properties of the `Item`, respectively. Finally, the subprocedure returns the Result property of the `ProductOfInterest` form field, which is a drop-down list box, and assigns it to the Categories property of the `Item`.

With the transfer of information complete, the subprocedure uses the `objWord` `.ActiveDocument.Close` statement to close the `ActiveDocument` object (closing the document), and then uses the `Quit` method on `objWord` to quit the session of Word. The `Set objWord = Nothing` statement then releases the memory that `objWord` was occupying.

All that remains is to hide the Import Information from Word command button, which will not be needed again for this new Contact form. The subprocedure assigns to the `objControls` variable the `Controls` collection for the General page of the form (`ModifiedFormPages("General")`), and then sets the Visible property of the `cmdImport-FromWord` control to `False`.

## Creating Outlook Contacts from Word

In this section, we'll reverse the example from the previous section and look at how to construct a subprocedure to transfer information from a sequence of Word documents to new Contact forms. This subprocedure runs in Word, where it is created in a VBA module in the Visual Basic Editor for Word.

For this subprocedure to work, first add a reference to the Outlook object model. Choose Tools ➤ References from the Visual Basic Editor to display the References dialog box, select the Microsoft Outlook 9.0 Object Library check box, and click the OK button.

Here is the code for the subprocedure:

```
Option Explicit


Sub TransferInformationToOutlookContacts()
'Transfer information from all the Word forms in the
'F:\CUSTOMERS\NEW\REGISTRATION\ folder
'to contact forms in Outlook
'Move the processed Word forms to the \CUSTOMERS\NEW\PROCESSED\ folder


    'Declare object variable to represent Outlook
    Dim objOutlook As Object
    'Declare object variable to represent a contact
    Dim objContact As Object
    'Declare string variable to contain name of form to open
    Dim strDocToOpen As String
    'Declare string variable to contain name for renaming form
    Dim strDocLoc As String
    'Declare string variable to contain current document
    Dim strCurDoc As String
    'Declare Boolean variable to store whether Outlook was running
    Dim blnOutlookWasRunning As Boolean


    'Return the (running) Outlook application
    On Error Resume Next
    Set objOutlook = GetObject(, "Outlook.Application")


    'Test for an error condition
    If Err = 429 Then
        'Outlook wasn't running; we need to start it
        Set objOutlook = CreateObject("Outlook.Application")
```

```
        blnOutlookWasRunning = False
Else
        blnOutlookWasRunning = True
End If

'Repeat the process while a file is found
Do While Dir("f:\customers\new\registration\*.doc") <> ""

    'Assign to strCurDoc result of Dir on target folder
    strCurDoc = Dir("f:\customers\new\registration\*.doc")
    'Proceed if strCurDoc is not a directory or a blank string
    If strCurDoc <> "." And strCurDoc <> ".." And strCurDoc <> "" Then

        'Assign document to open to strDocToOpen
        strDocToOpen = "f:\customers\new\registration\" & strCurDoc
        'Assign new name for document to strDocLoc
        strDocLoc = "f:\customers\new\processed\" & strCurDoc

        'Open strDocToOpen
        Documents.Open strDocToOpen
        'If strDocToOpen is protected, unprotect it
        If Documents(strDocToOpen).ProtectionType <> wdNoProtection _
            Then Documents(strDocToOpen).Unprotect
        'Create a new contact form in Outlook
        Set objContact = objOutlook.CreateItem(olContactItem)
        'Display the new contact form
        'This is not necessary, but it's useful to see what's going on
        objContact.Display

        With Documents(strDocToOpen)

            'Assign the telephone numbers to the contact's properties
            objContact.MobileTelephoneNumber = _
                .FormFields("TelephoneMobile").Range.Text
            objContact.BusinessTelephoneNumber = _
                .FormFields("TelephoneWork").Range.Text
            objContact.HomeTelephoneNumber = _
                .FormFields("TelephoneHome").Range.Text
```

PART

V

Building Customized
Outlook Applications

```
        objContact.BusinessFaxNumber = _
            .FormFields("TelephoneFax").Range.Text


    'Set the FullName property for the contact
    objContact.FullName = .FormFields("FirstName").Range.Text _
        & " " & .FormFields("MiddleInitial").Range.Text _
        & ". " & .FormFields("LastName").Range.Text


    'Return the street address and assign it to the
    'BusinessStreetAddress property
    objContact.BusinessAddressStreet = _
    .FormFields("Address1").Range.Text
    'If the Address2 field contains text, add that to the
    'address
    If .FormFields("Address2").Range.Text <> "" Then _
    objContact.BusinessAddressStreet = _
        objContact.BusinessAddressStreet & _
        vbCr & .FormFields("Address2").Range.Text


    'Return the City, State, and Zip, and assign them
    objContact.BusinessAddressCity = _
        .FormFields("City").Range.Text
    objContact.BusinessAddressState = _
        .FormFields("State").Range.Text
    objContact.BusinessAddressPostalCode = _
        .FormFields("Zip").Range.Text


    'Return the Job Title, Company, Email, and Web page, and
    'assign them
    objContact.JobTitle = .FormFields("JobTitle").Range.Text
    objContact.CompanyName = .FormFields("Company").Range.Text
    objContact.Email1Address = .FormFields("Email").Range.Text
    objContact.WebPage = .FormFields("WebPage").Range.Text


    'Return and assign the result of the Products of Interest
    'drop-down list
    objContact.Categories =
.FormFields("ProductOfInterest").Result
```

```
               'Close the Contact form, saving changes automatically
               objContact.Close 0
         End With

               'Close the strDocToOpen document without saving changes
               Documents(strDocToOpen).Close SaveChanges:=wdDoNotSaveChanges
               'Move the processed document to the \New\Processed\ folder
               Name strDocToOpen As strDocLoc
      End If
   Loop

      'If the subprocedure had to start Outlook, close it again
      If blnOutlookWasRunning = False Then objOutlook.Quit

      'Release the memory held by the objOutlook variable
      Set objOutlook = Nothing
End Sub
```

PART

**V**

Building Customized
Outlook Applications

The preceding code begins with an Option Explicit statement to force an explicit declaration of each variable used. The subprocedure then begins by declaring the variables it will use:

- The object variable objOutlook will represent the Outlook application.

- The object variable objContact will represent a contact.

- The string variable strDocToOpen will contain the name of the document to open.

- The string variable strDocLoc will contain the name under which the current document is to be renamed (in order to move it from the \Registration\ to the \Processed\ folder).

- The string variable strCurDoc will contain the name of the current document found by the Dir function.

- The Boolean variable blnOutlookWasRunning will be set to True to indicate that Outlook was running when the procedure started or to False to indicate that it was not running. The value of this variable determines whether the subprocedure closes Outlook at the end of the operation.

The On Error Resume Next statement starts error trapping before the GetObject statement attempts to return the running session of the Outlook application and assign it to the objOutlook variable. If Outlook is not running, GetObject will return an error 429. The current error condition is compared to error 429; if it matches (that is, if Outlook was not running), the subprocedure uses CreateObject to start an Outlook session and assigns it to objOutlook and sets the value of blnOutlookWasRunning to False. If there is no error 429, the Else statement sets blnOutlookWasRunning to True.

The Do While... Loop then runs while the result of the Dir function on f:\customers\new\registration\*.doc returns a result other than an empty string—that is, while the Dir function finds a .doc file in the f:\customers\new\registration\ folder. The subprocedure assigns to strCurDoc the result of running Dir on the folder, and if the result is not a folder (. or ..) or an empty string, builds the strings strDocToOpen and strDocLoc from the name of the file found and the appropriate paths.

The subprocedure then uses the Open method to open the document identified as strDocToOpen and unprotects the document if it is protected. It then uses the CreateItem method to create a new contact item in Outlook, assigning it to objContact, which it displays by using the Display method. As the comment in the code mentions, it's not necessary to display the Contact form, but having it displayed allows you (or the user) to see what's going on. Not only can this be reassuring, especially when you're testing an application, but it can help you tell when something's gone wrong.

The With statement then assigns to the properties of objContact the Text property of the Range objects of the text formfields in the form and the Result property of the ProductOfInterest drop-down list formfield. As in the previous procedure, the maneuvering with the BusinessStreetAddress property is complicated by needing to include the Address2 formfield if it contains text but not if it is empty. Otherwise, the transfer of information is straightforward. When the information has been transferred, the subprocedure uses an objContact.Close 0 statement to close the contact form and save changes without prompting.

At this point, the subprocedure closes the Word document without saving changes (the only change would be the unprotecting of a previously protected form; returning the Text property of the Range objects does not change them). It then uses a Name statement to move the document identified by strDocToOpen to strDocLoc, placing the document in the \Processed\ folder. The loop then continues for the next document in the \Registration\ folder until all the documents have been processed and moved to the \Processed\ folder.

After the loop ends, the subprocedure checks the value of blnOutlookWasRunning and quits Outlook if it is False. Finally, it releases the memory held by the objOutlook variable.

## Bringing Excel Information into Outlook

In this section, we'll look at an Outlook subprocedure that accesses information in an Excel spreadsheet and brings it into an Outlook message. We'll assume that the company involved creates a daily spreadsheet containing sales results. This spreadsheet is named automatically using a naming scheme featuring a four-digit year, a two-digit month, and a two-digit day, so the spreadsheet for September 10, 1999 would be named Results 1999-09-10.xls.

This subprocedure, which is run from a mail message customized with a command button named cmdAttachDailySpreadsheet, builds a string containing the name of the day's spreadsheet file. It then starts Excel, opens the file, returns the contents of a six-cell range named Synopsis, and inserts those results with accompanying text into the body of the message. Finally, it closes Excel and attaches the spreadsheet to the message, which is then ready for addressing and sending manually.

Here is the code for the subprocedure:

```
Option Explicit


Sub cmdAttachDailySpreadsheet_Click()

    'Declare the variables for the subprocedure
    Dim strYear, strMonth, strDay, strTodaysDate, strTodaysFile
    Dim objExcel
    Dim strTodaysResult1, strTodaysResult2, strTodaysResult3
    Dim strTodaysResult4, strTodaysResult5, strTodaysResult6

    'Return the four-digit year
    strYear = Year(Now)

    'Return the two-digit month
    If Len(Month(Now)) = 1 Then
        strMonth = "0" & Month(Now)
    Else
        strMonth = Month(Now)
    End If

    'Return the two-digit day
    If Len(Day(Now)) = 1 Then
        strDay = "0" & Day(Now)
    Else
        strDay = Day(Now)
    End If

    'Build today's date from the year, month, and day
    strTodaysDate = strYear & "-" & strMonth & "-" & strDay
```

```
'Extrapolate the file name for today's file
strTodaysFile = "f:\Sales\Daily Results\Saigon\Results " & _
    strTodaysDate & ".xls"

'Use the CreateObject method to start Excel
Set objExcel = CreateObject("Excel.Application")

'Make Excel visible
objExcel.Visible = True

'Open the workbook identified by strTodaysFile
objExcel.Workbooks.Open strTodaysFile

'Select the named range Synopsis
objExcel.Range("Synopsis").Select

'Assign information to the six strTodaysResultX variables
strTodaysResult1 = objExcel.Selection.Cells(1).Text
strTodaysResult2 = objExcel.Selection.Cells(2).Text
strTodaysResult3 = objExcel.Selection.Cells(3).Text
strTodaysResult4 = objExcel.Selection.Cells(4).Text
strTodaysResult5 = objExcel.Selection.Cells(5).Text
strTodaysResult6 = objExcel.Selection.Cells(6).Text

'Close the workbook
objExcel.ActiveWorkbook.Close

'Quit Excel
objExcel.Quit

'Release the memory
Set objExcel = Nothing

'Assign information to the Body property of the item
Item.Body = "Today's key results are as follows:" & vbCr & vbCr _
& strTodaysResult1 & ":" & vbTab & strTodaysResult2 & vbCr _
& strTodaysResult3 & ":" & vbTab & strTodaysResult4 & vbCr _
& strTodaysResult5 & ":" & vbTab & strTodaysResult6 & vbCr _
& vbCr & "The attached spreadsheet contains the full information." _
& vbCr & vbCr
```

```
    'Assign information to the Subject property of the item
    Item.Subject = "Key Daily Results: " & strTodaysDate

    'Attach the spreadsheet
    Item.Attachments.Add strTodaysFile
End Sub
```

The preceding code begins with an `Option Explicit` statement to force the explicit declaration of each variable. The subprocedure then begins by obediently declaring the variables it needs.

- `strYear`, `strMonth`, and `strDay` will contain the year, month, and day, respectively.
- `strTodaysDate` will contain the stylized version of today's date, and `strTodays-File` will contain the name of today's spreadsheet.
- `objExcel` will represent the Excel application.
- Six variables named `strTodaysResultn` will contain the information in the six cells of the named range `Synopsis`.

The subprocedure then uses the `Year` function with the `Now` function to assign to `strYear` the four-digit year. It performs a similar procedure with the `Month` and `Day` functions to assign to `strMonth` the two-digit month and `strDay` the two-digit year, complicated by needing to add a leading zero to each string if it is only one character long. Once this information is assigned, the subprocedure assembles the full stylized date by concatenating the `strYear`, `strMonth`, and `strDay` variables with hyphens between then, assigning the result to the `strTodaysDate` variable. It then uses `strTodaysDate` to build the `strTodaysFile` variable, preceding it with the path (`f:\Sales\Daily Results\ Saigon\`) and the word `Results` (with a space after it) and following it with the `.xls` Excel file extension.

Now the subprocedure uses the `CreateObject` method to start Excel, assigning it to `objExcel`. It then sets the Visible property of `objExcel` to `True`, displaying Excel. (This is primarily so that the user can see what is happening. There is no other practical benefit to displaying Excel.)

The subprocedure then uses the `Open` method with the `Workbooks` collection and the `strTodaysFile` variable to open the day's spreadsheet, and the `Select` method with the `Range` object to select the range named `Synopsis`, which is two cells wide by three deep. With the range selected, it assigns to the six `strTodaysResultn` variables the Text property of the six cells in the range. Next, it uses the `Close` method on the `ActiveWorkbook` object to close the spreadsheet and the `Quit` method to quit Excel. It then releases the memory that `objExcel` was occupying.

Now, back to the Outlook message. The subprocedure assigns to the Body property of the current item (the message) the contents of the six `strTodaysResultn` variables, formatting the message with tabs and carriage returns and adding explanatory text to it. It then assigns to the Subject property of the message the phrase "Key Daily Results: " and the contents of the strTodaysDate variable.

Finally, it uses the Add method with the Attachments collection to attach the file identified by strTodaysFile to the message. Figure 25.5 shows the resulting message.

**FIGURE 25.5**

*The Outlook message with the data from the day's spreadsheet and the spreadsheet attached*

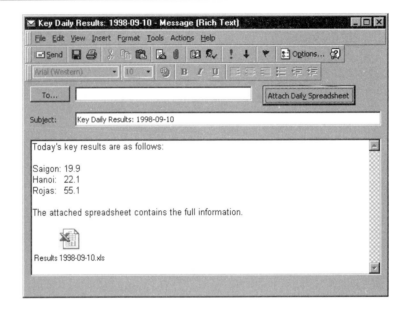

## Creating Outlook Items from Access

In this section, we'll look at an example of creating Outlook items programmatically from Access. If your company stores its information in Access, you'll often need to retrieve that information for use in other applications. The ExportTasksToOutlook subprocedure exports the records in the Schedule Details table of the Matrix Industries Resource Scheduling database, creating a task request from each and sending it to the person to whom the scheduled item is assigned.

Here is the code for the subprocedure:

```
Option Compare Database
Option Explicit

Sub ExportTasksToOutlook()
```

```
'Export the tasks in the Schedule Details table of the
'Matrix Industries Resource Scheduling database to Outlook tasks

'Declare the Access database
Dim objDB As Object
'Declare the RecordSet
Dim objRecSet As Object
'Open the database
Set objDB = _
    OpenDatabase("c:\My Documents\Matrix Industries Resource Scheduling.mdb")
'Assign the RecordSet
Set objRecSet = objDB.OpenRecordset("Schedule Details")

'Declare Outlook object
Dim objOutlook As New Outlook.Application
'Declare the Outlook NameSpace object
Dim objNameSpace As Object
'Declare the Tasks folder object
Dim objTasks As Object
'Declare an object for a task
Dim objTask As Object

'Assign the objNameSpace object
Set objNameSpace = objOutlook.GetNamespace("MAPI")
'Assign the Tasks folder
Set objTasks = objNameSpace.GetDefaultFolder(olFolderTasks)

With objRecSet
    'Move to the first record
    .MoveFirst

    'Use Do While loop to repeat for each record
    Do While Not .EOF
        'Create a new task item
        Set objTask = objOutlook.CreateItem(olTaskItem)
        'Assign the task (changing it to a Task Request)
        objTask.Assign
        'Assign the Subject to the task
        objTask.Subject = ![Description]
        'Assign the recipient for the task
```

```
            objTask.Recipients.Add ![Employee]
            'Assign the Due Date for the task
            objTask.DueDate = ![Due Date]
            'Assign the Start Date for the task
            objTask.StartDate = ![Start Date]
            'Send the task
            objTask.Send
            'Move to the next record
            .MoveNext
        Loop

    End With

    objOutlook.Quit
    Set objOutlook = Nothing
End Sub
```

This subprocedure is stored in a global module in Access. The following paragraphs describe how it works.

The code listing begins with an `Option Compare Database` statement (declaring the default comparison method for string data) and an `Option Explicit` statement to force explicit declaration of each variable used.

The subprocedure begins by declaring an `objDB` object variable to represent the Access database and an `objRecSet` object variable to represent the record set used. It then uses a `Set` statement to open the database involved (`c:\My Documents\Matrix Industries Resource Scheduling.mdb`) and assign it to `objDB`, and another `Set` statement to open the record set (`Schedule Details`) and assign it to `objRecSet`.

The subprocedure then declares the following: the variable `objOutlook`, assigning it to a new Outlook session; the object variable `objNameSpace`, which will represent the Outlook NameSpace object; the object variable `objTasks`, which will represent the Outlook Tasks folder; and the object variable `objTask`, which will represent the task currently being worked with. It uses the `GetNameSpace` method to return the Outlook NameSpace object and assign it to `objNameSpace`, and the `GetDefaultFolder` method to return the Tasks folder and assign it to `objTasks`.

The subprocedure uses a `With objRecSet` statement to work with the record set. After moving to the first record in the record set, it uses `Do While... Loop` to loop through the records until it reaches the end of the record set and the `EOF` property becomes `True`. Each iteration of the loop does the following:

- Uses the `CreateItem` method to create a new `TaskItem` object in Outlook, assigning it to `objTask`.

- Uses the `Assign` method to turn the task into a task request. (This is the equivalent of clicking the Assign Task button for the task when working interactively.)

- Assigns to the Subject property of the task the contents of the Description column in the record set.

- Adds the employee identified in the Employee column as a recipient for the task.

- Assigns to the DueDate property of the task the contents of the Due Date column in the record set.

- Assigns to the StartDate property of the task the contents of the Start Date column in the record set.

- Uses the `Send` method to send the task to the recipient.

- Uses the `MoveNext` method to move to the next record in the record set.

The loop repeats for each record in the record set, and then terminates. The subprocedure then quits Outlook and releases the memory held by the `objOutlook` variable.

PART

V

Building Customized
Outlook Applications

# APPENDIX A

## Installing Outlook

How you install Outlook depends a great deal on the type of environment you are working in and whether you have a previous version of Outlook installed on your system. However, whether you are installing Outlook over an existing version of Outlook or installing Outlook for the first time, you have a number of decisions to make that will significantly affect the features and options you have available to you when you run Outlook. This appendix will walk you through those considerations so you'll know exactly what you're getting and be able to explain why you have some features that your friends or colleagues don't have.

 **NOTE** Keep in mind that, for the first time in any Outlook version, you have the option to change the configuration of Outlook at any time. For example, if you install Outlook with the Internet Mail Only configuration and your office becomes Exchange-enabled, you can simply go to Tools ➤ Options ➤ Mail Services ➤ Reconfigure Mail Support and select the Corporate or Workgroup option. In earlier versions of Outlook, you were required to uninstall and then re-install Outlook.

# Preparing to Install Outlook

Before you install Outlook on your system, you need to make sure you have the equipment required to run it. Microsoft sets the minimum system requirements as a PC with a Pentium processor and at least 32MB of RAM for Windows 9*x* and 64MB for Windows NT. We want to emphasize that these are the *minimum* system requirements; you'll be happier with at least a Pentium II with 64MB of RAM for Windows 9*x* and 96MB of RAM for Windows NT. Of course, computer savvy people would suggest these amounts of RAM as minimum because of the performance benefits. You can try it with less, but if you're dissatisfied, hold off making too many judgments about Outlook until you have a more robust system to run it on.

## Readying Your Office Environment

At the time we are writing this, Microsoft has not announced a stand-alone version of Outlook 2000 that is separate from the Office 2000 suite of products. If a stand-alone version is released and you want to install it with Office 97, make sure you have all the Office 97 patches installed. If you have an early version of Office 97, or you installed the Office 97 SR-1 patch prior to 8/16/97, or you have a version of Office 97 that has an SR-1 item on the CD, you should definitely install the latest Office 97 SR-2 patch before installing Outlook. You can download this free from the Microsoft Web site (http://officeupdate.microsoft.com/Articles/sr2fact.htm) or you can call Microsoft and order a free CD (as long as you can validate that you already own Office 97) that contains a full version of Office with the Service Release included. If you install Outlook before upgrading to Office 97 SR-2, you have to install the full CD version of Office 97 SR-2.

There are no special considerations for users upgrading from Outlook 98.

 **MASTERING TROUBLESHOOTING**

### Running from Network or CD Modes

If you're installing Outlook 2000 *and* have Microsoft Office 97 or 2000 set to the Run from Network Server or Run from CD modes, you're going to have to make some changes before you can install Outlook. Both Office 97 and 2000 applications must be installed locally before Outlook 2000 can be installed on a machine. You may remove Office 97 or 2000 from your local machine after you install Outlook 2000.

## Running the Office 2000 Installer

Like other Microsoft installers, the Office 2000 Installer will guide you through the installation process. The CD-ROM loads automatically (unless you have turned off Auto Notification in the CD-ROM System Properties dialog), plays a familiar tune, and notifies you that it is loading. After it loads, the Office 2000 installer begins the first of several steps you will go through to install your software. Let's go through each of these steps in detail:

1. Enter your user and registration information and click the Next button in the lower right-hand corner to move to the next screen. It does not matter whether you enter the data in capitals or not; the Office installer won't know the difference.

2. Now you'll see the End-User License Agreement page (shown in Figure A.1). Microsoft suggests strongly that you read through the agreement, and you can check to make sure you entered your personal information correctly. Click the "I accept..." radio button, and then click Next to move on.

APP.

**A**

Installing Outlook

FIGURE A.1

Read the End-User
License Agreement
and click Next.

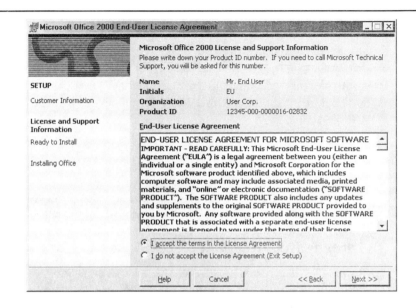

**3.** This takes us to the crossroads, shown in Figure A.2. You can either decide to Install Now, which will immediately install the default applications and components as determined by Microsoft, or you can click on the Customize button, which will take us to the screen *we* want. Click the Customize button to move on to the next screen.

**FIGURE A.2**

Choose to install the
default configuration
or to customize your
installation.

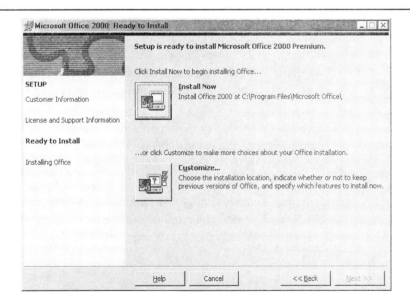

4. The dialog box shown in Figure A.3 lets you select the directory in which the software will be installed (the default is fine, unless you have a reason for installing it elsewhere) and choose a drive if you have either logical partitions or other physical drives. The columns in the table in the middle of the window tell you which drives you have, how much they hold in total, how much space is available, how much is needed, and what the difference is. Select your drive and click Next.

*Select a drive and a directory for Office 2000.*

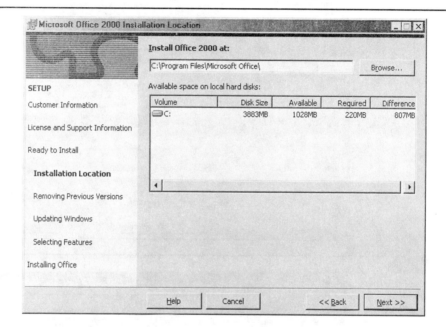

5. Here's where it gets a bit confusing, so watch the figures. As you can see in Figure A.4, the custom selection area looks similar to Windows Explorer. If you click on the small + to the left of an item, you will see another list of features. The button, a small rectangle with a small downward arrow and a little drive icon, is actually a menu that allows you to specify how the item will behave. The options (for most items) are:

- Run from My Computer
- Run All from My Computer
- Run from CD
- Run All from CD
- Installed on First Use
- Not Available

APP.

A

Installing Outlook

The Run All from My Computer option is often the easiest, but the other options can be helpful if you are low on disk space or rarely expect to use a feature. Click the + next to the Outlook item and you will see something similar to Figure A.5.

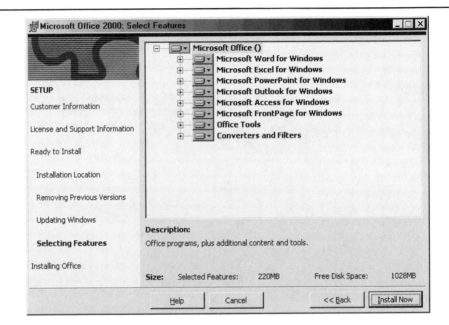

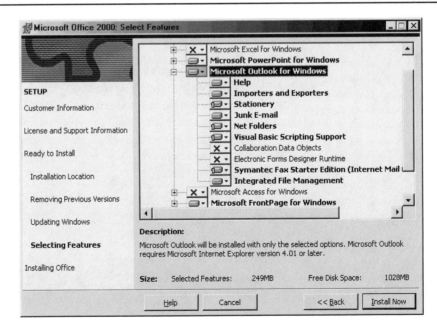

**6.** Select an installation option for Outlook by clicking the small button to the left of the Outlook option. As we mentioned before, clicking on the button gives you a menu of choices, as shown in Figure A.6. Select the Run All from My Computer option and release.

 **NOTE** The Run All from My Computer option we're using is merely for illustrative purposes only. If you need to make another selection, by all means do so.

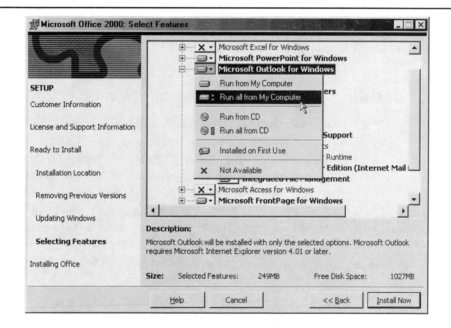

As you add or remove features from the various applications, you will note that the installation size shown near the bottom of the window changes to reflect your modifications. As we are in the Office installer, choose any other Office applications you would like to install at this time and click Install Now.

That's pretty much it. The installer grinds for a little while and then loads all of your choices onto your computer. When it has finished, it will tell you that you need to restart the machine before you can use your new software. Click Yes to do it now or No to do it later.

APP.

A

Installing Outlook

## Updating Internet Explorer

When you install Office, you also have the option to install Internet Explorer 5 if it's not already on your machine. Even if you don't plan to use Internet Explorer as your Web browser, you need to install it to give Outlook all of its functionality. Exceptions to this rule are if you already have Internet Explorer 4.01 installed on your Windows 95 OSR2 system or if you are using Windows 98, which comes with Internet Explorer 4.

## Upgrading Your Existing E-mail

When you run Outlook for the first time, Outlook examines your system and identifies any existing e-mail programs that you have on your computer. If it finds any, you are given the option of automatically importing e-mail messages, address books, and settings into Outlook. You can also choose to not upgrade these programs by choosing None of the Above.

## Deciding on the Type of Installation

When you install Outlook, you have a choice between three e-mail configurations, shown in Figure A.7. Each option gives you a slightly different list of features (to find out more about what is included with each installation, see Chapter 1). Make your selection based on how you intend to use Outlook and what your network supports (if you have one).

**Internet Only**   Choose this option if you have a modem and plan to dial into an Internet service provider and send and receive faxes on your PC, or if you are set up for an Internet-standard (for example, a POP3/SMTP or IMAP) server in your enterprise. This option gives you built-in access to LDAP servers on the Web and prompts you to install WinFax to send and receive faxes directly on your PC.

**Corporate or Workgroup**   This option is for users who primarily work with Exchange Server, MS Mail, or another third-party LAN-based mail system (such as cc:Mail). You can also use Internet mail in this configuration.

**NOTE**   The Corporate or Workgroup option gives you access to more sophisticated technologies and has a more complicated setup process as a result. If you choose this option, make sure you have your network's setup information or get it from your system administrator before beginning.

**No E-mail**   Choose this option if you plan to use Outlook to organize your data on a stand-alone computer but do not plan to use the electronic mail or fax features. You may also use this option to keep Outlook as a Personal Information Manager (PIM) if you use another application to manage your e-mail.

It is possible to change installations at a later time, but it's best if you know the type of installation you're going to need and set it up in that configuration from the beginning.

**FIGURE A.7**

*Outlook lets you choose between three E-mail Service Options.*

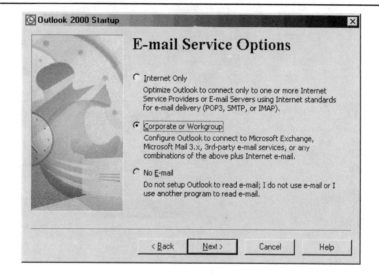

# Installing WinFax

When your computer reboots after setup, Internet Only users have the option of installing Symantec WinFax to send and receive faxes from their computers. The Symantec WinFax Starter Edition Setup Wizard, shown in Figure A.8, walks you through the process of configuring your modem and setting up a cover page for faxes you send. If you would prefer not to install WinFax, click Cancel.

In the second screen, enter the personal information, name, company, and other information that you would like to appear on your outgoing faxes. The next screen, shown in Figure A.9, is where you set up how you want your modem to interact with incoming and outgoing faxes. Here you set whether you want your modem to answer incoming calls and, if so, on how many rings. You can also set how many times you want to retry when a number is busy or there is no answer.

APP.

**A**

Installing Outlook

**FIGURE A.8**

*Use the Symantec
WinFax Starter Edition
Setup Wizard to
configure your
system to send and
receive faxes.*

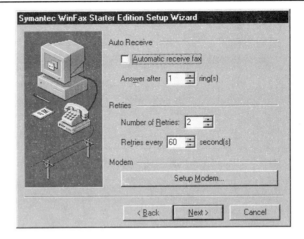

**FIGURE A.9**

*Use these options to
set up how you want
your modem to
operate.*

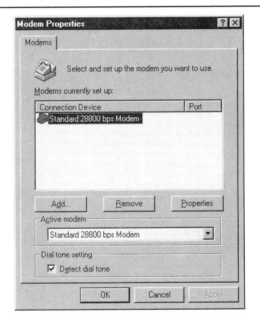

Click the Setup Modem button if you need to configure the modem you will be using. Choose Add to add a new modem or Properties to change the settings on an existing modem.

The next step lets you choose a fax cover page from among several templates. Make your selection and click Next and then Finish. Technically, you have now completed Setup. You are prompted to register the product either through the Symantec Web site, through a direct connection to Symantec, or by mail. Choose the country you are in and then the connection option you would prefer. The registration process includes several screens of questions that include your name and contact information and a series of marketing questions. When you have completed the survey, the Wizard will either print your survey so you can mail it or will connect to send the information online. Once the registration process is complete, you'll be able to send faxes just like sending e-mail messages. For more about using WinFax, see Chapter 5.

 **NOTE** If you choose the Corporate/Workgroup configuration, you won't have the option of installing Symantec WinFax. If you can dial out through a modem connection, you can set up Microsoft Fax as a service from within Outlook. See Chapter 12 for information about how to set up Outlook services.

# Reinstalling or Adding Components

If, at any time, you decide that you would like to add, remove, or repair any components of your Office 2000 installation, you can either insert the CD-ROM (if you have not turned off AutoStart) or go to Start ➤ Settings ➤ Control Panel ➤ Add/Remove Programs and double-click on the Office 2000 item. This will open the Office 2000 Installer. When the installer loads, it will be in Maintenance Mode, as you can see in Figure A.10. In the middle of the window are three buttons. The choices are Repair Office, Add or Remove Features, and Remove Office.

**FIGURE A.10**

*The Office installer in Maintenance Mode lets you add or change your Office (including Outlook) installation settings.*

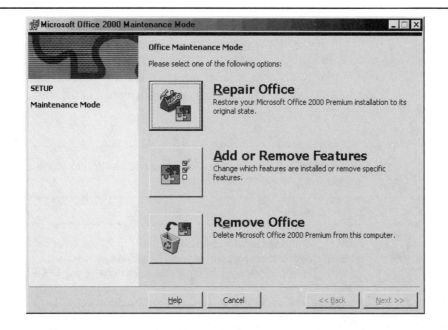

## Adding Features

When you click on the Add or Remove Features button, you are taken to the Update Features page where you can select or deselect individual items. This is just like the original installation, with the exception that it displays which items you already have installed. If you modify the set of applications and utilities that are installed, the installer will add or remove items as directed.

 **NOTE** For more detailed information on using the installer, see the Installing Office 2000 section earlier in this appendix.

## Changing Configurations

 If you want to change your configuration from, for example, Internet Only to Corporate/Workgroup, you can make these changes in Outlook itself. Open Tools ➤ Options ➤ Mail Services ➤ Reconfigure Mail Support and select your new support level. Outlook will ask for the installation CD-ROM and will add or remove components to suit your new configuration.

# Removing Outlook

Removing Outlook is simple. Go to Start ➤ Settings ➤ Control Panel ➤ Add/Remove Programs and double-click the Microsoft Office 2000 item. This will open the Microsoft Installer in Maintenance Mode. Click the Add or Remove Features button and locate the Outlook 2000 item. Clicking on it will reveal a menu. Select the Not Available item and click Update Now in the lower right-hand corner of the window. A few minutes later, Outlook will be gone.

 **WARNING** Do *not* click the Remove Office button to uninstall Outlook. This will remove your entire Office 2000 installation.

 **NOTE** Removing Outlook leaves all of your configuration and data files intact. If you reinstall Outlook thinking that you will get a clean installation, you're in for a surprise. When you start Outlook, everything will be back the way you had it before you removed Outlook.

# APPENDIX B

## Troubleshooting Outlook

**A**lthough you can expect Outlook to behave nicely most of the time, the complexity of the program and its interaction with other applications means that you will probably encounter an occasional unexpected problem. In this appendix, you will find answers to many of the most common Outlook problems, organized by category. If you review this appendix before you spend much time working in Outlook, you can avoid a number of problems from occurring in the first place. However, if problems do pop up, you should be able to solve them quickly and easily. Just scan the list of questions until you find what you're looking for. If you can't find the answer here or in the Outlook Help files, check out Microsoft's online support. Choose Help ➢ Office on the Web. Microsoft maintains an extensive library of articles on every aspect of Outlook, from the obvious to the obscure.

# Troubleshooting Common Outlook Problems

**Q: Why can't I see all the items in my folder?**

A: Look above the view list and you'll see the words "Filter Applied." You can either customize the view to change or remove the filter, or switch to another view to show all your items.

**Q: I just created a view; where is it?**

A: You access custom views from the View menu. Click on the folder you created the view in and choose View ➢ Current View; then choose the view from the menu.

**Q: I accidentally changed one of the predesigned views. How can I get the original view back?**

A: Select the folder that contains the view you want to reset. Choose View ➢ Current View ➢ Design Views to open the Design Views dialog box. Select the view from the list and then click the Reset button.

**Q: How do I change the default view on a folder?**

A: Right-click on the folder and choose Properties; then select the view you want from the Initial View drop-down list.

**Q: How do I restore the default settings for the Outlook toolbars?**

A: Choose View ➢ Toolbars ➢ Customize to open the Customize dialog box. Select the toolbar and click the Reset button.

# Troubleshooting Outlook Installation

**Q: How do I change my Outlook installation?**

A: Go to Start ➢ Settings ➢ Control Panel ➢ Add/Remove Programs and open the Microsoft Office 2000 item. Click on the Add or Remove Features button and you can make changes to Outlook from the hierarchical list of items under the Outlook 2000 item.

**Q: I used to use Outlook with Microsoft Exchange Server. Now, I want to use it in Internet Only configuration. How do I change configurations?**

A: Open Outlook and go to Tools ➤ Options ➤ Mail Services ➤ Reconfigure Mail Support and select your new configuration. Click OK and confirm the next dialog box. Outlook will close, but you can reopen it immediately afterward and begin using your new configuration.

# Troubleshooting Contacts

**Q: Why doesn't AutoDial work for some of my contacts?**

A: If AutoDial functions properly for contacts in your area code, but not in other area codes, check the long distance dialing settings in the Dialing Properties dialog box. (Choose Actions ➤ Call Contact ➤ New Call and then click the Dialing Properties button in the New Call dialog box.) If the problem isn't related to area code, check the number to make sure it contains only numbers, not letters.

**Q: Why doesn't my Contacts folder appear in the list of address books in the Select Names dialog box?**

A: Right-click on the Contacts folder and choose Properties from the shortcut menu. On the Outlook Address Book page of the Properties dialog box, enable the Show This Folder as an E-mail Address Book check box to use Contacts as an address book.

**Q: Why don't all my contacts appear in the Select Names dialog box?**

A: In the Workgroup/Corporate configuration, only contacts with e-mail addresses or fax numbers appear when you use the Select Names dialog box to address mail and faxes.

**Q: My current contact manager doesn't appear on the list in the Import/Export dialog box. How can I import my information into Outlook?**

A: In your contact management program, save your contacts in a supported format, such as a text file. Then, import the text file using the comma separated value format in the Import/Export dialog box. You will have to map the fields in your old program to Outlook, but take the time to do this.

# Troubleshooting the Calendar

**Q: Why does my appointment appear at the top of the Day view rather than at its scheduled time?**

A: You created an event rather than an appointment. To convert the event to an appointment, double-click on the event and then disable the All Day Event check box. Verify the starting and ending times and save and close the appointment.

**Q: Why did the times for all my appointments change?**

A: When you switch time zones, Outlook automatically changes all your appointments to reflect the change. (This often happens when you import items to a new computer before setting the system clock. The default Windows time zone is Pacific time.) Double-click on the time in the Windows Taskbar, set the correct time zone, and return to Outlook. The correct time will appear for your Calendar items.

**Q: How do I display the date navigator? It's not on the View menu.**

A: The date navigator is displayed by default. If you resize other items in the Calendar (such as the TaskPad or the Appointment list), there may not be room to display the date navigator. Use the adjustment tool to narrow the display window for the other elements and create room for the navigator.

**Q: How do I display the TaskPad in the Calendar?**

A: Resize the items that are displayed to create space for the TaskPad display.

**Q: Why do some holidays appear more than once in my Calendar?**

A: Many holidays are repeated from country to country and between countries and religious groups. For example, Christmas Day is shared by Christians and people in the United States, Ireland, and numerous other countries. If you choose to add all of these holidays to your Calendar, you will have multiple occurrences of these shared holidays on your Calendar. Outlook has no way to remove the holidays once you've added them, except by selecting and deleting them each individually.

**Q: Why don't I have a Delegates page in the Options dialog box?**

A: If you aren't connected to a Microsoft Exchange Server, you can't add delegates for your Calendar, so the Delegates page isn't an option. If you are on an Exchange Server network and the Delegates tab doesn't appear, Delegate Access hasn't been installed. In the Options dialog box, go to the Other tab, click Advanced Options, and click the Add-In Manager button. Select Delegate Access from the list of choices and click Install. Choose Dlgsept.cgf from the list of available add-ins and click Open. If Dlgsept.cgf does not appear in the list, you must install it using the Office Setup program.

# Troubleshooting Tasks

**Q: When I send a task to another user, they receive text instead of the task item. How do I send the task item?**

A: When sending a task to another person through Internet e-mail, make sure the properties for that person's e-mail address in Contacts is set to Always Send to This Recipient in Microsoft Outlook Rich-Text Format. This way, the recipient will be able to transfer the task directly into their Task List using copy and paste.

**Q: When I assigned one of my tasks to someone else, it disappeared from my task list. How do I get it back?**

A: You can't. If you cleared the Keep an Updated Copy of This Task check box in the Task Request form, Outlook deleted the copy of the task from your list. You can have the assignee send you a copy of the task.

**Q: The person I assigned to a task says they marked it as completed. Why didn't I receive a status report?**

A: To receive status reports, the Send Me a Status Report check box must be enabled when you send the task. Also, the assignee must be on your network. Status reports don't work with Internet mail.

**Q: Why isn't an assigned task being updated in Outlook?**

A: To receive updates on assigned tasks, you must have a copy of the original task in your task list. If you disabled the Keep an Updated Copy of This Task check box in the task request form, or have deleted the task from your list, you won't receive updates even if you re-create the task. Also, the assignee must be on your network. Status reports don't work with Internet mail.

# Troubleshooting Printing Options

**Q: Outlook doesn't print. How do I fix it?**

A: First, make sure that you've selected a valid printer (File ➤ Print to open the Print dialog box). If you have selected a printer, the problem is in Windows, not in Outlook. See Windows Help for information on troubleshooting printers.

**Q: Sometimes I can't find the print style I want to use. What am I doing wrong?**

A: Remember that views and print styles are linked. If the current view is a table view, the print styles will be table print styles. Change to a view similar to the print style you want and choose File ➤ Print Preview again.

**Q: Why can't I preview outbound mail messages before I print them?**

A: HTML and WordMail don't support Print Preview. Change your mail format to Plain Text or Microsoft Rich Text Format if you want to preview messages.

**Q: When I print the Calendar, long appointment descriptions are cut off. How do I get them to wrap?**

A: Calendar items only wrap in Daily view. If you're printing a monthly or weekly calendar, items are truncated if they're too wide. You can change the font (File ➤ Print ➤ Page Setup) or switch to Day in one of the Day/Week/Month views.

**Q: In the Calendar component, how do I set the range of days I want to print?**

A: Choose beginning and ending dates in the lower-left corner of the Print dialog box.

Q: How can I print noncontiguous days; for example, just the weekends or week-days in a month?

A: You can't do it as a single print operation. Print the first weekend, then the second, and so on.

# Troubleshooting Services and Mail Options

Q: Why can't I send and receive e-mail messages?

A: Outlook relies on a number of settings to send and receive e-mail messages. In the Internet Only configuration, you may have more than one e-mail service (for example, CompuServe and an ISP). Check each service by choosing Tools ➤ Send and Receive and then selecting the service you want to use. If one of them works, you can use that service to send mail. Try removing and reinstalling the service that does not work. Sometimes, walking through each step of a service configuration reveals a missing or misconfigured item.

 **NOTE** Remember, when Outlook is in Internet Only mode, the Services menu item is called Accounts.

If none of the services work, open the Windows Control Panel and check your modem. (It's also a good idea to make sure the phone line is plugged in!) Open the Dial-Up Networking folder in My Computer, and check the settings for the dial-up connection you're using. Launch the dial-up connection directly from the folder to see if it's the connection, rather than your Outlook settings, that's causing the problem. You'll find troubleshooting help for modems and dial-up connections in Windows Help.

In the Workgroup/Corporate configuration, your messaging is normally handled by a LAN-based mail server. When this mail server is down, you won't be able to send or receive messages. If other users on your network can send mail, check with your network administrator to see how your mail services should be configured.

Q: I can't find a mail message I received a couple of months ago. Where is it?

A: If you didn't move the message, there are three possibilities: you switched to another Inbox since you received the message, the message has been archived, or the message was automatically moved or deleted based on rules you created in the Rules Wizard. If you've installed a new set of personal folders, check the Inbox in the folders you used previously. The message should be there. To see if the message may have been archived, right-click on the Inbox, choose Properties, and see if Automatic Archiving is enabled on the AutoArchive tab. If you're using the Rules Wizard to move or delete items automatically, choose Tools ➤ Rules Wizard to change the rules so you don't move or delete messages accidentally.

**Q: I AutoArchive my messages. Can I mark individual messages so they won't be archived?**

A: Yes. Open the message and choose File ➤ Properties to open the message's Properties dialog box. On the General page, enable the Do Not AutoArchive This Item check box.

**Q: Why are the voting options disabled in my mail message form?**

A: You can't use voting in the Internet Only configuration. Voting options are only supported if you are using Microsoft Exchange as well as Outlook.

**Q: Why don't all of my recipients see the voting options in my messages?**

A: The voting options don't work for messages sent over the Internet.

**Q: Why does an e-mail message stay in the Outbox after I click Send?**

A: If you edit a message after it's in the Outbox, you must click Send again to send the message. If you simply close it, it remains in the Outbox. You can easily check to see if this is the problem. Messages that will be sent are italicized. If a message isn't italicized, open it and click Send.

**Q: Why does it take more time to send and receive mail when I change editors?**

A: You need to have a fair amount of memory to use Word as your e-mail editor; if you have less than 32MB of memory, it will take longer to send and receive Word mail messages. To speed things up, switch to Microsoft Rich Text Format or Plain Text mail format (Tools ➤ Options and change formats on the Mail Format page of the Options dialog box).

**Q: Why is the Signature Picker disabled in the Mail Format dialog box?**

A: You're using Word as your e-mail editor, so you can't create a custom signature in Outlook. You can create a template in Word that includes a custom signature, and then use that template for WordMail in Outlook. However, you can't include a digital signature in a WordMail template, so you might consider using one of the Outlook mail editors rather than Word.

**Q: I'm trying to find a specific e-mail option. Where should I look?**

A: Outlook's mail options are found in a number of locations. Table B.1 lists the more frequently used e-mail options by type.

**TABLE B.1: E-MAIL OPTIONS**

| Type of Option | Purpose/Action | Location |
|---|---|---|
| Accounts | Set to check for mail, Internet Only configuration | Account Properties dialog box: Tools ➣ Accounts ➣ Properties |
| Address Separator | Allow comma | Advanced E-mail Options dialog box: Tools ➣ Options ➣ Preferences ➣ E-mail Options ➣ Advanced E-mail Options |
| Automatic Name Checking | Toggle on or off | Advanced E-mail Options dialog box: Tools ➣ Options ➣ Preferences ➣ E-mail Options ➣ Advanced E-mail Options |
| Automatic Processing | Complete processing of mail on arrival | Advanced E-mail Options dialog box: Tools ➣ Options ➣ Preferences ➣ E-mail Options ➣ Advanced E-mail Options |
| Comments | Add your name | E-mail Options dialog box: Tools ➣ Options ➣ Preferences ➣ E-mail Options |
| Custom Signatures | Select or create | Mail Format, Options dialog box: Tools ➣ Options ➣ Mail Format |
| Digital Signatures | Obtain Digital ID | Security, Options dialog box: Tools ➣ Options ➣ Security |
| Digital Signatures | Set defaults | Security, Options dialog box: Tools ➣ Options ➣ Security |
| Encoding | Default format for Internet mail | Internet E-mail, Options dialog box: Tools ➣ Options ➣ Internet E-mail or Mail Format, Options dialog box: Tools ➣ Options ➣ Mail Format |
| Encrypted Messages | Set defaults | Security, Options dialog box: Tools ➣ Options ➣ Security |
| Forwarded Messages | Default font | Mail Format, Options dialog box: Tools ➣ Options ➣ Mail Format |
| Forwarded Messages | Include or exclude original text | E-mail Options dialog box: Tools ➣ Options ➣ Preferences ➣ E-mail Options |
| Forwarded Messages | Save or discard | Advanced E-mail Options dialog box: Tools ➣ Options ➣ Preferences ➣ E-mail Options ➣ Advanced E-mail Options |

*Continued* ▶

**TABLE B.1: E-MAIL OPTIONS (CONTINUED)**

| Type of Option | Purpose/Action | Location |
|---|---|---|
| Importance | Set default | Advanced E-mail Options dialog box: Tools ➤ Options ➤ Preferences ➤ E-mail Options ➤ Advanced E-mail Options |
| Importance | Set for this message | Message Options dialog box: View ➤ Options |
| Message Delivery | Automatically hang up when finished sending/ receiving | Internet E-mail, Options dialog box: Tools ➤ Options ➤ Internet E-mail |
| Message Delivery | Check for Internet messages at set interval | Internet E-mail, Options dialog box: Tools ➤ Options ➤ Internet E-mail |
| Message Delivery | Display a message box when new messages arrive | E-mail Options dialog box: Tools ➤ Options ➤ Preferences ➤ E-mail Options |
| Message Delivery | Play a sound or change cursor when new messages arrive | Advanced E-mail Options dialog box: Tools ➤ Options ➤ Preferences ➤ E-mail Options ➤ Advanced E-mail Options |
| Message Delivery | Prompt or don't prompt before connecting to ISP | Internet E-mail, Options dialog box: Tools ➤ Options ➤ Internet E-mail |
| Message Delivery | Warn before switching to dial-up connection | Internet E-mail, Options dialog box: Tools ➤ Options ➤ Internet E-mail |
| Message Format | Default stationery for HTML | Mail Format, Options dialog box: Tools ➤ Options ➤ Mail Format |
| Message Format | Set default | Mail Format, Options dialog box: Tools ➤ Options ➤ Mail Format |
| Original Message | Close on reply or forward E-mail | Options dialog box: Tools ➤ Options ➤ Preferences ➤ E-mail Options |
| Replies | Default font | Mail Format, Options dialog box: Tools ➤ Options ➤ Mail Format |
| Replies | Quote text, format quoted text | E-mail Options dialog box: Tools ➤ Options ➤ Preferences ➤ E-mail Options |
| Replies | Send replies to another person | Message Options dialog box: View ➤ Options |

*Continued* ▶

| Type of Option | Purpose/Action | Location |
|---|---|---|
| Sensitivity | Set default | Advanced E-mail Options dialog box: Tools ➤ Options ➤ Preferences ➤ E-mail Options ➤ Advanced E-mail Options |
| Sensitivity | Individual message | Message Options dialog box: View ➤ Options |
| Sent Messages | Delay delivery | Message Options dialog box: View ➤ Options |
| Sent Messages | Folder to save in | Advanced E-mail Options dialog box: Tools ➤ Options ➤ Preferences ➤ E-mail Options ➤ Advanced E-mail Options |
| Sent Messages | Save in location for individual message | Message Options dialog box: View ➤ Options |
| Sent Messages | Save or discard original | Advanced E-mail Options dialog box: Tools ➤ Options ➤ Preferences ➤ E-mail Options ➤ Advanced E-mail Options |
| Sent Messages | Save or discard copies | E-mail Options dialog box: Tools ➤ Options ➤ Preferences ➤ E-mail Options |
| Sent Messages | Set expiration for deletion of sent messages | Message Options dialog box: View ➤ Options |
| Services | Set expiration for deletion of sent messages | Mail Services, Options dialog box: Tools ➤ Options ➤ Mail Services |
| Spelling | General options | Spelling, Options dialog box: Tools ➤ Options ➤ Spelling |
| Spelling | Select custom dictionary, all other options | Spelling, Options dialog box: Tools ➤ Options ➤ Spelling |
| Tracking | Set defaults for Internet Only configuration | Tracking Options dialog box: Tools ➤ Options ➤ Preferences ➤ E-mail Options ➤ Tracking Options |
| Tracking | Set defaults for Internet Only configuration | Rules Wizard |
| Tracking | For this message, Corporate/Workgroup only | Message Options dialog box: View ➤ Options |

**TABLE B.1: E-MAIL OPTIONS (CONTINUED)**

*Continued* ▶

| TABLE B.1: E-MAIL OPTIONS (CONTINUED) | | |
| --- | --- | --- |
| **Type of Option** | **Purpose/Action** | **Location** |
| Unsent Messages | AutoSave | Advanced E-mail Options dialog box: Tools ➣ Options ➣ Preferences ➣ E-mail Options ➣ Advanced E-mail Options |
| Unsent Messages | Save in drafts or discard e-mail | Options dialog box: Tools ➣ Options ➣ Preferences ➣ E-mail Options |
| User Profile | Prompt or use default | Mail Services, Options dialog box: Tools ➣ Options ➣ Mail Services |
| vCard | Attach as signature | Mail Format, Options dialog box: Tools ➣ Options ➣ Mail Format |
| Voting | Corporate/Workgroup only | Message Options dialog box: View ➣ Options |

Q: **Why does an error message appear whenever I try to send digitally signed messages?**

A: Class 1 digital signatures include your e-mail address. If you change addresses (or your system administrator changes your address), you will need to obtain a new or updated certificate from your ID provider to send digitally signed messages.

Q: **Why can't I preview a message/an encrypted message?**

A: The message is encrypted. You can open the message, but you can't preview it.

# Troubleshooting Attachments

Q: **Why can't I open a file attached to a mail message?**

A: To open an attachment, you must have a program that can read the file format of the attachment. For example, if someone sends you a drawing created in Visio, you must have Visio on your machine to open the file or an application that can import the file. Ask the sender to save the file in a format you can open and send it to you again.

Q: **Why do some of my recipients receive a file called `Winmail.dat` attached to messages I send?**

A: This happens when you send a message that uses Microsoft Rich Text formatting to someone whose mail program can't read RTF. To change the format used to send all mail messages, choose Tools ➣ Options to open the Options dialog box and choose Plain Text on the Mail Format page. If you're using plain text or HTML, open the Contact form for the recipient and double-click on their e-mail address to open the Address Properties dialog box. Disable the Always Send to This Recipient in Microsoft Outlook Rich Text Format check box, and then click OK.

**Q: Why can't message recipients open attachments I send as shortcuts?**

A: The recipient must have permission to open the folder that contains the file that the shortcut points to. Consider attaching the file itself instead of a shortcut.

# Troubleshooting Categories

**Q: Why do categories I deleted from the Master Category list still appear in some items?**

A: Deleting a category from the list does not delete it from the individual items that you'd already assigned to the category.

**Q: How do I remove a category from multiple items?**

A: Use Find to locate all items that use the category, and then select the items. Choose Edit ➤ Categories to open the Categories dialog box. In the Available Categories list, turn off the check boxes for the categories you want to remove from the selected items.

**Q: Why do I have Categories that I didn't create?**

A: Outlook includes default categories, so the category may have been on the default list. If other users send you mail messages or items with custom categories they created, the categories are added to your list of available categories. This is why it's a good idea to remove your custom categories from items you send to other users.

# Troubleshooting Files and Folders

**Q: I created a custom view in a public folder. Why can't other users see it?**

A: When you create a view, you can let everyone see it, or hide it from other users by choosing In This Folder, Visible Only to Me in the Create View dialog box. While you can't change this setting, you can copy the view and make it visible by choosing the In This Folder, Visible to Everyone option in the Copy View dialog box.

**Q: Why can't I open a shared folder?**

A: If you can see the folder, but not open it, there are two possibilities: the server that the folder is shared on isn't available, or you don't have permission to open the folder. For permission to open the folder, talk to the folder's owner or your network administrator.

**Q: If I can open a public folder, why can't I create a new item in it?**

A: You have permission to read the items in the folder, but you don't have permission to create new items. (Either your system administrator or the folder's owner can give you permission to create items.) If you have the appropriate permissions, you may need a customized form to post to the folder.

**Q: Why can't I create a subfolder in a public folder?**

A: The default role for users of a public folder, Author, doesn't have permission to create subfolders. If you need to create subfolders in an existing public folder, ask the folder's owner or the system administrator to create a new subfolder for you or to give you permission to do it yourself.

# INDEX

**Note to the Reader:** Throughout this index **boldfaced** page numbers indicate primary discussions of a topic. *Italicized* page numbers indicate illustrations.